Greg J. Bamber is Professor in the Griffith Business School at Griffith University, Queensland, Australia. Russell D. Lansbury and Nick Wailes are Professor and Lecturer in Work and Organisational Studies, School of Business, at the University of Sydney, Australia.

This edition was facilitated by the Graduate School of Management in the Business and Law Group, Griffith University, Queensland, and Work and Organisational Studies in the Faculty of Economics and Business, University of Sydney.

Griffith University Graduate School of Management

Griffith University is a leading provider of business and management education and research. It has campuses in Brisbane (Australia's third-largest city and the Queensland state capital) and at the Gold Coast (Australia's premier tourist destination). Evaluations by the Australian government confirm Griffith's position as a premium quality teaching and research university. Griffith University belongs to the Australian National Business School (ANBS), a consortium of leading Australian universities. ANBS facilitates transfer between each university and offers exchange programs with international universities, intensive overseas study programs and executive development programs. The original Griffith MBA is for experienced professionals and managers. The MBA (International) is for recent graduates (with little or no work experience).

Griffith University has highly qualified staff teaching its programs, including one of Australia's largest groups of specialists in employment relations. People travel from all over the world to study at Griffith, with more than 40 nationalities and most professionals and managerial backgrounds represented. Professor Greg Bamber is the Director, Graduate School of Management.

For more information email: gsm_enquiry@griffith.edu.au or see www.griffith.edu.au/faculty/gsm

Work and Organisational Studies is within the Faculty of Economics and Business at the University of Sydney, which is Australia's oldest and pre-eminent research university. The Department of Industrial Relations was established in 1976, although Industrial Relations has been taught as a subject within the Faculty of Economics since 1953. Work and Organisational Studies, which evolved from the former Department of Industrial Relations, has one of the largest groupings of academics in this field in Australia, and has large undergraduate, postgraduate and doctoral programs. It conducts courses and undertakes research in areas such as Industrial Relations, Organisational Studies, Human Resource Management and Management. The Faculty of Economics and Business at the University of Sydney offers Masters programs in a wide variety of fields such as Economics, Business, Industrial Relations and Human Resource Management. Russell Lansbury and Nick Wailes teach in Work and Organisational Studies. The website for Work and Organisational Studies is www.econ.usyd.edu.au/wos

The **Australian Centre for Industrial Relations Research and Training** (ACIRRT) grew out of the former Department of Industrial Relations at the University of Sydney and was established by the Australian Research Council (ARC) in 1989 as a national key centre with a nine-year grant from the Australian Research Council. The foundation director of ACIRRT was Russell Lansbury and the current director, since 1991, is Ron Callus. The website for ACIRRT is www.econ.usyd.edu.au/ACIRRT

INTERNATIONAL AND COMPARATIVE EMPLOYMENT RELATIONS

GLOBALISATION AND THE DEVELOPED MARKET ECONOMIES

Fourth edition

Edited by

Greg J. Bamber, Russell D. Lansbury and
Nick Wailes

$SAGE Publications
London • Thousand Oaks • New Delhi

SAGE Publications Ltd
1 Oliver's Yard
London EC1Y 1SP

SAGE Publications Inc
2455 Teller Road
Thousand Oaks, California 91320

SAGE Publications India Pvt Ltd
B-42, Panchsheel Enclave
Post Box 4109
New Delhi 100 017

HD
6971
.I595
2004

British Library Cataloguing in Publication data

A catalogue record for this book is available from the
British Library

ISBN 1-4129-0124-3 (hbk)
ISBN 1-4129-0125-1 (pbk)

Library of Congress Control Number 2003115425

Set in 10.5/13 pt Garamond Book by Midland Typesetters, Maryborough
Printed by South Wind Production, Singapore

10 9 8 7 6 5 4 3 2 1

To Betty, Alex, Kate, Gwen, Owen, Nina, Sharon and Stella
In loving memory of Freda and Doug
(Royalties from this book will contribute to research on cancer)

FOREWORD

This new edition of *International and Comparative Employment Relations* is a welcome contribution to and timely update of the literature in this growing field of study and teaching. The book embodies the best principles of international scholarship. By assembling a premier group of experts from different countries to address a similar set of issues, Greg Bamber, Russell Lansbury and Nick Wailes have produced a book that provides rich and detailed country-specific knowledge and information, from which readers can make informed comparisons.

This new edition focuses more closely on the impact of globalisation on employment relations in developed market economies. I am pleased to see this, given the heightened sensitivities (and tensions) globalisation has generated in recent years and the growing role that it is playing in employment relations in all countries. Indeed, it is not too much to say that some of the biggest intellectual puzzles and practical challenges facing our field today and in the future lie in managing globalisation in ways that benefit the world economy and enhance the standards of living and employment rights and opportunities for people in developing and advanced countries alike. This will not happen by the workings of some invisible hand of market forces: it requires public policies and private practices and institutions, informed by experiences and evidence on the ground. The data and evidence included in this edition provide a good starting point for addressing these challenges.

The field of international and comparative employment relations is in the midst of a mild renaissance, having come alive in recent years following a long period when most researchers focused on developments within their national systems. We are now once again learning a great deal from each other, and the material in this volume advances this effort nicely. Continuing to support this cross-national and cross-cultural learning process is critical to the successful performance of world markets and regional trading blocs, as well as to the development of effective labour market and employment institutions in countries with new or fragile democracies in Europe, Asia, and Latin America. Moreover, experiences in these countries will need to be brought to bear if we are ever to build sustainable democracies and peaceful and prosperous societies in the Middle East and Africa. Meeting this challenge will feature prominently on the world agenda for many years to come.

Understanding these developments increases the range of options from which managers, union leaders and government policy makers can choose in shaping their own employment practices. Our challenge as teachers, researchers, students and practitioners is to determine which employment relations institutions and practices can be effectively transferred across international borders and can be adapted satisfactorily to different local settings. Yet, as the material in this book attests, there are significant limitations to this transfer process, given the desire by most parties to maintain well-established traditions and the fear of changing existing power relationships. *Understanding and appreciating the importance* of the country and culture-specific features of work and employment practices is therefore equally important for managers, union leaders and policy makers.

Greg Bamber, Russell Lansbury and Nick Wailes provide a useful guide to how we might go about this cross-national learning. They indicate that a variety of different analytical frameworks exist to support international comparisons. I believe these frameworks will become the focus of important debates in our field in the years ahead. This book should serve as a valuable empirical point of reference in those debates.

I am delighted that the authors and editors continue to use to good avail the meetings and members of the International Industrial Relations Association and draw on the results of the cross-national research teams and projects promoted by our Association in producing this book. My hope is that the Association will serve as host to similar international and comparative projects in the future.

Thomas A. Kochan
Sloan School of Management,
Massachusetts Institute of Technology;
Former President, International Industrial Relations Association
and Industrial Relations Research Association

CONTENTS

CONTRIBUTORS

Greg J. Bamber was educated at Manchester University, the London School of Economics, and Heriot-Watt University, Edinburgh. He is Professor and Director, Graduate School of Management, Griffith University, Australia. He is past President of the International Federation of Scholarly Associations of Management. Before working in Australia, he was at Durham University Business School; he also was an independent arbitrator for the Advisory, Conciliation and Arbitration Service (ACAS). His publications include many journal articles and books, for example: *Managing Managers* (Blackwell); *Organisational Change Strategies* (Longman); *Employment Relations in the Asia-Pacific* (Allen & Unwin/Thomson). His publications have been translated into several languages. He has won grants from the Australian Research Council, Economic and Social Research Council (UK) and other agencies. He researches and consults with international organisations, governments, employers and unions.

John Berridge trained in England and France in languages, business and social sciences. After eight years in production and chemical engineering, he taught, researched in HRM and administered in eleven universities across the world, including the University of Manchester, up to 2000. The author of eight books and over 40 articles, he edited *Employee Relations* for the decade of the 1990s. Now in part-retirement, he enjoys reverting to his roots by lecturing in the Department of Chemical Engineering in the University of Cambridge.

Janine Goetschy is Senior Research Fellow at the Centre National de la Recherche Scientifique (CNRS), attached to 'Travail et Mobilité' at the University of Nanterre (France). Her main research activities and publications are in the field of comparative industrial relations, labour relations at EU level and EU integration studies. She has been lecturing in a number of French and foreign universities. She currently is Reader at the Institute for European Studies, University of Bruxelles (Belgium) (since 1998), in charge of the postgraduate course on the social dimension of the EU. Her present research concerns new modes of governance at EU level.

John Goodman CBE is Emeritus Professor of Industrial Relations in the University of Manchester, UK. He has held visiting appointments at the Universities of Western Australia, McMaster and Auckland. A very experienced arbitrator and mediator, he was an independent member of the governing Council of the Advisory Conciliation and Arbitration Service 1987–98. The author or co-author of eight books and over 60 journal articles/book chapters, he has a wide range of research interests. He is currently a Deputy Chairman of the Central Arbitration Committee (CAC), and chair of the national joint negotiating committee and other bodies in professional football.

Olle Hammarström received an MBA from Gothenburg School of Economics and Business Administration, Sweden, in 1967. He worked as a consultant before joining the Sociology Department of Gothenburg University. He later worked with the Ministry of Industry and the Ministry of Labour as a policy adviser. He joined the Swedish Centre for Working Life as a Research Director in 1978 and became Head of Research Department at the Swedish Union of Clerical and Technical Employees in 1981. Since 1995 he has combined work-life research with consulting and worked as an entrepreneur. He has published several books and articles on industrial democracy and industrial relations and has been a visiting fellow with Work and Organisational Studies at the University of Sydney.

Tony Huzzard is a Research Fellow at the National Institute for Working Life in Stockholm, where his research activities include studies of social partnership and European works councils as well as organisational development in a regional health authority. He holds a PhD in Business Administration from Umeå University, Sweden.

Annette Jobert is Director of Research at the Centre National de la Recherche Scientifique (CNRS), and is teaching industrial relations at the University of Paris X-Nanterre. Her current research interests include collective bargaining in France and Europe, ways of classifying jobs and qualifications, employment and training policies, European works councils. Her publications include *Education and Work in Great Britain, Germany and Italy*, jointly with C. Marry and L.Tanguy, (Routledge); and *Les Espaces de la Négociation Collective, Branches et Territoires*, (Toulouse, Octarès, 2000).

Harry C. Katz is the Jack Sheinkman Professor of Collective Bargaining at the New York State School of Industrial and Labor Relations, Cornell University. He received his PhD in Economics from the University of California at Berkeley. His publications include: *Converging Divergences: Worldwide Changes in Employment Systems*, with Owen Darbishire, (Cornell University Press, 2000); and *Telecommunications: Restructuring Work and Employment Relations Worldwide* (Cornell University Press, 1997).

Berndt K. Keller is Professor of Employment Relations at the University of Konstanz, Germany. He received a Doctorate from the Ruhr-Universität Bochum in 1973, and Habilitation from the University of Essen in 1981. His fields of academic interest and research include public-sector labour relations and European integration. He is the author and editor of several books and volumes on German and European industrial relations, including *Arbeitspolitik des Oeffentlichen Sektors* (1993), and *Europaeische Arbeits- und Sozialpolitik* (2nd edn, 2001). He has published in leading journals, including *British Journal of Industrial Relations*, *European Journal of Industrial Relations*, and *Industrial Relations Journal*. He has been a visiting scholar at the University of California at Berkeley (1975–77, 1991) and was Leverhulme Visiting Professor at the University of Warwick in 1994.

Yasuo Kuwahara is President and Professor of Economics at Dokkyo University, Japan, and an acting Chairperson of the Board of Trustees at Dokkyo Academic Group, including three universities and two high schools and hospitals. He is a member of the Board of Trustees of the Japan Industrial Relations Association (JIRA). He is a graduate of Keio University, Tokyo, and the New York State School of Industrial Relations, Cornell University, USA. He has worked at Nippon Light Metal Co.; the Organisation for Economic Cooperation and Development; and the Japan Institute of Labour, as a senior research officer and adviser. Professor Kuwahara has published over 100 papers and books on labour markets, industrial relations, technological changes, and migration.

Russell D. Lansbury is Professor of Work and Organisational Studies and Associate Dean (Research) in the Faculty of Economics and Business at the University of Sydney. He holds degrees in Psychology and Political Science from the University of Melbourne and a doctorate from the London School of Economics, and is a Fellow of the Academy of Social Sciences in Australia. He has been a Senior Fulbright Scholar at both MIT and Harvard University in the United States and a visiting Research Fellow at the International Institute for Labour Studies at the ILO, Geneva, and at the Swedish Centre for Working Life in Stockholm. He is joint editor of the *Journal of Industrial Relations* and a board member of other leading international journals.

Chris Leggett is Professor of International Employment Relations at the University of South Australia and an Associate of the Korea-Australia Research Centre (KAREC) at the University of New South Wales. Professor Leggett has taught and researched industrial relations in the United Kingdom, Africa and the Asia-Pacific region and has published articles and contributed to texts on the region. His current endeavours include research on developments in the Korean conglomerates, jointly with colleagues at the University of New South Wales and the University of Western Australia, and on the relevance of Western models for explaining transformations in Singapore's industrial relations.

Mick Marchington is Professor of Human Resource Management at the University of Manchester. He has published widely on many aspects of HRM and industrial relations and is best known for his work on employee participation. He recently completed a major study on the Future of Work, financed by the ESRC. He is former editor of *Employee Relations* as well as editor and author of a number of books on industrial relations and human resource management.

Serafino Negrelli is Professor of Industrial Relations at the University of Brescia. He has taken part in many international comparative research projects on employment relations in the sectors of automobile, telecommunications and banking. He has been involved (with Tiziano Treu) in the project of the *European Employment and Industrial Relations Glossary* and in other research projects of the European Foundation for the Improvement of Living and Working Conditions. He has been editor (with Guido Baglioni) of the *Cesos Annual Report on the Industrial Relations in Italy*. His recent publications include:'Social Pacts in Italy and Europe: Similar Strategies and Structures; Different Models and National Stories', in *Social Pacts in Europe—New*

Dynamics (European Trade Union Institute, Brussels, 2000); and 'Italy', in *Collective Bargaining in Europe* (European Trade Union Institute, Brussels, 2002).

Tommy Nilsson has a PhD in Sociology from the University of Lund, Sweden, and is an Associate Professor in Sociology at Stockholm University. He is a Senior Researcher at the Swedish National Institute for Working Life, Stockholm. His research is mainly in the fields of work organisation, modern production systems, payment systems and local industrial relations. He has published articles and books on individual wage setting for blue-collar workers, and on shop floor workers' participation in continuous improvement programs. He recently completed a research project and a development program about how the exchange of experience in networking can help union activists improve their competence in organisational change.

Young-bum Park is a Professor of Economics at Hansung University in Seoul, Republic of Korea, where he teaches labour economics and industrial relations. He holds a PhD in Economics from Cornell University. From 1988 until 1997 he was a Senior Research Fellow at the Korea Labor Institute, a government-sponsored research institute which examines employment relations issues. Professor Park has published extensively on industrial relations, economics and related fields in Korea and Asia. He has also participated in many government committees related to labour issues. He has been a member of the Presidential Tripartite Commission of the Republic of Korea.

Shaun Ryan is a lecturer at Curtin University and a PhD candidate and researcher in Work and Organisational Studies at the University of Sydney. His current research focuses on employment relations and organisational culture in the commercial cleaning industry. Shaun has also published a number of articles comparing union organisation strategies in the shearing industry in Australia and New Zealand in the late 19th and early 20th centuries.

Peter Sheldon teaches in the School of Industrial Relations and Organisational Behaviour, University of New South Wales, Australia. After graduating from the University of Sydney, he lived for some years in Italy before completing a PhD at the University of Wollongong. He has taught at the Hebrew University of Jerusalem in Israel and at the universities of Sydney and Wollongong, and Griffith University. He teaches widely in employment relations and organisational behaviour and has been a visiting scholar in Italy, Israel and the USA. His main research interests are employer associations (with Louise Thornthwaite), industrial relations history and comparative international employment relations.

Daphne G. Taras is a Professor of Industrial Relations and Associate Dean (Research) at the University of Calgary's Haskayne School of Business. Her principal research interests are non-union employee representation and petroleum industry labour relations. She has published over 40 articles and book chapters and edited six journal symposia. She co-edited the book *Nonunion Employee Representation and Union–Management Relations in Canada*. She served on the executive board of the Industrial Relations Research Association and is on five editorial boards. She was her faculty's Outstanding New Scholar (1997) and recipient of the Dean's Research Excellence Award (2000).

Mark Thompson is Professor Emeritus of Industrial Relations, University of British Columbia, Canada. He was a faculty member there for 31 years and has been a visiting scholar in Mexico, Britain, Australia and the USA. He has co-edited two books on industrial relations in the public sector and a volume on regional differences in industrial relations. He has published articles in leading journals in Canada, the USA and Britain.

Nick Wailes is a lecturer in Work and Organisational Studies at the University of Sydney, where he teaches comparative employment relations and strategic management. He has published articles on globalisation and employment relations in a number of leading academic journals. He is currently involved in a research project which compares the impact of globalisation on employment relations in Australia and South Korea. He holds a PhD from the University of Sydney.

Hoyt N. Wheeler is a Professor of Management at the University of South Carolina, and holds a PhD from the University of Wisconsin and a JD from the University of Virginia. He is a former president of the Industrial Relations Research Association and a member of the National Academy of Arbitrators. His most recent book is *The Future of the American Labor Movement* (Cambridge University Press).

FIGURES AND TABLES

Figures

Tables

ABBREVIATIONS

ACAS	Advisory, Conciliation and Arbitration Service (UK)
ACCI	Australian Chamber of Commerce and Industry
ACM	Australian Chamber of Manufacturers
ACSPA	Australian Council of Salaried and Professional Associations
ACTU	Australian Council of Trade Unions
ACTWU	Amalgamated Clothing and Textile Workers Union (USA)
ADGB	*Allgemeiner Deutscher Gewerkschaftsbund* (General Federation of German Trade Unions)
AEU	Amalgamated Engineering Union (UK)—merged in 1992 to form Amalgamated Engineering and Electrical Union
AFAP	Australian Federation of Air Pilots
AFL	American Federation of Labor
AFL-CIO	American Federation of Labor-Congress of Industrial Organizations
AIG	Australian Industries Group
AIRC	Australian Industrial Relations Commission
ALP	Australian Labor Party
AMG	American Military Government (Korea)
AMS	*Arbetsmarknadsstyrelsen* (Labour Market Board) (Sweden)
AN	*Alleanza Nazionale* (National Alliance) (Italy)
ARAN	Agency for bargaining in the public administrations (Italy)
ASAP	*Associazione Sindacale Aziende Petrolchimiche* (Italian Employers' Association of Petrochemical Firms)
ASEAN	Association of South East Asian Nations

Assicredito	*Associazione Italiana Credito* (Italian Association of Employers in Credit)
ATP	Swedish old-age pension scheme
AWA	Australian Workplace Agreement
AWIRS	Australian Workplace Industrial Relations Survey
BCA	Business Council of Australia
BDA	*Bundesvereinigung der Deutschen Arbeitgeberverbände* (Confederation of German Employers' Associations)
BIAC	Business and Industry Advisory Committee to the OECD
BLS	Bureau of Labor Statistics of the US Department of Labor
BNA	Bureau of National Affairs Inc. (USA)
CAGEO	Council of Australian Government Employee Organisations
CAI	Confederation of Australian Industry (merged in 1992 to form ACCI)
CAW	Canadian Auto Workers
CBI	Confederation of British Industry
CCL	Canadian Congress of Labour
CDU	Christian Democratic Union (Germany)
CEEP	*Centre Européen des Entreprises Publiques* (European Centre for Public Enterprises)
CF	*Civilingerjörsförbundet* (Swedish Association of Graduate Engineers)
CFDT	*Confédération française démocratique du travail* (French Democratic Confederation of Labour)
CFE-CGC	*Confédération française de l'encadrement*-CGC (French Confederation of Executive Staffs, the successor to the CGC)
CFL	Canadian Federation of Labour
CFTC	*Confédération française des travailleurs chrétiens* (French Confederation of Christian Workers)
CGC	*Confédération générale des cadres* (French General Confederation of Executive Staffs)
CGD	*Christlicher Gewerkschaftsbund Deutschlands* (Confederation of Christian Trade Unions of Germany)
CGI	*Cassa Integrazione Guadagni* (Wages Integration Funds) (Italy)
CGIL	*Confederazione Italiana Generale del Lavoro* (Italian General Confederation of Labour)

CGT	*Confédération générale du travail* (French General Confederation of Labour)
CIA	Central Intelligence Agency (USA)
CIC	*Confédération internationale des cadres* (International Confederation of Executive Staffs)
CIDA	*Confederazione Italiana Dirigenti di Azienda* (Italian Confederation of Enterprise Managers)
CIG	*Cassa Integrazione Guadagni* (Italian Wages Integration Funds)
CIO	Congress of Industrial Organizations (USA)
CISAL	*Confederazione Italiana Sindacati Lavoratori Autonomi* (Italian Confederation of Unions of Autonomous Workers)
CISAS	*Confederazione Italiana Sindacati Addetti ai Servizi* (Italian Confederation of Unions in the Service Sector)
CISL	*Confederazione Italiana Sindacati Lavoratori* (Italian Confederation of Workers' Unions)
CISNAL	*Confederazione Italiana Sindacati Nazionali Lavoratori* (Italian Confederation of National Unions of Workers)
CLC	Canadian Labour Congress
CNPF	*Conseil national du patronat français* (National Council of French Employers)
CNTU	Confederation of National Trade Unions (Canada)
Confagri-coltura	*Confederazione Generale dell'Agricoltura* (Italian General Confederation of [Employers in] Agriculture)
Confapi	*Confederazione Italiana della Piccola e Media Industria* (Italian Confederation of Small and Medium Enterprises)
Confcom-mercio	*Confederazione Generale del Commercio* (Italian General Confederation of [Employers in] Commerce)
Confin-dustria	*Confederazione Generale dell'Industria Italiana* (General Confederation of Italian Industry)
CONFSAL	*Confederazione Sindacati Autonomi Lavoratori* (Italian Confederation of Unions of Autonomous Workers)
COPE	Committee on Political Education (USA)
CSU	Christian Social Union (Germany)
CWA	Communication Workers of America
DAG	*Deutsche Angestelltengewerkschaft* (German Salaried Employees' Union)

DBB	*Deutscher Beamtenbund* (Confederation of German Civil Service Officials)
DC	*Democrazia Cristiana* (Christian Democratic Party)
DFKTU	Democratic Federation of Korean Trade Unions
DGB	*Deutscher Gewerkschaftsbund* (German Trade Union Federation)
DME	Developed market economy
Domei	Japanese Confederation of Labour
DSP	Democratic Socialist Party (Japan)
EC	European Community
EETPU	Electrical, Electronic, Telecommunication and Plumbing Union (UK, merged in 1992 with Amalgamated Engineering Union)
EFA	Enterprise Flexibility Agreement (Australia)
EI	Employee involvement
EMU	European Monetary Union
ENI	*Ente Nazionale Idrocarburi* (Italian National Institute for Hydrocarbons)
ERM	Exchange rate mechanism (of EU)
ETUC	European Trade Union Confederation
EU	European Union
EWCs	European works councils
FDGB	*Freier Deutscher Gewerkschaftsbund* (Free German Trade Union Federation) in the former German Democratic Republic
FDI	Foreign direct investment
FDP	Free Democratic Party (Germany)
Federazione	CGIL-CISL-UIL, Italian Inter-union Federation
FEN	*Fédération de l'éducation nationale* (French National Federation of Education)
FIET	*Fédération internationale des employés techniciens et cadres* (International Federation of Commercial, Clerical, Professional and Technical Employees)
FIOM	*Federazione Italiana Operai Metallurgici* (Federation of Metal workers)
FKI	Federation of Korean Industries
FKTU	Federation of Korean Trade Unions
FO	*Force ouvrière* (Workers' Force); also known as CGT-FO (France)
Forza Italia	Go on Italy
FTA	Free Trade Agreement

GATT	General Agreement on Tariffs and Trade
GCHQ	Government Communications Headquarters (UK)
GDP	Gross domestic product
GHQ	General Headquarters of the Allied Powers (Japan)
GNP	Gross national product
HCM	High-commitment management
HR	Human resources
HRM	Human resource management
IBT	International Brotherhood of Teamsters (USA)
ICC	International Chamber of Commerce
ICEM	International Federation of Chemical, Energy, Mine and General Workers' Unions
ICFTU	International Confederation of Free Trade Unions
IG Chemie-Papier-Keramik	Union of Chemical, Paper and Ceramics Industry Workers (Germany)
IG Metall	Union of Metal Industry Workers (Germany)
ILO	International Labour Organisation
IMEs	Industrialised market economies
IMF	International Metalworkers' Federation
IMF-JC	Japan Council of Metalworkers' Unions
IOE	International Organisation of Employers
IPA	Involvement and Participation Association (UK)
IR	Industrial relations
IRI	*Istituto per la Ricostruzione Industriale* (Italian Institute for Industrial Reconstruction)
IRRC	Industrial Relations Reform Commission (Korea)
ITSs	International Trade (Union) Secretariats
IWW	Industrial Workers of the World (USA and Canada)
JCC	Joint consultative committees
JCP	Japan Communist Party
JSP	Japan Socialist Party
KCCI	Korean Chamber of Commerce and Industry
KCTU	*Cheonnohyup* (Korean Council of Trade Unions)
KEF	Korean Employers' Federation
KFTA	Korean Foreign Trade Association
KLI	Korea Labour Institute
KTUC	Korea Trade Union Congress
LDEs	Less developed economies
LDP	Liberal Democratic Party (Japan)

Ledarna	Association of Management and Professional Staff (Sweden)
LMC	Labour–Management Council (Korea)
LO	*Landsorganisationen i Sverige* (Swedish Trade Union Confederation)
LRC	Labour Relations Commission (Korea)
MBL	Act on Co-Determination at Work (Sweden)
MEDEF	*Movement des entreprises de France*
MNE	Multinational enterprise
MTIA	Metal Trades Industry Association (Australia)
MUA	Maritime Union of Australia
NAFTA	North American Free Trade Agreement
NCIR	New Conception of Industrial Relations (Korea)
NDP	New Democratic Party (Canada)
NIEs	Newly industrialising economies
Nikkeiren	Japan Federation of Employers' Associations
NLRA	National Labor Relations Act (USA)
NLRB	National Labor Relations Board (USA)
NMO	National Mediation Office (Sweden)
NMW	National Minimum Wage (UK)
NUM	National Union of Mineworkers (UK)
NUMM	New United Motor Manufacturing–Toyota–General Motors joint venture (USA)
OECD	Organisation for Economic Cooperation and Development
OH&S	Occupational Health & Safety
OPEC	Organisation of Petroleum Exporting Countries
OSHA	*Occupational Safety and Health Act 1970* (USA)
PATCO	Professional Air Traffic Controllers Union (USA)
PCI	*Partito Comunista Italiano* (Italian Communist Party)
PDS	*Partito Democratico della Sinistra* (Italian Democratic Party of the Left)
PGEU	Plumbers and Gasfitters Employees' Union (Australia)
PLI	*Partito Liberale Italiano* (Italian Liberal Party)
PPPs	Purchasing power parities
PRI	*Partito Repubblicano Italiano* (Italian Republican Party)
PSDI	*Partito Socialista Democratico Italiano* (Italian Social Democratic Party)
PSI	*Partito Socialista Italiano* (Italian Socialist Party)
PTK	*Privattjänstemannakartellen* (Federation of Salaried Employees in Industry and Services) (Sweden)

QWL	Quality of working life
Rengo	Japan Trade Union Confederation (JTUC)
Rodosho	Ministry of Labour (Japan)
RSA	*Rappresentanza Sindacale Aziendale* (Italian Firm Union Representative)
RSU	*Rappresentanza Sindacale Unitaria* (Italian Unitary Union Representative at Firm Level)
SACO	*Sveriges Akademikers Centralorganisationen*, also known as SACO (Swedish Confederation of Professional Associations)
SAF	*Svenska Arbetsgivareföreningen* (Swedish Employers' Confederation)
SAP	*Socialdemokratiska Arbetar Partiet* (Social Democratic Labour Party) (Sweden)
SAV	*Statens Arbetsgivarverk* (National Agency for Government Employers) (Sweden)
scala mobile	Wage indexation (Italy)
SDP	Social Democratic Party (Japan)
SED	*Socialistische Einheitspartei Deutschlands* (Former East German Communist Party)
SEIU	Service Employees International Union (USA)
Shunto	Spring labour offensive (Japan)
SIF	*Svenska Industritjänstemannaförbundet* (Swedish Union of Clerical and Technical Employees in Industry)
SKTF	*Svenska Kommunaltjänstemannaförbundet* (Swedish Union of Local Government Officers)
SLD	Social and Liberal Democrats (UK)
SMEs	Small and medium-sized enterprises
SMIC	*Salaire minimum interprofessionnel de croissance* (French national minimum wage)
SN	*Svenskt Näringsliv* (Confederation of Swedish Enterprise)
SNCF	*Société Nationale des Chemins de Fer* (French Railways)
SNECMA	*Société Nationale d'Etude et de Construction de Moteurs d'Aviation* (French Aerospace)
Sohyo	General Council of Trade Unions in Japan
Somucho	Management and Coordination Agency (Japan)
SPD	*Sozialdemokratishe Partei Deutschlands* (Social Democratic Party of Germany)

TCO	*Tjänstemännens Centralorganisation* (Swedish Confederation of Professional Employees) (Sweden)
TCO-OF	*TCOs förhandlingsråd för offentliganställda* (Confederation of Professional Employees, Public Sector Negotiation Council) (Sweden)
TDL	*Tarifgemeinschaft der Deutschen Länder* (German State Government Employers' Association)
TGWU	Transport and General Workers' Union (UK)
THC	Trades Hall Council (Australia)
TLC	Trades and Labour Congress (Canada)
TLC	Trades and Labour Council (Australia)
TQM	Total quality management
TUAC	Trade Union Advisory Committee to the OECD
TUC	Trades Union Congress (UK)
UAW	United Automobile Workers (USA)
UCC	*Union confédérale des ingénieurs et cadres* (Confederated Union of Engineers and Executive Staffs of CFDT) (France)
UCI	*Union des cadres et ingénieurs* (Union of Executive Staffs and Engineers of FO) (France)
UCR	*Union confédérale des retraites* (Union of Pensioners) (France)
UDF	*Union pour la Démocratie Française* (Union of Independent Republican and Christian Democratic Parties) (France)
UGICA	*Union générale des ingénieurs et cadres* (CFTC) (France)
UGICT	*Union générale des ingénieurs, cadres et techniciens* (General Union of Engineers, Executive Staffs and Technicians of CGT) (France)
UIL	*Unione Italiana del Lavoro* (Italian Union of Labour)
ULA	*Union der leitenden Angestellten* (German Union of Senior Managers)
UMW	United Mine Workers of America
UNICE	*Union des Industries de la Communauté Européenne* (Union of Industrial and Employers' Confederations of Europe)
UNSA	*Union nationale des syndicats autonomes* (National Confederation of Independent Unions) (France)
USWA	United Steelworkers of America

ver.di	*vereinte Dienstleistungsgewerkschaft* (Confederation of Service Sector Unions) (Germany)
VKA	*Vereinigung der Kommunalen Arbeitgeberverbände* (German Federation of Local Government Employers' Associations)
WARN	Worker Adjustment and Retraining Notification Act (USA)
WCL	World Confederation of Labour
WERS	Workplace Employee Relations Survey
WFTU	World Federation of Trade Unions
WIRS	Workplace Industrial Relations Survey (UK)
Zaibatsu	Group of holding companies based on a group's commercial bank (Japan)
Zenkoun	All Japan Council of Traffic and Transport Workers' Unions
Zenminrokyo	Japanese Private Sector Union Council

PREFACE

This book summarises traditions and issues in employment relations in ten significant developed market economies (DMEs)—the UK, the USA, Canada, Australia, Italy, France, Germany, Sweden, Japan and Korea. We discovered the need for this book while researching, consulting, and trying to encourage people to understand international and comparative industrial relations (IR) and human resources (HR) in Australia, Britain, the USA and elsewhere.

In this fully revised edition of the book, the introductory and concluding chapters explore trends across DMEs in general. The book begins by showing why international and comparative employment relations is an important area of study. It goes on to consider some of the relevant methodological problems and to evaluate some of the most influential theories in this field. (Some may prefer to read both of these general chapters before they read the more specific national chapters.)

A chapter is devoted to each of the countries, which all belong to the 'rich countries' club'—the Organisation for Economic Cooperation and Development (OECD). The first four of these countries have comparable adversarial traditions: the UK, the USA, Canada and Australia. The next four are on the European continent. Two are Latin countries, with strong postwar traditions of communist and Catholic unionism: Italy and France. The next two are from northwestern Europe and have developed distinctive approaches to industrial democracy and skills formation: Germany and Sweden. The other two countries are in

East Asia, and have tended to develop alternative patterns of employment relations from those in the West: Japan and South Korea. The commentary starts with the country where industrialisation began (the UK) and finishes with a newly industrialising economy (NIE), which has moved from being an agrarian to a developed economy in less than 50 years (Korea). To aid comparison, countries that display some similarities are considered in adjacent chapters. For example, the neighbouring chapters on the UK and the USA, Canada and Australia, France and Italy, Germany and Sweden, and Japan and Korea, can fruitfully be read alongside each other.

Each country is analysed according to a similar format, with an examination of the context—economic, historical, political, legal and social—and the characteristics of the major interest groups—employers, unions and governments. Then follow concise analyses of the main processes of employment relations, such as legislation, plant or enterprise bargaining, centralised bargaining, arbitration and joint consultation. Important and topical issues are discussed, such as novel forms of human resource management (HRM), labour law reform, technological change, employee participation, labour migration, labour market flexibility and incomes policy. Periodically, these issues are controversial in most economies, and valuable lessons can be learnt—and anticipated—from the experience of others. For each country there is a list of references and a historical chronology of major relevant developments, which is a helpful way of putting current events into perspective. The chapters also comment on prominent disputes and controversies (e.g. the 1992 German public-sector pay dispute in chapter 8 and the 1996–97 union protests against Korea's new labour laws in chapter 11). Chapter 9 describes the altercations about the wage-earner funds in Sweden, while chapter 10 illustrates how Japanese enterprises may differ fundamentally from those of most other countries. The Appendix includes a useful collection of comparative international economic and labour market data on these ten countries.

Earlier editions and the subsequent Japanese, Korean and Chinese editions of this book were repeatedly reprinted and have been widely read around the world. Other translations have been proposed for this edition. This book is one of the most widely prescribed texts in its field around the world. This success is a tribute to the perseverance and skill of all those who have helped. We much appreciate the constructive comments that readers have passed on. We are already planning to improve the next edition, so would be glad to receive any suggestions or corrections, please, to any of our inevitable errors (in spite of all the people who have cooperated), at the addresses below.

Despite the difficulties of working across different languages, cultures and disciplines, the contributors have patiently met our requests for updating, redrafting and sometimes our reinterpretation of their original material. We are grateful that the contributors to this new edition include most of the team that compiled the 1998 edition. We thank several new contributors, who are listed on the contents page. Oliver Clarke was an indefatigable help with earlier editions. Sadly, he died in 2001; he is greatly missed. We appreciate assistance with the Appendix from the Australian Bureau of Statistics; Office for National Statistics, UK; International Labour Organisation (ILO); Korea Labour Institute; OECD; and the US Bureau of Labor Statistics (BLS). Unless otherwise specified, currencies cited throughout the book are in $US at April 2003 exchange rates.

We are indebted to all those who have facilitated this project, including Tom Kochan, who wrote the Foreword. Many people have commented on parts of the draft manuscript of this edition and/or helped in other ways, including: Cameron Allan, Michael Barry, John Benson, Kaye Broadbent, William Brown, Duncan Campbell, Laurinda Cronk, Linda Dickens, Geoff Dow, Tony Fashoyin, Winton Higgins, Carola Frege, Muneto Ozaki, Andrew Pendelton, Dick Peterson, Gerry Phelan, George Strauss, Mike Terrry, Manfred Weiss and Helen Wright. Rawya Mansour provided very valuable secretarial and administrative support.

The Industrial Relations Research Centre, University of New South Wales, originally commissioned this book in its series with Allen & Unwin. We thank the former vice-chancellor of the university and the publisher for their longstanding personal interest and encouragement: John Niland and Patrick Gallagher.

We much appreciate the support of our colleagues (not least the library staff) in Australia at Griffith University and the University of Sydney. Institutions in several other countries have also augmented our efforts over several years, including: in Japan, Dokkyo University and the Japan Institute of Labour; in Korea, the Korea Labor Institute; in Sweden, the Arbetslivcentrum; in the UK, the University of Durham; in the USA, Harvard University and the Massachusetts Institute of Technology.

Our debts extend to other friends too numerous to mention, including all those who were associated with the first edition. But our greatest debt is to our families, to whom this book is dedicated.

Greg Bamber
Graduate School of Management
Griffith University
Brisbane
Queensland 4111, Australia
Fax: +61 7 3875 3900
Email: greg_bamber@yahoo.com.au

    and

Russell Lansbury
and Nick Wailes
Work and Organisational Studies, Faculty of Economics and Business
University of Sydney
Sydney
NSW 2006, Australia
Fax: +61 2 9351 4729
Email: r.lansbury@econ.usyd.edu.au
n.wailes@econ.usyd.edu.au

Note: We acknowledge that parts of this preface draw on Roger Blanpain's Foreword to this book's first edition.

Chapter 1

INTRODUCTION

Greg J. Bamber, Russell D. Lansbury and Nick Wailes

Most studies of industrial relations (IR) have focused on the *institutions* involved with collective bargaining, arbitration and other forms of job regulation. However, we see industrial relations as dealing with all aspects of the employment relationship, including human resource management (HRM).[1] Hence, the term employment relations is used in this book to encompass IR and HRM. On occasions where it is appropriate, however, the terms IR and HRM are also used.[2]

Although the study of employment relations focuses on the regulation of work, it must also take account of the wider economic and social influences on the relative power of capital and labour, and the interactions between employers, workers, their collective organisations and the state. A full understanding of employment relations requires an interdisciplinary approach that uses analytical tools drawn from several academic fields, including accounting, economics, history, law, politics, psychology, sociology, and other elements of management studies. Adams (1988) sees industrial relations as having a dual character: 'it is both an interdisciplinary field and a separate discipline in its own right'.

Adopting an *internationally comparative approach* to employment relations requires not only insight from several disciplines but also knowledge of different national contexts. Some scholars distinguish between *comparative* and *international* studies in this field. Comparative employment relations may involve describing and systematically analysing two or more countries. By contrast, international employment relations involves exploring institutions and phenomena that cross national boundaries, such as the labour market roles and behaviour of intergovernmental organisations, multinational enterprises (MNEs) and unions (cf. Bean 1994). This is a useful distinction, but again we incline towards a broader perspective, whereby *international* and *comparative* employment relations includes a range of studies that traverse boundaries between countries.[3] This book emphasises an internationally comparative approach, focusing on ten countries, which are all developed market economies (DMEs). In other words, it combines comparative and international approaches to the subject.

In this chapter we examine the ways in which comparative analysis can contribute to an understanding of the factors that shape national patterns of employment relations; identify the main features of comparative analysis; and discuss some of the conceptual frameworks that have been developed for comparing employment relations. We examine the long-running debates about tendencies towards convergence and divergence between DMEs in their employment relations. We also review arguments about the impact of globalisation on employment relations in the DMEs. Aspects of international employment relations issues are discussed in the national chapters. However, such issues are discussed more explicitly in chapter 12.

WHAT IS GLOBALISATION?

There is a rapidly expanding literature on globalisation and its impact on many aspects of people's lives—including their working lives. There are many definitions of 'globalisation'. These range from narrow technical definitions, associated with the structure of international trade, to those that define globalisation as a fundamental change in the ideological principles underpinning the international social, political and cultural order.[4] However as Wade (1996) notes, globalisation usually refers to changes in the international economy, which are associated with increases in international trade in goods and services, greater flows of foreign direct investment (FDI) and the growth of international financial transactions. These changes include higher levels of interconnectedness in international economic activity. Globalisation is a new word for an old phenomenon (Isaac 2003:1):

> At the end of the 19th Century, goods and services, money in the form of silver and gold, ideas, practices and people moved across state boundaries freely throughout most of the world. In recent years we have come

something close to that world, except that the movement of people is now restricted, and that technology, especially in the speed of travel and communications, has created a completely new dimension to the economic, social and cultural integration of the modern world we now term 'globalisation'.

Several authors, including Hirst and Thompson as well as Wade, have argued that national economies have become 'internationalised' rather than globalised, and that the pressures associated with globalisation are not as strong as others claim. However, as Perraton et al. (1997) demonstrate, there are contemporary changes in the international economy, which can usefully be summarised by the term 'globalisation'. These include changes in the extent and intensity of international trade, in international financial flows and in the operations of MNEs. On the basis of this evidence, Perraton et al. (1997: 274) argue that, while:

the world does fall short of perfect globalised markets . . . this misses the significance of global processes. Global economic activity is significantly greater relative to domestically based economic activity than in previous historical periods and impinges directly or indirectly on a greater proportion of national economic activity than ever before.

More detailed statistics on the contemporary wave of globalisation and its impact on the ten DMEs that are the focus of this book are in the Appendix. In the discussion that follows we adopt a relatively narrow definition of globalisation, as a description of recent changes in the international economy, but accept that these economic changes may be symptomatic of, and supported by, reconfigurations in the broader political and ideological context within which economic activity takes place.[5]

WHY STUDY INTERNATIONALLY COMPARATIVE EMPLOYMENT RELATIONS?

There are several reasons why it is beneficial to study internationally comparative employment relations. These include contributing to our knowledge about employment relations in different countries and as a source of models for policy development.[6] In addition, it is worth briefly noting that the increased economic interconnectedness associated with globalisation has produced a greater need for information

3

about employment relations practices in other countries and led to a resurgence of interest in comparative and international employment relations in recent years (Strauss 1998). This section focuses on the possibilities that comparative analysis offers for theoretical development in the field of employment relations and the particular contribution that comparative analysis can make in advancing our understanding of the impact of globalisation on national patterns of employment relations.

Another reason for studying internationally comparative employment relations is that it can help with the construction of theories (Bean 1994). Such an approach can be a useful way of verifying hypotheses or of producing generalisations derived from research findings from different national contexts. Industrial relations and human resource management, as fields of study, have often been criticised for being overly descriptive and for their apparent inability to develop straightforward causal explanations of relevant phenomenon (Barbash & Barbash 1989; Sisson 1994). This view was expressed clearly in Dunlop's (1958: vi) famous observation, that:

> The field of industrial relations today may best be described in the words of Julian Huxley 'Mountains of facts have been piled on the plains of human ignorance ... the result is a glut of new material. Great piles of facts are lying around unutilised, or utilised only in an occasional and partial manner'. Facts have outrun ideas. Integrating theory has lagged far behind expanding experience. The many worlds of industrial relations have been changing more rapidly than the ideas to interpret, to explain and determine them.

Many would argue that Dunlop's observation is as relevant in the 21st century as it was in 1958. There are various explanations for the descriptive nature of and relative lack of theory in the study of IR and HRM. These include the practitioner and policy orientation of these subjects.

While this tendency towards description has also been noted in comparative employment relations, it has been suggested that comparative research offers the potential for significant theory building (Shalev 1980; Bean 1994; Strauss 1998). This is because comparison requires the abstraction of concepts from particular contexts. As Kochan (1998: 41) puts it:

Each national system carries with it certain historical patterns of development and features that restrict the range of variation on critical variables such as culture, ideology, and institutional structures which affect how individual actors respond to similar changes in their external environments. Taking an international perspective broadens the range of comparisons available on these and other variables and increases the chances of discovering the systematic variations needed to produce new theoretical insights and explanations.

Nevertheless, a further factor adds to the complexity of this field: analysts have to collect much information about more than one country before being able to make generalisations. There is also a tendency to focus on the formal institutional and legal structures as a basis for comparison, rather than on the more complex informal practices and processes. Strauss (1998) advances the interesting proposition that it is fruitless to seek to design a complete, full-grown comparative theory at this stage of the field's development. Rather, he suggests it is more appropriate to 'creep towards a field of comparative industrial relations' by developing generalisations and testable hypotheses that explain differences among countries and may subsequently provide the basis for developing useful theories. He draws attention to advantages to be gained from studying close pairs of countries with similar economies, cultures and historic traditions. This permits the researcher to hold many characteristics constant and to examine those which vary between each country: 'By looking at differences we seek uniformities, universal rules which explain these differences' (Strauss 1998: 186).

As an illustration of such a comparative approach, Lansbury et al. (1992) matched Swedish and Australian plants in the automotive components industry. They examined productivity levels in each of the plants and sought to determine which variables explained differences in performance. The superior levels of productivity achieved by the Swedish plant appeared to be related not only to levels of investment but also to employment relations in the broadest sense including the degree of consultation between management and workforce, type of work organisation and degree of teamwork. However, the study also demonstrated the difficulty of seeking to hold all variables constant, even when the products being manufactured and the processes used are identical.

WHAT AND HOW TO COMPARE?

While an internationally comparative approach may provide the basis for establishing causal inference in employment relations research, the act of comparison itself does not necessarily ensure this outcome. One of the challenges of comparative studies is the choice of 'what' and 'how' to compare. As Schregle (1981: 16) argues: 'international comparison . . . requires the acceptance of a reference point, a scale of values . . . a third factor to which the industrial relations systems or phenomena of the countries being compared can be related'. He illustrates his argument by considering three examples: labour courts and labour disputes; collective agreements; and collective bargaining. In each case there are problems of distinguishing the formal institutions themselves from the functions they perform. Thus, a comparative study of labour courts in Western Europe immediately encounters the difficulty that the functions of these institutions differ so markedly. In France, for example, the labour courts deal with individual as distinct from collective disputes, while the Swedish labour court is competent to deal with little more than disputes arising from the interpretation of collective agreements.

Employment discipline or industrial justice is an issue in all countries, so is an especially appropriate focus for comparative analysis (see chapter 3), even though there are many international differences in terminology. There are challenges in communicating even between English-speaking countries: for instance, there are significant differences in the style and legal status of a British *collective agreement*, an American *labor contract* and an Australian *industrial award*. Nevertheless, each of these instruments has a broadly similar role. Hence, it is important to compare the role of particular institutions, irrespective of the terminology used.

The lack of a common language and terminology may create confusion. As Blanpain (2001) points out: 'identical words in different languages may have different meanings, while corresponding terms may embrace wholly different realities'. He notes that the term 'arbitration' (or *arbitrage* in French), which usually means a binding decision by an impartial third party, can also signify a recommendation by a government conciliator to the conflicting parties. And there can be difficulties in distinguishing between the law and the actual practice. For example, while Australia formally practised 'compulsory arbitration' from the beginning of the 20th century at least until the mid-1990s, there was relatively little 'compulsion' in practice, and the arbitration tribunal has relied mainly on advice and persuasion (see chapter 5).

6

An example of how similar institutions may be applied in different ways is provided by works councils. Despite the adoption of the European Works Council by the European Union (EU) in 1994, there remain a variety of approaches to works councils in the EU. For example, practices differ between Germany, Austria and the Netherlands. This is due to differences in history, legal frameworks, and relationships between unions, employers and the state in the various European countries in which similar concepts of works councils have been introduced (Rogers & Streeck 1995). In other regions of the world where works councils are being introduced, the differences are even greater. In Korea and Taiwan (where a process of democratisation was introduced after 1987), works councils have been introduced with very different consequences (Kim 1997). Yet it is possible that over time, as more experience is gained with the operations of works councils, they tend to become more similar. Streeck (1997) argues that European works councils are neither truly 'European' nor should they be described as 'works councils'. The same terms do not always have the same meaning in different contexts (see also Knudsen & Markey 2002).

The collection of comparative data also poses challenges for those studying this field; for example, the definition of industrial disputes differs significantly between countries (see Appendix). Conflicts of *right* concern the interpretation of an *existing* contract or award, such as which pay grade applies to a particular individual or group of workers. However, conflicts of *interest* arise during collective bargaining about an apparently *new* demand or claim, such as for a general pay rise or a reduction in working hours. In practice, conflicts of interest are usually collective disputes. In the USA, Sweden and many other countries, this distinction is important. In France, Italy and certain other countries, conflicts of right are further divided into *individual* and *collective* disputes. The general intention is that different settlement procedures will apply to different types of dispute. In some countries only conflicts of interest can lead to lawful strikes or other forms of sanction, but conflicts of right should be settled by a binding decision of a labour court or similar tribunal (see Bamber & Sheldon 2001).

An illustration of the way in which institutions are reshaped by different environments may be seen in the former British colonies. Although many of these countries inherited the English legal system and other institutions from Britain, most of them have subsequently modified or transformed this legacy. Many of the American (chapter 3), Canadian (chapter 4) and Australian (chapter 5) approaches to employment relations are as different from each other as they are from Britain's (chapter 2). In Japan (chapter 10), after World War II, the occupying forces imposed American-style labour laws and managerial techniques. These were not completely rejected, but were subsequently reshaped by the Japanese to suit their particular circumstances (Shirai 1983; Gould 1984). In practice, much of the Japanese industrial relations legislation was reinterpreted by Japanese courts. Under American military occupation, similar laws were introduced in Korea (chapter 11), where they were to be implemented in quite different ways.

Many of the problems associated with comparative analysis relate to the difficulties of establishing *conceptual equivalence* when operationalising comparative research. Linden (1998) distinguishes between *phenomenal equivalence* (where identical measures are used for the same concept regardless of context) and *conceptual equivalence* (where different measures are used for the same concept to reflect differences in contexts). He argues that comparative analysis can proceed only on the basis of conceptual equivalence (Linden 1998: 5–6). One of the reasons that the approach suggested by Strauss (1998), of comparing closely matched pairs of countries, may be effective is that in these cases the gap between phenomenal and conceptual equivalence is relatively narrow.

INTERPRETING CHANGING PATTERNS OF EMPLOYMENT RELATIONS

Having outlined some of the benefits of an internationally comparative approach to researching these issues and examined some of the challenges of comparative analysis, we now summarise some of the major conceptual frameworks that have been developed by comparative analysis, and assess the extent to which these frameworks can be used to examine the impact of globalisation on national patterns of employment relations.

Industrial relations systems

Perhaps the most famous conceptual framework is Dunlop's (1958) notion of an 'industrial relations system'. Dunlop argues that an industrial relations system includes three sets of 'actors' and their representative organisations ('the three parties'): employers, workers, and the state. (In some Western European countries, the parties are known as 'the social partners'.) These parties' relations are determined by three environmental contexts: the technology; market forces; and the relative power and status of the parties. Dunlop defines *the network of rules* that govern the workplace (e.g. the web of rules about pay and conditions) as the *output* of the industrial relations system. Dunlop's approach has been influential among scholars in the English-speaking countries and elsewhere: it was a notable attempt to identify a theoretical framework for industrial relations; for example, Walker (1967) was influenced by Dunlop, and urges that we should transcend the dominant descriptive approaches to 'foreign industrial relations systems' and concentrate on identifying the role, importance and interaction of different factors that shape and influence industrial relations in different national contexts. Others enlarge on Dunlop's approach (e.g. Blain & Gennard 1970; Craig 1975).

Various critics accept that Dunlop's framework is useful as 'a model within which facts may be organised, but stress that it must not be understood as having a predictive value in itself' (Gill 1969). Criticisms of the systems approach include its neglect of the importance of such behavioural variables as motivations, perceptions and attitudes (Bain & Clegg 1974). Dunlop ignores the insight into the importance of informal work groups developed by his Harvard colleagues, the 'human relations school' (e.g. Mayo 1949). Moreover, Dunlop's approach tends to concentrate on the rule-making institutions and the settlement of conflict, rather than examining the causes of conflict and the role played by *people* in making decisions about the employment relationship (Hyman 1975). In spite of many attempts to refine the systems approach, it is by no means a generally accepted theory.

Collective bargaining

Dunlop's approach has been a point of departure for others, who have compared various systems of collective bargaining. Clegg (1976: 118) draws on data from six countries to support his argument that:

> The extent and depth of collective bargaining and the degree of union security offered by collective bargaining are the three dimensions which influence trade union density. The level of bargaining accounts for the extent of decentralisation in union government, including the power and independence of workplace organisations, and decentralisation in turn helps to explain the degree of factionalism within unions ...

Clegg argues that dimensions of collective bargaining are mainly determined by the structures of management and of employers' organisations. However, he also emphasises the importance of the law in shaping collective bargaining, especially when introduced in the early stages of the development of an industrial relations system.

Clegg's approach is narrower than Dunlop's, in that he seems to ignore the importance of the economic, social and technological environment while concentrating on collective bargaining and the 'web of rules'. Clegg sees collective bargaining as the principal influence on union behaviour, yet unions are also part of the collective bargaining process. Clegg was writing during a period when centralised forms of collective bargaining, especially in Europe, were at their zenith. From 1945 until the late 1970s, collective bargaining expanded in most DMEs in terms of coverage of the workforce and the scope of issues. Elements of the employment relationship that had traditionally been regarded as the prerogative of management were drawn into the bargaining process. By the early 1980s, however, there was a change in bargaining relationships. Unions were losing power in the labour market as well as in the political arena; moreover, employers were demanding that labour markets be deregulated. By the mid-1980s the movement towards deregulation and decentralised bargaining had gained momentum in Britain and many other DMEs, though the trend was by no means uniform (Albeda 1984).

Adams (1981) and Sisson (1987) seek to develop the collective bargaining approach in an international context, but they both focus on the role of employers. Adams points out that employers' attitudes and behaviour towards unions differ significantly between Europe and North America. In the former, typically, employers are organised into strong associations that engage in collective bargaining with unions (and sometimes with the state). By contrast, in North America employers have generally not formed strong associations; even where they have, it is much less usual for them to engage in collective bargaining. Adams holds that these differences are attributable to the differing early political or economic strategies of the various labour movements and the resulting differing degrees of state intervention in industrial relations arrangements.

Sisson argues that there could be no adequate theory of collective bargaining that overlooked the interests of management. Furthermore, there has been widespread failure to appreciate how the role of employers in collective bargaining varies from country to country.

Sisson compares the role of employers and their organisations in the development of collective bargaining in seven DMEs. He also concludes that differences between the countries were rooted in historical experience, particularly flowing from the impact of industrialisation. Hence, in Western Europe, including Britain, multi-employer bargaining emerged as the predominant pattern largely because employers in the metal-working industries were confronted with the challenge of national unions organised along occupational or industrial lines. By contrast, single-employer bargaining emerged in the USA and Japan because the relatively large employers that had emerged at an early stage in both countries were able to exert pressure on unions to bargain at the enterprise or establishment level. When legislation was introduced requiring employers to recognise unions (in the 1930s and 1940s), such employers had already exerted a profound influence on the labour movement and were able to deny unions the platform from which to push for more effective national unionism, especially in Japan.

The key features of collective bargaining, whether single-employer or multi-employer, are not easily changed. Sisson instances the lack of success of attempts to extend the scope of collective bargaining at the workplace level in several Western European countries, excluding Britain. He also makes the important point that most attempts to change the collective bargaining system by legislation are unlikely to have the intended effect, unless they take into account the parties' wishes (as illustrated by the short-lived *British Industrial Relations Act 1971*). There are significant forces in most countries that tend to constrain major deviations from their traditions. Nonetheless, in the 1979–97 period, following determined and continuing attempts by the Thatcher and Major Conservative governments, there were fundamental changes in British industrial relations (see chapter 2).

Decentralisation of bargaining

Since the mid-1980s there has been a trend towards less centralised forms of collective bargaining in most DMEs. This has generally involved the locus of bargaining shifting downwards, from a national or industry level to an enterprise or workplace level. However, the degree of decentralisation and the means by which changes in bargaining structures occurred have varied between countries. Based on a comparison of experiences in six countries (Australia, Germany, Italy, Sweden, Britain and the USA), Katz (1993) reports many similarities in the process of decentralisation. In each country except Germany, there was a shift towards decentralisation in the formal structure of bargaining initiated by employers, and a consequent reduction in the extent of multi-employer bargaining. With the exception of Australia (where there was an Accord between the unions and the then Labor government; see chapter 5), most central union organisations opposed the decentralisation of bargaining.

Katz evaluates three hypotheses that have been suggested to explain the trend towards decentralised bargaining: first, shifts in bargaining power from unions to employers; second, the emergence of new forms of work organisation, which put a premium on flexibility and employee participation; and third, the decentralisation of corporate structures and diversification of worker preferences. Katz concludes that the second hypothesis is the most convincing, on the grounds that labour and management appear to have gained distinct advantages from the work restructuring that accompanied decentralisation. However, shifts in bargaining power, as well as the diversification of corporate and worker interests, are important contributing factors to the decentralisation process.

While we accept many of the criticisms that have been levelled at the notion of the industrial relations system and acknowledge some of the difficulties associated with classifying different 'collective bargaining' regimes, it is useful to have detailed information on the organisation of employees and employers and the role played by the state when comparing employment relations developments across countries. Similarly, it is useful to know about the nature of bargaining and the extent to which it is centralised or decentralised relative to other countries.

CONTROVERSIES ABOUT CONVERGENCE

While such information can provide useful background, probably the most relevant conceptual tools for examining the impact of globalisation on national patterns of employment relations are still those associated with debates about convergence and divergence. Debates about convergence and divergence have a long history in comparative employment relations and precede recent discussions about the impact of globalisation on employment relations. Reviewing the convergence and divergence debate helps reveal potential limitations in the way that contemporary students have approached the issue of globalisation.

The *convergence* thesis was developed by Kerr, Dunlop, Harbison and Myers in their book *Industrialism and Industrial Man* (1960). Their core proposition is that there is a global tendency for technological and market forces associated with industrialisation to push national industrial relations systems towards uniformity or 'convergence'. This conclusion is based on the view that there is a *logic of industrialism*, that as more societies adopted industrial forms of production and organisation this logic would create 'common characteristics and imperatives' across these societies. To accommodate these imperatives, Kerr et al. (1960: 384–92) argue that industrial societies had to create a means of developing a consensus and industrial relations systems embodying the 'principles of pluralistic industrialism' that played a central role in establishing this consensus.

Figure 1.1 illustrates schematically the logic of industrialism, showing how the various social changes are related to the prime cause: technology. Convergence between advanced industrial societies occurs most readily at the technological level, at workplace and industry levels, or at urban levels, and then at national levels. Kerr et al. do concede that total convergence is unlikely because of the persistence of political, social, cultural and ideological differences. Nevertheless, while the authors acknowledge that there were factors that could mediate the relationship between industrialism and the particular institutions that developed, including the timing of development and the nature of the modernising elite, they also argue that the logic of industrialism tended to override these sources of difference and would produce convergence on a particular set of institutional arrangements of labour market regulation.

Modified convergence

The convergence hypothesis based on the logic of industrialism has been widely contested, with many authors arguing that the theory had neither foundation in fact nor explanatory value and should therefore be discredited. Inspired by the influential book by Kerr et al. (1960), a range of empirical studies have sought to test the extent of convergence in industrial relations systems. While some studies claimed to show evidence of convergence, most of the empirical data showed persistent differences in national industrial relations systems. As Katz and Darbishire (2000: 8) note:

Figure 1.1   The logic of industrialism

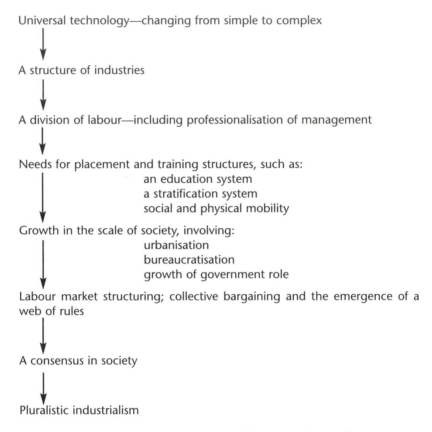

Universal technology—changing from simple to complex

A structure of industries

A division of labour—including professionalisation of management

Needs for placement and training structures, such as:
                        an education system
                        a stratification system
                        social and physical mobility

Growth in the scale of society, involving:
                        urbanisation
                        bureaucratisation
                        growth of government role

Labour market structuring; collective bargaining and the emergence of a web of rules

A consensus in society

Pluralistic industrialism

Source: Reproduced with permission from Brown and Harrison (1978: 129).

> The thrust of . . . much of the comparative industrial relations litera-
> ture . . . was that there was wide and persistent variation in industrial
> relations across countries in part due to the influence of nationally
> specific institutional factors.

There are two main strands to the theoretical criticisms of the industrialism thesis. First, several authors argue that what Kerr et al. refer to as
industrialism is a normative concept. Thus many writers criticise the
'liberal-pluralist' approach of Kerr et al. For example, Chamberlain
(1961) sees their book as:

> long on categories and classifications and impressionistic observations,
> but . . . short on analysis. It is perhaps best described as a latter-day

descendant of the 19th century German school of economic history, whose hallmark was a literary exposition of the transition from one idealised state of economic development to another.

According to Bendix (1970: 273), 'seldom has social change been interpreted in so *magisterial* a fashion, while all contingencies of action are treated as mere historical variations which cannot alter the logic of industrialism'. Arguably, Kerr et al. were too concerned with maintaining the status quo, controlling conflict, defending the existing institutions and imposing an ethnocentric, American perspective on the rest of the world. It is relevant to note that they were writing against the background of the Cold War.

Other critics question the assumption that industrialism is likely to produce convergence. Even though there may be strong pressures associated with industrialism, this does not necessarily imply that there would be convergence on a single set of societal institutions, much less on a single set of institutions that resembled those that had developed in the USA (see Berger 1996: 2–4). Cochrane, for example, rejects the 'deterministic view of the future' represented by industrialisation as an 'invincible process' (Cochrane 1976). Doeringer (1981) is less critical, but argues that convergence should be seen in a different form from that envisaged by Kerr et al. Doeringer argues that countries develop alternative solutions to common industrial relations problems; thus all industrialised countries show a tendency to institutionalise their arrangements for rule making about employment, even though their particular approaches vary. Differences between countries, therefore, are by no means random but are rooted in their responses to industrialisation. He analyses convergence using a three-part framework: first, as the result of responses to problems common to all industrial relations systems; second, as the process by which gaps in areas in the institutional industrial relations arrangements are filled; and third, as the realisation that, over time, the key decision makers in industrial relations systems selectively aim for multiple and often incompatible goals. Hence, what may appear as differences between systems may be due simply to differences in the goals that are being pursued at a particular point in time.

Piore (1981) also doubts that the convergence thesis is a general theory of comparative employment relations. He observes that certain aspects of industrial societies tend to converge while others diverge, depending on time and circumstances. An alternative approach suggested by Piore is to focus on the role of regulatory institutions in the industrial relations of different societies. He argues that capitalist economies pass through a distinct series of regulatory systems in the course of their historical development. As technology and industry change they outgrow the regulatory structures initially adopted, and the system is decreasingly likely to remain in some kind of balance. The result is an economic and social crisis which is settled only by the development of a new set of institutions.

Industrialisation appears to be occurring more rapidly in some of the newly industrialising economies (NIEs) than has been the case in the past; therefore, industrial relations institutions there have developed more quickly than in the DMEs. An example of this is the weak state of unions in most of the first four Asian 'tigers'—Hong Kong, Korea, Singapore and Taiwan. However, the growth of unions (official and unofficial) in South Korea since 1987 provides an exceptional case in the Asian region (see chapter 11; Verma et al. 1995), and in this book we regard South Korea in the 21st century as a DME.

Kerr later modified his views, to take into account some of these criticisms. Kerr (1983) argues that convergence is a *tendency* that is not likely to precipitate identical systems among industrialised countries. He also notes that while DMEs at the macro level might appear to be similar, differences at the micro level could be quite profound. Further, industrialisation on a world scale is never likely to be total because the barriers to it in many less developed economies (LDEs) are insurmountable. Nevertheless, he still holds the central assumptions of the original study: namely, that the basic tensions inherent in the process of industrialisation had been overcome by modern industrial societies and that there would be a growing consensus around liberal-democratic institutions and the pluralist mixed economy. Relations between 'managers and the managed' would be increasingly embedded in a web of rules agreed to by both parties, so that industrial conflict would 'wither away' (Ross & Hartman 1960).

Late development

Ronald Dore makes an important contribution to the debate about convergence. Drawing on a comparison of Britain and Japan, he argues that while there may be a tendency towards convergence in national patterns of employment relations, the tendency is towards convergence on Japan and not the USA (the implicit model that underpinned Kerr et al.'s analysis). Dore places less emphasis on technology than Kerr et al., and highlights the importance of other factors: the emergence of giant corporations and the spread of democratic ideals of egalitarianism.

In examining Japanese industrial relations, Dore (1973) identifies a 'late-comer' effect. As Japan began to industrialise relatively late (a century after Britain), it was able to learn from the experience of the countries that had already been through that process. He argues that late developers had been able to adopt organisational forms and institutions better suited to industrialisation than those of countries that industrialised relatively early.

There have been general criticisms of Dore's thesis and specific criticisms of some of his detailed interpretation, including the narrow basis of his empirical research; however, his approach has considerable potential in this field: 'By concentrating on only two country cases and dealing with these cases in a consistently and systematically comparative fashion, Dore succeeded in minimising the danger of lapsing into either vacuous description or superficial comparison' (Shalev 1980: 40).

Dore concludes that employment arrangements are becoming more alike, then, but that Japan, rather than any Western country, is the model on which other countries are converging. Support for this argument can be found in the so-called 'Japanese management practices', which have been incorporated under the umbrella of 'world best practice' in management and work organisation.

Since the 1970s, as they adopted more globally oriented strategies, Japanese MNEs have increasingly been exporting their approaches to managing, for example, output, human resources, work organisation and industrial relations. Although these approaches have been strongly criticised (e.g. Parker & Slaughter 1988), business leaders tend to see them as successful, especially in the manufacturing sector, so that many non-Japanese enterprises have tried to emulate Japanese role models. This is illustrated in a best-selling book on the automobile industry, a study of 'Japan's revolutionary leap from mass production to lean production (i.e. approximately the Toyota Production System), and what industry everywhere can learn from it' (Womack et al. 1990; also see Fucini & Fucini 1990; Bamber et al. 1992). Yet a study of the application of the 'lean production' concept by car companies around the world indicates that this has not resulted in exact convergence or imitation. Instead, there are important variations reflecting differences in the strategies and power of the parties involved, as well as the effects of local institutional and cultural forces (Kochan et al. 1997). Hence, it may be more accurate to refer to 'Mediterranean' or 'Scandinavian' forms of lean production, which have certain characteristics in common but also reflect important local differences (Camuffo & Micelli 1997; Brulin & Nilsson 1997). Furthermore, not all car companies have chosen to adopt lean production in some (or all) of their locations, because its organisational and employment relations requirements may not be consistent with their managerial values and traditions.

TOWARDS DIVERGENCE?

During the 1980s a series of authors refuelled the earlier convergence debates and predicted divergence and dualism in national patterns of employment relations. Goldthorpe (1984) argues that in confronting macroeconomic problems, far from converging, DMEs have followed divergent paths. On the one hand, there are countries like Norway, Austria, Germany and Sweden (see chapters 8 and 9), where inequalities between capital and labour have been mitigated by corporatist state policies; these seek to balance, to an extent, the interests of employers, unions and the state. By contrast, in countries like Britain and the USA (see chapters 2 and 3), traditional labour market institutions (e.g. collective bargaining) have been undermined by market forces that have operated to overcome perceived rigidities. This has resulted in a tendency towards dualism, in which the workforce is separated into core and peripheral employees. The former may remain unionised and within the collective bargaining framework, albeit in a more decentralised mode, while the latter are employed under more individualistic work arrangements characterised by contractual forms of control.

Goldthorpe (1984) is pessimistic about the long-term likelihood that such corporatist and dualist structures could continue to coexist within the same society. Rather, the logical and political implications of each approach were so dramatically opposed to the other that this would lead to increasing tension between them, resulting in the ultimate dominance by one of another. In other words, any compromise would be unstable and ineffective in resolving macroeconomic problems. Either the corporatist system would triumph or the more market-based, dualistic industrial relations system would become the norm. However, different societies find their own solutions depending on social, economic and political pressures.

Similarly, Streeck (1988) identifies several factors that operate in most DMEs to induce structural change, but hold that these are leading to diverse outcomes or 'divergent evolutionary trajectories'. Streeck likens this situation to the growing variety in the use of technology and the structure of work organisation, whose present trend has been described as an 'explosion', with different strands of development moving away from each other in different directions, as opposed to 'implosive' convergence towards one central 'best practice'.

The changes in the structure of employment are exacerbating the loss of unions' power. These changes include: shifts in employment from the industrial to the service sector; the growth of a 'secondary sector' of small subcontracting firms and of a marginal workforce in unstable employment; increases in part-time work and white-collar jobs; the increasing participation of women in the labour market; the growing use of HRM techniques, including worker-involvement schemes; and other individually oriented approaches. Although these changes are widespread, they are likely to have very different consequences for employers, governments and unions, depending on their organisational base. Where union density is low, it is likely to decline further; where density is high, it is more likely to remain stable.

Union strategies for coping with structural changes are also likely to vary in accordance with their current situation. Heterogeneity is increasing not only between, but also within, national employment relations systems. A growing 'individualisation' within the workforce (which is promoted by many employers) is eroding the membership base of unions and resulting in three alternative responses: first, de-unionisation, with unions organising a smaller proportion of the labour force; second, the decomposition of the labour movement resulting from the fragmentation of many enterprises; third, the preservation of formal organisational unity at the national or sectoral level, but at the price of heightened internal policy conflict. Streeck warns that the ability of unions to manage internal heterogeneity (and thereby preserve a strategic continuity) will be put to a severe test in the coming years in all DMEs. To maintain even a modicum of centralised decision making, unions will require major organisation and institutional change. Hence, unions in many countries appear to be implementing significant innovations.

Freeman (1989) identifies evidence of divergent trends in union membership and density across developed market economies. He argues that 'far from converging to some modal type, trade unionism . . . traditionally the principal worker institution under capitalism developed remarkably differently among Western countries in the 1970s and 1980s'. Since the 1980s union density has risen or at least was maintained at high levels in the Scandinavian countries but declined significantly in the UK, Australia and the USA (see Appendix). This divergence in density occurred despite such common factors as increasing trade, technological transfer and capital flows between countries, which might have been expected to exert pressure for similarities.

CONVERGENCE AND DIVERGENCE RECONSIDERED

Several studies, then, suggest that divergence rather than convergence has been taking place. Questions of convergence and divergence in national patterns of employment relations were reconsidered in the 1990s by researchers associated with the strategic choice approach at MIT as well as by critical political economists.

Strategic choice and the MIT project

The MIT project involved employment relations scholars from a variety of countries to consider changes in employment relations across DMEs and within a range of industries (see Locke et al. 1995a). For the MIT project, Kerr et al. (1960) was a point of departure.[7]

The MIT project aimed to test the generalisability of arguments made about changes in US employment relations and production systems. Kochan, Katz and McKersie (1984) was one of its main precursors. This argues that changes in US industrial relations from the late 1970s amounted to a *transformation*, and that at the heart of this transformation was a fundamental change in the strategic choices made by US managers about firm-level employment relations practices. They argue that to be able to conceptualise this change it was necessary to add a *strategic choice* dimension to Dunlop's framework. They proposed a framework that differentiated between three levels of decision making (macro, industrial relations system and the workplace) and three parties (employers, unions and governments), and which identified the relatively independent effects of the levels on employment relations. They used a matrix to encompass the three levels of strategic decision making. As shown in Table 1.1, the columns of the matrix represent the three key parties that make strategic decisions. The rows represent three levels at which these decisions can be made. The effects of particular decisions, however, may appear at levels other than those where the decisions are made.

Table 1.1 Employment relations strategy matrix

Decision level	Nature of decisions		
	Employers	Unions	Government
I. Macro or global level for key institution	The strategic role of human resources; policies on unions; investments; plant location; new technology; and outsourcing	Political roles (e.g. relations with political parties and other interest groups); union organising (e.g. neutrality and corporate campaigns); public policy objectives (e.g. labour law reform); and economic policies (e.g. full employment)	Macroeconomic and social policies; industrial policy (protection vs free trade)
II. Employment relationship and industrial relations system	Personnel policies and negotiations and strategies	Collective bargaining policies and negotiations strategies (employment vs income)	Labour and employment standards law; direct involvement via incomes policies or dispute settlement
III. Workplace individuals and groups	Contractual or bureaucratic; and individual employee/workgroup participation	Policies on employee participation; introduction of new technology; work organisation design	Regulation of worker rights and/or employee participation

Source: Reproduced with permission from Kochan, McKersie and Cappelli (1984: 23).

The MIT project was developed in response to criticisms of the strategic choice framework and questions about the extent to which the transformation thesis could be generalised across countries and sectors (see e.g. Burton 1988; Lewin 1988; Chelius & Dworkin 1990). This research sought to understand the impact on employment relations of increasing international competition and of new production technologies. It focused, in particular, on the effects of different competitive strategies on firm-level employment strategies. Key questions driving the research included the following. Are changes in employment relations in DMEs being driven by differences in the competitive strategies of firms or by differences in national institutional arrangements and public policies? Which are the relevant actors driving this process and at what level of political economy and the industrial relations system do they interact? What role do national institutions play in an increasingly global economy? How do they interact with micro-level actors so as to shape and/or restrict the range of strategic choices of individual firms and unions? Perhaps the most challenging question raised by the research, however, is whether it still makes sense to try to conceptualise distinct national systems of industrial relations when there appears to be almost as much variation in employment relations practices within countries as between them (Locke et al. 1995b).

The research project developed in two stages. The first stage involved identifying developments in the various countries and comparing them (see Locke et al. 1995a; Kitay & Lansbury 1997). The second phase involved examining employment relations within specific industries in these countries, including automobiles, banking, electronics, steel and telecommunications (e.g. Katz 1997a; Kochan et al. 1997; Regini et al. 2000). The analytical framework guiding the research is summarised in Table 1.1. At the core of the framework are four important firm-level employment practices:

1. changes in work organisation due to the introduction of new technologies and the adoption of new competitive strategies (e.g. decentralisation or team systems); linked to these changes are new work rules and patterns of employee participation within the firm;
2. changing patterns of skills acquisition and training to match the needs of firms; this takes account of the shifting balance between the public and private provision of education and training;
3. new compensation or remuneration systems that affect all employees in the firm;

4. staffing, employment security and recruitment, which affect the way in which firms adjust their workforce when faced with cyclical or long-term structural changes in demand for their output.

The framework used to explain variations in these employment practices includes two competing hypotheses for the degree of transformation in employment relations. One hypothesis stresses the importance of institutional structures (at the national, industry and firm levels) that limit the discretion of firms and other actors in employment relations. The alternative hypothesis emphasises the range of strategic choices available to firms and pressures associated with international competition and technological changes. In each country and for each industry, data are analysed to compare the explanatory power of these two hypotheses in relation to contemporary workplace developments.

The industry studies, while suggesting that there was evidence of changing employment practices within industries and across countries, also highlighted the continued importance of national-level institutional frameworks (see Kochan et al. 1997; Katz 1997a; Regini et al. 2000). Katz (1997a: 11–23), for example, in summarising the findings of research on the telecommunications industry in ten countries, argues that there are broad similarities across countries in relation to employment security, work organisation, training, compensation and governance. Yet there also remain important national differences.

The findings of the MIT project suggest at least four emerging trends in employment relations. First, the enterprise emerges as an increasingly important locus for strategy and decision making on employment relations. Management is generally the driving force for change, albeit sometimes in collaboration with unions or works councils. Second, decentralisation of firm-level structures is accompanied by the search for greater flexibility in work organisation and the deployment of labour. Third, many firms and governments in most countries appear to be increasing their investment in training and skills development, which is often associated with a trend towards skills-related pay systems. Fourth, unions are experiencing major challenges in most countries as the pace of restructuring intensifies, the workplace becomes more diverse and the average size of enterprises decreases (see Katz & Darbishire 2000).

Three types of tension are observed in patterns of adjustment to changing patterns of employment relations. First, in all the countries studied, cost-cutting and high-value-added competitive strategies coexist uneasily. Second, the drive for increased flexibility in work organisation and related employment practices has the potential for polarisation between workers with access to jobs and those without. Third, while unions in many countries are experiencing declining influence and membership, arguably there is a growing need for a stronger employee voice in corporate decision making as well as in industry-level interactions, and national policy making is growing. Yet there is little evidence that HR issues are attracting much greater attention in corporate decision making. A simple reconstruction of union membership and power along traditional lines appears unlikely in the foreseeable future, although new forms and approaches to employee representation might emerge.

Converging divergences

Building on the MIT project, Katz and Darbishire (2000) examined two industries (car manufacturing and telecommunications) in six countries. They concluded that there was increased diversity of employment patterns across the countries studied. They called this 'converging on divergence', and argued that it was characterised by the spread of four employment patterns: low wage, HRM, Japanese-oriented, and joint team-based (see Table 1.2). However, they note differences in the distribution of these patterns at the national level as well as in the extent of variation within countries. They attribute these variations to differences in national-level institutions. In particular, they argue that differences in employment patterns reflected the differential impact of national-level institutions on the degree of centralisation of bargaining, the extent of commonality of processes at a decentralised level and the degree of effective coordination between decentralised bargaining structures. Thus, Katz and Darbishire conclude that, despite evidence of divergence, 'the persistence of sizeable country differences in the relative mix of various employment patterns, and the role that national level institutions play in shaping that mix, suggest a continuing influential role for national employment-related institutions' (2000: 281).

There are criticisms of the converging divergences concept. Some authors suggest that the empirical evidence does not support the claim that four employment patterns are spreading across all six countries (Giles 2000c: 476; Hancke 2001: 306; Streeck 2001), and it is also suggested that these employment patterns are not mutually exclusive (de la Graza 2001; Wailes 2000b). More importantly, the Katz and Darbishire argument demonstrates the limits of the concepts of convergence and divergence in capturing the complexity of contemporary

Table 1.2 Emerging patterns of workplace practices

Low wage	HRM	Japanese-oriented	Joint team-based
Managerial discretion with informal procedures	Corporate culture and extensive communication	Standardised procedures	Joint decision making
Hierarchical work relations	Directed teams	Problem-solving teams	Semi-autonomous work groups
Low wages with piece rates	Above-average wages with contingent pay	High pay linked to seniority and performance appraisals	High pay with pay for knowledge
High turnover	Individualised career development	Employment stabilisation	Career development
Strong anti-union animus	Union substitution	Enterprise unionism	Union and employee involvement

Source: Adapted from Katz and Darbishire (2000): 17.

changes in employment relations. For example, the convergence criteria that Katz and Darbishire establish are so broad that it would be possible to conclude that the USA and Sweden have experienced similar changes in employment relations during the 1980s and 1990s. The consequence is that important differences between the cases (which can be seen by comparing chapters 3 and 9) are obscured (see Wailes 2000b: 542–3).

This criticism can be applied more generally. While the work associated with the MIT project demonstrates the need for more research focusing on the workplace and at industry level, it also demonstrates the continuing influence of Kerr et al.'s original convergence hypothesis on comparative employment relations scholarship. Since Kerr et al. (1960)'s work, comparative assessments of change in employment relations have tended to look for evidence of either convergence or divergence. However, too little attention has been devoted to exactly what convergence is and how it can be measured. As Seelinger (1996: 287) notes:

> Considering the convergence hypothesis' increasing prominence in the literature, it is surprising that much more space and thought has been devoted to the presentation of 'results' than to the rigorous conceptualisation of hypotheses, the design of appropriate research strategies, and the discussion of its potential to advance our general understanding of comparative public policy . . . Advancement of convergence research has been hampered by the vagueness of its underlying concepts, particularly the concept of similarity . . . Calling objects similar and in its consequence the determination of convergence, is no more than a subjective opinion about the magnitude of their differences.

Whether comparative analysis produces evidence of convergence or divergence may be most dramatically affected by the choice of dependent variable. Studies that focus on measures like wage inequality may find evidence of convergence, while studies that focus on participation rights between countries may find evidence of divergence. At the very least this suggests a need to be explicit about what would constitute convergence or divergence.[8] It may also suggest that the concepts of convergence and divergence are too limiting to capture all the nuances of the relationship between globalisation and national patterns of employment relations.

A CRITICAL POLITICAL ECONOMY PERSPECTIVE

The preceding review of controversies about convergence in comparative employment relations suggests that there may be some limitations to examining the impact of globalisation on national patterns of employment relations in a 'liberal-pluralist' framework. Critiques of such perspectives argue that the orthodox approaches are parochial and generally ignore the world outside a narrow definition of industrial relations (e.g. Mills 1959; Mandel 1969). They hold that, at most, the wider society is included in the pluralists' models only through narrowly circumscribed channels of 'adjustment' and 'feedback' (Hyman 1980).

Giles (2000a: 174–6) maintains that, because of this liberal-pluralist perspective, most industrial relations scholars have tended to treat globalisation as external to employment relations in two senses. First, he suggests that, because industrial relations scholars tend to 'draw a thick line around industrial relations', globalisation is treated as an external shock on otherwise stable national patterns of employment relations. Second, he suggests that globalisation is treated as external to employment relations, because comparative employment relations focuses overwhelmingly on the national sphere and largely ignores the impact of the international dimension. For this reason it can be argued that mainstream employment relations scholarship has been largely trapped in attempting to assess the relative convergence or divergence of aspects of employment relations patterns produced by globalisation.

As Giles (2000a) notes, there is another intellectual tradition in employment relations scholarship, which can potentially overcome these limitations and provide the basis for greater insight into the factors that mediate the relationship between international economic change and national patterns of employment relations. This is the critical political economy tradition. Giles and Murray (1997: 81–5) summarise the contributions of critical political economy to employment relations. These include defining the field as the study of the 'social relations in production'; adopting a view of the employment relationship as one of 'structured antagonism'; and regarding 'mechanisms such as collective bargaining . . . as institutionalized compromises between workers and employers' which may be affected by changes in the balance of power between them. They also argue that a key difference between the liberal-pluralist tradition and critical political economy is the way in which issues like globalisation are conceptualised (Giles & Murray 1997: 85):

> where mainstream researchers see a series of exogenous changes, politi-
> cal economists see patterns rooted in the dynamics of international and
> national social structures of production and accumulation; where the
> mainstream sees such changes as having an 'impact on' industrial rela-
> tions, political economy sees changing workplace relations as a central
> part of these patterns.

This suggests that changes in the international economy, associated with globalisation, need to be integrated into the analysis of national patterns of employment relations. However, while the critical political economy tradition offers a range of conceptual tools that would potentially provide insight into the relationship between globalisation and national patterns of employment relations, in many ways it has failed to live up to its promise. Such authors as Hyman (1980: 127–8) and Giles and Murray (1997: 100–1) suggest that this reflects the difficulty of integrating the different levels of analysis required of such an approach into a single framework.

This problem is particularly acute when it comes to integrating the international dimension into the analysis. Although most critical political economists would see international economic changes as of direct relevance to the domestic institutions of industrial relations, there have been few identifiably political economy attempts to examine the relationship between globalisation and industrial relations on a comparative or international basis.[9] Haworth and Hughes argue that political economy in employment relations simply replaced the overemphasis on institutions in the industrial relations orthodoxy with concern about control over work relations. As a result, they suggest that (Haworth & Hughes 2000: 200):

> the critical perspective was still firmly located in the enterprise, sectoral
> or national environments and its power relationships. Where opportu
> nities arose for engagement between radical industrial relations theory
> and international analysis . . . they were generally underdeveloped.

Murray et al. (2000) provide one example of how a critical political economy approach can be operationalised to provide insight into the relationship between globalisation and employment relations. Murray et al. argue that three vignettes illustrate that, rather than *deregulation*, there is a *re-regulation* of employment relationship taking place in

Canada in the context of an increasingly globalised economy. The first vignette recounts changes in the local collective agreement introduced at a car plant faced with competition from US plants and the threat of closure. The second vignette notes the increasing trend in Quebec during the 1990s towards long-term collective agreements—in one case up to eighteen years—in which new investment is tied to agreement by the union to joint resolution and no use of the strike weapon when renegotiating the contract. The third vignette notes the reduction of and in some cases abolition of awards extending collective bargaining conditions across entire industries in Quebec in the second half of the 1990s in the name of international competitiveness. For Murray et al. to understand the nature of the re-regulation of labour taking place, it is important to focus on how globalisation either alters or accentuates the following key relationships: the indeterminacy of the employment relationship; the uncertainty and contingency faced by the organisation; the power, scope for agency and level of interdependence of actors; and the interconnectedness of different sources of regulation.

While Murray et al.'s study focuses on Canada, these four key relationships could be used as a framework for international comparisons between cases. To this extent, their analysis illustrates that by working with critical political economy concepts it is possible to go beyond establishing whether the dominant trend in national patterns of employment relations is convergence or divergence. Rather, a critical political economy perspective makes it possible to specify a range of factors, including international economic change and historical and institutional traditions, which are likely to shape national patterns of employment relations.

HOW DOES GLOBALISATION INFLUENCE NATIONAL PATTERNS OF EMPLOYMENT RELATIONS?

We classify various perspectives on this issue in the literature into three categories: a *simple globalisation* approach, an *institutionalist* approach, and an *integrated* approach.

Simple globalisation approach

The *simple globalisation approach* assumes that international economic activity has become so interconnected and that the pressures associated with globalisation are so overwhelming that they leave little scope for national differences in patterns of employment relations. In many ways, it is this perspective which has dominated popular debate about the effects of contemporary changes in the international economy on working conditions and the relations between workers and their employers. In an extreme form, this approach predicts a 'race to the bottom' in terms of wages and other labour standards across most economies and the erosion of nationally specific labour market regimes, including those which may provide for union security or encourage the pursuit of equity as well as efficiency.

Tilly (1995) contends that globalisation threatens established labour rights because it undermines the capacity of the nation-state to guarantee these rights. The whole range of workers' rights that have developed over the past century have been heavily dependent on the state's capacity and propensity to discipline capital. Tilly argues that the re-establishment of labour rights depends on unions' ability to develop transnational strategies to counter the effects of globalisation, but doubts the likelihood of such a development.

Similarly, Campbell (1996) notes that increased economic interconnectedness may erode the market power of organised labour because of the increased ability of firms to move production from one country to another. Campbell refers to this as a 'shallow' effect of globalisation, which is related to increases in trade openness. By contrast, 'deep' effects on employment relations are associated with the interplay between the increased potential mobility of productive capital and the hypermobility of short-run speculative capital. The interaction of these factors may place limits on the ability of the nation-state to pursue, or even maintain, nationally specific employment relations policies because they reduce the power of nation-states over capital and make the state more dependent on private economic activity for macroeconomic performance. This may have significant implications for the diversity of employment relations institutions and outcomes across national economies, irrespective of the relative market power of organised labour. Although Campbell raises caveats, his broad conclusion is that, because of these pressures, there is likely to be a convergence of national labour standards due to the loss of national policy autonomy associated with such globalisation effects.

The simple globalisation approach, and particularly the view that globalisation has eroded national policy autonomy, has been widely criticised. Garrett (1998), for example, argues that just because national governments are faced with similar economic pressures, it does not follow that they have no choice over how to respond to these pressures. He supports this argument with evidence to show that there is considerable diversity in monetary and fiscal policy setting across countries. As the chapters in this book demonstrate, there is also considerable diversity in national patterns of employment relations. In line with arguments put forward by Evans (1997) and Weiss (1998), Garrett notes that there is evidence to suggest that the pressures associated with globalisation may increase the role the nation-state needs to play in some areas, including the labour market, to ensure the maintenance of international competitiveness.

Institutionalist approach

Criticisms of the simple globalisation approach and evidence of continued diversity in national patterns of employment relations have contributed to the development of the *institutionalist approach*—a second perspective on the impact of globalisation on employment relations. The institutionalist approach suggests that differences in national-level institutions are likely to refract common economic pressures in different ways. As Locke and Thelen (1995) put it, according to this view, 'international trends are not in fact translated into common pressures in all national economies but rather are mediated by national institutional arrangements and refracted into divergent struggles over particular national practices' (1995: 338). Because differences in national-level institutions are relatively enduring, this approach suggests that globalisation is unlikely to lead to a general convergence in national patterns of employment relations (Locke et al. 1995b). Rather, it predicts continuity and even increased divergence between national patterns of employment relations. This approach draws on arguments from a variety of disciplines about the independent role institutions play in shaping economic and political outcomes.[10]

Examples of the institutionalist approach in the industrial relations literature are studies by Turner (1991) and Thelen (1993) of German industrial relations in a comparative framework. Both argue that the 'dual system' of industrial relations in Germany has enabled German unions to withstand the pressures of globalisation better than their counterparts in the USA and Sweden. Turner (1991) compares the involvement of unions in industrial restructuring in Germany and the USA and places heavy emphasis on the role that differences in institutionalist arrangements have played in determining the reaction of employers and workers to international economic pressures. Similarly, according to Thelen (1993), the German system, with national- and industry-level bargaining plus separate legally enshrined rights for workers at the workplace level, has allowed pressures for decentralised bargaining to be accommodated within the existing institutional configuration. In Sweden, by contrast, the absence of institutionalised rights for workers at the workplace, and the divisions created between blue-collar and white-collar workers by the centralised bargaining system, has meant that pressures for decentralised bargaining could not be accommodated within the existing structure of bargaining.

The importance of differences in national-level institutions for explaining differences in patterns of employment relations is also emphasised by Ferner and Hyman (1998), in their comparative European studies. In particular, they point to the re-emergence of 'societal corporatism' in some European economies during the 1990s as evidence that 'states possess a key role in the reconfiguration of the relations between social regulation and markets (including labour markets)' (Ferner & Hyman 1998: xxi). They also develop the notion that some forms of labour market institutions can adapt to international economic changes better than others. Further support for the institutionalist perspective on globalisation and industrial relations is provided in an empirical study by Traxler et al. (2001), who argue that divergence is likely because 'market pressures affect labour relations institutions indirectly, in that they are processed and filtered by institutions' (2001: 289).

The institutionalist approach represents a useful corrective to the simple globalisation model. The focus on the mediating role of institutions helps to explain patterns of persistent national differences, and demonstrates that the relationship between globalisation and national employment relations is neither simple nor deterministic. It also points to key variables that play a decisive role in determining distinctive national patterns of industrial relations, many of which may be national in character. In particular, it suggests that to understand the impact of globalisation on employment relations in the ten DMEs which are the focus of this book, it is important to know many of the specific details outlined in the national chapters that follow.

However, while the institutionalist approach provides a correction to the convergence logic of the simple globalisation thesis, it has difficulty explaining similarities between cases. As a result, assessments of the impact of globalisation on employment relations tend to get caught in establishing the extent to which there is *convergence* or *divergence* in national patterns of employment relations.

Integrated approach

A third perspective on the relationship between globalisation and national patterns of employment relations is an *integrated approach*. While less developed than the other two approaches, an integrated approach draws on the insight provided by the globalisation and institutionalist views, and offers the possibility of explaining similarities and differences in national patterns of employment relations within the same analytical framework.[11] This approach is drawn from the political economy tradition, and stresses the importance of the interaction between interests and institutions in the context of international economic change.

Wailes et al. (2003) compare the impact of changes in the international economy on industrial relations policy in Australia and New Zealand during the 1980s and 1990s. Comparisons of policy developments in the two countries that focus entirely on the importance of institutional differences between the cases have tended to ignore small but important historical differences between them; have exaggerated the differences in policy outcomes in the two countries; and have been largely unable to explain recent developments in the two countries.[12] While acknowledging that institutional factors are important, it is necessary to take into account the similarities and differences between the countries and to examine the coalition of interests (consisting of elements of both capital and labour) that underpin the institutional arrangements in the labour markets of the two countries.

This approach can also help explain how these interests have been influenced by changes in the international economy. To do this it is necessary to develop a clear understanding of the ways in which the countries being compared are integrated into the international economy, and potential differences in the configuration of material interests that developed as a result. An explanation of the impact of globalisation on national patterns of employment relations needs to take into account not just the independent role that institutional factors may play in shaping political and economic decisions but also the role that the DME nation-states play in shaping relationships between employers, unions and employees in seeking to ensure economic growth and development.[13]

While there are difficulties associated with undertaking internationally comparative industrial relations research, it provides an ideal framework within which to analyse the impact of globalisation on national patterns of employment relations. Thus, if the simple globalisation approach provides an accurate description of the relationship between changes in the international economy and national patterns of industrial relations, we would expect to see evidence of common changes across a range of countries despite historical and institutional differences between them. Similarly, if the institutionalist approach tends to hold sway, we would expect to find evidence of persistent differences in patterns of national employment relations despite similar external economic pressures. However, evidence of a more complex pattern of similarity and difference across countries may suggest that an integrated approach provides a better explanation of how globalisation affects national patterns of employment relations. Thus a comparison of national cases and contexts makes it possible to examine competing accounts of the impact of globalisation on national patterns of employment relations.

CONCLUSION

This chapter has provided an introduction to ways in which international and comparative analysis can be used to examine how national employment relations are affected by globalisation. It has also been argued that an international and comparative approach, because it makes it possible to separate out the general from the specific, provides an excellent context within which to test these competing approaches. Nevertheless, there are practical and technical difficulties associated with international and comparative analysis, such as differences between countries in the way strikes are measured. This chapter has reviewed such challenges and suggested some of the ways they might be met.

This chapter has reviewed some of the conceptual tools that have been developed in debates about comparative employment relations and assessed their usefulness for examining the relationship between globalisation and national employment relations. While questions were raised about the assumptions on which it is based, as an organising device it is useful to base comparison between countries on information about the nature of the bargaining system; the organisation of workers, and their representatives, and employers, and their representatives; and the role that each of these and the state play in determining employment relations outcomes.

It has also reviewed debates about convergence and divergence, which have to some extent been reassessed by those examining the impact of globalisation on employment relations. While these debates identify variables that should be considered in comparative analysis, the convergence–divergence dichotomy and the 'liberal-pluralist' perspective within which they have taken place may be too limited to capture the range of factors that influence how national employment relations are affected by globalisation. A critical political economy perspective, which treats employment relations as a reflection of the broader political economy, may offer a better basis for examining national patterns of employment relations in the context of globalisation. Hence this chapter has identified three broad approaches to this issue in the existing literature—a *simple globalisation* approach, an *institutionalist* approach and an *integrated* approach—and pointed out that each of these approaches anticipates different outcomes in terms of national patterns of employment relations.

The national chapters that follow include an historical background on the development of the pattern of bargaining; information on how employees, and their unions, and employers, and their associations, are organised and interact; as well as information about the role of the state. Furthermore, each of the chapters contains information about changes in bargaining patterns. The Appendix provides useful comparative statistics, which complement each national chapter.

Chapter 2

EMPLOYMENT RELATIONS IN BRITAIN*

Mick Marchington, John Goodman and John Berridge

The United Kingdom[1] has a total population of 59 million people and a labour force participation rate of 74 per cent. While the participation rate for women continues to rise, the rate for men dropped markedly over the decade 1985–95. (Such statistical data cited in each chapter are elaborated and discussed in more detail in the Appendix.) The UK has fewer people employed in agriculture (2 per cent of civilian employees) than any other Organisation for Economic Cooperation and Development (OECD) country. About 27 per cent of its other civilian employees work in industry; the remaining 70 per cent work in services (according to OECD definitions). There has been a greater decline in its 'industry' category since 1970 than in any other OECD country. In spite of the relative growth of services, there was a steep rise in unemployment, from 1.2 per cent of the working population in 1965 to nearly 12 per cent by 1986, by which time the UK had a higher unemployment rate than any of the other countries discussed in this book. The unemployment benefits claimant rate, much redefined, fell in the late 1980s but rose again in the early 1990s, before subsequently falling to around 7 per cent in the late 1990s. In terms of gross domestic product (GDP) per capita—an approximate indicator of labour output—the UK ranks in the lower half of the ten countries (see Appendix). The rate of infla-

*This is a revised version of the chapter that was co-authored by Greg Bamber and Ed Snape in earlier editions of the book.

tion declined during the 1990s, with the UK rate being around the average for the ten countries during the 1990–96 period.

British politics has been dominated by two parties since 1945. The Conservative Party's support is strongest among the business and rural communities. In the general election of 2001, it had just one MP elected in Scotland and Wales. By contrast, the Labour Party's support is traditionally strongest in urban working-class communities, though this has broadened. A significant but reducing proportion of its funds still comes from affiliated trade unions. There are several other political parties, including the Liberal Democrats and nationalist parties in Scotland and Wales, all of which increased their representation in recent years. Increased devolution of powers to Scotland, Wales and Northern Ireland modified certain provisions in these countries.

There has been much change in employment and industrial relations in Britain over the past two decades. Successive Conservative governments over the period 1979–97 set the tone, with their radical step-by-step reform of industrial relations law, labour market deregulation and attempts to foster a competitive 'enterprise culture'. Labour governments since 1997 have continued to promote increased private-sector involvement in the public sector through a variety of initiatives, with potentially significant implications for employment relations.

After the postwar period of general labour scarcity, employers cut workforces, often substantially, and union membership has fallen by about 40 per cent since 1979. If there has been a single dominant thrust in employer strategies and policies in what is a diverse picture, it might be summarised as the promotion of the decentralisation and individualisation of the employment relationship, aimed at increasing flexibility but often also bringing perceived (and actual) job insecurity. 'Individualisation' has been pursued, for example through individual performance-related pay, and a managerially initiated employee involvement (EI) and other techniques (Cully et al. 1999). These are targeted at winning employee commitment to organisational goals, and at trying to redefine adversarial 'them and us' attitudes towards a more unitarist perspective. There has been growth in temporary and part-time work, a clearer distinction between the treatment of core and peripheral workers in some organisations, and an increasing incidence of multi-organisational arrangements through outsourcing, partnerships, franchises and alliances (Colling 2000; Rubery et al. 2002). There is little doubt that the landscape of British employment relations has changed substantially since 1979, although the WERS

37

(Workplace Employee Relations Survey) panel data show that this has been much less pronounced in 'older, continuing' than in new workplaces.

THE INDUSTRIAL RELATIONS PARTIES

Unions

Britain was the cradle of industrialisation, with the 'industrial revolution' taking place long before adult electoral suffrage. Workers were seen as 'hands', as expendable resources for whom the employer had no responsibility beyond the minimal legal obligations of contract (Fox 1985). The law and reality of master and servant was deeply embedded.

Many present unions can trace their roots back to this mid-19th century period or earlier, the earliest enduring unions being formed by skilled craftsmen. Widespread unionisation of semiskilled and unskilled manual workers began in the late 19th century, while relatively few white-collar workers joined unions until after World War II. British unions could be classified as craft, general, industrial or white-collar, but this categorisation was only approximate and has become blurred as unions have merged and/or broadened their membership. It is more useful to see unions as either 'closed' or 'open', according to whether or not they restrict recruitment to particular industries, sectors or occupational categories (Turner 1962). Although there were 1384 UK unions recorded in 1920, by 2002, mainly due to mergers, there were only 199. Union membership is highly concentrated, with the 22 unions with over 50 000 members accounting for 87 per cent of the total membership (*Labour Market Trends*, July 2000) (see Table 2.1).

Multiple unionism has diminished markedly. According to the WERS[2] in 1998, 55 per cent of workplaces employing 25 or more employees did not recognise unions. Of those that did, the largest proportion (43 per cent) recognised only a single union, with only 23 per cent recognising more than three (Cully et al. 1999: 91).

The level and density of union membership has fluctuated since World War II. Bain and Price (1983) identified three broad postwar phases. First, between 1948 and 1968 membership grew, from 9.3 million to 10.2 million, but lagged behind employment growth. This led to a 15-year union density plateau at around 43 per cent. Second, membership grew markedly in the 1970s as (particularly white-collar) workers were attracted into unions, in part by the 'threat' effect of rapidly rising prices and the 'credit' effect of big pay rises in a period of high inflation. Membership grew from 10.2 million in 1968 to an all-time peak of 13.4 million in 1979, when density also reached a record high of 55 per cent.

The beginning of the third phase in 1979 coincided with the election of a radical Conservative government led by Margaret Thatcher, an accelerated decline in manufacturing employment (falling to less than 20 per cent of overall employment), and the onset of the deepest postwar economic recession in the early 1980s. The sharp rise in unemployment contributed to reduced union membership. However, union membership continued to decline in periods of employment growth, largely because many new jobs were part-time or atypical, and were concentrated in private-sector services where unions had long found it difficult to recruit. Union density declined continuously during the 1980s and 1990s, as in most OECD countries. Between 1979 and 1997 union membership fell by well over 40 per cent (6.2 million) to 7.15 million, and density from 55 per cent to around 29 per cent. Structural and labour force compositional changes, such as the decline in manual work, manufacturing, public sector employment and large workplaces, plus the rise in service-sector employment, part-time work and self-employment, were important factors in the reduction (Green 1992), although they were not the only influences (Waddington & Whitson 1997). It remains open to conjecture whether a fourth phase began in 1997, following the election of the Labour government, with its different reform agenda in industrial relations and labour markets. Perhaps significantly, the eighteen-year continuous decline in union membership halted in 1998, and 1999 and 2000 both witnessed small rises. Small declines followed, but in 2002 trade union membership was 178 000 higher than in 1997 (*Labour Market Trends*, July 2002).

There are marked variations in union density. Non-manual workers have constituted an increasing proportion of total union membership, and are now as likely to be unionised as manual staff.[3] According to the 1999 Labour Force Survey (*Labour Market Trends*, July 2000) union density is higher among men (31 per cent) than women (about 28 per cent), and among full-time workers (33 per cent) than part-timers (20 per cent). Private-sector services have lower union density, for example, only 12 per cent in retailing and 6 per cent in hotels and restaurants, compared with 28 per cent in manufacturing. There is also a wide differential in union density between the public sector (60 per cent) and the private sector (19 per cent). The four WERS-type surveys show that the number of workplaces that recognised union(s) for collective bargaining declined from 66 per cent in 1984 to 53 per cent in 1990 and 45 per cent in 1998. However, union recognition (for collective bargaining) was more common at larger workplaces, such that 62 per cent of employees worked in workplaces with union recognition. Again there is a disparity between public and private sectors, with union recognition at 95 per cent of public-sector but only 25 per cent of private-sector workplaces (Cully et al. 1999: 92).

Unlike most other Western European countries, Britain has only one main union confederation—the Trades Union Congress (TUC), established in 1868. In 2000, 75 unions representing around 85 per cent of British union members were affiliated with the TUC. In contrast with its counterparts in many other countries, the TUC has no direct role in collective bargaining. The TUC's primary role has been to lobby governments, and in recent decades also the EU. During and after World War II the TUC's political influence grew, and it participated in many tripartite bodies and quasi-governmental agencies (Goodman 1994), a role that peaked under the 1974–79 Labour government. The TUC has also long played an important role in regulating inter-union relations. However, membership decline among affiliates after 1979 reduced TUC income, necessitating cost-cutting. The TUC's exclusion from the 'corridors of power' during the 1979–97 Conservative governments reduced its lobbying effectiveness with government to a lower level than it had experienced since the 1930s. This major turnaround induced debates about TUC policy; these debates were fuelled by successive election defeats for the Labour Party. In the 1990s there was an emphasis on 'partnership', i.e. building constructive partnerships with 'good' employers. This displaced the traditionally more adversarial orientation; adoption of a more continental European-style approach, pressing for broader statutory rights for *all* employees (including non-unionised), ousted the old voluntarist philosophy. These changes and other adaptations to new realities were associated with the relaunch of the TUC in 1994 as a more 'encompassing', more widely networking organisation, with a campaigning approach to 'world of work' issues relevant to all workers. The TUC sought to promote more effective recruitment strategies and set up an Organising Academy to train a new generation of union organisers (Heery 1998). The priority of recruiting new members led some unions to focus on broader services to individual members, and to adopt models closer to customer 'servicing' than to the traditonal

Table 2.1 The largest British unions

	Membership (000s)		% change 1980–2000	Summary description
	1980	**2000**		
UNISON[a,b]	1697	1272	−25	Public services; white-collar and manual
Transport and General Workers' Union	1887	872	−54	General/open; has white-collar section
Amicus—Amalgamated Engineering and Electrical Union[a]	1690	727	−57	Ex-craft; now fairly open
GMB (General, Municipal & Boilermakers' Union)[a]	1180	694	−41	General/open; has white-collar section
Manufacturing Science and Finance Union[a]	683	405	+41	White-collar, technicians and supervisors
Royal College of Nursing	181	327	+81	Professional union; largest union not in TUC
Union of Shop Distributive and Allied Workers	450	310	−31	Based in retailing, but wider
National Union of Teachers	273	295	+8	School teachers
Communication Workers Union[a,c]	334	281	−16	The 'industry' union for communications
Public and Commercial Services Union[d]	—	259	—	Civil servants/exec. agency staff
National Assoc. of School Masters & Union of Women Teachers[a]	156	252	+62	School teachers
Graphical Paper and Media Union	286	201	−30	Ex-craft, printing/paper industries
Association of Teachers and Lecturers	90	183	+103	School and some college teachers

a The 1980 membership figures for these unions have been adjusted to take account of amalgamations.

b Formed by the merger in July 1993 of three of the largest unions, namely the National and Local Government Officers' Association, the National Union of Public Employees, and the Confederation of Health Service Employees.

c Formed by the merger of the Union of Communication Workers and the National Communication Union in 1995.

d Formed by the merger of civil service unions.

Source: Calculated from Annual Reports of the Certification Office (1980–2000).

fraternalist ideals and collective consciousness (Salamon 2000). The return of Labour in 1997 presaged a more fruitful role for the TUC as a social partner with government, though this has proven much less close than under previous Labour governments, despite the moderate, 'modernised' stance the TUC adopted.

The unions were instrumental in the establishment of the Labour Party in 1906. This was seen as a necessary complement to the industrial activities of the unions, particularly after a series of adverse legal judgments meant that new legislation was required to re-establish union rights. Individual unions may affiliate to the Labour Party, contributing to its funds through a 'political levy' on members, from which individuals may 'opt out' if they wish. Since the mid-1980s, the Labour Party leadership has increasingly distanced the party from the unions, and their voting power at its policy-making annual conference has been reduced.

Most British unions have lost their militancy, in both rhetoric and action, and strikes are at record lows. Despite changes in both methods and emphasis, most unions are still perceived as being collectively oriented in an age of enhanced individualism, and as associations aiming to protect producers in an age of consumerism. Although the value of an independent and influential employee voice may be accepted by some employers, in practice unions continue to face difficulties in establishing their cost-effectiveness relative to other (sometimes more managerially favoured) systems of employee representation.

EMPLOYERS, ORGANISATIONS AND EMPLOYMENT PRACTICES

The Confederation of British Industry (CBI), formed in 1965, is the peak employer body in Britain. It is an important lobbyist in relation to the British government and EU agencies but, like the TUC, it does not participate in collective bargaining. During the 1980s the smaller Institute of Directors[4] grew in influence, being closer in ideological terms to the Thatcher and Major governments.

Historically, associations of employers played an important part in shaping the British voluntarist system of industrial relations (Gospel & Littler 1983). Initially at local level and then (more importantly) at national level, they acted as representatives for employers in each industry, reaching agreements with unions over recognition, disputes procedures and the substantive terms and conditions across member companies. They offered forms of mutual defence against union campaigns and to some extent took wages 'out of competition' among British employers competing in the same product market. Multi-employer, industry-level collective bargaining meant the numerous industry employers' associations were crucial actors in the 'formal system of industrial relations' (Donovan 1968).

There were many signs in the 1950s and 1960s that the agreements to which employers' associations were signatories were losing their regulatory effectiveness. The growth of workplace-based incentive payment and job evaluation systems, the escalation of overtime working, and the broadened scope of joint regulation into what were notionally areas of management prerogative, were led by workplace-based union shop stewards.[5] Between 1980 and 1990 private-sector firms' membership of employers' associations fell steeply, from 29 to 13 per cent (Millward et al. 1992), before rising slightly in the 1990s (Cully et al. 1999: 228). Although there are some exceptions, employers' associations have moved to the periphery of industrial relations, offering legal, advisory, training and other services, and are generally shadows of their former selves. Some have been wound up.

The steep rise in unemployment in the early 1980s, combined with sharper international competition in product markets and reductions in unionism, has greatly enhanced employer power and freedom of action. While employer objectives in the labour field continue to focus on control, productivity improvement and cost reduction, the mix of strategies and balance of methods is diverse. Many could be described as using pragmatic/opportunist (see Purcell & Sisson 1983) management styles.

Managements have sought more flexibility and employee commitment, with many developing direct employee communications arrangements, teamworking and other techniques associated with human resource management (HRM), and unilaterally introducing performance-related elements into pay, sometimes linked with individual performance appraisals. In certain sectors, notably financial services, major employers have undertaken collective bargaining with staff associations and in-house unions. However, many of these have subsequently merged with wider unions, so are different from the in-house unions seen elsewhere. Experience of redundancy has been widespread, and self-employment, part-time, limited-term and casual employment contracts have expanded in a relatively deregulated labour market. There has been a growth in direct investment in manufacturing and financial services by American, European, Japanese and other East

Asian companies. Given their association with earlier international competitive success, the employment practices of such multinational enterprises (MNEs) have had a significant influence on the policies of indigenous British firms (Grant 1997).

Almost one-third of workplaces have a personnel specialist at workplace level, and more than three-quarters have access to a specialist at a level above the workplace (Cully et al. 1999: 51). Not surprisingly, the likelihood of a personnel presence at workplace level is greater in larger workplaces and organisations. More than 60 per cent of organisations have a personnel presence on the board of directors (Cully et al. 1999: 225), though successive WERS reports show a slight reduction since 1980 in the proportion of private-sector organisations having a personnel director. Personnel representation on the board has become more extensive in large organisations and especially those that recognise unions (Millward et al. 2000: 77). Individual membership of the professional body (Chartered Institute of Personnel and Development) has risen fivefold since the early 1980s to more than 100 000.

Nevertheless, there is a threat to the future of the personnel function, both from line managers and from specialist consultancy firms. In many enterprises, line managers undertake a greater range of human resource activities, and this has led in some cases to the break-up of the specialist internal function (Hall & Torrington 1998; Gratton et al. 1999). This has occurred through outsourcing and shared service operations. The fragmentation of management support for employment relations is likely to accelerate as employers face sustained pressure to cut costs and focus on their core business.

The principal employee relations responsibilities of specialist managers remain concerned with issues such as grievance handling, recruitment and selection, equal opportunities and staffing. However, it is also clear that there has been a significant growth in the incidence of so-called 'new' management practices aimed at engendering employee commitment and promoting high performance. The WERS data indicated, for example, that more than half of British workplaces have employees working in formally designated teams, operate a team briefing system, and have formal performance appraisal for non-managerial employees (Cully et al. 1999). Significant questions remain, however, on the extent to which such policies are embedded within organisations, and whether their use is strategically based or merely pragmatic.

THE ROLE OF THE STATE

The state (including national and local government and their various agencies) plays a crucial role in employment relations, both directly and indirectly.

Legal reforms of industrial relations

During much of the 19th century the law was hostile to unionism. When this stance was modified towards the end of the century, the route chosen was not that of positively stated rights for either employees or unions (as in many other countries) but rather a system of immunities for unions from various areas of criminal and civil law. This process was completed by the *Trade Disputes Act 1906*, which provided the main principles of union law until the 1980s. These were broadly accepted by peacetime governments of different political complexions, giving rise to what became known as 'voluntarism'. The intervention of the state and of the law and lawyers was minimised, this being varied only by the imposition of some compulsory arbitration processes during and briefly after the two world wars. The three principal features of voluntarism were:

1. non-legally binding collective agreements;
2. voluntary union recognition by employers;
3. a light, voluntary framework of state-provided supplementary dispute resolution facilities, with no governmental powers to order suspension of industrial action or impose cooling-off periods.

By the 1960s there was increasing concern at Britain's relatively poor economic performance, and some commentators argued that Britain's industrial relations system was a major factor, with restrictive (or protective) working practices and unofficial strikes[6] making industry uncompetitive. Accordingly, after the late 1960s, industrial relations reform was high on the political agenda.

Although the Donovan Commission (1968) had argued for *voluntary* reform to formalise workplace bargaining, in subsequent years successive governments resorted to legislation. The Conservatives' *Industrial Relations Act 1971* sought to legislate for rapid and fundamental reform at a stroke. Following a US example, this ill-fated Act aimed, *inter alia*, to make collective agreements into legally enforceable contracts. The unions boycotted much of the Act and few employers used it, thereby rendering it largely ineffective. Most of the Act, apart from the unfair dismissal provisions, was repealed by Labour in 1974.

Between 1979 and 1997, Conservative governments successfully adopted a more gradualist but no less radical approach. They enacted important new laws at approximately two-yearly intervals through the 1980s and early 1990s. The legislation limited the ability of unions to organise lawful industrial action; it narrowed union immunities from legal action (principally injunctions) by employers and others through the courts, outlawed secondary industrial action, and restrained picketing. Since 1984, to be lawful, industrial action has had to be preceded by a secret ballot of the workers concerned, with a requirement since 1993 that ballots be postal. A union cannot lawfully discipline a member who refuses to support industrial action, even where the majority has voted in favour. Unions have also been made liable for unauthorised or unofficial industrial action by their officials—including workplace representatives.

Legislation prohibited the closed shop and made it more difficult for unions to consolidate and extend union membership by removing the statutory procedures to facilitate union recognition introduced by the 1974–79 Labour government (but see below). In addition, the Conservative laws intervened prescriptively in internal union governance: for example, members were given new rights to bring legal actions against their unions. Secret membership ballots were required to elect union executive committees and national leaders directly rather than indirectly via delegates, and to approve the continuation of a 'political fund' every five years. The espoused objective was to ensure that unions were responsive to the wishes of their members (Goodman & Earnshaw 1995). In the event, the unions won all of the political fund ballots. Compulsory pre-strike ballots have also proven double-edged, with the great majority of such ballots apparently supporting industrial action (ACAS 1991). In practice, such ballots are widely seen as an additional element in the bargaining game, aimed at securing improved offers, and, although influenced by many factors (Edwards 1995), the huge decline in strikes since the 1970s adds credence to this view.

Post-1997 Labour governments have not changed the broad framework of industrial relations law introduced by the Conservatives, though they have eased some details, such as arrangements for the deduction of union dues, and introduced a new mechanism for unions to secure recognition from employers (Simpson 2000). This intricate and protracted process, overseen by a revamped Central Arbitration Committee, emphasises the preference for voluntary agreements but residually enforces recognition and a bargaining procedure where the union(s) secures a majority in a secret ballot, amounting to 40 per cent of workers in the bargaining unit.[7] The *Employment Relations Act 1999* also introduced other collective rights for workers and unions (Smith & Morton 2001).

A further characteristic of the traditional British system was that minimum labour standards were established by statute in remarkably few areas, apart from the health and safety field. The main exception was in relation to low pay (see below). For most of the 20th century governments encouraged the parties to develop voluntary collective bargaining arrangements, although post-1979 Conservative governments abandoned this policy and pursued labour market policies targeted at reducing collectivism and regulation. Use of statutory measures to establish a broader platform of minimum employee rights on a universal basis (some subject to length of service qualifications) began selectively in the 1960s but has since increased considerably. To early rights, such as redundancy payments and remedies for unfair dismissal, have been added topics as diverse as protection of continuity of employment following a change of ownership; sex, race and disability discrimination; and maternity leave and pay arrangements. Some of these burgeoning statutory individual employment rights were established by British initiative, others flowed from the EU and the concept of 'Social Europe'. Conservative governments 1979–97 tended to resist the latter's approach and attempted to dilute its impact (e.g. in relation to the European Working Time Directive that set statutory maxima on weekly working hours, and minimum holidays and break times). Post-1997 Labour governments have further strengthened statutory employment rights, such as better unfair dismissal compensation, (unpaid) parental leave, and other 'family-friendly' employment rights. The Working Time Directive has been implemented, and a national minimum wage and measures to prevent discrimination against part-time workers have been introduced. There has been a remarkable shift from voluntarism towards juridification in the regulation of employment relationships in Britain, at least in terms of minimum rights and standards.

A key development after 1979 was the transformation in the nature and role of labour law, with the long-established voluntarist regime largely being superseded by statutory regulation. Industrial action and unions have been subjected to substantial new legislative restrictions. As unions and collective bargaining have receded, a wide-ranging body of statutory minimum labour standards and individual employment rights, enforced through regional specialist employment tribunals, has been introduced. Where the coverage of voluntary collective bargaining system was partial, the new juridified regime is wider and sometimes deeper.

Economic policies

Post-1979 Conservative governments took a radically different approach from their predecessors, adopting monetarist policies and fiscal restraint as a way of tackling inflation, backed by direct controls and 'cash limits' in the public sector. This strategy amounted to a rejection of the postwar Keynesian consensus. The defeat of inflation became the dominant priority, and the commitment to full employment (or indeed any specific employment target) was abandoned. During the mid- to late 1980s, and again after 1992, the government had some impressive success in restraining inflation. Earlier corporatist approaches (e.g. prices and incomes policies) were viewed as anathema, and the government opposed a range of EU social/employment legislation, securing an 'opt-out' from the Social Chapter of the 1991 Maastricht Treaty. This opposition to many aspects of 'Social Europe', together with the government's concern to minimise wage costs, 'social charges' and the 'burdens on business', gave the UK some advantage in attracting overseas direct investment (OECD 1997).

Since 1997, inflation rates have remained low, with the newly independent Monetary Policy Committee of the Bank of England adjusting interest rates to keep inflation at or below the 2.5 per cent target set by the government. The Blair government was committed to the Social Chapter, but reluctant to lose the advantages of Britain's restructured and relatively flexible labour markets and wary of adopting all the social policies pursued by France and Germany, in particular. Its 'third way' approach seeks to combine efficiency and fairness through an extended platform of statutory employment standards, although such increased regulation makes several concessions to employer opinion on matters of detail and remains light relative to most other DMEs (Undy 1999). It also chose to remain outside the launch phase of the common European currency project.

EQUITY AND DISCRIMINATION AT WORK

Equity as a labour market and social issue has attracted increasing attention since the 1960s. The *Equal Pay Act 1970* aimed to eliminate pay differentials based on gender. Under various statutes passed since then, discrimination in employment on grounds of race or gender is unlawful. In the 1970s the government established the tripartite Commission for Racial Equality and the Equal Opportunities Commission to provide information and help monitor and enforce these laws, though the lengthy procedures for individuals pursuing cases via complaints to employment tribunals require tenacity. In the late 1990s, legislation was extended to the area of disability with the establishment of a Disability Rights Commission following the 1995 Act. As yet there is no British legislation specifically targeting age discrimination or (excepting Northern Ireland) religious discrimination in the employment field. While the various agencies have helped to raise the issues and improve practice in their respective areas, much remains to be done. It is proving extremely difficult, for example, to reduce further the male–female earnings differential (EOC 2001).

Low pay and minimum pay

Between 1909 and 1993 the state played a limited role in fixing legally enforceable minimum pay and conditions in industries such as agriculture, clothing manufacture, retailing, hairdressing, hotels and catering, where effective voluntary collective bargaining had failed to develop. At its height this partial and selective approach through wages councils (earlier called trade boards) applied to no more than 15 per cent of workers, and contrasted with the less industry-specific statutory minimum wage systems of other countries.

In line with their deregulatory ideology the post-1979 Conservative governments regarded the wages councils' setting of wage floors as restricting 'flexibility' in the labour market and 'pricing people out of jobs'. They trimmed the powers and scope of wages councils in 1986, and abolished them in 1993—except in agriculture. The long-established Fair Wages Resolution was also rescinded. Thus the Conservatives sought to remove all regulatory constraints on employees' pay and conditions. This paved the way for cost-cutting before its large-scale program of compulsory competitive tendering for many elements of the public-sector work that had remained 'in house'. But the EU Transfer of Undertakings regulations tempered this program.

The new Labour government in 1997 acted quickly on its manifesto pledge to introduce a national minimum wage (NMW), with no industrial or regional variants. A tripartite Low Pay Commission made recommendations, and the new minima (there being a lower rate for younger workers aged 18–22) were introduced in 1999. There is no set mechanism for raising the NMW, such as earnings or price indexation or even a set annual review, but the Low Pay Commission has been retained. Its research suggests that, at the initial and subsequent levels, the NMW has had few of the negative repercussions predicted by many sceptics (Metcalf 1999; Low Pay Commission 2000). Unions remain critical of the level(s) at which the NMW is set, however, and of the uncertainty of periodic reviews.

Dispute resolution: conciliation and arbitration

Although third-party involvement in collective disputes has not been a prominent feature of industrial relations in peacetime, the British state has long provided conciliation and arbitration services as a supplement to voluntary collective bargaining and disputes procedures. These were provided by a government department until 1974, when the Labour government established the independent Advisory, Conciliation and Arbitration Service (ACAS). ACAS is governed by a tripartite council, consisting of employer and union nominees with a balance of independent members. By these means successive governments have sought to distance themselves from the settlement of particular industrial disputes, though their influence as an interested party in the public sector is still important.

ACAS services are free and include conciliation in complaints by individuals over alleged breaches of statutory employment rights (its principal and hugely expanded activity) as well as in collective disputes. It also offers information on employment matters and advice to the parties on all aspects of employment relations and policies. ACAS officials carry out individual and collective conciliation and advisory work, but they appoint independent experts to act as ad-hoc mediators and arbitrators. Unlike the position in many other countries, arbitration is neither compulsory (as it was in Australia) nor legally binding (as in North America and Australia). Although ACAS was established by a Labour government, it continued under the Conservatives; however, they did curtail the use of arbitration in the public sector, cut ACAS's role in conducting inquiries, and removed its earlier responsibility to promote the growth and reform of collective bargaining (see Goodman 2000).

Annual requests to ACAS for conciliation and arbitration in collective disputes are around 1200 and 60 cases respectively, both substantially lower than their peak levels in the 1970s. The decline in union membership and the coverage of collective bargaining since 1979, together with the growth of individual statutory rights, saw complaints against employers more than doubling to almost 100 000 in the decade to 1996, with a further rapid growth in subsequent years. ACAS has a statutory right to conciliate in more than 50 employment rights jurisdictions (see Dickens 2000; Dix 2000), prior to cases being heard at the regionally based employment tribunals.

THE PUBLIC SECTOR

The state plays an important role as a direct or indirect employer for a substantial proportion of the labour force, and less directly through its influence as an exemplar to other employers. For much of the 20th century the government aimed to be a 'good' employer, encouraging union membership, and offering broadly comparable terms and conditions and generally more secure employment than the private sector.

Over the 1979–97 period many of these traditions were rejected, as Conservative governments sought a transformation in the public sector, seeking to limit and reduce public expenditure and to reduce the role of the state. Most dramatic was the privatisation of publicly owned corporations (e.g. telecommunications, airways, coal, steel and railways) and utilities (e.g. gas, electricity and water). Public-sector employment fell from around 30 per cent to 22 per cent of the labour force (Winchester & Bach 1995). Second, strict cash limits and projected 'efficiency gains' were built into forward budgets to restrain public-sector pay settlements to below inflation rates in most areas (Beaumont 1987). Public-sector strikes were resisted, generally successfully, most notably the year-long miners' strike in 1984–85. Access to arbitration was withdrawn or restrained. Collective bargaining rights for teachers were withdrawn following lengthy industrial disputes, with pay and conditions in schools subsequently being set by Cabinet approval of recommendations from a Pay Review Body. Similar arrangements cover around a third of public-sector workers.

Deregulation was introduced in many areas (e.g. local bus passenger transport, local authorities and the National Health Service [NHS]). Many civil service functions were reorganised into more autonomous executive agencies, and other areas were subjected to substantial reductions in employment and to 'market testing' (Stewart & Walsh 1992). Local authorities were required, under the 'best value' provisions, to put services out to tender with the private sector, and public–private partnerships have been introduced into local government and the NHS with major implications for employment relations (Rubery et al. 2002; Grimshaw et al. 2002). This process introduced private-sector values and practices into what became a smaller and more fragmented public sector, which generally experienced improvements in pay and conditions below those in the private sector. Union density, however, remained high, with some of the traditionally moderate unions gaining sharp increases in membership (see Table 2.1).

The Labour governments have retained many of the Conservative reforms of public-sector industrial relations, with the tight monetary and 'prudent' fiscal policies continuing. Re-nationalisations have not been on the agenda. While decentralisation of public-sector bargaining has been advocated less forcefully, the Blair government has pressed performance-related pay in the face of union opposition, notably in teaching. In addition, it has offered larger rises only to tightly defined and relatively small groups in the public sector (e.g. 'consultant' nurses, and police in southeast England).

INDUSTRIAL RELATIONS PROCESSES

The terms and conditions that regulate levels of pay, working hours, methods of working, and procedures for resolving differences between workers and employers are central to the employment relationship. They can be established in various ways, including legal enactment, management decisions—with or without employee consultation—and collective bargaining between unions and employers. Collective bargaining has diminished in coverage and scope, and in the 2000s affects only a minority of employees. Increasingly since the early 1980s managements have set the terms, conditions and other employment matters directly, rather than bargaining with unions. Some writers have highlighted the vacuum left by the contraction of collective bargaining (and the general absence in Britain of a mandatory system of employee consultation such as the Works Council) by referring to a growing 'representation gap' (Towers 1997).

Collective bargaining

Collective bargaining has a long history in Britain, developing in several industries in the late 19th century and then through 'joint industrial councils' soon after World War I in others. By the early 1920s, multi-employer bargaining for manual workers was well established, and industry-level negotiations were encouraged by the government as a way of establishing orderly industrial relations. Though there were some exceptions, centralised negotiations across whole industries generally left little room for workplace bargaining.

After World War II, shop stewards increasingly became involved as workplace bargainers, supplementing the industry-wide negotiations conducted between national union officials and representatives of employers' associations. This was partly because centralised agreements could not specify workplace rules in sufficient detail, but it was also due to the increasing power of shop stewards in a context of tight labour markets. The Donovan Royal Commission, set up in 1965 to examine 'the industrial relations problem', argued for workplace bargaining to be formalised, as this would weaken the influence of multi-employer, national negotiations and at the same time remove the 'disorder' created by uncoordinated sectional agreements. To the extent that employers and unions took this advice, single-employer bargaining received a significant boost.

In 1970 collective bargaining covered approximately 70 per cent of the workforce, but it has since declined to around 40 per cent (Cully et al. 1999: 242). There are sizeable variations between sectors, with the public sector having the highest coverage (63 per cent) and private-sector services the lowest (22 per cent). The shape and character of collective bargaining also varies considerably between workplaces, in relation to the *level* at which bargaining takes place, the size/structure of the *unit* of employees covered by any agreement, and the *scope* (and depth) of the subjects determined by joint regulation.

Very little multi-employer negotiation remains in the private sector and it is also weakening in the public sector, although it is still twice as important there as single-employer bargaining. Bargaining units at work-place and company level have become wider since 1980. The moves to single unionism and to single-table bargaining have accelerated since 1990. WERS 1998 showed that a single union was recognised in just under half of the workplaces with union recognition. In the remainder—where two or more unions were recognised—three-fifths of these joint negotiations were conducted with *all* trade unions, i.e. single-table bargaining (Cully et al. 1999: 93–4).

The scope of collective bargaining has also shrunk since the early 1980s, leading Marchington and Parker (1990: 228) to suggest that union involvement in the regulation of workplace industrial relations had been 'marginalised'. Under this scenario, the institutions of collective bargaining remain intact but union representatives' involvement is reduced, because managers refuse to discuss issues with them and place restrictions on the time allowed for their union duties (Marchington 1995). Rather than bargaining about a wide range of issues, union representatives may be presented with a 'take-it-or-leave-it' offer (Kessler & Bayliss 1998). More recently the TUC and many leading unions have emphasised their adoption of a partnership approach, in place of power-based adversarialism. This more integrative, joint problem-solving orientation has enjoyed strong rhetorical support, though its detailed definition is rather fluid and its adoption not invariably successful in practice (Kelly 1996; Marchington 1998; Claydon 1998; Ackers & Payne 1998). The concept and practice are examined further below.

Employee involvement

Interest in participation and employee involvement (EI) has waxed and waned over the past century, with surges of activity at times when employers feel they are under threat from labour and a loss of impetus when this threat recedes (Ramsay 1977). This is illustrated by a growth in participation through profit sharing in the late 19th century, joint consultation during and just after the two world wars (1917–20; 1940s), and in worker directors through the TUC and the Bullock Committee of Inquiry during the 1970s. The most recent growth of interest and activity has occurred under the EI label since the 1980s, and it differs substantially from earlier variants. It tends to be individualist and direct (as opposed to collective and through representatives), it is initiated unilaterally by management, and it is directed at securing greater employee commitment to and identification with the employing organisation. Whether these initiatives have been successful remains an open question (Marchington 2001). Since the 1980s EI has grown without much pressure from employees or unions, but with some legislative support at various times for employee share ownership, profit-related pay, and elements of information and consultation. Despite a change of government in 1997, it continues to be pursued with a voluntarist tenor.

The growth in EI is apparent from an examination of the data from the successive WERS reports. Millward et al. (1992: 166) noted that 'management initiatives to increase EI were made with rising frequency throughout the 1980s', and this trend has continued throughout the last decade. The most recent survey (Cully et al. 1999) indicates that four of the top five 'new management practices and EI schemes' were forms of direct EI. These were teamworking (present in 65 per cent of workplaces), team briefing (61 per cent), staff attitude surveys (45 per cent) and problem-solving groups (42 per cent). Profit-sharing and share-ownership schemes for non-managerial employees were present at 30 per cent and 15 per cent of these establishments respectively. This picture of growth in direct EI is reinforced by case study and anecdotal evidence (Marchington et al. 2001), as well as from the surveys undertaken by Gill and Krieger (1999) and Industrial Relations Services (1999).

Direct EI takes several distinct forms in practice. First, there is downward communication from managers to employees, the principal purpose of which is to inform and 'educate' staff so that they accept management plans. This includes techniques such as team briefing and employee reports. Millward et al. (2000: 118) report that since the mid-1980s there has been a doubling in the number of workplaces where regular briefings occur, although the frequency and formality of these can vary substantially. Second, there is upward problem solving, which is designed to tap into employee knowledge and opinion, either at an individual level or through small groups; the best known of these techniques are probably quality circles and suggestion schemes. There is evidence of a 40 per cent growth in their incidence since 1990 (Millward et al. 2000: 118), so that approximately half of all workplaces report the use of problem-solving groups. The third category of direct EI initiatives is task participation, in which individual employees are encouraged or expected to extend the range and type of tasks undertaken at work. These are directed at individual employees, with some such initiatives having their roots in earlier 'quality of working life' experiments (Kelly 1982), although more recently the stimulus has been so-called lean production (Womack et al. 1990). Examples of task-based participation are job rotation, job enrichment and teamworking. Despite the claim that teamworking is present in a majority of workplaces, in only 3 per cent of these were team members able to select their own leader (Cully et al. 1999: 43).

There is also financial involvement, with schemes designed to link part of an individual's rewards to his/her own performance and/or that of the unit or enterprise as a whole. These take a variety of forms, including profit sharing and various employee share-ownership schemes. These appear to have peaked in the early 1990s, following a period of sustained growth due to concerted efforts by governments to foster entrepreneurial values and wider share ownership. The most recent WERS data show that nearly half of all workplaces had a profit-sharing scheme in 1998 while about one-quarter had an employee share-ownership program (Millward et al. 2000: 214).

Although direct EI has become much more prominent in recent years, representative participation has not disappeared. Joint consultative committees (JCCs) are an example of this form of EI, having had a long but mixed history comprising various periods of growth and decline. Although some commentators felt that they were unlikely to survive the development of strong shop steward workplace organisation, JCCs re-emerged during the 1970s before declining slightly during the 1980s (Millward et al. 1992). By the end of the 1990s JCCs were present in 29 per cent of workplaces, compared with one-third in the mid-1980s. They were more extensive in the public sector than the private, in larger workplaces than smaller, and where unions were recognised than where they were not. The decline is therefore principally due to the changing structural and sectoral composition of workplaces, in particular to the falling number of larger establishments. The WERS data (Millward et al. 2000: 111) suggest that consultative committees have not been introduced as an alternative to unions, and direct EI was as likely to be found in workplaces where management actively encouraged unions as in those where it did not. Accordingly, Millward et al. (2000: 126) suggest that 'the undermining of union influence may have been a motive for some employers, but it was clearly not in many cases'.

Non-unionism

Non-union firms received little attention in the literature until the 1990s, even though most small companies have never recognised unions. It was only with the growing awareness of what Beaumont (1987) refers to as the 'household name' group—large companies such as IBM, Marks & Spencer and Hewlett Packard—that academic interest started to blossom. These companies were praised for HRM policies designed to offer employees better terms and conditions than were generally achieved by unions through negotiations. However, it is misleading to assume all non-union enterprises are similar. Combining Guest and Hoque's (1994) categorisation of non-union firms with Hyman's (1997) typology of employer regimes, a broad twofold categorisation of 'soft HRM' and 'bleak house' can be identified.

The former are the relatively small number of sophisticated non-union firms that seek to avoid unions by offering what are supposedly 'superior' terms and conditions. These employers tend to have a clear strategy for managing people, making use of a wide range of human resource policies combined into a complete employment package (McLoughlin & Gourlay 1994; Marchington & Wilkinson 2002). This tends to include highly competitive remuneration packages, a strong focus on employee communications, single status and a commitment to career development.

By contrast, the 'bleak house' scenario is where unions are denied access to potential members by a mixture of managerial aggression and either a lack of response or a very adversarial response to union attempts to gain recognition. These firms are more likely to be the traditional, sweatshop employers, and they are often small, independent, single-site companies operating as suppliers to the large non-union enterprises analysed above. Their employment practices contrast sharply with those pursuing 'soft HRM': pay rates are likely to be low, fringe benefits are virtually non-existent, and employees typically lack any form of effective 'voice'. Such employers constitute the vast majority of non-union employers.

The number of non-union firms has grown since 1980 but the impact of de-recognition on union membership in general has been slight, and it has tended to relate to specific groups of employees rather than whole workforces (Claydon 1989; Gall & McKay 1994). The most recent panel data from WERS (Cully et al. 1999: 241) shows that between 1990 and 1998, just 6 per cent of 'continuing' workplaces reported a de-recognition during this period and 4 per cent a new recognition. Since then, there has been an increase in the number of recognition agreements, probably stimulated by the imminent legislation (McKay 2001: 300). The stock of non-union firms has grown mainly because 'new' workplaces are less likely to be unionised.

CURRENT AND FUTURE ISSUES

The changing pattern of British employment relations reflects some trends that are similar to those found in most DMEs. These include de-industrialisation, increases in the proportion of service and knowledge sector employment, and the growth of atypical employment. Particular national influences in the British context include fundamental changes in labour legislation, economic and labour market policy trends, sociodemographic and familial changes, and developments in managerial and union policies and practices.

Changing labour markets

In the first decade of the 21st century, Britain is predicted to see an increase of 2.1 million jobs (about 8–9 per cent), particularly in the professional, technical and personal service occupations. Around two-thirds of the additional jobs will be taken by women, raising their economic activity rate to about 80 per cent. Economic growth is likely to be strongest in southern England, and much of the growth will be in part-time jobs, with self-employment marginally declining but relatively high employment being maintained (IER 2001).

This scenario, if it is borne out, suggests a markedly different decade from both the 1980s and 1990s. As measured by claimant figures, unemployment fell almost continuously from around 9 per cent in 1991 to less than 5 per cent in 2001, a level not known since the 1960s. With inflation held at around 2–3 per cent per annum since 1997 and wage rate rises only a little higher, labour shortages began to appear in high-technology industries and in particular regions, such as parts of southeast England. However, structural unemployment remained high in Britain's older industrial areas, such as Wales, northeast England and Scotland. The impact of global trends in production costs and consumption patterns (Barrell & Pain 1997) was seen as MNEs and major employers retrenched or even disappeared from former flagship industrial sectors, such as in steel, shipbuilding, textiles, electronics and car manufacture, with the government reluctant to provide subsidies.

From the early 1990s, governmental policies have been directed primarily at the control of inflation, rather than at the goal of reducing unemployment. Nevertheless, numerous initiatives were aimed at reducing the (claimant) jobless total, moving away from passive policies (e.g. the use of benefits squeezes to 'price people back into jobs') towards active, supply-side policies of labour market intervention ('encouraging people off benefits back into work') (Schmid et al. 1992). These targeted especially the long-term unemployed through, *inter alia*, intensive retraining programs and youth unemployment initiatives. Despite the fall in unemployment, a number of deep-rooted problems remain. Long-run labour market shortages persist, such as in skilled areas of the National Health Service, in school teaching, in the police and prison services and in the military forces. The reasons for this are complex but include low salaries (especially for starters), work intensification, the erosion of job security, and a general loss of morale in many parts of the public sector (Colling 1997).

Employing organisations continue to face demands for improved competitiveness and enhanced pressures for quality and value, and these have led to substantial changes in employment practices. Employment legislation to curb unions encouraged the growth of individualised employment practices such as short- or fixed-term working, part-timing, outsourcing, annualised (or zero) hours contracts, or corporate divestment of specialist functions. Such flexibility was pursued also through early retirements, dispersion to subsidiary companies with fewer employment benefits, homeworking, or the use of interim management. In many cases, the pursuit of flexibility was not so much a coherent managerial philosophy as an exercise in opportunism in situations where custom and practice had disappeared or never existed, and the law placed few obstacles on cutting employment numbers and rights (Kessler & Bayliss 1998: 296–7).

The experience of work

Changing subjective experiences of work have become a prominent topic of debate for unions, employers and governments. A white paper, *Fairness at Work* (DTI 1998), articulated multiple concerns. The quality of the national labour pool was allegedly in decline. The costs of work-caused incapacity and invalidity were a rising call on the social security budget. Issues of work-life balance became prominent (with an increasing stream of EU directives and judgments), including rights for parents, women and atypical workers, as well as for pensions, training and individual dignity. The problem was to find the right mix of statutory, employer-led and workforce-originated steps (Kochan et al. 1986) to prevent or mitigate these personal and collective dysfunctions.

On the one hand, government policies from 1997 have been oriented particularly towards establishing recognition of the importance of work-life balance (Lobel 1996), both through employer-led family-friendly initiatives, such as parental leave, flexible hours, career breaks and crèches (Gottlieb et al. 1998: 1–23), and through legislation. On the other hand, government policies also placed great emphasis on getting the unemployed and the never-employed into the labour market, and reducing the social security burden. The methods were diverse, including special training for mothers with young families, an expanded nursery school program, the National Minimum Wage, a tightening up of eligibility for long-run disability allowances, and financial subsidies (Working Families' Tax Credit) for low-income working parents. All of these were designed to make work appear more attractive than unemployment and to encourage the inculcation of long-term working habits. Many employers (especially SMEs) have been vociferous in their opposition to such provisions, which they alleged would hamper job creation, flexible labour utilisation and competitiveness.

There is a growing body of evidence that employment is becoming more stressful and damaging to employees' physical and mental health (Berridge et al. 1997). This stress typically comes from raised levels of work output (e.g. caused through delayering and mergers), higher-quality standards in all sectors, augmented management control (often using information technology), or greater use of audits (as in teaching). Complaints from unions and professional societies have been supported by evidence of rising rates of incapacity and early retirement (Shephard 1996). Many responsible employers recognise the negative aspects of work-related stress, particularly in instances of organisational change and enhanced performance requirements. They implement secondary and tertiary stress-reduction methods (e.g. more favourable working environments, employee assistance and counselling) but generally fail to remove the primary stressors, which are often embedded in organisations' processes and practices.

The civil courts have awarded large financial awards in several cases of job-related stress, notably for professionals, in teaching and in social work. Courts judged that organisation structures were inadequate, supervisory systems had failed, and management had not taken the necessary steps to protect employees from unreasonable job pressures (Earnshaw & Cooper 1996). A further warning for employers came from pension fund providers, who claimed that reserves paid in by firms and individuals were most unlikely to generate the expected historical levels of company-funded pensions, due among other reasons to increased rates of ill-health and stress retirements (Blake 2000).

In spite of legislation over many decades, employment practices have been criticised as outmoded and discriminatory (Kramer 1998). Those most affected include disabled people, workers from black and other ethnic minorities, older employees, women and immigrant workers. These issues are probably more acute in SMEs and owner-managed firms than in large enterprises, where professional human resource managers often take the lead in promoting good practice above and beyond statutory requirements. Consequently, the current government has moved cautiously in reforming inherited legislation, also fearing that foreign MNEs, attracted to Britain in the past by its relatively unregulated labour market practices, will be discouraged from investing. This is a potentially severe problem, given that Britain continues to attract the largest share of inward foreign investment of all EU countries.

Yet, in spite of such repeated negative perceptions and evidence, the latest WERS study revealed a seemingly high degree of satisfaction among British employees regarding their work, their job and their management. A summary measure of job satisfaction across a wide range of factors showed 53 per cent expressing a high level of job satisfaction compared with 19 per cent dissatisfaction (Cully et al. 1999: 182). Interpretations of this apparently high level of job satisfaction and pride are necessarily complex. They may well centre on the high salience given to work in British society, almost regardless of how good or bad those jobs are. Alternatively, it may be the product of a new emphasis on high-commitment human resources practices as a key component in efforts to motivate and retain skilled and scarce labour (Guest & Conway 2000).

PARTNERSHIP AGREEMENTS

One of the most significant developments in the past few years in Britain has been the growth of partnership agreements between employers and unions. It is a concept and practice that fits well with the political discourse of the Labour government and the Third Way (Undy 1999). The government set up a Partnership Fund from which bids for money to support training and other initiatives can be claimed. The Involvement and Participation Association (IPA) has become more prominent through its advice to organisations, and the TUC has shown considerable interest in the development of partnership. The reaction of employers appears rather more mixed and fragmented. The TUC Partnership Institute acknowledges fewer than 100 formal agreements in 2000, although other evidence indicates that partnership can flourish without this formal title (Marchington et al. 2001). Certain schemes have continued for more than five years in the retail, finance and utilities sectors, as well as in MNE manufacturing companies.

There have been attempts to define partnership, most notably by the IPA and by the TUC. The IPA sees partnership in terms of mutuality—such as employee commitment to the success of the enterprise, organisational needs for flexibility, and long-term employment security

(Coupar & Stevens 1998). The TUC supports the principle of mutuality but, not surprisingly, also argues strongly for employment protection as a necessary precondition for the delivery of flexible working patterns, as well as for the importance of training for personal development, not just for organisational needs (TUC 1999). Marchington (1998) suggests that partnership is distinctive only if it combines three separate elements: a cooperative stance by both partners, a recognition that direct EI and representative participation work alongside each other, and a buttressing of partnership by a bundle of high-commitment human resource practices.

Questions about partnership revolve around its outcomes, in particular whether or not unions and workers gain from their involvement. The agreements analysed by Haynes and Allen (2001), Guest and Peccei (1998, 2001) and Knell (1999) agree that employers certainly gain from entering into partnership agreements. For example, Guest and Peccei (2001: 232) state that 'a bundle of partnership practices associated with direct and representative participation, job design and a focus on quality, and the additional use of employee share ownership, produce the most positive outcomes for all the partners'. The evidence in relation to union gains is more mixed and more open to disagreement. Kelly (1996) sees partnership as a major problem for unions, and he has argued forcefully that unions are not well served by engaging in this form of labour-management cooperation but would reap greater benefits for their members by pursuing a more militant line. Questions are raised in particular about the extent to which managers who have been used to operating in the traditional, adversarial climate of British employment relations can ever be trusted in the long term. Other writers disagree with the line that unions are naive to engage in partnerships, as employers are not inevitably hostile to unions (Ackers & Payne 1998: 545). The union representatives involved in the most high-profile partnership agreements do not feel that they have been 'incorporated' into a management agenda (Thomas & Wallis 1998; Haynes & Allen 2001). Nevertheless, Guest and Peccei express concern that mutuality in practice may be lopsided in many partnership agreements, with a greater emphasis on employee *responsibilities* than on employee *rights*. They argue that trust is a distinctive feature of partnership, and that it is in danger of failing if 'the balance of power errs too far in favour of the employer' (Guest & Peccei 2001: 231-3).

Throughout much of mainland Europe, social partnership finds expression in national and organisation-wide policies for regulating management–union relations. Successive governments have been reluctant to *require* British firms to set up consultation machinery. Recent surveys indicate that many large UK employers have voluntarily implemented Works Councils, while others have developed systems to provide consultation machinery for employees in other EU countries and sometimes in the UK (Marginson et al. 1998; Wills 1999). Waddington (2000: 610) also reports that slightly more employers appear to be in favour of compulsory Works Councils than are against them, although many remain undecided. The decision by the British government in 2001 to drop its opposition to the wide-ranging EU information and consultation directive should pave the way for new arrangements. The precise shape of these is not yet known, but enterprises with 150 or more employees will be required to consult on a range of issues connected with the operation, performance and future of the business at least once a year—and perhaps more often in the event of major changes—from 2005 (Burns 2001). These provisions are to be progressively extended to smaller firms, but only those employing 50 or more, during the following three years.

CONCLUSIONS

The British industrial relations system has a long history, but in recent years it has undergone much change. Union density is little more than half of its peak in 1979 and the unions are struggling to find a clear identity for the 21st century, both in their international and workplace profiles and in their traditional links with the Labour Party. Much will depend on the success of the 'organising' model in generating increases in union membership, the direct and indirect impact of the recognition legislation, and the ability of partnership to deliver improvements for workers as well as for employers. There are specific challenges for unions in the much-reduced public sector, and there are signs that discontent with growing private-sector involvement in public services (e.g. schools and hospitals) is high on the union agenda.

Despite increasing juridification, employer strategies for managing labour remain diverse. The absence of a strong centrally regulated system of employment relations has meant that employers have been relatively free to set or (less commonly) to negotiate pay and other terms and conditions of employment at levels that they deem to be appropriate for their own competitive circumstances. There appears to be a growing bifurcation of employer approaches along the lines of 'contract or status' (Streeck 1987), with some employers adopting policies of high-commitment management (HCM) and others opting for a cost-minimisation model. Union representation and HCM can and do coexist. Perhaps a greater challenge for HCM is the increasing likelihood of employers to outsource substantial elements of their personnel function and to rely more extensively on line managers for the implementation of employment relations.

The role of the state in industrial relations has also been subject to change. In some respects it has lessened through the decline in the size of the public sector, while expanding in others through an increased legal regulation of many areas of employment rights. Much of the latter has been driven by EU initiatives, especially in strengthening individual employment rights, and it will be interesting to see how this develops. The introduction of the NMW at a relatively low level initially is an example of a major policy change, the subsequent impact of which will be closely linked to the rate at which the NMW is increased. A wider range of statutory rights exercised via individual complaints to tribunals poses a potential threat to employers and unions who, for the most part, have managed recently to maintain a relatively consensual state of affairs.

Finally, what about the workers themselves? A rather mixed and confused picture emerges as to their experience of work and employment in contemporary Britain. Some studies show work intensification, job insecurity, low morale, high levels of stress, and increasing discontent with widening pay differentials between rich and poor. Other studies suggest that workers are relatively satisfied with their work, show high levels of commitment and loyalty to their employer, and feel that they have an improved standard of living. To some extent, subjective experiences are positively related to occupational and hierarchical level, but not necessarily so—doctors' frustration with lack of funding being a prime example. Despite the picture of relative calm that is portrayed by low levels of industrial action, employment relations continue to be characterised by tensions and contradictions. Managing these issues will remain a major task for employers, unions and governments.

A CHRONOLOGY OF BRITISH EMPLOYMENT RELATIONS

1349	Ordinance of Labourers sets up pay determination machinery (the first recognisable labour legislation).
1563	Prohibition of workers' 'conspiracy' and 'combination' to raise wages.
1780–1840	Period of primary industrialisation.
1799–1800	Combination Acts provide additional penalties against workers' 'combinations'.
1811–14	'Luddites' begin smashing machines.
1824–25	Repeal of Combination Acts.
1834	'Tolpuddle martyrs' transported to Australia for taking a union oath.
1851	'New model unions' formed, mainly of skilled craftsmen.
1868	First meeting of TUC.
1871	Trade Union Act gives unions legal status.
1891	Fair Wages Resolution of the House of Commons.
1899	TUC sets up Labour Representation Committee (which became the Labour Party in 1906).
1901	House of Lords' Taff Vale judgment holds that a union could be liable for employers' losses during a strike.
1906	Trades Disputes Act gives unions immunity from such liability, if acting 'in contemplation or furtherance of a trade dispute'.
1909	House of Lords' Osborne judgment rules that unions could not finance political activities.
1913	Trade Union Act legalises unions' political expenditure if they set up a separate fund, with individuals able to 'contract out'.
1917–18	Whitley reports recommend joint industrial councils.
1926	General strike and nine-month miners' strike.
1927	Subsequent legislation restricts picketing and introduces criminal liabilities for political strikes.
1945	Election of Labour government.
1946–51	Repeal of 1927 Act; nationalisation of the Bank of England, fuel, power, inland transport, health, steel etc.
1951	Election of Conservative government.
1964	Election of Labour government.
1968	Donovan report advocates voluntary reform of industrial relations.
1969	Labour government proposes legal reforms, but is successfully opposed by the unions.

1970	Equal Pay Act. Election of Conservative government.
1971	Industrial Relations Act legislates for reform; most unions refuse to comply. It also introduces the concept of 'unfair dismissal'.
1974	A miners' strike precipitates the fall of the Conservative government.
1974	Trade Union and Labour Relations Act replaces the 1971 Act, but retains the 'unfair dismissal' concept, sets up ACAS and signals a new Social Contract.
1974	Health and Safety at Work Act.
1975	Employment Protection Act extends the rights of workers and unions; Equal Pay Act implemented.
1976	Race Relations Act.
1978–79	'Winter of discontent'.
1979	Election of Conservative government led by Mrs Thatcher.
1980–92	Employment Acts restrict union rights to enforce closed shops, picket and strike; weaken individuals' rights (e.g. in relation to unfair dismissal and maternity leave).
1984	Trade Union Act requires regular secret ballots for the election of officials, before strikes, and to approve the continuance of political funds.
1984–85	Miners' strike.
1986	Wages Act restricts the scope of Wages Councils.
1988–90	Employment Acts remove all legal support for closed shops, further restrict unions and their scope for invoking industrial action.
1991	UK opts out of Social Chapter of Treaty of Maastricht.
1992	Re-election of Conservative government under John Major (the fourth consecutive defeat for the Labour Party).
1993	EC establishes a single European market.
1993	Trade Union Reform and Employment Rights Act.
1995	EC becomes European Union (EU); Department of Employment merged with other departments.
1997	Labour government, led by Tony Blair, elected with a large majority.
1998	National Minimum Wage introduced, initially at £3.60 per hour.
1999	Employment Relations Act introduces new union recognition provisions, among other things.
2001	Re-election of Labour government under Tony Blair, again with a large majority.
2002	EU Information and Consultation Directive.

Chapter 3

EMPLOYMENT RELATIONS IN THE UNITED STATES OF AMERICA

Harry C. Katz and Hoyt N. Wheeler

In accord with the relatively strong role that market forces have played in American economy history, the United States has long been noted for a high degree of diversity in the conditions under which employees work. Yet in recent years the amount of labour market diversity has increased markedly, spurred in part by the share of the labour force represented by unions continuing to decline (from a peak of 35 per cent in the early 1950s, to 20 per cent in 1983, and to 13.5 per cent in the early 21st century).

Diversity also appeared, insofar as, while union representation declined, the American labour movement engaged in vigorous revitalisation efforts. Thus, although facing continuing difficulties organising new members, the American labour movement has been engaged in innovation and experimentation. Diversity was also apparent in collective bargaining outcomes as, although some workers and unions lost devastating strikes or were forced into severe concessions, other unions were winning significant contractual gains, in some cases as a result of innovative collective bargaining strategies.

As shown by its GDP of $US10 039 billion and labour force of 142 million, the American economy is the largest of any considered in this book. Because of the size of its economy and its important role in global political affairs, the USA has played an important role in the development of other national systems.

THE HISTORICAL CONTEXT

American skilled craftsmen started to form unions even before industrialisation, which began in the 1790s. The skilled trades nature, practical goals and economic strategy of these early, pre-factory unions had a lasting legacy in American unions (Sturmthal 1973). Yet, from the time of the American revolution in 1776, there has also been a strong element of radical egalitarianism in the US labour movement. Also, in the early years of the 19th century many workers were attracted to various utopian schemes (Foner 1947).

The widespread establishment of the factory system in the 1850s and 1860s brought into the industrial system large numbers of rural women and children, and many immigrants from Ireland, Britain, Germany and other countries. These early factory workers did not unionise. This may have been partly because their pay was generally comparable to American farm earnings and higher than those of factory workers in Europe. It may also be that the high rate of worker mobility to other jobs, and considerable social mobility, hindered the development of the solidarity among workers that would have facilitated widespread organisation of unions (Lebergott 1984: 373, 386–7; Wheeler 1985). In addition, as often occurred later in US history, vigorous repression of unionisation by employers, both directly and through government action, inhibited unionisation (Sexton 1991).

In spite of these difficulties, skilled craftsmen did form national unions in the 1860s. These pragmatic 'business' unions quickly drove competitors from the field, and in 1886 the craft unions organised on a national basis into the American Federation of Labor (AFL) (Taft 1964).

Around 1900, building on a large home market made accessible by an improved transport system, large corporations achieved dominance in American industrial life. These complex, impersonal organisations required systematic strategies for managing their workers. Responding to this need, Frederick Taylor, the father of 'scientific management', and his industrial engineer disciples gained a powerful influence on the ideology and practice of management in the USA (Hession & Sardy 1969: 546–7). These ideas became widely accepted before they became influential in Europe and other parts of the world. By declaring 'scientific' principles for the design of work and pay, the Taylorists undermined the rationale for determining these matters by power-based bargaining by unions. Added to this difficulty for the unions was the continuing vigorous opposition of the capitalists, who had enormous power and high prestige (Sexton 1991).

The craft unions survived and prospered in the early part of the 20th century, partly because of cooperative mechanisms put in place during World War I and their patriotic support of the war. Yet by the 1920s a combination of the influence of Taylorism, employer use of company-dominated unions as a union-substitution device, tough employer action in collective bargaining, widespread use of anti-union propaganda by employer groups, and a hostile legal environment, had reduced even the proud and once-powerful craft unions to a very weak position, although unions in a few industries such as railroads and printing continued to have some success.

It was not until the 1930s, during the Great Depression, that US unions first arose as a broadly influential and seemingly permanent force. Then, for the first time, they penetrated mass production industry, organising large numbers of factory workers. A fateful conjunction of circumstances led to this. Working conditions and pay had deteriorated. There was a changed political environment with the election of Franklin D. Roosevelt as President in 1932. A wave of strikes, many of which were successful, took place in 1933–34. The *Wagner Act 1935* gave most workers a federally guaranteed right to organise and strike for the first time. Under these conditions, the strategy of mass campaigns by unions organised not by craft but by industry (United Automobile Workers, United Mine Workers, United Steel Workers), and united in a new labour movement—the Congress of Industrial Organizations (CIO)—led to unionisation of the car, steel, rubber, coal and other industries (Bernstein 1970; Wheeler 1985).

In the 1940s and 1950s the unions continued to grow, although federal legislation of this period restricted and regulated them. It was during this time that they developed the collective bargaining system. The post-World War II period saw general prosperity and constantly improving standards of living, accompanied by industrial peace. Union automatic wage rises (cost of living [COLA] clauses) in major industries contributed to the rise in living standards during this period. A wave of organising in the 1960s and 1970s, led by school teachers, transformed government employment in many parts of the country into a sector with strong unions.

THE MAJOR PARTIES

In the USA, all of the participants in the employment relations system retain some influence. However, it is the employers that have generally been the most powerful of the actors and, as will be argued below, are becoming increasingly dominant.

Employers and their organisations

As large corporations expanded in the 20th century in the USA, structured and bureaucratic 'internal labour markets' appeared within those 'primary-sector' enterprises. This included well-defined job progressions, also formal pay and fringe benefit policies (Doeringer & Piore 1971; Jacoby 1985). Jobs found in the union sector, even in industries such as construction that faced substantial cyclical economic volatility, led the way in developing structured and high-pay employment practices.

Yet the USA retained more unstructured employment practices, often in smaller or rural firms, where pay was lower and administered in a less formal manner. Furthermore, job progressions, dispute resolution procedures, and other employment practices were relatively informal and of lower quality in these 'secondary-sector' enterprises, especially when compared with the work practices found in large private- or public-sector employers.

Employers' organisations are relatively unimportant in the USA (Adams 1980: 4). In contrast to many other countries, there have never been national employers' confederations there engaging in the full range of industrial relations activities. There have, however, long been employers' organisations that have the mission of avoiding the unionisation of their members' employees. The National Association of Manufacturers was formed for this purpose in the 19th century. In addition, many regional Chambers of Commerce include union avoidance in their activities. These employer groups and others engage in anti-union litigation, lobbying and publicity campaigns. They, along with management consultants, engage in the lucrative business of educating employers in techniques of union avoidance.

The unions

The US labour movement is generally considered an exceptional case because of its apolitical 'business unionism' ideology, focusing rather narrowly on benefits to existing members. The most convincing explanations for this are historical (Kassalow 1974). First, there is no feudal tradition in the USA, which has made the distinctions among classes less obvious than in much of Europe. Second, US capitalism developed in a form that allowed fairly widespread prosperity. Third, the diversity of the population, divided particularly along racial and ethnic lines, has hampered the organisation of a broad-based working-class movement. Fourth, the early establishment of voting rights and free universal public education eliminated those potential working-class issues in the 19th century. Fifth, social mobility from the working class to the entre-preneurial class blurred class lines, creating a basis for the widely held belief in the 'log cabin to White House' myth. In consequence, the labour movement has seldom defined itself in class terms. Additionally, the historic experience of unionists was that class-conscious unions (i.e. those that assumed the 'burden of socialism') tended to be repressed by the strong forces of US capitalism (Sexton 1991).

American unions have relied on collective bargaining, accompanied by the strike threat, as their main weapon. This strategy has influenced the other characteristics of the labour movement. It has provided the basis for an effective role on the shop floor, as the day-to-day work of administering the agreement requires this. It has required unions to be solvent financially in order to have a credible strike threat. It has resulted in an organisational structure in which the power within the union is placed where it can best be used for collective bargaining, the national union (Barbash 1967: 69).

Centralisation of power over strike funds in the national union has been a crucial source of union ability to develop common rules and to strike effectively. It has facilitated, and perhaps even required, an inde-pendence from political parties that might be tempted to subordinate the economic to the political. It is one reason why there is a relatively low total union density, as collective bargaining organisations need to have a concern about density only as it pertains to their individual economic territories.

Although unions have emphasised collective bargaining, they have also engaged in politics. Their political action has for the most part taken the form of rewarding friends and punishing enemies among politicians and lobbying for legislation. They have avoided being involved in the formation of a labour party. The American Federation of Labor–Congress of Industrial Organization's (AFL-CIO) Committee on Political Education (COPE) and similar union political agencies are major financial contributors to political campaigns. The goals of such political activity have often been closely related to unions' economic goals, being aimed at making collective bargaining more effective. However, the labour movement has also been a major proponent of progressive political causes, such as laws on civil rights, minimum wages, plant closing notice, social security, and other subjects of benefit to citizens generally.

The structure of the labour movement is rather loose compared with that of other Western union movements, as the national unions have never been willing to cede power over the function of collective bargaining to the AFL-CIO. The AFL-CIO is a federation of national unions that includes a substantial share of union members. It serves as the chief political and public relations voice for the labour movement, resolves jurisdictional disputes among its members, enforces codes of ethical practices and policies against racial and sex discrimination, and is US labour's main link to the international labour movement.

A major change in the AFL-CIO occurred in 1995 with the unprecedented election challenge for the federation's presidency by John Sweeney. As president of the Service Employees International Union (SEIU), Sweeney successfully organised a coalition of union leaders within the federation's member unions and defeated the chosen successor of the previous president, who had retired as a result of the Sweeney-led challenge. In an effort to address the decline in union density, the Sweeney administration of the AFL-CIO has emphasised organising new membership through a variety of new initiatives. The most innovative of these measures are described in more detail later in this chapter.

Within the labour movement, the national unions have been described as occupying the 'kingpin' position (Barbash 1967: 69). They maintain ultimate power over the important function of collective bargaining, in large part through their control of strike funds. The national unions can establish and disestablish local unions. They can, as the Carpenters did, withdraw from the AFL-CIO if they wish (Bureau of National Affairs 2001).

Continuing a trend that began in the early 1980s, several mergers and proposals for mergers among national unions have occurred. Recent examples of mergers include the combination of the two largest textile unions. In addition, many small independent unions have begun to choose to be absorbed into national unions, further consolidating the union structure of US unionism (McClendon, Kriesky & Eaton 1995).

The local unions perform the day-to-day work of the labour movement. They usually conduct bargaining over the terms of new agreements and conduct strikes, although in some industries national unions do this. They administer the agreement, performing the important function of enforcing the complex set of rights that the collective bargaining agreement creates. Social activities among union members take place at the local level, where there is a union culture (Barbash 1967: 26–41).

Government

The rapid increase in public-sector unionisation in the 1960s and 1970s was probably the most important development in the US labour movement since the 1930s. Teachers led the way as they successfully protested about declines in their salaries and benefits relative to those of other workers. Rapid expansion in public-sector union membership and militancy followed.

In the mid-1970s a taxpayers' revolt emerged and slowed the gains of public employee unions, although union representation, as a share of the total public-sector workforce, held steady. Then in the mid-1980s, teachers and other public-employee groups benefited from public concern over the inadequacy of public services and saw their bargaining power rebound. In the 1990s, calls to reinvent the public sector led to diverse strategies, ranging from downsizing and privatisation to efforts to bring empowerment and a quality focus to public service provision.

Federal, state, and local government employees are excluded from coverage under the National Labor Relations Act (NLRA). Separate legal regulations govern collective bargaining in each of these sectors. Federal employees received the rights to unionise and to negotiate over employment conditions other than wages or fringe benefits through Executive Order 10988, signed by President Kennedy in 1962. In 1970, as part of its effort to reform the postal service, Congress provided postal employees the right to engage in collective bargaining about pay, hours and working conditions. Then in 1978 Congress replaced the executive orders of President Kennedy (and a related order of President Nixon) with the first comprehensive federal law providing collective bargaining rights to federal employees. Subsequently, collective bargaining in the federal sector has been regulated by the Federal Labor Relations Authority. Responsibility for impasse resolution is vested in the Federal Services Impasse Panel. The panel may use mediation, fact-finding or arbitration to resolve disputes. The right to strike is prohibited.

As of 1997, all but nine states had legislation that provided at least some of their state or local government employees with the rights to organise and to bargain collectively. Twenty-five states have passed comprehensive laws that cover a range of occupational groups; the others that have not yet enacted public-sector bargaining laws are primarily in the south.

In addition to its role as employer, the US federal government has two other main roles in industrial relations—direct regulation of terms and conditions of employment, and regulation of the manner in which organised labour and management relate to each other.

The direct regulation of terms and conditions of employment was limited to the areas of employment discrimination, worker safety, unemployment compensation, minimum wages and maximum hours, and retirement (Ledvinka & Scarpello 1991). In 1964, the government prohibited discrimination in employment on the grounds of race, colour, sex, religion, or national origin. This law was subsequently strengthened and broadened to prohibit discrimination against disabled workers.

In the 1980s and mid-1990s, there was a great deal of legislative activity in the broad field of employment relations, in part to fill gaps created by the weakening influence of unions. Legislative initiatives in the areas of minimum wages, termination of employment, race and sex discrimination in employment, pensions, health and safety, plant closing, drug testing, race and sex discrimination, discrimination against disabled workers, polygraphs (lie-detector machines), and family and medical leave have all attracted attention and produced a plethora of new laws.

Unemployment benefit, for example, is provided for on a state-by-state basis, but with some federal control and funding. It involves payments to persons who have become involuntarily unemployed and are seeking work. The duration of payments is shorter than in most other countries. Federal and state wage and hour laws provide for a minimum level of pay and a premium pay rate for overtime work, although many workers are excluded from the coverage of these laws.

Retirement benefits are regulated in two main ways. First, through the Social Security system, employers and employees are required to pay a proportion of wages into a government fund. It is out of this fund that pensions are paid by the government to eligible retired employees (Social Security Act). The second way in which government controls pensions is by regulation of the private pension funds that are set up voluntarily by employers. The *Employee Retirement Income Security Act 1974* requires retirement plans to be financially secure, and insures these plans. It also mandates that employees become permanently vested in their retirement rights after a certain period.

Government regulation of the labour–management relationship consists largely of a set of rules through which these actors establish, and work out the terms of, their relationship. Through the NLRA 1935, as amended in 1947 and 1959, government provides a structure of rules that establishes certain employee rights with respect to collective action.

The process and rules established by law for union certification and bargaining in the private sector represent one of the more unusual features of US labour–management relations. The NLRA specifies a multi-step organising process, ordinarily culminating in a secret ballot election by employees to determine whether they want union certification. The objective of the law regulating union representation elections is to ensure employees have a free choice. To achieve this objective, the National Labor Relations Board (NLRB) determines the appropriate voting unit, conducts the secret ballot election, certifies the union as the exclusive bargaining agent for the unit when the union achieves a majority of the votes cast, and rules on allegations of unfair labour practices such as employer retribution against employees who support the union. When the union is victorious in the election, the NLRB issues a certification that requires the employer to bargain in good faith with the union. The union has the same obligation.

Much controversy has focused on whether or not the election process is working in accordance with the original legislative intent. This has led to a continuing debate over the adequacy of laws protecting workers' rights to form and join unions. The Commission on the Future of Worker–Management Relations (Dunlop Commission), reporting in 1994, reached the conclusion that the labour laws should be changed to facilitate union organising. Little has come from these and other related recommendations to reform US labour laws, however—in part because most employers remain reasonably satisfied with the outcomes of the present legal framework.

The government plays a very limited role in the collective bargaining process in the private sector. Although it requires 'good faith' bargaining efforts, government generally takes a 'hands-off' position (with notable exceptions such as the railroad industry) in influencing contract outcomes achieved between labour and employers in private-sector collective bargaining.

THE MAIN PROCESSES OF EMPLOYMENT RELATIONS

In the *non-union sector*, employers have devised a set of management practices to determine pay and conditions of work systematically. In

terms of pay, a combination of job evaluation and individual performance evaluation systems is widespread. The range of possible pay rates
for workers in, say, a clerk's job are determined by an assessment of the
worth of the job to the firm (i.e. job evaluation). A particular employee
is assigned a pay rate within this range depending on seniority, performance or other factors. In addition to pay, fringe benefits such as health
insurance, pensions, vacations and holidays are determined by company
policy. All of this is done with an eye to the external labour market, with
total compensation having to be adequate to attract and keep needed
workers (Gomez-Meija, Balkin & Cardy 1995).

In the *union sector* the structure of collective bargaining is highly
fragmented, and this fragmentation is increasing. As is the case in many
other DMEs, trends discussed in more detail below suggest that the locus
of collective bargaining is shifting downward towards the enterprise or
workplace level (Katz 1993). Single-company or single-workplace agreements are the norm in manufacturing. Most collective bargaining takes
place at such levels. Even where there are national agreements, as in the
car industry, substantial scope is left for local variation.

While the government plays only a very limited role in determining
collective bargaining agreements in the private sector, mediators
employed by the national government through the Federal Mediation
and Conciliation Service (FMCS) are active in the negotiation of new
agreements, and their work is generally popular with the parties. In
negotiations involving government employees, many state laws provide
for binding arbitration of unresolved disputes over the terms of a new
agreement. This is especially common where the government employees involved, such as fire fighters or police officers, are considered to be
'essential'. Interest arbitration of the terms of a new agreement is very
rare in the private sector.

Although there is considerable variety in collective bargaining agreements (contracts), nearly all of them share certain features. Most are
very detailed, although the craft union contracts are less so. Agreements
generally cover pay, hours of work, holidays, pensions, health insurance,
life insurance, union recognition, management rights, the role of seniority in determining promotions and layoffs, and the handling and arbitration of grievances. Most agreements have a limited duration, usually
of one to three years (Bureau of National Affairs 1995).

In both the private and public sectors, the majority of agreements
provide a formal multi-step grievance procedure that culminates in
rights arbitration. The formal procedure specifies a series of steps

through which the parties can settle disagreements about the application and interpretation of an existing collective bargaining agreement. The procedures are almost always capped by the provision for an independent arbitrator to be selected jointly by the union and the employer. Compared to most DMEs, the emphasis on formal grievance arbitration represents one of the more unusual features of employment relations in the USA. A substantial body of private 'law' has grown up through arbitral decisions, providing employment relations with a set of norms that are used in the non-union sector as well as the union sector. Decisions of arbitrators have historically been treated by the courts as final, binding and unappealable (Feuille & Wheeler 1981: 270–81).

In 1991, through its decision in the Gilmer case, the Supreme Court allowed statutory employment rights claims to be solved in arbitration. This spurred the spread of 'alternative dispute resolution' procedures, particularly in the non-union sector, to settle disputes over matters such as dismissals or racial discrimination. In 2001, further impetus to so-called employment arbitration was provided by the Supreme Court's Circuit City decision. Some analysts charged that the replacement of court procedures with private justice violates employee rights (Stone 1996).

Major changes also occurred in recent collective bargaining, primarily in response to economic pressures. The process of change began with developments in the 1980s. Those and subsequent events are reviewed in detail below.

The 1980s: experimentation and change

The election of Ronald Reagan as President in 1980 reflected a strong conservative shift in the political climate. This shift was vividly illustrated early in Reagan's administration when he fired and permanently replaced air traffic controllers (members of the Professional Air Traffic Controller Union, PATCO) who had gone out on strike in August 1981.

PATCO had been engaging in an illegal strike over the terms of a new collective bargaining contract. Although the President's actions were directed at employees of the federal government, those actions sent a strong message to employers that the unions had lost not only much of their political power but also the public's support. The firing of striking controllers and the demise of PATCO strengthened the resolve of employers to seize the initiative in collective bargaining.

The economic recession of 1981–83 further mobilised many employers to sidestep or even abolish collective bargaining. The rise in the value of the US dollar against foreign currencies further reduced the competitiveness of US producers operating in foreign markets. Many layoffs in key, highly unionised sectors resulted, reaching deep into union ranks and thereby cutting off the unions' primary source of bargaining power. Plant closings and mass layoffs spread to the point where some analysts argued that a deindustrialisation of America was underway. Thus began the era of concessionary bargaining that entailed unions agreeing to wage cuts or freezes or in other ways giving back previous gains.

Union concessions along with other factors led to particularly difficult times for poorly educated workers, and this contributed to a growing inequality in income distribution. The rate of decline in union membership accelerated during the 1980s. By 1985 the labour movement acknowledged the depth of its membership crisis and called on its leaders to consider a variety of new strategies.

At the same time, new forms of employee participation and new concepts of how to organise work appeared in some workplaces. Thus, on the one hand unions were negotiating concessionary agreements and losing members; on the other hand some of the concessionary contracts included gains, by providing employees with employment security or direct participation in business decisions. Employers were taking benefits away from unions at the same time as offering unions other benefits some of them had been asking for. By the late 1980s better times appeared in some manufacturing industries, such as cars and aerospace, and elements of traditional collective bargaining including pattern bargaining began to reappear.

Although these contradictory pressures did not hit all bargaining relationships with equal force, their cumulative effects posed fundamental challenges to the basic principles underlying the New Deal industrial relations system that had been established in the 1930s. There were changes occurring at all three levels of the traditional bargaining system.

At the workplace level, unions were challenged by new forms of worker and union participation and by more direct communication between workers and management. At the middle enterprise level, unions were making major concessions to their pay settlements and work rules (e.g. fewer job classifications). Meanwhile, at a higher level, substantial strategic level changes were occurring that often involved greater union involvement in strategic business issues.

The nature and extent of these changes varied considerably across the range of bargaining relationships in different industries and companies.

They were not universal, and they may not prove to be lasting features of collective bargaining. But the new practices were in use in enough bargaining relationships to lead many managers and unionists to discuss whether these new practices were superior to collective bargaining. Thus, the 1980s proved to be a period of experimentation and of new strategic choices for management, unions, and government decision makers.

The 1990s: income and collective bargaining polarisation

Even though the economy experienced a strong recovery that started in the early 1990s, there was growing polarisation in collective bargaining and in employees' labour market experiences. In the early 1990s, corporate downsizing and re-engineering led to layoffs and insecurity, particularly among middle managers and white-collar employees, who bore an uncharacteristically large share of the brunt of these initiatives. Income bifurcation continued in the face of large rewards to those employees that were highly educated (and particularly large rewards to top corporate management), while poorly educated workers fared badly as new technologies and heightened international competition spurred industrial changes.

Unions became concerned about employment security, a concern that helped spur the negotiation of modest pay rises, which in turn helped produce low rates of inflation and unemployment in this period. Meanwhile, labour–management relations also became more polarised. At some enterprises, unions and management further developed participatory styles that included team forms of work organisation and union involvement in business issues. On the other side there were high-conflict relationships where strikes involved the use of permanent striker replacements and union decertification.

Pressures from globalisation became particularly acute by 2000, even though exports of goods constitute only 11.6 per cent of US GDP—smaller than any other OECD country (*Economic Report of the President* 2001). The relative unimportance of exports to the economy reflects the USA's large home market, which creates a considerable potential for self-sufficiency. However, international trade and investments have become increasingly important to US-based MNEs. The wage and other cost control pressures resulting from increased international competition have led to more aggressive management behaviour towards unions. Regional trade pacts, particularly the NAFTA accord, helped spur further globalisation.

NAFTA, which took effect in January 1994, removes tariffs and other trade barriers between the USA, Mexico and Canada during a fifteen-year period. Both the passage and the continuing effects of NAFTA have been controversial. NAFTA has been widely criticised by unions claiming that Mexico's low wages cause many US companies to relocate south of the border. Meanwhile, environmentalists worry that companies flee south in order to take advantage of weak pollution controls and lax enforcement of environmental regulations. On the other side of this debate, Presidents Clinton and Bush, the business community and many economists support NAFTA, on the grounds that it provides gains through trade to all three countries. NAFTA supporters claim that it will help integrate Mexico more fully into the world economy and thereby address Mexico's social problems and their spillover effects on the USA (e.g. high immigration and the drug trade).

To silence its critics, side agreements were added to NAFTA concerning the environment and labour rights. The labour side agreements create National Administrative Offices authorised to investigate public charges that one of the NAFTA countries is not enforcing its own labour laws. NAFTA also includes a 'Transitional Adjustment Assistance' program to provide training to workers who lose their jobs because of the trade pact. Yet unions complain that this assistance program fails to meet the needs of the much larger number of workers harmfully affected by NAFTA, while others argue that many assisted workers lost their jobs for reasons that had nothing to do with NAFTA or trade. There is continuing debate regarding the effects of NAFTA on workers and the US and Mexican economies.

CHANGING EMPLOYMENT RELATIONS

The non-union sector has continued to grow in the private sector, as management has aggressively resisted union organisation and taken advantage of new technologies and relatively lax enforcement of labour laws to shift work within or outside the USA, or relies on outsourcing or 'contingent labour' to meet competitive pressures and union organising efforts.

Union revitalisation

Faced with a growing non-union sector, since the mid-1990s the labour movement has initiated innovative efforts to stimulate new organising.

Union organisers have been elected to leadership positions of several unions. National unions and the AFL-CIO have begun to spend more on organising; and innovative organising tactics, including efforts to organise on a community or regional basis outside the NLRB procedures, have been launched (Turner, Katz & Hurd 2001).

The 'Justice for Janitors' campaign is a noteworthy example of the innovative union organising activities taking place. Since the late 1980s, the SEIU has led a campaign to organise janitors in a number of regions of the country, using non-traditional tactics that in some cases have sought to go outside the NLRA and NLRB procedures to gain union representation. This Justice for Janitors campaign tries to organise on a multi-employer (regional) basis and often avoids normal NLRB-style representation elections by inducing employers to voluntarily recognise the union. The campaign puts pressure on the primary employers that typically rely on subcontractors to provide janitorial services in their buildings. The Justice for Janitors campaign also tries to use alliances with community groups such as churches to gain public support for union organising efforts.

Other important steps in union revitalisation are the AFL-CIO Organizing Institute and the restructured AFL-CIO Organizing Department. The Organizing Institute focused on recruiting members, and through the clinical programs used to train new organisers. After Sweeney's election to the presidency of the AFL-CIO in 1995, a new Organizing Department in the AFL-CIO was given a sizeable budget and the task of extending the sort of activities begun in the Organizing Institute. In addition to recruitment and training of organisers, the Organizing Department provides affiliated unions with strategic planning and analysis for organising campaigns. The AFL-CIO's Union Summer program has been funding college interns on summer union organising projects.

One of the purposes of the AFL-CIO organising initiatives is to diffuse some of the successful organising strategies used by affiliated unions. Unions such as the Union of Needletrades, Industrial, and Textile Employees (UNITE) and the SEIU have had above-average success in their organising. The campaigns of these unions use young, well-educated organisers and involve extensive direct communication with prospective members and links to community groups such as churches.

This approach to organising has been labelled a 'rank-and-file' style and contrasts with the more top-down traditional organising that relied on appointed organisers and formal communication strategies. Rank-and-file organising also tries to modernise and broaden the issues around which employees are attracted to unions by confronting child care, equal pay and other issues of concern to the current workforce. Research suggests that this method of union organising has been more successful than traditional methods in the private sector (Bronfenbrenner 1997).

It is too early to tell whether the AFL-CIO will be able to increase greatly the use of rank-and-file organising and whether this and other revitalisation measures will have a significant impact on union organising success.

Variation in employment practices

Economic pressure has induced a substantial increase in the amount and nature of the variation in employment practices. Some of the increased variation has been spurred by a decline in unionisation and the differences between the union and non-union sectors. Perhaps most striking is the fact that even within the union and non-union sectors variation has been increasing through the spread of a diverse array of employment practices. Another divergent aspect of collective bargaining is that union representation is much more substantial in the public sector, where the unionisation rate was 37.5 per cent (versus 9 per cent in the private sector) in 2000 (Bureau of Labor Statistics 2001).

A key factor promoting variation in employment relations has been a substantial decline in the level of unionisation and growth in various types of non-union employment. Unionisation in the USA never approached the levels found in many other countries. As a result of a lower level of unionisation, and the limited influence of other constraints on managerial behaviour, the USA generally has had a relatively large low-wage employment sector. Nevertheless, there were other non-union firms that chose to pay more, often as part of employment strategies following bureaucratic, HRM or Japanese-oriented employment patterns.

The downward trend in unionisation increased the variation in employment conditions given that, where it existed, unionisation brought a high degree of standardisation in employment conditions. Job-control unionism put a high premium on contractual rules and pattern bargaining linking contractual settlements within and between industries (Katz 1985: 38–46). In contrast, a common feature of non-union employment systems has been procedures that relate pay and other employment terms to individual traits. The resulting 'individualisation' of the employment relationship in non-union settings has produced much higher variation in employment practices across individuals, companies and industries when compared with union employment systems.

The future of career jobs?

A key current debate spurred by the diversity found in the labour market concerns whether career jobs are a thing of the past. Will employees spend much, if not all, of their working life with a single employer, or will they often move across jobs and firms? In the hi-tech sector, and particularly in California's Silicon Valley, hypermobility appeared in the labour market for computer programmers and other professional employees, as employees moved relatively easily between enterprises in part to take advantage of attractive stock option offers. In other parts of the labour market, such as the new media industry, the lack of employment continuity reflects the programmer/graphic artists who provide Internet design services, usually working as independent subcontractors, whose link to any particular company may last only as long as a particular project. Some observers claim that frequent inter-firm mobility has, or will shortly, become a common feature of the labour market as employees experience 'boundary-less' careers (Cappelli 1999).

When the hi-tech bubble burst in mid-2000, the attractiveness of inter-firm mobility lost some of its appeal, and there is debate among economists about the extent and permanence of 'hypermobility'. Economic analysis has revealed that while there is some shortening in the average job tenure experienced by workers, the sort of job hyper-mobility found in Silicon Valley or among media workers is not typical (Farber 1998). Rather, as Osterman (1999) notes in his careful analysis of the evidence, what seems to have changed is that workers and managers now fear the possibility of layoff, and do so even if their employer is doing well (also see Jacoby 1999). A significant number of workers now face heightened, if not hyper-, labour market mobility. The way to reconcile these findings is to recognise the diversity of labour market experience (Katz & Darbishire 2000).

Many US workers still have relatively long work careers with a single employer, while some employees do often change employers. This diversity exists not only with regard to the frequency of cross-employer labour market mobility but also in terms of a significant variety in employment practices and systems. The labour market, for example, has a large and growing number of low-end jobs, characterised by low wages, high turnover, ad-hoc and autocratic personnel practices, and little training. Yet there are also progressive employers, who use work teams, pay high wages, use contingent compensation, and have formalised complaint and other personnel practices.

COLLECTIVE BARGAINING INITIATIVES

Unions have struggled in recent years to extend their membership and maintain their influence in unionised settings. To do so, unions have made significant changes in the process and outcomes of collective bargaining, including corporate campaigns and the linking of collective bargaining to organising and political strategies. While corporate campaigns historically had been used sporadically by the US labour movement, the use and intensity of these campaigns increased in the 1990s as unions struggled to find ways to counteract the power advantages management had gained through such factors as the availability of outsourcing, globalisation, and the use of permanent striker replacements.

Corporate campaigns are characterised by the use of media, political, financial, community and regulatory pressures to build bargaining power. The United Steel Workers of America (USWA) have been particularly aggressive in developing these tactics, and successfully used corporate campaigns in disputes with the Ravenswood Aluminum Corporation (Juravich & Bronfenbrenner 1999) and, after their merger with the United Rubber Workers, in the Bridgestone dispute (settled in 1996). Unions learned painfully, through lost strikes at Phelps Dodge (Rosenblum 1995) and International Paper (Getman 1998), that corporate campaigns had to be well developed and started early in order to succeed.

The revitalisation efforts of the Communications Workers of America (CWA) highlights the advantages of a triangular agenda linking organising, politics and collective bargaining (Katz, Batt & Keefe 2000). In such a triangulation strategy, union activities in any one of these three spheres interact with and complement activities in another sphere. It is, for example, through novel language won in collective bargaining agreements in the telecommunications industry (with the Regional Bell phone companies) that the CWA gained card check recognition and employer neutrality in representation elections, key parts of the union's organising initiative. Similarly, the CWA has linked political actions towards public agencies that regulated pricing and access in the telecommunications industry with efforts to strengthen the union's strike leverage (and win more at the collective bargaining table).

The labour movement will have to find ways to extend triangulation linkages into the international arena. The expansion of international trade and the accelerated expansion of MNEs extend the market internationally. John R. Commons explained, in his classic analysis of early union formation among American shoemakers, that as the extent of the market expanded, to counteract 'competitive menaces' and retain bargaining power, unions at the beginning of the 20th century shifted to a national structure (Commons 1909). This provided a structure of representation that was parallel to the emerging national structure of markets.

Labour movements all over the globe confront the need for cross-national unionism, but their efforts to create such unionism face substantial barriers. These barriers include divergent interests (i.e. each labour movement wants the employment) and national differences in language, culture, law and union structure. Yet unions will need to find an international parallel to the sort of domestic sphere linkages being pursued by the CWA. There are some recent signs of increased international activity among US unions. Several cases where American unions have engaged in cross-national pressure campaigns involve NAFTA provisions (Katz & Kochan 1999: 373–4). However, union gains on this and related fronts in the USA are limited and the barriers remain daunting.

While it is important to note the extent of innovative bargaining strategies being developed by unions, unions still successfully use traditional collective bargaining pressure tactics such as strikes (or strike threats) to make gains. Recent examples include the United Automobile Workers (UAW) bargaining with the Big Three car companies, pilots bargaining at Delta and other major airline carriers (before 11 September 2001), and bargaining involving IAM-represented machinists at Boeing. In these firms unions retained significant membership and benefited from the effects of the strong macroeconomic growth experienced in the USA in the 1990s. The UAW, for example, gained 3 per cent annual base pay rises on top of income security guarantees and plant closing moratoriums in its four-year agreements signed with the Big Three in the latter part of 1999.

The UAW's success at gaining the restoration of traditional 3 per cent base pay rises in its Big Three contracts is a telling illustration of the symbolic importance of the 3 per cent figure and the amount of bargaining power the union had regained. The UAW, like other US unions, did not use its renewed bargaining power to push excessive wage claims. In contrast, the moderate nature of collective bargaining settlements in the 1980s and 1990s contributed to the strong economic expansion experienced in the USA.

Pay is perhaps the most important employment outcome, and there is clear evidence of growing earnings variation (Levy & Murname 1992: 1333). While increasing income inequality is a trend common to many countries, the gap is particularly large in the USA. There is accumulating evidence that a mixture of market and institutional factors (most importantly the low level of unionisation and decentralised structure of collective bargaining) have caused income inequality to rise to such levels in the USA (Blau & Kahn 1996).

The decentralisation of collective bargaining structures

While there were diverse outcomes in collective bargaining, there were also significant changes underway in the structure of US collective bargaining, perhaps the most important of which was decentralisation. Until the early 1980s, the structure of bargaining affecting unionised employees was a mixture of multi-employer, company-wide and plant-level bargaining. But after that, the structure of collective bargaining began to crumble as formally centralised structures broke down, the locus of bargaining shifted to the plant level within structures that maintained both company- and plant-level bargaining to some degree, and pattern bargaining weakened.

In some cases multi-employer bargaining in the United States was ended. This was the fate of the basic steel agreement in 1986. In some other industries, the number of companies and unionised employees covered by a multi-firm agreement declined as companies withdrew from master agreements—as in the trucking industry (eroding the influence of the Master Freight Agreement negotiated by the Teamsters and an employers' association which had set employment terms for inter-city truck drivers) and in the underground coal-mining sector (eroding the influence of a master agreement negotiated between the United Mineworkers and the Bituminous Coal Operators' Association) (Kochan, Katz & McKersie 1994: 128–30).

Simultaneously, there has been a shift to plant-level, and away from company-wide, collective bargaining agreements. In many cases, such as the tyre and airline industries, this involved the negotiation of local pay and/or work rule concessions. Often these negotiations included whip-sawing by management, with local unions and workers being threatened with the prospect of a plant closing if adequate concessions were not granted (Cappelli 1985; Kochan, Katz & McKersie 1994: 117–27). In some cases, concessions on work rules have been accompanied by new arrangements providing extensive participation by workers and local union officers in decisions that were formerly made solely by management. With increasing frequency, work rule bargaining has come to involve a decision whether or not to implement a joint team-based approach or involve disputes that arise during the implementation of that type of work organisation.

Even where company-level collective bargaining has continued, greater diversity in collective bargaining outcomes has appeared across companies. This diversity has replaced the pattern bargaining that had informally served to centralise bargaining structures to the multi-employer level. In the aerospace and agricultural implements industries, for example, pattern bargaining weakened, and significant inter-company variation in wages and other contractual terms emerged in the 1980s and 1990s (Erickson 1992, 1996).

There was even wider variation appearing in work practices across companies and industries in light of the uneven spread of work re-organisation. Some plants adopted team systems of work, while others did not. Wide differences appear in the form and role of any work teams. In some places there was much bargaining at the plant and work group level, involving team systems, pay for knowledge, and other contingent compensation mechanisms, and changes in work time arrangements (Kochan, Katz & McKersie 1994: 146–205). Also, more direct communication between managers and workers spread in many parts of the union sector. The increased role for localised bargaining and work rule adjustment contributed to the emergence of a 'participatory' employment system in a number of unionised settings. The best-known example of such participation was the Saturn subsidiary of General Motors, where workers and the UAW continue to engage in extensive involvement in business decisions, even in the face of changes in union leadership and debates about the appropriate role and form of union participation (Rubinstein & Kochan 2001).

Although participation programs spread first in the manufacturing sector, by the late 1990s they were more obvious in the service sector. Perhaps the most elaborate service-sector example of a participatory employment pattern is the Kaiser Permanente–AFL-CIO partnership (Katz & Kochan 1999: 304; Bureau of National Affairs 2000).

However, in some workplaces, employee and union participation in business decisions or other forms of work restructuring has been limited. Osterman (1994: 177), for example, finds that 36 per cent of enterprises use none of a long list of innovative work practices. Applebaum and Batt (1994) provide a rich description of the diversity of work practice changes and an insightful analysis of why there has been sluggishness and variation in the diffusion of new work practices.

CONCLUSIONS

Diversity in employment relations is growing as a product of the growth in non-union employment and the variety of union and non-union employment practices. The breakdown of pattern bargaining across enterprises and industries in the union sector, and the spread of contingent forms of pay and associated greater reliance on individualised rewards, are all contributing to greater variation in work rules and pay. The changes in pay practices have contributed to the unusually large growth in income inequality in the USA.

While team systems have spread and operate as a critical part of the employment systems in some firms, more traditional forms of work organisation continue in other firms. Decentralisation, more direct management–employee communication, and increased employee (and union) involvement in business decisions all have contributed to the wide variation of work practices.

There is also wide variation in the tenor of recent collective bargaining. In some companies heightened conflict has appeared, while in some others extensive partnerships have been forged. While some workers suffered greatly as management took advantage of a power imbalance provided through non-union growth and globalisation, in some other contexts unions used innovative bargaining or traditional strike leverage to make gains.

Unions have shown a willingness to cooperate with workplace changes that attempt to raise productivity and product/service quality—where the innovations also include attention to the union's goals. As such, consistent with US 'business unionism', the collective bargaining process has shown flexibility in responding to competitive pressures. The challenge faced by the labour movement is to find ways to combine collective bargaining successes and revitalisation efforts to further promote high-end employment outcomes and limit the growth of low-wage employment patterns and income inequality.

A CHRONOLOGY OF US EMPLOYMENT RELATIONS

1794	Federal Society of Cordwainers founded in Philadelphia—first permanent US union.
1828	Working Men's Party founded.
1834	National Trades Union founded—first national labour organisation.
1866	National Labor Union formed—first national 'reformist' union.
1869	Knights of Labor founded—a 'reformist' organisation dedicated to changing society, which nevertheless was involved in strikes for higher wages and improved conditions.
1886	Formation of the American Federation of Labor (AFL), a loose confederation of unions with largely 'bread-and-butter' goals. Peak membership of the Knights of Labor (700 000 members), which then began to decline.
1905	Formation of the Industrial Workers of the World, the 'Wobblies', an anarcho-syndicalist union.
1914–22	Repression of radical unions because of their opposition to war, and during the 'Red scare' after the Russian Revolution.
1915	Establishment of the first company-dominated union, Ludlow, Colorado.
1920s	Decline and retrenchment of the American labour movement.
1932	Election of Franklin D. Roosevelt as President —a 'New Deal' for unions.
1935	National Labor Relations (Wagner) Act gives employees a federally protected right to organise and bargain collectively. Also, formation of the Congress of Industrial Organizations (CIO), a federation of industrial unions.
1935–39	Rapid growth of unions covering major mass-production industries.
1941–45	Growth of unions and development of the collective bargaining system during the war.
1946	Massive postwar strike wave in major industries.
1947	Enactment of the Taft-Hartley Act prohibits unions from certain organising and bargaining practices.
1955	AFL and CIO merger to form the AFL-CIO.
1959	Landrum-Griffin Act regulates the internal operations of unions.
1960	New York City teachers' strike—the beginning of mass organisation of public employees.
1962	Adoption of Executive Order 10988 by President John F. Kennedy, providing for limited collective bargaining by federal government employees.

1960–80	Growth of unionism of public employees. Decline in union density in the manufacturing sector.
1977–78	Defeat of Labor Law Reform Bill in Congress, as employer movement in opposition to unions gains strength.
1980	Election of President Ronald Reagan—new federal policies generally adverse to organised labour.
1981	Economic recession.
1988–89	Federal legislation on drugs, lie detectors, plant closing, minimum wages. Court decisions on drug testing and termination of employment.
1991	Federal legislation prohibiting discrimination against disabled workers. Federal legislation strengthens employment discrimination laws.
1991	Through the Gilmer and related decisions the Supreme Court allows statutory employment rights disputes to be resolved through (private) arbitration. Alternative dispute resolution then spreads, particularly in the non-union sector.
1991–92	Extended economic recession.
1992	Election of President Bill Clinton. A more labour-friendly national administration comes to power.
1992–2000	Sustained economic growth with low unemployment, low inflation, and limited real wage growth.
1994	The Commission on the Future of Worker–Management Relations (Dunlop Commission) recommends that a number of changes be made in the nation's labour laws, but these recommendations are ignored by the US Congress.
1994	Republicans win Congressional elections. A very conservative Congress comes into being.
1994	NAFTA removes tariff and other trade barriers between the USA, Canada and Mexico.
1995	Increases in the minimum wage voted by Congress.
1995	John Sweeney elected president of the AFL-CIO, spurring accelerated union revitalisation.
2000	George W. Bush becomes President after an extremely close election. Republicans gain control of the Senate in mid-2001.

Chapter 4

EMPLOYMENT RELATIONS IN CANADA

Mark Thompson and Daphne G. Taras

Employment relations in Canada rest on several fundamental character-istics. A large proportion of the labour force is subject to the influence of collective bargaining, directly or indirectly, and legal protection for collective bargaining is strong. There are traditions of adversarialism and high levels of strike activity. The structures of employment relations are less centralised than other nations. Canada has incorporated employers, unions and public policies that originated in the USA but produced a distinctive employment relations system.

THE HISTORICAL, POLITICAL AND SOCIOECONOMIC CONTEXT

Canada's federal system of government is one of the most decentralised in the world, vesting authority for most employment matters with the ten provinces. Except for wartime crises, the federal authority is limited to regulation of the federal civil service and employment within national industries such as interprovincial transport. Less than 10 per cent of Canadian workers falls within this domain. This decentralisation has led to considerable public policy experimentation: Canada has not experienced the American political gridlock on labour law reform. However, national companies must comply with different labour and employment laws depending on the location of their employees, and unions must be sensitive to local differences in law when they organise, bargain and strike.

To this already complex mix is added the history and traditions of French Canada, with the province of Quebec having alternative social, economic and legal traditions that are different from those elsewhere in North America. Quebec is the second most populous province, after the neighbouring Ontario. The strong nationalism of many in Quebec has reinforced the already powerful decentralising forces within Canada. Canada is well known for its bilingual and bicultural image, but the country is regionally fractured into a primarily French-speaking province of Quebec and parts of adjacent provinces, and primarily English-speaking provinces known colloquially as 'the rest of Canada'.

Immigration continues to be important. While the 1996 government census shows that 62 per cent of Canadians learned French or English as a first language at home, 38 per cent cited more than 70 other primary languages. The largest source of immigrants was Britain, followed by other European countries. In the 1960s and 1970s there were many migrants from developing countries, especially from the British Commonwealth. Most of the early immigrants came to improve their economic status, but many also brought a tradition of working-class politics. Simultaneously, the relatively conservative political tradition of the USA has been a powerful model to Canadians. These influences, combined with a Westminster parliamentary political system (and its acceptance of third parties), have combined to produce a value system that includes US-style individualism of an expanding capitalist economy and the collectivism of mature industrial nations in Western Europe.

Politically, Canada has a multi-party system reflecting regional inter-ests. The political structure reflects strongly held regional sentiments, accentuated by distance and language. For decades, the country was dominated by a rivalry between two parties, the Liberals and Conserva-tives, with a powerful third party, the New Democratic Party (NDP), able to achieve some of its left-of-centre agenda when it occasionally held the balance of power. Since the 1930s, the Liberals have dominated federal politics, occasionally forming a minority government or yielding power to the Conservatives, who won large majorities in 1984 and 1988. The Liberals are a pragmatic, reformist party, with a traditional base of support in Quebec. The Conservatives are a right-of-centre party, normally drawing votes from the eastern and western regions. While it had a market orientation, the Conservative government did not embrace the social and economic policies of the Thatcher or Reagan administrations. Canadian politics allow political platforms to be conservative fiscally but simultaneously embrace responsibility for the social welfare of the citizenry. Thus, Conservative governments occasionally have nationalised private companies and NDP regimes have encouraged SMEs. Even political parties that govern for long periods of time, such as the Liberals nationally, may alternate between conservative and liberal economic policies.

Elections in the 1990s dramatically changed the nature of party politics. In a stunning reversal of fortune, the Conservatives were almost eliminated from parliament in the 1993 election and unable to rebuild the party to its former level of support during the rest of the 1990s. The NDP, with a social-democratic philosophy and strong union support, traditionally had held a small number of parliamentary seats and 15–20 per cent of the popular vote. It too lost much ground in 1993, its support falling to 7 per cent of the popular vote. The New Democrats were forced to the margin of federal politics after 1993. Significant numbers of voters turned their allegiance from these three parties to regionally based new parties. In the early 1990s, a pro-independence party from Quebec (*Bloc Quebecois*) and a conservative party (Canadian Alliance) from the western provinces both gained substantial representation in parliament. Quebec provincial referendums in 1980 and 1995 favoured remaining in Canada, but the 1995 referendum vote was close. In the late 1990s the Alliance Party became the official opposition in parliament, and its agenda of extreme fiscal and social conservatism helped swing the Canadian public policy agenda more towards the right. It is becoming more difficult for unions to find allies in federal politics.

The politics of each province are distinct, reflecting regional differences in the various economies of Canada, immigration patterns, and political attitudes. None of the federal parties is strong in all the provinces, and provincial parties have normally governed in two large provinces, Quebec and British Columbia. While the NDP never gained power in the federal arena, it has won elections in four provinces, and while in power was able to influence the development of labour policy.

Canada enjoys a standard of living equal to the more prosperous nations in Western Europe, but depends heavily on the production and export of raw materials and semi-processed products—mineral ores, food grains and forest products. Although Canada enjoys a comparative advantage in the production of most of these commodities, their markets are unstable and primary industries do not generate substantial direct employment. There is a large manufacturing sector in Ontario and Quebec, but manufacturing accounts for only 21.5 per cent of the

GDP. Because Canada lacks a large domestic market, it signed a Free Trade Agreement (FTA) with the United States and the North American Free Trade Agreement (NAFTA) with Mexico and the USA, in 1988 and 1994 respectively. The immediate impact of free trade was to accelerate the integration of the manufacturing sector into a larger North American economy. Levels of activity in traditional industries, such as textiles and furniture, fell substantially, while other sectors, such as car manufacturing and chemicals, expanded.

Canada usually exports about 33 per cent of its GNP and imports about 25 per cent. The USA accounts for approximately 75 per cent of Canada's exports. Trade with Mexico is relatively modest. Apart from proximity and a natural complementarity of the two economies, Canadian–American trade relations are encouraged by extensive US ownership in many primary and secondary industries as well as the free trade agreements.

Canada has a mixed economy, with active roles for the public and private sectors, often in the same industries. Older public enterprises typically came into being for pragmatic reasons—provision of a necessary service, development of natural resources or the preservation of jobs. Thus, government owned many public utilities, transport and communications companies. Privatisation gained favour in the mid-1980s, as the federal and provincial governments disposed of natural resources and transport companies, in addition to smaller holdings. This trend continued in the 1990s.

Canada's most pressing economic problems in the 1990s were high government deficits and unemployment, difficulties it shared with most other developed nations. After a period of inflation in the mid-1970s, unemployment—always substantial by international standards—rose sharply and began to drop off only in the mid-1990s, as Table 4.1 demonstrates. Canadians were less well off financially in 1999/2000 than a decade earlier, with real disposable income falling over the previous decade. More Canadians took part-time jobs than ever before. Unemployment rates in 2001 hovered at about 7 per cent, lower than in the previous decade, but nevertheless were higher than in many developed economies. One of the balancing acts of government policy is the exchange rate. A high Canadian dollar increases citizens' purchasing power for foreign goods, but a lower Canadian dollar reduces the unemployment rate. The Canadian dollar fell from a rate slightly above the American dollar in the 1970s to about 67 cents to the US dollar in 2003.

Table 4.1   Earnings, prices and unemployment 1974–99,
             forecasts to 2002

Year	Change in wages major collective agreements (%)	CPI annual rate of change	Annual rate of unemployment
1974–78	11.4	9.2	7.1
1979–83	9.8	9.7	9.0
1984–88	3.8	4.2	9.6
1989	5.3	5.0	7.5
1990	5.6	4.8	8.1
1991	3.6	5.6	10.3
1992	2.1	1.5	11.3
1993	0.6	1.8	11.2
1994	0.3	0.2	10.4
1995	0.9	2.2	9.5
1996	0.9	1.6	9.7
1997	1.5	1.6	9.0
1998	1.7	0.9	8.2
1999	2.2	1.7	7.6
2000	2.5	2.7	6.9
2001	3.1	2.6	6.8
2002	2.9	3.9	7.5
2003	NA	4.6 (Feb.)	7.3 (Mar.)

Source: Statistics Canada 2002, 2000.

During the inflationary periods of the 1970s, governments inter-vened directly to reduce pressures on prices. Between 1975 and 1978, the federal government and nine of ten provinces imposed an anti-inflation program, which included comprehensive wage and price controls, limits on growth in government spending, and restrictive monetary and fiscal policies. The weight of controls fell most heavily on public-sector workers (and their unions). Although opinions differ about the impact of the program, the rate of inflation declined during its life, and the rate of wage rises fell even more sharply. However, labour and management resented the restrictions in the program, so it was not extended.

When a recession hit in 1982, federal and provincial governments again imposed temporary public-sector wage controls, then to reduce government spending. In the following decade, Canada experienced slow economic growth. In a departure from past policy, in the 1990s the federal government allowed the Canadian dollar to slide to unprecedented lows in relation to the US dollar, and kept the Canadian bond rate lower than that offered in the USA. By 2003, Canada's inflation rate of about 2.5 per cent was among the lowest of any industrialised nation.

Government efforts to deal with economic problems are restricted by the nation's political structure. Like Australia, Canada is a confederation with a parliamentary government. The ten provinces hold substantial powers, including the primary authority to regulate industrial relations, leaving only a few industries, principally transport and communications, to federal authority. The provinces, often led by Quebec, not only have resisted any efforts to expand federal powers but gradually have gained greater powers at the expense of the federal authorities.

A fundamental change in Canadian political life occurred in 1982. The Liberal government produced the nation's first written constitution, which included a *Charter of Rights and Freedoms*. The Charter guarantees certain fundamental freedoms, including freedom of association, thought, belief, opinion and expression. But these individual rights are not paramount and absolute (as they are in the USA under the Bill of Rights). In Canada, the Charter allows courts to use a clause to achieve a balance between individual rights and the collective good. The Charter holds that individual rights are subject to 'such reasonable limits as can be demonstrably justified in a free and democratic society.' There is a presumption within the Canadian constitution that a fettering of individual rights is necessary for democracy, and that there must be a way to subordinate some rights for the good of the country. Achieving this delicate balance is important in the employment relations arena, where the ability of unions to represent members, collect union dues, and exercise the right to strike on behalf of the bargaining unit as a whole depends on a legal regime that allows for collective action, even over the protests of individuals who believe that their own rights are diminished by their representation by unions.

THE PARTIES IN EMPLOYMENT RELATIONS

Unions

The Canadian labour movement has displayed steady, though unspectacular, growth since the 1930s, despite longstanding patterns of disunity. The number of employees covered by union bargaining arrangements was approximately 4 million throughout the 1990s, which at the start of the 21st century constituted 32 per cent of paid non-agricultural employees. While absolute numbers of employees represented by unions had grown by 1.4 million since 1960, the proportionately greater increase in the labour force as a whole has meant that the union density figure has declined moderately since 1984, in contrast to the USA. This membership is divided between two national centres and a large number of unaffiliated unions. The Canadian density figure reflects growth in female union members and high union density rate in the public sector. The greatest penetration of unionism is in primary industries, construction, transport, manufacturing, plus the public sector. In the late 19th and early 20th centuries, Canadian unions were established first in construction and transport, mostly on a craft basis. During the 1930s and 1940s, industrial unionism spread to manufacturing and primary industries, without including white-collar workers in the private sector. Since the late 1960s, the major source of union growth has been the public sector. More public servants, then health and education workers, joined unions. Professionals, notably teachers and nurses, had long been members of their own associations, and these transformed themselves into unions as their members' interest in collective bargaining grew. By 1980, nearly all eligible workers in the public sector had joined unions. Public-sector employees are almost four times more likely to belong to unions than private-sector workers. Table 4.2 shows the relative rate of unionisation by industry, sector, gender, age, work status and province.

Unionisation of the public sector raised the proportion of female union members. By the late 1990s, nearly half of all union members were women. Unionisation rates in the public sector are about 72 per cent for women, while for men they are about 69 per cent. The labour movement, including the large congresses discussed below, made special efforts to include women in senior leadership roles. Many unions have close ties with women's organisations.

There are approximately 275 unions in Canada, ranging in size from less than 100 members to nearly half a million. Two-thirds are affiliated with one of the central confederations, with the remainder, principally in the public sector, independent of any national centre or in Quebec. The ten largest unions contain 54 per cent of all members. Mergers have created 'mega' unions, concentrating union membership in fewer

Table 4.2 Union membership by selected characteristics 2002

	Density (%)*
By industry	
Education	73.6
Public Administration	72.3
Utilities	67.9
Health Care and Social Assistance	56.7
Transportation and Warehousing	43.1
Construction	33.8
Manufacturing	32.7
Information, Culture and Recreation	28.2
Natural Resources	26.8
Management, Administration and Support	14.9
Trade	14.5
Finance, Insurance, Real Estate and Leasing	10.8
Other	10.2
Accommodation and Food	8.3
Professional, Scientific and Technical	5.4
Agriculture	3.6
By sector	
Public	75.9
Private	19.7
By gender	
Men	30.3
Women	30.2
By age (years)	
15–24	15.4
25–44	32.5
45–54	43.0
55+	36.7
By work status	
Full-time	34.1
Part-time	24.8

By province

Newfoundland	40.5
Prince Edward Island	31.4
Nova Scotia	28.3
New Brunswick	29.0
Quebec	40.9
Ontario	28.1
Manitoba	35.8
Saskatchewan	36.0
Alberta	24.7
British Columbia	34.9

*Union density is measured as the percentage of Canadian workers who are covered by collective agreements. This 'coverage' figure is slightly higher than the union-members-only figure, as some Canadians are not union members (e.g. due to religious exemptions) but are represented by unions. In 2002, Canadian density measured by membership was 30.3 per cent. Measured by coverage, it was 32.4 per cent.

Source: Statistics Canada (2002).

and larger organisations. Table 4.3 lists the various unions, their sizes and their affiliations. A variety of union philosophies are represented. Most of the old craft groups still espouse US-style apolitical 'business unionism'. A larger number of unions see themselves as fulfilling a broader role, and actively support the NDP and various social causes. A few groups, principally in Quebec, are highly politicised and occasionally criticise the prevailing economic system from a socialist perspective. But rhetoric aside, the major function of all unions is collective bargaining

The role of US-based 'international' unions is a special feature of the Canadian labour movement that has affected its behaviour in many ways. Most of the oldest labour organisations in Canada began as part of American unions—hence the term 'international'. Most of these unions are affiliated with the American-based AFL-CIO. The cultural and economic ties between the two countries encouraged the union connection, while the greater size and earlier development of US unions attracted Canadian workers to them. For many years, the overwhelming majority of Canadian union members belonged to such international unions, which often exerted close control over their Canadian

Table 4.3 Canadian union membership (000s)

	Affiliation	2002
Canadian Union of Public Employees	CLC	522
National Union of Public and General Employees	CLC	325
National Automobile, Aerospace, Transportation and General Workers Union of Canada	CLC	238
United Food and Commercial Workers' International Union	AFL-CIO/CLC	220
United Steelworkers of America	AFL-CIO/CLC	18
Public Service Alliance of Canada	CLC	150
Communications, Energy and Paperworkers Union of Canada	CLC	150
International Brotherhood of Teamsters	AFL-CIO/CLC	102
Fédération de la santé et des services sociaux	CSN	101
Service Employees International Union	AFL-CIO	90
Federation des syndicats de l'enseignement	CEQ	81
Laborers' International Union of North America	AFL-CIO/CLC	73
International Brotherhood of Electrical Workers	AFL-CIO/CLC	55
United Brotherhood of Carpenters and Joiners of America	AFL-CIO/CLC	53
Canadian Union of Postal Workers	CLC	51
Elementary Teachers' Federation of Ontario	Independent	64
Ontario Secondary School Teachers' Federation	Independent	48
Federation des infirmières et infirmiers du Quebec	Independent	46
International Association of Machinists and Aerospace Workers	AFL-CIO/CLC	44
Ontario Nurses' Association	CLC	45
British Columbia Teachers' Federation	Independent	53
Industrial Wood and Allied Workers of Canada	CLC	43
International Union of Operating Engineers	AFL-CIO/CLC	38
Other		1040
Total union membership		3650

Sources: Workplace Information Directorate, *Workplace Gazette*, Vol. 3, No. 4, p. 115; Akyeapong (2000), Statistics Canada, *Special 2000 Labour Day Release.*

locals. But the spread of unionism in the public sector during the 1960s and 1970s brought national unions to the fore, as internationals were seldom active among public employees. Since the 1970s, many Canadian unions have seceded from internationals. This reflected their perception that they received poor service in Canada, the protectionism of American unions and Canadian nationalism. A particularly wrenching breakaway was the 1985 withdrawal of Canadians from the American-based United Automobile Workers to create the Canadian Auto Workers (CAW). Subsequently, the CAW absorbed Canadian locals of internationals. As a result of these factors, the proportion of international union membership declined from more than 70 per cent in the mid-1960s to less than 30 per cent in the early 21st century.

In the past, internationals encouraged a conservative form of business unionism in Canada, discouraged political involvement and exerted powerful influence over the policies of national centres. While a role in these areas continues, the impact of policies originating in the USA is low and seems destined to decline further.

The most important central confederation is the Canadian Labour Congress (CLC), representing almost 69 per cent of all union members belonging to 93 national and international union affiliates. Members of CLC affiliates are in all regions and most industries. It is the principal political spokesperson for Canadian labour, but is weaker than confederations in many other countries. It has no role in bargaining, for instance, nor does it have any substantial powers over its affiliates, unlike confederations in Germany and Scandinavia. The CLC's political role is further limited by the constitutionally weak position of the federal government (its obvious contact point) in many areas the labour movement regards as important, such as labour legislation, regulation of industry or human rights. In national politics, it has supported the NDP. The poor electoral record of the NDP federally further weakens the CLC's political role. The CLC has chartered federations in each province to which locals of affiliated unions belong. Some of these bodies wield considerable influence in their provinces.

The Confederation of National Trade Unions (CNTU) represents 6.2 per cent of all union members, nearly all in Quebec. It began early in the 20th century under the sponsorship of the Catholic Church as a conservative French-language alternative to the predominantly English-language secular unions operating elsewhere in Canada and in Quebec. As Quebec industrialised during and after World War I, members of the Catholic unions grew impatient with their lack of militancy and

101

unwillingness to confront a conservative provincial government. Following an illegal strike against a powerful employer supported by the provincial government in 1949, the Catholic unions abandoned their former conservatism and moved into the vanguard of rapid social change in Quebec. In 1960, the federation adopted its present name and severed its ties with the Catholic Church. Since then, ideological competition has prevailed in the Quebec labour movement, and the CNTU has probably become the most radical and politicised labour organisation in North America. It has supported Quebec independence and has adopted left-wing political positions. Unlike the CLC, it has a centralised structure, which gives officers considerable authority over member unions. Because of its history, current political posture and the large provincial public sector in Quebec, the CNTU membership is concentrated heavily among public employees.

Management

The majority of unionised firms grudgingly accept the role of unions, and open attacks on incumbent unions are rare. In industries with a long history of unionism—for example, manufacturing or transport—unionism is accepted as a normal part of the business environment. However, non-union enterprises strive to retain that status, some by matching the wages and working conditions in the unionised sector, others by combinations of paternalism and coercion. Some enterprises have union substitution policies, which replicate many of the forms of a unionised work environment with grievance procedures, quality circles or mechanisms for consultation. Management-influenced forms of employee representation for non-union workers are not illegal as in the USA. Almost 20 per cent of Canadian non-union workers have a formal non-union employee representation plan at their workplaces and of those workers more than half (i.e. 10 per cent of workers) are covered by that representation plan. Thus, although the number of workers represented by unions is slightly more than 32 per cent, the number of workers who experience some form of collective representation is considerably higher.

Unionised companies in Canada usually have a full-time industrial relations staff, though seldom a large one. Collective bargaining rounds usually occur at intervals of between one and three years, so most companies do not maintain a large staff for such purposes, and many staff have non-industrial relations duties. Major industrial relations decisions, such as decisions to take strikes or the level of pay offers, are highly centralised—that is, taken at the corporate level. In general, Canadian managers do not have much industrial relations expertise. Few staff have formal industrial relations training; the cadre of specialists is not large; and key decisions may be taken by senior executives with little sensitivity for the issues.

The high degree of foreign ownership in the Canadian economy affects the Canadian economy generally, but seldom affects industrial relations directly. About 25 per cent of the assets of all industrial enterprises are foreign-owned, chiefly by MNEs. Foreign ownership affects strategic managerial decisions, such as product lines or major investments. But there appears to be little impact of non-Canadians on industrial relations decisions in unionised sectors. Foreign owners prefer to remain in the mainstream of industrial relations for their industries rather than imposing corporate policies.

The organisation of employers varies among regions. No national group participates directly in employment relations, although some present employers' viewpoints to government or the public. As most employment relations law falls under provincial jurisdiction, few industries have national bargaining structures. In two provinces, Quebec and British Columbia, local conditions and public policy have encouraged bargaining by employers' associations formed specifically for that purpose. Elsewhere, single-plant bargaining with a single union predominates, except in a few industries with many SMEs, such as construction, longshoring or trucking, where multi-employer bargaining is the norm.

Government

The government in Canada has a dual role in employment relations: it regulates the actors' conduct, and employs about 18 per cent of the labour force, directly and indirectly.

There is extensive government regulation, though it rests on an assumption of voluntarism. Each province, and the federal government, has at least one Act covering employment relations and employment standards in the industries under its jurisdiction. Employment standards legislation generally sets minima for such areas as pay or holidays. In a few areas, such as maternity leave, the law has led most employers. Although the details vary considerably, much legislation combines many features of the US National Labor Relations Act (Wagner Act) and an older Canadian pattern of reliance on conciliation of labour disputes. Each statute establishes and protects the right of most employees to form unions, setting out a procedure by which a union may demonstrate majority support from a group of employees to obtain the right of exclusive representation for them. The employer is required to bargain with a certified union. A quasi-judicial labour relations board administers this process and enforces the statute, although the legislation often specifies the procedural requirements in detail.

Legislation imposes few requirements on the substance of a collective agreement, though the exceptions are significant and expanding. For many years, Canadian laws have prohibited strikes during the term of a collective agreement, while also requiring that each agreement contain a grievance procedure and a mechanism for the settlement of mid-contract disputes. Despite these restrictions, as many as 15 per cent of all stoppages occur while a collective agreement is in force. Most of these stoppages are brief and seldom attract legal action. Several statutes require the parties to bargain about technological change and that management grant union security clauses.

There is separate legislation federally and in all ten provinces for at least some employees in the public sector. These statutes may apply to government employees and occasionally to quasi-government employees, such as teachers or hospital workers. They are patterned after private-sector labour relations Acts except in two broad areas. The scope of bargaining is restricted by previous civil service personnel practices and broader public policy considerations. In a majority of provinces, there are restrictions on the right to strike of at least some public employees. Police and fire fighters are the most common categories affected by such limits, but there is no other common pattern of restrictions. Employee groups without the right to strike have access to a system of compulsory arbitration. While a statute requires arbitration, the parties can normally determine the procedures to be followed and choose the arbitrator.

THE PROCESSES OF EMPLOYMENT RELATIONS

The major formal process of Canadian employment relations is collective bargaining, with union power based on its ability to strike. Joint consultation is sporadic. Health and safety legislation in all jurisdictions requires joint consultation on those subjects for all but the smallest employers. The parties have initiated consultation outside any legislative framework in about a quarter of enterprises covering such subjects as product quality, technological change or performance. Other formal systems of worker participation in management are rare, although in an era in which employee involvement systems have become popular more collective agreements have developed novel clauses reflecting this thrust, including some relaxation of strict work rules, multiskilling and cross-crafting, pay for education and training and so on. Arbitration of interest disputes is largely confined to the public sector.

Collective bargaining

Collective bargaining is decentralised. The most common negotiating unit is a single establishment–single union, followed by multi-establishment–single union. Taken together these categories account for almost 90 per cent of all units and more than 80 per cent of all employees. Company-wide bargaining is common in the federal juris-diction, where it occurs in railways, airlines and telecommunications, and in provincially regulated industries concentrated in a single province, such as car or lumber manufacturing.

Despite the decentralised structure of negotiations, bargaining often follows regional patterns. National patterns in bargaining are rare. Instead, one or two key industries in each region usually influence provincial negotiations. In larger provinces, such as Ontario and Quebec, heavy-industry patterns from steel, paper or cars often predominate.

The results of bargaining are detailed, complex collective bargaining agreements. Few of the terms are the result of the law; negotiated provi-sions typically include: pay, union security, hours of work and holidays, layoff provisions, and miscellaneous fringe benefits. Grievance proce-dures are legal requirements and invariably conclude with binding arbi-tration. In addition, there are often supplementary agreements covering work rules for specific situations or work areas. Seniority provisions are prominent features in almost all collective agreements, covering layoffs, promotions or transfers, with varying weight given to length of service or ability.

Given the detail in collective agreements and the parties' preference for litigation, rights arbitrations are frequent and legalistic. In turn, this emphasis on precise written contracts often permeates employment relationships.

Strikes and settlement methods

Another outcome of collective bargaining is labour stoppages, the most controversial feature of Canadian industrial relations. In most years

Canada has lost more working days due to industrial disputes than any other country in this book. From 1986 to 1995 Canada's strike rate was about 2.5 times higher than the average of the 24 nations of the OECD. There have been frequent allegations, never really proven, that labour unrest has hindered the nation's economic growth seriously. As did other industrialised nations, Canada experienced a steady decline in strikes during the 1990s. Nevertheless, in this decade Canada still lost more working days than any country in this book.

Historically, strike levels have moved in cycles. There was a wave of unrest early in the 20th century, another around World War I, a third beginning in the late 1930s and a fourth in the 1970s (see Table 4.4). The latest wave abated in 1983, and most measures of disputes have fallen sharply since then. By international standards, the two salient characteristics of Canadian strikes are their length and the concentration of time lost in a few disputes. Involvement is medium to low (3–10 per cent of union members annually), and the size of strikes is not especially large (350–450 workers per strike, on average). The largest five or six strikes typically account for 35 per cent of all days lost. In recent years, the average duration of strikes has been 12–15 days. These characteristics have not been explained fully, but may be due to the presence of major MNEs, such as General Motors or International Nickel, and large unions that can withstand long strikes at individual production units without the parent enterprises suffering major economic loss.

Conciliation and mediation efforts have long been a feature of Canadian collective bargaining. There are two models: a tripartite board may be appointed and given authority to report publicly on a dispute; alternatively, single mediators function without the power to issue a report. In most jurisdictions participation in some form of mediation is a precondition for a legal strike. Although elements of compulsion have diminished, more than half of all collective agreements are achieved with some type of third-party intervention.

Outside the public sector, compulsory arbitration of interest disputes is rare. However, there may be special legislation to end particular disputes in the public sector or essential services. Back-to-work laws are unpopular with the labour movement and have contributed to the politicisation of employment relations in some areas. In the public sector, interest arbitration is common. Arbitrators are usually chosen on an ad-hoc basis from among judges or professional arbitrators, who are usually lawyers or academics. The process is legalistic without the use of sophisticated economic data. When collective bargaining first appeared in the public

Table 4.4   Strikes and lockouts in Canada (annual)

Year	Number	Workers involved	Days lost	% of working time
1966–70	572	291 109	5 709 000*	0.35
1971–75	856	473 795	7 309 000*	0.38
1976–80	996	620 876	7 834 142	0.34
1981–85	784	296 836	5 200 454	0.21
1986	748	484 255	7 151 470	0.27
1987	668	581 882	3 810 170	0.14
1988	548	206 796	4 901 260	0.17
1989	627	444 747	3 701 360	0.13
1990	579	270 471	5 079 190	0.17
1991	463	253 334	2 516 090	0.09
1992	404	149 940	2 110 180	0.07
1993	381	101 784	1 516 640	0.05
1994	374	80 856	1 606 580	0.06
1995	328	149 159	1 583 061	0.05
1996	330	281 816	3 351 820	0.11
1997	284	257 644	3 610 206	0.12
1998	381	244 402	2 443 876	0.08
1999	413	158 612	2 445 740	0.08
2000	377	144 000*	1 662 000*	0.05
2001	379	224 000*	2 240 000*	0.07

* Data rounded by thousands.

sector, there was concern that compulsory arbitration would cause bargaining to atrophy. Experience has demonstrated that collective bargaining and compulsory arbitration could coexist successfully, though the availability of arbitration does reduce the incidence of negotiated settlements.

CURRENT AND FUTURE ISSUES

The future of collective bargaining is being questioned in most DMEs. In large measure, this debate revolves around the ability of unions to retain, or even expand, their traditional bases of strength in heavy-industry and blue-collar occupations. Though union density in these industries in Canada has declined, it has not declined materially and is still twice as high as that of the USA, for instance. However, Canadian unions have had similar difficulties to their counterparts elsewhere in extending their membership base into the more rapidly growing areas of the service sector and technologically advanced industries. As employment shifts from the goods-producing sectors to services, the historic base of collective bargaining gradually shrinks as a proportion of the labour force. For example, from 1976 to 1998 the number of employed Canadians in the bastion of traditional unionism, the goods sector, fell from 32 per cent to 22 per cent. Compared with the non-union employers, the organised elements of the labour force have played a leading role in the expansion of employee rights and improvement in pay and conditions of employment. If collective bargaining becomes confined to declining sectors of the economy, this leading role will also diminish.

Traditional centres of collective bargaining are also under pressure from foreign competition and deregulation, factors common among DMEs. Canada has long relied heavily on foreign trade, so foreign competition is not new. Tariff barriers were reduced slowly in the 1960s and 1970s and more rapidly after the FTA took effect in 1989. The Canadian manufacturing sector, aided by a depreciating currency, responded well to these challenges. The decentralised structure of collective bargaining seems to have facilitated adaptation to economic change. Exports rose steadily, while manufacturing employment was stagnant. These developments were sources of stress for employment relations institutions, but changes were incremental.

Similar results occurred after deregulation. Governments deregulated most of the transport and communications sectors in the 1980s and 1990s. In addition, several public enterprises in these sectors were privatised. Employment in the unionised firms in these industries shrank, while new competitors were largely non-union. These developments occurred gradually and generally did not provoke disputes.

The immediate future of collective bargaining will be a function of the actions of governments and managers in the face of union economic and political power. Federal and provincial governments continue to respect the legitimacy of collective bargaining and an active labour movement. A review of labour relations in federally regulated industries completed in 1995 found strong support for the institution of collective bargaining among the employment relations parties, for instance. Legislation and other public policies reflect that commitment, even when most right-of-centre political parties govern. There were few major changes in labour legislation in the 1980s. When a conservative government in British Columbia made sweeping changes to the basic labour relations statute (without eliminating the basic protections that had been part of the legislative framework since World War II), the labour movement reacted vigorously. Ultimately, the government was replaced by the NDP, which returned most legislative provisions to their previous state and added a number of protections for the labour movement in 1992. In 2001 the NDP lost to a right-of-centre government committed to stability in labour policy. Ontario also experienced instability. In the early 1990s, the NDP government of Ontario, the largest and most industrialised province, passed a new labour law that substantially assisted organised labour. When the NDP was ousted by an extremely right-wing and arguably anti-union Conservative party, the pendulum swung back, and legislative reforms made unionisation more difficult and reduced protections for labour generally.

On balance, it appears that the legislative support for collective bargaining will not change markedly across Canada. However, there is little political support for reform that would appreciably strengthen union power. Given Canada's tilt towards a right-wing agenda, a more likely scenario is further modest reductions in the unions' legal position without a wholesale dismantling of the collective bargaining regime.

Management and collective bargaining

Canadian employers faced similar market forces to reduce costs in the 1980s and 1990s to their private-sector counterparts in other DMEs: foreign trade, increased domestic competition in services, and deregulation. Public-sector employers were required either to limit or to reduce labour costs. The FTA (with the USA) and NAFTA added to competitive pressures. Many employers responded to these changes by initiating layoffs, which dramatically reduced employment in many industries. The use of part-time and casual workers rose substantially. But there was no general movement to escape unionism.

In industries where unionism was well established, a combination of tradition and legal forces induced Canadian employers to work within the collective bargaining system to meet competitive pressures. Militant anti-unionism is not a popular public position among Canadian employers, although many managers privately express hostility towards labour organisations. Major employers' organisations usually advocate cooperative relations with unions and have not called for a deregulation of labour markets. At the company level, surveys of industrial relations and human resource managers show little interest in unseating incumbent unions, although resistance to the spread of unionism may have strengthened.

Legal restrictions on employer tactics make deunionisation very difficult, and protections for unionism are effective. Employer success in bargaining has diminished pressure for structural changes. The decentralisation of bargaining structures in the private sector, driven by employers, effectively put wages into competition. Negotiated changes in work rules have been frequent, and in the mid-1990s negotiated wage freezes and concession bargaining became more common. In a few industries, the parties have negotiated collective agreements with terms as long as six years, typically incorporating wage freezes followed by modest wage rises coupled with employment guarantees for most bargaining unit members. With low rates of inflation, it is difficult for unions to bargain for anything other than very modest pay rises.

At the workplace level in unionised industries, radical reorganisation of work and the implementation of work systems based on high levels of employee commitment have been limited, due to both union resistance and lack of management commitment. Labour generally is concerned that these initiatives have the effect, and perhaps the goal, of reducing workers' support for their unions. Where initiatives have been introduced, the failure rate is relatively high. However, many employers are seeking to move away from the traditional adversarial system of employment relations, especially in manufacturing. Increased consultation and communication by managers with their unions is a common development, for instance. There have been many modest changes in work practices, often outside formal collective bargaining. However, the life span of many of these initiatives appears to be limited.

It is unclear how much Canadian employers' acceptance of collective bargaining in the face of difficult economic conditions is due to legal protections for unions and collective bargaining or to a philosophical acceptance of the legitimacy of these institutions. If employers are merely obeying the law, then support for collective bargaining obviously is subject to changing political and legal circumstances. If the support for collective bargaining is cultural, then industrial relations institutions will probably survive and evolve gradually.

Industrial disputes

Historically, the most important issue in Canadian industrial relations has been the working time lost due to strikes. Beginning in the late 1960s, Canada became known for the high levels of working time lost due to strikes. By most measures, strike levels fell sharply after 1982, as the economy suffered a severe recession and unemployment rose, though the number of strikers declined much less. Time lost and the number of strikes remained lower throughout the 1980s and 1990s. Despite public concern about strikes, there have been few efforts to deal with their underlying causes or even to understand them better. Certainly, the fragmented structure of bargaining is one factor that contributes to the pattern of strikes. Yet the causes of fragmentation lie in Canada's governmental structure and politics. Provincial governments resist most efforts to limit their powers, and the paramount importance of Quebec separatism on the national political agenda has restrained any impulses of the federal government to extend its authority over economic issues.

Governments have attempted to deal with labour unrest in a variety of ways. One model is to encourage consultation. During the 1970s and 1980s, several governments took initiatives directed at establishing labour-management consultation as practised in Western Europe. In cases of large-scale layoffs, joint labour-management committees (in union and non-union workforces) were mandated. Later the federal government sponsored tripartite sectoral committees to deal with the effects of restructuring. These committees function well, and their number has expanded, slowly, but there still is no evidence that cooperation at this level of the employment relations system affects the parties' actions at other levels.

Every province requires joint health and safety committees in most workplaces. In unionised organisations, such committees are an avenue of influence outside collective bargaining. These committees operate in large workplaces, and stoppages or serious disputes over health and safety are rare. However, employers resist vigorously any initiatives to strengthen the statutory authority of health and safety committees. Mandating labour-management cooperation represents a sharp departure from the North American traditions of a limited role for government in the workplace and the maintenance of a clear distinction in collective representation between the unionised and non-union segments.

A second model for dealing with labour unrest has been to impose legislative controls on the exercise of union power. Two provinces enacted labour relations amendments along those lines, and others considered the same policies. As in Britain and other countries, even though governments in these jurisdictions may legislate against unions, most substantial employers seem to be reluctant to invoke such laws against their workers or the unions that represent them. Hence, the long-run prospects for this model are not good. There is little groundswell of support that would seriously threaten the legitimacy of the current collective bargaining regime.

By the start of the 21st century the incidence of disputes had fallen considerably, as Table 4.4 indicates. The decline in labour unrest diverted interest from this issue and labour relations in general. Beginning the mid-1980s, unions demonstrated that they could mount a few large strikes and win concessions on significant issues, almost invariably involving job security. But later, in a time of low inflation and high unemployment, the incentives to strike on other issues fell and the confrontation costs rose. Although there were situations in which organised labour responded decisively in a concerted effort to achieve specific outcomes, there was a general decline in militancy. It became significantly more difficult for unions to make advances through the use of strikes.

Public-sector employment relations

The public sector is the area of Canadian employment relations most subject to change. From the mid-1960s through the 1980s, mature systems of collective bargaining developed in all provinces and the federal government. Beginning with the 1982 recession, governments in several jurisdictions addressed budgetary shortfalls by restricting public-sector pay levels. In general, governments dealt with their fiscal problems by legislation rather than bargaining. By 1987, legal restraints had been removed. Early in 1991, the federal government led another round of restrictions on public-sector bargaining and compensation. By 1995, a majority of all provinces had imposed restrictions on public-sector bargaining as part of their programs of fiscal restraint.

One of the most comprehensive restraint programs was the misnamed a 'Social Contract', in Ontario. In 1993, an NDP government attempted to negotiate substantial reductions in compensation with more than 100 public-sector bargaining agents. When negotiations failed, the government threatened to impose cuts legislatively if agreements were not reached. Under such pressure, nearly all unions agreed to cuts in labour costs that did not entail reductions in rates of pay. Compulsory unpaid holidays, for example, became a common feature in the Ontario public sector. These policies split the Ontario labour movement, which had supported the government, generally along public-versus private-sector lines. The vigorous action by an NDP government marked a shift in the politics of restrictions on public-sector collective bargaining. No longer were severe policies regarded as aberrations of right-wing governments. This made it easier for more conservative regimes to impose similar or more severe controls. For example, in 1994 the province of Alberta cut public-sector salaries by 5 per cent and cut funding of most social services, including those in health care and education. The split in the Ontario labour movement contributed to the election of an anti-union Conservative government.

Public-sector unions protested all the restraint programs, but generally in vain. Governments found restricting public-sector wages and bargaining rights politically popular. Reliance on legislation or other means to impose freezes or reductions has brought into question the commitment of Canadian governments to collective bargaining systems enshrined in many statutes. Under these circumstances, unions' responses to government initiatives are likely to be political. In the 1980s, public-sector unions in Quebec, Ontario and British Columbia (the three most populous provinces) organised major demonstrations and work stoppages that brought pressure on governments to moderate their policies. A major national strike by a federal public-sector union with a tradition of moderation showed that public-sector workers could be mobilised when they faced restrictions they regarded as unfair. In the end, however, the government employers prevailed. Led by the federal government, controlled by the Liberal Party since 1993, deficit reduction became a dominant theme in the nation's political orthodoxy. Federal government employment fell substantially, and several provincial governments also cut employment as well as pay. In these conditions the unions could do little to resist the losses.

Political role of the labour movement

Although many unions and union leaders are active in partisan politics, the labour movement has been unable to define a political role for itself. Officially, the CLC supports the NDP, but this alliance has presented problems. Federally, the NDP has been unsuccessful in raising its share of the popular vote (and legislative seats) beyond about 20 per cent and was left without official party status in the parliament elected in 1993. The labour movement has been unable to deliver large blocs of votes to the federal NDP, though financial contributions and the diversion of staff to the NDP are invaluable. In Quebec the NDP has minimal influence, as most labour leaders support pro-independence parties. Even when the NDP enjoyed greater success, the CLC has been left to deal with governments whose election it had opposed. For example, labour opposed the US–Canada Free Trade Agreement, a central issue in the 1988 national election. When the pro-free trade Conservatives triumphed, the CLC was in a poor position to secure assistance for workers who lost their jobs as a result of new trade patterns. The tensions created by this situation have hampered consultation on economic policies.

Provincially, the situation is different. The NDP has governed in Ontario and three western provinces. Labour's political role is better defined when the NDP is a viable option provincially. However, the labour movement's partisan position provincially risks making labour issues more political and subject to sharp variation after changes of government. Quebec unions have supported independence for the province and have enjoyed great political influence when pro-separatist parties have governed the province.

The aftermath of the Social Contract in Ontario sharpened labour's dilemma. Public-sector unions withheld all support for the NDP in the 1995 election, contributing to the NDP's defeat. This experience revealed that the labour movement had no alternative to the election of the NDP. Punishing the NDP improved the electoral chances of more anti-labour parties. Yet the Ontario NDP proved willing to override valid collective agreements, attacking one of the fundamental principles of the Canadian employment relations system.

The practical result of these problems is that the CLC has vacillated between wholehearted commitment to the NDP and a more independent posture as workers' lobbyists before governments of any party. To further complicate the situation, some public-sector unions avoid political endorsements. The founders of the NDP had the British Labour Party as a model, but were unsuccessful in achieving their goal. The American tradition of labour acting as an independent political force has adherents in Canada, despite its limited relevance in a parliamentary political system. It thus appears that the labour movement will continue to search for an effective political role.

CONCLUSIONS

The employment relations system is caught up in Canada's central concerns—the division of powers between provinces and the national government, the relative importance of the public and private sectors, relations with the USA and other trading partners, and the performance of the economy. While employment relations will contribute to the resolution of these issues, the future direction of the system is likely to be determined by broader trends in Canada. But decisions on economic policy, changes in industrial structure and a new constitution will ensure the continuation of flux and unrest in Canadian employment relations.

The employment relations system itself displays few of the overt signs of structural changes found in other DMEs. Unlike the USA, Canadian unionism and collective bargaining have not been subjected to an attack by management. By contrast with Britain, it is rare for governments to undertake a sustained anti-union campaign. (The most concerted efforts to limit the power of unions through legislation occurred after 1996 in Ontario.) The labour movement has a high degree of legitimacy in Canada. It has close ties with the women's movement and consumer groups, for instance. The labour movement is recognised as the spokesperson for workers in economic and social consultations.

Canada's record of slow but steady economic growth, combined with more than a decade of stagnant wages, provides scant support for politicians or employers wanting to blame collective bargaining or unionism for the economy's performance. The collective bargaining system has responded successfully to most of the changes in economic conditions. Yet a decade of high unemployment has reduced the militancy of Canadian workers, except when job security is the central issue in dispute. The elimination of trade barriers undermines the bargaining power of Canadian workers in their manufacturing and transport sectors, two major sources of industrial strength. Continued reductions in government service employment affect another pillar of collective bargaining. The lack of perceptions of crisis in employment relations has stifled debate over the broader questions of worker representation outside the traditional strongholds of unions. In the absence of a direct challenge to the employment relations system, the recent pattern of incremental adaptation seems destined to continue.

A CHRONOLOGY OF CANADIAN EMPLOYMENT RELATIONS

1825	Strike by carpenters in Lachine, Quebec for higher wages.
1825–60	Numerous isolated local unions developed.
1867	Confederation—Canada became an independent nation.
1872	Unions exempted from criminal and civil liabilities imposed by British law.
1873	Local trade assemblies form the Canadian Labour Union, the first national labour central.
1886	Trades and Labour Congress (TLC) is formed by 'international' craft unions.
1900	Department of Labour established under the Conciliation Act. William Lyon Mackenzie King named first deputy minister; first issue of *Labour Gazette* published.
1902	'Berlin Declaration', TLC shuns unions not affiliated to international unions.
1906	Canadian chapter of Industrial Workers of the World is founded.
1907	Canadian Industrial Dispute Investigation Act—first national labour legislation, emphasising conciliation.
1908	Under the Government Annuities Act, the federal Department of Labour administers a plan to help individual Canadians provide for their old age.
1909	Labour Department Act creates a separate labour portfolio in the federal government. William Lyon Mackenzie King becomes the first minister of labour.
1919	Winnipeg General Strike—most complete general strike in North American history. The International Labour Organization is established and Canada is a founding member.
1921	Canadian and Catholic Confederation of Labour formed, Quebec federation of Catholic unions.
1927	All-Canadian Congress of Labour founded.
1930	Fair Wages and Eight-Hour Day Act for workers in the federal jurisdiction. The Great Depression leads to the passage of the Unemployment Relief Act for a system of relief payments to provinces and municipalities.
1935	Following the National Labor Relations (Wagner) Act in the USA, there are demands for similar Canadian legislation.
1937	Auto workers strike at General Motors, Oshawa, Ontario, establishing industrial unionism in Canada.

1939	TLC expells Canadian affiliates of US Congress of Industrial Organizations (CIO).
1940	CIO affiliates join All-Canadian Congress of Labour to form the Canadian Congress of Labour (CCL). The Unemployment Insurance Commission comes under the direction of the federal Department of Labour.
1944	Order-in-Council PC 1003 guarantees unions' right to organise (combining principles of US Wagner Act with compulsory conciliation); imposes a legal obligation on the employer and the employees' bargaining agent to negotiate in good faith. (Many provinces begin extending PC 1003 to their own labour relations situations or drafting similar legislation between the late 1930s and mid-1940s.)
1948	Industrial Relations and Disputes Investigation Act. Collective bargaining rights firmly established in law. Canada Labour Relations Board is created in the federal jurisdiction.
1949	Miners in Asbestos, Quebec, strike in defence of law, initiating 'quiet revolution' in Quebec.
1954	Establishment of the federal Women's Bureau to advance opportunities for women in the workforce.
1956	Merger of TLC and CCL to form the Canadian Labour Congress (CLC).
1958	Full-time workers in the federal jurisdiction are guaranteed two weeks' of paid vacation per year under the Annual Vacation Act.
1960	Canadian and Catholic Confederation of Labour severs ties with the Catholic Church to become the Confederation of National Trade Unions.
1965	Canada Labour (Standards) Code establishes minimum standards for hours of work, wages, vacations and statutory holidays for workers in the federal jurisdiction.
1967	Federal government gives its employees bargaining rights; other jurisdictions follow suit.
1975	Federal government imposes first peacetime wage and price controls.
1977	Canadian Human Rights Act is passed, forbidding discrimination against certain groups.
1982	Federal government enacts Charter of Rights.
1984	Protection from sexual harassment is added to the Canadian Labour Code.
1986	Joint employer–employee safety and health committees in the workplace is required under the CLC. Employment Equity Act is passed to deal with issues of discrimination.

1987	Charter of Rights and freedoms (enacted in 1982) take effect.
1991	Legislated pay freeze is imposed on federal government employees.
1994	North American Agreement on Labour Cooperation between Canada, the US and Mexico; commits countries to protection of labour standards and enforcement of their own labour laws.
1999	Federal employees receive $4 billion pay adjustment to compensate for gender-based discrimination in pay.

Chapter 5

EMPLOYMENT RELATIONS IN AUSTRALIA*

Russell D. Lansbury and Nick Wailes

Like Canada, Australia was colonised by the British, has a wealth of mineral and energy resources, and is sparsely populated. Australia has a population of 19 million people and in 2000 had a GDP of $US508 billion. Australia has developed a services sector which is almost as predominant as those in the USA and Canada. Thus, out of its total civilian employment of approximately 9 million people, 73 per cent are employed in services, 22 per cent in industry and 5 per cent in agriculture (also see Appendix). Nevertheless, Australia's economy remains highly dependent on raw materials and rural products.

Strong economic growth in the middle of the 1980s and a reduction in real wages enabled the labour market to expand and reduced the rate of unemployment. However, as shown in Table 5.1, deteriorating economic conditions in the late 1980s and early 1990s resulted in a rise in the unemployment rate to 11 per cent in the period 1991-93. With a tightening of government economic policy and a sharp downturn in 1990/91, inflation fell to 1 per cent in 1992/93 but after this began to rise again, although it generally remained between 2 and 5 per cent throughout the 1990s. Unemployment in the mid-1990s persisted at levels of 8-11 per cent but fell in the second half of the 1990s and was 6.7 per cent in 2001. However, the structure of employment has changed radically in recent years with the decline of full-time permanent work and the expansion of various kinds of non-standard forms of

* This is a revised version of the chapter that was co-authored by Ed Davis in earlier editions of the book.

Table 5.1   Selected economic variables 1986–2001

Year	Real GDP (% change)*	Inflation % change in CPI**	Current account (% of GDP)	Unemployment (% of the workforce)
1986/87	2.5	9.4	–3.0	8.0
1987/88	5.4	7.3	–2.7	7.5
1988/89	4.0	7.3	–4.2	6.1
1989/90	3.7	8.0	–4.8	6.6
1990/91	–0.1	5.3	–3.7	9.3
1991/92	0.3	1.9	–2.8	11.0
1992/93	3.4	1.0	–3.1	11.0
1993/94	3.9	1.8	–3.1	9.9
1994/95	4.2	3.2	–5.3	9.3
1995/96	4.2	4.2	–3.9	8.8
1996/97	3.7	1.3	–3.0	8.9
1997/98	4.5	0.0	–3.8	8.6
1998/99	5.0	1.2	–5.3	7.8
1999/2000	4.3	2.4	–4.9	6.8
2000/01	1.9	6.0	–2.7	6.6

*Real GDP figures show percentage change in the chain volume gross domestic product from previous year. For example, 1990/91 shows percentage change between 1989/90 and 1990/91.

**Inflation figures show percentage change in the Consumer Price Index since the end of previous financial year. For example, 1988/89 shows percentage change from June 1988 to June 1989.

Sources: ABSa (various years); ABSb (various years); ABS (2003).

employment. This has occurred as a result of increases in casual work, temporary jobs, outsourcing, and the use of agencies and other labour market intermediaries. As Burgess and Campbell (1998) have noted, the majority of all new jobs created in the 1990s were casual, while part-time jobs were the fastest-growing area of employment (see also McCallum 2000).

THE LEGAL, ECONOMIC AND POLITICAL BACKGROUND

Australia achieved its federation in 1901. When the former colonial governments agreed to establish the Commonwealth of Australia, the new federal government was given only a limited jurisdiction over employment and industrial relations. Under the Constitution of the Commonwealth of Australia (1901), federal government was empowered to make industrial laws only with respect to 'conciliation and arbitration for the prevention and settlement of industrial disputes extending beyond the limits of any one State' (Section 51, para. xxxv).

The Australian system of conciliation and arbitration, adopted in the federal jurisdiction in 1904, was part of a policy response to a series of political and economic crises that hit the Australian colonies in the late 19th century. These colonies experienced rapid economic development during the second half of the 19th century, benefiting from free trade between Britain and her colonies and the ready availability of capital on the London market. Debt-financed, export-led development created the conditions for immigration to the Australian colonies and the development of domestic manufacturing and service industries (Denoon 1983). However, instability in the international economy and declining prices for commodity exports in the late 19th century produced conflict both between capital and labour and between different elements of capital over who would bear the costs of adjustment associated with international economic change (Schwartz 1989). In particular there was a series of strikes in the agricultural export sector, which produced significant defeats for emerging unions of semi- and unskilled workers in the mining, wool and maritime industries (Bray & Rimmer 1989).

The introduction of arbitration in some colonies, and its subsequent inclusion in the Australian Constitution, was an attempt to use the power of the state to prevent the widespread reappearance of class conflict. As Macintyre (1989) notes, arbitration was introduced by predominantly middle-class politicians, closely aligned to domestic manufacturing interests, who were influenced by concepts of social liberalism. Employers were initially hostile to the Commonwealth Court of Conciliation and Arbitration, established under the *Conciliation and Arbitration Act 1904*, as it forced them to recognise unions registered under the Act and empowered these unions to make claims on behalf of all employees in an industry. The operation of the federal arbitration system was severely restricted in its early years by a series of employer-led Constitutional challenges (Hancock 1984).

Nonetheless, despite their initial opposition to the system, employers came to accept the system of compulsory arbitration for several reasons. These included the tendency for arbitration to take wages out of competition and thus limit unfair competition based on wage costs. Although very different in form, the arbitration system had a similar impact to the classic compromise between labour and capital in some European countries (e.g. Sweden), where employers recognised unions in return for retention of managerial prerogative, and in order to take wages out of competition. It has been argued that employers came to accept arbitration as a quid pro quo for tariff protection. Furthermore, employers felt that arbitration tribunals would help contain industrial disputes and militancy in periods of economic prosperity, when labour was in short supply and unions had greater bargaining power (Plowman 1989).

While initially hostile to the notion of compulsory arbitration, unions changed their stance after some disastrous defeats during the strikes of the 1890s. Under the 1904 Act unions could force employers to compulsory conciliation and arbitration even if they were unwilling to negotiate, and once there was an arbitrated award (i.e. ruled on pay or other terms of employment), such provisions were legally enforceable.

The establishment of systems of conciliation and arbitration marked an important departure from the British-style industrial relations imported into Australia before the 1890s. That British tradition, more influenced by classical liberalism, played a large part in Australian industrial relations was unsurprising. British law and notions of unionism were major imports in the 19th century, when the foundations of Australia's contemporary employment and industrial relations system were established.

The system of arbitration includes federal and state industrial tribunals. Until 1956, the Court of Conciliation and Arbitration carried out both arbitral and judicial functions. After this, the industrial division of the Federal Court administered the judicial provisions of the Act while the Conciliation and Arbitration Commission (hereafter referred to as the Commission) carried out non-judicial functions. Federal awards, which cover approximately a third of the workforce, have tended to set the pattern for all other tribunals, so that a high degree of uniformity has emerged despite the multiplicity of tribunals. Although the Commission is empowered to intervene only in disputes extending to more than one state, most important cases fulfil this requirement or can be made to do so. Either party to a dispute may refer a case to the Commission, or it may intervene of its own accord 'in the public interest'. Thus, the powers of the Commission have become more extensive than was originally intended. Some states have expressed concern at the drift of control to the federal level; others have been in favour. Attempts by the federal government to persuade all of the states to cede their industrial relations powers to the federal level have so far failed. Although the state government of Victoria did so in 1996, this was reversed with the election of a state Labor government in 1999. Most national industries, however, are covered by federal awards.

Since the late 1980s there have been major changes to the Australian arbitration system. In 1988 the Labor government replaced the *Concili-ation and Arbitration Act 1904* with the *Industrial Relations Act 1988*. The name of the Commonwealth Conciliation and Arbitration Commission was changed to the Australian Industrial Relations Commission (AIRC), but its function remained largely the same. However, the new Act was similar in approach in many ways to its pred-ecessor. More significant change was introduced in the *Industrial Rela-tions Reform Act 1993* (the Reform Act) and the *Workplace Relations and Other Amendments Act 1996* (the Workplace Relations Act). The Reform Act, introduced by a federal Labor government, among other things made it possible to certify non-union collective agreements in the federal jurisdiction for the first time (Bennett 1995). As well, this Act incorporated a right to industrial action during the designated 'bargaining period', and thus introduced to Australia the familiar distinction between disputes of 'interest' and 'rights'. The election of a Liberal/National conservative coalition government in 1996 after thirteen years of Labor governments heralded further change to the arbitration system. The Workplace Relations Act (discussed below) attempted to limit the power of the AIRC and for the first time made it possible to register individual contracts, known as Australian Workplace Agreements (Pittard 1997; McCallum 1997a). Despite attempts by the Howard government to introduce further deregulatory reform, a hostile Senate (upper house) has so far prevented more dramatic change. While commentators have suggested that recent changes have fundamentally altered the operation of the Australian arbitration system (Gardner & Ronfeldt 1996; McCallum 1997a, b), there remain distinctive features of Australian industrial relations that reflect the impact of compulsory arbitration.

It has been argued that the introduction of arbitration in Australia in the early 20th century was just one element in a broader social settlement in Australia that included tariff protection, a restrictive immi-gration policy and a minimal welfare state (Castles 1988). This policy pattern, which Castles calls *domestic defence*, significantly influenced the economic development of Australia. The tariff policy was originally designed to insulate the Australian economy from cheap imported goods and to provide employment for an expanding labour force. It also enabled wages to be determined by tribunals more on social and equity grounds than in accordance with productivity and market forces. However, the viability of tariff protection depended largely on the terms of trade for the commodity exports and the competitiveness of the domestic manufacturing sector. Commodities traded in world markets exhibit high levels of price volatility in the short run and tend to exhibit long-run decline in price relative to manufactured goods.

While Australia enjoyed favourable terms of trade in the immediate post-1945 period, since the late 1960s it has suffered significant decline in its relative terms of trade for commodity exports. At the same time, tariff protection, along with relatively lax controls on investment by MNEs in Australia behind the tariff wall, have produced a manufacturing sector that was domestically focused and largely uncompetitive in international terms. As Ravenhill (1994: 79) puts it, this 'left Australian industry ill-equipped for the increasingly competitive global economy of the 1970s'.

The move by the Whitlam Labor government (1972–75) to reduce tariffs by 25 per cent 'at a single stroke' was strongly criticised by both Australian unions and employers as having led to higher levels of unemployment, especially in industries vulnerable to overseas competition. The federal Labor government, between 1983 and 1996, sought to 'phase in' tariff reductions and stimulate competition, especially in such key manufacturing industries as automotive assembly and components (see Lansbury 1994). Since its election in 1996, the Coalition government has looked to accelerate the reduction of tariffs and has recently entered into talks with the US government about a free trade agreement. With the decline of tariff protection, groups of employers have begun to question their acceptance of arbitration.

While the six state governments are important in Australian politics, the federal parliament remains the formal and symbolic focus of Australian political democracy. Since Federation, conservative political parties have generally dominated federal government. During their intermittent periods in office at the federal level, Labor governments made significant changes in the economic management of the nation and were more sympathetic to union interests than their conservative counterparts. Australia had a Labor government in office from 1983 to 1996. It was the longest-serving Labor government at a national level in

Australia's history. Another interesting development in Australian politics is the increasing tendency for the federal government not to hold the balance of power in the upper house—the Senate. While the powers of the Senate are limited to review, it does have the power to hold up legislation. Since 1996 this has had an increasingly significant impact on employment relations legislation, with moves by the Coalition government to extend federal control over industrial relations though powers held under the Constitution to regulate corporations.

THE MAJOR PARTIES

Employers' associations

The early growth of unions in Australia encouraged the development of employers' associations and led them to place greater emphasis on industrial relations functions than their counterparts in some other countries. Numerous employers' associations have a direct role or interest in industrial relations (Plowman 1989). However, there is variation in the size and complexity of employers' associations, from small, single-industry bodies to large organisations that attempt to cover all employers in a particular state. In 1977, the Confederation of Australian Industry (CAI) was established as a single national employers' body, almost 50 years after the formation of the Australian Council of Trade Unions (ACTU). In 1983 a group of large employers set up the Business Council of Australia (BCA), partly as a result of their dissatisfaction with the ability of the CAI to service the needs of its large and diverse membership. Membership of the BCA comprises the chief executive officers of Australia's largest corporations, which has given it a high profile and significant authority when it makes pronouncements on matters such as employment relations.

Since the mid-1980s there have been several important secessions from the CAI. These included large affiliates, such as the Metal Trades Industry Association (MTIA) in 1987 and the Australian Chamber of Manufacturers (ACM) in 1989. One repercussion has been employers airing different viewpoints at events such as National Wage Case hearings. In 1992 the CAI attempted to present a more united front and to attract back former affiliates by merging with the Australian Chamber of Commerce to form a new organisation, the Australian Chamber of Commerce and Industry (ACCI). However, employers' organisations have generally appeared to be less united than the unions, under the umbrella of the ACTU, especially during the period of federal Labor governments (Mathews 1994).

There has been further change in employer representation since the election of the pro-business Liberal/National coalition government in 1996. One major development has been attempts by employer associations to shift from providing industrial advocacy and introduce a range of fee-based services for members. This shift can in part be said to reflect the decline of the centralised bargaining system, and the need for advocacy. Sheldon and Thornthwaite (1999) argue that this has produced growing competition between employers' organisations for members and encouraged the consolidation of employers' associations. Most notable among these was the 1998 merger of the MTIA and ACM to form the Australian Industries Group (AIG). At a policy level, while generally supportive of the Coalition government's industrial relations policy, business groups like the BCA have criticised the federal government and the minor parties in the Senate for not going far enough. A particular source of annoyance for employers has been repeated rejection by the Senate of proposed weakening of the unfair dismissal provisions of the Workplace Relations Act.

Unions

The establishment of the arbitration system encouraged the rapid growth of unions and employers' associations. By 1921, approximately half of the Australian labour force was unionised. Union density has fluctuated: during the depression of the early 1930s it dropped to around 40 per cent; the 1940s witnessed a steady increase in density and a peak of 65 per cent was achieved in 1953.

As in Britain, unionism originally developed on a craft basis, but with the growth of manufacturing, general and industrial unions became more common. The basic unit of organisation for the Australian union is the branch, which may cover an entire state or a large district within a state. Workplace-level organisation tends to be informal, but shop floor committees and shop steward organisations have developed more rapidly in recent years, in blue- and white-collar sectors (see Peetz 1990).

Nevertheless, unionism in Australia tends to be comparatively weak at the workplace level, reflecting a past reliance of many unions on the arbitration system rather than enterprise-level bargaining to achieve their objectives (see Lansbury & Macdonald 1992). The Australian Workplace Industrial Relations Survey (AWIRS), conducted in 1990, revealed that while 80 per cent among workplaces with 20 or more employees had at least one union member, in one-third of workplaces there was no workplace union representative, and only 26 per cent of workplaces had what could be described as an active union at the workplace (Callus et al. 1991: 48–53). A second AWIRS, conducted in 1995, showed a significant decline in the number of Australian workplaces with union members. It also demonstrated the key role that workplace union structures played in preventing the decline in unionisation (Morehead et al. 1997: 139–41; Alexander et al. 1998).

Union membership in Australia has been steadily declining over the past two decades or more. Union density fell from 49 per cent in 1990 to 23 per cent in 2002. The reasons for the decline of union membership are complex and varied. A major study by Peetz (1998: 82) concluded that 'a reasonable estimate is that around half of the decline in union density in the decade to 1992 can be explained by . . . [structural] factors'. These include changes in the structure of the economy, which has seen contraction of employment in manufacturing (in which unions have traditionally been well organised), and the growth of the service sector (in which unions have been weaker). A related change has been the decline in full-time employment and the rise of non-standard employment. Yet these phenomena have characterised most advanced industrialised countries, not all of which have experienced so steep a decline in membership as Australian unions. Other factors contributing to the decline of unionism include the growing anti-unionism among employers, and the removal of institutional arrangements, enshrined under the centralised system of arbitration (e.g. de-facto compulsory unionism), which artificially inflated union membership numbers. It has also been suggested that the unions' policies, particularly their participation in the Accord (discussed below), may have contributed to the decline in union membership (see Peetz 1998; Cooper et al. 2003).

The main confederation for manual and non-manual unions is the ACTU. It was formed in 1927 and covers around 95 per cent of all unionists. The ACTU expanded considerably after its merger with two other confederations that formerly represented white-collar unions: the Australian Council of Salaried and Professional Associations (ACSPA) joined the ACTU in 1979 and the Council of Australian Government Employee Organisations (CAGEO) followed in 1981.

Thus, as in the UK and USA, there is now only one main central union confederation. This is in contrast to some Western European countries, which have several confederations. In each of the states, trades and labour councils also play a significant role in industrial relations. And, although the state trades and labour councils are formally branches of the ACTU, they generally have a much longer history than the ACTU and display some independence in the way they conduct their affairs.

Nevertheless, in comparative perspective, the ACTU is relatively powerful—in terms of both the percentage of union members it represents and its control over its affiliates. The ACTU's considerable influence over its affiliates was reflected at ACTU congresses and conferences throughout the 1980s and early 1990s, which saw executive recommendations, almost without fail, endorsed by affiliates (Davis 1996). Officers of the ACTU also play key roles in the presentation of the unions' cases before the AIRC and in the conduct of important industrial disputes. The authority of the ACTU, in part, explains why the Australian union movement, unlike many union movements in other countries, was able to participate in a social compact from 1983 until 1996 (Briggs 1999).

Under the direction of the ACTU, strategies aimed at reversing membership decline have been put in place by Australian unions in recent years. During the 1990s the union movement focused on restructuring and amalgamations, which resulted in the merger of 360 federally registered unions into 20 industry-based 'super unions'. The rationale for the creation of these unions was that it would release resources for improved provision of services to members. While the strategy was successful in changing the structure of Australian unions and reducing their number, it did not halt the decline of membership density.

The strategy adopted by the union movement since the election of the Coalition government in 1996, and the demise of the Accord, has been to focus on the principles of 'organising'. Unions have been encouraged to build workplace activism, build alliances with the broader community and develop capacities for strategic campaigning. The objective is that unions should redefine themselves as more autonomous and less dependent on the state. In 1994 the ACTU initiated an 'organising works' program, based partly on the experience of US unions, in order to build the organising skills and capacities of the Australian union movement and to give effect to an 'organising model'. At the ACTU Congress 2000, a new strategy was launched, Unions@Work, which emphasised the central role of the organising model in building a more inclusive, social movement approach to unionism and thereby increasing membership. During 2001, the ACTU mounted various campaigns aimed at the broader workforce, rather than union members exclusively. Focused on issues of equity and fairness, a policy document, *Our Future at Work*, was launched by the ACTU in 2001, based on evidence of a national survey undertaken by the ACTU that highlighted workers' concerns about family issues. The campaign focused on problems caused by the increased casualisation of the workforce, inequality of wealth, job insecurity and perceived unfairness in the industrial relations system (Cooper 2002).

While the ideal of improved social conditions had been pursued by the union movement through the Accord process under the Labor government, the new strategies adopted by the ACTU have marked a more independent approach, in which the unions are pursuing their own agenda for social reform regardless of which government is in power. The union movement is therefore moving away from policies that stressed cooperation between government and unions and is eschewing any discussion of a new Accord should Labor be returned to government. Although they retain a formal relationship with the Australian Labor Party (ALP), there is a strong desire in the unions to forge a more independent role so that they do not find their interests subordinated to that of a Labor government or business (see Cooper et al. 2003).

Government

The powers of the federal government over industrial relations, as noted previously, are limited under the Constitution. The lack of legislative power, particularly over prices and incomes, has frustrated federal governments of all political persuasions. During the period of the Fraser Liberal/National government (1975–83) there were occasional strong exchanges between the federal government and the Commission. For instance, in 1977 the Fraser government argued strenuously that its economic policy would be prejudiced unless the Commission's decisions on wage adjustments were framed in accordance with government wishes. The Commission responded that it was 'not an arm of the government's economic policy [but] an independent body . . . required under the Act to act according to equity, good conscience and the substantial merits of the case' (Isaac 1977: 22).

A feature of industrial relations during the period 1983–96 was the strength of ties between senior ministers in the federal Labor government and senior union officials. Contributing factors were that Bob Hawke, Prime Minister in 1983–91, was a former president of the ACTU, and two of the four ministers for industrial relations during this period were former ACTU officials. Paul Keating became Prime Minister in December 1991. Although Keating developed a strong personal relationship with

Bill Kelty, secretary of the ACTU, he was not so closely aligned with the union movement as his predecessor.

During the period of the Keating Labor government (1991–96), there was a shift towards decentralised bargaining at the enterprise level and a greater focus on achieving higher labour productivity. The union move- ment was on the defensive, finding little comfort in general policy devel- opments but seeing little alternative to the Accord with the government. Furthermore, the emphasis of the Keating government's 1993 Reform Act was on strengthening individual legal rights rather than collective advances for the unionised workforce. To achieve its objectives, the 1993 Act drew on other constitutional powers—namely, the corporations power and the external affairs power. This was a departure from tradi- tional reliance on the conciliation and arbitration power (Section 51, para. xxxv). By the time of its defeat in 1996, the Keating government had moved away from the policy of the Hawke government in 1983. The emphasis on state intervention and centralisation of the first Hawke Labor government had been replaced by greater reliance on market forces and decentralisation, as well as an expansion of the federal govern- ment's industrial relations powers.

The Howard Coalition government not only eschewed any formal negotiations with the unions but has also sought to hasten the move to a more deregulated employment relations system through its Work- place Relations Act. The main policy changes in the Act included: a reduction in the role and importance of awards, which would be limited to an enforceable safety net of minimum wages and conditions; new arrangements for enterprise bargaining, which included individual agreements without union intervention; and removal of restrictions on the use of particular types of labour and hours of work. Although the minor parties holding the balance of power in the Senate forced a number of amendments to the government's original Bill, the principal reforms were retained in the new Act.

Although the Howard government was re-elected for a second term in 2001, it was continually frustrated by the Senate's unwillingness to pass additional legislation that would fulfill the government's industrial rela- tions reform agenda. It also faced a situation where all state governments had passed into the hands of the Labor Party by the end of 2001, and most of these Labor-controlled state governments undertook reform of their industrial relations legislation to strengthen the rights of unions and the role of industrial tribunals. This is significant in the most populous state of New South Wales, where more workers are covered by state than federal awards and agreements and where recent reforms have been more favourable towards the unions (see Patmore 2003).

EMPLOYMENT RELATIONS PROCESSES

Although federal awards have had precedence, the state systems of employment and industrial relations are still very important. Problems arising from overlapping jurisdiction of the state and federal tribunals have long been a source of concern to reformers, but changes have been difficult to achieve. In the late 1980s, agreements were reached between the state and federal governments on the dual appointment of heads and other members of the state industrial tribunals to the federal commission. This was a step towards the possible development of an integrated national industrial relations system. However, reforms introduced by the Howard government and the election of Labor governments in all states and territories have reversed this trend.

Historically, the Australian system of conciliation and arbitration was based on the assumption that the processes of conciliation would be exhausted before arbitration was undertaken. The system of arbitration was compulsory in two senses. First, once engaged, it required the parties in dispute to submit to a mandatory procedure for presenting their arguments. Second, tribunal awards were binding on the parties in dispute. Awards specified minimum standards of pay and conditions that an employer must meet or else face legal penalties. However, unions and employers were free to negotiate above these minimum standards. It is necessary to distinguish between the formal provisions of the arbitration system and the way it worked in practice. In reality, there has always been a considerable amount of direct negotiation between the parties. Agreements directly negotiated between employers and unions coexist with or take the place of arbitrated awards. If these agreements were ratified by the Commission, they were known as 'consent awards', and could deal comprehensively with the terms and conditions of work in particular workplaces or supplement existing agreements. In this way, awards were more flexible in practice than they appeared to be in a formal sense.

There was considerable growth of informal direct bargaining in Australia during the 1970s (Yerbury & Isaac 1971; Niland 1976). While this was halted by attempts by the Commission to control wages in the early 1980s, by the late 1980s there were attempts to foster more industry and enterprise bargaining within limits set by the Commission

(Rimmer & MacDonald 1989). The trend towards greater decentralisation of employment relations processes intensified during the 1990s in response to economic recession and growing political pressures. The *Industrial Relations Reform Act 1993* extended the scope for enterprise bargaining by reducing the ability of the Commission to vet union-negotiated enterprise agreements and by introducing Enterprise Flexibility Agreements (EFAs). These allowed workplace agreements to be negotiated in non-unionised workplaces. The Commission retained a role in ensuring that the terms and conditions of EFAs did not disadvantage employees when compared with the relevant award. Although there was a significant growth in the number of enterprise agreements during the 1990s, these largely supplemented rather than replaced existing awards. However, the effects of these changes were to widen the opportunities for employers, employees and unions to opt out of the traditional award system (Ludeke 1993).

This tendency was further enhanced by the Workplace Relations Act. A key element of the Workplace Relations Act was the introduction of Australian Workplace Agreements (AWAs), which enabled (and sought to encourage) employers to enter into individual (non-union) contracts with their employees. Although AWAs have played only a minor role in regulating wages and conditions and cover less than 2 per cent of the labour force (Waring 1999), arguably their significance lies in their use by employers as a threat or bargaining lever to force concessions from employees and unions during the bargaining process (Ellem 2001).

THE SETTLEMENT OF DISPUTES

One of the principal motivations behind the introduction of compulsory arbitration was to render strikes unnecessary. The 'rule of law' provided under arbitration was supposed to displace the 'barbarous expedient of strike action'. For many years the Conciliation and Arbitration Act contained a provision making strike activity illegal and subject to penalties. Although this provision was removed in 1930, Australian workers in the federal system were granted a qualified and limited right to strike only in 1993.

The Reform Act 1993 provided unions and employers with a period of immunity from common law and the secondary boycott actions associated with strikes and lockouts. Under this Act, either party could notify the other of its intention to use industrial action during the designated bargaining period. The Commission could intervene and make use of its traditional arbitral functions if it believed that the parties were not acting in good faith, if there was little likelihood of an agreement being reached, or on the grounds of public interest. In seeking to resolve the dispute, parties that engaged in unlawful strikes could be fined as well as have their awards suspended or cancelled. The Howard government has maintained a limited right to strike during the designated bargaining period in its Workplace Relations Act, but it has sought to strengthen the Commission's powers to address illegal industrial action, prohibited the payment and acceptance of pay or wages for workers when involved in strike action, and restored secondary boycott provisions to the Trade Practices Act, with substantial fines for breaches.

Another sanction, used sparingly by tribunals, has been to deregister a union that has acted in defiance of a tribunal order. As deregistration has tended to be difficult and complex, tribunals have generally hoped that its threat would be sufficient. Threats, though, made little impact on the Builders Labourers' Federation, deregistered in 1986; its members were quickly absorbed by other unions, leaving only the shell of a once powerful union.

One of the main effects of arbitration has been to shorten the duration of strikes and to increase their frequency. During the 1960s and 1970s, Australia was among those countries with a relatively high number of strike days per 1000 people employed. A relatively adversarial style of employment relations prevailed in Australia then; countries such as Japan, Germany and Sweden recorded many fewer strike days each year per 1000 employees (see Appendix).

After 1983, the federal Labor government presided over a more peaceful employment relations climate. During the 1980s, average working days lost through disputes per 1000 employees were halved. Beggs and Chapman (1987) have argued that while changing macroeconomic conditions played a part in this absolute and relative decline in the impact of industrial stoppages, so too did the Accord (see later in this chapter). While the Australian strike rate in 2000 was above the OECD average, it was much lower than in the decade previously and almost ten times lower than in 1980. However, it is doubtful whether the reduction in industrial disputation in Australia can be ascribed to activities of the Howard government, as the decline in strike activity occurred before the introduction of the Workplace Relations Act.

There has been an increase in the use of employer-initiated industrial action to support non-union agreements among private-sector employers (Ellem 2001). Several high-profile disputes have been sparked by employers attempting to introduce non-union agreements in areas such as mining and the maritime industries, which were traditionally strongly unionised. Such employers have been actively seeking to eliminate unions from their operations and activities.

One such attempt led to the most significant industrial dispute in recent years—the 1998 waterfront dispute. The publicly stated view of the company, Patrick, was that overpaid dockworkers (or stevedores) and their union, the Maritime Union of Australia (MUA), enjoyed a monopoly of labour supply on the waterfront and that the union fostered restrictive practices. After a series of disputes with the union, in April 1998 Patrick decided to appoint an administrator and withdraw financial support from its subsidiary labour hire companies. Patrick thereby hoped to avoid its debts and lay off its employees. New companies were contracted to replace former Patrick employees with non-union labour. The government had been encouraging Patrick to take a strong line against the MUA and announced a levy on the movement of cargo at the docks to raise $US99.8 million to fund redundancies.

The AIRC was restricted by the Workplace Relations Act from becoming involved in attempting to resolve the dispute by conciliation. Instead, the dispute was adjudicated on the docks, in the media, and in the political and legal arenas. Ironically, although the intention of the federal Coalition government's *Workplace Relations Act 1996* was to remove the role of 'third parties' (e.g. unions and the AIRC), this dispute saw a greater use of the courts (also third parties) than has usually been the case. This may in part reflect the parties' lack of experience in settling disputes autonomously. The MUA received support from waterside and longshoreman unions from other countries and the international union movement during the dispute.

The government and Patrick found themselves facing the likelihood of massive financial and even criminal penalties for allegedly conspiring to dismiss unlawfully the workforce because they were union members. On the condition that the union would not proceed with legal action, Patrick agreed to reinstate about half the unionised workforce and to stop using non-union replacement labour. The union also agreed to accept changes to work practices designed to raise productivity.

As it was being settled, all of the parties to the dispute claimed to have achieved their objectives, but there were no clear winners. The government and Patrick both pointed to reduced numbers of employees on the waterfront and the likelihood of higher productivity, but this had been gained at great economic and political cost. The union claimed that it had maintained the rights of waterfront workers to remain unionised and had retained a union shop. Yet the level of employment on the waterfront was significantly reduced after the dispute. The waterfront dispute demonstrated the lengths to which the Coalition government has been prepared to go in order to support employers in their quest to create non-union workplaces (Dabsheck 2000).

THE DETERMINATION OF WAGES

The arbitration system led to the development of a relatively centralised wages system in Australia. This has been achieved by extending the influence of the federal tribunal over key wage issues, despite constitutional limitations. The federal tribunal initially became involved in fixing a minimum wage in 1907, when it described the 'basic wage' as intended to meet 'the normal needs of an average employee, regarded as a human being living in a civilised community'. The basic (male) wage was set at a level sufficient to cover the minimum needs of a single-income family unit of five, and became the accepted wage for unskilled work. The rate for women workers was set at 57 per cent of the basic wage. The custom of wage differentials (margins) for skills was formalised in the 1920s, based largely on historical differentials in the metal and engineering trades (Hancock 1984).

The Commission and its predecessors thus began to regulate wages and differentials through decisions on the 'basic wage' and 'margins' at National Wage Case hearings. These are much-publicised rituals and occur at regular intervals, with usually one National Wage Case decision per year. The employers, unions (through the ACTU) and governments (at federal and state levels) each make submissions to the Commission, which later hands down a decision. These have, in the past, determined changes to wages and conditions. Depending on the nature of the decision these have at times, through a 'pipeline' effect, applied rather generally to employees throughout Australia.

In 1967, the Commission ended the system of a basic wage and margins in favour of a 'total' wage. It also introduced the concept of national minimum wages, representing the lowest wages permissible for a standard work week by any employee. During the early 1970s, the Commission sought to adjust the relative structure of award wages in different industries and to limit over-award rises. But by 1973/74, the contribution of increases determined at National Wage Case hearings to total wage rises had declined to approximately 20 per cent as unions bargained directly with employers for large over-award payments (Howard 1977). This, Clegg (1976) argued, made Australian compulsory arbitration more analogous to a system of collective bargaining. Collective bargaining had therefore become the dominant force in wage rises, its leading settlements being generally extended to the whole economy (Isaac 1977: 14).

Faced with rapidly rising inflation and unemployment, efforts were made to restore the authority of the Commission (Lansbury 1978). Between 1975 and 1981, partial rather than full indexation was the norm. In other words, the wage rises determined by the Commission were regularly below the rises in the Consumer Price Index. However, because of lack of cooperation from employers and unions, the Commission abandoned wage indexation in 1981 (Dabscheck 1989). In the context of rapid rises in wages and a sharp fall in economic growth, the Fraser government then initiated a 'wage pause' within the federal public service and successfully sought its general implementation by the Commission.

Perhaps the dominant feature of Australian wage determination was a social compact called the Price and Incomes Accord (the Accord), originally negotiated between the ALP and the ACTU prior to the 1983 election (Accord Mk 1) and renegotiated seven times between 1985 and 1996 (Accords Mk 2–8; for details of the agreements, see Wilson et al. 2000: 283–407). Under the Accord, the government and the ACTU presented a joint submission to the National Wage Case. For most of this period, with the notable exception of Accord Mk 6 in 1990/91, the Commission largely accepted these proposals and introduced wage principles designed to give them effect.

In its initial stages the Accord led to centralisation of wage determination in Australia. The first Accord was essentially a voluntary incomes policy, in which the ACTU pledged the union movement to making no extra claims in wage bargaining in return for the reintroduction of wage indexation. For its part the government pledged, among other things, to introduce a range of reforms to the taxation system, to raise the 'social wage' and to implement a range of industry policies (Lansbury 1985; Rimmer 1987: 106–7). In late 1983 the Commission agreed to reintroduce wage indexation, and National Wage Case decisions in 1983, 1984 and 1985 provided for full wage indexation, although these simultaneously delivered reductions in real wages through a mixture of delays in the adjustment of money wages and other factors. As Dabsheck (1989) notes, between September 1983 and December 1985, 96 per cent of nominal wage rises in Australia resulted from the decisions of the AIRC in NWC decisions.

The economic crisis of 1985/86, however, seen in the rapid and largely unanticipated fall in the exchange value of the Australian dollar, the accompanying stimulus to inflation, soaring levels of foreign debt and escalating interest rate levels, led the government to abandon its commitment to full wage indexation. Wage fixing became a more complicated business thereafter. In 1985 (Accord Mk 2), the ACTU and ALP agreed to a shift to partial indexation in response to the deteriorating external economic environment.

Since 1986 there has been a steady movement towards the decentralisation of wage determination in Australia. The initial phases of this process have been called 'managed decentralism' (Rimmer & MacDonald 1989). In Accord Mk 3, negotiated in 1986, agreement was reached on a two-tier wages system. The first tier was to provide a minimal rise in wage levels covered by federal awards, while the second tier of wage rises were to be made available only where it could be demonstrated that agreement between employers and unions had been reached on improving efficiency and productivity. The AIRC translated this agreement into a wage principle (known as the Structural Efficiency Principle) in the 1987–89 NWCs.

Faced with continued economic uncertainty, mounting employer criticism, political opposition and increased dissatisfaction among some groups of workers at the slowness of the second tier, the ACTU and the ALP agreed in February 1990 (Accord Mk 6) that 'enterprise bargaining' would become the main source of wage rises. The AIRC, however, rejected the parties' submission and argued that employers and employees were not prepared for this step. The AIRC eventually accepted the enterprise bargaining principles in the October 1991 NWC, which introduced a safety-net increase for all awards and limited wage rises through enterprise bargaining to cases where increases in efficiency or productivity could be demonstrated.

In reaction to the position taken by the AIRC over enterprise bargaining, the Labor government, in consultation with the union movement (Accord Mk 7), introduced legislation designed to speed up the introduction of enterprise bargaining and limit the power of the Commission to vet wage outcomes from enterprise bargains. The Reform Act 1993 established a wage determination system with two distinct streams—an award stream and a bargaining stream. The award stream was intended to provide safety-net increases for those workers who were unable to gain access to wage rises through enterprise bargaining. The bargaining stream included both union and non-union elements.

These changes produced a dramatic increase in enterprise bargaining, although most of it was union-based and supplemented rather than replacing award coverage. By November 1994 there were 2700 federally registered union-based enterprise agreements, which covered 58 per cent of employees registered under federal awards. However, there were only 20 non-union enterprise agreements, covering only 3000 employees federally registered (Short & Buchanan 1995: 124). Changes in wage determination during this period produced increased wage dispersion in Australia. In 1996, employees covered by enterprise agreements had average annual wage rises of between 4 and 6 per cent, whereas employees covered solely by awards received a mere 1.3 per cent rise (ACIRRT 1999: 77).

The election of the Howard government in 1996 ended the Accord and its role in shaping wages policy. The Workplace Relations Act has further decentralised wage determination in Australia. The Workplace Relations Act retained the award stream and the mechanism of safety-net adjustments but reduced the ability of the AIRC to vet outcomes of non-union enterprise agreements—also introducing AWAs, which are a new non-union individual stream of wage bargaining.

This continued decentralisation of wage bargaining has led to a further increase in wage dispersion in Australia. In 1997 the AIRC established a federal minimum wage across industries and occupations, set at the lowest level of the Metal Industries Award. However, minima have continued to fall behind average weekly earnings and, in 2000, the basic federal minimum weekly rate for adult full-time workers was 46 per cent of average weekly earnings, compared with 58 per cent for women (OECD 2000). Indeed, during the past fifteen years, wages dispersion in Australia have grown at a faster rate than in most continental European members of the OECD (Wooden 2000).

CURRENT AND FUTURE ISSUES

The emerging bargaining structure under the Workplace Relations Act

As a result of the legislative and institutional reforms since the early 1990s, the arrangements for determining wages and conditions of work are complex and fragmented. There are four main streams of regulation:

1. *Awards* are determined by the AIRC, and generally cover an industry or sector, following negotiations between a union and employer.
2. *Enterprise Bargaining Agreements* (*EBAs*) are negotiated between a single employer and a union. These are specific to a company or enterprise and supplement the award for that industry. In most cases the EBA is negotiated with a union, but there is provision for non-union collective agreements.
3. *Australian Workplace Agreements* (*AWAs*) are contracts negotiated with an individual employee or group of employees. Each contract must be signed individually and registered with the office of the Employee Advocate.
4. *Individual non-registered agreements* operate outside the formal industrial relations framework and rely on the common law of contract.

Approximately 25 per cent of all employees have their wages and conditions entirely regulated by awards, while 35 per cent rely on a combination of awards and collective agreements. The remaining 40 per cent of the labour force have their wages and conditions determined largely by individual arrangements, mostly relying on the common law (ABS 2000). This marks an important shift from the early 1990s, when up to 80 per cent of employees had their terms and conditions set by awards or collective agreements (Campbell 2001).

While AWAs represent a change in the federal employment relations system, it remains unclear how significant their impact will be. The adoption of AWAs has been slower than many expected, especially in the private sector, where they cover less than 1 per cent of the workforce (Waring 1999). This may in part reflect the view of employers that they are too onerous and costly to implement (Creighton 1997).

Nevertheless, AWAs may be more significant than their numbers indicate. O'Brien and O'Donnell (1999) have argued that the federal government has used AWAs in the public sector to force a shift towards non-union and individualised employment agreements despite the resistance of unions.

Of perhaps greater significance has been the increase in the number of employees covered by individual common law contracts of employment, which are neither registered nor necessarily formalised. Many employers appear to prefer these contracts, as they are simpler to adopt and do not have to be vetted by a government agency. It is estimated that up to 38 per cent of employees have their pay set by such contracts, and these are overwhelmingly in the private sector

(Wooden 1999). Related to growth of unregulated individual employment contracts has been the dramatic increase of non-standard forms of employment in Australia. Approximately 45 per cent of the Australian labour force was classified as being in non-standard forms of employment by the late 1990s (ACIRRT 1999). Almost half of this group of workers were employed part-time (i.e. fewer than 35 hours per week), while the other half were causal workers and did not have formal employment protection. While causal employment has long been a feature of the Australian labour market, the number of casual employees has doubled since the mid-1980s. Of all the new jobs created since that time, 60 per cent have been casual (Burgess & Campbell 1998).

Since the late 1980s, there have been significant shifts in the bargaining structure. Australia has a system of formal and informal streams of bargaining and employment regulation. It seems likely that the trend towards increased fragmentation of bargaining and growth in the unregulated sector is likely to continue for the foreseeable future.

Relations between the industrial and political wings of the labour movement

While Australia was almost unique among the DMEs in being able to sustain a social compact for more than a decade, from the mid-1980s until the mid-1990s, the prospects of the reintroduction of an Accord-like compact if a federal Labor government is elected seem increasingly unlikely. This reflects a reassessment by both the union movement and the ALP of the benefits derived from the Accord.

ACTU officials involved in the Accord contended that the impact of the fall in real wages was more than offset by increased employment (thereby raising household incomes), tax reform, improved superannuation and a raft of more generous social welfare provisions. These, it were claimed, had led to higher standards of living. The Accord also allowed union representatives to have greater influence over economic, industry and social policies, and it consistently provided the framework for union influence on these areas of government policy. The Accord, for instance, set out 'agreed policy details' on the treatment of prices and non-wage incomes, on taxation, and on supportive policies covering industrial relations legislation, social security, occupational health and safety, education, health and Australian government employment.

However, in the post-Accord period, commentators have argued that involvement in the Accord had adverse consequences for the unions. It is, for example, claimed that the rapid decline of union membership during the period of the Accord reflected growing dissatisfaction by rank-and-file members with their union's participation in a policy that lowered real wages. More generally, it has been argued that the focus by the ACTU on achieving improvements in the social wage prevented unions from developing effective mechanisms for workplace bargaining (Wilson et al. 2000).

There are indications that the ALP is moving away from cooperation with unions. In the aftermath of the 2001 election defeat, it was argued—in a manner reminiscent of arguments made by reformers in the British Labour Party—that close association with the unions was an electoral liability and there was a need to broaden the appeal of the ALP. One of the recommendations of a review of the 2002 federal party commissioned by the new Labor leader Simon Crean was the abolition of the 60:40 rule, which guaranteed unions a majority in party policy formation. The attack on the 60:40 rule met with a mixed response from unions. Somewhat ironically, it was right-wing unions that objected most strongly, while left-wing and militant unions, which were seeking to increase their independence from the Labor Party, were generally unconcerned with the change (Cooper 2003).

Alternative forms of employee representation

Some employers and unions have considered means by which employees might be given a greater influence in decisions affecting them in the workplace. Evidence from the Australian Workplace Industrial Relations Survey in 1990 and 1995 revealed that the proportion of workplaces with joint consultative committees increased from 14 to 33 per cent during this period, although they were more prevalent in large workplaces with 500 or more employees. However, when managers were asked whether they had consulted workers about important changes that had affected their workplaces during the previous year, only 29 per cent responded positively and only 18 per cent said that employees had a significant input into decisions (Morehead et al. 1997: 244).

This has stimulated debate about the merits of statutory mandated works councils as a means for employees to gain greater influence in decision making at the enterprise level (Gollan et al. 2002). McCallum (1997a) has argued that legislation is needed to strengthen 'industrial citizenship' and to give employees the right to participate in workplace governance. He has proposed the establishment of electoral works councils in enterprises with 100 or more employees. These councils would consult with employers on a wide range of issues, including the introduction of technological change, rostering agreements and amenities (see also McCallum & Patmore 2002).

Opposition to works councils in Australia has been based on concern that there is an absence of preconditions that would enable them to function as effective vehicles for collective representation and social protection. Buchanan and Briggs (2002) argue that the resurgence of unilateral managerialism and employer militancy, as well as the lack of commitment among employers to 'social partnership' strategies, means that works councils are likely to entrench managerial prerogatives rather than reverse the 'representation gap' left by declining unionisation. Their view is that works councils should be considered only after there have been measures implemented to address deepening inequalities and the rebuilding of coordinated bargaining structures and collectivism. Yet there is a growing concern, even among union leaders, that it is necessary to look beyond traditional union and workplace structures 'to secure for employees a genuine democratic right to information and consultation' (Combet 2001). Unless there is union support for mandated works councils, it is unlikely that they will be successful. Yet simply waiting for a revival of union membership will forgo an opportunity to consider alternative forms of employee voice and representation, which may strengthen the role of workers in decision making within the enterprise (Lansbury & Wailes 2003).

CONCLUSIONS

The 1990s were a period of significant change in Australian employment relations, as the shift towards a more decentralised form of labour market regulation, begun by a Labor government, gained momentum under a Liberal/National coalition government. By the turn of the new century, the emphasis was on individualistic (rather than collectivist) approaches to employment relations, in which industrial tribunals played a diminished role and unions were increasingly marginalised. There was less consensus between employers, unions and government about future directions of employment relations than had existed under a more centralised system. With the decline of unionisation, employers' organisations became less powerful and employers adopted more enterprise-based approaches to employment relations. Employers continued to place greater emphasis on human resource strategies with a diminished role for unions. While there was increased involvement of employees in informal participation activities, employers were reluctant to establish more formal mechanisms of joint consultation with employees. Unions attempted to arrest their decline in membership by focusing more directly on organising and strengthening representation at the workplace level. There was also growing support among some union leaders for the statutory introduction of works councils, which could provide an institutional focus, albeit imperfect, for union action at this level of the workplace.

Whichever political party gains power in the future, there is a need to establish a more appropriate framework for employment relations in Australia. The existing system has not provided adequate protection for the most vulnerable members of the labour market. Nor has it facilitated a cooperative approach between unions and employers to enhance national economic performance while providing fair and equitable distribution of gains. A key policy challenge is how to meet the demands of increasing competitiveness while maintaining desirable social standards of living for all citizens. A more inclusive model of employment relations is needed. This will require new approaches to the changing status of workers, the regulation of work and working time, as well as the pooling of risks and responsibilities between workers, employers and the state. As the nature of work changes in response to changing global, technological, competitive and corporate conditions, new labour market and employment relations policies are needed to address these realities.

A CHRONOLOGY OF AUSTRALIAN EMPLOYMENT RELATIONS

1788	European settlers arrive in New South Wales, with separate British colonies established subsequently.
1856	Unions win recognition of the eight-hour day. The Melbourne Trades Hall Council (THC) is formed.
1871	Sydney unions create a Trades and Labor Council (TLC); Brisbane and Adelaide unions follow.
1879	First Inter-Colonial Trade Union Conference.
1890–94	The Great Strikes. Following defeat by combined employer and colonial government power, unions found Labor parties in each colony.
1901	Commonwealth of Australia founded.
1904	Commonwealth Conciliation and Arbitration Court established under the Commonwealth Conciliation and Arbitration Act, with powers of legal enforcement.
1907	The *Harvester* case establishes the principle of the basic wage, above which the Court may award a margin for skill.
1916	Widespread union opposition to the Labor government's conscription policy.
1917	The All-Australian Trade Union Congress adopts a socialist objective.
1927	Founding of the Australian Council of Trade Unions (ACTU).
1929	The conservative government is defeated in a federal election called over proposed weakening of the Conciliation and Arbitration Court.
1949	A major coal strike, begun around economic demands, sees the federal Labor government take strong action to defeat the Miners' Union.
1950	Penal provisions, known as bans clauses, written into awards, enable employers to seek an injunction from the court restraining unions from taking industrial action.
1955	The Australian Labor Party splits, with a breakaway group becoming the Democratic Labor Party.
1956	Following the *Boilermakers*' case, the Arbitration Court is disbanded. The Conciliation and Arbitration Commission is set up with arbitral functions and the Industrial Court with judicial responsibility.
1967	*Metal Trades Work Value* case—the determination of a basic wage and margins is discontinued and a 'total wage' is introduced in lieu.
1969	The gaoling of a union official for failure to pay fines for contempt of court leads to extensive strike action throughout Australia.

1972	A federal Labor government is elected after 23 years of a Liberal coalition government.
1975	Wage indexation is introduced; Labor government is dismissed.
1977	The CAI is established as a national employers' confederation.
1979	The Australian Council of Salaried and Professional Associations is affiliated with the ACTU.
1981	The Council of Australian Government Employee Organisations merges with the ACTU; wage indexation is abandoned.
1983	Hawke Labor government is elected; ALP-ACTU Prices and Incomes Accord becomes the linchpin of government policy. Return to centralised wage fixation and full wage indexation. The Business Council of Australia is formed.
1985	Report of Committee of Review of Australian Industrial Relations Law and Systems.
1987	Landmark National Wage Case decision.
1988	Elaboration of structural efficiency principle. New federal Industrial Relations Act.
1989	Award restructuring. Domestic airline pilots' dispute.
1990	Accord Mk 6 is agreed between the ACTU and federal government.
1991	Acrimony over the April National Wage Case decision; October National Wage Case decision condones shift to more enterprise bargaining. Paul Keating replaces Bob Hawke as Prime Minister.
1992	Further movement towards decentralisation of bargaining, including amendments to the *Industrial Relations Act 1988*.
1993	Keating Labor government re-elected for an unprecedented fifth consecutive term of Labor government.
1994	The *Industrial Relations Reform Act 1993* comes into operation and extends the scope of enterprise bargaining.
1995	Amendment of unfair dismissal provisions of the Reform Act 1993 to simplify procedures.
1996	Election of the Liberal/National coalition government led by John Howard.
1997	The Workplace Relations and Other Legislation Amendment Act is proclaimed.
1999	The Howard government's attempts to introduce further industrial relations reforms through the More Jobs Better Pay Bill is rejected by the Senate.
2001	The Liberal/National coalition government is elected for a further three-year term.
2003	Further decline in the level of unionisation to 23 per cent of the labour force in Australia.

CHAPTER 6

EMPLOYMENT RELATIONS IN ITALY*

Serafino Negrelli and Peter Sheldon

Of the countries examined in this book, Italy has been one of the most volatile politically, economically and in its employment relations. Such volatility, apparent for more than a century, is common in southern Europe (Sapelli 1995). Historical causes, including the forcible retention of power by elites who governed processes of industrialisation that developed later than in the UK, USA, Germany or France, had geographically very uneven results that left most rural people impoverished. These factors encouraged an economic 'dualism' in which more democratic, modernising sectors—mainly in the north and centre—coexisted with feudalistic, premodern ones in the south. Reinforcing this dualism has been a state tradition that is simultaneously invasive in its social control yet mostly inefficient and ineffective at providing necessary services. These trends have helped provoke particular political responses: widespread hostility towards the state; deep-seated localist sentiments; the growth of a labour movement that was militantly class-conscious and open to spontaneous revolts; a central role for Catholicism in political and social life; and recurring tendencies towards right-wing political authoritarianism. This has led to intensely ideological politics and employment relations.

Italy has also shared strong modernist (and, more recently, post-industrial) impulses with its neighbours to the north and west. Tensions

*The equivalent chapter was authored by Claudio Pellagrini in earlier editions of the book.

between 'Latin' and 'European' patterns have long been part of Italian history, and policy debates centre on shifting Italy towards a more 'European' trajectory of pluralist employment relations, political stability and public-sector integrity. 'Anglo-Saxon' notions of the primacy of market relations also increasingly influence policy debate. Overall, contemporary Italy presents itself as a sophisticated, urbane consumer society with one of the world's leading economies and a vibrant democracy. Yet problems of dualism, corruption and cynicism remain, most obviously in the continued existence of a large clandestine (informal) economy and diffuse organised crime, particularly in the south. As these activities go unrecorded (as well as unregulated and untaxed), official statistics (as below) often understate economic activity and employment.

Italy has a population of 58 million and an official employment participation rate of 60 per cent (see Appendix). Reflecting developmental dualism, employment participation in the south is only 42 per cent, compared with 60 per cent in the centre-north, a level similar to the Euro-country average. Among working-age (15–64-year-old) men in the centre-north, the level is 72 per cent. Despite growth in female employment since the 1960s, employment of women remains low. In 2000, the official female working-age participation rate was 40 per cent. Again, dualism is marked. The rate in the centre-north was 48 per cent but only 25 per cent in the south.

Of the 24 million working people, there are almost 6 million self-employed—a very high level for the EU. Until very recently, Italy officially had very few people in 'atypical' employment, but this has been changing. There are 1.6 million part-time employees (low for the EU) and 1.4 million fixed-term or temporary workers. The majority in both categories are women. Further, more than 1.6 million are (employer-coordinated) consultancy and freelance workers. The inflow of young people and women—particularly in the south—into this category has raised suspicion that their independence from employers is a fiction aimed at regulatory evasion (Fellini et al. 2001). Temporary agency work, legally available only from 1997, has grown very rapidly to employ 0.7 million people.

High unemployment—particularly youth and long-term unemployment—has bedevilled Italy since the 1980s. Unemployment was at 12 per cent in 1996, more than half of this figure comprising young people in search of their first job (Pellegrini 1998: 144). Public policy since 1996 has achieved some successes, and total employment grew by 1.4 million (of whom almost a million were women), with a particular boost during

2000. Much recent growth has come via 'atypical' employment; however, in 2001 full-time employment grew. Unemployment fell to 9.4 per cent in 2001, the lowest level since 1992. Again, dualism has meant unemployment in the south continuing to rise while largely disappearing in the northeast.

Italy's compliance with EU monetary union criteria in 1998 surprised domestic and overseas pundits but, partly as a result, Italy's economy between 1990 and 1999 grew more slowly than the average in the other Euro-zone countries and than its own 1980s rates (Banca d'Italia 2000). While 'social pacts' helped guarantee broad acceptance of deflationary programs and extensive structural change (Negrelli 2000), there have been clear winners and losers.

THE HISTORICAL, POLITICAL AND SOCIOECONOMIC CONTEXT

Modern Italy came into being as a unified whole only in 1861. Reunification elevated northern political and economic interests at the expense of the southern poor, and papered over an array of longstanding local differences that derived, partly, from geography. For example, alpine northern Italy abuts Austria, Switzerland and France, while the far south is close to North Africa. Differences in topography also made for many 'Italies'. Further (and leaving aside ancient Rome), Italy had urbanised and developed sophisticated craft production very early—during mediaeval times, when densely populated, complex, self-governing cities controlled populous rural hinterlands. This encouraged self-sufficiency and strong senses of localism that centuries of foreign invasion and domination reinforced. Further, familial relationships have long been central to social, political and economic organisation at all socioeconomic levels (Ginsborg 1990; Sapelli 1993).

Until recently, rural life dominated most Italians' experience. In 1881, agricultural workers represented some 60 per cent of the workforce, and even in 1951 agriculture remained by far the largest employment sector. During this period, distinct systems of agricultural property relations prevailed. These influenced the development of employment relations. On the Po plain, running west to east over most of northern Italy, masses of agricultural proletarians (including many women) worked, on call, for large, more capitalised estates. Sharecropping families lived and worked on smaller holdings in the hill regions of central Italy. In the south, feudalistic absentee landlords dominated, whether providing harsh day labour on large, coastal estates or grinding poverty for peasants who lived in small towns and rented tiny pockets of impoverished hillside to farm (Ginsborg 1990: 210; Maraffi 1994: 137; Clark 1996).

The period 1895–1914 was crucial for economic take-off, political development and fashioning modern employment relations. In common with other DMEs, industrialisation involved an early, driving role for food-processing, textile and clothing industries followed by steelmaking and metalworking. Industrialisation depended on family entrepreneurship and provoked antagonism among craft workers. Five factors marked Italy's modernisation as fundamentally different. First there was the continuing dominance of agriculture. Second, heavy industry was concentrated in a very restricted area—the northwestern 'industrial triangle' of Milan, Turin and Genoa. Third, industry elsewhere remained small-scale, labour-intensive and under family control. Fourth, to over-come lack of private initiative, governments invested heavily in crucial industrial sectors. Finally, and not by accident, northern modernisation exacerbated southern underdevelopment, misery and exasperation. For example, leading reformist, liberal politicians like Giovanni Giolitti, while expressly tolerating northern unions and agricultural strikes, sided with reactionary southern landlords in their repression of peasant activism (Candeloro 1977; Castronovo 1980; Sapelli 1995).

What options did rural and urban masses have at this time to change their impoverished lives? Parliamentary politics remained a marginal strategy, as voting rights came with wealth. All men (over 30) received the right to vote only in 1912 and all women only in 1946. Emigration was one response used massively. Sporadic insurrectionary revolts were another. Unionism, despite its risks, was the most accessible strategy. Its rapid growth from the 1880s owed much to massive enrolment among northern agricultural labourers through local 'leagues of resistance', which federated into a national agricultural workers' union (*Federterra*) in 1901. This was by far Italy's largest union in 1914 (Candeloro 1977, 1978; Clark 1996).

A critical spur to unionism was the formation, after a decade of localised activities, of the Italian Socialist Party (PSI) in 1892. Although a national party, its activists also reinforced localist tendencies. Socialists promoted extensive networks of local producer and consumer coopera-tives. From the early 1890s, they also organised local labour chambers (*camere del lavoro*) as solidaristic labour exchanges and coordinating bodies for local unions. In 1893 a number of *camere* federated. From 1900, PSI activists also systematically reorganised craft unions into industry unions—such as the metalworkers' federation (FIOM), which became the leading union after 1945. *Camere del lavoro* and industry unions have been the twin bases of Italian union structures ever since. Socialists formed a national union confederation, the CGL (General Confederation of Labour), in 1906. It gathered industry unions and *camere del lavoro* but could not dent their local autonomy. By then, the PSI was the dominant labour movement tendency. In these years its main left-wing competitor, anarchism, also developed an influential strand of locally based, revolutionary unionism (Candeloro 1977; Castronovo 1980; Procacci 1991; Clark 1996).

When social Catholicism belatedly provided socialism with competition to its right, it too reinforced labour movement localism. The 1891 papal encyclical *Rerum Novarum* attacked socialism and enjoined Catholic activists to provide organisational alternatives—cross-class bodies seeking social justice through social harmony and state intervention. In the north and northeast, activists established local producer and consumer cooperatives on a vast scale, local mutual aid societies (and eventually unions) and, in support, local banks (Candeloro 1977, 1978; Clark 1996).

As Italian employers largely contended with local markets, employer associations developed late and haphazardly. Until the early 1900s, localism, trade sectionalism and a focus on governmental economic policy marked business combinations. Employers counted on governmental repression to deal with union threats. However, when Prime Minister Giolitti's neutrality in (northern) industrial conflicts encouraged greater localised strike activity, employer organisations developed local industrial relations strategies and coordination across trade sectors. The first, local, all-industry employer federation was founded in Monza (near Milan) in 1902, and became a prototype. Local federations constituted regional ones, and in 1910 these combined to form a (still tiny) national employers' confederation, Confindustria. Employer organisation and most strikes remained localised, as did collective bargaining when it developed in the early 1900s (Maraffi 1994).

Subsequent events lessened localism but intensified volatility. World War I encouraged nationally oriented political, economic and social trends. The birth of the centrist People's Party in 1919 gave Catholic initiatives a national focus. That year too there was resounding PSI electoral success and a massive upsurge in union militancy. Revolutionary militancy intensified and in 1921, in the expectation of soviet-style revolution, PSI dissenters formed the Italian Communist Party (PCI). However, the tide had already turned and brought a bloody, employer-backed reaction that developed into fascist seizure of state power in 1922.

Benito Mussolini's fascist state outlawed independent unions and opposition political parties. For some 20 years, those organisations that survived did so underground or in exile. In the meantime, the centralising fascist regime developed national industry through extending state ownership, militarisation and a rigid policy of self-sufficiency. It also restructured employment relations on top-down, interclass lines that provided employers with total control at work and gave the Fascist Party enormous power in the labour market. For workers, apart from obedience there was a range of welfare and social activities (Procacci 1991).

Allied liberation of southern Italy came in 1943. With the aid of local partisans, the Allies had liberated the centre and north by 25 April 1945. In the interval, workers in northern factories again began to chance strikes and protests despite the presence of murderous Nazi occupation troops. With final liberation, PCI emerged dominant among resistance forces that had included all antifascist factions, from anarchists to social Catholics, which in 1942 had formed the Christian Democratic Party (DC). In a spirit of democratic unity, many of these forces established: the CGIL as a single, non-party union confederation; a multi-party coalition government in 1945; a 1946 national referendum that chose to replace the monarchy with a republic; and the Constitution of 1948. That year, however, domestic and Cold War politics brought this unity undone. The DC used its new parliamentary majority to oust the left-wing parties from government, and DC supporters left the CGIL and set up their own competing Catholic confederation, CISL. In 1950, supporters of the Republican and Social Democratic parties also left the CGIL and set up UIL (Ginsborg 1990; Procacci 1991). Each confederation had a clear ideological character and political alignment. The largest, the CGIL, came under communist domination.

After 1945 Italian employers enjoyed low wage costs and promoted product quality and innovation. As government policies and entrepreneurial strategies focused on exports, the Italian economy gained from international growth. From the early 1950s to the mid-1960s, the 'Italian economic miracle' consistently produced among the world's highest annual economic growth rates despite continuing stagnation in the south. Italy shifted from being largely an agricultural society with extensive premodern areas to an industrial economy and largely modern society. By 1961, 38 per cent of the workforce worked in industry, 32 per cent in services, and (a still relatively high) 30 per cent in agriculture.

Industrialisation extended well beyond the industrial triangle, also depending heavily on state enterprises. Clothing, textiles and food processing remained significant but renewed industrialisation reinforced the leading role of machine tools, transport vehicles, white goods, office equipment and chemical products.

Northern employers took advantage of large-scale migration of low-cost workers from the rural northeast and south, and coped with increasing scale and complexity by intensifying task specialisation and deskilling. During the 1960s, Fordist methods encouraged an emerging dominance of semiskilled workers (often from the south) at the expense of craft workers. This, management speed-ups and abysmal housing for immigrants gave a particularly exasperated tone to the growing worker militancy that exploded in the 'hot autumn' of 1969 and continued through radicalised workplace and street politics over the following decade (Castronovo 1980; Ginsborg 1990; Sapelli 1995).

During the 1970s and early 1980s, international economic crises, political corruption and industrial militancy caused the Italian economy great problems. Large companies and state enterprises suffered most, while many small and medium-sized family companies of the centre and northeast—the 'Third Italy'—garnered great success. Whether in traditional or emerging sectors, as subcontractors to large companies or as direct suppliers, smaller employers have boosted Italy's export performance. Some became substantial MNEs themselves, while others remain small but take advantage of customised infrastructure available in their specialised industrial districts. These smaller employers have gained from a range of flexibilities, including those they enforce on their workforces (Ginsborg 2001).

As the DC held power from 1948 until its collapse in 1993, perceptions of governmental instability overlook remarkable immobility. While always the largest party, the DC rarely won more than 40 per cent of votes in a proportional electoral system, and during the 1980s won substantially fewer (Ginsborg 1990: 442). Sometimes holding power alone, it mostly depended on coalitions with small centrist or centre-left parties. Some 1980s coalitions had prime ministers from the PSI or the Republican Party but the DC retained ultimate control. Dependence on other parties was one source of coalition volatility. Another was the DC's internal volatility. The DC was a cross-class party, riddled with internal factions headed by powerful leaders. This factionalism had some ideological basis. For example, through the CISL, left-wing factions had a strong foothold in unionism (and vice versa), while those on the right were closely linked to employer positions. Mostly though, DC factionalism derived from personal opportunism and the use of localist patronage to 'balkanise' state entities under broader DC control, particularly in southern Italy. Its minor coalition partners developed similar appetites (Ginsborg 1990, 2001).

After 1948, with its huge, informed and activist rank and file, the PCI became Italy's second-largest and core opposition party. In important regions it also dominated regional, provincial and local government, where its administration was mostly efficient and honest. Yet, and despite gradually shifting to the centre, its links to the Soviet Union made it anathema to Italy's power elites and the USA. Even when its 1976 vote went to 34.4 per cent, the PCI was unable to share national government. The absence of any other opposition created a 'blocked democracy' of long-lasting DC rule in which fierce factionalism and pervasive corruption flourished (Ginsborg 2001).

The Cold War's end encouraged political realignments. The DC, PSI and minor government parties collapsed over corruption scandals and the PCI (after splitting) reconstituted itself as a non-communist, 'Left Democratic Party' (PDS). Two new groups emerged on the right. The Northern Leagues are an employer-led surge of northern localism hostile to the centralised state, Rome's profligacy and immigration. Into the DC's vacuum also stepped media magnate Silvio Berlusconi. His new mass party, *Forza Italia* ('Come on Italy'), linked astutely marketed national pride, 'antipolitical' cynicism and neoliberal economics. In coalition with the hypernationalist but now more respectable heirs of fascism (National Alliance) and the 'anti-Italy' Northern Leagues, Berlusconi won the 1994 election. Like the DC, all these parties have cross-class aspirations but, unlike the DC's left, none have real empathy for workers' rights or unionism. In particular, Berlusconi is committed to employer unitarism and neoliberal economics. Coalition disunity brought Berlusconi's government down later that year, and his troubles with corruption inquiries helped keep him out of power until his coalition won the 2001 election. In the meantime, a succession of centrist and centre-left *'ulivo'* ('olive tree') coalition governments, with the PDS at their core, delivered major structural change to Italy's economy, political system and employment relations (Ginsborg 2001).

THE PARTIES IN EMPLOYMENT RELATIONS

Within Italy's relatively voluntarist collective industrial relations, unions and employers' associations are 'non-recognised' associations. This, however, does not preclude them from acting as legal entities, concluding collective agreements, calling strikes and having legal standing in courts of law and specialist tribunals. On the whole, 'non-recognition' has kept them free from judicial and governmental interference. It has also made it easier for dissident groups to establish alternative organisations.

There have been three recent turning points in Italian employment relations. The first, the 'hot autumn' of 1969, signalled the rise of militant worker and then union power. The second, FIAT's 1980 defeat of metal-working unions, marked the decline of that power and management resurgence. Third, the 1993 tripartite accord[1] represented an accommodation that has systematically institutionalised employment relations for the first time.

Management, employers and their associations

After a number of generations, founding families still largely control many of the major northern firms. Led by FIAT's Agnelli family, they make up Italy's industrial and financial elite, with immense political and economic influence. Their firms and their foreign MNE neighbours are also the principal areas of professionalised management. The successful smaller firms of the Third Italy are mainly family businesses that their founders, often former skilled workers or farmers, still control. FIAT, long Italy's dominant employer, has traditionally committed itself to workplace control and cost containment through engineering, organisational and political means— whether through Fordist mass production or, more recently, robotics. Leadership among Italian employers on issues of quality of working life, employee participation and human relations at work has come from elsewhere. After liberation, it came from Olivetti and, to some extent thereafter, from some state-owned corporations. In recent years it has come from appliance-maker Electrolux-Zanussi[2] (Ginsborg 1990, 2001; Sapelli 1993; Boldizzoni et al. 1996).

Employer organisation and representation involve overlap and competition among confederations. Divisions flow from sectoral identity, firm size and even political orientation. Thus, for example, Confcommercio and Conferscenti represent employers in retailing and other branches of commerce. In agriculture, there is Confagricoltura as well as Coldiretti and Confcoltivatori (small farmers). Confapi represents small and medium-sized enterprises and Confartigianato the still-strong sphere of artisan production.

Confindustria is by far the most important association. It covers manufacturing, building and construction, and some service industries.

Individual firms cannot join Confindustria directly but join its horizontal (territorial) and sometimes vertical (industry) affiliate associations. As the pre-eminent voice of organised capital, Confindustria has played a central role in tripartite economic policy making, economy-wide collective bargaining, coordinating industry bargaining, as well as in lobbying, policy development and propaganda. Confindustria owns an influential daily newspaper (*Il Sole 24 Ore*) and other media through which to disseminate its philosophies, perspectives and policies. In 2003, Confindustria had 259 territorial and sectoral affiliates that together represented more than 110 000 employers employing 4.2 million people (Confindustria 2003).

Territorial associations still control Confindustria and, of these, the association of Milan's industrialists and that of Turin are the largest and most influential. Confindustria formed its industry affiliates only during the 1970s and 1980s in an effort to deal with particular bargaining challenges. The most important industry associations cover engineering employers, the chemical industry and the textile industry. Each represents employers in industry-level bargaining, but they have different membership structures that help determine their ranges of activity and limited autonomy from Confindustria. In other sectors, Confindustria's territorial affiliates are more important.

SMEs constitute the vast majority of Confindustria's affiliates, and Confindustria suffers recurrent internal conflicts between groupings of large employers and SMEs. In particular, since the late 1960s, the dominant role of FIAT and its allies in employer politics has been a recurring theme. From 1958 Intersind (manufacturing) and from 1960 ASAP (petrochemicals), specialised associations separate from Confindustria, represented enterprises in the very large state-owned sector. They re-entered Confindustria in 1994 after decades of having proven more amenable to political interference, also to innovations in employment relations (Lanzalaco 1998).

FIAT's 1980 victory strengthened management's new employment relations activism. Influential employers' association officials argued for a non-union or individual bargaining stream but, in the face of underlying union strength and the real possibility of renewed worker militancy for anticapitalist agendas, employers' associations instead sought two connected ends: the regularisation of pluralist industrial relations around mutually accepted 'rules of the game'; and the subordination of union bargaining agendas to the logic of profit-seeking enterprises. In this way, employers sought to overcome Italy's historic volatility. Their reward was the 1993 accord (Sheldon et al. 1997).

Confindustria traditionally had strong ties to the DC but became more independent on the DC's dissolution and the series of left-leaning governments during the 1990s. The March 2000 election of Antonio D'Amato as Confindustria president suggests another significant political realignment. D'Amato, a young, southern SME employer, won despite strong opposition from FIAT's coalition of large, northern employers. FIAT's tradition since the late 1960s has been to mix its own maximum workplace employer prerogative with the legitimation of tripartite bargaining (or partnership) as a mechanism for policy change and social peace in the public arena. D'Amato's election represented a victory for employer opinion opposed to privileging tripartism in politics. In this, D'Amato garnered support not only from vast numbers of SMEs but also from a few large, northern, 'new' entrepreneurs. One, Berlusconi, was happy to take these understandings into government in 2001. For both D'Amato and Berlusconi, governments are elected to govern (not to indulge in social partnerships), business is the privileged interlocutor and a freeing of business from external constraints a necessary priority. If unions wish to contribute to these conceptions of modernisation, partnership has value—otherwise not (Pellegrini 1998; Pedersini 2000; Paparella 2001a, 2001b).

Unions and other forms of employee representation

Given their history of deep politicisation, Italy's principal unions have long identified themselves as having class leadership and representational missions rather than a vocation for servicing financial memberships. In Italy, this identification has received repeated legitimation from governments and political parties. Moreover, it receives legitimation from that (elsewhere) most unlikely source, non-unionists, who often join one-off union action in large numbers and vote for those unions in workplace elections (Regalia & Regini 1998; Baccaro et al. 2003).

Italy presents external observers with a bewildering multiplicity of unions and union structures. The vast majority of members belong to one of the three union confederations—the CGIL, CISL and UIL. Each of these is composed of territorial bodies based on *camere del lavoro* as well as industry unions (that have their own local sections). Thus, for example, there are three (potentially competing) industry unions in metalworking: FIOM (CGIL); FIM (CISL); and UILM (UIL). There is a similar situation in other sectors. While territorial associations remain more important for employer organisation, industry unions have become more influential within unionism. The CGIL has 5.4 million members, the CISL more than 4 million and the UIL some 1.7 million. A majority of CGIL and CISL members are pensioners, suggesting deep commitment to the union movement but also union difficulties with recruiting among younger employees (Baccaro et al. 2003: 46, 57). Apart from the confederations, there is an array of 'autonomous' and rank-and-file organisations. Even as political party influence over union affairs has lessened or disappeared, union fragmentation and competition continues, further complicating an already complex picture.

In the early years after 1945, employer intransigence and union fragmentation and weakness meant little workplace union presence. Unions remained centralised and deeply party-politicised. Blocked electorally, the PCI attempted to exercise opposition and policy-making influence through the CGIL. Short 'demonstration' general strikes and street protests raised broad-ranging social, economic and political demands aimed at governments more than employers. CISL, the first confederation to slip tight party shackles, began to experiment with plant-level productivity bargaining during the early 1950s, but general lack of operational purpose helps account for heavy overall falls in union density before the late 1960s. Post-liberation euphoria had brought total union density to 50.8 per cent in 1950. After a decade of frustrations, this had dropped to 28.5 per cent (Ginsborg 1990; Regalia & Regini 1998: 472). CISL's autonomy allowed it to pioneer industry bargaining from the early 1960s, spurring competitive emulation from the CGIL. As industry affiliates gained more bargaining autonomy, they extended it into formally decentralised bargaining at the enterprise level. In some sectors, industry unions began to overshadow territorial bodies. CISL also gained from its DC links at executive levels of state-owned industries (Pellegrini 1998).

Nevertheless, unions still lacked workplace structures. These emerged spontaneously in the months leading up to the 'hot autumn' of 1969. Expressions of militant direct democracy and anticapitalist egalitarianism, their innovative and far-reaching demands threatened employer control and profits but also the hierarchical, institutionalised union confederations. But the confederations were able to harness this 'workerist' wave to make gains through collective bargaining, to greatly augment their power in industry and their influence in politics.

The Workers' Charter 1970, a PSI-sponsored legislative response to the 'hot autumn', provided some of the most advanced employee rights anywhere, including powerful support for workplace-based union activity. In particular, it provided for enterprise-level union representative structures (or RSA) that unions then combined with rank-and-file activism in the form of factory councils (*consigli di fabbrica*). Alongside protection against employer victimisation of union representatives, the statute provided the rights to hold mass meetings and ballots on company time, a room for union activities and noticeboards for union information, paid time off and leave of absence for union delegates. Significantly, election to factory (or delegates') councils came via a vote of all employees at the workplace, irrespective of union membership status. Thus while industry unionism overshadowed territorial bodies, within the former, initiative had swung to workplace structures (Alacevich 1996; Regalia & Regini 1998).

Successful militancy ignited workplace optimism and activism, encouraging greater solidarity 'from below' across confederal borders. Union density rebounded to 38 per cent in 1970 and rose to 49 per cent in 1980 (Regalia & Regini 1998: 472). Union autonomy from political parties created increasing pressure from below for greater unity 'from above'. This crystallised in the 1972 federation of the three confederations into CGIL-CISL-UIL and agreement to weaken party influence in unions. This unity came undone in 1984, when CGIL alone refused government and employer pressures to weaken wage indexation.

'FIAT 1980' ended the cycle of union resurgence and cast a pall of gloom over confederal unionism that lasted for much of the 1980s (Galli & Pertegato 1994). Debate arose over unions' loss of representativeness, particularly in regard to white-collar and supervisory workers. These trends most concerned CGIL, the most ideological confederation and the one with the most strongly ingrained sense of its historic mission. With Italy a (mostly) prosperous society dependent on international trade, what was the future for a confederation with a tradition of anticapitalist analysis and class mobilisation? In reality, however, employers' associations were aware that employee class consciousness still ran deep and wide and that unions retained a substantial threat effect. Recurrent economic crises still generated intense industrial volatility. In search of social consensus for austerity measures and economic and workplace restructuring, governments and *Confindustria* appeared more open again to dealing with confederal unions as 'social partners', but only on two agreed conditions: respect for the 'rules of the game', and recognition of employers' agenda for enterprise competitiveness.

Since the late 1970s, even CGIL had formally accepted that unions shared responsibility for macroeconomic stability. A decade later, confederal leaders were even more convinced and again open to tripartite bargaining. Tripartism also appealed for reasons relating to their representational legitimacy. First, union density had again fallen heavily: by 1990 it was less than 39 per cent and in 1998 only 35 per cent. An increasing number of retirees (pensioners) who maintained their membership helped disguise the real decline. Thus, while absolute union membership rose from 9 to 10.7 million in the 1980s and 1990s, confederal membership among the economically active fell by 28 per cent, from about 7.4 million in 1980 to 5.3 million in 1998. Part of this had to do with the recomposition of the workforce within an economy increasingly based on private services. In 1998, unionisation was high in agriculture (87 per cent), moderate in the manufacturing industry (40 per cent) and non-market services (45 per cent), and still low in market services (20 per cent) (Codara 2000).

Second, there was the rise of competing and hostile forms of employee representation. The three confederations had long had other competitors. CISNAL, a small fascist union, had been around for decades, house unionism had been a major challenge at FIAT, as had 'autonomous' unions with a strong sectional bent in banking. However, autonomous unionism became more pervasive during the 1980s in unionism's public-sector heartlands—railways, hospitals, airlines, schools and police—and this trend intensified during the 1990s. Thus, about one-third of all union members in the public sector now belong to some 714 non-confederal organisations (Carrieri 2000). Some autonomous unions are tiny, some are employer-oriented, and others are aggressively and selfishly sectional. Reasons for joining them include political dispositions opposed to those of the confederations; and sectional, occupational and craft-like jealousies and chauvinisms. There has also been greater consolidation and coordination among them recently. UGL, successor to fascist CISNAL, is an almost wholly public-sector union, with about 2 million members. CISAL, a quasi-public-sector union with 1.8 million members, has its base in sectors such as the railways, education and public administration, and often undercuts confederal agreements. Over the past decade too there has been significant diffusion of autonomous rank-and-file committees ('Cobas', 'Cub' and 'Rdb') in the wake of protest and dissension against confederal compromises. Cobas-style unionism shares aspects of *pre*-earlier anarchist unionism. Strongest in the public sector, it also has some influence in private industry, where it has claimed former CGIL militants (Bordogna 1998).

Confederal unions have responded by reinvigorating workplace representation and marginalising their opposition. Support from employers and government helped. One way was to replace factory councils, which had become relatively autonomous, open to take-over by dissidents and opponents. A 1991 confederal framework agreement introduced a model of 'unitary union representation' (RSU) that gained express recognition under the 1993 accord as private-sector employers sought to prevent the spread of Cobas contagion (Sheldon et al. 1997). RSUs retain all rights granted to predecessor structures—including to information, consultation, and to bargain at company level. However, only two-thirds of RSU seats are filled by election of the workforce as a whole via electoral lists. The rest can be appointed by unions that sign the relevant industry-wide agreement in proportion to their lists' electoral success. RSU elections since then suggest high levels of employee engagement and a rising representative status of confederal unions far beyond official membership statistics (Regalia & Regini 1998; Baccaro et al. 2003).

Improved confederal representativeness was also to come from greater interconfederal unity, and a 1997 agreement was supposed to lead to a single, unified confederation in 1999. Yet, once again, differences in perceptions of mission, strategy and tactics and political affiliation made each confederation wary of sacrificing its autonomy. Since then, there have been contrasting moves towards unity at both industry and central levels, where differences often reflect divergent attitudes to dealing with (hostile) governments (Paparella 1999: 5; 2001a, 2001b).

The government and state agencies

We now look at the role of the state as employer, provider of the employment relations framework, and as a party—with unions and employers' associations—to tripartite agreement making. Although liberation and the 1948 Constitution appeared to herald a new era of state involvement, political corruption re-emerged under the DC, as did sporadic violent government repression of union activism. Over time, this repression declined. A DC-controlled state adopted patronage and corruption to build its own spheres of support and, later, engaged in forms of political exchange to mollify worker militancy. Given Italy's parliamentary (but not electoral) volatility, this often took legislative form though executive decrees rather than parliamentary majorities (Ginsborg 2001).

DC governments fragmented a public administration in which legislation traditionally set employment terms and conditions. More recently, there has been a growing tendency to 'privatise' employment relations in public administration. One element is outsourcing but, more fundamentally, it involves explicitly importing private-sector assumptions and processes. Some reflect managerialist preferences, but a major change came at confederal union insistence: replacing legislative regulation of public administration employment relations with a regulatory regime based on collective bargaining (Mania & Orioli 1993). A 1993 legislative decree created ARAN, to represent public administration employers as signatories to framework agreements and to national agreements. ARAN also assists, on request, with decentralised bargaining. This decree has separated the 'technical' bargaining role of the state as an employment relations actor from its role as employer at a time when its managers are required to meet results-based targets and hold powers corresponding to those possessed by private-sector employers. Collective agreements subsequently established important frameworks for union voice (EIRR 2002a)

The DC also greatly expanded fascist-era public ownership and control of industry through vast holding companies, notably IRI and ENI, that controlled substantial enterprises in steelmaking, engineering, ship-building, car manufacture, newspapers, banks, the wider oil industry, chemicals, pharmaceuticals—even ice-cream and confectionary. Some enterprises played crucially important roles in Italy's economic miracle and their holding companies became employment relations pace-setters. During the 1970s their finances worsened, often dramatically, as they came to include many failed private enterprises and politically related corruption expanded. Effective reform efforts during the 1980s were insufficient to prevent the privatisation boom of the 1990s (see below) (Ginsborg 1990, 2001).

Italy's antifascist legacy has remained most apparent in relation to its legal framework for collective industrial relations. The Constitution reflected an identification of independent unionism with democracy (and employers' shameful collaboration with Mussolini) by delineating the new republic as 'founded on labour' and guaranteeing individuals' rights to unionise and to strike. Until recently, wariness from governments, employers and unions has meant that there was little legislation expanding on these clauses, and collective industrial relations remained largely voluntarist. Indirect effects, however, were evident as governments developed broad if complex regimes of individual labour rights and employment-related, contributory social security, in which unions play pivotal formal roles. One of the main markers of the clandestine economy is that its employers do not provide social security payments on the employees' behalf.

Enhancing the 'positive rights' aspect of Italy's voluntarist system has been the application of the Constitution's Article 39(4). A 1959 extension (*erga omnes* law) has since served as a basis for giving collective agreements legal status and allowing their extension to all employees in an industry, unionised or not (Alacevich 1996). This effectively blocks formation of a formal non-union sector and renders union avoidance an irrelevant option, even for MNEs that actively seek to remain non-union elsewhere (Boldizzoni & Lorenzet 1996). However, this measure governs outcomes, not the processes that produce them or the parties involved. In the absence of a prescriptive legislative framework, it is therefore industry agreements that mostly establish procedural frameworks. The Workers' Charter, despite being such advanced legislation, also set no bargaining framework.

In the shadow of the 'hot autumn', reform from the left often came through collective agreements that resulted in legislative ratification. This interpenetration of employment relations and parliamentary politics encouraged repeated ad-hoc government intervention to resolve disputes with a national dimension. From the mid-1970s and particularly during periods of endemic stagflation, class conflict and domestic terrorism, these interventions became less ad-hoc as governments became more involved in tripartite arrangements linking employment relations and economic policy through 'political exchange'. PCI influence over CGIL also allowed it to dampen more spontaneous workplace conflict in the 'national interest' in exchange for concessions from DC governments. Industrial conflict sometimes became a cipher for parliamentary politics, with levels of volatility linked to party political agendas (Golden 1988; Ginsborg 1990).

As tripartism (and union concessions) proved useful for mounting effective incomes policies while minimising industrial and political conflict, governments also began to seek union consent prior to legislating in certain areas. This began a trend to 'negotiated law' that re-emerged in the 1990s as 'social pacts' for facing tough EU convergence criteria (see below). During the 1990s too, EU pressure and directives as well as examples in other EU countries encouraged centre-left governments to rethink labour market policies. Apart from wider legislative legitimation of atypical employment, this has included responding to redundancies more through active labour market policies that emphasise training and better job matching than through cash benefits. Other innovations deriving from EU directives include extension of parental leave (Regalia & Regini 1998; Trentini 2000).

THE PROCESS OF EMPLOYMENT RELATIONS

Bargaining and 'social pacts'

Collective bargaining, sometimes with subsequent legislative ratification, has remained the prevalent regulatory mechanism within Italian employment relations. Yet there is no one 'Italian model'. Below we trace and explain oscillations in bargaining level and the scope of issues involved, highlighting the changing role of governments in bargaining and the development of tripartite social pacts to deal with crises.

From the late 1940s to the early 1960s, employers largely imposed economy-wide (or national multi-industry) agreements on a deeply divided and weakened union movement. Since the early 1960s there has been a series of shifts in bargaining level in Italy. At any time, two of three levels of bargaining—economy-wide, industry- and company-level—have tended to be more prominent for manufacturing. In other sectors, bargaining at a regional or provincial level retains its historic prominence. Between 1969 and 1993, choices of and relationships between bargaining levels were often the result of crude industrial relations power, reactions to intermittent crises and jockeying for advantage.

(National) industry agreements have been the fulcrum of the system since the 1960s. They cover general pay and working conditions, establishing the standard arrangements open to supplementation at company level. The leading industry agreements are in metalworking, chemicals and textiles. Under the influence of the 'hot autumn', the scope of 1970s industry agreements extended to include health and safety, workloads, labour mobility, and previously untouchable areas of company policy. Between 1968 and 1975, the growth of company- and plant-level bargaining greatly widened the scope of issues under discussion—work intensity, health and safety, hours of work and works canteen food quality—and the number of those involved in negotiations. With no clear framework determining a division of labour between bargaining levels, worker revolt created unmanaged decentralisation, wherein 'double-dipping' by militant workplace unionism repeatedly added to industry-level agreements. Rapid wages drift and militant challenges to employer legitimacy at the workplace provoked intense employer dissatisfaction.

To regain order and predictability, employers' associations sought to recentralise bargaining. Given the worsening economic crisis, they found governments, confederal union leaderships and the PCI available as partners (Golden 1988). Between 1975 and 1984, economy-wide bargaining re-emerged as dominant, but with a much more powerful union presence and direct government involvement. Governments gained union acceptance of voluntary wage restraint and industrial peace as well as of employers' demands for greater flexibility. In exchange, governments offered a range of concessions to employees and broader working-class interests. Tripartite bargaining on incomes policies severely restricted lower-level bargaining, particularly after 'FIAT 1980' encouraged employers to regain workplace control. At economy-wide level, employers' associations also won important victories in wage determination.

When unity among the union confederations collapsed in 1984, economy-wide pay bargaining gave way to industry- and company-level bargaining. Although ascendant, larger employers saw the usefulness of a union voice during an era of considerable workplace restructuring and technological change. At workplace and local area levels, employers and unions experimented with informal, flexible forms of joint regulation. All this encouraged a search for a stable procedural framework. From 1992, economic crisis again prompted governments and Confindustria to seek restructuring and reform via bargained (tripartite) social pacts that gained subsequent legislative ratification. EU pressure to reduce public debt meant governments had much less to offer by way of political exchange but the confederal unions were more vulnerable to competition and employer attack, and thus accepted calls for concessions on national (incomes policy) and employer (enterprise flexibility and productivity) goals (Baglioni 1991; Sheldon et al. 1997; Regalia & Regini 1998; Negrelli 2000).

Social pacts have brought together three linked spheres: collective bargaining, the welfare system, and employment generation. Together, they have largely introduced employer demands for reductions in labour costs and government expenditure and increased flexibility via atypical employment. The 1993 accord, which continues to govern collective bargaining, institutionalised collective industrial relations so as to guarantee consistency, accountability and predictability. It stipulated only two levels of bargaining: industry and company. Moreover, for the first time in the private sector, it clearly stipulated the bargaining scope of each level and the links between them. Industry agreements, renewable for pay every two years (and for other matters every four years), determine minimum pay levels for industry classifications. Its incomes policy function is to simultaneously protect real pay levels, overcome inflation and reduce strikes. The accord has also restricted company-level pay bargaining to company-related criteria such as quality, productivity and profitability.

Confederal unions gained approval for RSUs, a new form of company-level employee representation (see above) that strengthen the unions against competitors and increase the likely consistency of employee voice. For the first time too, the accord formally provided that company agreements were to have jurisdiction over technological and organisational change, strengthening the unions' workplace role. Parties to the accord appear happy with its outcomes, and its implementation has achieved most of the aims set for it, including the previously forlorn hope of meeting EU criteria (Mania & Orioli 1993; Bordogna 1997; EIRR 2002a). Radical changes to the pension system through a social pact became law in 1995. A 1996 social pact for employment generation became law in 1997 and another, for Milan in 2002, also focused on integrating socially marginal people into the workforce (EIRR 2002b).

Criticism of this model largely comes from SME circles and Cobas. Some employer representatives call for the abolition of industry bargaining (while others want only an industry level). In their favour, they now have a Berlusconi government, and confederal unions have split on issues related to bargaining structure. By 2000, CGIL appeared to have exhausted the compromises that its rank and file would accept and began to rebut negotiated positions of government, Confindustria, and CISL and UIL that weakened employee rights. It has strongly opposed CISL's openness to more decentralised bargaining at the expense of the national industry level, and during 2001, in breach of the 1993 accord, it sought productivity-related pay rises through industry bargaining (Paparella 2001a; Pedersini & Trentini 2002).

National industry bargaining still strongly prevails. In 2001, 66 industry-wide agreements then in force covered almost 11 million out of a total 15.7 million employees. Another half-million came under a further fourteen agreements awaiting renewal. These coverage figures represented a substantial increase over 2000 as a result of hard union bargaining for renewals. The vast majority of strikes were connected to agreement renewals that continued in 2002 (Pedersini & Trentini 2002: 2, 7; EIRR 2002a).

In terms of coverage, significant extensions in bargaining during 2001 demonstrate the ability of Italian unions and collective bargaining to penetrate such areas as private services, SMEs and the 'new economy'. One has provided the first single national collective agreement covering the 1 million employees working in the 'professional offices' of lawyers, engineers and architects. Another, part of a national agreement for journalists, covers online journalism. The third, this time between confederal unions and Confapi (SMEs), is an economy-wide agreement to regulate teleworking that will operate in tandem with more detailed industry- and enterprise-level agreements (Pedersini & Trentini 2002).

Disputes and dispute settlement

Italy has long had one of the highest levels of industrial conflict by international standards. Industrial conflict in Italy also follows particular patterns. First, 'demonstration' strikes are extensive in coverage but of short duration (a few hours), and are often related to renewal of agreements, particularly in a leading sector (e.g. metalworking). Second, there is a high proportion of strikes linked to party politics and government policy. Third, continuing localism generates a significant number of local strikes. Fourth, many strikes are spontaneous in nature or led by unofficial bodies. Fifth, since the 1980s, many strikes have involved public-sector employees. Finally, many strikes also involve street marches and demonstrations.

Nevertheless, in line with the experience of many other DMEs, the strike record has been declining in recent years. The average annual number of recorded strikes between 1995 and 1998 (with 1974–79 in parentheses) was 867 (3185); these involved 0.81 million strikers (7.803 million) and meant 0.995 million days not worked (15.46 million) (Bordogna 2000). One set of explanations of Italian strike patterns links the interpenetration of party politics and industrial relations, high levels of class consciousness and militancy in extensive sections of the workforce, and employer and state traditions of high-handed autocracy. Before the 1993 accord, leading Italian academics also often pointed to the lack of an institutional dispute resolution framework or sanctions for strikes (Giugni 1987; Treu 1987; Cella 1990). Political strikes have received Constitutional Court protection, while top-down, confederal union attempts to self-regulate strikes during the 1980s failed before the determined action of militant rank-and-files, competition from autonomous unions, and sectional groups seeking to maximise their strategic positions (Golden 1988). Since then, 1990 legislation restricting strikes in essential public services and union adherence to the 1993 accord have gone some way to overcoming these factors. However, confederal unions maintain their ability to mobilise massive participation in strikes and demonstrations.

Wage determination and payment systems

The 'hot autumn' raised insistent pressure for more egalitarian income distribution, and subsequent industry agreements reflected this pressure, raising pay rates of the unskilled relative to skilled and of blue-collar relative to white-collar employees. They also harmonised pay scales across Italy to the advantage of employees in the south. Revisions to wage indexation (*scala mobile*) formulae furthered these tendencies and increased the proportion of pay rates open to automatic adjustment at a time of high inflation. The results included strong compression of relativities and, during periods of high inflation and economic crisis, reduced opportunities for employers to customise pay for enterprise circumstances. During the 1980s, Confindustria pressured governments and unions to reverse these trends. In 1984 its efforts brought a weakening of the *scala mobile* and in 1992 the demise of the *scala mobile* (Ginsborg 1990; Baccaro & Locke 1998; Pellegrini 1998).

The 1993 accord delivered the most important innovations in wage determination in recent decades. Wage indexation under industry bargaining is now based on government projections of inflation over the following three years, allowing room for discounts for certain factors plus any differences between projected and actual rises over the preceding period. While this incomes policy has depressed real wages, very high levels of indirect labour costs have continued to keep total unit labour costs higher than in other EU countries. Wage earners have thus made most of the sacrifices to cure Italy's economic ills. Further, there is continuing evidence of substantial gender-based pay gaps, to the particular disadvantage of women in the south (EIRR 2001; Pedersini & Trentini 2002).

Employee involvement and consultation

A 1906 company agreement with the FIOM introduced formal employer recognition of workplace employee representation through a works committee (*Commissione interna*), but Mussolini's fascist regime destroyed all forms of independent employee involvement. With fascism's collapse, a 1943 CGL-Confindustria agreement re-established the *Commissione interna* structure which, however, lost its initial extensive bargaining powers and became mainly responsible for monitoring and implementing outcomes of negotiations (Della Rocca 1998). For many years after World War II, with notable exceptions like Adriano Olivetti, Italian employers were generally as hostile to workplace-level employee participation as to company-level bargaining. They feared the inroads that militant employees might make on their managerial prerogatives. Politicised, class-conscious unions too were wary of the potential compromises involved. The situation was different in the public sector, where the cross-class tradition among DC managers and CISL unionists encouraged participation through combined committees of employees and management.

The 'hot autumn' unleashed a torrent of demands for workers' control that the Workers' Charter partially absorbed (Terry 1994). Since the mid-1970s, industry agreements have provided unions with rights to information regarding far-reaching and hitherto confidential aspects of enterprise management: investment programs; technological innovation; decentralisation of production; and the general impact of restructuring on employment and work organisation. Certain agreements provide for joint examination of these matters (Treu & Negrelli 1985). Unions have regarded information rights as supplementing collective bargaining, not supplanting it. The IRI Protocol 1984 combined both methods in seeking to reduce and manage conflict in state-owned enterprises (Regalia & Regini 1998). Since the 1980s too, many industry agreements have provided for joint consultation or bilateral committees regarding, for instance, health and safety, equal employment opportunity, work reorganisation, training, flexible working hours and payment by results (Negrelli & Treu 1992).

From the employer side, Electrolux-Zanussi has been a leader through its numerous agreements instituting a wide range of participatory mechanisms (Cesos 2000), while at Melfi, FIAT broke with its Fordist traditions by accompanying its new 'lean production' model with sophisticated forms of individual and collective participation (Camuffo & Volpato 1997; Negrelli 2000). In general, whether in the public or private sectors, these practices result from collective bargaining and not from the individualistic HRM model common in Anglophone countries.

CURRENT ISSUES

New forms of work and employment

Since the 1980s, Italian employers have introduced old and new forms of labour flexibility in response to pressure from product and financial markets and from technological change. Their strategies have included those pertaining to entry-related numerical flexibility, management of internal labour markets through greater functional flexibility and the more controversial exit-related numerical flexibility. As employers face union resistance and other institutional restraints against unilateral action, they have pursued their strategies through collective bargaining, partnership and social pacts.

Employers have made strong legislative gains under centre-left governments in their demands for greater numerical flexibility, receiving still greater encouragement since Berlusconi's re-election. As well, they have been bargaining hard—at enterprise and territorial levels—to exchange the creation of new jobs for union concessions that allow management greater flexibility in labour use. An EU directive encouraging the spread of (regulated) forms of fixed-term employment became law in 2001 despite CGIL opposition. More generally, confederal unions have acquiesced to employer demands for greater flexibility in types of hiring, but have done so through collective agreements that provide a series of regulatory protections to employees. Fuelling their wariness is the awareness that rising incidences of atypical employment in DMEs have grown in parallel with rising levels of workplace injuries and fatalities (Pedersini & Trentini, 2000: 2, 5, 2002; Ginsborg 2001; Quinlan et al. 2001)

Development of the south and employment relations

Decades of heavy state spending have contributed to relatively modest amelioration of southern underdevelopment and social disadvantage. Huge emigration in the 1950s and 1960s—to northern Italy and abroad—helped relieve southern underemployment and poverty. However, Italy's political and social ills persist in their most intense and interconnected forms in the south—social inequality, political corruption and patronage, the informal economy and organised crime (Ginsborg 1990, 2001). Union bargaining (and political exchange) platforms during the 1970s and 1980s often sought greater private- and public-sector investment in the south. More recently, unions have bargained for other, more innovative forms of employment generation. Nevertheless, despite impressive development in limited zones, labour market conditions for employees remain far more unfavourable than those in the north—particularly the northeast, where labour shortages abound (Fellini et al. 2001; Pedersini & Trentini 2002).

Under the Employment Pact 1996, to encourage investment and employment in depressed areas of the south, governments have promoted a variety of local, tripartite collective agreements that 'discount' labour costs compared to the national industry standard. 'Gradual alignment' agreements have had success in encouraging 'clandestine' SMEs to emerge from the informal 'black economy' and regularise their employment practices in exchange for discounts that decline over three years. 'Area agreements' and 'territorial pacts' between local organisations of confederal unions and Confindustria allow local exceptions to industry agreements on pay, job security, working-time flexibility and job classifications. They thus align with Confindustria policy to decentralise bargaining to reflect local labour market realities. D'Amato's election to head Confindustria gave this greater resonance, as it made southern economic development a central Confindustria objective linked to others that weaken legislative protections for employees (Pedersini 1997, 2000).

Privatisation and employment relations

As in many other DMEs, Italian governments have embraced the extension of external market forces into areas previously under state control. Italy's case was particular, given the crippling public debt that derived from the DC's long, corrupting hold on power. Longstanding domestic pressure to resolve these issues met intense resistance from political and employment relations spheres. Yet during the 1990s and through largely technocratic, centre-left governments, Italy closely followed the UK at the head of the EU privatisation ladder (Pedersini 1999: 3–4). Domestic and EU pressures combined to produce large privatisations in the competitive sector (steel, engineering, chemicals, oil and oil products, banks and insurance companies) as well as widespread privatisations and corporatisations of previously monopoly utilities (railways, telecommunications, water supply and sewerage) sometimes within new 'competitive regimes' (Pedersini 1999; Zanetti 1999; Ginsborg 2001).

The effects of all this on employment relations are still unclear. Heavy job losses have hit some sectors, like the partially privatised state railways (Zanetti 1999). There will certainly also be a shift in public-sector patterns to those resembling the private sector, including more aggressive linking of performance management and pay. This has recently occurred by collective agreement in the railways. Complicating this process have been situations where formerly state monopolies operated under enterprise agreements that were, in effect, industry agreements. Under new, competitive regimes, this lack of a formal industry agreement allows 'new entrant' employers to evade the existing, more expensive agreement of their privatised competitor. Fragmentation of employee representation and decentralisation of collective bargaining suggest that some new entrants are pursuing a 'low-road' approach (i.e. using low pay and low skills). On the other hand, some unions have reacted energetically and cohesively. Starting with the privatised and 'liberalised' telecommunications industry in 2000, confederal unions gained an industry-level agreement direct from Confindustria. In 2001 they gained a single, industry agreement for electricity generation and distribution, and in 2002 for a water supply and gas sector that includes private- and public-sector employers (Pedersini 1999; Paparella 2000; Pedersini & Trentini 2000, 2002; EIRR 2002a).

CONCLUSIONS

For more than a century, uneven economic development, the role of the state and localism helped make Italian employment relations and politics more ideological and volatile than in other DMEs. The 'hot autumn' of 1969 and successive years represented the high point of these features. These features, in turn, shaped the complexity of aims, forms, strategies and behaviours among employers' associations and among unions, including their tendencies to fragmentation and competition. They also created a fluid bargaining structure that experienced pronounced shifts in bargaining level and scope, reflecting the relative power of the parties and the degree of economic or political crisis. More recently, the role of the state has been important in quietening these tendencies but it has done this through a largely voluntarist framework that incorporates unions and employers' associations through centralised bargaining and social pacts. In particular, the watershed 1993 accord provided an agreed set of mechanisms for resolving many of the longstanding areas of volatility, fragmentation and conflict in bargaining and representation.

The recent Italian tradition at the central level has been one where trilateral agreements receive legislative confirmation. This response, the driving of fundamental change to incomes policy, tax and welfare policy and employment policy through bargained union involvement, significantly differentiates recent Italian experience from that of many other DMEs. So too has much of the informal company- or territorial-level union–employer bargaining that maintains union voice over organisational and HRM issues and that has contributed to the flexibility of the SMEs. The 1993 accord also institutionalised this bargained change process through company-level bargaining. This institutionalisation of union bargaining is an important bulwark against government or employer temptations to foster non-union or individualised strategies. Thus, the implementation of HRM in Italy has largely come via collective bargaining and union voice.

Repeated crises have encouraged the confederal unions towards compromises that favour the competitive survival of Italian capitalism together with continuing external labour market regulation. The confederal unions' inclusion in these processes and the powerful symbolic and institutional roles they lend unionism reflects recognition by larger employers and governments of a continuing and viable union threat effect. At the same time and in the face of competition from autonomous unions and Cobas, this inclusion presents confederal unions with inevitable difficulties regarding responsiveness and representativeness towards politically aware rank-and-files aware that they are paying the price for decades of DC corruption. This appears to be one of the challenges facing the maintenance of the 1993 accord. Larger employers and governments need union involvement to manage militant or sectionally oriented workforces towards agreed national and enterprise goals. For confederal unions (and particularly CGIL), this means maintaining levels of internal discipline unattainable during the 1970s and 1980s despite the costs of compromise. At the same time, any dramatic decline in rank and file militancy may mean that larger employers adopt a more unitarist approach to employment relations.

A CHRONOLOGY OF ITALIAN EMPLOYMENT RELATIONS

1848	First printing workers' associations. Ad-hoc development of craft unions.
1850s	Mutual aid societies, localised cross-class unions, dominant union form.
1861	Reunification of Italy (*Il Risorgimento*). Spurs diffusion of unionism.
1868	First city-wide general strike, at Bologna.
1870s	Class-conscious but local and sectional 'leagues of resistance' supplant mutual aid societies as dominant model. Multi-unionism at work.
1880s	Growth of local union organisation and socialist organisation, particularly in northern agricultural areas.
1891	First *camera del lavoro* (labour chamber), in Milan (based on French model), as worker and union-controlled local labour exchange. Horizontal, inclusive, localist unionism. *Rerum Novarum* (papal encyclical) fosters Catholic labour movement activism.
1892	Formation of the Socialist Party of Italy (PSI).
1893	Federation of *camere del lavoro*.
1900	Industry union of railway workers.
1901	Socialists active in formation of: *Federterra* (agricultural workers' union federation), the largest and most influential union; FIOM (federation of metal workers); and other important industry unions.
1902	First local, all-industry employers' federation (Monza).
1906	General Confederation of Labour (CGL), composed of *camere del lavoro* and industry unions.
1910	Confindustria, the national employers' confederation.
1918	Formation of Catholic union confederation (CIL).
1919	People's Party (Catholic).
1920	First national industry collective agreement—for gas workers.
1921	Communist Party of Italy (PCI).
1922	Mussolini and Fascist Party seize power.
1925	Fascist government abolishes freedom of association, bans all non-fascist unions. Strikes and other forms of union action are forbidden.
1943–45	Liberation of Italy, starting from southern Italy: many strikes in northern Italy against fascist regime and Nazi occupation. Final liberation, 25 April 1945.

1944	Pact of Rome (antifascist forces) for the creation of a single, non-party union confederation (CGIL).
1945–48	Coalition government of antifascist parties.
1946	National referendum abolishes the monarchy for a republic.
1948	New constitution guarantees rights to union freedom and to strike. DC wins parliamentary majority and excludes PCI and PSI from government. Catholics leave CGIL to form CISL. Start of decades of intense political rivalry among unions and their decline.
1949	Social Democrats and Republicans leave CGIL and later form UIL. Subsequently, PCI increasingly controls CGIL.
1959	Law (*erga omnes*) allows legal exension of collective agreements to the entire sector.
1962	Protocol between metalworkers' unions and ASAP and Intersind (public-sector employers' associations) for enterprise-level collective bargaining.
1968–73	Long wave of intense industrial conflict, including 1969 'hot autumn' (*autunno caldo*). Unions gain and entrench workplace presence. Factory councils (*consigli di fabbrica*), new horizontal forms of workplace representation. Workers' Charter (*Statuto dei diritti dei lavoratori*), advances protection of employee and union rights at work. Formalises new phase for Italian employment relations: union ascendancy at all levels. Employers under siege.
1972	Unified union federation CGIL-CISL-UIL.
1975	Economy-wide agreements between Confindustria and CGIL-CISL-UIL on wage indexation (*scala mobile*) favours lower-paid employees. Start of decade of tripartism.
1976–79	PCI supports DC government at time of economic crisis and domestic terrorism but without governmental participation.
1980	FIAT dispute. Revolt of FIAT technicians and super-visors against union policy ('March of the 40 000'). Metalworking unions vanquished. New phase: employer ascendancy and union crisis.
1983	Tripartite agreement on labour costs and wage indexation. New law formalises collective bargaining in public employment.
1984	Inconclusive tripartite negotiations on wage indexation leads to collapse of CGIL-CISL-UIL federation. Government decree codifies agreement with CISL and UIL.
1987–89	Rise of rank-and-file committees (Cobas) challenges leading role of union confederations in the public sector.

1990	First legislative protection from unfair dismissal for employees in 'micro' enterprises (fewer than fifteen employees). Law restricting strikes in public-sector essential services. Tripartite agreement abolishes *scala mobile* (wage indexation).
1992	Tripartite central agreement reshapes incomes policy, bargaining structure, union workplace representation structures and rights. New phase: more institutionalised employment relations.
1993	First Berlusconi (right-wing) coalition government elected, soon collapses.
1995–2001	Centre-left governments with leading role for PDS (ex-PCI). Structural changes and reforms to employment and labour market policies, welfare and collective bargaining via tripartite 'social pacts' that subsequently gain legislative form.
1998	Italy fills criteria for entry into European monetary union. 'Christmas Social Pact' confirms the 1993 central agreement with new forms of decentralised concertation.
2001	Berlusconi's right-wing coalition regains power after seven years in opposition. New Berlusconi government presents '*Libro bianco*' on more labour market flexibility for employers.
2002	'Pact for Italy' on competitiveness and social inclusion, but CGIL refuses to sign. Includes a partial temporary abolition of the application of the Workers' Charter for new hiring in smaller firms.

Chapter 7

EMPLOYMENT RELATIONS IN FRANCE

Janine Goetschy and Annette Jobert

France has a population of 59 million, and its population continues to rise but at a slower pace than previously. The population is ageing: the proportion of people over 60 years old is 20 per cent, while those under 20 years old account for 26 per cent. After severe difficulties between 1990 and 1997, France's economic situation improved considerably; it increased its economic growth rate while maintaining low inflation. The average annual growth rate was 3 per cent between 1997 and 2001. However, its economic situation started to deteriorate in 2000, in parallel with several other EU economies.

From the 1980s until the end of the 1990s, there was high unemployment. This induced the development of public employment and training measures. Unemployment affects most significantly the most vulnerable groups—young people and those aged over 50, manual rather than white-collar workers, the unskilled rather than the skilled, women rather than men. The share of long-term unemployment (those unemployed for more than one year) has declined but remains at a high level (35 per cent in 2001). However, the share of long-term unemployment in France has remained lower than the EU average since the mid-1980s.

There are about 26 million people in the labour force: 14 million men and 12 million women. The labour market participation rate was 55 per cent. It has risen because of the increase in female labour market participation, from 37 per cent in 1963 to 48 per cent in 2000. It has reached 80 per cent for the 25–49 age bracket. By contrast, the participation rate for young people 15–24 years old has been in decline for the past 25 years (it declined from 12 per cent in 1990 to 8 per cent in 2000) because of the trend towards longer schooling. The participation rate for young people is among the lowest in the EU. In line with international trends, since the 1970s the forms of employment in France have been changing substantially. Temporary employment represents about 14 per cent of the labour force, while about 14 per cent are in part-time employment (5.3 per cent of men are part-time compared with 24 per cent of women).

Before the advent of the Fifth Republic in 1958, politics in France were more volatile than in most of the other European countries discussed in this book. There are four main political parties in France. The *Rassemblement pour la République* (mainly Gaullists) and the *Union pour la Démocratie Française* (UDF; a combination of Independent Republican and Christian-Democrat parties) are broadly towards the right of the political spectrum, while the Communist Party and the Socialist Party are to the left of centre.

Between 1958 and 1981, France was governed by governments of the right. The socialists made a decisive gain in 1981 when F. Mitterrand, a Socialist president, was elected. Since then, France has been characterised by alternate right and left governments, as well as a periodic 'cohabitation' between a right government and a left president. This was the case several times during the Mitterrand presidency. After 1997 there was a 'cohabitation' of a left government and J. Chirac, a right president. In 2002, in the first ballot of the presidential elections, L. Jospin, the socialist prime minister, was defeated. In the second ballot, J. Chirac was re-elected as president in a contest with J.M. Le Pen, the extreme right-wing leader. In the following parliamentary elections the socialists were defeated; this ended the period of 'cohabitation' and confirmed the supremacy of President Chirac.

THE INDUSTRIAL RELATIONS PARTIES

Industrialisation and urbanisation developed in France during the mid-19th century, rather later than in Britain. Strikes were not permitted until 1864, but even then unions were still illegal. However, many informal unions were organised during this period on a local level. There were some parallels with the origins of unions in English-speaking countries. Craftsmen were the first to organise, but craft unions were soon displaced by industrial unionism. The early unions were often involved in violent clashes with state agencies and employers, which tried to suppress them. Unions were eventually legalised in 1884.

The present features of French unions derive partly from their early history and their ideological complexion. The importance of anarchists and revolutionary socialists within the labour movement and the specific characteristics of French employers, who tended to be either paternalistic or reactionary in their attitudes, heavily influenced French employment relations. This helps to explain the traditional lack of mutual recognition between the employment relations parties (the social partners) and the interventionist role of the French state in industrial and social matters.

There are several factors that contribute to the low membership of unions and employer associations. These include: divisions within and between the organisations; the peculiarities of the collective bargaining system, which does not provide particular benefits to members; and lack of incentives to join.

The unions

The French union movement has been characterised by pluralism, rivalry and fragmentation on the one hand, and paucity of financial and organisational resources on the other. Since the 1970s, these structural weaknesses have been particularly apparent. Union density has long been low in France. It was around 23 per cent in the mid-1970s, fell to about 14 per cent by 1985 (Mouriaux 1994), then declined to around 10 per cent by the mid-1990s (see Appendix).

There are five national union confederations (see Table 7.1). These are the *Confédération générale du travail* (CGT); the *Confédération française démocratique du travail* (CFDT); the *Force ouvrière* (FO); the *Confédération française de l'encadrement–confédération générale des cadres* (CFE-CGC); and the *Confédération française des travailleurs chrétiens* (CFTC). The CGT, the oldest French confederation, was established in 1895. With the 1906 Charter of Amiens, the CGT adopted an anarcho-revolutionary program, with members being wary of political parties and political action. Interestingly, in the same year the British unions turned in the opposite direction, by forming the Labour Party. The coexistence of Marxists with anarchist and social-reformist elements led to a major split in the CGT in 1921, with an expulsion of the Marxists following the split in the Socialist Party after the Russian Revolution. The two wings reunited during the 1936 Popular Front; however, another split occurred in 1939 after the Germano-Soviet pact. A further reunification took place during the 'resistance', but they again split in 1948 when the minority group rejected Marxism, as well as the strong ties between the CGT and the Communist Party, and established the current FO (see later). Since the 1940s, most of the CGT's leaders have been Communist Party members, at both the top and intermediate levels. The CGT has remained faithful to the ideology of class struggle. With the end of the Cold War and the collapse of the Berlin wall, its independence vis-à-vis the French Communist Party has been growing. With its 40th Congress held in 1999, there was a turning point of CGT strategy: without renouncing industrial action, it seeks negotiations. As a result, the CGT has improved its relations with the CFDT. Its new secretary general, elected in 1999, Bernard Thibault, the former secretary general of the powerful CGT rail workers' federation, came to prominence as the leader of the 1995 strike movement against the welfare reform policies of the conservative Juppé government. The CGT, via its unemployment committees, was also the union most involved in supporting the locally based unemployment associations active during the 1990s.

The CGT's membership has gone through four phases since the 1940s. After reaching a peak in 1947, it declined until 1958; it then grew between 1959 and 1975, and declined again after the mid-1970s. Between 1976 and 1990 the CGT lost two-thirds of its members; however, the CGT has grown since the mid-1990s, to about 800 000 members. As with the other confederations, the CGT is organised into industry federations and into geographically based local unions. It is especially active in public enterprises in which employees are protected by a special statute (railways, gas and electricity, mines and hospitals). Whereas manual workers were traditionally its main strength, they currently represent only 39 per cent of the members, while the share of white-collar employees and technicians has been growing respectively to one-third and one-fifth of its membership. It is relatively weak in the more dynamic sectors of the economy, and now has a smaller membership than the CFDT. In addition, more specific organisations of the CGT represent certain broad categories of members. Among the most important is the UCR for pensioners (*Union confédérale des retraités*) created in 1969 with 240 000 members. The UGICT (*Union générale des ingénieurs, cadres et techniciens*) was also established in 1969 and has 57 000 members. These are mainly technical, managerial and professional staff.

The CGT was a member of the World Federation of Trade Unions (WFTU), and held the post of WFTU secretary general continuously from 1947 until 1978. Krasucki, former head of the CGT, also held the post of vice-president of the WFTU. Since 1977, the CGT has tried without success to join the European Trade Union Confederation (ETUC). The ETUC refused to admit the CGT in view of its lack of independence from the Communist Party and its membership of the WFTU. In the elections for the ratification of the Maastricht Treaty, the CGT gave its support to the 'no' vote. During its 45th Congress in December 1995, the CGT decided to leave the WFTU to improve its chances of joining the ETUC, which admitted it in 1999. Its admission to the ETUC was also a result of its change of attitude vis-à-vis EU integration.

The FO was established in 1948 as a reaction to communist interference in the CGT. It claims to be the true heir of the CGT's traditional policy of political independence and is staunchly anticommunist. In earlier times the FO was influenced by a small but well-organised Trotskyist group, which provoked internal conflicts and defections. Although the ideological tension between the CGT and the FO has declined with the end of the Cold War, a degree of friction remains. Its membership has been decreasing since the mid-1980s and is estimated to be at about 280 000. It has traditionally included diverse political elements, and in the 1990s internal conflict led to defections in favour of the *Union nationale des syndicats autonomes* (UNSA) (see later). It sees collective bargaining as the main element of union action, and aims to defend workers' job interests, independently of any political party. It emphasises the importance of the union's role in representing the interests of employees and distrusts direct forms of employee representation and participation. Since the election of Marc Blondel as general secretary in 1989, the FO has adopted a more radical strategy, asserting its opposition to certain governmental reforms (such as in 1995), and has regularly led strikes and protests. It is strongest among white-collar workers, particularly technical and professional groups in the public sector. The FO has also a small cadre (managerial) section, the *Union des cadres et ingénieurs* (UCI). The heterogeneous membership of the FO has impeded the development of an efficient organisational structure and hampered recruitment.

At the international level, the FO has been a member of the anti-communist ICFTU since its creation in 1949, and an affiliate of ETUC since it began in 1973. Since the 1950s, the policy of the FO has been favourable towards European integration. However, in recent years the FO has been critical of the EU, on the grounds that the EU is mainly an instrument for economic integration and the free circulation of capital.

During the vote on ratification of the Maastricht Treaty in 1992, the FO did not provide any voting guidelines.

Confessional unionism began in 1919 with the formation of the CFTC. Its main objective was to promote peaceful collaboration between capital and labour, according to the social doctrine of the Catholic Church. The CFTC split in 1964, when the minority group retained its religious orientation and kept the name CFTC. Its centres of strength are among miners, Christian school teachers and health workers. Its total membership is around 100 000. It emphasises the development of contractual relations, the rejection of the politisation of unions, and the defence of the family. The CFTC has a tiny cadre section, the UGICA (*Union générale des ingénieurs et cadres*), with some 20 000 members, and a specific union for retired members, with 55 000 affiliates. As a member of the World Confederation of Labour (WCL) from its inception and of the ETUC since 1990, the CFTC favours the development of a 'Social Europe' and was in favour of the ratification of the Maastricht Treaty in 1992.

Following the CFTC's 1964 split, the majority group formally abandoned the Catholic connection and formed the CFDT. Between 1948 (as the old CFTC) and 1976, membership of the CFDT nearly doubled to more than 800 000, but it declined from 1977 to about 600 000 in the early 1990s. Since then it has grown to about 840 000 members.

In 1970, it adopted elements of a socialist-Marxist ideology with elements of Gramscism and favoured workers' control. The radicalisation of its ideology put it in closer competition with the CGT. But after 1979 the CFDT played down its former ideological emphasis. It began to emphasise union adaptation to economic change and aimed at a process of 'resyndicalisation', which meant establishing closer links between union issues and the rank-and-files. From the mid-1980s, this back-to-the-centre strategy (*recentrage*) entailed keeping a greater distance from the left and developing closer links with the reformist unions. While it favours independence of political parties, it also encourages constructive dialogue with government and employers; its policies are in many respects similar to those of the Socialists. Its links with the CGT have been strengthened during negotiations on the implementation of the 35-hour week. But the CFDT experienced some internal factional conflict in the 1990s. Compared to the other unions, the CFDT is present in a more balanced way in the private and public sectors and includes the highest proportion of women (40 per cent), which reflects its presence in health and commerce. The CFDT has a small cadre section, the *Union confédérale des ingénieurs et cadres* (UCC), with about 42 000 members. However,

Table 7.1 Membership figures of the main union confederations (000s)

Union Confederations[e]	1976	1983	1987	1995[a]	2002
CGT	2074	1622	1031	630	800
CFDT	829	681	600[a,c]	600[d]	850
FO	926	1150	1108	400	270
CFE-CGC	325	307	241[b]	110	80
CFTC	223	260	250	100	100
UNSA[f]	526	493	394[c]	140	350
FSU	—	—	—	140	150

[a] Estimate.
[b] 1986.
[c] 1988.
[d] Early 1990s.
[e] The full name of each confederation is included in the text—see also list of abbreviations.
[f] Includes FEN and others.

Sources: Adapted from Bibes and Mouriaux (1990); Labbé (1996); Andolfatto (2002).

UCC membership is restricted to 'senior' cadres, which explains partly why it is smaller than other unions' cadres sections.

At the international level, the CFDT is a member of ETUC, and has played an active role in the EU in the arguments in favour of a Social Europe. Some of its previous leaders have held key posts in several EU institutions. In 1978, the CFDT left the WCL and joined the ICFTU.

The *Confédération générale des cadres* (CGC) was formed in 1944. In 1981 this confederation changed its name to CFE-CGC (*Confédération française de l'encadrement-Confédération générale des cadres*), given that about half of its members were not really managers but included engineers, salesmen, supervisors, technicians and commercial agents. In the late 1970s its membership was around 300 000, but its membership declined by nearly half during the 1980s, and it had only 80 000 members by the early 2000s. It is strongest in the metals and chemical industries and among salespeople. Its goals focus on issues such as winning more participation for cadres; maximising their pay differentials; and protecting their interests in relation to tax and social security. It claims not to be associated with any political parties.

All these confederations are known as 'representative unions' at national level. This is a legal attribute granted on the basis of five criteria, the most important of which is proving that the union is independent from the employer. This confers on the union some exclusive rights, such as the nomination of candidates in the system of employee representation within the firm, in representation on governmental and other consultative bodies. This also empowers unions to negotiate on behalf of larger groups of workers than their members (see later).

Except for the CGC, unions from all these five confederations recruit across all industries and trades and across all categories of employees. Thus, they compete with each other. However, they each have their traditional strengths in their own specific sectors, occupational groups and regions.

The FEN (*Fédération de l'éducation nationale*) is another important specialist union, which is also 'representative' but only on a sectorial level—the education sector. The FEN decided to remain independent at the time of the CGT split. It recruits staff in most types of state educational institutions. Its main component comprises primary school teachers of a socialist orientation. Whereas the FEN had 500 000 members at the end of the 1970s, its membership fell to 140 000 due to internal tensions which led, in 1992, to the eviction of two left-wing federations. Seriously weakened, the FEN had been looking for alliances with other groups, mainly from the civil service, which led in 1993 to the foundation of UNSA (*Union nationale des syndicats autonomes*). The UNSA has yet to obtain official recognition as a nationally representative union. It has about 350 000 members. In 1999 it became a member of the ETUC. It has built a close relationship with the CFDT.

In 1993, the left-wing federations evicted from the FEN founded the FSU (*Fédération syndicale unitaire de l'enseignement, de la recherche et de la culture*), which has about 150 000 members. The FSU rejects the collaborative attitude of FEN, condemned the 1995 Juppé proposed reforms of the social security system, when it joined the CGT and FO in large-scale protests and strikes, and resisted successive government reforms of the educational system.

Beside these confederations, a looser gathering of unions called the 'group of ten' was formed in 1981. Its objectives were to have the capability to carry out united action, to function more democratically, and to defend previously excluded groups such as the unemployed and the poor. It was, therefore, not created to cater exclusively to the interests of employed workers. The 'group of ten' played an important role in the

1995 strikes. It includes eighteen unions and 80 000 members, while its two major union affiliates are the tax collectors (SNUI) and post and telecommunication workers' (SUD-PTT) unions. The SUD grouping (post, railway, banks, education) has recruited ex-members of the CFDT (who left the CFDT in 1989 and 1996). Some of the unions among the 'group of ten' are considered 'representative' in their respective sectors.

There are also several other 'autonomous' unions which organise specific sectors, such as air traffic controllers, train drivers, truck drivers and journalists. They are called 'autonomous' unions because they do not belong to any of the larger groups that benefit from being legally defined as 'representative'.

'Representative status' for unions has been subject to considerable debate since 1998. In the past, representative status used to provide unions with rights and roles in enterprises even when they had little real membership. The 'Aubry law' on working time intended to introduce some changes in that respect by making state aid conditional. For unions to benefit, plant-level agreements would have to be signed by unions having obtained a majority of votes at elections, or those agreements would have to require the assent of employees through a ratification procedure based on a referendum. This new prescription was a serious breach in French labour law, as it invalidated previous practices where a collective agreement was valid—as long as the union had 'representative status'—even if signed by only one union and even if it represented only a minority of the workforce. The debate pitted the CGT and CFDT, which defended the 'majority principle' in the case of collective bargaining at sectoral and company level, against the FO, CFTC and CGC, which were hostile to any change of rules that would threaten their negotiating power. The smaller confederations such as the UNSA and the 'group of ten', which do not yet enjoy representative status, are in favour of the 'majority principle'.

The employers

Although small and medium-sized enterprises (SMEs) were traditionally important in the French economy, since the late 1950s large companies have had a more important role. Such SMEs are usually family businesses and often have a strong Catholic tradition of paternalism. Three employers' organisations are seen as representative at the national level.

By contrast with the plurality of unionism within the various union confederations, at a national level the employers are more united in their main confederation, the *Conseil national du patronat français*

(CNPF), which became the *Mouvement des entreprises de France* (MEDEF) in 1999. The employers began to organise in the early 19th century and established their first formal national association in 1919, which was the forerunner of the CNPF (which was established in 1945). The MEDEF includes more than three-quarters of all French enterprises. However, MEDEF members differ in terms of their size and sectoral interests, diversity of capital ownership and range of management origins. They have, then, a heterogeneous range of interests. There has been tension between being merely a liaison body for its sectoral affiliates, which was the case in the 1950s and 1960s, and becoming a real decision-making centre, which was the case after the organisational reforms of 1969. Unlike its counterparts in Britain and Germany, the CNPF has engaged in negotiation on certain broad issues since the late 1960s, though not on wages or working hours, with rates of pay being determined at the industry level.

The post-1973 economic crisis stimulated important changes in the employers' strategy. After this they sought to convince the government, the unions and public opinion more generally that there was a crisis and that business was vulnerable. The employers' objective at the micro level was to increase the flexibility of the workforce, a choice they preferred to drastic employment reductions. At that stage the employers did not see flexibility being achieved through training. Flexibility was reached partly through quantitative *external* flexibility—that is, by introducing shorter-term contracts of employment and more temporary work. Employers were especially enthusiastic about such employment practices as they disliked the constraints imposed by the 1976 law on redundancies introduced by the Chirac government. This law, requiring prior administrative permission before implementing redundancies, was abolished in 1986, also under a Chirac government.

Another method used from the end of the 1970s was quantitative *internal* flexibility of working time. The average length of the working week could vary and could be calculated on a yearly basis until the 1990s. This led to developments such as weekend work, shiftwork and flexitime, although this trend was slowed down somewhat by the Aubry laws. In the mid-1980s, the CNPF launched a campaign in favour of more *wage* flexibility.

With regard to *functional* flexibility, such as new job content and work autonomy for specific groups of workers, there have been many experiments. Since 1977, the CNPF has exhorted managers to pursue an active social policy at plant level and to take more initiatives to facilitate the implementation of this whole range of flexibility practices. Managers have been encouraged to abandon their old autocratic behaviour, to bypass union channels and to enter into direct dialogue with employees. Having to face a socialist government for years after 1981, the CNPF adopted a policy of 'conflictual cooperation' with the government, rather than one of ideological confrontation. The election of Gandois as president of CNPF in 1994 led to expectations of more cooperation with the unions. The election of Mr Seillière in 1997 inaugurated more conflictual relationships both with the government and with the unions, reflecting the MEDEF's fierce opposition to the law on the 35-hour week, which it sees as a disaster for enterprises' costs and detrimental to job creation. (By changing its name to MEDEF, the latter wanted to stress the greater weight given to enterprises. It had often been criticised for representing primarily major sectoral federations such as the metal industry employer federation.) In 1998, structural reforms were agreed to increase the influence of smaller companies and to include better representation of local and regional employers.

The Confederation of Small and Medium-Sized Enterprises, or CGPME (*Confédération générale des petites et moyennes entreprises*), is a rival employers' organisation, which nevertheless has common roots with MEDEF and often cooperates with it. Founded in 1944, its history has been marked by some of its members violently opposing taxation, technocracy, Marxism and the nationalised sector. Since the 1970s, public authorities have taken greater care of SMEs' interests. Further, an array of measures were adopted in the 1990s to encourage the setting up of new small businesses. The *Union professionnelle artisanale* (UPA) is a third employer organisation: it includes about 250 000 very small enterprises with 2 million employees.

The state

State intervention is important in French employment relations. This reflects the traditional reluctance of unions and employers to use voluntary collective agreements. In periods when the left has been in the ascendancy, unions have pressed for new laws: in 1936 with the Popular Front; in 1945 after liberation; in 1968 following the events of May; and in 1981 with the advent of the Socialist government.

Since the late 1960s, there have been closer links between the law and collective bargaining. Certain laws are based on the results of previously negotiated agreements or on earlier discussions between the employment and industrial relations parties and the state. The state, then, does not play an authoritarian role in labour relations. Moreover, the state has tended to enhance the social partners' autonomy by transforming the legal framework for collective bargaining in 1971 and 1982.

The state and public authorities are also major employers, with about 5 million civilian employees working in the three public services (central administration, hospitals, local and regional government). In spite of a trend towards privatisation, notably in telecommunications, the French public sector embraces a wider range of nationalised industries than is usual in most Western countries. As an employer, the state also exerts great influence on pay settlements in the private sector. It influences wages through legislated rises in and index-linked adjustments to the national minimum wage (SMIC). Unlike its British counterpart, the SMIC is adjusted according to the price index of consumer goods when the latter has risen by 2 per cent. Moreover, the government can raise the SMIC independently whenever it wishes; in 1997 the SMIC was raised by 4 per cent, double the rate of inflation. From a legal point of view, the SMIC should not constitute a basis for remuneration packages as a whole, but inevitably it exerts a general ratchet effect on all wages. However, since 1981 successive governments, of the left and the right, have tended to avoid using the SMIC to raise average wage levels. In July 2000 only 13.6 per cent of workers received the SMIC, which reflects the difficulty of improving low wage levels through sectoral collective bargaining. In certain sectors, minimum wages remain lower than the SMIC.

Throughout the 1980s, Socialist government policies aimed to reduce unemployment through special programs, especially to help the young and long-term unemployed find work. They encouraged employers to recruit by reducing their social security contributions rather than through macroeconomic measures, as France had chosen monetary stability. When the right was in power again (1986–88), its main preoccupation was to introduce more flexible employment relations rules for employers by amending the laws on redundancy, working hours, fixed-term and part-time hiring. After 1988, the socialist Rocard government launched three successive 'employment plans' with an array of policy measures—among others, the introduction of a 'minimum integration income' (RMI), intended to ease the most vulnerable into work. There were sharp cuts in unemployment benefits in 1992 and 1993 due to decisions made by the social partners that jointly manage the unemployment insurance scheme. By the late 1980s, the government had abandoned its expectation that unemployment would disappear with economic recovery and believed that a continuing significant level of unemployment was unavoidable.

The 1986 legislation, which had abolished controls on redundancies, was reformed by the Socialist government in 1989 to enhance works councils' rights to information and consultation with regard to redundancy. Whatever their size, all companies had to prepare a 'social plan' before implementing redundancies. While the government did not reinstate official controls over redundancies, the High Court has since recognised the duty of lower courts to check not only their legality but also the substantive contents of the 'social plans'. This is largely equivalent to the former control, and is tantamount to a regulation of dismissals. The courts also gave employers a 'duty to retain' redundant employees before they could lawfully consider dismissing them.

The conservative Balladur government, which gained power in March 1993, introduced a 'five-year' employment law in December 1993 that aimed to remove the rigidities it perceived as barriers to job creation. Among its provisions, the legislation included such items as: a reduction in employers' social security contributions; encouraging work-sharing through cuts in hours and pay; simplifying company-level employee representation procedures and reducing their costs; and vocational training for young people, especially at regional level. The 1993 law was followed by a long implementation phase, lasting more than 30 months. The process entailed the publication of decrees and a reliance on collective bargaining developments at various levels. One of the most important and successful implementation measures was the 1996 'de Robien law'. Concerned with the reduction of working time, working-time flexibility and job creation, it provides financial incentives for employers to reduce their employees' collectively agreed working time. Despite fierce opposition from the CNPF, which believes it is too costly for the state and employers, the de Robien law has been successful at an enterprise level. This success (160 agreements covering 100 000 employees), but also the limited coverage of the law (because it was based on voluntarism), induced the Socialist Jospin government to undertake a more radical 35-hour-week reform.

After 1997, the employment policy of the Jospin government pursued earlier tendencies, such as targeted policies in favour of young people, older workers and the long-term unemployed as well as the reduction of indirect labour taxes so as to encourage employers to recruit. But two more major decisions marked his employment policy. First, the setting up of the 'Jobs for Young People' program: 350 000 jobs were to be created within five years, essentially in the public and community sector. The aims of the program were to provide youngsters with a full-time five-year contract from the start in sectors with unsatisfied social needs (education, police, family, culture, sport and the environment). This program provided government funding representing 80 per cent of pay, and youngsters were to be paid at least the SMIC. Since its implementation, 267 000 such jobs for youngsters have been created and the experiment has been 'consolidated' after the five first years.

Second, the 35-hour-week law dominated the Socialist government's social policy. The so-called Aubry law on the 35-hour week (1998) was to become effective within two years for enterprises with more than 20 employees and within four years for the others. Social partners at sectoral level and at enterprise level were invited to reach collective agreements, which would maintain wages, favour recruitment, and should not be detrimental to enterprises' competitiveness. Financial support would be given to enterprises that would sign such agreements in advance of the law's implementation deadlines. In the case of enterprises without union delegates willing to negotiate, wage earners or workplace delegates could be 'mandated' by a representative union organisation to engage in negotiations. This law has generated harsh criticism from the MEDEF, on the grounds that it is compulsory and applicable in a generalised manner throughout the country, and has led to a destabilisation of the industrial relations system.

However, the new law gave a decisive boost to collective bargaining at sectoral and enterprise level, where about 48 000 agreements on working time were signed between 1999 and 2000. By mid-2001, 50 per cent of full-time employees in firms with more than ten employees worked less than 36 hours. The assessment of those agreements has generated controversy. According to the Ministry of Employment, the agreements enabled the preserving and creation of 347 000 jobs, a figure contested by the law's opponents, who consider that improved employment results are primarily due to economic growth. If on the whole wages have been maintained, working time has been reduced in numerous enterprises by work reorganisation as well as more working-time flexibility through 'annualisation' (a trend most unions had initially opposed). Subsequently, the right-wing government legislated to make the 35-hour-week law less constraining for SMEs.

Employee representation within the enterprise

At enterprise level, there is a range of representative bodies that have been set up by governments, in some cases in response to particular social events. Workplace delegates (*délégués du personnel*) were instituted by the Popular Front in 1936; works councils (*comités d'entreprise*) in 1945, following the liberation; and workplace union branches (*sections syndicales*) after May 1968. As a generalisation, workplace delegates deal with individual employee grievances, works councils deal with workplace consultation, while union branches and stewards represent their union and participate in collective bargaining at the workplace. There is a legal framework for all these institutions.

Unlike shop stewards or workplace delegates in the English-speaking countries, who are union representatives, French workplace delegates are not union representatives. However, in practice, a majority of them are elected from a union 'platform'. Delegates must be elected every second year by the total workforce in all enterprises employing ten people or more. The 1982 Act stipulates that delegates may also be elected in those workplaces with fewer than ten employees where several firms operate on a common site, such as a building site or commercial centre, and if there are at least 50 employees in total. Most of the private sector is covered by this Act.

Workplace delegates deal with individual claims for wages, working conditions, the implementation of labour law and collective agreements. They may also call the Labour Inspector in cases where there is disagreement. The number of delegates elected varies according to the size of the firm. The employer must meet them collectively at least once a month. To fulfil their duties, they are allocated fifteen hours' paid working time per month.

Delegates are elected by proportional representation. Manual workers and lower clerical staff vote separately from technicians and cadres. The election procedures must be agreed between the employer and the unions. There is no exclusion of foreign 'guest workers' from voting or from being candidates.

Unlike other countries, under these election procedures there is a two-round secret ballot. In the first round, candidates can be nominated only by one of the main union confederations, or by any other affiliated union that is recognised as 'representative' within the firm. If less than half of the electorate votes in the first round, then any employee may stand as a candidate for the second round. In practice, a second round is rarely required.

Works councils are required in all firms employing at least 50 employees. They use election procedures similar to those summarised above. These councils have little real decision-making power, except in relation to welfare issues. They do have the right, however, to be informed and consulted at specific periods on the general management of the business, particularly in relation to the number and organisation of employees, their hours of work and employment conditions.

Each quarter, the employer is required to inform the works council about the general progress of orders, output and finances. Employers should also provide employment data including details of any short-term contracts and subcontract work. The employer must justify the use of such measures. Once a year, the employer has to submit a general report in writing to the works council, covering the business's activities, turnover, losses or profits, the production achievements, substantial capital transfers, subcontracting, the allocation of profits, subsidies from the state or other public authorities and their use, investments, and salaries. To help it examine the annual accounts, the works council may choose an accountant. Further, on an ad-hoc basis, the council must be informed and consulted on all changes in the economic or legal organisation of the business, in such cases as sales or mergers, for instance. Moreover, under the 1982 Act, the council has to be informed and consulted prior to the implementation of any large project involving the introduction of new technologies, whenever there may be consequences related to employment, qualifications, pay, training and working conditions. In firms with at least 300 employees, an expert can be co-opted to advise. Recently, works councils have seen their role strengthened on employment matters: in 2000, new rights were awarded to works councils in the case of take-over bids, which was part of the wider Act concerning 'New Economic Regulations'; in 2001, the 'Social Modernisation Act' stipulated that 'Social Plans' should reflect the new emphasis on redeployment measures as an alternative to redundancy, and strengthened the works council information rights on redundancies.

The works council does not only have to give its opinion, but its agreement is required on such issues as profit-sharing arrangements and changes in working hours. If the employer requests it, the representatives have to maintain confidentiality about the employer's information on production processes and finances. The works council is composed of the employee representatives and the employer, or deputy. The employer chairs the meeting, which takes place at least monthly. Each representative union can appoint a union observer to the council. To fulfil his/her duties each employee representative can use 20 paid working hours per month. The works council can create subcommittees to examine specific problems. Health, safety and improvement of working conditions committees are compulsory in firms with at least 50 employees. Firms with at least 300 employees have to set up an employment-training committee. Many employers initially resisted works councils, but most have gradually come to accept them as having a legitimate role.

Since 1968 there have also been workplace union delegates in parallel with the representative bodies. Before 1968 unions had no legal right to establish such union delegates. In firms of a certain size, they can have an office and other facilities. According to the law, workplace union delegates are appointed by the local union branch, but the designated union delegate must be an employee working in the firm. Each union appoints its own union delegates, their number varying according to the size of the firm. Union delegates can collect dues during working hours, use noticeboards, distribute leaflets, and organise monthly meetings (outside working time). All employee representatives are legally protected against dismissal. Hindering a representative or the various representation institutions is unlawful.

The representative institutions are not a coherent system but have grown in an ad-hoc way. Moreover, with their complex and occasionally imprecise legal framework, there is some confusion of functions, not least because individual representatives may fulfil several functions. Often there is a lack of candidates to fill the various elected positions. In the larger firms, these representatives often coordinate the activities of the works councils as well as being workplace delegates. Although this may be accepted by managers in big firms, in smaller firms managers may resent what they see as union interference.

A major innovation of the 1982 Act was to set up a *group committee* in large multi-plant companies with registered offices in France. The function of such committees is to receive, at least once a year, information about the financial and employment situation within the group. With the national implementation of the 1994 EU directive on European Works Councils defining information and consultation rights for employees in multinational firms, those group committees have become less necessary and less relevant.

According to research published by the Ministry of Employment, unions are present in only 37 per cent of companies with more than 20 employees. This varies, however, according to the size of the firm and the length of time a firm has been established (DARES 2000).

The 1993 'five-year employment' law sought to simplify the legislation on employee representation, especially for SMEs. The mandate of the workplace delegate, elected in enterprises with ten or more employees, was extended from one year to two. This brought delegates into line with employee representatives on works councils elected for two years, and was compulsory in firms with 50 employees and more. Elections held simultaneously were intended to reduce the administrative burden on the employer. In SMEs, the monthly minimum paid time for workplace delegates to accomplish their duty was reduced from fifteen to ten hours. With regard to works councils, enterprises with fewer than 300 employees were entitled to provide information in a single document once a year rather than in four written reports. In firms with fewer than 150 employees, works council meetings could be held every two months rather than every month—the previous requirement. Further, firms with 50–199 employees could opt for a single representative structure instead of two, with workplace delegates taking over the works council representatives' role. Many firms have chosen this option for a single representation structure.

Employee participation and collective bargaining

The Employee Participation Act of February 1982 (part of the Auroux laws) gave employees the right to withdraw from dangerous working conditions if they considered the job to be dangerous, but not to stop the machinery. The Act was further extended in August 1982 to give employees the right to have a say in the content and organisation of their work and, more generally, their working conditions. The Act prescribed that employees' views should be expressed 'directly' and 'collectively' on these matters (*groupes d'expression directe*). The statutes on collective bargaining (1919, 1936, 1946, 1950, 1971 and 1982) illustrate typical French labour law prescriptions. These attempt to compensate for the unions' organisational weakness and the lack of effective collective bargaining. For example, all employees, whether or not they are unionised, may benefit from a collective agreement. Furthermore, French labour law reinforces union pluralism and in some ways even favours the minority organisations (e.g. the CFTC, CGC and formerly the FO). Thus, a collective agreement is valid even if only one representative union has signed it. To what extent has this provision divided the union confederations? Before the mid-1970s, the most radical unions (CGT and CFDT) tended to adopt an uncompromising approach during the negotiation process, while the reformist ones (FO, CFTC, CGC) were usually more willing to compromise and sign agreements. In many instances, however, such an arrangement seems to have suited both categories of unions. The CGT and CFDT members could thus benefit from an agreement even though their leaders had not compromised themselves by signing it. This system is challenged by several unions arguing for the introduction of the 'majority principle' for a collective agreement to be valid (as mentioned earlier).

Collective bargaining used to take place mainly at industry level. Employer and union organisations preferred such bargaining for ideological as well as tactical reasons. This practice also reflected the lack of mutual recognition between unions and employers at plant or company level. Industry agreements covered the maximum number of employees, which was an advantage to the unions when their membership was low. The employers have favoured industry agreements, which establish only minimal standards for a given industrial sector. Furthermore, for a long time this spared employers from having to recognise unions at plant level.

After 1968 there was a significant development in multi-industry bargaining and plant-level bargaining. Both practices were reinforced by the 1971 amendments to the 1950 Collective Bargaining Act. Innovative multi-industry bargaining dealt with such issues as job security, vocational training, the introduction of salaried status for manual workers, unemployment benefits following redundancies, and working conditions. Such national agreements provided a framework that aimed to encourage collective bargaining at lower levels, such as in a specific industry or firm.

The increasing number of workplace-level agreements resulted from: first, the demands from employees after the extensive protests of May 1968; second, new strategies used by employers to reduce labour turnover by granting employees specific company benefits; and third, the 1968 statute, which legalised union delegates at plant level and gave them a legitimate function within collective bargaining. The workplace-level agreements were generally not innovative but rather improved on or adapted higher-level agreements. In practice, such domestic bargaining was generally confined to larger firms, but following the 1973 energy crisis there was a decline in the number of workplace-level agreements.

In the 1980s, the election of the Socialist government induced a different political and legal context for collective bargaining. It was outlined in the *Report on the Rights of Workers* by the then minister of labour, Jean Auroux (1981). This *Auroux report* aimed to provide employees with real 'citizenship within the firm' and to create new opportunities so that 'employees may become actors of change within the enterprise'. The report was not completely new; it adopted a gradual rather than a radical approach and partly reflected the 1975 *Sudreau report*. Though the report paid heed to the unions' platforms (especially the CGT's and CFDT's), it followed the government's own industrial relations policy and thus received varying responses from the different union and employer organisations (Goetschy 1983).

The 1982 Collective Bargaining Act followed the Auroux report. The 1982 Act included many prescriptions, most of which aimed to improve the existing system, but some of them were innovative. For instance, in firms with union branches, employers were obliged to open negotiations every year on pay and working hours. Since 2001, compulsory bargaining at plant level has been extended to such issues as equal employment rights between men and women, sickness benefits, and saving schemes for employees. However, there is no obligation to reach an agreement, and the employer has the final say. Unlike in the USA, there was no requirement to bargain 'in good faith'.

Such provisions aimed to foster collective bargaining within the firm. The intention of the government may have been to induce more 'integrative' attitudes, whereby employers would become more aware of their social responsibilities and unions more attentive to economic constraints. But the various political parties that comprised the government at this time were deeply divided over the objectives of the Auroux law (Howell 1992).

As another innovation, non-signatory unions could veto a workplace-level agreement—for example, if an agreement included an 'opt-out' clause in relation to shorter working hours. Before using a veto, the non-signatory opponents had to win more than half of the votes in the works councils or workplace delegates' elections. Granting such veto rights to the largest opposition unions was expected to lead to more legitimate agreements.

Further, in national industry agreements, there was an obligation to meet once a year to negotiate wages, every fifth year to discuss job classifications, and every third year to discuss equal opportunities to bring the agreed basic minimum pay rates and other conditions closer to actual practice. At the firm or industry level, the frequency of meetings (for a compulsory 'social dialogue') was expected to make the negotiators more responsive to their constituents when the negotiators engaged in collective bargaining.

After the 1982 Collective Bargaining Act, employers raised fierce criticisms of the new obligation on them to negotiate at company level. However, their criticisms seemed to fade as the Act was implemented.

There were also several prescriptions that aimed to enlarge unions' rights to information and to provide expert help in the bargaining process. The Act further improved the existing procedures whereby the minister of labour could extend certain collective agreements to non-signatory firms. These extension procedures were important, given that the employer might initially refuse to sign an agreement.

Both the Act and some other 1982 ordinances gave priority to collective bargaining rather than the law. The search for a new balance between state intervention and collective bargaining was a hallmark of Mitterrand's post-1981 reforms.

The attempts by the early Mitterrand government to promote collective bargaining became entangled with its 'austerity plans' of 1982 and 1983. Nevertheless, workplace-level bargaining was subject to a new boost, not only by the Auroux laws but also because it suited employers' interests in a context of technological change, increased competitive pressure, and difficult redundancy or redeployment decisions for which it was useful to obtain union support. In 2000, of the total number of company agreements signed, 71 per cent were concerned with work-time issues while 14 per cent dealt with pay. About a third of wage agreements at enterprise level contained individualised pay-rise clauses, most often linked to a general pay rise. About 30 000 company agreements were signed in 2000, covering more than 4 million employees (about 25 per cent of the workforce). Such a boost (company agreements were more than doubled) was largely due to the 35-hour-week law. Six out of ten company agreements were linked to working-time reductions and employment levels. The upsurge in company-level bargaining affected SMEs as well as larger firms. It is likely that such a high degree of negotiation activity will decrease after the full implementation of the 35-hour-week law.

In spite of the moves towards decentralisation, collective bargaining is still mainly at industry level. The latter continues to play a central role in employment relations despite the wish of some employers to decentralise (Jobert 2000). Initially limited to wages and job classifications, compulsory sectoral bargaining every third year has been extended to equal opportunities. About 97 per cent of workers employed in firms with more than ten workers are covered by sectoral or company agreements or by a public-sector statute.

Another trend in collective bargaining has been the development of financial participation, which was subject to major laws in 1959, 1967 and 1986. France has one of the most developed patterns of employee financial participation. The number of employees covered by voluntary profit-sharing schemes (*accords d'intéressement*) has increased significantly. There has been a growing number of agreements on employee participation involving company results or growth, known as capital sharing (*accords de participation*). The schemes became so popular that legislation was passed in the late 1990s to curb their growth. In 2001, a new law was passed to extend financial participation to SMEs and to introduce a new partnership plan for voluntary financial participation.

After a decline in multi-industry bargaining in the late 1970s and early 1980s, it increased in importance in the 1990s. The development of multi-industry bargaining was supported by the government and the CNPF, which favoured a 'consensus approach' for achieving the modernisation of French enterprises. Among the unions, the CFDT has been most prominent in supporting such an approach. In 1988 a national agreement on technological change was signed, with the aim of encouraging negotiations on this issue. The consensus approach also inspired the 1989 national framework agreement on the flexible organisation of work time.

There have been similar agreements on such issues as equal employment, working environment and occupational training, supplementary pensions and welfare. Sectoral and multi-industry bargaining activity were given new impetus by the 'five-year' employment law of the Balladur government. In 1995, three major multi-industry agreements were reached on vocational integration for young people. Whereas the CGT has opposed such 'enabling' arrangements, the CFDT and CGC have supported these arrangements being agreed with the CNPF. By contrast, the FO and the CFTC have been critical and refused to sign some of the agreements.

Training has been one of the main issues of multi-industry bargaining (Gehin & Jobert 2001). It was initiated by the law of 1971, which was influenced by Jacques Delors, then social adviser to the government. Originally the law made it a collective bargaining issue, and required employers to pay at least 0.9 per cent of their wages bill towards vocational training (raised to 1.5 per cent in 1994). This has induced a growth in the number of public and private organisations providing courses. Most of the multi-industry agreements provide frameworks which imply further industry-level bargaining. They are generally signed by all union confederations. (In practice, companies spend around 3.2 per cent on employee training.)

The procedural agreement on 'the articulation of bargaining levels and the possibility of negotiations in companies without union representatives' (1995) was signed by employers, the CFDT, CFE-CGC and CFTC, but not by the CGT and FO. This agreement entails two key changes for the system of collective bargaining. Its first aim is to ensure that the three usual bargaining levels (multi-industry, industry and enterprise) would be complementary rather than hierarchical. The second objective makes it possible, in situations where union delegates are absent, for company agreements to be signed either by employees specifically mandated by unions or by elected employee representatives (e.g. works council members or workplace delegates). Implementing the options would be left to industry bargaining.

However, the agreement, on trial for a three-year period, is intended to involve the representative unions in an experiment, by combining in a new way industry- and enterprise-level negotiations. Its aim is to circumvent two specific features of employment relations: first, to develop collective bargaining in SMEs where there is often no union presence; second, to counter increasing legislative intervention from the five-year employment bill. Moreover, the agreement is an attempt to answer the numerous economic pressures linked to globalisation. A draft bill of May 1996 provided legislative support for company agreements to be signed where there were no union representatives. The national agreement was renewed in 1999. Such sectoral agreements on mandating were introduced mainly in agriculture and services in which SMEs predominated. Before the 35-hour-week legislation, there was only a modest impact at workplace level, partly because of the opposition of many employers. The 35-hour-week legislation (1998) made it possible for mandating to take place without prior sectoral agreement, but only in respect of the negotiation of working time. This practice has been developing fast in relation to working-time agreements: more than half of the company agreements on working time have been reached through such a mandating procedure.

The industrial relations system is characterised by national social-protection institutions, some of which are jointly managed by the employers and the five representative unions. This is the case with social security funds (health, pensions, family allowances), supplementary pension funds, unemployment insurance and vocational training for employees. This involves the state to a greater or lesser degree, depending on the issue. Since at least the 1980s there have been serious problems, reflecting the weakness and division of the unions, the lack of transparency of the joint management, the social partners' inability to undertake reforms without state pressure, and the tense relations

Table 7.2   Results of works committee elections, as a
             percentage of the votes cast

	1990	1992	1994	1996	1998	2000
CGT	24.9	24.3	24.1	23.6	24.3	24.4
CFDT	19.9	20.3	20.8	21.5	21.7	22.9
CFTC	3.6	4.3	4.3	4.5	4.9	5.3
CGT-FO	12.8	12.2	12.2	12.1	12.1	12.4
CFE-CGC	5.6	5.8	5.6	5.8	5.8	5.7
Other unions	6.5	6.7	6.8	7.3	7.0	7.4
Non-unions	26.6	26.4	26.1	25.1	24.1	21.9

Source: DARES (2002).

between the state and the social partners that often prevailed. In 1999 the employers threatened to withdraw from the social security agencies to protest at the state's increasing interventionism.

Representative elections

Besides their formal membership, then, unions' support can be assessed on the basis of the results from 'social' elections, such as the representatives on works councils, social welfare boards (*Sécurité sociale*) and industrial tribunals (*Prud'hommes*).

The works council election results for 1993 show that, in total, the five representative unions obtained nearly 65 per cent of the votes (see Table 7.2). Thus the unions have a much higher degree of support than might be inferred from their low membership. However, between 1981 and 1993 there was a significant increase for non-union representatives as shown by the voting results.

The participation rate for works council elections remains fairly high, being 65.7 per cent in 1998, though it has been declining. As Table 7.2 shows, the support obtained by the CGT, in percentage of votes received, declined from 27.4 per cent in 1985/86 to 21.5 per cent in 1998/99. By the 1990s, the CGT's percentage of the vote had fallen behind the non-union representatives, and was at a similar level to the CFDT's results. Support for the CFDT, the CFTC, the CGT-FO and the CFE-CGC remained relatively stable over the 1985–99 period. The non-unionised list of candidates, which grew between 1985 and 1995, appears to have declined since 1995.

Table 7.3   Elections for industrial tribunals, as a percentage of the votes cast

Year	CGT	CFDT	FO	CFTC	CGC	Others
1979	42.3	23.2	17.3	7.2	5.2	4.8
1982	37.0	23.5	17.7	8.5	9.6	3.7
1987	36.5	23.0	20.4	8.3	7.4	4.5
1992	33.3	23.8	20.4	8.5	6.9	6.8
1997	32.8	25.3	20.5	7.5	5.9	7.7
2002	32.1	25.2	18.2	9.6	7.0	7.4

Source: MES

Turning to industrial tribunals (see Table 7.3), it appears that although the CGT has remained the leading confederation, its support has declined greatly since 1979. Despite their low membership, the support unions obtain through such 'social' elections is important. (When comparing these results, keep in mind that the voting constituencies are different for the three types of elections. Those for social welfare boards and industrial tribunals cover a much larger electorate than those of the works councils.)

WHY IS UNION DENSITY LOW?

Following the left's 1981 electoral success, an increase in the CGT and CFDT membership might have been expected, as was the case in 1936 and 1945, but throughout the 1980s these unions continued to lose members. Why has French unionism declined since the 1970s even though the political environment was apparently beneficial to unions, with the Socialists in government for much of the period (apart from 1986–88, 1993–97 and since 2002)?

First, major restructuring has taken place in the French economy. There has been a movement away from unionised industrial sectors (e.g. coal, steel, metals and shipbuilding) to new industrial sectors, and a shift of jobs from industry to the services sector. The growing number of SMEs has also contributed to the decline in union membership.

Second, high unemployment was detrimental to unionisation. And there were changes in employment contracts and employment practices, which precipitated an increase in the number of people working on a part-time basis and on a temporary basis. Both these categories are

200

difficult to unionise. By the late 1990s more than 70 per cent of all new recruits were working under fixed contracts or with agencies.

Third, young people seem to be more sceptical about the efficiency of union action versus their own individual capacity to negotiate. The decline in unionisation also appears to have been higher among women than among men.

Fourth, employers' social policies have been changing a great deal since 1977. The CNPF sought to establish a direct dialogue with employees and aimed to mobilise middle managers. Employers, then, were increasingly aiming to communicate with the workforce outside the formal employee representation system. Therefore unions were often bypassed, and this tended to diminish their role even further. Employers developed a more participative style of management and introduced innovations. This led, for instance, to the number of quality circles growing to a greater extent than in many other European countries. In practice, though the CNPF had expressed some initial fears, employers welcomed the Auroux law granting employees the right to direct participation (Goetschy 1991). Moreover, employers initiated a whole range of flexibility practices on working time and recruitment such as flexible hours, short-time and part-time work. Such practices often met employees' wishes, but led to the individualisation of employment relations. In 1987, the CNPF issued guidelines promoting the individualisation of pay, including the deindexation of wages and the development of merit pay, which impinged on the unions' wage bargaining function.

Fifth, there was increasing concern among unions about their strategies being ineffective in the face of new challenges. On the one hand, the gap between the union leadership and the rank-and-files appears to have been widening. This is due to the unions' workload, including the numerous duties resulting from the Auroux laws (see below), their increasing participation in welfare state institutions (social security, unemployment insurance, training, employment and administrative committees in the public sector), and to the developing trend of multi-industry bargaining. Such an 'institutionalisation' of unionism seems to have isolated unions from those they were supposed to represent (Adam 1983; Labbé 1995).

On the other hand, union fragmentation was exacerbated during the 1980s due to conflict and animosity between unions. Rivalry between the CGT and CFDT led to the breaking up of their 'Union of the Left' in 1977. After the left's 1978 electoral failure, the CGT and CFDT both initiated a process of self-criticism. The CFDT admitted that it had been too dogmatic and that it had been insufficiently attentive to workers' preoccupations. The CGT was less self-critical and did not question its fundamental strategies or links with the declining Communist Party, which had exacerbated its own decline. Inter-union rivalry became even more acute when confronted with the Socialist government's austerity, modernisation and flexibility policies. The CGT was isolated, whereas the CFDT continued to follow its reformist *recentrage* strategy that had begun in 1979, and it developed the idea of the merger of non-communist unions.

In 1990, leaders of the CFDT and the FEN called for a 'labour axis' plan that required a united front between non-communist confederations, excluding the CGT. This call did not generate much enthusiasm among the other unions. Part of the aim of such an axis would be to counterbalance the influence of the large national federations in the EU, such as Germany's DGB (see chapter 8) or Britain's TUC (see chapter 2). This represented a move away from the 'unity of action' practices of the 1970s, when the CGT and CFDT managed to agree on a range of issues.

In short, the decline of unionism is explicable in terms of several factors, including the unions' work overload, their fragmentation, the disappointing results of the CFDT's *recentrage* strategy, and the leftist unions' policy disarray when confronted with a leftist government in power.

Even before the problems of declining support in the 1980s, the weakness of the French union movement was a major issue, for the following six reasons. First, closed-shop practices were prohibited, to safeguard individual freedom to choose whether to join a union. (However, there are some de-facto closed shops in sectors such as the docks and printing.) Second, as a legacy of their anarcho-syndicalist roots, French unions have traditionally put more emphasis on having an active core of 'militant' organisers, rather than recruiting a stable mass membership. This also explains why they have rarely built up bureaucratic organisations on the scale of those in Germany, for instance. Following this early ideological choice, militants tended to see their role as fostering strikes and political action, rather than engaging in collective bargaining with employers, which made it difficult to demonstrate clear bargaining results to their members. Third, all wage earners benefit from any improvement won by the unions: after it is signed, a collective agreement applies to all employees, whether unionised or not. Fourth, in general, no specific welfare benefits accrue to a union member, as may be the case in other countries. Fifth, employers have often opposed any extension of union influence, and have long used paternalistic practices, particularly in the numerous SMEs. Sixth, the fragmentation of unions on ideological and political grounds has hampered the recruitment and retention of members.

The low union membership creates other problems, such as poor financial resources and small organisational infrastructures in comparison to many other European unions. Their financial resources are strained, given that dues are paid irregularly. On average, a union member pays only half the required dues per year and union dues are relatively low, being on average less than 1 per cent of wages.

Nevertheless, unions do have more political and industrial influence than their low density implies. They play an important role in collective bargaining and in representative elections. They also play a role in public tripartite or bipartite institutions, transforming unions into a 'public service agency' (Rosanvallon 1988). However, there has been a recent tendency for the CGT and the CFTD to increase their membership. This seems to be associated with the strategic *'rapprochement'* between the two confederations.

INDUSTRIAL DISPUTES

The right to strike is guaranteed by the French Constitution but, as with any other right, it is qualified. In the public sector since 1963 the unions have had to give five days' notice before a strike. But there is little legal regulation of strikes in the private sector. The courts distinguish between legal and illegal strikes. In the private sector, a strike is legally defined as a stoppage of work. Hence other actions such as industrial sabotage, working to rule or slowing down are unlawful. A lawful strike has to concern 'industrial relations issues'. Despite legal constraints on sit-ins, such actions are permitted when their primary aim is to seek negotiations, rather than merely to disrupt output. Nevertheless, excessive disruption of output through strikes is illegal and lockouts are generally illegal.

Although there is little legislation on strikes, there are elaborate procedures for the settlement of disputes, including conciliation, mediation and arbitration, but these procedures are rarely used in practice. Industrial disputes tend to be unpredictable in France, but, as in Australia, they are usually short-lived (see Appendix). Strikes tend to be short because, as a legacy of the anarcho-syndicalist tradition, French unions have few financial reserves and generally do not grant strike pay.

Moreover, France loses relatively few days due to stoppages, compared with Italy and the English-speaking countries (see Appendix).

When comparing strikes over a longer period the following trends can be noticed. First, compared to the 1970s, there was a significant decline in the number of working days lost during the 1980s. This tendency continued in the 1990s. On average, there were 3.6 million days lost per year in the 1970s, 1.2 million days lost per year in the 1980s and fewer than 600 000 days lost per year in the 1990s (the trends concern market-sector strikes—private- and public-owned companies—but the general picture does not change much when civil servants are included). The year 1995 is an exception, with 5 million days lost (private and public sectors). Second, the proportion of 'generalised conflicts' (multi-employer strikes) decreased significantly in the 1980s and 1990s to only about 10–15 per cent of the level of such strikes occurring in the 1970s. Third, the public non-market sector was more strike-prone than the private sector (Jefferys 1996).

Strikes in the public sector accounted for around 45 per cent of strikes in the late 1980s and 1990s. Some of the public-sector strikes were characterised by the establishment of rank-and-file 'coordination groups' to organise strikes alongside or in opposition to official union channels, such as administration workers and nurses. These coordinated activities were reflected deficiencies of French unions. In the public sector, claims were a combination of pay claims and demands to improve working conditions, career opportunities and human resource policies. Certain sectors are particularly strike-prone, such as transport (private- and public-sector), which in 1999 accounted for one-third of the total number of days lost.

Another feature of strikes is the growing importance of wider employment issues as the motive for strike action. It is very difficult to attribute precise causation, as many disputes may have multiple causes and involve several issues. Nevertheless, the negotiations on the 35-hour week have been generating a growing number of strikes: in 1998, a quarter of the strikes were apparently about working-time issues, whereas wages and employment matters apparently precipitated only half of the total number of strikes. There was also a growing number of disputes due to MNE restructuring and plant closures, which were publicised by the media.

Around 80 per cent of strikes seem to be initiated by union action, whereas 20 per cent are triggered by employees' initiatives. In 1999, one-third of strikes were initiated by the CGT, 10 per cent by the CFDT, and 40 per cent by more than one union. Strikes on employment issues are more likely to be the result of the initiatives of several unions, compared with strikes about pay issues.

In December 1995 there were strikes against the reform plan of Prime Minister Alain Juppé. The aims of this reform were: (a) to reduce the deficit arising from the social security system through fiscal measures; and (b) to align civil servants' pensions with those in the private sector and to end certain more favourable pension systems enjoyed by some public-sector categories, such as railway workers. The strikes were launched by the unions in the public sector (public transport, post, electricity and education), mainly the CGT and FO. Apart from their length, these disputes had three major characteristics. First, they were mainly restricted to the public sector and generally did not spread to the private sector. Second, the strikes took place throughout France, and mobilisation was high in certain large towns in the provinces. Third, they obtained much public support despite the great inconvenience. While their immediate cause was the Juppé plan, the strikes reflected fears of increasing unemployment and job insecurity. Fourth, the strikes were a reaction against the threat to 'public services'. More generally, these strikes illustrated the weaknesses of the French employment relations system and its difficulty in concluding collective agreements. Last, these strikes reflected a lack of confidence between the state and its experts on the one hand and the French population on the other.

With the Juppé social security reform plan and the 1995 strikes, union divisions at national level became accentuated. While the FO came closer to its former enemy—the CGT—during the strikes, tensions grew with the more reformist CFDT. Further, the 1995 strikes reflected tensions within the FO and within the CFDT. The former has been accused by some of its affiliates of becoming too influenced by internal Trotskyist and/or external communist interests. The leader of the CFDT, Nicole Notat, has been attacked from the left opposition within the CFDT for supporting part of the Juppé plan and for trying to attain a privileged position with the government and employers. In 2002, Nicole Notat was replaced by François Chérèque, who continued to follow a similar policy.

CONCLUSIONS

Although France had a Socialist president from 1981 to 1995 and a Socialist prime minister between 1997 and 2002, and despite labour legislation tending to reinforce their position, French unions have continued to be weak in terms of membership. Nevertheless, the precipitous fall in union membership from the late 1970s to early 1990s appears to have been stemmed, and there has even been a slight growth in membership. After the 1995 strikes, rivalries between and inside unions increased, which further weakened them. However, the end of the Cold War and the CGT joining the ETUC have helped to improve the relationship between the two largest unions (CFDT and CGT).

Competitive pressures, the increasing number of mergers/takeovers, restructuring plans, the expansion of the service sector, changes in the labour market, high unemployment, the growth of flexible labour contracts, proactive employers' policies and unsatisfactory union strategies are all factors that have made the unions' role even more difficult. French employment relations remain characterised by a contrast between on the one hand large companies, where unions are active participants in company-level bargaining and where representative institutions exercise their rights, and on the other hand SMEs, where unions and representative institutions are rarely present, making company-level bargaining impossible. The reforms undertaken by governments or implemented through collective agreements have not changed this situation. This is largely because of the opposition by some unions and the large number of employers who consider the presence of unions in their enterprises as having a negative effect.

But the unions have an influence greater than their low membership density might imply. Strikes still take place, with significant disruption to public services (e.g. transport, education, health care and postal services). This is one of the reasons why, in comparison with other EU countries, France has not yet reformed its pension and health-care systems, and why France is lagging behind in the privatisation process of its public utilities (e.g. gas, electricity, post and railways) as required by the EU internal market program.

Despite decentralisation policies towards enterprises and towards the regions since the 1980s, the system of employment relations has relied on the state to initiate developments in collective bargaining and the whole process of social dialogue. The state has long been active in compensating for the structural deficiencies of industrial relations and the lack of social dialogue. But the high levels of unemployment throughout the 1990s induced governments to intervene in the labour market. Such interventions were fairly successful after 1997, with the creation of more than half a million jobs in some years, though it is difficult to prove to what extent either economic growth or labour market structural reforms do most to stimulate job creation.

State interventionism was considered, though, to have reached its zenith in the eyes of the employers with the adoption of the 35-hour law and the state's increasing interference in some of the social protection agencies jointly managed by unions and employers. MEDEF was angered by the government's attempt to use the unemployment benefit funds to help finance the introduction of the 35-hour law. This led MEDEF, in 1999, to criticise 'the constant attempts of the law and the government to dominate the social partners' and to propose to the unions negotiation of a new 'social constitution' (*la refondation sociale*) for reforming employment relations. In 2000, MEDEF suggested eight issues to the unions for negotiating reforms: (a) unemployment insurance and social inclusion of youth, (b) pension schemes, (c) occupational health and safety issues, (d) the social protection system (sickness benefit and family benefit), (e) vocational training, (f) the role of management, (g) gender equality, (h) collective bargaining and the social dialogue in SMEs.

By the end of 2001, four issues had been discussed and three agreements were signed (on unemployment insurance, occupational health and collective bargaining) with all key union confederations except for the CGT. The negotiations on unemployment insurance were most difficult. The state intervened directly to refuse approval to the agreement negotiated between MEDEF, the CFDT, CFTC and CGC. The agreement sought to oblige the unemployed to sign a contract whereby they would commit themselves to search actively for work or lose their unemployment benefits. However, the state imposed a revision of this controversial part of the collective agreement to safeguard the rights of the unemployed. This illustrates how difficult it is to reform French industrial relations. For the time being, MEDEF reduced its ambitions for reform, but it continues to seek an alternative system whereby contractual relations between autonomous social partners will progressively replace the role of legislation.

Despite the changes of government, in certain areas of political and social life there has been a reasonable continuity in approaches. For example, the decentralisation of the state and public action was initiated by the Socialists in 1983 and has been continued by both right and left governments. There has also been continuity of education and training policies as well as of employment policies, such as the reduction of indirect labour costs, which previously were highly contentious issues. Nevertheless, there has continued to be conflict about the notion of the 35-hour week.

In a context of increasing unemployment and growing numbers of redundancies, the post-2002 right government cancelled 'the job for youth program'. Instead it introduced a program to encourage private firms to recruit unqualified youngsters. The government undertook a reform of the pension system, not least to bring the civil service pension system into line with the private-sector system, which had been reformed in 1993. In spite of such moves towards economic liberalisation, wage earners and most unions remain committed to the state's continuing to exercise a strong regulatory role in employment relations.

A CHRONOLOGY OF FRENCH EMPLOYMENT RELATIONS

1791	Le Chapelier law forbids strikes and unions but not employers' associations.
1821	Building industry employers' association is established.
1830s–40s	Many illegal combinations of workers and some collective agreements.
1864	Abolition of Le Chapelier law.
1871	Paris Commune.
1884	Unions are entitled to organise on a craft or industry basis, but not at enterprise or plant level.
1895	The anarcho-syndicalist Amiens Charter asserts the CGT's independence of political parties.
1919	The CFTC is established following the Pope's 1891 encyclical (see chronology in chapter 6 on Italy). First national industrial employers' confederation founded.
1920	Peak of union density—approximately 25–30 per cent.
1921	CGT split, following Russian Revolution.
1934	General strike called by the CGT.
1936	Election of the Popular Front coalition of socialists, communists and radicals; many strikes and sit-ins. Agreements between the employers' association and the reunited CGT herald major social reforms, including the introduction of employee delegates.
1944	The CGC is established.
1945	The liberation government initiates works councils within enterprises.
1946	The CNPF is established as the main employers' association.
1948	Creation of the FO after a split within the CGT.
1950	Law on collective bargaining and the establishment of a minimum wage system.

1958	Multi-industry unemployment insurance agreement introduces the principle of national agreements.
1964	CFDT established as a secular breakaway from CFTC.
1965	Multi-industry four-week holiday agreement.
1966	Works councils' role extended in relation to training and profit sharing.
1968	Events of May precipitate a general strike; workplace union branches permitted.
1970	Multi-industry job security agreement; a multi-industry *mensualisation* agreement grants 'single status' for blue-collar workers.
1971	Amendment to 1950 Act to permit plant-level bargaining.
1974	A multi-industry redundancy agreement, including a continuation of 90 per cent of previous job's pay levels.
1981	Mitterrand's socialist–communist coalition forms the government. 39-Hour working week ordinance.
1982	Auroux laws are enacted. Prices and incomes policy initiated. Retirement age reduced from 65 to 60.
1983	Major strikes in the car factories.
1984	Abortive multi-industry negotiations to introduce more flexibility in employment protection laws (initiated by CNPF). Communists leave 1981 coalition.
1986	Socialist government replaced by a right-of-centre government.
1987	New Redundancy Act repeals the earlier requirement for administrative approval before redundancies; new flexible work-time law.
1988	Socialist government returns to power and announces its first social program. Bill on minimum integration income (*Revenu minimum d'insertion*).
1989	Socialist government announces its second social program.
1990	Important multi-industry agreements are reached.
1991	Restructuring of the national employment office.
1992	The government launches significant job-creation programs to counter long-term unemployment.
1993	Socialist government overwhelmingly loses the legislative elections. A right-wing coalition government takes office under Prime Minister Balladur, but President Mitterrand continues in his post.
1994	Implementation of the 'five-year employment plan' of the Balladur government.
1995	Jacques Chirac elected President; major public-sector strikes against policies of the Juppé government.

1997	General election called prematurely by President Jacques Chirac; advent of a left-wing government headed by Prime Minister Lionel Jospin.
1998	New laws introduce the 35-hour week.
1999	The main employees' confederation (CNPF) is replaced by the *Mouvement des Enterprises de France* (MEDEF). Bernard Thibault is elected general secretary of the CGT.
2000	Industrial relations reforms (*la refondation sociale*) launched by MEDEF; second law on 35-hour working week.
2001	The Social Modernisation Act strengthens the information rights of works councils on redundancies.
2002	Re-election of Jacques Chirac as President of France; the right wins parliamentary elections, thereby ending the 'cohabitation'.

Chapter 8

EMPLOYMENT RELATIONS IN GERMANY*

Berndt K. Keller

THE SOCIOECONOMIC ENVIRONMENT OF EMPLOYMENT RELATIONS

The fast and unexpected recovery of the German national economy began after the destruction caused by World War II and led to the 'economic miracle' (*Wirtschaftswunder*) of the 1950s and 1960s. The creation of a high-productivity, high-added-value and high-wage model of production based on a highly skilled workforce lasted until the mid-1970s. Over several decades, the Western part of Germany was not only reconstructed but developed into the strongest economy of Europe, as well as one of the leading nations in world trade. In political terms, prosperous West Germany was one of the six founding members of the European Economic Community (EEC) in the late 1950s. Since then it has strongly supported the idea of economic, political and social integration. In the late 1990s, Germany became one of the founding members of the European Monetary Union.

The Bretton Woods system of fixed but adjustable exchange rates collapsed in the early 1970s, and the two oil crises in the mid- and late 1970s led to sudden drastic rises in crude oil prices. As a result, the German economy stagnated and even suffered decline in some years;

*This new version of the chapter that was authored by Friedrich Fürstenberg in earlier editions of the book.

in addition, unemployment began to rise rapidly. The 'golden age' of the economic miracle had come to a sudden end. In the mid- to late 1980s there was a modest economic recovery. This period included not only new record export surpluses but also the creation of additional jobs in new sectors of employment. *Modell Deutschland* seemed to be a successful solution for the difficult challenges of strategic modernisation and necessary processes of rationalisation. However, there was relatively high and persistent unemployment (averaging about 8 per cent), which had not been experienced for more than two decades.

Since 1990 and the end of the Cold War, the unification of the Federal Republic of Germany (FRG) (*Bundesrepublik Deutschland*) and the German Democratic Republic (GDR) (*Deutsche Demokratische Republik*) has been the main problem. The economic, political and social consequences of the sudden integration of a socialist, centrally planned economy into a specific variant of capitalist economy (*soziale Marktwirtschaft*) have become unique and long-lasting challenges for the political economy. In the very early 1990s, after the relatively short 'unification boom' in the West, unemployment in the unified Germany rose and there was the most severe economic crisis experienced since World War II. Since the mid-1990s, unemployment has remained at a high level despite the shrinking supply of labour, caused primarily by the changing age structure of the population.

The employment to population ratio is the other crucial indicator of the development of labour markets and overall employment. Germany's ratio of just over 81 per cent corresponds almost exactly to the West European norms, which are themselves far below those of the USA and Japan (at about 75 per cent). This ratio was previously much higher and will, in the forthcoming years, have to be increased again in order to improve the financing of the pension system and the changing age structure. The labour force participation rate of women (at about 63 per cent) has almost reached West European average. However, differences between the eastern and western parts of the country persist.

The broader political conditions in Germany are characterised by a high degree of continuity and stability. There are only about four periods to be distinguished. Between 1949 and the late 1960s, the conservative Christian Democratic Union (CDU/CSU) was in power, in most cases in coalition governments with the Free Democratic Party (FDP). In the period between 1969 and 1982, coalition governments forged between the Social Democratic Party (SPD) and the FDP ruled the country and changed the system of employment relations in various ways. Between 1982 and 1998, the CDU was back in power, again in coalition with the FDP, and promoted labour market flexibilisation and deregulation. In 1998 the SPD and the Greens, the ecological and environmental party, formed the coalition government and have been in power since then.

Until recently, German employment relations were seen as an integral part of the virtuous circle of the political economy and the postwar compromise. The legal infrastructure dates back to the post-1945 period, although its institutional roots extend from the period of the Weimar Republic (1919–33) (Baethge & Wolf 1995; Visser & van Ruysseveldt 1996; Jacobi et al. 1998). According to the German Constitution, the Basic Law (*Grundgesetz*) of 1949, Germany is a federal system. The states (*Bundesländer*) have been granted autonomous rights in different fields of public policy (e.g. cultural affairs, education and science). In employment relations, however, the legal foundations are the same for all federal states and/or municipalities, while the states have very few rights. Germany is, like some other West European countries, a developed welfare state with all-encompassing systems of social protection (including unemployment insurance, health insurance and pension schemes). This extensive social regulation, which has focused on occupational status and the insurance principle, has always been regulated by legal enactment and not by collective bargaining (Leibfried & Wagschal 2000; Manow & Seils 2000).

THE EMPLOYMENT RELATIONS PARTIES

Employers and their associations

Germany shares with Switzerland and Scandinavian countries the prevalence of various types of interest organisations, namely general business or trade associations (*Wirtschafts- or Unternehmensverbände*) as well as specific employers' associations (*Arbeitgeberverbände*) (Bunn 1984; van Waarden 1995a, 1995b). In theory, there is a task differentiation between these interest organisations. The first category represents more general economic interests vis-à-vis the government and parliament (or general product market interests), whereas the second is concerned in particular with social policy and employment relations, including collective bargaining (or specific labour market interests). The economy-wide peak associations are the Federation of German Industries (*Bundesvereinigung der Deutschen Industrie*—BDI) and the Confederation of

German Employers' Associations (*Bundesvereinigung Deutscher Arbeit-geberverbände*—BDA). These 'associations of associations' are representative of a wide range of industries and sectors, and cooperate very closely in their everyday activities. Private-service-sector associations are, however, underrepresented by comparison with their counterparts from manufacturing (the sectors exposed to global markets). Third, there are chambers of industry and commerce (*Industrie- und Handelskammern*) and chambers of trades (*Handwerkskammern*), with compulsory membership.

These three pillars of interest representation perform a variety of public and semigovernmental tasks that are outside employment relations. Multiple membership by enterprises in different associations is a frequent consequence of this organisational structure, and their membership in central confederations is indirect.

Interests are organised according to sectors (*Fachprinzip*), as well as regions (*Regional*), the latter reflecting the federal system. These structures are vertically and horizontally integrated and lead to a network of a large number of organisations representing differing interests. As in most other countries, the most important exemptions are public-sector employers' associations, although those of the German steel industry are also excluded because of the existing system of co-determination in this sector. The sectoral member associations, not BDA, are responsible for collective bargaining.

Membership densities of employers' associations are difficult to determine because of a lack of reliable information for all sectors, in addition to the lack of time-series data. It is, however, reasonable to assume that these ratios have always been, as in the majority of other countries (except for the Scandinavian countries and Ireland), much higher than those of employees. The most often quoted density figures are between 75 and 80 per cent (Visser & van Ruysseveldt 1996; Bispinck & WSI-Tarifarchiv 2000).

Since the 1980s, however, employers' associations and the unions have experienced a problem of declining membership in terms of companies as well as employees. This is in contrast to the stability of general business associations. Engineering is the most important and a relatively well-documented sector of private industry. Membership density of the regional member associations of *Gesamtmetall* have decreased from almost 80 per cent in West Germany in the early 1980s to about 62 per cent of employees (and one-third of enterprises) in unified Germany towards the end of the 1990s (Table 8.1).

Table 8.1 Development of membership and density ratios of member firms in the Metal and Engineering Employers' Federation

Year	Member firms		Employees of member firms	
	Overall	Density ratios	Overall	Density ratios
Former West Germany				
1960	9 626		2 755 264	
1965	9 935		3 040 108	
1970	9 594		3 264 598	76.3
1975	9 471		2 865 519	73.3
1980	9 108	57.5	2 950 325	75.6
1990	8 173	46.4	2 936 637	72.9
1991	8 168	45.2	2 920 487	71.6
1992	8 081	44.0	2 738 722	69.0
1993	7 752	42.8	2 458 665	67.4
1994	7 458	43.1	2 305 423	68.2
1995	7 094	39.2	2 210 511	66.7
1996	6 731	37.7	2 109 019	65.7
1997	6 504	37.2	2 072 480	65.3
1998	6 307	34.5	2 078 935	64.8
Former East States				
1991	1 365		535 066	65.7
1992	1 278		270 942	63.3
1993	1 111		204 458	59.4
1994	983		163 725	52.3
1995	792	28.0	141 748	36.2
1996	655	22.4	119 713	43.7
1997	540	18.7	100 423	37.8
1998	503	16.0	88 271	32.2
Germany				
1991	9 533		3 455 553	70.6
1992	9 359		3 009 664	68.4
1993	8 863		2 663 123	66.7
1994	8 441		2 469 148	66.8
1995	7 886	37.7	2 352 259	65.2
1996	7 386	35.6	2 228 732	63.9
1997	7 044	34.6	2 172 903	63.2
1998	6 810	31.8	2 167 206	62.2

Source: Müller-Jentsch & Ittermann (2000).

There are significant differences in stability between sectors. In some, such as chemicals and/or the public sector, the established system of interest representation has remained comparatively stable, whereas in others (e.g. construction or printing) the erosion has become fairly obvious. Available data show that larger companies are much more likely to be organised in comparison with small and medium-sized enterprises (SMEs), and that all membership densities in the East are much lower than in the West (Müller-Jentsch & Ittermann 2000).

Internal cohesion has become a concern, and certain members have been less willing to comply with the goals of their associations. The particular interests of SMEs (or *Mittelstand*) on the one hand and those of larger enterprises on the other are more difficult to coordinate than previously. Tensions between these member groups and tendencies of fragmentation within their organisations have been on the increase. Associational policies that manage to balance differing interests are almost impossible to agree on. In the main, SMEs have been generally dissatisfied with their organisations' collective bargaining policies and particularly dissatisfied with their working-time policies (the shortening of the working week). They consider their associations' central policies to be dominated by the interests of the large enterprises and that they pay insufficient attention to the interests of other groups. After considering the changing costs and benefits for them, SMEs have left their organisations more often than have larger companies.

Legally, all member companies have to adhere to the conditions of the current collective contract until it expires (*Nachwirkungspflicht*). They can come to a different decision later, but they usually take the terms and conditions of existing collective contracts as a general frame of orientation, even though there is no legal necessity to do so.

From the associations' point of view, their capacity for self-discipline and authority vis-à-vis their members have been weakened. In some sectors (e.g. engineering) and regions one recent strategy to counter loss of members has been the development of so-called split memberships. Individual enterprises are allowed to join associations (or at least not to leave them) without having to accept the binding stipulation of collective agreements. Nevertheless, the variety of all other 'private' goods and services will be provided as for all other regular members. The question is: will the creation of this compromise solve the problems of declining membership, or will it lead to a new type of association and further erode the foundation of the existing ones and collective bargaining in general?

Unions

The principles of industrial unionism (*Industriegewerkschaftsprinzip*) and unitary unions (*Einheitsgewerkschaft*) were introduced in the period of restructuring shortly after World War II. The first principle means that there should be only one union per enterprise, which all employees are supposed to join irrespective of characteristics such as occupation or blue-collar versus white-collar status. The second principle includes the rule that unions should not be affiliated with political parties. The peak association of unions is the comparatively weak German Trade Union Federation (*Deutscher Gewerkschaftsbund—*DGB), which is responsible for political activities including lobbying. It does not, however, conduct collective bargaining, which is conducted by its member unions.

There are some exemptions from these principles of inclusive unionism. The small (not to say marginal) Confederation of Christian Unions (*Christlicher Gewerkschaftsbund—*CGB) has about 300 000 members, and the German Civil Service Association (*Deutscher Beamtenbund—*DBB) has about 1.2 million members. The DBB exists solely for the public sector and organises mainly, but not exclusively, civil servants. This was the only association with growing membership in the 1990s. Neither the CGB nor the DBB is affiliated with the peak organisation DGB; they are, therefore, regarded as rival confederations. The former German Union of Salaried Employees (*Deutsche Angestelltengewerkschaft*) was also independent; it had about 460 000 members, all of whom belonged to the specific group of white-collar employees. It became part of the most important merger of unions, and ceased to exist in 2001. The following analysis will focus on DGB affiliated unions, because more than 80 per cent of union members were members of DGB affiliates.

The principle of industrial unionism dominated for more than four decades and remained basically unaltered, even throughout periods of turbulence. Organisational competition and inter-union rivalries, including demarcation and/or jurisdictional disputes, were not completely excluded. They are, however, relatively rare in comparison with other countries in which there are stronger legacies of craft or occupational unionism.

There have been major changes within this surprisingly stable organisational structure of around seventeen DGB affiliated unions since the mid-1990s. Mergers and takeovers (a phenomenon formerly unknown in Germany) have been encouraged by shrinking membership, decreasing financial resources and structural changes in the economy,

Figure 8.1   Union mergers in Germany

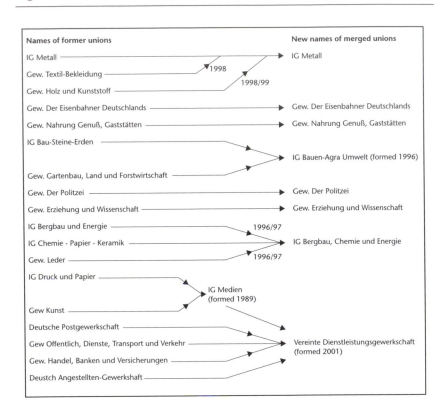

Source: Waddington & Hoffman (2000).

including labour market flexibilisation and deregulation. These mergers have gradually replaced the old system of industrial unionism and have led to an even smaller number of 'multi-sectoral unions' and a higher degree of concentration.

The result of these most recent processes was the launching of the biggest union in the world, the Unified Service Sector Union (*vereinte Dienstleistungsgewerkschaft*—ver.di), in 2001. It consists of five unions in both the public and the private sectors and has about 3 million members (Keller 2001a). It is likely that the mergers and internal restructuring will continue, so the number of unions will further decrease (Figure 8.1).

While union membership has increased in absolute terms, membership density has remained fairly constant because of the growing total number of employees. German unions survived the 1980s, which was a critical decade for their counterparts in many other European countries, without fundamental problems. However, they did not start to reform during this period of relative organisational stability and uncontested status (Ross & Martin 1999). The period of relatively favourable conditions lasted longer than in other major countries, but finally ended around 1990.

After unexpected increases in membership immediately after unification (from 8 to almost 12 million), all unions experienced significant losses of membership during the early 1990s. The loss of about 4 million members (or 30 per cent) during the 1990s contributed to a decline in union bargaining power—and contributed to a trend towards 'de-unionisation'. The density of unionism had fluctuated around 35 per cent for several decades, but it fell to a historical low of less than 30 per cent by the end of the 1990s (Müller-Jentsch & Ittermann 2000). In comparative perspective, the present German union density is comparable to the European average (Ebbinghaus & Visser 1999).

Another problem facing unions is that the structures of union membership and employment do not correspond. The present membership structure reflects the industrial and employment structure of the 1960s. Since then, the number of part-timers has expanded to about 20 per cent of the labour force. Underrepresented in unions are women, younger employees, highly educated and qualified employees, private-service-sector employees, foreigners, and the 'new economy', as well as so-called atypical employment or contingent workers. In contrast, the fairly well-educated, prime-age men working full-time (*Facharbeiter*), the public sector and the 'old economy' in general are overrepresented in unions.

This unequal distribution of members exerts a major impact on union strategies. Furthermore, it creates serious problems for differentiated future policies within the emerging service economy. Organising the unorganised, especially salaried employees (*Angestellte*), in the service sector will continue to be of major concern in the future for the long-term survival of unions (Traxler et al. 2001).

The state and public-sector employment relations

In contrast to the more voluntaristic systems of Anglo-Saxon countries, the German system is characterised by a high degree of juridification (*Verrechtlichung*) (Weiss & Schmidt 2001). Examples are the Works Constitution Act, the Co-Determination Acts, the Collective Bargaining Act and the Social Security Act. The only major exception concerns collective labour disputes, which are not constrained by special legislation but by so-called 'judge-made law'. These are enshrined by a whole series of binding decisions from the independent Federal Labour Court as well as the Constitutional Court.

Until the 1980s, this juridification was often criticised by insiders as well as outsiders because of its 'restrictive', legally binding character. More recently, the positive outcomes have been more obvious. It has contributed to relative stability and limited the likelihood of sudden, drastic changes to the system.

The Constitution, the Basic Law, guarantees all individuals the fundamental right of freedom of association. Hence, membership of interest associations is voluntary, and union security arrangements, such as closed shops and union shops, are illegal. The social partners are granted the right of bargaining autonomy or free collective bargaining (*Tarifautonomie*) as specified in the Collective Agreement Act (*Tarifvertragsgesetz*) of 1949, amended in 1969 and 1974. Collective bargaining takes place within the responsibility of autonomous private actors and without any active state interference. Collective agreements are absolutely binding on both signatory parties. They are protected by a strict peace obligation during their currency. This rule limits the opportunities of industrial action.

There are mediation agreements in all major sectors of industry. They are always the procedural results of voluntary negotiations between the social partners and are not determined by legal enactment or any other form of state interference. By contrast with many other countries, federal and/or state mediation and conciliation services are of little importance. State intervention in this crucial period would be incompatible with the fundamental principle of free collective bargaining. Arbitration of collective disputes of interest is, unlike in the period of the Weimar Republic, completely unknown. There is a clear and undisputed legal distinction between disputes of rights and disputes of interest (*Rechts- und Regelungsstreitigkeiten*).

The state, at the federal (*Bund*), state (*Bundesländer*) and local levels (*Gemeinden*), is the most important employer in Germany. Public-sector employment relations are still characterised by the traditional legal differentiation between wage earners (*Arbeiter*) and salaried employees (*Angestellte*) on the one hand, and civil servants (*Beamte*) on the other. This so-called 'duality of employment relations' dates back to the Bismarck Constitution of the late 19th century. It was incorporated in the Basic Law of the FRG and has not been substantially changed.

Growing public deficits have led to high interest rates. Strict rules concerning new public debts (of no more than 3 per cent of GDP) were established for those countries that intended to participate in the European Monetary Union. These rules favoured different measures of privatisation and placed increased pressure on public-sector budgets. Therefore, the overall number of public-sector employees (currently about 5 million) is much smaller than it used to be (Keller 1999). As in other countries, the number of public employees grew after World War II, especially in the 1960s and 1970s. However, the number has been declining since a short period of growth in the early 1990s, which was caused by the unification with the overstaffed equivalent of the public sector in the former East Germany. Differences in labour market strategies between private- and public-sector employers have been diminishing as both pursue greater flexibility and take advantage of the present labour market conditions (Keller & Henneberger 1999). Seen from the perspective of other DMEs, Germany has only a medium-sized public sector (Bach et al. 1999; Dell'Aringa et al. 2001).

Public-sector employees enjoy the same rights as their counterparts in private industry. Civil servants and their interest organisations, however, are not allowed to bargain collectively or to strike. Their employment conditions are determined by law and not by collective bargaining. However, interest associations exert political influence through lobbying (Keller 1993). Both processes lead to similar results. This practice of equal treatment of different status groups has changed since the late 1980s.

Collective bargaining is still highly centralised, and takes place at the national level. This structure is in contrast with growing decentralisation tendencies in the public sectors of other major European countries (Bach et al. 1999). Collective disputes are rare; major strikes took place only in 1974 and 1992. Furthermore, there are specific regulations for co-determination at the federal as well as at the regional and local levels, but there is no equivalent for the co-determination of private industry.

Privatisation had been on the political agenda for many years. Some privatisations took place during the 1990s and were mainly at the local level (e.g. refuse collection and cleaning). However, privatisation also affected some former state monopolies, including the postal service and the railways. Privatisation has had some impact on employment practices in Germany, but it has been less important than in other countries such as the UK. In addition, other strategies of rationalisation, including new public management techniques, have been tentatively introduced, especially at the local level (Naschold 1995; Schedler & Proeller 2000). The public sector is, however, in contrast with those of other major industrialised countries (Dell'Aringa et al. 2001), not the focus of fundamental change.

On comparative scales of corporatism in DMEs (Siaroff 1999), Germany always scores somewhere in the middle, between non-integrated pluralism (as in the Anglo-Saxon world) and integrated corporatism (as in Austria or the Scandinavian countries). The late 1960s and 1970s were the heydays of neocorporatism as a specific mechanism of interest intermediation between the state and major economic interest groups, whose power resources and general political impact were enhanced by state action and their inclusion in processes of socioeconomic policy making.

Within the institutionalised form of 'concerted action' in Germany, voluntary wage restraint (and non-binding or statutory incomes policy as in many other countries) was at the top of the political agenda. This 'weak form of macro-level coordination' (Iversen 1999: 159) also included macroeconomic goals such as the relative stability of prices, high levels of employment/full employment, steady economic growth, and a foreign trade balance. Tripartite management of the economy by means of Keynesian instruments of macro-steering and 'demand-side economics' was the aim of the SPD-FDP coalition government. Unlike its counterparts in some other countries, the German central bank, the *Bundesbank*, was a completely independent institution. Its top priority was the maintenance of strict price stability and the dampening of inflation, even if these options contradicted the governments' general economic policy, opposed unions' wage policies or risked increasing unemployment.

As in the majority of other European countries, this classical form of centralised, macrocorporatist arrangement gradually declined. Underlying causes included the decline of Keynesianism and its macro-steering capacities, shifting political preferences towards conservative majorities, and the rise of neoliberal ideologies and 'supply-side economics' that had been introduced after the second oil crisis. More recently, however, there have been, as in some other Western European countries, preliminary signs for a revival of neocorporatism at the macro level (Fajertag & Pochet 1997, 2000). National pacts have been concluded in several countries. This 'competitive corporatism' takes non-classical, network forms of macro coordination and intends to increase national competitiveness and employment. All corporatist arrangements include the government as the third corporate actor, which takes the initiative to coordinate differing goals and to set incentives for closer cooperation between unions and employers' organisations (Traxler 2000).

In the mid-1990s, during the conservative Christian Democratic-led government, first attempts to introduce such new mechanisms failed. It remains to be seen whether the SPD-led government will be more successful on a broader range of employment-related issues after the launch of its 'alliance for jobs'. This seeks to achieve not only less over-time work, more part-time work, more opportunities for vocational training and more jobs for the long-term unemployed, but also a general reorientation of social and fiscal policies. Modest wage demands and rises even below the level of productivity growth are supposed to stimulate investment and to generate more employment. The crucial relationship between the unions and the renewed, 'third way' Social Democrats is, of course, different from the close relations between the unions and the 'old' SPD. Tensions and frictions are both more likely and more frequent (Arlt & Nehls 1999).

Other tripartite institutions have been of major importance in employment relations. At least since the late 1960s, when the Work Promotion Act was passed, the state has also been actively involved in labour employment policies. The tripartite Federal Agency of Employ-ment and its offices at the federal, state and local levels are in charge of implementing a range of policies. Costs are primarily financed by unem-ployment insurance contributions, paid by employees and their employers and not by the federal budget.

The first active strategies (e.g. further education, training and retrain-ing, creation of additional, temporary jobs) were relatively short-lived. Passive strategies (first of all, unemployment benefits) began to domi-nate in the mid-1970s, when unemployment began its rise to previously unforeseen heights. Expenditure on labour employment policies has increased considerably since the mid-1970s—especially, however, after unification (to almost 3 per cent of GDP per year). It became obvious that the Work Promotion Act and its set of instruments had not only become less effective but were designed for a period of full-employment and labour scarcity. It was difficult to adapt them to long-term high unemployment.

In the late 1990s, some of the major instruments were changed, and new ones (e.g. integration contracts) were introduced. Furthermore, the system of labour administration was decentralised. Last but not least, the responsibility of individuals for their own 'employability' was strengthened in contrast to the collective obligations of the general public and the state.

The dual system of vocational training, a peculiarity of the German-speaking countries, is a tripartite, 'corporatist' institution (run by employers, unions and the state). It constitutes a competitive advantage over the less integrated training in other DMEs. This system provides most young people (about two-thirds of the age group) with two kinds of qualification: general training and skills are taught in highly specialised, part-time vocational schools; specific skills and training are acquired at the workplace level in individual companies. This sophisticated system of creating human capital (especially at the level of intermediate skills) has positive outcomes. It creates large pools of qualified labour, and leads to the continuous supply of employees with standardised, theoretical as well as practical qualifications. The acquisition of broad skills constitutes a necessary prerequisite for a 'high-skill/high-wage' economy.

From an international perspective, this dual system of vocational training results in a comparatively low percentage of youth unemployment, because it eases the transition from school to the labour market. Additionally, it provides ample opportunities not only for horizontal mobility but for high degrees of broad functional flexibility in the workforce. The peculiar segmentation structures of German labour markets (the so-called 'three-tier labour markets') result from this institutional setting of providing human resources. Different forms of internal flexibility (e.g. within relatively stable internal labour markets) are generally more important than external ones. This specific labour market segmentation constitutes a clear contrast to 'hire-and-fire' markets or, more accurately, the markets with external numerical flexibility, that are typical in some other DMEs (e.g. the USA, UK and Australia).

THE MAIN EMPLOYMENT RELATIONS PROCESSES

Co-determination: employee participation in management

The two major characteristic features of the labour management cooperation system or 'employee participation in management' are the following. Different provisions for mechanisms not only of 'collective voice' but also of unitary representation of employees and 'co-decision making' have been institutionalised by legal enactment. By contrast with some other countries (e.g. Italy and Sweden), central collective bargaining has played no role (Adams 1995; Thelen & Turner 1999). This sophisticated system of 'industrial democracy' dates back at least to the Weimar Republic. It comprises two interrelated levels—the workplace, and the company.

The *Works Constitution Act 1952* was amended in 1972 by the SPD-FDP coalition government, and again to a lesser extent in 1988 by the CDU-FDP coalition. Another major reform was introduced by the coalition government between the SPD and the Greens in 2001. It simplified the complicated election procedures for small enterprises (up to 50 employees), increased the number of works councillors, included some formerly excluded groups (e.g. workers with temporary contracts), and broadened and strengthened works councils' rights (further training, securing of employment, among others).

On the one hand, the Act defines the sets of rights (e.g. information, voluntary consultation, and binding co-determination with veto rights). On the other, the Act relates to different fields of interest (e.g. social policy issues, such as payment methods and systems, work schedules, regulation of overtime; personnel or staff matters, such as recruitment, transfers, dismissals; and economic or financial affairs). These substantive as well as procedural rights are legally guaranteed and enforceable. The general rule is that these rights are stronger in social matters than they are in employment relations and in economic or financial matters. Thus, a fairly sophisticated web of constraints and opportunities for works council action limits what has been called 'managerial prerogatives' in other countries.

Negotiations that take place between management and works councils lead to company or works agreements. These are not allowed to contradict the provisions of the industry-wide collective contracts.

Because of its legal foundation, the system is difficult and costly to alter. According to Wever: 'If they could, some German employers—perhaps many—would circumvent or do away with the dual system, operating without any employee representation. But because that path is not open to them, many German employers prefer to work actively with the works councils' (1994: 479). Therefore, mutual concessions are likely to emerge. Management and the works council are obliged to cooperate 'in a spirit of mutual trust for the good of the employees and of the establishment'. Due to this and the fact that short-term opportunistic behaviour does not reward the parties in the long term, cooperative instead of conflicting relations have been institutionalised.

The legal constraints and opportunities are identical for all actors. However, there is an enormous diversity of practices, and these change over time. In SMEs, management's acceptance of the principle of joint decision making has increased (Kotthoff 1994). In most works councils, the interests of male, middle-aged, well-educated employees are better represented than others (e.g. those of foreign workers or women).

First, the overall participation rate in elections has always been rather high (at almost 80 per cent; see Table 8.2). Second, re-election of works councils happens often (in more than two-thirds of all cases). Third, their union density ratios are fairly high in comparison with regular employees (about two-thirds of regular members and up to three-quarters of chairpersons are union members). The Works Constitution Act does not apply to very small enterprises (with up to five permanent employees as the threshold), nor to all public-sector employees who are covered by separate Acts, the Staff Representation Acts, that provide less encompassing rights. Furthermore, enterprises that serve political, religious, charitable, educational and scientific aims are only partially covered.

In many other enterprises (mostly SMEs) there are no works councils. Works councils are mandatory, then, but not automatic, and high coverage rates can by no means be taken for granted. The most significant determinant of the likelihood of an election and later existence of works councils is the number of employees. Works councils generally arise only in companies with 1000 and more employees, and the average number of employees per company has been falling. Recent data indicate that only about one-quarter of all eligible private enterprises have elected works councils. These cover, however, the majority (of 60 per cent) of the private-sector workforce (Frick & Sadowski 1995; Addison et al. 1997). But others have estimated that 60 per cent of all private-sector employees are *not* covered by works councils. This percentage has been rising since the mid-1980s (Bertelsmann-Stiftung & Hans-Böckler-Stiftung 1998).

In contrast to widespread assumptions about the 'German system', the majority of all private-sector employees have no access to shop-floor interest representation. Thus, there is a growing 'representation gap' despite legal guarantees. This has serious consequences for the implementation of collective contracts and their results. In older industrial relations textbooks there was usually a chapter on administering the contract, and to fulfill this important task an enterprise-level institution is required.

Works councils are being weakened by tendencies towards smaller company sizes created by the processes of reorganisation. They are more likely to be elected in the older industrial sectors. However, the relative size of the labour force in the poorly covered service sectors has increased—and is likely to continue to increase. Low coverage rates also undermine the important channel of recruitment of union members through works councils' initiatives (Hassel 1999).

Table 8.2 Results of the works council elections in Germany 1975–98 (in percentages)

		1975	1978	1981	1984	1987	1990	1994	1998
Turnout	blue-collar	82.6	81.9	79.9	82.59	82.50	79.14	78.8	64.6
workers	white-collar	72.7	80.8	79.3	82.53	83.60	75.85	76.6	68.4
Re-elected	member	72.3	72.8	65.6	70.28	68.38	68.43	67.1	67.9
candidates	chair	69.9	75.9	75.4	73.11	71.51	72.19	71.1	71.2
Newly elected	member	27.8	27.2	34.3	29.72	31.62	31.57	32.9	32.1
candidates	chair	30.1	24.1	24.6	26.89	29.44	27.81	28.9	28.8
Degree of	member	67.9	58.6	63.2	63.90	65.39	69.25	66.7	61.9
unionisation (DGB)	chair	78.8	71.4	79.9	75.10	74.81	78.37	74.7	73.2
DAG	member	10.4	14.6	8.5	8.90	5.56	3.98	4.3	3.2
	chair	2.6	14.4	5.2	6.81	3.56	3.79	4.5	3.0
CDB	member	2.6	0.7	3.7	0.80	1.04	1.04	1.6	0.5
	chair	0.0	0.1	0.5	0.14	0.26	0.45	0.2	0.4
ULA	member	—	—	0.4	0.30	0.14	0.06	0.0	0.1
	chair	—	—	0.5	0.04	0.01	0.09	0.1	0.0
Others	member	1.6	2.8	0.9	0.70	0.36	0.52	0.9	1.0
	chair	0.6	0.7	3.4	0.87	1.22	0.67	0.7	1.5
Not	member	17.5	23.3	23.3	25.40	27.51	25.15	26.5	33.3
unionised	chair	1.5	13.1	10.5	17.04	20.09	16.45	19.8	21.9
Independent	member	—	—	—	—	—	—	12.8	15.2
	chair	—	—	—	—	—	—	12.2	11.8
Members not	member	—	—	—	—	—	—	13.7	18.1
on a trade union list	chair	—	—	—	—	—	—	7.6	10.1

Source: Niedenhoff (1999).

The impact of participation of employees and their interest organisations on indicators such as productivity, fluctuation, innovation and earnings has been controversial. The econometric evidence is inconclusive: 'the findings do not closely support the simple assertions of protagonists or antagonists of this form of worker representation' (Addison et al. 1996: 581). Due to the specific 'dual' structure of the German system of employment relations, the discussion deals, in contrast to other countries, more with the consequences and effects of works councils than of unions. This literature has been independent from the conventional industrial relations studies that are primarily qualitative, emphasise processes rather than outcomes, and refer to sets of institutional structures instead of particular variables. Traditionally, co-determination has been justified as a basic political right rather than on grounds of economic efficiency.

Co-determination has been characterised by specific features, namely: its legalistic, indirect representative, collective and union-driven nature. This formerly well-established system has been challenged by the decreasing importance of Taylorist-Fordist, standardised mass production, increasing flexible specialisation, Japanese-style 'lean' forms of production and management, and the 'new concepts of production' (Kern & Schumann 1986). Since the mid-1980s different forms of management-driven, economically motivated, direct individual participation have been introduced. The best-known examples of this kind of 'worker involvement' are quality circles and semiautonomous work groups. By the mid-1990s, 15 per cent of all companies in manufacturing had introduced quality circles and 14 per cent teamwork (Dreher et al. 1995). In Lower Saxony, one of the federal states, 48 per cent of all enterprises (covering 60 per cent of all workers) had introduced group work (Addison et al. 2000).

The diffusion of different forms of direct participation in the individual workplace contrasts with the gradual retreat of different traditional forms of co-determination. Some unions as well as works councils tried to resist these changes towards 'managerial' participation, which they saw as a threat. However, the majority of unions became accustomed to these direct forms of participation, and works councils have even made use of them to further their own goals.

Representative co-determination and direct participation supplement each other. 'Bilateralism' or bargaining, and not the restoration of 'managerial prerogative', has been the dominant mode according to Müller-Jentsch (1995: 75):

Sooner or later the structural characteristics (of the German system) will be modified: The dual system might give way to a triple system of interest representation with sectoral bargaining between trade unions and employers' associations, enterprise negotiations between works councils and management, and direct participation by work-groups with elected team leader ... And there is no guarantee that the integration of the formal and representative institutions with the emerging decentralised and informal structures will succeed.

Co-determination at the upper (or company) level can be correctly understood only within the specific legal setting of German companies. This is because of the two-tier board structure that differs from the unified structure of the Anglo-Saxon counterparts. All strategic decisions are taken by the larger supervisory board (*Aufsichtsrat*), which also appoints the members of the smaller management board (*Vorstand*). The latter is required to execute and implement all strategic decisions, and to monitor and control all everyday affairs. In reality, however, its impact is more encompassing.

Employee participation in decision making typically refers to institutions and levels of 'corporate governance'. A percentage of members of the supervisory board (from one-third to almost one-half, depending on specific Acts) are representatives of employees as well as of unions. Furthermore, one member of the management board, the labour director (*Arbeitsdirektor*), is supposed to represent employees' interests. In the majority of companies, the labour director is in charge of employment relations and social policy.

There are different Acts on co-determination at the company level (*Mitbestimmungsgesetze*).

The sector-specific Act for the coal and steel industries (*Montanmitbestimmung*) 1951 established the most far-reaching form of 'full parity' between the representatives of capital and labour within the supervisory board. Therefore, it is still of enormous symbolic value and significance to the unions. In quantitative respects, however, it is only of minor importance because of the decline of these dominating industries. Only about 50 companies (with about 300 000 employees) are still covered by its special provisions (Müller-Jentsch & Ittermann 2000).

The *Works Constitution Act 1952* granted comparatively weaker rights (one-third of the seats of the supervisory board). It still covers all enterprises with from 500 to 2000 employees with a specific legal form

Table 8.3   Forms of co-determination in Germany: proportion of employees represented in the private sector and the national economy (in percentages)

	Private sector		National economy	
	1984	1994/96	1984	1994/96
Double co-determination (works councils and employees representation on company boards of directors)	30.5	24.5	22.2	18.2
Single co-determination (works councils only)	1.9	15.0	40.8	36.9
Companies with no co-determination	50.6	60.5	37.0	44.9

Source: Bericht der Kommission Mitbestimmung (1998).

of joint stock company and limited liability company. This Act applies to about 2600 enterprises.

The *Co-Determination Act 1976* (*Mitbestimmungsgesetz*) grants rights close to parity. It is the most important Act because it is valid for all limited liability companies with more than 2000 employees. Throughout the 1980s the number of companies was fairly stable at about 500, with few changes throughout the years. In the early 1990s this number grew considerably (to about 700), and has not significantly changed since then. Unification was the prime cause for this major growth. Splitting of large companies into smaller ones, and privatisation of former public enterprises, were other major causes.

As shown in Table 8.3, by the mid-1990s only one-quarter of all employees were covered by 'double co-determination'—that is, work councils and representatives on the supervisory board. Another 15 per cent had only works councils, and the majority (about 60 per cent) had no representation at all. In the recent past, coverage rates, which positively correlate with firm size, have declined (Bertelsmann-Stiftung & Hans-Böckler-Stiftung 1998):'The shrinking presence of co-determination in the German economy has not appreciably weakened organized labor so far, but if codetermination continues to erode unabated, it would inevitably impair the trade unions too' (Silvia 1999: 82).

These different channels of co-determination have generally contributed to the gradual development of the sophisticated forms of formal as well as informal cooperation, instead of open or covert conflict at the enterprise and/or shop-floor level. Because differentiated mechanisms of collective 'voice' (and improved channels of communication) have been provided, forms of individual 'exit' (e.g. voluntary quits) have become less prevalent. The notion of mutual recognition within 'social partnership' is a more accurate description of reality than concepts of class antagonism between 'capital and labour' or 'adversarial' traditions in employment relations. According to Adams (1995: 146):

> There is general agreement that the requirement to consult and reach consensus rather than submit disputes to third parties . . . has substantially modified managerial style . . . The institutions of codetermination have resulted in a much more collaborative managerial approach. Employee representatives, on the other hand, have been able to become acquainted first hand with the difficult and complex decisions continually facing management. This greater understanding has helped to ensure more cooperation and commitment to decisions taken.

Works councils are required to represent the interests of the entire workforce (with the only exception being the small tier of senior executives/*leitende Angestellte*), and they are formally independent and separate from the unions. They are obliged to follow a strict peace obligation and the dominating principle of 'trustful cooperation' with management. Co-determination at enterprise and collective bargaining at sectoral level is supposed to be separate, and works councils are required to be detached from all 'quantitative' problems of wages and income distribution. These two broad arenas of interest representation encompass not only differing means of collective action but also different actors, works councils and unions, which represent either specific enterprise-related or more general industry-wide interests.

Most works councillors (between two-thirds and three-quarters, depending on their status as members or chair) are also loyal members of 'their' union, even if they are not union activists. Throughout the 1990s, the percentage of independent works councillors, who are not members of unions, has grown to more than one-quarter. Unions provide different services (e.g. training, legal expertise and advice, and general information) that facilitate the everyday activities of works councillors. However, unions depend on the actions of works councils at enterprise level, where recruitment of new members has to take place. Recruiting is not an official duty of works councillors but it is tolerated by employers, primarily in the larger enterprises. In this regard, works councils show some functional similarities with 'company (or enterprise) unions' in other countries.

Thus, despite the legal separation of both institutions and their arenas of interest representation, a system of 'give and take' or mutual dependence has developed over several decades. According to Thelen (1991: 2):

> The central argument is that the institutional arrangements within which conflicts between labour and capital are resolved have contributed to stable, collaborative adjustment. West Germany's distinctive 'dual system' of labour relations has been a key source of institutional resiliency through the economic turmoil and political changes of the past decades.

Collective bargaining

The basic procedures of collective bargaining are regulated in the Collective Agreement Act. There are three kinds of collective agreement: first, wage agreements fix the level of wages and their periodic changes; second, framework agreements specify wage-payment systems; third, umbrella agreements regulate all other conditions of employment (e.g. working time, overtime, holidays). There are 52 000 valid contracts (Bispinck & WSI-Tarifarchiv 2000). In contrast to some other countries Germany has no explicit minimum wage legislation. The wage floor in an enterprise, which can be voluntarily surpassed but not undercut (*principle of favourability*), is determined by collective bargaining. The 'reservation wage' under which no individual will accept job offers is defined by the social security system.

According to the Collective Agreement Act, contracts can be extended and declared to be legally binding for all enterprises in a specific sector or region. However, this so-called *erga omnes* rule is rarely used, and then only in a few sectors (mainly in the construction, textiles, food, retail and wholesale trade). Towards the end of the 1990s this option applied to only about 600 collective contracts, or 1.2 per cent of all valid contracts (Clasen 2000). The only recent exception of some importance is the construction industry, because of its sector-specific problems of foreign migrant workers, who are supposed to be protected from 'social dumping' by minimum pay and working conditions.

There is a close relationship between the organisational structures of social partners and the system of collective bargaining. In most industries, collective bargaining takes place at the regional and sectoral level (e.g. between unions and employers' associations). These regional activities take place, with very few exceptions, annually, and are centrally coordinated by the national organisations on both sides of industry (e.g. Gesamtmetall and IG Metall). The degree of centralisation and intra-associational coordination had been increased in the late 1960s and 1970s.

In most cases this peculiar structure led to pattern bargaining, especially in engineering. On the one hand, 'pilot agreements' concluded in specific, carefully selected bargaining districts are transferred to other districts of the same industry. On the other hand, they also predetermine the results in all other major sectors (through inter-associational coordination). Therefore, there is a high degree of de-facto coordination. As in most other West European countries (the main exception being the UK), 'multi-employer' or 'industry-wide' bargaining is still the dominant form. This structure of 'flexibly coordinated wages' (Iversen 1999: 159) is perhaps surprising, because it was criticised by employers' organisations throughout the 1990s.

Changes in labour costs or nominal wages are similar for all companies in a particular industry. Pay differentials between individuals as well as groups of employees, sectors, regions, and levels of qualifications are relatively narrow. There is a high degree of standardisation of working conditions (mainly compression of pay differentials and working time) in comparison with decentralised systems. Furthermore, savings in transaction costs are an obvious economic advantage of the system of sectoral bargaining.

Enterprise (or 'single-employer') bargaining that includes unions and not works councils as agents is possible. It grew in the 1990s and has been correlated with the declining membership of some major employers' associations. The increase in the number of enterprises, which doubled in the 1990s to almost 6000, is much higher than that in the percentage of employees covered (8 per cent in the West and 13 per cent in the East). The explanation for this distribution is that it is mostly SMEs that are engaged in this type of bargaining. There are also significant differences between West and East, as well as between sectors (Schnabel 2000). Two-thirds of all contracts are sectoral, and one-third is enterprise-specific. However, the first group covers 22 million employees (Clasen 2000). Changes between both possible levels of bargaining occur in both directions.

233

In the early 1990s, when Volkswagen was in financial trouble, it introduced an innovative strategy of job-saving reductions in working time. The unions made concessions not only in regard to standard working hours but also on wages. Management gave temporary 'employment guarantees' to the workforce (Promberger et al. 1999). Furthermore, measures to increase productivity and competitiveness were taken, such as the introduction of new shift systems and continuous improvement processes. The consensus between the actors can be interpreted as a rather late, German variant of what has been called 'concession bargaining' in other countries.

The major features of this unusual experiment were copied in some other sectors in both parts of Germany (Rosdücher 1997a). But this new form of '*quid pro quo* bargaining' never became the dominant 'new paradigm'. It proved a helpful instrument to overcome the short-term problems of companies in some sectors without having to make use of the traditional instrument of massive layoffs (Seifert 2000). Some concessions also included the introduction of 'two-tier wage structures' differentiating between 'insiders' and 'entrants'. However, these created the internal problems that are well known in other countries (e.g. the USA).

In this 'crisis of sectoral collective bargaining', the former high overall coverage rates of sectoral collective bargaining has decreased since the early 1990s. Towards the end of the 1990s they had declined from more than 80 per cent of employees (in the 1980s) to about 66 per cent of all employees (and fewer than half of all companies) in the West (Kohaut & Schnabel 1999). There are significant variations. The public-sector/social insurance, mining/energy, construction as well as banks/insurance companies are highly integrated, whereas other private-service sectors have much lower coverage rates. Larger companies are covered to a considerably higher degree than SMEs. Higher savings in transaction costs (e.g. bargaining and industrial conflict) seem to be the main explanation for these differences. Furthermore, younger companies are less likely to be covered than older ones. Companies in the West are also covered to a much higher degree than their counterparts in the East. In the transformation process of the East, the deterioration in coverage rates has been even greater, with only one-half of employees and one-quarter of all companies covered by collective bargaining (Bellmann et al. 1999). Throughout the 1990s, there was a trend towards the decentralisation of collective bargaining.

An indicator of the disintegration of the German system is the combination of the coverage rates of both forms of interest representation, that is to say the system of works councils as well as collective bargaining. As both have been on the decline, the percentage of covered employees has also diminished. Only a minority of all companies (about 14 per cent in the West and 12 per cent in the East), with 55 per cent of all employees, are covered by both forms of representation. The most decisive determinant of coverage is the number of employees (WSI-Projektgruppe 1998). There is a problem in that the results of sectoral collective bargaining cannot be implemented and monitored under the control and surveillance of works councils, particularly in SMEs. Any kind of strict decentralisation would be incompatible without works councils.

The 'duality' of the German system, one of its basic characteristics, has been gradually weakened. Decentralisation can be managed effectively only if both institutional forms of interest representation coexist. Works councils are necessary to implement and supervise the results of sectoral bargaining. There are problems in sectors with a high percentage of SMEs and therefore a small number of works councils (Bellmann et al. 1998).

One topic discussed in the comparative literature since the late 1980s has been the impact of different degrees of centralisation on macroeconomic performance (e.g. unemployment, inflation and economic growth). The early studies seemed to indicate that highly centralised as well as highly decentralised systems of collective bargaining would perform much better than intermediate ones (Calmfors & Driffill 1988). Germany seemed to belong to the least favourable group of intermediate countries that were supposed to be unable to deliver moderate pay rises. Recommendations for governance institutions and public policy were obvious, and demanded further decentralisation of wage bargaining and more enterprise-specific bargaining.

More recently, this non-linear, so-called 'hump-shaped' relationship was questioned when studies showed that it was not so much centralisation but different forms of coordination that influenced macroeconomic performance (Soskice 1990; Dell'Aringa & Samek Lodovici 1992; Traxler 1997; Traxler et al. 2001). 'Centralisation' and 'coordination' are not identical, and should not be confused for analytical reasons. It is not only the (high) degree of centralisation but also the (high) degree of horizontal and vertical coordination that has enormous (positive) impact on the overall performance of the institutions involved in employment relations. Germany belongs to the group of market economies with intermediate levels of centralisation but comparatively high degrees of coordination within, as well as between, sectors. The specific form of pattern bargaining provides high degrees of de-facto coordination.

Industrial disputes

There are only limited opportunities for German unions to take industrial action. Unions have been curtailed by a series of decisions by the courts. Ballots of union members before and after strikes ensuring the necessary support for collective action are prescribed by unions' statutes and not by legal enactment. Furthermore, according to the Basic Law and its enshrined principle of freedom of association, industrial conflicts include strikes, as well as lockouts, as legal weapons. From an employer's point of view, the logic of a lockout is to extend the collective conflict in order to exhaust the unions' resources.

In a historical as well as a comparative perspective, there has generally been a relatively low level of industrial disputes. Only relatively small countries such as Switzerland, Austria and the Netherlands have had lower rates (Clarke et al. 1998; Eaton 2000). This comment applies whatever the selected indicator (e.g. companies affected, employees involved or working days lost).

While there has been a pattern of occasional, major disputes every few years, these have had only limited aggregate economic impact. The sectoral distribution has changed according to the changes of industrial structure, but conflicts have been confined to a small number of industries (e.g. engineering and printing). So-called wildcat and spontaneous strikes are illegal but have occurred—in particular during the late 1960s and early 1970s, a period of increased worker militancy in many countries.

In view of the structure of collective bargaining, lockouts have to be organised and coordinated by employers' associations. In most cases they are reactions against strikes, and intensify a current dispute. They mainly took place between the 1950s and early 1980s and were concentrated in a few industries, primarily engineering. Since then, they seem to have been more difficult to implement due to the increasing differences within employers' associations (Hege 1999).

Why is there a relatively low degree of industrial conflict in Germany? First, relatively centralised systems of collective bargaining tend to result in less industrial conflict than in the more decentralised ones. Germany fits very well into this general pattern. Second, the 'dual' system of employment relations promotes long-term cooperation and mutual trust rather than industrial conflict. Third, there is a crucial legal distinction between individual and collective disputes of rights about the interpretation of existing agreements, and disputes of interest about the terms and conditions of new contracts. For the first group, either the existing arbitration committees at the company level operate as efficient 'grievance machinery', or these disputes are solved by the system of independent and specialised labour courts at the local, regional and national levels. Only conflicts of interest can be the subject of legal industrial action.

CURRENT AND FUTURE ISSUES

Flexibility and deregulation

Deregulation and flexibility should be differentiated. In all DMEs, deregulation of product as well as labour markets has been on the political agenda since at least the 1980s. There are, however, significant differences between ideological orientation and political demands on the one hand, and real measures and outcomes on the other. Furthermore, there are differences not only between conservative and Social Democratic governments but also between the different conservative governments themselves. Deregulation, initiated by the conservative coalition governments in Germany (1982–98), was in most ways different from the consequences of Thatcherism and Reaganomics. Supply-side policies and monetarism never dominated Germany, despite more or less vigorous demands from several quarters, and organised labour relations were never seriously challenged.

Legislative foundations of labour market deregulation include the following (Keller & Seifert 1998):

- The *Employment Promotion Act 1985* has been the most prominent and controversial example of deregulation. It reduced the former level of protection from dismissal and extended the opportunities for fixed-term contracts, to promote employment. Studies that cover different periods of the business cycle indicate that the Act's employment impact has been modest. The Act is infrequently used and only by a few companies, its main purpose being to extend periods of probation and to increase 'numerical flexibility' in certain segments of the labour market.
- Minor adjustments in the Works Constitution Act in 1988 have included the introduction of special-interest representation for senior executives.
- The privatisation of placement services in 1994 replaced the previous monopoly of the Federal Agency of Employment. The number of private licences has risen, but the placement activities of private firms has remained at a rather low level (about 2 per cent), and has been limited to narrow segments of the labour market.

• The *Working Time Act 1994* replaced regulations that began in the 1930s. It defined fairly broad limits for daily (eight) and weekly (48) working hours, which can even be extended (to ten and 60 hours respectively). It lifted restrictions on night work and granted more opportunities for work on Sundays and holidays. In general, collective bargaining has played a more decisive role in the flexibilisation of working time than legislation.

The limited degree of deregulation in Germany is surprising, given that conservative governments have been in power for extended periods. Traxler et al. (2001) argue that: 'making deregulation work in favour of sensitivity to externalities would thus require disorganizing not only the labour market but also product markets. Even die-hard neo-liberals shrink from embarking on such a project' (Traxler et al. 2001: 283). There has been no coherent strategy for procedural as well as substantive deregulation. The results can be described as a patchwork of cautious deregulation measures and even mild re-regulation. The far-reaching aims proclaimed by the supporters of deregulation were never achieved, despite fears voiced by the unions and others (Keller 1998; Fuchs & Schettkat 2000).

This result is in line with the observation by the OECD that employment protection legislation 'appears to have a greater impact on the *dynamics* and *composition* of unemployment than on its *level*' (OECD 1999: 86). Complete deregulation or dismantling of the legal foundations of overtly 'rigid' labour market institutions did not occur, probably because the political costs of its implementation would have been too high. After these measures had been introduced by the conservative government, some of them were withdrawn by the SPD–Greens coalition government and replaced with more union-friendly rules. Even cautious steps of re-regulation have taken place.

As in most other countries, it was management and not the unions that was the 'prime mover' in employment relations reforms after the early 1980s. Various demands for more 'flexibility' have been voiced by managers as well as employers and their associations. The reasons advanced have included the changing conditions of labour and product markets, as well as new patterns of work organisation following the demise of the Taylorist-Fordist age of standardised mass production. 'Flexibility' has various meanings and differing impacts (Esping-Andersen & Regini 2000). There are at least four forms: temporal flexibility, flexibility of wages and salaries, functional flexibility, and flexibility of forms of employment and contracts.

Flexibility of working time was the main topic in the 1980s after the major unions, principally IG Metall, demanded shorter weekly hours (e.g. the 35-hour week). Unions sought to decrease the supply of labour in order to create additional employment opportunities. The outcomes of the bargaining rounds included the gradual introduction of shorter hours, greater flexibility, and more differentiation in the allocation of working times at the enterprise level. While shorter hours were sought by the unions, the other issues were mainly but not exclusively in the interests of employers.

Working hours can be flexibly arranged. They can be unequally distributed in terms of days, weeks or even seasons, with long periods of equalisation of about one year or, in some cases, even longer. Working hours have been decoupled from the operation time of the enterprise by means of new shift systems, including weekends, and variable working hours over longer periods of time. Enterprise-specific productivity and production hours have been increased, despite shorter working hours for individuals. The management of working-time arrangements has become a new field of specialisation and has led to a diverse array of models, particularly in larger companies.

Since the early 1990s, the working-time bargaining agenda has changed considerably. Further collective reductions of working time are no longer on the agenda. Employers have strongly opposed further reductions, and employees have to find a balance between wage rises and shorter hours. Individualisation of working hours has become the main focus of attention. Short-term or even longer-term individual working-time accounts have been introduced for at least 40 per cent of employees (Bundesmann-Jansen et al. 2000). These arrangements in all major sectors of the German economy can be used for different purposes, such as extended leave, further training or early retirement. Their negotiation and implementation are of major concern to works councillors.

Flexibility of wages and salaries (including fringe benefits) became a major topic only after the introduction of temporal flexibility. Wages should correspond to the individual company's 'ability to pay'. In the 1990s unions were unable to increase real wages, and in some cases there were reductions in real wages. Issues of wage redistribution have declined in importance, and labour's share of the national income has fallen again to the level of the early 1970s (around 72 per cent). The incidence of wages drift has declined. It had previously resulted from an additional or 'second' round of informal bargaining at the enterprise level after the formal round at sectoral level. In the 1990s, differences between the low-paid and high-paid, as well as between blue- and white-collar workers, widened to some degree. The 'working poor' can no longer be ignored in certain sectors. Rates of return on capital and investment have begun to rise without the expected creation of a high number of additional jobs.

In comparison with the other forms of flexibility, functional flexibility is of minor concern and importance. The main reason is the dual system of vocational training. It provides a high degree of general as well as specific training, fosters a multiskilled workforce, and increases the internal as well as external flexibility of the employees. Following the shift from mass production to diversified quality production, greater flexibility in work organisation, work rules and production processes have been less controversial than in many other countries. Job demarcation and strict seniority rules have never been prominent in Germany.

Since the early 1980s, the dominant employment structure has moved away from the so-called regular employment relationship that comprised full-time, uninterrupted, lifelong individual contracts to be covered by social insurance schemes (including pensions). As in other DMEs, various forms of contingent work or atypical employment have increased (Delsen 1995). These include not only variants of part-time work but also 'new' forms of self-employment, homeworking and telework, fixed-term contracts and (temporary) agency work. With the exception of agency work, women are overrepresented in all these atypical forms of employment. Currently, 'non-standard work' accounts for almost one-third of all employment contracts, and will most likely continue to grow.

The long-term consequences of these recent developments for the system of employment relations have not been completely analysed (Keller & Seifert 1995). However, they include lower union density for 'peripheral' workers, compared with 'core groups' of employees. Interest representation by works councils is less prevalent, and unilateral decision making by management is more dominant (Düll & Ellguth 1999).

More fragmentation and new segmentation lines, instability and less employment security for these rather heterogeneous groups of 'semi-outsiders' have accompanied the emergence of more market-driven arrangements. Tendencies have been increasing towards dualisation, between unionised and protected versus unorganised and unprotected segments. Serious negative consequences are more likely than before, not only for the composition of the labour force but also for social cohesion, the degree of inequality and the employment-related social insurance schemes (particularly pensions).

Flexibility (pursued by employers) and deregulation (initiated by conservative governments) are not necessarily interrelated. In reality, however, they happened simultaneously and contributed to decentralisation. Decentralisation has become a frequent though by no means universal trend, and has varying consequences for employment relations (Katz 1993; OECD 1997; Traxler et al. 2001).

The German path of development towards decentralisation differed from that in other countries, and has been categorised as 'organised' as opposed to 'disorganised' decentralisation (Traxler 1995). So-called opening clauses have been agreed in the collective contracts of major sectors (e.g. engineering, chemicals, retail, textiles and printing) to secure, innovate and reform the system of relatively uniform sectoral bargaining. This introduction of 'strategic choice' and more 'flexible' opportunities for the actors at the level of the individual enterprise is relatively new in Germany. These opening clauses, however, have rather differing impacts (Rosdücher 1997b; Bellmann et al. 1999; Tüselmann & Heise 2000).

The primary goal of employers' associations has been to change or modify the introduction of opening clauses, rather than abolishing the current system of industry-wide bargaining in favour of enterprise bargaining. This could be due to self-interest, because these organisations would become less influential if far-reaching decentralisation occurred. Opening clauses have become the major instrument of reform within processes of 'centrally coordinated adjustment'. Collective contracts negotiated between unions and employers' associations continue in most sectors and regions. But they define only general options for managers and works councils. Different issues, such as the distribution of working time, work organisation and wages, can be specified according to enterprise-specific conditions. Decentralisation has been more successful in regard to some issues (e.g. working time) than others (e.g. wages) (Bispinck 1997).

Company or works agreements are a form of flexibility under the Works Constitution Act. They are of increasing importance. Their number and quality grow with the enterprise's number of employees. In most cases they have been limited to social and personnel issues, covered by enforceable co-determination rights such as payment systems, working time, vacations and social affairs. They have increased since the mid-1980s, when flexibility of working time and decentralisation became major issues. The impact and power of managers and works councils have gradually intensified, while that of unions and employers' associations have been constrained and weakened. The balance of power between both levels of employment relations has shifted towards the lower level. So-called 'micro-corporatist arrangements' have developed and strengthened between managers and works councils at the enterprise level (Windolf 1989, 1990). Factors influencing these developments include technological change, new forms of work organisation, and the transformation of world markets. The establishment of such 'high-trust, low-conflict relations' by means of bipartite internal agreements has aimed to stabilise the company's product markets as well as its labour markets.

Works councillors have indicated that they have to cope not only with their traditional duties but also with many new responsibilities. The continuation of decentralisation, such as the introduction of more individual working-time accounts and plant-level implementation of agreements on security for temporary employees, adds to the workload of works councillors (WSI-Projektgruppe 1998). One implicit precondition for this less centralised pattern of interest representation is the existence of works councils. However, the declining unionisation rates will cause problems for the functioning of works councils, particularly in SMEs.

The peace obligation of works councils prevents them from taking industrial action. This would make no sense under decentralisation that included, almost by definition, negotiations about substantive issues of distribution at the company level. Any fundamental change towards a devolution of bargaining authority would have to grant works councils the right to industrial action. But this step would most likely lead to less cooperation and more conflict. On the other hand, the idea of a general prohibition of strikes is neither in line with the Basic Law nor is it politically feasible. However, we should not overestimate the degree of decentralisation (Ross & Martin 1999: 380). Formal institutions and procedural arrangements at the sectoral level have remained intact, but final decisions about substantive issues (e.g. working time) have gradually been shifted to the enterprise level. The outcomes and functions, then, but not the formal structures of bargaining have changed significantly.

Thus, the 'German postwar industrial relations regime' (Silvia 1999: 114) has lost its original power to set and determine not only pay but also all other working conditions. The crucial balance of power between the specific actors at both levels has decisively shifted. The formerly narrow scope of negotiations at the enterprise level has been broadened and widened by working-time arrangements and problems of work organisation. The previously balanced division of labour and authority, between the institutions and actors of collective bargaining at the sectoral level and co-determination at the enterprise level, has become blurred. This can lead to increased tension and conflict.

The degree of heterogeneity and diversity between as well as within sectors has heightened since the early 1990s. The construction industry is towards the disintegrating end of the continuum, engineering is somewhere in the middle, while chemicals are towards the relatively integrated end. Differences between SMEs and MNEs (multinational enterprises) have increased. Even in the public sector, which is assumed to be relatively stable, some segments such as public mass transport have begun the process of disintegration.

Unions and most employers' associations intend to preserve the existing bargaining system despite the growing tendency towards decentralisation. The key question is whether these trends will replace the institutional frameworks and rules of the highly legalised system. Alternatively, will the institutional infrastructure be compatible with the higher degree of autonomy at the enterprise level?

German unification: the internal challenge

The post-1945 political and economic division of Germany came to a sudden end in 1990, shortly after the collapse of the Berlin wall. Since then, the integration of a socialist, centrally planned economy into a capitalist, social market economy has caused difficulties. The policy makers underestimated the unprecedented and lengthy task of privatisation and reorganisation. In terms of employment relations, new developments in the East have also had major repercussions for the West. A laboratory for the creation and testing of new regulatory mechanisms has been created.

Employment in the East fell soon after the collapse of the old regime, by about one-third (from more than 9.5 million to about 6 million). The main reasons included: antiquated and highly inefficient means of production and infrastructure; misallocation of major parts of the labour force; sudden introduction of the monetary, economic and social union with West Germany; unexpected collapse of foreign trade partners and export markets (COMECON) in central and eastern Europe; decline in sales of domestic products because of increasing competition from the West and changing preferences of consumers in the East; not to mention the ecological damage of the environment (Sinn & Sinn 1994).

The profound de-industrialisation had to be stabilised by some other means than active labour market policies. First, a system of labour market administration had to be developed. Initially, this involved the implementation of early retirement programs and short-term work. Later, it involved training and retraining as well as subsidised agencies for employment promotion and structural development. More than 1 million people migrated to the West, which constituted a 'brain drain' from the East (Silvia 1999).

The officially registered unemployment (including about one-third long-term unemployed) in the East is almost twice as high as in the West, being particularly high in the East's industrialised regions and in the low-skill segments of the labour market. Continuing unemployment contributes to the deterioration of the unions' bargaining power. High unemployment also creates problems of social disintegration, and militates against political radicalisation.

The transfer of the legal system from West to East included not only state and constitutional law but also social and labour law. The strategy to give both currencies equal value led to a 'cost shock' in the East German economy. In contrast to the societal and economic transformation of all other member states of the former Soviet bloc (the 'transition countries'), the new East German federal states soon had a comparatively stable framework of legal regulation and institutional infrastructure. There are now identical legal frameworks in both parts of Germany, although there are still major differences in everyday practice, which will probably continue for the foreseeable future.

The deteriorating membership density ratios of unions and employers' associations in the East are of concern. The old union movement, the Free German Trade Union Federation, was closely affiliated with the old communist regime. Consequently, it was completely discredited and collapsed immediately. West German unions' membership grew to an unexpected high of about 50 per cent in 1991. This was due to massive inputs in terms of money and human capital.

Since then, however, unions have been losing members. The reasons include increasing and persistent unemployment, disappointment and disillusionment of members with the unions in a capitalist market economy, as well as the failure of industrial restructuring after wide-ranging de-industrialisation. These drastic losses after the short 'unification boom' and 'unification euphoria' caused the unions serious financial trouble in both parts of Germany. It led not only to freezes on hiring but also to layoffs and reductions in staff levels. Expenses in the East, to cover problems such as unfair-dismissal litigation, were much higher than membership fees, and drained union funds. Union-free plants and even non-union sectors (or sectors without interest representation) have become a reality, in at least some sectors in the East.

There have been similar problems in employers' organisations, which expanded their organisational domains and transferred their institutional structure to the East without making consequential modifications (Henneberger 1993). During the first phase of transition, West German associations supported the founding of their counterparts in the East. They had not existed under the old communist regime due to the lack of private ownership of the means of production since World War II. Autonomous East German organisations were not established. A public trustee institute was established to privatise the formerly state-owned companies of a bankrupt economy and then to transform them into a market economy (Fischer et al. 1996). It urged all 'its' enterprises to become members of employers' associations, and paid their fees for them. This favourable practice came to an end after the privatisation of formerly state-owned companies had been successful (or non-viable ones had been liquidated).

Subsequently, new companies and SMEs, in particular, preferred not to join 'their' associations because they were primarily seen as representatives of large companies' interests. Thus, the lasting problem is not so much the active 'exit' of the associations but rather abstinence or avoidance. Aggregation and mediation of heterogeneous, widely differing interests (not only between East and West but also between large firms and SMEs) create enormous internal difficulties and prevent the formulation of homogeneous associational policies. Vigorous demands for further decentralisation of collective bargaining have been implemented. In 1993 a current contract was terminated in manufacturing. This event was unique in the history of German collective bargaining; it indicated a new offensive strategy of employers' associations as they sought to change the established standards (Artus 2001). This strategy led also to the introduction of far-reaching opening clauses, such as the hardship clause, which permits, under specific economic circumstances, pay levels below the contractually agreed minimum. However, this clause has not often been used (Hickel & Kurtzke 1997).

The so-called 'tacit escape from collective bargaining results' has become another important problem for the stability of the system of employment relations. Enterprises belong to employers' associations, but, in contrast to undisputed legal requirements, they do not comply with the standards agreed on in bargaining contracts. This has been mainly in the case of working hours, but has also involved wages and fringe benefits. It is not only works councils but also 'their' unions which acquiesce to practices involving the undercutting of current collective standards in individual companies. They tolerate this non-compliance quietly to save scarce jobs in times of high unemployment (or to prevent the reallocation of employment opportunities), or to increase the productivity of 'their' company. According to Tüselmann and Heise (2000: 169), 'Despite being illegal, this wildcat co-operation or disorganised decentralisation has so far received the tacit acceptance of the sectoral parties. However, there is a danger that the problems in eastern Germany may feed back to the western region, thereby undermining the system as a whole'.

Another consequence of this 'tacit escape' is that the official bargaining coverage rates overestimate the real scope of coverage. This creeping, internal erosion of sectoral bargaining has accompanied the 'exit' from employers' associations. It indicates tendencies of growing segmentation between included and excluded firms and sectors.

The viability and legitimacy of collective bargaining and its key players have been undermined and challenged. Collective agreements are no longer able to fulfill their original function to take 'wages out of competition'. Informal and uncoordinated 'wildcat cooperation' between managers and works councils seems to be widespread, and grew during the 1990s. Even in the early 1990s, only 60 per cent of East German enterprises (with about 83 per cent of all employees) paid the contractually agreed levels of wages (DIW 1994). Pay levels in most industries and sectors increased to a considerable degree, particularly in the early years after unification (up to 1993/94).

After these 'political agreements', wage growth declined. Wages are still lower than in the West (at about 90 per cent on average), whereas working hours are longer and social benefits (such as Christmas or vacation bonuses) are lower. Differences in real wages are larger than in nominal ones (Clasen 2000). Such discrepancies are difficult to justify in terms of equality of living conditions and social justice. The 'orbits of coercive comparison' are always set by West German standards and not by those in the former member states of COMECON. Labour productivity, however, is still considerably lower in the East than in the West (at about 60 per cent, but with considerable variance between sectors).

Cooperation between managers and works councils seems to be even closer in the East than in the West. Works councillors have turned into 'co-managers'. They fear the loss of additional jobs; the pressure to compromise comes from both sides of industry. On the other hand, the relationship between works councils and unions, so crucial to the survival of the 'dual system' of interest representation in Germany, is less institutionalised than in the West (Schmidt 1998).

Huge financial transfers (of up to 4 per cent of German GDP in some peak years) from the West's richer states to the East continued throughout the 1990s, and seem likely to continue for an indefinite period. Despite these huge payments and enormous progress in some regions, a self-sustaining economic upswing has not yet taken place. Prospects for the future were overestimated at the beginning (Wever 1995; Turner 1997, 1998). The politically motivated promises that 'nobody will be worse off' did not come true, and led to major disappointments and frustration. Since the end of the 1990s catch-up processes have stagnated, and growth rates have been lower than in the West.

European integration: the external challenge

Additional pressures and challenges for national systems of employment relations have been created by internationalisation. These include Europeanisation in particular and globalisation in general. About 90 per cent of the GDP of EU members remains in the EU, which is equivalent to the ratio of trade within Japan or the USA. Furthermore, foreign direct investment (FDI) remains largely within the EU. FDI takes place more often in other EU member countries than in other regional blocks (such as South-East Asia or North America). Trade between EU member states has gradually increased over the last decades and has grown faster than trade with outsiders. More than 60 per cent of all exports of the EU member states remains within the EU. Evidently, processes of Europeanisation are more important for the future development of national employment relations than is the less definite impact of 'globalisation' (Keller 2001b).

German employers' organisations and unions are members of their European confederations, the UNICE and ETUC. Both agree on the ultimate goal of further European integration but differ on the most appropriate means to achieve this. The political regulation of the 'social dimension of the internal market' is supposed to complete the process of economic and monetary integration. Yet this goal is still far from being achieved. During the 1990s, the organisational capacities of German social partners were absorbed by the more urgent problems of coping with unification. Employers' organisations and unions still have difficulties in transferring resources from the national to the supranational level. European confederations remain comparatively weak, particularly on the employers' side. The top priority of interest representation is still at the national level, and 'solidarity' at the international level is difficult to organise. The shift towards 'Europe' implies a loss of power and impact, especially for the unions.

Recent developments at the supranational level or, to be more precise, at the enterprise, sectoral and macro levels, have had major impacts on national employment relations. At the level of MNEs, European works councils (EWCs) are required according to the EU Directive of 1994, which was transposed in Germany by legislation in 1996, not by collective bargaining. EWCs are not designed to replace national organisations but to represent employees' transnational interests in MNEs (with more than 1000 employees within the EU and more than 150 in at least two EU member states). EWCs should not be confused with the comparatively powerful German works councils. EWCs have rights only to information, rather than co-determination. Their impact therefore will remain fairly limited in the overwhelming majority of MNEs. On the other hand, EWCs are the main institution in an emerging system of European employment relations. There are no counterparts (or functional equivalents) at the sectoral and/or macro level.

The number of EWCs is difficult to assess, but it is estimated that there are more than 1700 MNEs, 400 of which have their headquarters in Germany (Kerckhofs 2000). It is surprising that the so-called rate of agreements concluded is much lower in Germany than in most other EU members. Implementation has taken much longer than originally expected. Since the late 1980s, various German unions (particularly IG Metall) have actively supported the establishment of voluntarily concluded and, later on, mandatory EWCs. This support required a significant input of resources. The majority of EWCs in German-based MNEs are composed exclusively of workers' representatives, following the German model of works councils. Although most EWCs follow the French-Belgian pattern of equal representation of 'both sides of industry', differences in the everyday activities of both forms are less significant than is often assumed (Marginson et al. 1998).

Despite increasing pressure because of the growing interdependence of national economies, collective bargaining still does not take place at levels higher than the national. The introduction of the third and final step of the European Monetary Union (EMU) in 1999 meant the ultimate centralisation of the monetary policy but not of the fiscal policy. It terminated the existence of exchange mechanisms, particularly devaluation, as a mode of adaptation to the fluctuating economic activities. National central banks, such as the previously independent German *Bundesbank*, lost their importance and power because the European Central Bank is now in charge of monetary policies (and the maintenance of strict price stability) for the Euro zone. In contrast to national banks, it cannot take the specific conditions of individual countries into consideration.

The EMU has increased the necessity of wage moderation and coordination. From the unions' point of view, it has launched processes of transnational coordination of national collective bargaining policies to avoid downward spirals and wage cost competition ('beggar-my-neighbour policy'). The general idea is that wage claims should be based on the sum of cost-of-living changes and improvements in labour productivity. The first experiments with the 'European coordination rule' (in engineering and construction) started only in the late 1990s. They are still in their early stages of development and cover only a limited number of countries (Schulten & Bispinck 1999).

Genuine European collective bargaining is not on the political agenda. The necessary institutional, legal and factual prerequisites are missing, and employers' associations are not interested in creating them, because the status quo of national regulation better fits their interests. Furthermore, it is questionable as to whether such a European-wide system, which should not be confused with harmonisation, would be the most appropriate. This growing pressure towards coordination is intensified by the fact that other possible modes of adaptation do not exist. In contrast to some other regions of the world, the transnational mobility of 'labour' within the EU is still surprisingly low (about 2–3 per cent of the labour force). This is the case despite the fact that all legal barriers to free movement, which constitutes one of the four basic goals of 'free movements of goods, persons, services and capital', have been repealed.

At the macro level, more binding social dialogues have been conducted—first, according to the Social Protocol of the Maastricht Treaty and, later, the Amsterdam Treaty. They are, however, by no means sufficient surrogates or equivalents of collective bargaining. In quantitative terms, the issues voluntarily agreed by the social partners are very few in number (parental leave, part-time work and fixed-term contracts); in qualitative terms, they suffer from a lack of substance. It always requires the initiative of the Commission to get voluntary negotiations of the social partners started, and then, in cases of failure, to finalise the proposed project. UNICE is not interested in binding results, only in purely voluntary recommendations and joint opinions. Employers' associations often refer to the dominating principle of *subsidiarity* that was renewed in the Maastricht Treaty and, as such, take a wait-and-see position for as long as possible.

Furthermore, social dialogue at the sectoral level, due to the structure of collective bargaining in the EU's members, is supposed to be of greater importance. However, as it is voluntary in character, and lacks implementation at the national level, social dialogue is not the functional equivalent of collective bargaining. European industry federations either have no sectoral counterpart at all on the employers' side or associations are unwilling to negotiate binding solutions (Keller 2001c).

In national 'dual' systems of employment relations, such as that in Germany, collective bargaining takes place mainly at the sectoral level. Such systems can be particularly hit by the processes of Europeanisation, because there is no equivalent for their upper level, which is 'the cornerstone of the edifice' (Hege 1999: 49). In the EU, a 'monistic' system, with forms of interest representation only at the enterprise level, is more likely to emerge than a dual structure. If this is the case—and the introduction of EWCs by legal enactment clearly points in this direction—the important sectoral pillars of national, 'dual' systems could gradually erode. This development would exert destabilising effects not only on sectoral bargaining but on the whole system of employment relations (Marginson & Sisson 1998).

The economic and social consequences of the Eastern enlargement of the EU are difficult to assess. Not all, but certainly some national labour markets (e.g. those of Austria and Germany) will experience an inflow of foreign labour that will create additional problems, at least in certain segments or sectors. The introduction of the principle of 'freedom of movement' could be delayed for some years, but not for an indefinite period. The establishment of new rules for the allocation of regional and social funds will be necessary but difficult to achieve, because they will include a major redistribution of resources.

CONCLUSIONS

The 'dual system' of German industrial relations, which has been called 'the paradigm of the highly regulated industrial relations system' (Ferner & Hyman 1998: xiv), has not ceased to exist but is in deeper and more serious difficulties than ever before. Since the early 1990s, fundamental processes of gradual disintegration have taken place and partially replaced the formerly integrated system. This development has been caused by internal factors (e.g. German unification and changing modes of production) as well as external developments, including Europeanisation and globalisation. The consequences of unification in Germany have accelerated the already existing trends towards destabilising the system of employment relations.

The system of German employment relations that developed in the decades after 1945 will not collapse or disintegrate. However, institutional arrangements can change. The 'German model' is in the midst of a transformation of its key institutions and procedural rules, and in some ways is developing similarities to the Anglo-American model. Gradual development towards a larger degree of disintegration, if not dualisation between core and periphery (or highly and poorly covered segments of employment and employees), is looking more likely. Furthermore, the neoliberal orientation towards short-term maximisation of shareholder interests, dominating in the UK and the USA, appears to be gradually replacing the more long-term multiple stakeholder interests approach that formerly dominated the German version of capitalism.

This gradual erosion of the key institutions that supported the 'dual system' in Germany is leading to an uncertain future, with less coordinated decentralisation, less legal interference and institutional constraints, more heterogeneity and fragmentation. There is increasing differentiation between sectors as well as between enterprises of different sizes. We may be witnessing the decline of of the 'German model of negotiated adjustment' (Thelen 1991) or 'negotiated approach to industrial adjustment' (Wever 1995), with its emphasis on long-term cooperation.

A CHRONOLOGY OF GERMAN EMPLOYMENT RELATIONS

1844	Silesian weavers' revolt.
1848	Year of revolutions.
1848–54	General German Worker's Fraternity.
1848–53	Association of cigar-producing workers.
1849–53	Printers' association is formed.
1863	Foundation of the General German Workers' Association.
1865–67	First national associations of cigar workers, printers and tailors.
1869	Foundation of Social Democratic Workers' Party.
1869	Prussian Trades Law grants freedom of coalition.
1873	First collective agreement (in the printing trade).
1878–90	Antisocialist legislation.
1891	First industrial union—German Metal Workers' Association.
1892	First trades union congress.
1894	Foundation of first large Christian trade union (coal miners).
1899	Congress of Free Trade Unions recommends collective agreements.
1904	Main employers' association founded.
1905	First long strike by the German miners' union.
1913	Association of German Employers' Federations is established.
1914–18	World War I.
1916	Law to enforce works committees in all production establishments with more than 50 workers.
1918	Law on collective agreements.
1918–24	Central Working Commission of employers and workers in manufacturing industries and trades.
1919	Foundation of General German Trades Union Federation (ADGB).
1920	General strike against rightist riot (Kapp-Putsch).
1920	Works Councils Act.
1927	Law on labour courts.
1928	Law on collective agreements.
1928	Thirteenth ADGB Congress discusses co-determination.
1933	Unions abolished by National Socialist government.
1939–45	World War II.
1949	Founding Congress of DGB.
1951	Co-determination Act for coal and steel industries.

1952	Works Constitution Act.
1955	Staff Representation Act (for employees in the public sector).
1963	Foundation of Christian Trade Union Movement.
1963	Lockout of metal workers.
1967	'Concerted action' begins.
1972	Revision of the Works Constitution Act.
1974	Strike in the public sector.
1974	Revision of the Staff Representation Act.
1976	Co-determination Act for firms with more than 2000 employees.
1978–79	Steel strike: dispute about a shorter working week
1984	Metalworkers' dispute about shorter working week.
1989	Amendment of the Workers Constitution Act.
1990	Reunification of West and East Germany. Dissolution of the FDGB
1992	Public services strike.
1995	Failure of attempts to establish a joint platform between government, employers and unions to confront increasing unemployment.
1998	Alliance for work, education and competitiveness.
2001	Revision of the Works Constitution Act. Merger of five service-sector unions, foundation of ver.di.
2003	Failure of the alliance for work, education and competitiveness.

Chapter 9

EMPLOYMENT RELATIONS IN SWEDEN

Olle Hammarström, Tony Huzzard and Tommy Nilsson

Sweden became an industrial society later than most other countries covered in this book. At the start of the 20th century, Sweden was a poor agrarian society with high emigration. In the early 21st century it is a relatively wealthy, welfare-oriented, service society. Sweden has 25 per cent of its civilian workforce employed in industry, only 2.4 per cent are still in agriculture, while 73 per cent are in services (see Appendix), partly as a result of the strong growth of local and regional government since the 1960s.

Swedish employment relations have long fascinated foreign observers. With a total population of 9 million and with 4.4 million in the labour force, Sweden is the smallest of the countries discussed in this book. However, 76 per cent of its women are in the labour force, which is the highest female participation rate of any OECD country.

After the 1998 election, there were seven political parties represented in the parliament. The percentage of the popular vote they each received is given in brackets. Four of them are liberal conservative (*bourgeois*) parties: the Conservative Party (23 per cent); the Centre Party (5 per cent); the Liberal Party (5 per cent); and the Christian Democratic Party (11 per cent). The Social Democratic Party was returned to office in 1994 and in 1998 it again formed a minority government. The relatively new 'green' party, the Environment Party, received 4 per cent. The small Left Party (12 per cent) has never been part of any Swedish government, but it has often been an ally of the much more important Social Democratic Party (38 per cent), which formed the government for 53 years of the 59-year period from 1932 to 1991—including a continuous period of 44 years between 1932 and 1976 (Hammarström & Mahon 1994).

During the 1970s and 1980s the Swedish economy was characterised by a high level of inflation. But after a shift in economic policy in the early 1990s, the inflation rate fell below the European Union (EU) average. At the same time, the previously low levels of unemployment (1.8 per cent in 1990) rose and reached 10 per cent in 1996. By the early 21st century it had declined significantly. For most of the post-1945 period, Swedish unemployment has consistently been lower than in most of the other countries discussed in this book. In some years it has been even lower than that in Japan.

HISTORICAL CONTEXT

Following its relatively late industrialisation, Sweden became unionised somewhat later than other countries. The union movement started to develop during the 1880s. At first, the Social Democratic Party, which was established in 1889, functioned as a union confederation, but then the Swedish Trade Union Confederation (LO) was formed in 1898. The Swedish union movement began with craft unions, but by 1910 the concept of industry unions was dominant. The employers' organisations developed as a response to the growth of the unions. The Swedish Employers' Confederation (SAF) was established in 1902 (Korpi 1978).

Initially, the right to organise and bargain collectively had no legal basis and was strongly contested by the employers. The first industrial disputes were combined struggles for the right to organise and for higher pay in the 1870s. These struggles intensified in the early years of the 20th century—for example, in a lockout in the engineering industry in 1905. These conflicts led to the recognition of union rights in the so-called 'December compromise' of 1906. In an agreement with the LO, the SAF acknowledged the unions' right to organise and bargain collectively. For its part, the LO accepted that all collective agreements were to include a clause giving the employer 'the full right to hire and fire and to organise production'. The agreement was seen as a major step forward by the unions. The right to organise had been achieved, even though employers' rights were then generally seen as the natural state of affairs. This was the first example of a major agreement reached by the central organisations on behalf of their affiliated unions and employer associations.

However, the 'December compromise' was not fully recognised by all employers; therefore, some of them continued to implement anti-union policies. The first nationwide dispute was in 1909. The legendary 'great strike' started as a lockout by employers as an attempt to weaken the unions. The dispute ended with the workers returning to work without an agreement. It was a heavy defeat for the unions whose membership declined from 162 000 members in 1908 to 85 000 members in 1910 (Tilton 1990).

Industrial relations legislation developed slowly. It was reactive rather than promotional of reform. In 1906 an Act on voluntary mediation was passed and a small mediation office was established. During the 1910–20 period, employers and conservative politicians tried on several occasions to introduce legislation that would restrict unions' rights to strike. These attempts were blocked by socialist and liberal interests. As strikes continued to be seen as a major social problem, Acts on Collective Bargaining and the Labour Court were passed in 1928, despite union opposition. These Acts were the first legal recognition of union rights (Johnston 1962; Hanami & Blanpain 1987).

In 1932, after the election of the first Social Democratic government with a workable parliamentary majority, the situation changed. The unions adopted a new strategy, as they no longer saw the government as inevitably an ally of the employers. The new relationship between capital and labour led to the Basic Agreement on Industrial Peace 1938 (also known as the Saltsjöbaden Agreement, named after the place where the negotiations took place), which laid the foundation for labour management cooperation and consultation. Subsequently, this spirit of cooperation became known as the 'Swedish model'.

There are no official definitions of the 'Swedish model'. Various writers have given it different meanings (e.g. Rehn & Viklund 1990). Common to all definitions, however, is the philosophy that unions and employers should take full responsibility for pay determination and industrial peace, whereas the government should take responsibility for upholding full employment and economic stability. The interests that brought unions and employers together to develop the Swedish model was the common interest to stimulate economic rationalisation and productivity growth and the desire to avoid government interference in collective bargaining (see Olsson 1989; Brulin & Nilsson 1991; Brulin 1995; Erixon 2000; Huzzard 2000).

This cooperative spirit was codified in the Basic Agreement 1938. After that, other agreements followed that together formed the collective bargaining base for the Swedish model. They included the Industrial Welfare Agreement 1942; the Works Council Agreement 1946; the Vocational Training Apprentices Agreement 1947; and the Time and Motion Studies Agreement 1948.

Before World War II, the Social Democratic government largely followed a Keynesian economic policy, which used budget deficits to fight unemployment. After 1945, a modified version of Keynesian policy was developed. In 1951, the LO Congress adopted a policy based on the so-called 'Rehn-Meidner' model, named after two prominent LO economists who proposed a new approach to economic policy. The LO advanced the view that unions should take into account the government's economic policy when formulating their wage demands. In exchange for union support, the government agreed to pursue a policy of full employment. Economic growth was secured by union commitment to rationalisation and technological development. This government also gave support to an 'active labour market policy', which encouraged geographical and skill mobility for displaced workers. The Labour Market Board (AMS) was established in 1948 and has subsequently assumed a strong role in developing labour market policies (Meidner 1983). But this national and largely centralised 'active labour market policy' was, more recently, regarded as less effective. Hence, there have been changes to decentralise labour market policy, involving local politicians and representatives of unions and employers.

In adopting the program based on the 'Rehn-Meidner' model, the unions assumed partial responsibility for national economic performance, thereby changing their policy from the early 1930s. This involved, for example, support for the employers in their programs for technological and structural change. Thus, industrial conflict was partly transferred to the political arena, with the state taking an active part in income redistribution through taxation and social security legislation. The period from 1950 to the end of the 1960s was one of stability in the labour market. Steady economic growth, particularly through the 1960s, meant that pay disputes were settled without great difficulties. Unions accepted management's right to 'hire and fire' and to rationalise production in the expanding sectors of the economy. This transition process was facilitated by the government's active labour market policy. The main emphasis of union demands during this period was on improved social security.

During this period, the LO implemented its policy of a 'solidaristic' wage policy, which was an essential element of the 'Rehn-Meidner' model. The policy had two ingredients. One was 'equal pay for equal work', regardless of industry or company. That meant that company profit levels were not the main basis for negotiations. Subsequently, poor economic performers were forced out of business, while the profits in the most successful companies were not challenged by the unions. The other dimension of the 'solidaristic' wage policy was the narrowing of the gap between the lower-paid and the higher-paid workers. The gap was attacked by a progressive taxation system and by pay contracts that gave extra wage rises to low-income earners (Delsen & Van Veen 1992).

The harmonious pattern of employment relations that emerged in Sweden during the 1950s and 1960s was facilitated by steady economic growth. The industrial development of Sweden was originally based on natural resources: iron, timber, and hydroelectric power. In addition, some important innovations allowed some Swedish firms to become major players in world markets, including AGA (lighthouses), ASEA (power generation, electrical and diesel motors), SKF (ball bearings), Nobel (explosives), Ericsson (telephones), Electrolux (refrigerators), Atlas Copco (rock drilling) and Alfa-Laval (separators). Sweden became the home base for MNEs, rather than merely a host country. Sweden is more dependent on international trade than any of the countries discussed in this book. Around 30 per cent of Sweden's GDP is exported. This includes approximately half of the production of the engineering industry, which is dominant in the Swedish economy. The figures are even higher for other sectors such as the iron, steel and wood industries, although the IT and telecommunications sectors have increased in their relative size in the recent period. Sweden's dependence on international markets inclined Swedish unions in the private sector to accept productivity improvements. Technological and administrative rationalisation have usually been accepted and often welcomed by Swedish unions.

THE PARTIES

Unions

The establishment of a union in Sweden does not require any registration or acceptance by government authorities or courts. Any group of employees is free to form its own union and will automatically be covered by industrial relations legislation. The more advanced union rights are, however, reserved for unions holding contracts. The most significant of these rights is access to company information and the right to initiate bargaining on any major changes before they take place. There are very few new unions in Sweden, mainly because the existing unions appear to serve their members effectively and protect their area of interest from competing unions.

There are three main union confederations: the LO (the Swedish Trade Union Confederation) and the TCO (the Swedish Confederation of Professional Employees) dominate the blue- and white-collar sectors respectively. A third confederation, SACO (the Swedish Confederation of Professional Associations), consists of professional unions organising employees who generally possess an academic degree.

LO's sixteen affiliated unions have a total membership of more than 2 million people, including retired members. This means that the LO covers around 90 per cent of blue-collar employees—a very high density by international standards. Most affiliated unions are organised on an industrial basis, with one union at each company or site. The largest unions are the Swedish Municipal Workers' Union (610 000 members) and the Swedish Metal Workers' Union (420 000 members). The LO represents its affiliated unions in the areas of social and economic policy. Until recently, it also bargained collectively on behalf of all members in the private sector. In the public sector, however, the two major unions bargain directly, without the direct involvement of the LO.

The TCO was formed in 1944 by the merger of two organisations, one covering private-sector employees and the other covering public-sector employees. The eighteen unions affiliated with the TCO have 1.2 million members. It does not take part in collective bargaining, but is active in training and represents its unions in consultation with the government on general economic and social policies. The largest member unions are the SIF, the Swedish Union of Clerical and Technical Employees in Industry (366 000 members); the SL, the Teachers' Union (215 000 members); and the SKTF, the Swedish Union of Local Government Officers (176 000 members). The largest member unions are 'vertical' industry unions, which means they organise all white-collar employees at all levels in an enterprise. They constitute three-quarters of total TCO membership. The other member unions are organised on an occupational basis.

The SACO is the smallest of the three confederations, albeit the fastest-growing. The 25 member unions of the SACO have around 540 000 members. The unions are organised primarily on the basis of members having a similar academic background. The largest unions are those which organise teachers in secondary education and graduate engineers.

Union organisation changed during the 1990s. Significant mergers, coalitions and alliances took place, and more are likely. One example is in the private-sector manufacturing industry, where the unions Metall, SIF and CF, affiliated to the three different central confederations, have formed a joint bargaining agency.

There have been strong links between the LO and the Social Democratic Party (SAP). The LO's financial support to the party is of prime importance, particularly in election campaigns. A significant part of local electoral work is also carried out by union activists. The strong links between the LO and the SAP were demonstrated through the system of collective membership, though this was abolished in 1991. The links continue, but both organisations have found reasons to operate with more independence since the early 1990s. In contrast to the LO's affiliation with the Social Democratic Party, the TCO and SACO have no formal political affiliation.

Most employees in Sweden are members of unions: about 79 per cent of blue-collar employees and 78 per cent of white-collar employees and professionals are unionised. This exceptionally high union density by international standards is explained by several factors. One is that the unemployment benefit system is administered by the unions. Most workers regard it as sensible to belong to a union for protection against possible unemployment. Other benefits offered by the unions help them further in recruiting members. It is also true that the Swedish employers in general have not displayed hostile attitudes to unions; the union-busting seen in the USA is uncommon in Sweden. Thus, most Swedes see joining a union as normal when entering the labour market.

Employers' organisations

Employers in Sweden are as well organised as the employees. There are four employer confederations: one for the private sector and three for the public sector. The Swedish Employers' Confederation (SAF) used to organise employers in the private sector. The SAF acted for more than 40 000 affiliated companies organised in 38 sectoral associations. SAF-affiliated companies employed about 1.2 million people. In 1991, the SAF decided to withdraw from engaging in central wage negotiations on behalf of its members, and in 2001 it was wound up. Instead, a new employers' organisation was founded, the Confederation of Swedish Enterprise (SN). This was a merger between parts of the old SAF and the

Federation of Swedish Industries. The national government authorities are represented by the Swedish Agency for Government Employers (SAV). The local government sector has two confederations: the 278 municipalities collaborate through the Swedish Association of Local Authorities, and the 23 county councils through the Federation of County Councils. The public sector has more than 1.3 million employees, of whom around 230 000 are national government employees.

Characteristics of the social partners

One important feature of Swedish unions is the high degree of centralisation of decision making. Decisions about strikes and accepting collective agreements are normally taken centrally, for instance by executive committees. Even in cases where centralisation in decision making is not formally regulated in statutes, members usually follow the recommendations of their leaders. Although Swedish unions are centralised, this does not mean that they are weak or inactive at the local level; in comparison with unions in other countries there tends to be a great deal of local activity (Kjellberg 1992). Some researchers, moreover, have attributed the high level of union density in Sweden not only to strong local organisation but also to how local union organisations interact with the national level (Sandberg et al. 1992; Huzzard 2000).

Wherever there are ten or more members, it is usual that a local branch of the union will be formed. Approximately 10 per cent of union members hold an elected position in their union organisation, and 15–20 per cent of the membership receives some form of union training each year. Participation in union meetings, however, is usually low. It is common to find only 5–10 per cent of members in attendance at regular meetings. Typically, there is an attendance of 50 per cent or more only for annual meetings or when decisions are to be taken on collective agreements or strike action.

The role of the government

The private sector has been the traditional pace-setter in Swedish pay negotiations. It is also widely accepted that the production costs and productivity of the export sector are of prime importance in pay determination. Nevertheless, the government exerts its main influence on employment relations through its political role. Traditionally, industrial relations has been left to the employers and unions. However, during the 1970s new laws were introduced, constituting a new employment relations framework. These laws have dealt with issues such as industrial democracy, the work environment, security of employment, and union rights. They generally limit the rights of employers and strengthen those of employees and their unions. After the advances for unions in the 1970s, there was a period of employers' offensives in the 1980s and a dramatic rise in unemployment in the 1990s. These have contributed to a major setback in the status and influence of unions, as discussed later.

THE MAIN PROCESSES OF EMPLOYMENT RELATIONS

Every national union has its own statutes, including rules about how to enter into collective agreements. It is common practice that the right to conclude agreements is entrusted to a union's executive committee. A union may give its mandate to a central union council to bargain on its behalf. Central agreements, negotiated at the confederation level, were the general practice between 1956 and 1982. A central agreement was normally a recommendation that had to be endorsed by each participating union before it was binding.

The central agreements included a peace obligation, whereby the employers agreed to increase economic rewards in exchange for a guaranteed period of labour peace. Once an agreement was ratified, the detailed implementation was worked out through industry-wide and local agreements. Any disputes had to be referred to the central level rather than settled by industrial action.

Dispute settlement

The Swedish government plays only a limited role in settling disputes. The Swedes differentiate between 'interest' disputes and 'rights' disputes (see chapter 1). In the case of interest disputes, parties have the right to engage in industrial action after giving proper notice (usually a week). A small state agency provides mediation. However, the mediator has only an advisory role and there is no formal obligation for the parties to accept the mediator's proposal or to withdraw industrial action if requested by the mediator. In most years there are 30–40 cases of mediation. Parliament can in theory legislate to seek an end to an industrial dispute, but such action has been very unusual (Olsson 1990).

In the case of rights disputes, there should be no industrial action. Disputes about the interpretation of laws or agreements must be referred to the National Labour Court or, in some cases, to regional lower civil courts or magistrates. Verdicts of the lower courts may be appealed to the Labour Court, which is the final arbiter for all labour disputes. The Labour Court hears at most around 250 cases per year, including individual grievances. Unlike the position in most other countries, individual workers are usually precluded from making claims other than through a union.

The right to engage in industrial action includes lockouts as well as strikes. In addition, there are milder forms of industrial action, such as bans on overtime and new recruitment, as well as blacklisting of certain jobs. However, industrial action is allowed only when contracts have either expired or been properly terminated. Industrial action undertaken during a contract period is prohibited by law. Actions in support of other unions (secondary conflicts) are always allowed. If a union engages in an illegal strike, at either local or central level, the employer may sue the union for damages. To avoid responsibility for an illegal strike, union officials must actively discourage their members from taking part. Only in this way can they avoid being fined or sued for damages. Individual union members who take part in unlawful industrial action can also be fined by the Labour Court. These fines have traditionally been limited to a maximum of about $US23, but this has recently been raised to $US580.

Industrial and economic democracy

Industrial democracy is a broad term, which refers to the influence of employees on their working lives or, more precisely, *what and how they produce*. The debate in Sweden has concentrated on two areas: first, work organisation and the individual's influence over his or her job; second, union influence over top management decisions via collective bargaining and through representation on company boards (Schmidt 1976; Brulin 1995).

Towards the end of the 1960s, demands for increased employee influence were raised within the unions. The debate was influenced by the effects of technological change in the workplace, the growing awareness of work environment issues, health hazards, and the wave of radical political ideas that were current in Europe. Some union demands were heeded in the political arena and reforms were introduced (Olsen 1992).

The union strategy on industrial democracy can be summarised as follows. Mobilisation of interested members and union activists was achieved by focusing on problems of health and safety at work. This created a political climate in which laws and regulations in support of industrial democracy could be introduced. Accordingly, the industrial relations legislation was revised by the passing of an Act on Co-Determination at Work. These laws were supplemented by financial support for training and research which, to a large extent, was channelled through the unions.

The MBL prescribed that management should be a joint effort by capital and labour—that is, managers and union representatives (Sandberg et al. 1992). Both sides should have equal rights to information, which means that unions should be able to obtain all the relevant information available from the company. Further, MBL 1976 stipulates that management has to consult the unions before any decision is taken on major changes in the company (such changes ranging from reorganisation to the introduction of new technology). Although management is not obliged to reach agreement, it has to allow time for unions to investigate the matters being decided, and to consult at either local or central level before it implements decisions.

The introduction of the MBL and other laws that constituted the legal base for a reform of working life was very controversial in the 1970s. The employers strongly opposed most of the laws, and predicted that reforms would lead to inefficiency, raise costs and inhibit the decision making process. The employers also argued that this legislation would be preferable if it promoted *individual employee involvement*, rather than *union activity*. In spite of this resistance, the SAF reached a new basic agreement on efficiency and participation with the LO and the national unions of salaried employees in the private sector in 1982. This agreement was an attempt to implement MBL in the private sector by setting up a joint development council, which would promote efficiency and participation in individual firms. Significantly, this agreement provided for considerable adaptation, depending on local circumstances—for instance, in relation to technological change (Hammarström 1978b; Brulin & Nilsson 1991).

The legal reforms had limited impact. From the unions' perspective, there was a general feeling of disappointment about the reforms. They concluded that the reforms did not precipitate a significant change in the power situation at most workplaces. While the reforms were seen as a definite step forward, the step was too short and too slow for most union activists. However, MBL did lead to an improved provision of information by management to the local unions. Consultation by management with the unions before deciding on changes has become standard procedure.

Economic democracy was a dominant issue in the Swedish political debate, especially during the 1970s. The LO saw economic democracy as a necessary complement to the 'solidaristic' wages policy, whereby wages are related to the profits not in an individual company but in the economy as a whole. In view of the limitations of industrial democracy, the LO argued in favour of expanding workers' power through 'wage-earner funds'. Employees would exert more genuine influence, it was argued, if they were part-owners of their firms through the funds (Olsen 1992; Pontusson 1992).

The first radical proposal for wage-earner funds, the Meidner Plan, was adopted by the LO in 1976. It aimed, in the long run, to make the unions the majority shareholders in all major industries in Sweden. The proposal was for the compulsory issuing of new shares based on excess company profits. These shares would then be transferred to funds controlled by the unions. The logic of the policy also meant that less profitable firms would have automatic incentives to improve efficiency and to undergo structural change. Five regional wage-earner funds were established to operate in a similar manner to insurance companies and pension funds. There were few signs, however, of their precipitating a 'fundamental change of the economic system in the direction of state socialism', as had been predicted by earlier opponents of the funds. The funds were used for research and for incentives for savings. Following the defeat of the Social Democratic government in 1991, the incoming Conservative–Liberal coalition government abolished the wage-earner funds (Pontusson & Kuruvilla 1992). Despite the return of Social Democratic governments, the LO does not seem inclined to put this issue onto the agenda again.

CURRENT AND FUTURE ISSUES

The Swedish model worked well until the early 1970s, then came under increased strain (Huzzard 2000). The unions' radical demands for economic and industrial democracy met with strong employer resistance. The political and economic scene changed when 44 years of Social Democratic government ended in 1976. In common with other OECD countries, Sweden was then confronting considerable economic turbulence in the wake of the oil crisis. The employers felt that it was politically and economically necessary to fight back. The unions' demands for 'economic democracy' in the form of wage-earner funds were strongly opposed by the three Conservative-Liberal political parties and by the SAF, which has played an increasingly visible role in politics since the late 1970s. Current discussions on ownership have a rather different focus: at the central level, some union leaders have considered their members' pension funds and whether a more proactive union role in their administration might be a means of exerting greater union influence on the economy at the level of the firm.

Sweden experienced its largest industrial dispute in 1980. A strike was met by an employer lockout of 80 per cent of the workforce. The dispute was settled after two weeks on the basis of a mediated proposal. Some commentators claimed that this conflict symbolised the end of the Swedish model and its spirit of cooperation. The dispute symbolised the end of an era of relatively peaceful central collective bargaining. However, the Swedish model had never precluded the possibility of industrial disputes.

An important development is the move towards decentralised bargaining. Following the failure of their 1980 lockout, the private employers realised that such tactics would no longer be effective in opposing union power. The employers gradually adopted the view that wage solidarity had gone too far and that employers were losing ground within the central model. Therefore, they decided to break with centralised bargaining. The first step was in 1983, when the influential Engineering Employers' Association and its counterpart unions reached agreements outside of the central round of negotiations. Subsequently, the Engineering Employers' Confederation and the Metal Workers' Union continued to negotiate without the involvement of the SAF and LO. Increasingly, the other employers' associations and unions followed a similar strategy. By 1990 the SAF had decided that it would no longer take part in any central wage bargaining with the LO.

The industrial agreement

By the mid-1990s, the leaders of the employers and unions had come to the conclusion that Sweden's system of wage formation was increasingly unsustainable. The Swedish economy has historically been dependent on large firms trading in conditions of tough global competition. The perceived difficulty was the absence of any mechanisms for keeping labour costs in line with Sweden's international competitiveness. Accordingly, the government pressed the employers and unions to improve the collective bargaining process in an attempt to facilitate lower unemployment and stable prices and to boost competitiveness. In response, in 1996 a group of union leaders wrote an article in a national newspaper. Noting that a third of jobs in industry had disappeared in the 1990s, the authors of the article invited the employers to enter negotiations on a new agreement that embraced procedures for dialogue on industrial development as well as the more usual bargaining issues of distribution.

As a result of these initiatives, a new 'Agreement on Industrial Development and Wage Formation' was signed in 1997. Signatories included the SAF led by the Engineering Employers' Federation, the ALMEGA Industrial and Chemical Employers' Federation, six unions belonging to the LO, including 'Metall', as well as the industrial unions affiliated with the TCO and SACO. The agreement has been described as 'an entirely new model for collective bargaining and conflict resolution' (Elvander 2001). In effect, the agreement covers the entire competitive sector in the Swedish economy, comprising nineteen bargaining arenas, and aims to facilitate joint dialogue and consensus on Sweden's economic and to some extent political conditions for industrial enterprise and put distributional issues into such a context. This was supplemented by a subsidiary procedural agreement for collective bargaining and conflict resolution in the industrial sector, aimed at constructive negotiations that sought to avoid conflict. The agreement is overseen by a Joint Industry Committee consisting of equal numbers of representatives from both sides. An impartial chair is appointed jointly by the parties. An Economic Council for Industry, consisting of independent economists, has been set up that can make statements for the Joint Industry Committee, the chair or either party on request.

Each new agreement has a fixed time scale. Three months before the expiry of an agreement, negotiations commence on its successor. Claims are tabled, negotiations begin and the independent chair is appointed. One month before the expiry date, the chair takes an active role and can call for reports from the Economic Council and propose a draft agreement. At the expiry date, if no agreement is reached, either side may give fourteen days' notice of industrial action. In response, the chair is empowered either to postpone the dispute or to order the continuation of the former agreement. The intention is to establish a long duration for each agreement, typically at least three years. Two such agreements have been in force since the procedure began in 1997.

The dialogue on general conditions that precedes negotiations on the distributional aspects seeks consensus in a number of areas. These include competence development, research and development, and energy policy. Moreover, the routine application of the Industrial Agreement has been institutionalised through the appointment, by the Joint Industry Committee, of subcommittees that meet in between the bargaining rounds. These subcommittees discuss the economic and political context and conditions faced by Swedish industry as well as the procedural aspects of the agreement itself. Although differences between the parties remain, for example on issues associated with job security, the agreement is a very significant development.

Many so-called 'Cooperation Agreements' signed in sectors not covered by the Industrial Agreement in the mid-1990s (including central and local government) have also sought to introduce a two-stage process model whereby dialogue on the prerequisites for rewards distribution precedes negotiation on the bargain itself. Typically, a central framework is established for local-level (joint) activity. The role of the national unions is to encourage, train and diffuse best practice. However, it remains to be seen how robust such agreements are, given the attempts of the Swedish Municipal Workers' Union to take industrial action in spring 2003 in support of a pay rise before the expiry of the then prevailing agreement.

Employment relations at workplaces: 'boxing' and 'dancing'

One shortcoming of the Industrial Agreement is that the parties have yet to succeed in implementing the agreement at local levels. On the other hand, in many enterprises local bargaining shares many features of the emerging national procedures. Before beginning negotiations on distributional aspects, several employers and unions have established the practice of entering dialogue on the competitive conditions faced by the enterprise, as well as prerequisites for future development. As with the Industrial Agreement, local bargaining is a two-stage process. The first involves fostering social partnership on a broad range of enterprise issues. These typically include the core business, business development, training and possibly individual staff development among professional and white-collar staff.

In many cases, local negotiations occur in parallel with those being conducted centrally. The purpose of the latter is to provide a 'safety net' that can be applied if local-level agreement is not possible. The safety net may consist of a centrally agreed across-the-board rise or a 'lump sum' that the parties locally can then decide to distribute in ways they see fit. There is greater scope for individual negotiation and application of salary reviews for white-collar staff than there is for their blue-collar counterparts. Collective agreements generally apply to the latter.

During the 1990s the unions were engaged increasingly in various types of partnership at the local level (Nilsson 1999). Such partnership arrangements, characterised by attempts at consensus with the employers and the pursuit of mutual gains (Kochan & Osterman 1994), have been termed 'dancing'—as opposed to the practice of 'boxing' that better describes the more adversarial positional exchanges of traditional negotiation.

As early as the 1950s, forms of dancing could be seen at the shop floor, related to work rationalisation and the development of piece-rate systems (Johansson 1989). And during the 1970s, bipartite development projects were conducted in some workplaces, connected with the issue of co-determination (Sandberg et al. 1992). But in the 1990s the dancing between the unions and management developed in scope and deepened.

One feature that appears to characterise both the Industrial Agreement and the more recent developments at the local level described here is a prolonged and sometimes continuing dialogue on developmental issues and the prerequisites for pay determination. This engagement, a form of dancing, is seen by both sides as a means of curtailing lengthy episodes of 'boxing' and, at the same time, making less likely the possibility of subsequent disputes. There are a number of locally based dancing activities, ranging from more formalised agreements, including the centrally negotiated safety-net agreements, to informal arrangements based on mutual trust.

One union motive for dancing is the increasing importance being attached to production and development issues in union agendas (Huzzard 2000)—in particular, the aim of eliminating as many repetitive (short-cycle), high-strain jobs as possible. This is a central aspect of the unions' 'good work' policy. Boxing has not worked as a means of pursuing the policy. Another motive is the prospect of gaining an *earlier* influence in change processes. This is a particular aim of the various Cooperation Agreements of the mid-1990s.

The employers also see advantages in dancing. They can gain tactical advantages by establishing, centrally, rules for local conduct on company development, for example the Cooperation Agreements. Managing change is a key issue and this requires the development of new competencies, a process that is usually better facilitated by dancing than by boxing.

Mediation

The 1906 law on mediation in labour disputes continued to apply until 2000. After the 1980 dispute, there was a debate on the need to review the rules for settling disputes. The employers led the debate, claiming that the rules were outdated and favoured the union side. The political parties were concerned that the system did not prevent disputes and that the bargaining system did not operate as well as it used to in the 1950–70 period.

The 1990 recession led to severe strains on the collective bargaining system. The government attempted to prevent inflationary wage rises through special laws and by establishing a Negotiation Group during the 1991–93 period as a new basis of mediation.

It was, however, an initiative from the employers and unions in manufacturing industry that paved the way for a reform of the mediation system. The 1997 Industrial Agreement included new elements that also become part of the new law on mediation introduced in 2000. The new law on mediation replaced the old Office for Mediation and Conciliation with the National Mediation Office (NMO). The new rule on mediation is a supplement to the MBL legislation, and the NMO is regulated by an ordinance that supplements the 1977 Act.

The NMO has two functions: to mediate in labour disputes, and to promote an efficient pay determination process. The latter requires that the NMO keep in touch with the negotiating organisations, and keep track of possible disputes and when agreements expire. The NMO also has a responsibility to ensure that adequate statistical data on pay are available and to give guidance and information to the unions and employers' organisations on bargaining and collective agreements.

The law on mediation distinguishes between voluntary mediation and compulsory mediation. Voluntary mediation is performed when requested by the negotiation parties. The NMO may appoint one or two mediators to assist the parties in reaching an agreement. Should one of the parties oppose mediation, the NMO is prevented from appointing a mediator. If a dispute is initiated or if the NMO decides that there is a risk of industrial action, the NMO may appoint a mediator without the agreement of the parties concerned. In such a case the parties have an obligation to meet with the mediator, present their arguments and contribute to the settlement of the dispute. If a party fails to play a constructive role in the process, it runs the risk of having to pay a penalty. Mediators must also try to persuade the parties to postpone or cancel industrial action. If the mediator's recommendation is not observed, the mediator may ask the board of the NMO to order the parties concerned to postpone any action for up to fourteen days.

The NMO has a board of three people and a small administrative staff. There are no full-time mediators, but the NMO has a list of about 25 people willing to act as mediators on request. Most of these are senior government officers or retired leaders from labour market organisations. The role of the NMO does not significantly change the traditional system of free collective bargaining. The parties are not obliged to accept the proposals put forward by the mediator, and the right of industrial action remains unaffected by the 2000 law.

By mid-2001, one year after the new law came into force, around two-thirds of the labour market was covered by private mediation through collaborative agreements. This now applies to private manufacturing industry as well as local and state governments. Sectors covered by the new 2000 law on compulsory mediation include construction and retailing and several smaller sectors.

The experience drawn from the two wage rounds under the Industry Agreement (1998–2001 and 2001–04) and the first wage round under the 2000 Mediation Act is that it has generally been possible to reach agreements peacefully and in line with agreed wage targets. Mediators have been used in many sets of bargaining, and there seems to be wide acceptance of the proposals presented by both private and public mediators. By mid-2001 there had been no case of compulsory mediation.

The Confederation of Swedish Enterprise

In 2001, two employers' organisations, the SAF and the Federation of Swedish Industries (representing service employers and smaller businesses), ceased to exist, and the Confederation of Swedish Enterprise (SN) was born. Both had been established for around 100 years, but their boundaries had become less distinct. Accordingly, a unified central industry organisation was seen as appropriate. The formation of the new organisation also meant that the SN could become better at utilising its member companies' interests and avoiding duplication of work in certain areas.

The SN represents approximately 46 000 large and small member companies, which are organised in 52 sector and employer associations. The overall goals of the new organisation are the same as those of the old organisations: to create the best possible conditions for companies and business, to create the world's best business climate in Sweden, and to help the country once again hold a top position in the international prosperity league table. In turn, these goals cover such sub-goals as reduced taxation, improved education and research, internationalisation and reforming legislation. SN leaders also sought an efficient infrastructure, changed attitudes towards entrepreneurs and a relatively deregulated economy.

It was recognised that the SAF had not generally been a negotiating party in recent years, other than for certain agreements (e.g. service pensions and insurance agreements). On such specific matters, the SN assumed the SAF's earlier role on an 'as and when required' basis. Otherwise, the individual member associations continue to handle the central (sector) pay negotiations.

The SN's operations cover a broad field, and focus in particular on influencing opinion leaders, as well as the diffusion of knowledge, developing new ideas, and preparing proposals for the creation of a better business climate. Core target groups include its member organisations and individual companies, as well as journalists, the government, the parliament, ministries, agencies, the EU Commission, EU agencies and UNICE.

CONCLUSIONS

Employment relations in Sweden have passed through three broad stages since the 19th century. The first stage was from the beginning of the union movement in the 1890s to the mid-1930s. During this period the unions were established. The relationship between capital and labour was antagonistic, and there was a high level of industrial disputes. The government was either passive or supported the owners of capital.

The second stage lasted for most of the 44 years of Social Democratic government, from the mid-1930s to the early 1970s. The 'Swedish model' was established during this period, with a low level of industrial conflict, a 'solidaristic' wage policy, an active labour market policy and labour–management cooperation. An economic policy reliant on economic growth subsumed many of the pay-related problems for the unions and paved the way for a pattern of employment relations with few industrial disputes.

Emergence of a third stage can be traced to the 1970s. More radical union ambitions, the election of a non-socialist government in 1976, severe economic problems, and a strategy based on free enterprise and a market economy, on the employer side, represented significant changes. The 1980 dispute symbolised these developments. Wage-earner funds were introduced after a bitter conflict, but were not seen as a complete victory by the unions. The wage-earner fund system became a political burden for the Social Democratic Party and did not result in a basic change in Sweden's economic system. The employers tried to reverse the trends as much as was practicable. Their prime objective was to deregulate Sweden and facilitate more market influences. Their policy initiatives included fragmentation of the bargaining structures, more flexible working-time arrangements, profit sharing, and payment-by-results systems.

During the 1980s a new collective bargaining structure emerged. The centralised bargaining structure which had been dominant during the 1960s and 1970s was replaced by a more fragmented and decentralised bargaining structure. This development was led by the Engineering Employers' Association, despite opposition from most unions and some of the employers' organisations. The SAF's 1991 decision to withdraw from the central bargaining process marked the end of the bargaining pattern that had begun in 1956. The 1991–93 agreement was reached only after pressure from a special government commission. Since then, wage negotiations have taken place at industry level.

During the 1980s, the SAF withdrew from most of the cooperative institutions that had been established during earlier decades. Yet there were still some cooperative approaches that focused on work organisation, technological change and competence development. However, arrangements in the non-pay areas were hampered by disagreements between employers and unions about the locus of wage negotiations.

After the Social Democratic Party returned to government in 1982, the direction of economic policy changed. Devaluations led towards an expansionist, export-led recovery. This proved successful for a few years, but it delayed tougher structural decisions that the government was forced to make after 1989. Sweden subsequently reduced its budget deficit and restored balance to its foreign trade. The unemployment rate, which was already low by international standards, was cut to a very low level (1.2 per cent in mid-1989). The government gave high priority to measures to restructure industry and stimulate labour force flexibility. By 1990, however, fighting inflation had become the government's main priority, and unemployment grew dramatically during the early 1990s. It was not until the early 21st century that the unemployment was again cut to less than 4 per cent.

There was a slightly higher level of industrial disputes in the 1980s than in previous decades. A new element was that white-collar workers accounted for the majority of the working days lost in stoppages. White-collar unions, particularly those organising public-sector employees, were more often involved in industrial disputes. Groups that have participated in major disputes include nurses, fire-fighters and physicians. The involvement of public-sector employees in industrial conflict resulted in the government playing a larger role in industrial relations. However, the Social Democratic government did not attempt to change or interfere with the basic rules. Unions and employers still took primary responsibility for negotiating agreements and settling disputes.

Does the Swedish model still exist? This question has been debated on numerous occasions since the 1980 dispute. Several commentators announced the death of the model after this dispute. The model has changed, and employers are continuing to distance themselves from it. However, there are still basic common values between employees and employers. Both parties have a joint interest in efficiency and rationalisation of production and a commitment to take responsibility for industrial peace. This is illustrated by the 1997 Industrial Agreement and development in local cooperation—social partnership. The Swedish government, in turn, still accepts responsibility for an active labour market policy and gives high priority to maintaining relatively full employment.

One novel feature is the role of the employers. Through the 1980s and onwards, they were more interested in changing pay relativities and increasing pay differentials than in limiting total employment costs. This put pressure on governments to fight inflation without the support of the employers. Other new elements in employment relations are the increasing prominence of white-collar unions and the growth of the service sector. It is no longer possible for blue-collar unions to dominate the unions' agenda. The existence of more than one powerful union confederation complicates the employment relations system. The death of the SAF and birth of the SN, an employer organisation that has lobbying as its main duty, underlines the tendencies towards less centralised employment relations.

In 1994 Sweden joined the EU, and a debate on harmonisation of employment relations began. It is possible that employment relations in Sweden will move in a 'continental European' direction, which could lead to more fragmented bargaining structures, greater government intervention, and a consequent weakening of the unions (Higgins 1996).

A CHRONOLOGY OF SWEDISH EMPLOYMENT RELATIONS

1898	LO founded.
1902	SAF founded.
1906	December Compromise Agreement. Employers accept the right for workers to organise.
1909	General strike of 1909 followed by a severe decline in union membership.
1928	Establishment of Labour Court and a Collective Bargaining Act.
1936	Law regulates unfair dismissal for union activity and the social partners' rights to negotiate.
1938	SAF-LO Basic Agreement at Saltsjöbaden, which sets a cooperative 'spirit' for labour relations.
1944	TCO founded.
1946	SAF-LO-TCO Works Councils Agreement revised in 1966 and ended in 1977 by MBL.
1956	Beginning of LO-SAF central bargaining.
1971	LO and TCO adopt policies for industrial democracy.
1972	LO-SAF Rationalisation Agreement on productivity, job satisfaction and job security.
1973	Initial law on board representation for local unions.
1974	Law makes it difficult to dismiss employees, and for companies to hire workers on probation without union approval. Law gives local union representatives time off for union work with pay.
1975	The wage-earner funds debate begins. Law to give employees educational leave.
1976	Non-socialist coalition government replaces the Social Democratic Party.
1977	Co-Determination at Work Act (MBL) implemented.
1980	Lockout/strike throughout most of the private sector. Largest labour market conflict.
1981	LO and Social Democratic Party congresses approve principles for wage-earner funds.
1982	Social Democratic Party re-elected. SAF-LO-PTK Agreement on Efficiency and Participation.
1983	Wage-earner funds implemented. Industry-wide bargaining replaces the 1956–83 centralised pattern.
1984	Government initiative to introduce new three-party model for central wage fixation based on 'social contract'.
1986	Major public-sector conflict leads to a break-up of a traditional, rigid wage structure in the public sector.

1989	New leadership in SAF seeking a final breakaway from centralised wage formation models.
1990	SAF decides that it will no longer take part in wage bargaining. A new form of wage commission (*Rehnberg-gruppen*) manages to establish a two-year wage agreement covering almost the entire labour market.
1991	SAF decides that it will no longer nominate representatives to decision-making state authorities, including the Labour Market Board (AMS). Change of government to a four-party Conservative–Liberal coalition.
1992	The new government changes the composition of boards and statutory organisations; representatives from union and employer groups are replaced by members of parliament and independent experts. Changes in the industrial relations laws to meet employer demands.
1993	Unemployment reaches a record high level for the post-1945 period.
1994	Election of a Social Democratic government. Re-establishment of industrial relations rules that applied before 1992. Entry by Sweden into the European Union.
1995	Major reforms of the social welfare system; reduced levels of compensation in several benefits, from the traditional 90 per cent of earnings, to between 75 and 85 per cent of earnings.
1996	Major reductions in employment in the public sector. Strict budget restrictions in the public sector.
1996–97	Policy oriented towards small and medium-sized companies.
1997–2001	Several national agreements on social partnerships concluded.
1997	Agreement on Industrial Development and Wage formation is signed.
1998	The Social Democratic Party forms a new government.
2000	The Law of Mediation is enacted and the National Mediation Office (Medlingsinstitutet) is founded.
2001	SAF ceases to exist and the Confederation of Swedish Enterprise (SN) is born.
2002	The Swedish Municipal Workers' Union seeks to renegotiate its three-year agreement before its expiry date.

Chapter 10

EMPLOYMENT RELATIONS IN JAPAN

Yasuo Kuwahara

This chapter starts by putting Japanese industrial relations into context, sketches some historical background, then discusses the changing roles of unions and employers and the Japanese approach to collective bargaining and labour–management consultation. The issues discussed include: changing aspects of job security, inflexibilities in matching unemployed with the available employment opportunities, foreign workers, and technological change.

With its population of 127 million people and a GDP of $4765 billion (see Appendix), Japan is the second-largest economy of the ten countries discussed in this book (the USA is the largest). Since the early 1990s, the Japanese economy has endured a period of economic downturn and low economic growth. This poor economic performance is often referred to as 'the lost 1990s'. In 1998, financial collapse and other adverse factors caused economic growth in Japan to fall to minus 0.7 per cent over the previous year. This was the second time that the Japanese economy had a negative growth over the previous year in the postwar period. Japan faces a difficult task to improve its economy in the face of increasing global competition.

Japan has a labour force of 68 million; the labour force participation rate was 73 per cent in 2000. Some 83 per cent of the labour force are employees. Japan's labour force in 2000 grew by 1 million over 1995, with the number of job-holders dropping by 110 000. In 2000, about 7 per cent of the labour force worked in primary industries, including agriculture and fisheries. Manufacturing, mining and construction industries employed 33 per cent, while 60 per cent worked in the tertiary industries, including services, wholesale and retail, finance, utilities and government.

In many respects Japan appears to be different from most other countries. On average, the Japanese enjoy the longest life span (85 years for women and 78 years for men in 2000). It is estimated that the Japanese ageing ratio (the total of people 65 years old and over divided by the total population) will be the highest among the major DMEs by the year 2025 (Kosei-Rodosho 1989). The structure of Japan's population will change substantially from the pyramid shape of the 1950s to a top-heavy shape by 2025. Population ageing is a serious issue on both the supply and demand sides of the Japanese economy.

There has been a remarkable change in the labour market. Unemployment was about 1.1 per cent at the end of the 1960s, when the economy enjoyed high growth. The unemployment rate, one of the lowest of the ten countries until mid-1990s, rose to 3.4 per cent in 1997 and 5.0 per cent in November 2001, the highest in postwar Japanese history. Discouraged by the deteriorating employment conditions, many elderly workers have given up searching for jobs, and an increasing number of young people are unable to find career positions that match their expectations. On the other hand, a few firms in IT industries and low-wage firms in manufacturing and services find it difficult to hire workers.

Another indicator of the labour market—that is, the ratio of job openings to job-seekers (for regular workers)—fell from 1.51 in 1990 to 0.64 in 2000, aggravating the disparity between jobs and job-seeker profiles. The yearly average for 2001 was 0.59. The ratio of 1.0 may be taken as a sort of labour market equilibrium. The ratio was above 1.0 in 1967–74, peaking at 1.76 in 1973. Then the labour market balance collapsed, and fluctuated around 0.6 between 1975 and 1987. It rose above 1.0 again in 1988–92, peaking at 1.40 in 1990–91. Since then, the ratio has remained low, at slightly above 0.5.

This ratio indicates the difficult position of older workers. In 2000, the ratio was favourable for young workers below nineteen years of age (2.31) and for the prime-age workers in the age ranges of 35–39 and 40–44 (1.17 and 1.04 respectively), while it was very low for workers of over 45 years (below 0.5).

A significant feature of the post-1945 period has been a reduction in the number of working hours. In the prewar period, twelve-hour workdays were common. The number of hours per day was cut substantially. However, when the slow growth period started, hours declined further to around 2100 hours per year. By the start of the 21st century, a reduction in legal working hours and a boom in part-time work had pushed this figure down to 1853 at enterprises employing more than five people. Although Japanese working hours are shorter than those in the USA, the Japanese still tend to work more hours than Europeans.

The post-1945 period has seen Japanese politics dominated by the conservative Liberal Democratic Party (LDP). Opposition parties have exerted influence from time to time; however, apart from a brief period after the war, none obtained enough power to hold office in national politics. In this context, a remarkable change occurred in the election of the House of Councillors (*Sangiin*) in 1989, when the Japan Socialist Party (JSP) and other opposition parties won more seats than the LDP. However, in the more important House of Representatives (*Shugiin*), the LDP maintained its majority. Both the LDP and JSP substantially increased their numbers at the 1990 elections, at the expense of the other parties. In the election of July 1993 the JSP had a historic victory, when the leftist and rightest factions integrated. The LDP, the JSP and the *Sakigake* (Harbinger) Party formed a coalition cabinet. While a leader of the JSP initially became prime minister, this position was assumed by Ryutaro Hashimoto from the LDP in January 1996—in the same month the JSP changed its name to the Social Democratic Party of Japan (SDP).

Depending on their dominant ideology, unions are associated with various parties, including the SDP (formally JSP), the Democratic Socialist Party (DSP) and the Japan Communist Party (JCP). Successful candidates from these parties may be recommended or supported by a union, or may have been associated with a union in the past. Despite these relationships between parties and unions, rank-and-file members of unions tend to vote for candidates of their choice. A recent notable change has been the increase in voters who do not adhere to particular parties. As a result, the influence of unions on voters has clearly declined.

Changes in politics have been dramatic. In April 2000, following the hospitalisation of Prime Minister Obuchi Keizo, who later died, Mori Yoshiro of the LDP established his first Cabinet, a coalition government of the LDP, New Komeito and Hoshuto (New Conservative Party), which split from the Liberal Party. In the June 2000 general election the LDP secured a majority and, following the resignation of the first Cabinet, the second Mori government was formed. However, this Cabinet was unpopular among the voters and dissolved itself. At the election in July 2001, the LDP, led by Junichiro Koizumi, won a significant victory. Koizumi emerged as a leader in a very short period.

Koizumi has inherited the Mori cabinet with a high level of support. His popularity decreased in 2002, however, due to his political mis-handlings of the conflicts between the minister of foreign affairs and the bureaucrats of the ministry.

THE 'JAPANESE' MODEL

Given the continued stagnation of its economy, is the Japanese model of employment relations still viable? Since the mid-1970s, Japan has attracted much attention for its favourable economic performance and its 'cooperative' approaches to employment relations, which have allegedly supported this economic performance. The international interest in Japanese management and industrial relations was perplex-ing to Japanese people, as throughout the 20th century Japan has tried to follow models derived from the West (e.g. Britain, the USA and Germany). Before the 1973 oil crisis, the Japanese tended to see such countries as much more advanced, so that various management tech-niques and technologies were imported from them.

Because some of the Western countries that had once led Japan in economic prosperity had sluggish economies for some time, some of these countries lost their legitimacy as models. Moreover, when the former models went looking for a new model themselves, ironically, Japan was often the source of inspiration, as the Japanese economy seemed to be a success story. Although the interest in Japan waned after the failure of its economy in the post-bubble period of the early 1990s, a few coun-tries in Asia are still eager to 'import' the 'Japanese' model. In the current adversarial economic climate, management systems of some Japanese companies (e.g. Toyota, Honda, Sony) have been refined so as to survive in competitive world markets. Not only these large companies but also many smaller companies are shifting their production bases to other Asian countries, including China. To what extent are Japanese production and employment relations systems transferable to other countries?

To begin to answer such a question, some historical background is required. Japan's feudal era ended with the Meiji Restoration of 1868. Hitherto, Japan had had little contact with Western countries. Industri-alisation began in the following decade, a century later than in Britain. Japan's early factories in major industries were begun by the state, but in 1880s it sold most of them to a few selected families. These were the origin of what later became the powerful *zaibatsu* groups of holding companies, which were based on these groups' commercial banks.

Although some unions, such as those covering printers and iron-workers, began during this period, the familial basis of industrialisation continued well into the 20th century. Many factories had their own dormitories, especially in the textiles industry. In many industries they had master workers (*oyakata*), who were subcontractors, like the early British foremen. After World War I there was an acute shortage of skilled workers. Firms wanted to recruit workers directly. Hence, many large enterprises intervened in the *oyakata*'s prerogative to recruit. With the rapid development of industries, the system of skills formation through apprenticeship was absorbed into internal training within enterprises.

As the paternalistic tradition developed in the 1920s and 1930s, the unions did not exert much sustained influence. In the face of pressure from a militaristic regime, unions were dissolved between 1938 and 1943 and the employers' associations were absorbed into the mobilisation for war production.

After Japan's unconditional surrender in 1945, the Allied powers' General Headquarters (GHQ) sought to reshape the organisation of work and employment relations as part of the postwar reconstruction. The main elements of the present model, then, were established after the war under American influence.

Employees and unions

The Japanese labour movement developed rapidly under GHQ's democratisation program. Although much of Japan's industrial base was destroyed during the war, only four months after its end union membership had reached prewar levels, and by 1949 there were 6.6 million union members, a peak density level of 56 per cent. There were, nevertheless, some setbacks for the unions. For instance, their plans to hold a general strike in 1947 were suspended by order of GHQ. But the unions continued to grow, and recorded a peak membership, in terms of absolute numbers, of 12.6 million members in 1975, a density of 34 per cent.

After this peak, membership and density of union organisation stagnated. By the start of the 21st century, membership density had declined to its lowest level, of around 22 per cent. The total number of union members was about 11.5 million, a decline from a peak of 12.7 million in 1993. One of the main causes of this decline was the change in industrial structure, especially the shift towards the service sector. Union density varies by industry. The industry average was 22 per cent in 2000, but it was 62 per cent in civil services, and 56 per cent in public utilities such as electricity, gas and water. By contrast, union density in wholesale, retail and restaurants was only 9 per cent. There are very few unions in enterprises that have fewer than 30 employees. Union density in these SMEs is below 10 per cent.

During the decade after the 1973 oil crisis, there was substantial rationalisation in the highly unionised manufacturing sector. As most larger establishments adopt union shop clauses, union membership varies with the rise and fall of the unionised firms or industries. When the firm is expanding, union membership generally rises and vice versa. Although there has been a rise in the number of employees in the service sector, the average size of enterprises (in terms of employment) in the service sector tends to be relatively small, and it is generally more difficult and costly for unions to organise SMEs than large enterprises. Smaller ones tend to employ more contingent workers, who are usually not interested in unions.

Another cause of union decline has been the general improvement in living standards, which has tended to make employees less enthusiastic about union activities. Pay rises fluctuate according to prevailing macroeconomic conditions. The next year's rises tend to be lower when the economy is in a recession. Since the peak in 1990, when the pay rise in the central negotiations was 5.9 per cent, such pay rises have been minimal. These unfavourable outcomes might have discouraged workers' interest in unions. Thus, it is widely believed that unions have outlived their usefulness, and that the centralised mode of wage negotiations is outmoded.

Although the level of unemployment in Japan has remained lower than in most Western countries, it has more than doubled since 1970. In the recession after the 1973 oil crisis, many companies adopted a tougher stance towards unions, claiming public support for such policies. Employees have become more concerned about the competitive position of the companies for which they work, and most seem to have a high degree of commitment to the enterprise.

This reflects their expectation of 'lifetime employment' and seniority-based wages; such practices were consolidated after World War II. Permanent manual and non-manual staff are employed not for specific jobs or occupations but as company employees. Companies prefer to employ new school leavers or university graduates rather than experienced workers who have been trained in other firms. Their induction program is designed to encourage them to conform to the company's norms.

Young recruits start at a comparatively low level of pay, which is based on their educational qualifications. Their pay rises in proportion to their length of service in the enterprise. Promotion is largely based on length of service, which is assumed to correlate with the employee's level of skill developed within the enterprise. Therefore, it is disadvantageous for workers to change employers and for employers to lay off employees who have accumulated specific skills required in that particular enterprise. Typically, in the so-called primary labour market, comprising permanent or regular employees working for large enterprises, there is a tacit understanding about the long-term commitment between employer and employee. However, this is not confirmed in a written contract. Although the length of service among female workers is steadily increasing, 'lifetime employment' generally applies to male rather than female workers.

Most unions in Japan are organised not by occupation or by job but by enterprise or establishment. An enterprise union consists solely of regular employees of a single company, regardless of their occupational status up to lower management levels. As enterprise unions usually include both blue-collar and white-collar workers as members, the union density among white-collar workers is relatively high. These employees are expected to stay in the same company until their mandatory retirement age, unless they are made redundant or leave voluntarily (both acts being less usual than in most Western countries).

An increasing number of companies have extended the retirement age from 55 to 60 years, in accordance with the lengthening average life span of the Japanese, while adjusting age-wage profiles of employees not to give an automatic pay rise with length of service. By 2000, about 99 per cent of enterprises had adopted a retirement age of 60 years of age or over. Many workers remain in work even after reaching their mandatory retirement age. They find other jobs in subsidiaries or similar enterprises by recommendation of the parent companies, or they start small businesses by investing their retirement allowances and other financial resources. However, the number of retirements grew in the long-continued recession of the 1990s.

The primary core of regular employees constitutes only about one-third of all employees. This is an estimate of the proportion of employees working in the public sector (civil servants) and in large enterprises compared with the total number of employees, including those who work for SMEs. Regular employees with longer job tenure are typically found in the primary labour markets, where large organisations operate. Many of the remaining two-thirds of the labour force work for SMEs, or on a temporary or part-time basis, and are often not union members.

Therefore, union density among women, who constitute the majority of part-time workers, is lower than among male employees. The density is generally low in SMEs. However, in SMEs that are stable or expanding, there are many regular employees who stay in the same company for most of their working lives. In practice, therefore, it is difficult to make a precise distinction between the primary and secondary labour markets in Japan. The prevalence of SMEs is a notable factor in maintaining flexibility in the Japanese labour market.

As enterprise unions include non-manual staff and manual workers of the same enterprise, a worker leaving the company automatically loses union membership. The same is true for employees promoted to managerial positions. In spite of its name, an enterprise union functions not only for the benefit of the enterprise: it has legal protection against employer interference into its affairs and from other unfair labour practices.

Many enterprise unions grew sporadically in the period of turmoil after 1945. Some of them developed from the factory- and company-based wartime production committees. As most Japanese unions are organised for whole enterprises or individual plants, there are many unions—more than 68 737, according to one estimate (Rodosho 2001). About 97 per cent of enterprise union members work in firms employing more than 100 employees. Although there are other types of union organisations, such as industrial, craft and general unions, these are exceptions. *Kaiin*, the Seamen's Union, is a rare example of an industrial union.

Most enterprise unions within the same industry join an industrial federation of unions. There are more than 100 such federations. The major functions of the industrial federations include coordinating the activities of the member enterprise unions with the aim of improving wages and working conditions; dealing with problems common to a whole industry; guiding and assisting member unions in specific disputes; and political lobbying in the interest of workers. These industrial federations themselves belong to national centres, of which *Rengo* (JTUC, Japan Trade Union Confederation) is the largest.

After the two oil crises of the 1970s, unions at industrial and national levels led what they called a 'policy-oriented struggle', with the aim of ensuring stable employment and maintaining their members' standards of living. Another movement 'to unite the labour front under the initiative of private sector unions' emerged in 1982—*Zenminrokyo*, the Japanese Private Sector Union Council. It was formed by the labour federations in the private sector and reflected their enthusiasm for further unification to increase their strength. This organisation developed into a larger union centre, *Rengo*, which integrated the public-sector unions. The new *Rengo* was established in 1989, when it had 78 industrial federations with nearly 8 million members. Public-sector unions used to have more power than those in the private sector. But, in general, union membership has fallen since 1978, and certain unions in the private sector are also powerful.

Rengo has pursued cooperative labour–management relations. In terms of politics, it supported the establishment of a coalition cabinet in 1994 and sought to form an expanded liberal democratic league. However, it has had to endure the fragmentation of the political parties. Unions have been regarded as a source of voters for the new political parties. The defeat of the Social Democrat Party (the former JSP) has aggravated the situation. *Rengo*, which is an association of enterprise unions and their umbrella organisations, has found it difficult to represent the interests of union members at the grassroots level. And although *Rengo* has focused on political campaigns, these have further widened the gap between union leaders and members. The structure of *Rengo* has been seriously challenged by the unfavourable economic climate, high unemployment, university graduates' difficulties finding employment, and the restructuring of industries and enterprises.

Although the national confederations play important roles, the enterprise unions have more resources and are more powerful. The latter are autonomous in running their organisations and in promoting their members' interests. Furthermore, they are financially independent and self-supporting. Most union activities occur at the enterprise level, rather than at federation level. As the company's success greatly influences members' working conditions and employment opportunities, enterprise unions generally have a cooperative attitude towards management. Employees generally identify with their employer in making decisions that would enhance the employer's competitiveness. Thus, a key aspect of the work environment in Japanese companies is this interdependence and the belief that the company is a 'community of shared fate', where 'everyone is in the same big family'. In addition, the relatively modest wage differentials between managers, white-collar workers and blue-collar workers tends to reinforce the workers' sense of identification with the enterprise. This contrasts with some Western countries, where there is a more rigid class differentiation and much greater wage differentials.

Are enterprise unions really independent of the control of the employer? If a company is unionised, the enterprise union is usually the only organisation that is recognised as representing the employees at the enterprise. Employers usually offer various facilities to the union, including an office, but such facilities are offered on a voluntary basis after negotiations between the parties. To a certain extent, the availability of these facilities helps establish a basis for cooperative labour–management relations in enterprises.

It is generally believed that an advantage of enterprise unionism lies in its policies being adapted to each enterprise, rather than reflecting any broader craft, ideological or political issues. Employment relations based on enterprise unionism tend to be more flexible than those based on, for example, craft unionism. On the other hand, there are disadvantages from a union's point of view. Newly employed workers automatically acquire union membership and their union dues are 'checked off' from their pay automatically, thus their 'union consciousness' is generally less than their 'enterprise consciousness'. Union membership usually ceases on retirement, which also reduces the workers' commitment to the union.

Furthermore, a serious barrier to unionisation is that membership of an enterprise union is usually limited to those who are regular employees, or core workers. Non-regular employees such as part-time workers seasonal workers and immigrant workers are usually not organised by unions. Some part-time workers are unionised (mainly in the retail sector), but the percentage is low. Although some new types of unions for female workers are emerging, they are exceptions. During the recession, in an effort to reduce surplus workers, companies specifically designated middle-aged and older employees for redundancy. Such employees had already retired from unions after becoming managers, so they cannot gain support from the unions in their efforts to keep their jobs. Some unions are emerging for managers, although they are still on the periphery of the established unions.

Employers and their organisations

During the period immediately after 1945, there were many violent labour disputes in Japan. These tended to reflect the economic disorder and the shortage of food and daily necessities. Neither employers nor workers then had much industrial relations experience. To cope with this labour offensive and to establish industrial peace and order, employers organised regional and industrial associations. However, partly because of the so-called 'democratisation' policy of GHQ, employers were often obliged to yield to union pressure, thus facing an erosion of their managerial prerogatives.

Although most bargaining takes place at the enterprise level, some industries engage in collective bargaining at the industry level in parallel with the enterprise level—for example, in private railways, bus services and textiles.

Nikkeiren, the Japan Federation of Employers' Associations, was founded in 1948. It is the most important employers' organisation from an industrial relations point of view, and has many functions. It coordinates and publicises employers' opinions on labour problems, selects employer representatives to the various government commissions, councils and International Labour Organisation (ILO) delegations, and provides its member organisations with advice and services on labour conditions and employment practices. *Nikkeiren*'s members include employers' associations organised at regional and industry level. Every year at the time of *Shunto*, the Spring Labour Offensive, *Nikkeiren* releases guidelines for employers to follow when dealing with demands from the various unions during collective bargaining. Thus, although many of them do not have a direct role in bargaining, the employers' associations seem to have an important role behind the scenes (Levine 1984: 318ff).

Three factors strongly influence the magnitude of *Shunto*: (a) demand and supply conditions in labour markets; (b) consumer price levels; and (c) business conditions (a company's performance) (Ministry of Labour 1975). The main determinant of the outcome of collective bargaining is a shifting towards the individual company's business performance. As compared with the declining power of unions, employers have increased their influence over employees. Many large enterprises, for example in the automobile, electrical machineries, construction and banking sectors, have planned downsizing, which was rare in the past. Nevertheless, most unions are relatively quiet.

Employee-managed firms?

The structure of Japanese companies, particularly the large ones, is quite different from the structures found in most North American and European companies. The corporate structure of large Japanese companies may be closer to a model of 'employee-managed firms', unlike large companies in Western—particularly Anglo-American—countries, which are often characterised as 'shareholders' prerogative firms'. The structural characteristics of Japanese companies should not be seen as barriers to international competition; the Japanese corporate system is legitimate, even though it is different.

The literature on employee-managed firms usually distinguishes them from other firms by assuming that they have a distinct functional objective. It is assumed that employee-managed, or *Illyria*, firms seek to maximise the dividend or net income per worker, while capitalist firms seek to maximise total profit (Ward 1958).

In addition, an employee-managed firm implies a type of participatory management. Although various definitions could be formulated, a generally acceptable one would be that an employee-managed firm is a productive enterprise whose ultimate decision making rights are held by member-workers on an equal basis, regardless of job, skills grade or capital contribution. Using this definition, the typical Japanese firm might be called 'quasi-employee-managed', even if, strictly speaking, it is not managed by all the workers. Although board directors are not officially elected or nominated by employees through a system of voting, most directors are ex-employees. They are recommended as candidates for a directorship to the shareholders' meeting by the president, who has usually been promoted from within. Thus, most decisions are executed by board directors promoted from within the same corporation. Independent directors representing large shareholders such as banks, insurance companies and parent companies are also included as members of the board when the company is a subsidiary or is financially supported by the parent company, banks or insurance companies.

Directors are usually promoted from among the senior managers, who have worked for the company for a long time, often 25–30 years, after graduating from university or high school. Some of these people were leaders of enterprise unions when they were rank-and-file employees. Many employees that have been promoted to supervisory and/or managerial positions were previously union members. When promoted from senior managerial positions to board directors, individuals are asked to adopt a different role, as members of the senior executive. However, this change takes place on a continuum from being an employee to being a top manager. Directors that have been promoted internally after a long career might be expected to place the interests of the enterprise community, consisting of executive members and employees, above the interests of shareholders. Even if there are few independent directors, however, the interests of large shareholders are rarely neglected, and senior executives, such as the CEO, generally consult them before making important decisions. Larger shareholders are generally more interested in capital gain than in increasing dividends.

As internal promotion is the usual path for advancement, most employees have a strong commitment to the firm. In Japanese companies, the word *shain* is often used. (It literally means 'member of the company'.) This word contains nuances that do not have an equivalent in Western terminology. It means more than a mere hired worker, and implies belonging to a community formed by people with the same interests.

Substantial changes are developing in Japanese corporate governance with the recession that has continued for many years. Some advocate that Japanese companies should transform themselves into a more shareholder-based corporate governance. Some changes following this direction were introduced in the recent revision of company law and governance. For example, a revision of company law was proposed to the Diet in 2002 that obliges about 10 000 large companies to have at least one outside director. Japanese companies are in the midst of developing a new governance system, different from that of US and European companies. There were revisions of company law in 2001 and 2002. One of the most remarkable changes was the introduction of committees in companies, that is a committee for nominating director candidates, an audit committee and a directors' remuneration committee, which would also nominate officers who are responsible for particular aspects of the business. This organisation is similar to the American model. Large companies can choose either this new model or the traditional Japanese model. (In 2003, Matsushita and Toyota decided to introduce a slightly modified version of the Japanese model.) The outcomes are not yet clear. It is difficult to transform corporate governance so quickly, as the system has a long history.

In quasi-employee-managed enterprises, employees participate in the various stages of the decision making process. Small-group activities such as quality control circles (QCC) or total quality control (TQC) are widespread. With a reduction in the degree of explicit industrial conflict and the increasing development of 'internal labour markets', the difference between collective bargaining and joint consultation is becoming blurred.

Most blue-collar workers as well as white-collar workers are paid on a monthly basis. Performance-related remuneration is important. In addition to their regular pay, most Japanese workers receive two large seasonal payments, worth about 2.8 months' salary a year. Stable industries, such as public utilities, pay bonuses worth about 4.4 months' salary a year, while competitive industries such as wholesale, retail and restaurants pay about 2.4 months' salary a year. This practice originated from the employers' consideration of the extra expenditure required for the Buddhist 'bon festival', a kind of ancestor worship ritual observed in summer, and for the end-of-year and New Year celebrations. The amount of the payment fluctuates according to the performance of the company or industry and according to the merit of employees. However, it does not fluctuate a great deal, and workers assume that the payments are an integral part of their annual income. Despite the relative stability of the amount, employees do relate any small changes to variations in the company's profit. This increases employees' interest in the operation and performance of the company for which they work. The bonus system has attracted the interest of some Western economists as an effective measure to combat stagflation. One school of thought regarded bonuses as a form of profit sharing between the firm and its workforce (Weitzman 1984). Other studies have not always supported Weitzman's view. According to others, the bonus is a mixture of: (a) a disguised form of regular pay, (b) a means of compensating effort, (c) a type of profit sharing, and (d) the workers' share of investments in firm-specific human capital. The size of the bonus has gradually reduced since the business climate deteriorated in the 1990s.

Collective bargaining

Pay agreements may be concluded separately from agreements on other matters. Most unions conduct pay negotiations during *Shunto* in April and May each year, while negotiations on more comprehensive labour agreements may be conducted at other times. However, an increasing number of unions also make other claims during the *Shunto*—for example, for rises in overtime rates, revisions of allowances, shorter working hours, raising the retirement age and expanding private pensions. A decline in union density and a sluggish economic climate have helped change the characteristics of the *Shunto*. Its relative importance in national wage bargaining has declined, with the locus of wage bargaining shifting towards the enterprise level. Increasing differences in the profitability of enterprises, reflecting increased global competition, have been a major cause of this change.

The structure of enterprise unions usually corresponds to the organisation of the enterprise and its establishment, department or divisional groupings. Grievances are often settled informally, with formal procedures rarely used. Managers often attempt to subdue tensions and conflict and to reinforce a feeling of community. Despite this context, there were many large-scale and long disputes in mining and major manufacturing industries in the 1940s and 1950s. Some strikes were led by radical, leftist leaders. Many of these disputes left wounds in employment relationships that were not easily healed.

Such disputes taught the unions and employers some important lessons. Although there were many stoppages in 1974, there was a substantial reduction subsequently. Disputes are usually settled directly between the parties concerned, but sometimes a third party conciliates. Conciliation machinery for the private and public sectors is provided by the central and local labour relations commissions. Special commissions act for public-sector employees and for seamen. Nearly all the disputes brought before these commissions are settled either by conciliation or mediation; few disputes go as far as arbitration. Most disputes presented to the labour relations commissions are those which go beyond the limits of labour–management relations at the enterprise level. The relative importance of the commissions has declined, as there has been an improvement in cooperation between labour and management at the enterprise level.

Contemporary Japanese employment relations are relatively stable, and relations between the parties can generally be characterised as cooperative. Some see this in a positive light. Others have a more negative view, arguing that enterprise unions are too dependent on employers, and that the relationship is one of collaboration and incorporation. However, enterprise unions may be more appropriate than occupationally based unions in 'quasi-employee-managed firms', in terms of decision making and in fostering workplace democracy and employee morale. It is open to question to what extent Japanese firms fulfill this description; the pursuit of company profits tends to come before consideration of the individual employee.

Unions represent sectional interests, and enterprise unions are no exception. As many employees expect to work for many years for the same enterprise, they tend to place considerable emphasis on the improvement of their own working conditions, and do not pay as much attention to the interests of the temporary workers at the same establishment. This may be an unfortunate characteristic of quasi-employee-managed firms, where regular employees want to maintain their positions even at the expense of non-regular employees, such as part-time workers, and temporary workers, who are disproportionately likely to be women.

Why has the relationship between unions and employers changed so fundamentally since the 1950s? There has been increased global competition, improved standards of living, a shift towards a service-oriented economy, and public opinion is more conservative than it was in the 1950s. The 1970s' oil crises further accelerated the trend in this direction. Despite the long recession since the early 1990s, the number of industrial disputes has shown little sign of increasing. In 1975, the total number of industrial disputes recorded a peak of 8435. However, there were only 1102 in 2000. Where has all the discontent about redundancies during the recession gone? One of the remarkable changes is that the weight of disputes is shifting from the collective to the individual. There have also been higher levels of labour turnover. These developments represent challenges to unions as well as the employment relations system. Can they properly respond to these challenges?

CURRENT ISSUES

The Japanese economy is facing its most difficult period since the postwar era. Except for a few exceptional periods, the Japanese economy since the war has grown at an extremely steady pace. Negative growth was recorded in 1974 in the first oil crisis, and 1998 turned out to be a negative year. The high levels of unemployment make the picture rather gloomy. Having known only steady growth, Japanese leaders may understand what needs to be done, but taking the necessary action will prove extremely difficult. Japan's economy is too large to change quickly.

In 1999, however, advisers to the prime minister issued a ten-year economic plan outlining the ideal economic society and policies for economic rebirth. They proposed that the value from knowledge and intelligence become the source of strength to take Japan into the age of wisdom. They also forecast that Japan has a latent economic growth rate of about 2 per cent. So, while there are problems, the future is not all gloomy.

The social and economic environment in Japan is still changing rapidly. There is an ageing population, an increasing proportion of highly educated workers, growing participation by women in the labour market, increased immigration of foreign workers, and moves towards an 'information society'. One impact of globalisation is that in several sectors Japanese economic prowess is increasingly being challenged by competition from other countries.

A major issue is the appreciation and volatility of the yen, which has induced changes in product and labour markets. In 1980 the rate was

227 yen to the US dollar, but by 1995 this had fallen to 94 yen per US dollar. The rate rebounded to 131 yen in 1998, and fell to 108 yen in 2000. By 2002 the rate bounced to about 130 yen, but it fell to 117 yen in 2003. To cope with the difficulties caused by the volatility of the yen, many Japanese firms shifted their production bases to other Asian countries, particularly China. The major reason for shifting production to China is the wide difference in labour costs. According to the White Paper on Trade in 2001, the yearly average wage in China in 1999 was $US1008, while that in Japan was $US37259 (Keizai-Sangyo Sho 2001). Japan's average manufacturing wage is approximately 30 times higher than that of China.

Thus, the overseas production activities by Japanese firms have substantially expanded since the 1980s. Sales of Japanese manufacturing firms operating abroad exceed exports. These Japanese firms employ about 2.9 million workers abroad, which amounts to a quarter of domestic employment in the manufacturing sector (Fukao 2002).

Another consequence of globalisation has been the rise in migrant workers, attracted to Japan by high wages. Although the value of the yen has fallen, there has been little change in the trend of foreign direct investment and immigration.

Globalisation has affected many industries. This has been particularly apparent in the finance, communication and service sectors. An example is the remarkable development of the information and communication industries. Japan is not behind, compared with other advanced countries, in the diffusion of IT (Kosei-Rodosho 2001).

The development of information and communication technologies is transforming patterns of employment by generating new working styles, such as working at home, telework and satellite offices. The Internet is changing the world of work. During the 1990s, about 2 million jobs were created by IT innovation. Many new jobs were created in service industries, although there was job creation in most other industries too.

Job security and employment practices

Substantial changes are developing in labour markets in the recession that has continued since the 1990s. Job security and employment practices are two areas where major change is taking place.

Nearly all enterprises with compulsory retirement set 60 years as the mandatory retirement age. However, many workers want to continue to work beyond 60. Among those who were defined as 'not in the labour force' in the age category of 60–64, more than 60 per cent replied that they were healthy. In the 'not in the labour force' category beyond 60 years of age, about 40 per cent are healthy and able to work on a full-time basis (Rodosho 2000). This desire is so strong that there is a 34 per cent labour force participation rate among male workers aged over 64. A law was passed in 1986 with the aim of encouraging firms to raise the retirement age towards 60. More recently, the law was revised to give firms with retirement systems the objective of setting the age of retirement at 60 or higher from 1998, with a longer-term aim to set the age at 65. This upward adjustment of the retirement age is related to the fate of the life-time employment system and the state of the social security system.

However, with the ageing of the population, the original pay and retirement system can no longer be maintained. The average labour cost will rise if the present age-wage profile is maintained. Various efforts are made to reduce the burden of labour cost. These include downsizing, the introduction of temporary workers, foreign workers, outsourcing, computerisation, and relocation of production sites overseas. There are also voices in favour of abolishing the mandatory retirement. A common theme is how to enhance labour market flexibility to cope with the changing circumstances.

If enterprises were to lay off people, this could destroy the 'high trust relations' that usually prevail between managers and employees. Hence, one strategy adopted in Japan was to boost flexibility by minimising the number of regular employees, and by employing more temporary and part-time workers instead. Many companies are modifying their practices to achieve more flexible employment relations. The innovations include 'plateauing' the age-wage profile after a certain age so that an automatic seniority pay rise is not expected after, say, 45 years of age, and introducing selective career paths that induce early retirement. Many enterprises have reduced their total number of employees by 'natural wastage' or attrition.

From 1987, the job opening versus job-seekers ratio (the number of job offers divided by job-seekers) rose as the Japanese economy overcame the yen's appreciation and grew again. The labour shortages in the early 1990s gradually spread to many industries, and were especially serious in construction, retailing and other elements of the service sector, as well as in the machinery and metals segments of the manufacturing sector. Many of these industries had working conditions that were not attractive to young workers, and many companies encountered difficulties caused by a shortage of young people.

Since the mid-1990s, the labour market has been sluggish. To cope with the surplus of labour force, many firms have reduced the number of employees in various ways. But the situation is complex. In view of their poor working conditions, some SMEs had difficulties hiring adequate numbers of Japanese workers, allowing immigrant workers to find openings in these relatively low-skilled jobs. A mismatch of workers by skills and industry developed. How did industries respond to this mismatch? Among the various strategies adopted by firms, the employment of foreign workers has attracted wide attention.

The foreign labour issue

When faced with a serious shortage of labour, many firms have employed foreign workers, who were often 'illegal labourers' from developing countries. Until the mid-1980s, there was little discussion about the employment of foreign workers. However, given the subsequent appreciation of the yen and the tight labour market, particularly in the boom period, the wage differentials between Japan and developing countries have widened.

An increasing number of foreigners have entered Japan with tourist or student visas but then unlawfully entered the labour market. This includes those who are engaged in activities not allowed by law, or who have stayed in Japan longer than permitted by their visa. By the early 21st century, among the estimated 700 000 foreign workers in Japan, about 40 per cent of foreign workers are employed unofficially in construction, some aspects of manufacturing and the service sector. They are especially engaged in jobs that are demanding, dirty and dangerous. When legal immigrant workers are included, about 670 000 workers from various countries are working in the labour market.

In the construction sector, for instance, foreign labourers are employed through personal connections or through employment agencies, including brokers. Many are in the day-labourer market. Regrettably, an undercover network of brokers has been established that provides bridges between Japan and other countries. Many immigrants who look for employment opportunities in Japan depend on such a network. The trade in foreign workers often involves the use of smugglers, who extract exorbitant fees for transport and for providing false documents, such as visas and passports. Workers who find employment opportunities through these channels are often exploited and forced to work in substandard conditions for low pay. A substantial number of cases involving illegal foreign workers are reported each year.

Under these circumstances, the Japanese government has introduced an amendment to the Immigration Control and Refugee Recognition Act, which was implemented in 1990. The amendment expands the categories of authorised legal residence and employment, while introducing penalties against employers and brokers who employ illegal workers or who facilitate such employment. The government's policy is to prohibit unskilled workers, or those looking for simple jobs, from seeking employment in Japan. The amendment has not changed this. This policy is rationalised by arguing that if there is an abundant supply of cheap labour, it will obstruct the progress of industrial restructuring in desirable directions, such as the high-value-added or high-technology industries. Unless there is strong support for the maintenance of fair working conditions for foreign workers, it may be necessary to continue to prohibit the inflow of unskilled workers.

There is strong pressure from Asian developing countries to meet the demand for labour in Japan. Evidence includes the increase in illegal landings by Chinese stowaways since 1996. This has attracted much attention from the Japanese Maritime Safety Agency and the National Police Agency, because of a perceived link between such illegals and the rise in serious crime. In this environment, Japan must develop policies to accommodate the increasing number of immigrants who are attempting to adapt to Japanese society, while also preparing measures that will stem the arrival of illegals. Such policies should cover not only working conditions but also broader issues, such as housing, education, social security, regional issues, police, and political rights. This will allow foreign workers to be satisfactorily absorbed into Japanese society for the benefit of all concerned.

Sources of flexibility: technological innovations

Technological change is the most vital factor in economic growth. A country's productivity will grow through (a) technological innovations, (b) increases in capital intensity, and (c) transfers of resources from low-productivity to high-productivity industries. All three may occur simultaneously when there is strong economic growth.

Japan has fully utilised new technology in many ways, and enjoyed the benefits of technological progress in the past. New industries have been innovators of the economy, replacing the declining industries. Unemployment did not develop through technological change and the labour-saving effects of new technology. Despite concern in the 1950s and in the 1970s that technological change and innovation would so improve productivity and save labour that it would lead to decreased employment opportunities and higher unemployment, the movement towards a service-based economy and the introduction of new technologies have not been seen as reducing job opportunities in Japan.

Japan is leading the world in the diffusion of labour-saving technologies. A variety of technologies (factory automation and office automation) have been introduced. According to a survey by the Association of Industrial Robot Producers, by 1987 Japan was ahead of the other major DMEs; it had a more than 60 per cent share of all the industrial robots in the OECD.

Since the diffusion of the Internet in 1994, a new period of technological innovation has begun on a global basis. In Japan, the start in 1999 of the service to connect the Internet through mobile phones greatly expanded the number of Internet users, up 60 per cent on the previous year. According to a government White Paper on Telecommunications, by about 2005 the Internet and mobile communications will be the major source of communication, replacing televisions and telephones. The number of subscribers for mobile phones and car phones has risen dramatically, while the number of subscribers for landline telephones has begun to fall a little. Along with the spread of the Internet, the higher performance and lower cost of personal computers have driven companies into making greater use of IT. Almost all medium-sized and large companies use the Internet in one way or another.

It is difficult to estimate the number of jobs generated and destroyed by the diffusion of IT. However, according to an estimate by the Ministry of Welfare and Labour, more than 2 million jobs were generated by IT between 1990 and 1999. In estimating the number of jobs generated by the impact of information technology, the ministry made four assumptions. The number of jobs generated is the sum of the following effects:

1. job destruction due to the rise in labour productivity through the introduction of IT;
2. job generation due to the rising demand in the sectors utilising IT;
3. job generation due to expansion in the production sectors of IT, including the hardware and software; and
4. job generation (or destruction) through the income of employees.

If the combined effects of the last three are positive, employees' income is expected to boost household consumption and vice versa. The use of IT induces changes not only in numbers of jobs but also in the quality of jobs. The relative importance of jobs that require creative and specialised skills grows, while regular and monotonous jobs become less important.

Increasing labour mobility

Another way to cope with the mismatch of labour and job opportunities is to introduce greater labour market flexibility. Since the late 1970s there has been a considerable expansion in the employment of part-time workers and those available from temporary agencies. Most part-time workers are female, particularly middle-aged married women. About 36 per cent of women workers were part-timers in 1995. Such workers are more likely to enter and leave the labour force. The motivation of these employees is changing. Increasing numbers of them are entering the labour market not only for economic but also for socio-cultural reasons—such as to escape from the tedium of being a 'house-wife'. Employers are also increasingly seeking to employ more part-time workers to gain greater flexibility in their labour force. In addition, the average length of service for part-time workers with one employer has gradually extended. The rate of turnover among part-time workers has remained stable in recent years.

By contrast, the rate of turnover in young workers has tended to rise. Furthermore, it remains high against the backdrop of the tight labour market. Approximately 20 per cent of young workers with high-school diplomas left their initial place of work within a year, and 40 per cent left within three years. An increase in the number of young workers (known as *freeters*) who do not want to stay with a single firm is contributing to such changes. These young workers change their jobs for various reasons, some for better jobs, others finding difficulties in staying at their former jobs. These changes since the beginning of the 1990s in labour mobility among young workers are remarkable.

Simultaneously, the average length of service among 'core workers' (regular employees) is extending: it is around 12.4 years for men and 7.1 years for women (Rodosho 1987). Hence, changes are taking place in Japan's so-called 'lifetime' employment practices. The new mobility among young workers may be seen as an expanding period of 'job shopping'. This does not signal the 'collapse' of lifetime (long-term) commitment, although substantial changes are developing.

Many firms are trying to introduce HRM policies based on performance rather than length of service or age of employee. Some companies have introduced annual salaries based on the performance of each employee. They also classify employees according to their characteristics, such as core workers, specialists, and temporary (flexible) workers. The stereotypical Japanese employment practices mentioned above (e.g. long-term commitment and enterprise unions) are usual for most *large* employing organisations, but may also be found, albeit to a lesser extent, in SMEs.

The majority of Japanese workers work in SMEs, usually defined as establishments with fewer than 300 employees. For the purposes of international comparison, an SME is defined here as having fewer than 250 employees (fewer than 200 for the USA). SMEs had 74 per cent of all Japanese manufacturing employees. Comparable figures were 46 per cent in the UK, 25 per cent in Germany, and 46 per cent in the USA (Chusho Kiggyocho 1991). In terms of establishment numbers, SMEs constitute a high percentage share in every country. However, Japanese SMEs account for larger shares in respect of employment.

There are wide differences in wages and working conditions, depending on a company's size, capital/labour ratio, and other factors, which result in higher-value-added productivity in large firms. SMEs are not an inefficient and declining sector. SMEs account for a wide range of economic activity, and support for them is emerging from many quarters because they can be innovative and more flexible.

It is difficult to generalise about the characteristics of employment relations in SMEs because of their wide variety.

Subcontractors are one type of SME that plays an important role in manufacturing industries, although the percentage of subcontractors in other industries is low. It is hard to obtain an exact picture, but about 66 per cent of manufacturing firms are subcontractors. Industries with many subcontractors include the motor vehicle, textiles, clothing, general machinery, electrical machinery and metal industries. However, as a firm grows in size, it tends to be less dependent on other firms (Chusho Kigyocho 1983).

Independent firms constitute another type of SME; they compete with each other in the market. In this category there is a growing number of SMEs based on high technology. This type of firm typically combines advanced technology with high levels of business acumen and technical ability. There are still relatively few of these firms compared with the traditional type of SME, but they are expected to have a significant impact on their product and labour markets.

As union density is low in SMEs, the terms and conditions of employment are generally determined by market factors. In the case of subcontractors in very competitive areas, profit margins are low. Wage levels in the primary labour market do not correspond directly with those in SMEs, although there is a spillover effect.

When considering the dynamic role of SMEs, and the characteristics of Japan's part-time or temporary workforce, the simple stereotype of a dual labour market should not be automatically applied to the Japanese situation. Japanese labour markets are complex and segmented. Even the so-called primary labour market in the manufacturing sector has stagnated since the 1970s, especially in basic industries such as steel, non-ferrous metals and chemicals. On the other hand, many SMEs have emerged as being more dynamic and profitable, though they are often characterised as using secondary labour markets.

SMEs are playing a larger role in the Japanese economy. The growth of the service sector has led to an increasing diversity in workers' conditions; these reflect their employers' specific business conditions. By the early 21st century, more than 60 per cent of civilian employees were in the service sector. The future of unionism in Japan greatly depends on whether unions can recruit such employees.

CONCLUSIONS

Japanese employment relations are being transformed. Certain changes are parallel to those seen elsewhere (e.g. historically high unemployment, less lifetime commitment, declining union density, shift of production base to less developed economies [LDEs], and increased numbers of foreign workers). The globalisation of economic activities along with the rapid diffusion of IT is generating various changes in industries, management and employment relations. When parts of a whole system are changed, the system as a whole tends to change too. Can Japanese-style capitalism remain intact under changing conditions?

The Japanese economy has undergone a series of drastic changes. With primary industries diminishing (5.1 per cent in terms of number of employees), the tertiary sector will continue its expansion (64.2 per cent). The secondary (production) sector is likely to shrink (30.7 per cent) (Somucho 2001). The importance of the financial sector grows, while the production sector diminishes. This transformation will accelerate if Japan loses international competitiveness in manufacturing, with Japanese industries relocating overseas in search of cheaper production costs.

With increased imports by manufacturers, Japan's trade balance will move from a surplus to a deficit. At the same time, population ageing will reduce household savings, resulting in a decline in the domestic surplus. It is uncertain to what extent the government's policies towards 'structural transformation' will change Japanese society.

The Japanese savings rate has been falling since 1990. In 1998, the rate was 29.6 per cent. But this figure remains high relative to savings rates in the USA (17.2 per cent), the UK (18.2 per cent) and Germany (21.3 per cent). Since the collapse of the bubble economy, the amount of money being put into savings and insurance has been rising progressively. In contrast, the holding rates for stocks and investment funds have declined. Compared to most other DMEs, Japan has an unusually high portion of investments in funds and fixed deposits, while stocks account for only a small percentage. Individuals' holding rates for stocks are only 4.5 per cent in Japan, compared with 20.8 per cent in the USA, 15.6 per cent in the UK and 8.7 per cent in Germany (Bank of Japan 1999).

Apart from these macroeconomic aspects, the success or failure of the Japanese economy depends on political dimensions. Since the LDP's overwhelming victory at the 2001 election, there has been some turmoil around the coalition government led by Prime Minister Koizumi. His popularity has declined, particularly since the resignation of Minister of Foreign Affairs Makiko Tanaka. But the chief cause of worry for the Koizumi government is the economy.

Continuing recession enhanced the chaos in the banking system by adding to the bad debt situation. It also made prices fall. (Falling prices make the real value of debt grow, so that overborrowed businesses in Japan's construction, property and retail industries grow weaker still, adding further to the banks' burdens.) Opposition parties argue that Koizumi's painful changes would increase unemployment. Koizumi and his party assert that the pains are necessary for transformation. Koizumi insists that unemployment is an inevitable burden that should be faced to achieve a more competitive economy.

One of the most important characteristics of Japanese society, reflected in employment relations, has been its adaptability. There are various characteristics of Japanese employment relations that help maintain flexibility and facilitate adaptation to change. Some examples are relatively vague and wide job descriptions; flexibility of workforce allocation; lack of rigid work rules compared with those found in other DMEs; widespread use of annual payment (bonus) systems; and long-term merit ratings for managers and employees. These are not exclusive to Japan, but are generally more prevalent there in combination. Japan will combine these characteristics of HRM with the increasing flexibilities of the labour market to reform its economic structure.

By comparison with most other DMEs, Japan enjoyed consistently high rates of economic growth until the early 1990s. This may have been an unexpected result of World War II, which destroyed most of the special-interest organisations—which, as Olson (1982) argued, may hinder the growth of an economy. However, various constraints in the supply of oil and other raw materials have impeded Japan's growth, particularly since 1973. By the mid-1980s, then, Japan had entered a stage of slower growth, though it continued to grow more rapidly than most other DMEs until 1991. After then, there was the most serious stagnation that Japan has experienced since 1945.

Mismanagement in recent years has slowed the recovery of the economy. In addition, lower rates of economic growth, the ageing of the population and strict dismissal regulations for supporting the lifetime commitment system have introduced more rigidity into Japanese society. A smooth reallocation of resources will be difficult to achieve. In the past, the emphasis of Japan's employment policy was on the prevention of unemployment. Subsidies were given to the enterprises that maintained surplus employees (labour hoarding), keeping Japan's unemployment quite low until the early 1990s. This policy has been strongly criticised for its negative effect of hampering the transfer of workers from declining industries to expanding ones. Subsequently, emphasis was placed on removing the barriers to smooth job changes between industries or companies. This change of policy inevitably presaged a rise in unemployment.

The future of the Japanese model of industrialisation depends on its ability to continue to adjust to change by eliminating barriers to economic growth, with the help of various innovations. The model is changing, as there is continuing structural change in the face of strong global competition. New technologies are being used widely to thwart rigidities in the labour market and in the wider society. Hitherto, the process of 'creative destruction' of jobs has generally had a positive impact on the Japanese labour market and has had favourable consequences for employers and most workers in the longer term. Confronted with increased global competition and technological advances, Japan faces more change.

In spite of the many criticisms that have been voiced, the Japanese economy is not 'fragile'. It has overcome many difficulties and still maintains robust and flexible characteristics. Recent opinion polls suggest that more than 60 per cent of Japanese are satisfied with their lives, a figure that has not much changed in 20 years (Naikakufu 2001).

A CHRONOLOGY OF JAPANESE EMPLOYMENT RELATIONS

1868	*Meiji* Restoration ends the feudal era.
1880	Early government factories are sold to family groups, the genesis of *zaibatsu*, or holding companies.
1887	Unionisation movement among printers, ironworkers and other craft workers (which soon disappears).
1892	Formation of National Federation of Chambers of Commerce.
1894–95	Sino-Japanese War.
1897	Founding of *Rodokumiai-kiseikai*, the first successful union in Japan. Ironworkers' Union and Japan Railway Union (*Nittetsu Kyoseikai*) organised.
1900	Enactment of *Chian-iji-ho* (Maintenance of the Public Order Act) with provisions to prohibit workers' right to organise.
1901	Government-owned Yawata Ironworks opened.
1903	Ministry of Agriculture and Commerce issues 'Status of Factory Workers'.
1904–05	The Russo-Japanese War.
1906	Japan Socialist Party organised.
1907	Violent strikes at the Ashio and Besshi copper mines.
1911	Factory Law promulgated.
1912	Founding of *Yuaikai* (Friendly Society).
1914–18	World War I.
1920	Great Depression. Large-scale labour disputes at Yawata Ironworks. First May Day.
1921	Founding of *Nippon Rodo Sodomei* (Japan Labour Foundation).
1922	Japan Communist Party organised.
1925	General Election Law and Public Peace Maintenance Law promulgated.
1927	A large-scale strike at *Noda Shoyu*.
1929	Lifting of the gold embargo. *Showa* panic.
1931	Prewar record for the number of labour disputes. The Manchurian Incident starts.
1937	Sino-Japanese War starts. Founding of *Sangyo-hokokukai* (Association for Services to the State through Industry), a labour–management cooperative association.
1940	Organisations of workers and farmers dismissed. *Dainihon Sangyo Hokokukai* (Great Japan Federation of Patriotic Industries) inaugurated. *Taisei Yokusankai* (Imperial Rule Assistance Association) organised; merges with *Dainihon Sangyo Hokokukai* in 1942.

1941–45	World War II.
1945	Hiroshima and Nagasaki reduced to ashes by atomic bomb explosion. The Potsdam Declaration accepted. Japan's unconditional surrender. Trade Union Law promulgated.
1946	Workers' control of Tsurumi Works, *Nippon Kokan K.K.* Six labour unions, including the labour union of Tsurumi Workers, *Nippon Kokan* and the labour union of Toshiba Corporation, start production control. Labour disputes at the *Yomiuri Shimbun*. Japanese Confederation of Labour (*Sodomei*) organised. Labour Relations Adjustment Law promulgated. Constitution of Japan promulgated (effective on 3 May 1947). *Nichirokaigi* (Congress of Labour Unions of Japan) organised.
1947	General Headquarters orders the suspension of 1 February general strike. Constitution of Japan comes into effect. *Densan* (Japan Electric Industry Workers' Union) and *Tanro* (Japan Coal Miners' Union) organised. Ministry of Labour set up.
1948	Japan Federation of Employers' Association (*Nikkeiren*) organised. Revised National Public Service Law and Public Corporation and National Enterprise Labour Relations Law promulgated. Trade Union Law and Labour Relations Adjustment Law revised.
1949	Dodge Line introduced. US envoy Dodge indicates the guidelines for economic independence.
1950	Korean War breaks out. Conference for organising the General Council of Trade Unions of Japan (*Sohyo*). GHQ is ordered to expel communists from public offices (Red purge). Peace Treaty with Japan signed; Japan–US Security Treaty signed.
1952	Third May Day; bloodshed at the Palace Plaza. Third labour law revised.
1954	Human rights disputes at Omi Kenshi Co. Ltd. All Japan Federation of Labour Unions (*Zenro*) organised. *Sohyo* consolidates five industry-level offensives into a united wage rise in spring.
1956	Japan joins the United Nations.
1958	Labour disputes at Oji Paper Co. Ltd.
1959	Minimum Wages Law passed by the Diet. United movement to stop the revision of the Japan–US Security Treaty. Labour disputes at Miike Coal Mines.
1964	Japan joins the OECD. Federation of IMF-JC.
1965	Japan ratifies ILO's Convention 87.
1973	First oil crisis.
1974	The biggest strike in the history of the Spring Offensive—about 6 million participants.

1980	UAW (International Union, United Automobile, Aerospace and Agricultural Workers of America) asks for the Japanese automobile manufacturers' direct investment in the USA.
1982	Japanese Private Sector Trade Union Council (*Zenminrokyo*) formed.
1986	Equal Employment Opportunity Law (amended) is introduced.
1987	Japanese Private Sector Trade Union Confederation (*Rengo*) formed. Revision of Labour Standard Act (promotion of shorter working hours).
1988	Start of new *Rengo* (Japan Trade Union Confederation), which merges the public-sector unions.
1990	Revision of the Immigration and Refugee Recognition Act.
1991	Japan International Training Cooperation Organisation (JITCO) is established.
1992	Child Care Leave Law introduced.
1993	Skill Training System for Foreign Workers established.
1994	Yen records its highest rate against US dollar. The LDP, JSP and *Sakigake* (Harbinger) Party form a coalition cabinet. Law for Improving Working Conditions of Part-Time Workers passed.
1996	The LDP forms a new Cabinet.
1997	Agreement between universities and employers on new graduates. Mitsui Miike Coal Mine closed. Introduction of harsh penalties in Immigration Control Act against brokers who assist in illegal landings. Equal Employment Opportunity Act protecting women.
1998	Prime Minister Ryutaro Hashimoto resigns. Obuchi Keizo replaces him. Subsequently, Mori Yoshiro becomes prime minister. Nissan launches a drastic restructuring plan.
2001	Junichiro Koizumi becomes prime minister; law on settlement of individual labour disputes. In December, unemployment ratio records a high level: 5.5 per cent.
2002	Work sharing to respond to the urgent needs of enterprises in difficulties. Agreement between *Keidanren* (employers' organisation), *Rengo* (labour union centre), and Ministry of Welfare and Labour.

Chapter 11

EMPLOYMENT RELATIONS IN THE REPUBLIC OF KOREA

Young-bum Park and Chris Leggett

The Republic of (South) Korea (hereafter Korea) has a population of around 48 million; almost 80 per cent is urban, up from 30 per cent in 1962. This compares with urbanisation rates of almost 100 per cent in Hong Kong and Singapore and 58 per cent in Taiwan, the other Asian newly industrialised economies (NIEs) often compared with Korea. Ethnically homogeneous, about half of Koreans are Buddhist, although there is a substantial and significant Christian presence; all have inherited Confucian values. The labour force is about 22 million, with a participation rate of 64 per cent (77 per cent for men and 52 per cent for women).

Unemployment was not much above 2 per cent before Korea was hit severely by a major financial crisis in late 1997, so that it peaked at 8.5 per cent in February 1999. Since then it has dropped to below 4 per cent as the economy has begun to recover. Nevertheless, weekly working hours remained the longest for any country reported by the International Labour Office (ILO), and the employment of foreign workers has continued to increase, as it has in other Asian NIEs.

Rapid industrialisation through export-oriented manufacturing resulted in a rise in Korea's per capita GNP from $87 in 1962 to $9700 in 2000, an annual average growth rate of 8 per cent, but within a range of between –6.7 per cent in 1998 and +12.3 per cent in 1987, the extent of which reflects political crises and Korea's sensitivity to changes in the world economy. Korea became a member of the Organisation for Economic Cooperation and Development (OECD) in 1996.

Since World War II, Korea has been governed by an American Military Government (AMG) until 1948 and six republics: the first from 1948 to 1960 under Syngman Rhee[1], during which the Korean peninsula was devastated by a civil war that ended with the 1953 armistice and the division between the People's Republic of Korea in the North and the Republic of Korea in the South; the second from 1960 to 1961 under Chang Myeon; the third from 1961 to 1972 under Park Chung-hee; the fourth from 1972 to 1980 under Park Chung-hee and, in an interim, Choi Kyu-ha; the fifth from 1980 to 1987 under Chun Doo-hwan; the sixth since 1987 under Presidents Roh Tae-woo, Kim Young-sam, Kim Dae-jung and currently Roh Moo-hyun. Rhy was ousted by student demonstrations and Park assassinated, and in 1996 Roh and Chun were tried and sentenced for crimes committed during their presidencies. Although Rhee started the process, Presidents Park and Chun were the political driving forces of Korea's rapid industrialisation. Apart from a brief spell during the Second Republic, after the 1960s Korea began to function democratically only in 1987, and an opposition leader was not elected to the presidency until 1997.

THE DEVELOPMENT OF KOREAN EMPLOYMENT RELATIONS

In 1876, when it was opened to the outside world by the Kangwha Treaty, and until 1910, when it was colonised by Japan, Korea was the 500-year-old feudal kingdom of Chosun, ruled by the Yi Dynasty according to the Confucian code of personal, social and civic behaviour. Its society was rigidly stratified into *Yangban* (ruling class), *Jungin* or *Seoin* (middle class), *Sangmin* (peasant farmers and craftsmen), and *Cheonmin* (underprivileged class). Although handicrafts were made in *Sangmin* and *Cheonmin* family workshops, wage labour was rare. Organised labour can trace its origins to the late 18th century, but its extent was minimal until Japanese imperialism in the late 19th century resulted in workforce expansion in mining, stevedoring, transport, municipal services and trade-related occupations.

Under the Japanese colonial administration (1910–45), Korean industrial relations were restrained. The labour movement drew support from nationalist and socialist leaders, but their incompatibilities led to communist-backed unions being driven underground, the others tending to accommodate to the colonial regime.

In spite of a brief renaissance after liberation in 1945, unionism was restructured according to the division of the Korean peninsula. As a result, the leftist *Chun Pyung* (General Council of Korean Unions) was banned in 1947 by the AMG and soon replaced by its rival, the *Daehan Nochong* (General Federation of Korean Trade Unions, or GFKTU). Another attempt at independent unionism was made with the formation of the *Cheonkuk Nodongjohab Hyeobuiehyo* (National Council of Trade Unions, or NCTU) in 1959, but in 1960 the GFKTU and the NCTU were merged. In 1961, unions were obliged to affiliate with industry federations under a government-sponsored national centre known as *Hankuk Nochong* (Federation of Korean Trade Unions, or FKTU). Meanwhile, the government of Park Chung-hee incorporated the family businesses known as *chaebol*, which had been beneficiaries of state largesse under the First Republic, as capitalist partners in development. This completed the basic institutional character of Korean employment relations until the re-emergence of an independent union movement in the mid-1980s. Because the success of Korea's industrialisation was dependent on a supply of cheap labour to ensure the competitiveness of *chaebol* products in world markets, for Korean governments and the *chaebol* the control of industrial relations was of central importance.

Protests in the 1980s led by students and union activists against the Chun Doo-hwan government came to a head in June 1987 when the presidential candidate and Chun protégé, Roh Tae-woo, presaged political liberalisation, including direct elections. This was a turning point in Korean employment relations, with government subsequently withdrawing from its authoritarian approach to become more of a conciliator within its legal framework while remaining committed to the maintenance of economic growth (Woo 1996: 165). There followed immediately a revival of the labour movement, with substantial increases in the number of unions, in union membership and in industrial disputes (Table 11.1). Trade unionism has since become a powerful institution in Korea's employment relations, and collective bargaining has become an important means of defending and improving the working conditions of Korean workers.

Although union membership declined in the first half of the 1990s, partly reflecting changes to the economy, union influence has not waned, as demonstrated by a general strike to protest the government's unilateral labour law amendments in December 1996. In amending the Trade Union Act, the government had failed to meet the demands of unofficial unions for recognition and freedom of association. The amended legislation had permitted unions to engage in politics, but the

Electoral Law confines participation to registered political parties. Recognition of federations, other than the official FKTU, was postponed until 2000, but 'third-party involvement' was to be limited to people 'officially' linked to unions and/or management. The prospect of multi-unionism in workplaces was deferred until 2003 and in 2000 was deferred again, this time until 2007. In return, the Korean Employers' Federation (KEF) agreed to employers paying the wages of full-time union officials for a further five years. Teachers continued to be denied the rights to form a union and take industrial action, with collective relations in education confined to joint consultation. However, what prompted the largest outcry, including from the FKTU, was the easing of restrictions on employers laying off workers.

When confronted with public opinion and a series of strikes by the Korean Trade Union Congress (KTUC), the government postponed the introduction of the 1996 amendments, and in March 1997 the National Assembly amended the labour legislation to enable recognition of a rival national union federation (see below) and to delay the relaxation of restrictions on layoffs until 1999.

In November 1997, before even the most controversial provisions of the 1997 labour law amendment had become effective, Korea was hit by a severe financial crisis, and the government decided to approach the International Monetary Fund (IMF) for a rescue plan. With its offer of relief, the IMF demanded that further steps be taken to increase labour market flexibility. The then president-elect, Kim Dae-jung, established a Tripartite Commission, which in February 1998 agreed to allow dismissals when absolutely unavoidable and during mergers and acquisitions from April 1998, a year earlier than originally agreed.

The Tripartite Commission also agreed on developments that it had failed to agree on in 1997. These were that:

- government establish a substantial unemployment fund;
- public servants be allowed to form a workforce consultation body and teachers a union in 1999;
- unions be allowed to engage in political activities, starting in the first half of 1998; and
- contract labour be allowed.

Management–union confrontation over collective dismissals had been escalating, as had the level of unemployment since the 1997 financial crisis. By early 1999 unemployment had risen by more than 1 million, and employed and unemployed workers alike were calling for job security guarantees. Although the impact of the 1997 financial crisis on the unions has been generally negative, Korean unions have adopted defensive strategies that have enabled them to survive (see below).

THE MAIN PARTICIPANTS

There are three main participants in Korea's employment relations: workers and their organisations, employers and their associations, and government and private agencies (see chapter 1, also Dunlop 1958). The Tripartite Commission advising the president on the reform of Korea's employment relations also includes academics, lawyers, religious leaders and members of the press. It is therefore important to note the influence on industrial relations of organisations such as the Korea Labour Institute (KLI) and academics from the economics and law faculties of Korean universities. Nor should it be overlooked that before 1987 the Korean Central Intelligence Agency (KCIA) played a covert but significant role in the repression of labour activism.

Unions

Although Korean unions are structured on three levels (local, regional and national), most function at the plant or enterprise level, where all union members, regardless of their occupation, join the one local union. Local union leaders are directly elected by the members and bargain collectively with their employer. In consequence, collective bargaining issues tend to be enterprise-specific. The right to negotiate is vested in the local unions, with regional councils and industrial federations having only the right to consult and discuss. However, some occupational unions, such as the Korean Federation of Communication Trade Unions and the Federation of Korean Taxi Transport Workers' Unions bargain collectively at regional and national levels.

There are about 1.5 million union members (11.6 per cent of the total employed), who belong to nearly 6000 local unions (Table 11.1). Union membership peaked at nearly 2 million in 1989, but since then there has been a continued decline, attributed to Korea's economic restructuring, the union movement's failure to cope with new environments, and the financial crisis of the late 1990s (see below).

Korean union membership comprises predominately male production workers in heavy industry. Men constitute 72 per cent of total membership but only about 40 per cent of the workforce. *Chaebol* local

Table 11.1   Selected employment relations indicators in Korea

	Unions			Industrial disputes		
	Membership (000s)	Density (%)*	No. of unions	No. of strikes and lockouts	Workers involved (000s)	Unemployment rate (%)
1970	473	12.6	3500	4	1	—
1975	750	15.8	4091	52	10	—
1980	948	14.7	2635	407	49	5.2
1985	1004	12.4	2551	265	29	4.0
1986	1036	12.3	2675	276	47	3.8
1987	1267	13.8	4103	3749	1262	3.1
1988	1707	17.8	6164	1873	294	2.5
1989	1932	18.6	7883	1616	409	2.6
1990	1887	17.2	7698	322	134	2.4
1991	1803	15.9	7656	234	175	2.3
1992	1735	15.0	7527	235	105	2.4
1993	1667	14.2	7147	144	109	2.8
1994	1659	13.5	7025	121	104	2.4
1995	1615	12.6	6606	88	50	2.0
1996	1599	12.2	6424	85	79	2.0
1997	1484	11.5	5733	78	44	2.6
1998	1402	11.5	5560	129	146	6.8
1999	1481	11.8	5637	198	92	6.3
2000	1527	11.6	5898	250	178	4.1

*With respect to total employees.

Source: Korea Labour Institute (various issues), *Quarterly Labor Trend.*

unions, such as those at Hyundai, LG and Daewoo, play a key role in determining the country's employment relations climate.

An important development in Korean unionism since 1987 has been the emergence and rise of a movement independent of the officially recognised FKTU (Kim 1993: 133; Park 1993: 159; Kwon & Leggett 1994: 20; Moon 1994: 142; Wilkinson 1994: 5; Ranald 1999: 303–11). Since 1987 there have been many attempts to organise a separate national centre by union activists who do not follow FKTU policy lines, although Korean law allowed only one national centre until 1997. *Cheonnohyup* (the Korean Council of Trade Unions, KCTU) was formed in January 1991. It and other non-recognised unions formed *Minjunochong* (the Korea Confederation of Trade Unions, KCTU) in November 1995, and in November 1999 the KCTU was officially recognised by the government.

The leaders of the new union movement have been critical of the FKTU, which had close ties with government and employers under the authoritarian regimes of Presidents Park and Chun. In 1999 the KCTU claimed a membership of 568 000, compared with 400 000 at its foundation in 1995 (Park 1996), and was organised in 1256 affiliates, while the FKTU had 888 000 members in 4501 local unions. Although the KCTU membership is smaller than that of the FKTU, the KCTU is as powerful as the FKTU, as its enterprise affiliates include those of the large *chaebol* in key sectors of the Korean economy. *Minjunochong*-affiliated unions are based in the large manufacturing firms that were unionised after 1987. The average membership of the KCTU unions is more than twice that of those of the FKTU. Its unions, in tune with contemporary developments, tend to be more assertive and independent than those of the FKTU.

An important development in the 1990s was the increased unionisation of white-collar workers. With teachers allowed a union and the public sector and banking industry subject to severe structural adjustment following the 1997 financial crisis, Korea's white-collar union movement gained momentum (see below). The KCTU has a particularly strong white-collar union membership.

Kim (1993) makes a number of points concerning union membership in Korea. First, as noted above, with the growth of heavy industry, in general men have led unions. Second, white-collar workers have become increasingly unionised as their numbers in the workforce have grown, particularly since 1987. Third, there is the development of structures within unions that promote 'solidarity' and 'cleavage', for example the formation of joint councils based on region, occupation and industry, as well as enterprise. It is also noteworthy that the membership of Korean enterprise unions in manufacturing is mainly of blue-collar employees; white-collar employees above first-line supervision are more or less excluded.

A response to the difficult-to-counter divisive tactics of the *chaebol* has been the formation of enterprise councils to promote solidarity. Hyundai, in particular, has adopted a confrontational approach to the new unionism. The labour militancy of the late 1980s and early 1990s appeared to have subsided, until in late 1996 amended legislation provoked its revival (see below). It is possible, however, that the human resource management (HRM) policies of some *chaebol*, like Samsung and other exemplars, such as the government-owned Pohang Iron and Steel Corporation (POSCO), have had an influence on those who might otherwise have followed Hyundai's confrontational strategy.

The slight decline in union membership in the 1990s may be partly due to economic restructuring. First, employment in mining and manu-facturing, where unionisation is traditionally strong, has been declin-ing—by about 150 000 between 1990 and 1995—and many small firms in these sectors have collapsed. Consequently, between 1989 and 1995 the number of unions fell by 1287—from 7893 to 6606 (Table 11.1). Nevertheless, the union presence is strong in large companies, and the average membership of a union has remained at about 250.

Following the 1997 financial crisis, union membership appeared to be relatively stable—an illusion, however, in which the 88 000 teachers who joined their newly allowed union in 1999 hid a loss of almost 100 000 members elsewhere. The membership loss was mostly in chemi-cals, the metal industry and postal communications, while banking and the public sector increased their union memberships.

Union density grew from 11.2 per cent to 11.8 per cent during the same period, reflecting the reduction in the total number of employees. Because the number of unions also grew—from 5373 to 5637—many large unions must have experienced membership losses.

After the 1997 financial crisis, the power of the KCTU increased while that of the FKTU decreased. The FKTU lost 49 000 members, while the KCTU gained 112 000 between 1997 and 1999, which again included 38 000 teachers. Many unions in banking shifted their affilia-tion from the FKTU to the KCTU, but both federations enjoyed large increases in membership in the public sector. Before the financial crisis, neither banking nor the public sector had been subjected to large-scale employment adjustment, but both had to reduce their workforces substantially in the post-1997 restructuring (see below).

Employers

Korean employers are organised in several associations, the oldest of which is the Korean Chamber of Commerce and Industry (KCCI), founded in 1884. It represents all business sectors, and membership is mandatory. Membership of the Korean Foreign Trade Association (KFTA), established in 1947, is compulsory for all businesses engaged in import and export. The Federation of Korean Industries (FKI), founded in 1961, represents its (voluntary) member organisations on business and labour matters and the Korean Employers' Federation (KEF) deals exclusively with labour matters, being the official counterpart of the FKTU (Park 1993: 142–3). However, because of the workplace locus of collective bargaining, the employer role in Korean employment relations is best understood by focusing on the companies themselves, especially the *chaebol*.

As the government's chosen agency for the country's economic development, symbolically and industrially, the *chaebol* distinguish Korea from the other NIEs. It is in the *chaebol* that economic activities are highly concentrated: the top 30 *chaebol*, each a concentration of large firms, contribute about 95 per cent of the nation's GNP and the top five, that is Hyundai, Samsung, LG, Daewoo and Sunkyong, contribute about 60 per cent (Bank of Korea 1990). It follows that they are a major influence on the character of Korean employment relations. Hence, the *chaebol* constitute a major employer of Korean workers and, as indicated by the post-1987 enterprise union activism, employ a substantial proportion of Korean unionists (Chun 1989: 318–21): around 60 per cent of strikes occur in large corporations (Korean Chamber of Commerce and Industry 1988: 56–9).

The government's growth strategy—gaining economies of scale for low-cost competition through the agency of the *chaebo*—expanded employment, especially of blue-collar workers, and promoted the development of internal labour markets (Chun 1985: 247). Further, some *chaebol* businesses, such as those of Hyundai, were under a unified control, called a 'one-set approach', through the concentration of related industries or factories in one region (Kong 1992: 138–42). Similar workers doing similar work under similar conditions were concentrated by *chaebol* in one place or region. Further, government development plans often concentrated plants in industrial parks. All this enabled the formation of a collective consciousness that enhanced the power of workers and their unions. Structurally, the unions, often large, developed along regional or *chaebol*-based lines—for example, the Mansan-Changwon Union Coalition and the Hyundai Group Union Association (HGUA), respectively. With the support of the government, Hyundai established its related heavy manufacturing, including car assembly, and its shipyards in the city of Ulsan (Chun 1985: 319–22). It was in this city, the first industrial park in Korea, that in 1987 Hyundai workers first unionised the workplace before going on to organise at the Hyundai group level.

In line with its diversification and expansion and the requirements of mass production, the founders of the *chaebol* formalised their employment frameworks for workers into paternalistic, hierarchical and authoritarian structures. Typically, family members of the *chaebol* founders are appointed to key management positions (Kuk 1987: 144–58).

Reinforced by the threat of North Korean communism and the legacy of immediate post-1945 militant unionism, the government had built a legislative framework for Korean industrial relations (discussed below), but the *chaebol* aimed to control the unions directly. On the one hand, they attempted to incorporate unions into the framework of their management structure as compliant and subordinated labour agents for settling industrial conflicts. On the other hand, with the support of the state, they expelled militant unionists and workers from the workplace, being unwilling to accept what they saw as intermediary-political agents in their organisations. For them, the activities of unions should align with the hierarchical structure of the organisation rather than constrain the authority of management, a view especially reflected in the employment relations of Samsung and Hyundai (Ogle 1990). Therefore, although the *chaebol* suppressed the activities of unions, they also sought their compliance as 'company unions'.

After 1987, as we have seen, Korean employment relations began to change fundamentally. Broad social influences enabled workers and unions to regain their rights from the *chaebol*, while the *chaebol* maintained a decentralised approach to collective bargaining in order to retain managerial prerogatives at the highest level.

The effect of the new vitality of the Korean unions on the *chaebol* has varied. Many *chaebol* have met union demands to end or avoid strike action and have lost some of their direct control over production workers. The larger companies had generally employed permanent workers whose job security was assured, and layoffs from restructuring had been limited in Korea. Since 1987, unionised workers have become even more protected, often at the insistence of the union, without being subject to either individual or team performance evaluation. In some cases, bonus payments are made without reference to performance (Park & Lee 1996). Unlike the Daewoo shipping company in the early 1990s, small and medium-sized enterprises (SMEs) not cushioned within a *chaebol* and not eligible for government assistance when in difficulty have generally not had to make the same concessions as *chaebol* companies, partly because of the relative weakness of the unions outside the *chaebol*. Reflecting these developments, one study proposes a substitution of emphasis on the central role of employers, including the *chaebol*, for the conventional emphases on rapid industrialisation, Confucian values and anticommunist ideology in explanations of post-1987 employment relations in Korea (Kwon & O'Donnell 1999).

The role of the state

Due to its dominant role in economic development through industrialisation, the prevalent theme of most analyses of Korean employment relations has been the role of the state. The assumption is that the state is a central authority in shaping employment relations and, in particular, the character of the country's union movement. Tangential to the main theme is the corporatist nature of the state and its changes (Choi 1989; Park 1992; Frenkel 1993), although the structural limitations of unions (Deyo 1989), the level of industrialisation (Sharma 1991) and the relative timing of the development process are sub-themes (Dore 1979; Vogel 1991).

After 1961, the purpose of the state's dominant economic role in Korea was rapid growth in volume through export-led, low-cost competition. By intervention, referred to as 'traffic control', the state determined the growth strategy of the *chaebol* (i.e. by exploiting the economies of scale). The purpose of this strategy was achieved first by the *chaebol* diversifying their businesses, horizontally and vertically, within and across industries (called the 'octopus tentacle style'), and second by the *chaebol* exploiting their assigned monopolies in the market (Lee 1985: 122–36).

The most obvious role of the state is as a labour legislator, and since the end of the 1950s, as in some other NIEs, labour legislation in Korea has sought to regulate industrial relations to promote export-led industrialisation.[2] Statutes promulgated under the AMG were essentially labour protection, and those passed at the cessation of the Korean War under the First Republic—the Labour Union Act, the Labour Dispute Adjustment Act, the Labour Relations Commission Act and the Labour Standards Act—were replicas of the pluralist labour legislation imposed on Japan by the Occupation Authority after 1945 and incompatible with the unitarist approach of Korean governments. Consequently, they were amended in 1962 and 1963 by the Park government when the scope of collective activities, including political activities, was restricted, but there was a tightening of the protection for individual workers, and in 1967 there was legislation to promote vocational training.

Although the labour law revision of the early 1960s has been challenged as unconstitutional, it caused few problems because of the state of the labour market at that time. In 1970, foreign-owned firms were substantially excluded from unionisation. (The Act providing for this exclusion was repealed in 1981.) The 'Yushin' Constitution of 1972 and the 1.14 State Emergency Act Concerning Economic Affairs following the first worldwide oil price hike in 1973 were the preludes to further revisions of labour law in the 1970s. The revisions were part of a repression of labour that also involved the police and the KCIA. However, in recognition of the need to obtain employee commitment to the government's development plans, some of the legislation aimed at improvements in workers' welfare. This included the extension of the provisions of the Labour Standards Act to companies with five or more employees, and of the scope of state industrial accident insurance.

While the government pursued worker welfare improvements, the FKTU and the state failed to meet workers' concerns for better working conditions. Disenchantment with the FKTU spawned an underground labour movement led by intellectuals, human rights activists and religious leaders. However, repression did not prevent about a hundred industrial disputes occurring each year. It was such a dispute that was the catalyst for the political crisis, the 'Seoul spring', in 1979 and 1980 following the assassination of President Park.

The 'Seoul spring' included 407 disputes. It ended in May 1980 with the military coup of General Chun Doo-hwan and the establishment of the Fifth Republic. The labour laws were amended, unions restructured, union leaders suspended and the Labour–Management Council Act passed, with the intention of weakening unions at the workplace and making employment relations non-confrontational. On the welfare side, the Industrial Safety and Health Act and the Minimum Wage Act were passed and the scope of the Industrial Accident Compensation Insurance Act was extended.

In spite of repressive laws, the underground labour movement was active and growing in the 1980s. It drew much of its leadership from university students, who took jobs in factories as 'disguised workers' and mobilised the unions at workplaces to strike in 1984 and 1985 and again in 1987 and 1988 following the '6.29 [June 29] Democratisation Declaration'. Partly as a result of these endeavours, some minor amendments were made to the labour laws, including the Labour Dispute Adjustment Law, to facilitate unions following legal procedures.

Since 1987, the government has sought to apply a national incomes policy to the private sector, variously named the 'one-digit policy', the 'total wage system' and the 'social accord between the FKTU and the KEF'.

Attempts to keep pay settlements anti-inflationary have not been easy because of the de-facto deregulation of unions. Thus, pay rises in Korea from 1989 to 1993 were 21.1, 18.8, 17.7, 15.2 and 12.2 per cent respectively, well outside the guidelines and in contrast to pre-1987 rises. Then the annual rate, except for 1985, declined each year, from 20.7 per cent in 1981 to 8.2 per cent in 1986 (Korea Labour Institute 1994: 31). Pay restraint has been more easily achieved in the public than in the private sector (Park 1996).

A tripartite approach was initiated by the state when in April 1996 a presidential address from Kim Young-sam announced a New Conception of Industrial Relations (NCIR), with the purpose of reform through the deliberations of a multi-representative Presidential Industrial Relations Reform Commission (PIRRC). In spite of the official non-recognition of their centre, some KCTU leaders were invited to join the PIRRC as representatives of a single union. However, despite extensive discussions many key issues were not resolved, and the Korean government drafted its own Bill based on the Commission's interim report, the passage of which immediately provoked the strikes referred to above.

The 1998 Tripartite Commission established by President Kim Dae-jung produced significant results, yet, after a landmark agreement was reached, its progress suggests that Korea needs more time and experience for this kind of arrangement to be fully institutionalised. The KCTU kept out of the Tripartite Commission once union rights were given to teachers, while the FKTU has repeatedly vetoed the Commission's decisions.

THE MAIN PROCESSES

Collective bargaining and industrial disputes

The Trade Union Act regulates collective bargaining in Korea. The representatives of a union (or others appropriately authorised) may negotiate a collective agreement or other matters concerning employees with an employer or employers' organisation. A union may also entrust to a federation of unions with which it is affiliated the authority to negotiate on its behalf, and the law allows multi-employer bargaining to be conducted at enterprise and industry levels. Most collective bargaining takes place at the enterprise or plant level, but multi-employer regional and national wage bargaining is conducted in transport and textiles, where firm sizes are relatively small, and in mining, where the number of employers is few.

Since 1987, collective bargaining has become a more important means of regulating industrial relations. However, in only a few SMEs are employment relations regulated by a collective agreement (only 3 per cent of establishments employing 99 workers or fewer in 1990), and only about 7 per cent of them have Labour–Management Councils (see below). More than 90 per cent of small establishments have no collective arrangements.

Disputes peaked in 1987 and remained relatively high in 1988 and 1989—3749, 1873 and 1616, respectively. After 1989, the number fell, to as few as 322 in 1990 and fewer than 100 in 1995 (Table 11.1). The decrease was due to four factors. First, the Korean economy went into recession in 1989, and public sympathy for militant unionism declined. Second, union activists continued to be harassed and imprisoned. Third, strikes, although fewer, tended to be longer. Employers and unions were less inclined to use strikes or lockouts as weapons in collective bargaining, other than as a last resort. Fourth, the government became more assertive in requiring orderly workplaces and compliance with established procedures.

However, after December 1997 labour disputes increased sharply as the threat of job losses mounted, and Korea implemented a serious reform program aimed at overcoming the economic crisis. There were 129 industrial disputes in 1998, an increase of 65 per cent on the previous year. Workers participated in 146 000 disputes, three times as many as the previous year, and the trend continued in 1999. There were almost 1.5 million working days lost in 1998, compared with 444 000 days in 1997.

Labour–Management Councils

The *Labour–Management Council Act 1980* stipulates that a Labour–Management Council (LMC) should be created and meet four times a year in any establishment employing 50 or more persons. In 1997, its scope was expanded to establishments with 30 or more employees.

The LMC is required to consult with employee representatives on productivity increases, employee welfare, education and training, and grievance handling. Enterprises are required to submit the rules of their LMCs to the minister of labour, who has the authority to dissolve them or order the re-selection of their members (Kim 1984: 123). Before 1987, the LMCs were largely the means by which the government and the *chaebol* sought to legitimise their power over workforces, and in many cases they remained more symbolic than consultative. After 1987, the LMCs began to take on a more active role. Although by the legislation LMCs are not required to include wages and welfare on their agenda, in practice they do, and in non-unionised establishments they negotiate wages.

Where there is a union presence and an LMC, it has become usual for union leaders to be the workers' representatives on the LMC. But Korean unions generally regard LMCs as inhibiting unionism, and there are calls for the 1980 Act to be amended or repealed. On the other hand, employers and the government are inclined to favour the retention of LMCs as agencies for handling non-collective bargaining matters.

Dispute settlement

Mechanisms for settling labour disputes have long been formalised in Korea. In 1953, legislation established a Labour Relations Commission (LRC) to provide for the conciliation, mediation and arbitration of disputes. Besides the Central LRC and Regional LRCs, which come under the Ministry of Labour, there are nine Special LRCs, which are under the Ministry of Transport. When they cannot reach a collective agreement and the union intends taking industrial action, under the *Labour Dispute Adjustment Act 1953* both parties are required to notify the appropriate LRC of their intentions at least ten days before commencing the industrial action (for essential services the notice period is fifteen days), during which period industrial action is prohibited. Meanwhile the LRC commences mediation, at first by designating a conciliator and then, if the conciliator is not successful, forming a tripartite (labour, employer and public) mediation committee. After unsuccessful mediation, one or both disputing parties (depending on the terms of the collective agreement) may request arbitration by the LRC, which appoints a neutral arbitration panel. An arbitration award may be appealed against but is otherwise binding on the parties. In cases where the public interest is involved, or the economy or the daily lives of the public are deemed to be threatened, the Ministry of Labour may request the Central LRC to undertake emergency measures, during which a cooling-off period applies and there are conciliation, mediation and arbitration processes. A dispute in an 'essential public enterprise' requires a longer cooling-off period and compulsory arbitration. (The designation of an 'essential public enterprise' was extended by the December 1996 legislation.) The regulations for 'major defence industries' are such that a legal strike by their employees is virtually impossible.[3]

CURRENT ISSUES

Structural adjustment and job security

Unemployment grew substantially after the 1997 financial crisis. Before it began, unemployment was 2.6 per cent. In little more than a year it had jumped to 8.5 per cent, and 1.8 million Korean workers were out of work, of whom approximately 74 per cent had been forced to leave their workplace.

The government adopted measures to cushion the shock of the layoffs that would inevitably occur in the wake of Korea's application for an IMF bailout. From 1998 to 2000, it spent about 21 trillion won ($US16 billion) on projects to help the unemployed. However, employed and unemployed workers called for guarantees of job security, the suspension of unilateral layoffs in the name of structural reform, and subsistence payments for those retrenched. Less than 10 per cent of the unemployed received any primary social protection (Park 2000) and less than 20 per cent benefited from any of the government social protection programs (KLI and KIHASA 1999; Hwang et al. 1999). An example of the confrontation between union and management that occurred over collective dismissals for economic reasons was the dispute that took place in June 1998 in the Hyundai Motor Co., Korea's largest car manufacturer. The outcome was a compromise, so that dismissals were minimised and allowances to the laid-off exceeded the legal requirement.

In June 1998, for the first time in Korea's history, banks (five in all) were closed as an initial step towards restructuring the financial sector. The government also closed 55 private companies that were in financial trouble, and some 30 000 public-sector workers had been dismissed by 2000. Many state-run enterprises were privatised and 30 000 (10 per cent) local government employees had been retrenched by the end of 1998.

Tension between unions and the government over economic restructuring peaked in April 1999, as the Seoul Subway Workers' Union went on strike to protest the restructuring plan that presaged mass dismissals of Seoul subway workers. However, the strike ended without the union achieving any of its demands, as other unions did not join a general strike called by the KCTU. In May 2000, the KCTU experienced another defeat when it unsuccessfully called a general strike in support of claims for a reduction in working hours and, among other things, the protection of casual workers.

There has been some increase in employment levels as the economy has recovered. Since February 1999, the unemployment level has been falling, to below 4 per cent by 2001 from a high of close to 7 per cent in 1998.

There continues to be much tension between labour and management about structural adjustment, especially in the public sector. In three years the public-sector workforce was cut by 25 per cent. Nevertheless, when the FKTU called a general strike to prevent the government's privatisation of the Korean Electric Power Corp (KEPCO), a bridgehead for the FKTU's public sector unions, in December 2000, it was obliged to back down. The big unions have found it difficult in the private sector too. The government demanded that Daewoo Motors' union unconditionally agree to an employment adjustment program for the troubled manufacturer, which had been receiving government financial support. When the union refused, the government withdrew its support and Daewoo went bankrupt. The union, one of the most militant KCTU affiliates, was obliged to capitulate and accept the employment adjustment program.

Labour market flexibility and unions

The PIRRC reviewed legislation concerning the protection of the individual at work, including the *Labour Standards Act 1953*. Employers claimed that some of the protective legislation made labour inflexible and thereby undermined Korean companies' competitiveness in international markets when other countries were increasing the flexibility of their labour markets through deregulation. They argued that more flexible rules should apply to layoffs induced by restructuring. In 1996, however, the government's amendment to the legislation to supply more flexible rules for collective dismissals resulted in protests that in turn led to a withdrawal of the amendment.

Employers also sought to reduce labour costs and increase human resource flexibility by employing contract labour known as 'dispatched workers'. The contract is with the job agencies that employ the 'dispatched workers' and which, therefore, are responsible for their employment costs, such as welfare provisions. The employment of dispatched workers is technically illegal, but the employers argued that it should be legalised and government-regulated. The unions oppose the legalisation of 'dispatched workers', fearing that it will undermine their bargaining power.

The provisions for more market flexibility were introduced in 1998, when Korea received rescue funding from the IMF. The introduction of flexibility measures was made easier with the IMF rescue package, although large enterprises with their strong unions and employees with enterprise-specific skills encountered greater resistance than did non-union SMEs. A short-term outcome was the further polarisation of working conditions between large enterprises and SMEs.

With the improved performance of the Korean economy, unionised workers now expect their officials to negotiate hard for improved terms and conditions, including for job security. However, the demands of rank-and-files present a challenge for union leaders in what are more flexible labour markets than before the 1997 financial crisis.

Labour law changes

When the PIRRC reviewed proposals for labour law amendment in 1996, one of the key issues was the removal of the prohibition on multiple unionism in the workplace. The 1997 law granted workers the right to join a union of their choice, thereby allowing the independent KCTU to gain legal status and achieve multiple unionism at the industry level. To avoid conflict among unions over claims to bargaining rights, the ban on multiple unions at the enterprise level was not to be lifted until 2002. Likewise, another controversial issue, making the common practice of company payment to full-time union officers an unfair labour practice, was not to be effective until 2002. However, in November 2000 the Tripartite Commission agreed to postpone the implementation of these two controversial labour law amendments, which would adversely affect the FKTU, for a further five years. Details of an amendment gradually to reduce the standard working week to 40 hours have still to be worked out.

When these labour law changes become operational in 2007, they will have a significant effect on Korean unions. In particular, prohibiting the payment of wages by employers of full-time union officials will be a crucial factor in determining Korea's future bargaining structure. Most small unions will not be able to survive without the financial support of their employers. Even large unions, say ones with more than 1000 members, might find it difficult when they have to pay the wages of their officials themselves. In anticipation of difficulties, some unions have been promoting an organisational shift from an enterprise to an industrial structure. To this end they are seeking to strengthen solidarity within their federations by concentrating pay bargaining into the same time period, and by entrusting bargaining to upper-level leaders.

The prospect of unions competing for bargaining rights at the enterprise level is the focus of debate in many unions and is of concern to employment relations experts. In the Tripartite Commission, employers have been arguing for the US-style of single-union representation, but the unions have opposed this. On the other hand, multi-unionism may have a divisive effect on unions that employers will be able to turn to their advantage.

Foreign labour

As with the other Asian NIEs, a tight labour market has led to Korea employing migrant labour, mostly unskilled and especially in such labour-intensive industries as textiles, fabricated metal and machinery, electrical and electronics, and rubber and chemical products. For Korea, this phenomenon has been relatively recent, mostly since the early 1990s, and represents a reversal of when Korea was a major exporter of labour. Legal labour immigration is restricted to those engaged in journalism, technology transfer, business, capital investment, education and research, entertainment, or employment approved by a government minister, and amounted to nearly 11 000 people in 1996. Unskilled foreign workers are admitted only as 'trainees', and there were nearly 58 000 of them in 1996. Originally, foreign 'trainees' were just that—foreign workers in Korea to upgrade their skills—but intensified labour shortages has led to the scheme being used to meet the shortfalls. China, the Philippines, Vietnam and Indonesia are the source countries for more than half of the 'trainees', but there are also foreign workers from the Indian subcontinent, notably Nepal, and from other countries.

There may have been about 150 000 illegal migrant workers in Korea in December 1997. They comprised former trainees who had over-stayed their visas and foreign nationals, including some of Korean ancestry, who had entered Korea on tourist visas. Because of their illegal status, such foreign workers are vulnerable to employer exploitation and tend to live and work in substandard conditions. Government policy remains ambiguous, as it recognises the need for foreign workers as a means of preventing the cost of labour rising, but it fears that an employment pass system might increase the negative economic and social effects of migrant labour.

Although there was a popular call for the repatriation of foreign workers after the 1997 financial crisis, many Koreans had come to realise that the country still needed unskilled foreign workers. Not many Koreans want to work in 'three-D [difficult, dangerous and demanding] jobs'. SMEs in labour-intensive manufacturing still have difficulty finding

Korean nationals to work for them, and therefore government measures to replace foreign labour have not met with much success.

Hoping to remedy negative side-effects of the foreign trainee scheme, in July 2002 the government introduced an employment management scheme for unskilled foreign labour. Under this scheme foreigners are admitted as a workers, but only qualified foreigners with Korean ancestors are allowed in the service sector. There are also age limits. The Roh Moo-hyun government, the most pro-union among recent Korean governments, has been trying to introduce the employment permit scheme whereby all foreign workers without regard to their nationality are treated as equals of Korean workers.

Working hours reduction

With the 1997 financial crisis, unions proposed to reduce standard working hours with the aim of creating more jobs for displaced workers, but when Korea recovered from the crisis sooner than expected, the parties reconsidered the proposals. In 2001, the KEF and the FKTU proposed to reduce standard weekly working hours from 44 to 40, but the details have yet to be agreed. One obstacle is that many Korean workers do not take their full paid leave entitlement and, as the paid leave days would also be reduced with the reduction in standard working hours, many Korean workers would lose out. Another problem is that the current working hours are longer than the standard working hours, so the labour cost for employers would rise unless workers were willing to work fewer actual hours.

President Roh promised to reduce working hours as soon as possible when he campaigned for the presidency, and is therefore expected to make a determined effort to do so, especially with the KCTU participating in the process. In September 2002 the Korean government, unsuccessfully because it does not command a majority in the National Assembly, tried to introduce its own working-hour reduction policy.

CONCLUSIONS

It has been the historical circumstances in which Korean industrial relations institutions emerged and the unique significance of the *chaebol* that in part explain contemporary industrial relations in Korea. With the industrialisation of the East and South-East Asian countries since the

1960s, there have been distinctive national features of industrial relations that have not received due attention in the literature. Researchers intent on finding commonalities may have assigned less importance to national differences than subsequent observation warrants. While some of the characteristics of Korean industrial relations have their antecedents in the Japanese colonial period and under the immediate World War II AMG, it has been only since the end of the Korean War that they have been formed.

The industrialisation of Korea has unique characteristics, deriving from the contribution of the *chaebol* to economic development and from the nature of the state–*chaebol* relationship. With the selection of the *chaebol* as the agency for industrialisation, the unions were required to be compliant with *chaebol* prerogatives, and the state saw to this. However, with successful industrialisation, the legitimacy of the authoritarian state began to be challenged and, in a climate of democratisation, workers' rights and union rights were included in the reform agenda.

Most observers concur that in all four of the Asian NIEs (Korea, Taiwan, Hong Kong and Singapore) the union movement was subordinated in one way or another to state-initiated economic development priorities. However, in Korea (and in Taiwan, for that matter) there has been a renaissance of independent unionism. The structure of unions in Korea partly reflects the ownership structure of industry, and the new unions aspire to free collective bargaining with the *chaebol* employers. They also seek greater freedom of association (from the state) and the restoration of full rights of recognition (from the employers). Because of the extent of *chaebol* employment, industrial relations have become focused on *chaebol* unionisation and the levels at which collective bargaining takes place. The existence of rival trade union centres, their histories and *modus operandi* contribute to a struggle for legitimacy, even where legality has been achieved and more so where it has been put on hold to meet the contingencies for recovery from the 1997 financial crisis.

A CHRONOLOGY OF KOREAN EMPLOYMENT RELATIONS

1876	Japan forcefully opens up feudal *Chosun*.
1888	First unionised strike, by goldminers.
1898	Korea's first union, Seongjin Stevedores' Union, is formed. *Chosun* mining strike.
1910	Japan occupies Korea. Three-One National Independence Movement.
1920	The first national organisation, *Chosun Nodongkongjeahoe* (Chosun Labour Fraternal Association), is initiated by the liberal intelligentsia.
1922	The socialist-oriented *Chosun Nodongyeonmeainghoe* (Chosun Labour Confederation) is formed.
1924	*Chosun Nonong Chongyeonmeaing* (Chosun Labour and Farmer Confederation) is formed.
1925	Law and Order Maintenance Act represses national unionism.
1929	First general strike, in Wonsan.
1938	Unions prohibited with onset of China–Japan war.
1945	Korea is liberated from the Japanese, and the US Army Military Government in Korea (USAMGIK), known as the AMG, is established in Korea. National and Provincial Mediation Boards are set up. *Chun Pyung* (General Council of Korean Trade Unions) is formed.
1946	The Child Labour Law and the Basic Labour Law are enacted. The Labour Department is established. The September National Strikes are called. *Daehan Dogrib Chockseong Nodong Chongyeonmyeng* (General Federation of Korean Trade Unions, or GFKTU) is formed.
1947	*Chun Pyung* is banned by the AMG.
1948	Syngman Rhee is elected president of the First Republic of Korea. The Five-Year Economic Rehabilitation Plan aims at economic independence from consumption aid.
1950–53	Korean War.
1953	The Trade Union Act, the Labour Standards Act, the Labour Dispute Adjustment Act and the Labour Relations Commission Act are enacted.
1957	The Chosun Textile Company dispute in Pusan in December splits the FKTU.
1959	*Cheonkuk Nodongjohab Hyeobuiehyo* (National Council of Trade Unions, or NCTU) is formed.
1960	The 'Four/Nineteen Revolution' of 19 April deposes Syngman Rhee. The Chang Myeon government is elected. The FKTU and the NCTU merge to form a new national centre known as *Cheonnohyeob*.

1961	General Park Chung-hee seizes power in a military coup in May. The FKTU is restructured into twelve industrial union associations.
1963	Park Chung-hee elected president of the Third Republic of Korea. Labour laws revised.
1970	Restrictions on unionism in foreign-owned firms.
1971	Law Concerning the Special Measures for Safeguarding National Security (LCSMSNS) give Park Chung-hee lifetime presidency. Compulsory arbitration extended to all industries. Korea Employers' Federation (KEF) established.
1975	Labour Standards Act extended to companies with 5–15 employees.
1979	Park Chung-hee assassinated.
1980	Successful military coup by General Chun Doo-hwan.
1981	The Labour–Management Council Act, the Industrial Safety and Health Act and the Minimum Wage Act are passed, and the scope of the Industrial Accident Insurance and Compensation Act is extended.
1987	29 June Democratisation Declaration.
1991	*Cheonnohyp*, the Korea Trade Union Congress (KTUC), is formed. Korea joins the ILO.
1995	*Minjunochong*, the Democratic Federation of Korean Trade Union (DKFTU), is formed.
1996	The Presidential Industrial Relations Reform Commission (PIRRC) is formed. Korea joins the OECD. December amendments to the labour laws provoke a public outcry.
1997	Wave of strikes organised by the DKFTU is followed by the postponement and revision of the amended labour legislation.
1998	Presidential Tripartite Commission agreed to introduce more labour market flexibility measures, including collective dismissals for managerial reasons.
1999	Unemployment rate jumps to 8.5 per cent by February, which is a record high. The KCTU's general strike to protest the IMF's structural adjustment programs fails.
1999	Teachers are given union rights. The KCTU is officially recognised by the government.
2000	The Tripartite Commission agrees to postpone the enforcement of the 1997 labour law amendment concerning multiple unions at workplaces and the prohibition of payment of full-time union officials.
2001	The Tripartite Commission agrees in principle to reduce standard working hours to 40 hours per week.
2003	Roh Moo-hyun government is elected. President Roh Moo-huyn is considered to be supportive towards the labour movement.

Chapter 12

CONCLUSIONS

Greg J. Bamber, Russell D. Lansbury and Nick Wailes

Earlier chapters of the book have provided detailed analysis of employment relations in ten developed market economies (DMEs). This chapter draws together some of the major elements from these chapters. The first section examines international influences on national patterns of employment relations. The second provides an overview of changes in employment relations in these DMEs since 1945. The last section reflects on the implications of the analysis provided in the national-level chapters for evaluating the three approaches to globalisation and national patterns of employment relations outlined in the introductory chapter.

INTERNATIONAL DIMENSIONS OF EMPLOYMENT RELATIONS

In each of the national-level chapters the authors note the importance for national employment relations patterns not only of economic but also of political and institutional developments beyond the level of the nation-state. For example, Leggett and Park (chapter 11) note the significance of Korea's accession to the International Labour Organisation and the OECD in shaping Korea's labour legislation. Marchington et al. (chapter 2) discuss the impact the European Works Council Directive appears to be having on workplace participation in the UK. Thompson and Taras (chapter 4) touch on the efforts of Canadian unions to coordinate bargaining with unions in the USA, and to a lesser degree Mexico, in response to the challenges associated with the North American Free Trade Agreement (NAFTA). Lansbury and Wailes (chapter 5) note the impact of international solidarity campaigns by US longshoremen on the 1998 Waterfront Dispute in Australia. There are many more examples pointing to the complex nature of the international dimension in this book.

One of our main conclusions is that there is a need for students of comparative employment relations to go beyond treating the international dimension only in economic terms and to rethink the relationship of the international to the national. One way to reconceptualise the international dimension, and to integrate it into the analysis of national patterns of employment relations, is to identify elements of the *international industrial relations regime.* The concept of *regime* is derived from the international political economy literature and is based on the notion that national-level employment relations practices do not exist in isolation but rather develop in and are reinforced by an international set of rules or system of governance (Haworth & Hughes 2002: 13–18). By focusing on recent debates, which highlight elements of the international dimension, this section identifies several features of the emerging international industrial relations regime and ways in which the international dimension influences national patterns of employment relations.

The WTO, ILO, and international labour standards

One recent debate that has highlighted the potential impact that the international dimension may have on shaping future patterns of employment relations relates to the role labour standards ought to play in the rules of the World Trade Organisation (WTO). Hitherto, the International Labour Organisation (ILO) has been the main agency for developing and enforcing international labour standards, via its conventions and recommendations (Engerman 2003). The ILO is the major forum for international employment relations activities by governments, employers and unions (Servais 1996). It was founded in 1919 under the World War I peace treaty and was associated with the League of Nations. Unlike the League, it survived World War II and became associated with the United Nations. The ILO has 174 member states; its structure is illustrated in Figure 12.1.

As the major source of international labour law and of data on international and comparative employment relations, the ILO has adopted 184

**Figure 12.1   The structure of the International Labour
Organisation**

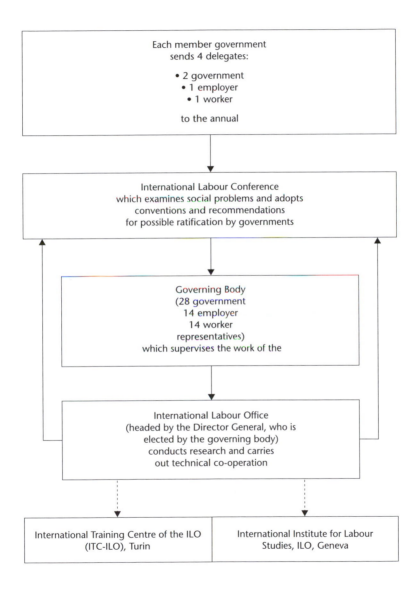

Source: Adapted from Smith (1984: 23). Thanks to Tayo Fashoyin from the
InFocus Program on Social Dialogue, ILO, Geneva, for amendments.

conventions and around 194 recommendations, which have had more than 7000 ratifications. It should be noted that recommendations are basically advisory standards which are designed to assist member states to apply conventions (whether ratified or not) to their local setting. These instruments deal with a wide range of issues, including: (a) fundamental human rights, such as freedom of association, equality of treatment and abolition of forced labour; (b) occupational health and safety; (c) working conditions; (d) social security and workers' compensation; (e) labour administration; (f) migrant workers; and (g) the specific needs or circumstances of particular occupational groups. Collectively, these standards are referred to as the International Labour Code.

Although it constitutes 'a gigantic exercise in transplantation' (Kahn-Freund 1976), like most other international agencies the ILO is cautious about offending its members, and so its recommendations are drafted carefully. It is significant that many of the ILO's conventions and recommendations relate to issues that are seen as not directly impinging on the power relations between labour, capital and the state, such as protective standards, discrimination in employment and general conditions of work. The ILO cannot compel its members to adhere to particular standards, and it is left to governments to decide which ones they will ratify. Conventions may also be denounced.[1]

The ILO suffers from budgetary constraints. It has been criticised as being too bureaucratic and cautious. But, as Creighton (1992) puts it:

> there is abundant evidence to suggest that the ILO can and does play an important role in protecting basic human rights and in combating the exploitation of the economically and socially disadvantaged.

It is, for example, widely recognised that the ILO played a major part in protecting union rights in Poland in the 1980s, when the authorities in that country were intent on suppressing the Solidarity union. The ILO is actively involved in helping the emerging democracies in Asia, Eastern Europe, Africa and Latin America to adopt labour laws and systems of labour administration that conform to accepted international standards (Creighton 1992: 39).

Moreover, the ILO can have a considerable impact—for instance, through its freedom of association standards (especially in relation to the right to strike and to engage in autonomous collective bargaining). And these are standards that cannot be avoided simply by non-ratification. Respect for the principles of freedom of association is an obligation associated with ILO membership. At the 1998 International Labour Conference, an overwhelming majority of delegates adopted the 'Fundamental Principles and Rights at Work Declaration and its Follow-up'. This obliged all member states of the ILO to introduce national legislation and practices to fulfill the purpose of the ILO's core conventions, irrespective of whether these had been ratified. In 2002, the ILO established a World Commission on the Social Dimensions of Globalisation to address some of the unfavourable social effects of globalisation and to examine the links between trade and labour standards.

Nonetheless, against the background of the liberalisation of international trade, serious questions have been raised about the ability of the ILO to enforce labour standards. Some have sought other mechanisms for protecting labour. The globalisation of the international economy has, in part, been underpinned by changes in the formal rules of international trade, which allow for increased access to markets and put fewer constraints on international trade. These changes, often referred to as trade liberalisation, have been introduced through bilateral and multinational free trade agreements. NAFTA forms a free trade zone between the USA, Canada and Mexico; it represents one example of this type of agreement. Another example is the formation of the WTO. Like the ILO, the WTO is a United Nations agency. Its aim is to promote free trade and to provide mechanisms for the resolution of trade disputes between member countries. The formation of the WTO in 1996 represented the culmination of negotiations over international trade which had been taking place since the early 1940s and which produced the General Agreement on Tariffs and Trade (GATT) (see Wilkinson 2002a).

It may be argued that issues of trade are separate from employment relations and labour standards, and that the WTO and the ILO have equal status as UN organisations. But there has been growing concern about the ILO's lack of effectiveness at policing international labour standards and growing awareness that rules for international trade would have a significant impact on national patterns of employment relations. Such awareness has precipitated arguments for the direct inclusion of labour standards in the rules of the WTO. This is often referred to as a 'social clause' (see Staiger 2003).

Despite this pressure, the WTO has rejected a social clause. As Wilkinson (2002b) notes in the lead-up to the formation of the WTO, the USA (supported by France) sought the inclusion of minimum labour standards in the new rules of world trade. They did so because their policy makers argued that without enforceable minimum labour standards, American (and French) workers would be faced with unfair competition from countries with no protections against child labour and other practices. One of the main sources of opposition to the social clause came from developing countries, which argued that minimum labour standards would be used as a form of non-tariff barrier and would limit their access to the markets of developed economies.[2] In these circumstances, it was agreed that the WTO would defer making a decision on labour standards and other 'additional items' until after its formation.

The concern of developing countries' governments about labour standards being used to prevent their access to developed market economies dominated discussion at a meeting of the WTO in 1996 designed to resolve 'additional items'. The ministerial declaration gave responsibility for these matters to the ILO, which seemed to counter the notion of a social clause in the WTO rules. However, campaigns by labour movements from developing and developed economies, and a growing anti-globalisation movement, forced the issue of labour standards onto the WTO agenda in subsequent meetings in Geneva in 1998 and Seattle in 1999 and led to acknowledgment by some members of the WTO that the ILO and other bodies might not be able to police labour standards effectively. Nevertheless, in a ministerial statement issued after its meeting in Dohar in 2000, the WTO reaffirmed its view that there was no need for direct inclusion of labour standards in the rules of the WTO or for social items to be the grounds for trade disputes between countries (see Hughes & Wilkinson 1998; Wilkinson 2002b, 2002c). Wilkinson (2002c: 20) argues that:[3]

> the closure of the labour standards debate within the WTO, coupled with the ILO's exclusion from the contemporary system of global political governance, ensures that organised labour lacks an appropriate political voice [in these increasingly important international organisations] . . . Given that within these circles a consensus has emerged on the divorce between trade and work rights, labour's role in the contemporary global economy remains precarious.

While not all commentators are as pessimistic as Wilkinson about the future of international labour standards, the important point to note is that there are several international organisations and a system of international agreements that have an impact on international economic activity and the relationship between international trade and national employment relations practices. While changing international political and economic forces do not appear to be favourable to organised labour, it may be possible for labour to influence the relevant agencies and thereby affect the balance between capital and labour at the national level.

International dimensions of union activity

How can national-level actors act effectively beyond the level of the nation-state and add an international dimension to their activities? This question has been at the heart of recent debates about the possibilities for international action by unions.

It has generally been assumed that workers and their unions are the victims of globalisation, and that they are relatively helpless in the face of developments in the international economy. There is considerable evidence to support the view that globalisation has had a negative effect on unions' bargaining power and political influence. Jacoby (1995) argues that competition from lower-cost producers, especially LDEs, has exerted downward pressure on wages and employment in many unionised industries of DMEs, from steel to apparel. In DMEs, many employers have shifted towards producing higher-value, more technology-intensive goods and services to secure a competitive advantage further up the value chain, thereby reducing the demand for less-skilled labour. International currency speculation has also inhibited nations from pursuing Keynesian-style economic strategies. Governments have been less willing to use deficit financing to confront unemployment in case this triggers an anticipatory run against the nation's currency. Similarly, Campbell (1992) has argued that globalisation appears to be associated with a widening of the gap between 'core' and 'peripheral' workers in internal labour markets. Those on the periphery of the labour market often work under temporary or part-time contracts or as subcontractors, and are difficult for unions to organise.

However, while much of the emphasis in recent debate has been on the consequences of globalisation *for* labour, there is a small but growing literature that reconsiders the options available *to* labour in the context of globalisation. Some such studies have assessed whether globalisation creates new options for agency on the part of labour and have examined ways in which organised labour might be able to internationalise its campaigns. As with the debate about labour standards, this literature points to the important role that the international dimension may play in shaping national employment relations outcomes.

One strand of this literature has focused on the activities of international union organisations and attempts by these organisations to develop more effective mechanisms for representing workers' interests in the context of a globalised economy. Since the 19th century, unions have forged links across national boundaries in an effort to counter the influence of international capital. But during the Cold War period the international union movement was divided between the International Confederation of Free Trade Unions (ICFTU), which was dominated by the interests of the USA and its allies, and the World Federation of Trade Unions (WFTU), which was dominated by state socialist and communist interests. The WFTU collapsed in the aftermath of the disintegration of the Soviet Union in the early 1990s, and the ICFTU became the dominant international union confederation.[4]

Nearly all of the main union confederations in the countries discussed in this book belong to the ICFTU, which plays a major role in organising the workers' group at the ILO. It claims about 158 million members, represented by 231 union affiliates from 150 countries and territories. Most ICFTU activities fall into one of three categories. First, in its representational activities, the ICFTU calls attention to injustices committed by governments or employers. Second, its services, and especially its organisational activities, are largely directed to LDEs and NIEs, where unionism is weak. Third, the ICFTU has fairly self-sufficient regional organisations for Asia and for North and South America. Since the 1970s, the ICFTU has also become stronger in Africa.

On a regional basis, the biggest union grouping is the European Trade Union Confederation (ETUC), which coordinates union activity relative to the EU and meets with its employer counterpart, the Union of Industrial and Employers' Confederations of Europe (UNICE). The ETUC, founded in 1973, has not confined its membership to member countries of the EU but has included other European union confederations. There are 76 confederations, from 35 countries, and eleven European federations affiliated with the ETUC, covering some 60 million workers. A complementary grouping with the same membership is the European Trade Union Institute (ETUI), which conducts research on subjects of union concern.

Covering a wider geographical area is the Trade Union Advisory Committee to the OECD (TUAC), which ensures that the OECD has a union viewpoint on its work. A notable activity of the ICFTU, and particularly of the TUAC, has been to formulate views on the desirable form of international economic and social policies, which they have then put before heads of government at their various summit meetings. The union officials involved in this work come from a variety of national and international collectivities. An official from one of the Swedish union centres, for example, might also be active in the Nordic Trade Union Council, the ICFTU, ETUC, TUAC, the workers' group in the ILO, and indeed other bodies. The international councils have consultative rights with a range of other international organisations as well as with those mentioned.

There have been international trade union secretariats (ITSs) for particular crafts, occupations or industries since 1889 (Northrup & Rowan 1979). The ITSs bring together individual national unions, in particular sectors of industry. They are sometimes referred to as the 'industrial internationals', as they focus on particular industries or occupations and concentrate on sectors or major companies rather than on wider political issues. For example, they coordinate research on health and safety hazards and technological change in their sectors. They also seek to gather information and to maintain international union solidarity in relation to certain large MNEs. The latter is an almost impossible task, as workers' interests in one country may seem to conflict with those in another (e.g. if an MNE aims to retrench in one country but expand in another—see Ramsay 1997). The ITSs are autonomous organisations, but most generally follow the ICFTU on broad policy issues. Mergers and recruitment have considerably increased the size of the main ITSs; they have also broadened their activity, particularly as a response to the growth of MNEs and the internationalisation of production. The two largest ITSs each claim to cover about 25 million workers. These ITSs are the Education International, which has affiliates in 159 countries, and the International Metalworkers' Federation (IMF), with more than 200 affiliated unions in 100 countries. The IMF has established 'world councils', mirroring particular major MNEs, to provide a forum for representatives of workers employed by those firms in different countries (e.g. Ford, Nestlé, Philips, Shell and Toyota). Other large ITSs include the Commercial and Clerical Workers (FIET), the Public Service Employees, the Chemical Workers, the Textile Workers, and the Transport Workers. A general conference of ITSs meets about once a year to review common problems and interests (Windmuller 1995).

Much of the recent debate about international unionism has focused on whether the various organisations will be able to respond to the challenges posed by globalisation and effectively represent the interest of workers. This can be illustrated in relation to the ICFTU. In part because of the role it played in the Cold War, the ICFTU has representation and official status at international fora, which are potentially important for shaping the system of governance for the international economy and would be otherwise difficult for representatives of the labour movement to access. However, as Wills (1998) notes, in the past international union bodies including the ICFTU have been dominated by national unions and national concerns. Wills argues that to become more effective in the contemporary period, national concerns need to be replaced with a more genuine international perspective. Since the 1990s, the ICFTU has been reorganised in an attempt to minimise its national focus and to become more effective for representing the interest of workers in a globalised economy.

There is debate about how successful these union bodies have been in the international arena. Some, like Breitenfeller (1997), argue that global unionism is likely to be a player in shaping the international economic order. The ICFTU, for example, was able to use its official representation at the meetings associated with the WTO to force the social clause back on the agenda. However, this did not result in a major change to the WTO rules. Furthermore, Jakobsen (2001) suggests that the election of the ICFTU's head, Bill Jordan, from the UK, and the limited nature of the reforms introduced by the ICFTU during the 1990s, illustrate that it is still dominated by the concerns of officials from rich and developed countries, and that this may prevent it from developing an effective global vision.

Wills (1998: 116) notes attempts to develop an international focus in some of the ITSs, including the International Federation of Chemical Energy, Mine and General Workers' Unions (ICEM). Similarly, research on the ETUC has questioned the extent to which the ETUC has been able to go beyond competing national union agendas and present a Europe-wide dimension to its activities (e.g. Ramsay 1997). Yet some evidence suggests that, in response to globalisation, there has been a reorientation and rein-vigoration of international union organisations. This signals a possibility that the international labour movement can play some role in establish-ing the governance mechanisms for international industrial relations, and may provide national labour movements with opportunities to act beyond nation-states in shaping patterns of employment relations.

Cross-border mobilisations of workers and the development of inter-national solidarity campaigns represent another important means by which international trends can influence national patterns of employ-ment relations in the context of globalisation. While it is generally accepted that there are inherent limitations to multinational collective bargaining, even between developed economies, there are a few examples where organised labour has succeeded in exploiting the interconnected character of national economies to put pressure on companies that operate across national borders. Many of these relate to attempts by groups in DMEs to aid workers in LDEs. Besides labour movements, there are a range of other non-labour non-government organisations (NGOs) that play an active role in these campaigns.

Armbruster-Sandoval (1999) examines the campaign by apparel workers at Phillips Van Heusen (PVH) in Guatemala to gain union recognition and collective bargaining rights during the 1990s. Despite being faced with a domestic political regime hostile to labour organisation in the export sector and a mobile form of capital, PVH workers were able to invoke forms of international pressure. In 1992 some US unions used US tariff regulations to file a workers' rights complaint on behalf of PVH workers. As a result, PVH recognised the workers' union STEMCOSA. However, PVH used the Guatemalan labour code to avoid negotiating with the union. In 1995 STEMCOSA requested assistance from the ITS representing garment workers. The ITS sent a full-time organiser to coordinate an organising campaign. Despite attempts by PVH, the Guatemalan Labour Ministry and the US embassy to frustrate this campaign, it was successful in increasing union membership. At the same time US-based labour organisations and non-labour NGOs (e.g. Witness for Peace) distributed leaflets to shoppers in US department stores during the Christmas shopping season outlining the working conditions of the Guatemalan workers. This campaign directly affected PVH's attempt to present itself as a socially responsible company. As a result, PVH entered negotiations with STEMCOSA in 1997. When it was ratified in 1997, the PVH agreement was the only collective bargaining agreement in the entire Guatemalan export processing sector. Ambruster-Sandoval (1999: 121) argues that the PVH case is a model for 'strategic cross-border labor organising'.[5]

While there are inherent difficulties for labour organising at the international level, especially in developing countries, union interests can exploit the connections between national economies created by globalisation to advance their interests. Hence, rather than eroding its potential influence, globalisation arguably requires labour to rethink its modes of representation and action (see Wills 1998).

It is has been argued that grassroots forms of cross-border mobilisation indicate a new form of union agency that may be more viable in the contemporary context than the official international forms of unionism, which developed under different conditions. Moody (1997), for example, argues that examples like STEMCOSA represent a new *social movement unionism*, where local groups of workers draw on patterns of organisation and agency developed by the women's movement, environmental groups, religious organisations and human rights groups. For Moody and others who champion the notion of social movement unionism, the current international union structure is too cumbersome and bureaucratic to meet the challenge of globalisation.

Carr (1999) argues, however, that there is an excessive triumphalism in much of the literature on social movement unionism. He suggests that in many cases cross-border mobilisation continues to be dominated by the concerns of the union leaders in the DMEs. Furthermore, there may be some limitations to the stark juxtaposition of grassroots mobilisation and the official international labour movement. Most of the case studies of local campaigns suggest that organisations such as the ITSs play a crucial role in ensuring the success of local campaigns. For example, in the PVH case, the ITS provided crucial resources to support the campaign. There are only a few examples of successful local-level mobilisation, and it may be too early to suggest that this represents a viable form of agency in the face of transnational capital. In the PVH case, the company closed the factory and moved production to another country after the spotlight of publicity had receded.

If the ITSs are going to help workers confront globalisation through cross-border mobilisations, they will need to undergo dramatic changes. But while these may be difficult to develop and sustain, there are options available to labour and its representatives beyond the level of the nation-state that potentially help shape national patterns of employment relations.

European Works Councils

Developments in the EU, and particularly the European Works' Council (EWC) directive, illustrate another way in which the international dimension can influence national patterns of employment relations. As Carley and Hall (2000: 103–4) put it, 'the EWC directive is widely seen as one of the most significant developments in the regulation of transnational employment relations'. The EWC directive has had more impact on employment relations practices in some countries than in others. There is a complex interaction between national and supranational forms of regulation.

It has often been argued that economic interests, particularly those of capital, have been at the heart of the economic integration of Europe.

Nevertheless, the formation of a single European market has been accompanied by a social dimension (e.g. Streeck 1998; Keller 2001). The 1992 Maastricht Treaty, which created the conditions for a single European market, committed the member states to upholding certain social rights (the Social Charter) and gave the European Commission power to regulate these social rights. In 1994, the European Commission issued a directive giving workers in companies in Europe with more than 1000 employees and at least 100 workers in two or more member states a set of consultation and information rights. This is widely known as the European Works Council (EWC) directive (Knutsen 1997). A directive is the strongest form of EU regulation, and requires member states to introduce national-level legislation to implement it.

Some have raised doubts about the likely effectiveness of EWCs. Streeck (1997) argues that the consultation mechanisms created by the EWC directive are neither European nor works councils. In particular, he notes that the directive does not attempt to harmonise consultation rights across member states but rather creates new and, in comparison with those existing in many Northern European countries, fairly weak consultation rights.

Consultation rights contained in the EWC directive are weaker than those of Germany and Sweden, for example (chapters 8 and 9), and are unlikely to produce a significant shift in the balance of power between workers and managers in these countries. But, the EWC directive has established a transnational aspect to labour regulation in the EU. Furthermore, in some countries the EWC directive has created conditions for at least some workers to gain access to consultation rights that they were previously unable to achieve under their national systems of regulation.

Britain provides an interesting example of this phenomenon. Britain, under its pre-1997 Conservative government, opted out of the Social Charter and was not therefore required to introduce legislation to establish EWCs in companies operating in Britain. However, the election of a new Labour government in 1997 produced a significant shift in Britain's relationship to the EU. In the Treaty of Amsterdam, Britain opted into the Social Charter and agreed to adopt the provisions of existing directives, including the EWC directive. These directives were implemented by the British Labour government in 2000 (Carley & Hall 2000).

Research on EWCs established in the UK prior to these regulations suggests that they were limited as a mechanism for consultation and that their operation was constrained by management (e.g. Wills 1998; Sterling & Fitzgerald 2001; Addison & Belfield 2002). Commentators have suggested that the minimalist and voluntarist form of regulations introduced by the Labour government are unlikely to change the situation. Yet Britain's involvement in the EU has resulted in the introduction of consultation rights for employees which most British workers had been unable to secure under national regulations (Strange 2002). Furthermore, while the EWCs are limited in scope, this form of representation may not always remain constrained (Lucio & Weston 2000). As Wills (2001) notes, there are steps that organised labour can take to try to shift the balance of power within the EWCs.

There are many other aspects of the international dimension, but the aspects exemplified above illustrate ways in which the international dimension can influence national patterns of employment relations. Therefore, as Giles (2000) suggests, employment relations students should take the international dimension seriously.

CHANGING EMPLOYMENT RELATIONS IN INTERNATIONAL PERSPECTIVE

From the national-level chapters it is possible to identify general trends in employment relations in the DMEs. World War II is a useful starting point for examining some of the factors that have shaped employment relations in the ten DMEs. After 1945, war-devastated Germany and Japan reconstructed many of their labour market institutions. In Italy and France, where unions had led an underground existence during the war, some elements of the prewar pattern carried forward but with significant new features (chapters 6 and 7). In the USA, the exigencies of war production induced practitioners and public-policy makers to refine the Wagner Act procedures. Although the strike wave of 1946 led to what unions saw as the repressive Taft-Hartley Act of 1947, much of the prewar New Deal system continued (chapter 3).

Sweden did not participate in the war. It had laid a new foundation for employment relations in the late 1930s. The parties had ensured that its employment relations system was well adapted to the postwar world (chapter 9). The active labour market, solidaristic wage policies and centralised collective bargaining were implemented. Korea's current approaches to employment relations have been developed since the end of the Korean War in 1953. The influence of the *chaebol* represents a continuity with the prewar period (chapter 11).

By the early 1950s, the postwar systems of employment relations in our sample of countries (apart from Korea) were broadly in place, in forms that would remain essentially unchanged for around two decades in some cases—and for a longer period in others. Until the early 1970s there was insufficient pressure to induce fundamental change in employment relations structures. However, their operation was increasingly influenced by two factors: the changing attitudes of workers and their consequent expression in their unions; and a growing conflict between the outcome of pay-determination processes and governments' economic policies.

First, a new generation of workers came into the labour force: better—and less conservatively—educated; more confident of their bargaining power in a context (in most countries) of relatively low unemployment; and expecting that, due to apparently continuing economic growth, they could come to expect regular improvements in wages and working conditions without extra effort on their part. The acceptance of a subservient role that had to some extent characterised earlier generations of workers was replaced by an apparently growing militancy, a demand for more say in decisions within enterprises, and less willingness to accept boring, repetitive or otherwise unpleasant jobs. Workers protested in manifestations that seemed to herald a new era—the French 'events' of 1968, the 'hot autumn' of 1969 in Italy, the wildcat strikes in Germany, Belgium and Sweden in 1969-70, and the new militancy shown by African-American workers in the 1970s in the USA. In Britain, in 1969, unions forced a Labour government to withdraw its industrial relations reform proposals, and in 1974 a miners' strike precipitated the end of the subsequent Conservative government and its Industrial Relations Act (chapter 2).

The late 1960s and early 1970s, then, was a period of worker militancy in many DMEs that seemed set to continue, at least in some of the countries under discussion. However, in the early 1970s the economic environment deteriorated sharply following the collapse in 1971 of the Bretton Woods monetary stabilisation arrangements and after the first large rise in oil prices by OPEC in 1973. That rise was, in terms of economics, a supply-side shock, which dramatically raised prices in non-oil-producing countries. If recompensed by equivalent pay rises, these would add to inflation. The subsequent behaviour of the collective bargaining partners varied between countries. In Germany there was relatively little inflation. In Japan there was major inflation, but only for one year. In Britain and Australia pay rises were generally seen by economic policy makers as too high. The USA and Canada tried incomes policies in the 1970s. In Italy, and in other countries where indexation of wages in relation to prices was an important component of wage-fixing machinery, there was serious inflation.

It took time for the industrial relations parties to adjust to the new and tougher economic context, and some of them had not fully done so at the end of the 1970s when the Islamic revolution in Iran induced the second large rise in oil prices. By then, however, although the responses again varied between countries, the governments of several countries were determined to rely to a greater extent on non-accommodating monetary policies—stronger measures that would make it more difficult for employers to concede wage rises—to lessen pressures of wage-rise inflation. These policies proved effective, though they also had a dampening effect on economic activity in a world that was already moving into the 1980–82 recession.

This recession was not just a cyclical phenomenon but marked a shift in the world economy. The long-term competitive advantage of the DMEs had been increasingly challenged in the postwar years. MNEs were globalising production to expand markets and to make use of low labour costs in some countries. Some of the newly industrialising economies (NIEs), notably Korea (chapter 11), Taiwan, Singapore and Hong Kong, appear to be performing better than the countries that had industrialised earlier. Also, the adoption of new technologies was facilitating the globalisation of production.

For several DMEs this recession also heralded a new phase in employment relations. A phase of union growth (in most countries), of relatively full employment, of experiments with industrial democracy, and of regular annual improvements in pay and working conditions, was giving way to a phase of difficulty for unions, of much higher levels of unemployment, and of concession bargaining (discussed later). Let us now consider how industrial relations parties fared after the recession of the early 1980s.

The unions

Across our ten countries union development has been uneven, though in almost all cases total membership failed to keep pace with the growth of the labour force (on the concept of union density, see Appendix). In the USA membership *density* has declined almost continuously since 1955, though *absolute membership numbers* peaked as late as 1979, since when they too have declined. In Japan, density declined slowly but steadily from 1975. Australian union density dropped from 51 per cent in 1976 to 25 per cent in 2000, while union density in the UK fell from 45 per cent in 1985 to 29 per cent in 2000. Membership density also fell substantially in France. On the other hand, Swedish membership density grew steadily from the 1960s until the 1990s (when it fell slightly); density in Canada held up relatively well; German density remained fairly steady; while that in Korea grew rapidly in the late 1980s, before declining in the early 1990s.

That unionisation should fall is hardly surprising. Unemployment rose in most countries—and unemployed workers are more likely to leave rather than join unions. Union membership was generally strong in the older manufacturing and extractive industries, but these industries were among those most severely hit in the recessions of the early 1980s, early 1990s and early 2000s. Employment growth was usually in the service sector, much of which is hard to organise. Unionisation tends to be relatively easy to achieve in large establishments with a stable full-time (and especially male) workforce; but the size of establishments has tended to fall, and there has been a considerable influx of women workers and workers on 'atypical' conditions—part-time, temporary, subcontract and fixed-term workers—who are more difficult to unionise. Furthermore, in more competitive global product markets, unions are less able to attract members by achieving large improvements in pay and working conditions, as this can have the consequence of pricing such members out of work.

What accounts for the differences in the fortunes of unions between countries? What common elements emerge when one looks at the countries in which levels of membership have been maintained or even improved (e.g. Germany, Sweden and Korea in this book, as well as Belgium, Luxembourg, and some of the other Nordic countries)? In these countries, unions are generally influential in public policy, and some are involved in the administration of unemployment and other social security benefits, although this by no means guarantees maintenance of membership.

Comparisons between the USA and Canadian experiences are interesting (chapters 3 and 4). These two countries have comparable labour legislation, and most of the bargaining is at enterprise level. Further, despite some defections in 1988, a number of Canadian unionised workers are still affiliated to US unions (Chaykowski & Verma 1992: 21). Whereas in 1965 membership density was a little higher in the USA than in Canada, by 2000 the unionisation rate in the USA was less than half of the Canadian rate (31 per cent). The explanation for this significant difference reflects the more favourable union recognition procedures of Canadian legislation; the more union-accommodating stance of Canadian employers (which have no southern 'sunbelt' to escape to); and the more vigorous strategies of Canadian unions, including their political strategies (Lipsig-Mumme 1989: 254).

In the UK, relatively militant union behaviour in the 1970s, culminating in the 'winter of discontent' of 1978/79, reinforced the determination of employers and right-wing politicians to curb union power. Labour law reforms enacted by post-1979 Conservative governments had a negative impact on union membership (chapter 2). Also, the drastic decline of industries such as steel, engineering, coal mining, the docks and rail transport, which were union strongholds, resulted in the loss of many members. This loss was exacerbated by the privatisation of many public-sector industries.

There was a similar decline in union density in Australia, even though federal Labor governments from 1983 to 1996 were sympathetic to unions' interests (chapter 5). This decline is partly explained by significant structural changes in the economy, including a sharp decline in the proportion of the workforce in manufacturing (Peetz 1998).

The employers

As economies became more integrated into the global economy, employers were faced with new challenges and new opportunities. Many industries had to restructure, and competition became increasingly fierce. Hence, employers perceived a greater need to ensure efficient work practices and to restrain labour costs. Governments were gradually persuaded that industries' struggle for survival precluded adding to their cost burdens, and sought to lighten their load. Moreover, growing unemployment sapped the bargaining strength of workers and their unions. There was a tendency in most countries for employers to take a tougher stance in collective bargaining and to try to increase the efficiency of work practices. Employers made more use of human resource management (HRM) techniques, some of which discouraged unionisation. There were, however, interesting differences in employers' policies between countries.

In the USA, union gains in the prosperous years and widespread cost-of-living clauses induced a substantial number of employers to take aggressive action to lower their labour costs. And, in a political climate favourable to them, employers' resistance to union recognition intensified. The employers' tactics included 'concession bargaining', involving some mixture of pay reductions, reductions in holidays, cutbacks in fringe benefits, and in some cases the introduction of 'two-tier' structures, with new workers being engaged on less favourable terms than those applying to existing employees. A substantial number of US employers moved labour-intensive operations to parts of the south, where unions and labour laws were weaker (chapter 3). Many US enterprises also sourced supplies from lower-cost countries (e.g. Mexico or in Asia). Canadian employers were much less aggressive than US employers, despite the prevalence of US-owned firms and the many similarities between the employment relations systems of the two countries.

Of all our sample countries, it was particularly in the USA that a large number of employers took an overtly anti-union stance. In many other countries, by contrast, employers tended to pursue cost reduction by improving productivity, reducing employment levels and enhancing operational flexibility, rather than targeting pay, working conditions and unionisation. Perhaps the key factor dictating the tougher stance of US employers was the extent to which pay levels, particularly in the unionised sector, had overtaken those in other sectors in the USA and in other countries. Such differences had been supportable when American industrial and technological superiority were almost unchallenged, but as other DMEs and the NIEs moved towards American levels of efficiency or beyond, it was more difficult for US enterprises to sustain such high labour costs.

Until the early 1990s, economic growth was more rapid in Japan and Korea than in any other of the countries under discussion. There is little evidence of aggressive anti-unionism being adopted by employers in Japan, even where their enterprise was confronting difficult times. Some Japanese enterprises responded to the changed market conditions by expanding their labour-intensive operations in low-cost countries, but in Japan they continued to pursue efficiency coupled with workplace harmony. Unemployment, though higher than it used to be, has continued at lower levels than in any of the other countries except Korea. By contrast, with the support of the government, Korean employers were generally successful in opposing the growth of independent unions, until the success of the democratisation movement in 1987 and widespread strikes in 1996/97 (chapter 11).

In continental Europe, many employers strengthened their resistance to union claims and tried to foster more efficient working, but there were few attacks on unions; employers generally still saw their relationship with unions as a continuing one. Although some employers' associations lost members, there was not a general change in the role of the employers' associations or the extent of their influence on governments. Nor was there a substantial shift in their policies, except in Sweden. There, under pressure from its member organisations, the SAF—the central organisation of private-sector employers—abandoned its bargaining role and moved away from the centralised tripartism that had characterised Swedish industrial relations for so long (chapter 9).

Developments elsewhere in Europe were broadly similar, but there were some differences. Since 1979, British employers have implemented more reform of workplace practices than those of most of the other European countries (and, arguably, had more incentive to do so). Nevertheless, though there were some cases of withdrawal of union recognition and more determination to reduce the number of strikes, most employers were less strongly opposed to unions than their US counterparts. When faced with problems where they could have used the new legislation against the unions, most British employers preferred merely to draw workers' attention to the current legal position.

The governments and the legal frameworks

After World War II, many governments adopted a more active role in regard to employment relations. The roles undertaken by governments may be categorised in terms of five components: maintaining protective standards; establishing rules for the interaction between the parties; ensuring that the results of such interaction were consistent with the apparent needs of the economy; providing services for labour and management (e.g. advice, conciliation, arbitration and training); and as a major employer.

During the early postwar years of economic growth, all of these roles were extended. Protective legislation became more detailed, adding appreciably to unit labour costs. The volume of legislation concerned with the relations of the parties increased too, though less so than protective legislation and in different ways and times in different countries. Services to employers and workers expanded—notably in the field of work organisation and the quality of working life in the 1970s. In several countries, the conflict between collective bargaining outcomes and economic policies induced government intervention. There was widespread extension of the right of public-service workers to organise and to have forms of collective bargaining rights.

From the early 1980s there was a clear shift in such developments. Governments became cautious about extending protection, and some started to reduce protection—assessing whether the benefits justified the costs. France abolished the need for administrative authorisation for dismissals, and several countries relaxed rigid rules about working time and the rules about the employment of women on night work. There were some attempts to change employment relations rules through legislation. First, in Britain, Conservative governments sought, through a series of new laws, to reduce the volume of unofficial strikes and to strengthen the members' control of unions. The legislation helped change British employment relations: it made workers and their unions more hesitant about going on strike (chapter 2). Second, in France, the Auroux reforms of 1982 sought to establish more cooperative employ-ment relations at the workplace. Although that legislation effected a number of changes, it did not transform French employment relations (chapter 7). A third case of change is Australia. From 1987, the several revisions of the Accord placed increasing emphasis on employment relations at the enterprise level, while the sweeping changes of the post-1996 conservative Coalition government's Workplace Relations Act further decentralised employment relations (chapter 5). Fourth, New Zealand until the 1980s had a century-old centralised arbitration system. However, vast changes to individual and enterprise bargaining were introduced by the *Employment Contracts Act 1991*. Although the subsequent Labour government has attempted to roll back many of these changes, employment relations in New Zealand remains funda-mentally changed (Rasmussen & Lamm 2003).

In their role as employers, governments had tended to follow prac-tices equivalent to those of recognised 'good' private employers, but were subsequently faced with rapidly rising costs and restricted income. Hence, they found it necessary to cut their labour costs by reducing numbers and by limiting salary rises. Prime Minister Margaret Thatcher in Britain initiated the privatisation of publicly owned indus-tries and enterprises, which took workers out of the public and into the private sector. A series of other countries followed this path, including Australia, even under a Labor government. A perceived need to restrain public-sector labour costs and the number of public employees contin-ues to be widespread.

The dynamics of change

Let us consider the development in post-1945 employment relations by reference to 1960, 1980 and the early 2000s. Comparing employment relations in 1980 with those in 1960 for countries in this book, there were few significant structural changes to note, other than legislation to strengthen industrial democracy in Germany and Sweden, the Italian Workers' Charter of 1970, and the failed British *Industrial Relations Act 1971*. Union membership had declined steadily in the USA and had started to decline in France and Japan, but in other countries it had increased or remained steady. There were few significant comparable changes on the employers' side, although their activities had declined at the central level as bargaining had become more decentralised.

Various forms of collective bargaining continued to be the most widespread way of regulating pay and working conditions in most of the countries, but the level at which it was conducted was generally shifting from the industry to the enterprise in Britain, and there was an increase in workplace negotiation in some other countries. Several countries had problems reconciling the results of collective bargaining with their economic policies, and some of them responded with incomes policies (which were mostly only minimally effective). Real wages and working conditions generally showed steady improvement. Industrial disputes increased over the period but were starting to decline. Unionisation grew in the public sector; the USA, Sweden and Canada strengthened the rights of public employees.

Interest in promoting industrial democracy grew, peaked and then largely dissipated (Poole et al. 2001). It was mainly concerned with expanding workers' and union rights institutionally, by such means as putting workers' representatives on company boards and strengthening works councils. There was little change in the traditional organisation of work, though Japanese innovations were already attracting attention and a few enterprises had experimented with semiautonomous work groups. In several countries regulations were introduced that made dismissals more difficult and expensive for the employer.

The contrast between the early 2000s and 1980 is much more substantial. Britain made significant changes in its legal framework; France introduced the Auroux laws of 1982; Italy had significant changes in the early 1990s; and there was the decline of the traditional 'Swedish model'. Australia experienced first the government–union Accord of 1983, then moves towards decentralisation until the Accord ended in 1996, after which the incoming Coalition government sought further to decentralise and deregulate the industrial relations system. Korea announced major and controversial changes to its labour laws in late 1996. Otherwise, there were relatively few systemic changes. Changes in the balance between employers and unions within the systems, reflecting globalisation, higher unemployment and a more difficult economic context, were more widespread in the 1980s and 1990s than was usual in the period before the early 1970s.

Between 1980 and 2000, union membership declined in most countries, but not in Sweden. Employers were induced by intensified international competition to press more strongly for efficient working practices and to limit labour costs. Occasionally national-central and, more often, national-industrial levels of collective bargaining remained, but enterprise negotiations became more important. The volume of strikes fell significantly in nearly all of the countries.

During the 1990s, at least for employees in the primary core labour market, pay and working conditions continued to improve in most countries, albeit more slowly than before. However, pay differentials, which earlier had tended to narrow, became wider. Working time was reduced in several countries, partly as a government response to high unemployment. Interest in institutional forms of industrial democracy was still generally low, but managements increasingly discussed ways of promoting more worker involvement, often as part of HRM programs. Managements also experimented with new methods of production and adopted increasingly varied patterns of employment. In the public sector, governments became more resistant to pay claims as a result of pressure to reduce taxes.

For most European countries, the increased involvement of the EU in the labour field added to the degree of regulation. This was despite arguments that, in comparison with the USA, the costs of such regulation in Europe were a cause of the higher and obdurate unemployment from which most European countries suffered. After decades of debate, European Works Councils were implemented. Yet, as EWCs have become more established, the importance of worker representation at the enterprise level is growing and the role of works councils may further expand. Another continuing theme has been the attempt to give workers more involvement in workplace decisions and to make their jobs more interesting. Such moves were fuelled, especially at times of labour shortages, by some opinion leaders among employers who believed that such reforms would facilitate the recruitment and retention of workers.

The forces underlying the changes in employment relations systems in DMEs in recent years are interrelated. They include the global redistribution of industry, consequent on the entry into international markets of NIEs and also some LDEs; the impact of new technologies; the growth of MNEs, facilitated by the free movement of capital; lower

351

real transport and communications costs; and the removal of barriers to international trade.

Changes in attitudes also influence employment relations. In the support for collectivism, public ownership, state planning and regulation of working arrangements seem to have declined in most DMEs, in favour of individualism, privatisation, the working of the market, and more flexible use of labour. However, while they may bring forth similar responses in different countries, there is little to suggest that this is inducing convergence in employment relations systems. Employment relations systems will continue to adapt and to be imperfect. There will always be conflict and calls for accommodation at workplaces. Will there be significant further structural change in employment relations systems in the near future? Reforms will probably require political changes as well as greater motivation to change among employers and union leaders. The most successful employment relations systems will be those that preserve a degree of equity between managers and workers, and develop their human resources. Successful systems will also prove to be most adaptable to external challenges, not least in terms of enhancing their efficiency and effectiveness.

CONCLUSION

This book has focused on employment relations in DMEs during a period of higher levels of competition across a broad range of markets and higher levels of interconnectedness in international economic activity. It began with a review of arguments about the impact of globalisation on employment relations and examined the ways in which comparative analysis can contribute to understanding how national patterns of employment relations are shaped by wider developments. Three major conceptual frameworks have been developed for comparing employment relations.

First, the simple *globalisation* approach, broadly defined, argues that economic changes are likely to produce pressure for convergence of national labour policies and practices. The proponents of this approach claim that globalisation produces significant increases in competitive pressure across national borders in nearly all product and factor markets and results in increased locational mobility of capital. At its extreme, the simple globalisation approach predicts a 'race to the bottom' in terms of labour standards across all economies, which leaves little scope for nationally specific institutional forms of labour market organisation.

According to the second perspective, the *institutionalist* approach, national-level institutions are important in mediating the common economic pressures that may result from globalisation. Despite significant common pressure from the international economy, the mediating role played by national-level institutions, it is argued, explains the persistence of cross-national differences across a range of variables, including patterns of labour market regulation. The institutionalist approach, then, suggests that the relationship between international economic changes and the domestic institutions of employment relations is more complex than the simple globalisation approach implies. It also suggests that most variables that explain differences in national patterns of employment relations are likely to be mainly domestic and institutional rather than external and economic in character.

The third perspective, the *integrated* approach, focuses on the interaction between market and institutional variables, and seeks to explain similarities and differences between countries. It rejects the convergence/divergence dichotomy as too crude and provides a potentially stronger framework for explaining continuities and changes in countries over time. This approach suggests that external economic factors and national institutional factors do not exist separately from each other. Rather, complex interactions between economic factors, institutional arrangements, and the strategic decisions made by corporate managers, state officials and union leaders, all shape employment relations outcomes to a greater or lesser degree.

The national-level chapters of this book provide little evidence to support the more extreme version of the simple globalisation approach. While it is possible to identify common developments in employment relations across the countries analysed—including a tendency for bargaining to become more decentralised and the erosion of union power—important and enduring differences between the countries remain. While there have been reductions in union power in Australia and Canada, the scale of the decline of unionisation has been more acute in Australia than in Canada. Similarly, while there has been pressure for a decentralisation of bargaining in Sweden and Germany, the extent of this decentralisation has been more pronounced in Sweden than in Germany. These developments suggest that change in employment relations in the DMEs has by no means been uniform.

In addition, in spite of widespread change, there is considerable evidence of continuity in national patterns of employment relations in ways not predicted by the simple globalisation approach. This can be illustrated by the Australian case. Despite dramatic changes in Australian employment relations since the early 1980s, there are aspects of the Australian institutional heritage that remain in place—including industrial tribunals and award regulation—and these continue to have significant consequences for the determination of employment relations outcomes. For example, the particular character of non-standard employment in Australia, with high levels of casualisation, can be attributed largely to the continued impact of award regulation on employment status. Rather than Australia converging towards a US-style deregulated labour market, the current Australian employment relations system has become a hybrid, with multiple streams of bargaining—centralised and decentralised, regulated and deregulated. To this extent Australian evidence supports the argument that the simple globalisation approach pays inadequate attention to the role of institutions and the range of policy choices governments and other parties have in their responses to globalisation (Weiss 1998; Evans 1997).

This book provides little evidence to support the simple globalisation approach, however, it also raises doubts about the potential of the institutionalist approach to account for the contemporary patterns of change in national employment relations. While the earlier chapters in this book support the view that 'institutions matter', they also suggest that institutions are not the only factors that influence the relationship between international economic change and national patterns of employment relations. There are similar developments in national patterns of employment relations, despite differences in key institutional arrangements. There has been a significant growth in non-standard employment across countries despite differences in bargaining systems. There is also evidence of considerable change in institutional arrangements themselves across DMEs, ranging from fundamental reform of bargaining structures (as in Australia) to dramatic reorganisation of unions (Italy) and employer groups (France). The institutionalist approach has difficulty explaining these developments fully.

The institutionalist approach represents an important alternative to the simple globalisation thesis, and points up the importance of institutional arrangements in shaping the relationship between international economic change and the domestic institution of industrial relations. However, the inability of the institutional approach to explain change as well as continuity in national patterns of employment relations suggests a need for further theoretical development. In its current form, the debate about the relationship between international economic change and national patterns of industrial relations revolves around establishing the relative importance of international economic and domestic institutional factors. Evidence of convergence between countries is taken as support for the explanatory significance of international economic change and the relative unimportance of domestic institutional factors. By contrast, continued diversity between countries is taken as evidence of the explanatory significance of institutions and the relative lack of importance of economic factors. As noted in chapter 1, however, this deadlock can be regarded as a consequence of the way in which globalisation has been conceptualised in the current debate. Globalisation theorists and institutionalists generally accept that globalisation creates similar economic pressures across all countries. But they disagree about the extent to which such similar pressures are determinant.

An integrated approach, outlined in chapter 1, represents an attempt to advance beyond the simple dichotomy of convergence and divergence. One of the key features of this approach is that it questions the extent to which globalisation creates similar economic imperatives across all countries. By highlighting the roles of and differences in interests across countries, an integrated approach suggests that pressures associated with globalisation are likely to be felt differently across different countries and sectors. Thus, for example, it suggests that a small country heavily dependent on exports (e.g. Sweden) is likely to experience globalisation differently from a large economy with a huge domestic market (e.g. the USA).

The evidence in this book suggests that national patterns of employment relations are characterised by a complex pattern of continuity and change. An integrated approach, which focuses on the interaction between interests and institutions in the context of changes in the international political economy, provides a promising framework for understanding and explaining these patterns. This approach still needs further development.

A challenge for international and comparative employment relations students is to develop a more sophisticated set of arguments about the various interactions between factors that shape national patterns of employment relations. For example, there is a need to include those aspects of the international dimension, identified earlier in this chapter, in the analysis of national patterns of employment relations. Perhaps the best context for theoretical development is a close comparison of aspects of employment relations across countries. By providing detailed over-356,304,views of employment relations in ten developed market economies, this book aims to contribute to this task.

Appendix

GLOBALISATION, EMPLOYMENT AND LABOUR: COMPARATIVE STATISTICS

Shaun Ryan, Nick Wailes and Greg J. Bamber*

This Appendix provides background statistical information on globalisation, employment relations and labour market outcomes in the ten DMEs which are the focus of the book. Chapter 1 outlined three competing views about the impact of globalisation on national patterns of employment relations—the simple globalisation approach, the institutionalist approach, and an integrated approach. In conjunction with the detailed historical and qualitative material to be found in the national chapters of this book, data reported in this Appendix can be used to test the explanatory power of these three approaches to globalisation and employment relations. However, this Appendix does not aim to provide a comprehensive data set nor a definitive set of figures. Rather, its aim is to provide easily accessible statistical tables of selected characteristics which can be used to draw initial comparisons between countries. It also includes details of some standard sources so readers themselves can elaborate and update these data. The website associated with this book provides up-to-date links to data sources.

This Appendix is organised in four sections. Section one provides basic statistical information on population, employment and economic structure. Section two focuses on measures of the contemporary wave of globalisation and its impact. Section three contains comparative data on employment relations institutions and practices. The fourth section focuses on labour market outcomes.

POPULATION, ECONOMY AND EMPLOYMENT

An important starting point for comparing countries is the size, relative development, structure and pattern of growth of the national economies being compared. One of the

---

*This is a substantially revised version of the Appendix that was co-authored variously by Peter Ross, Greg J. Bamber and Gillian Whithouse in earlier editions of the book.

Table A.1 Population and gross domestic product

	Population (millions)				GDP ($US billion): current prices & exchange rates				GDP ($US billion): current prices & current PPPs[d]			
	1970	1980	1990	2000	1970	1980	1990	2000	1970	1980	1990	2000
Australia	13	15	17	19	42	166	310	388	50	138	286	508
Canada	21	24	27	31	85	266	576	700	79	245	515	861
France	51	54	56	59	147[c]	682	1216	1294	185	513	1001	1463
Germany	61[a]	62[a]	63[a]	82	213[b,c]	935[b,c]	1689[b,c]	1866	249[b,c]	664[b,c]	1306[b,c]	2128
Italy	54	56	57	57	108	449	1102	1074	161	465	929	1452
Japan	104	117	123	127	206[c]	1073	3052	4765	302[c]	950	2263	3296
Korea	31	38	43	47	8.8	62	253	457	23	91	318	711
Sweden	8	8.3	8.6	8.8	35[c]	129	238	229	31[c]	77	151	220
UK	56	56	58	60	124	536	990	1427	179	442	925	1458
USA	205	228	250	275	1025	2771	5751	9810	1025	2771	5751	9810

[a] Former West Germany only. [b] Aggregated for the whole of Germany. [c] Estimate. [d] PPPs, Purchasing power parities.

Sources: OECDb, c (various years), d, f (2002); Korean National Statistical Office (NSO).

Table A.2   Gross domestic product per capita

	1970		1980		1990		2000	
	CPEX	PPP	CPEX	PPP	CPEX	PPP	CPEX	PPP
Australia	3.3	3.9	11	9.4	18	17	20	26
Canada	4.0	3.7	11	10	20	19	23	28
France	2.8[b]	3.5[b]	11[b]	9.2[b]	21	17	21	24
Germany	2.7[a,b]	3.2[b]	12[a,b]	8.5[b]	21[a,b]	16[a,b]	22	26
Italy	2.0	3.0	7.9	8.2	19	16	18	25
Japan	2.0[b]	2.9[b]	9.1	8.1	25	18	37	26
Korea	0.2	0.7	1.6	2.4	5.9	0.7	9.7	15
Sweden	4.3[b]	3.9[b]	15	9.3	28	18	26	25
UK	2.2	3.2	9.5	7.9	17	16	24	24
USA	5.0	5.0	12	12	23	23	36	36

GDP per capita ($US000)

CPEX, current prices and exchange rates.
PPPs, purchasing power parities.
[a] For the whole of Germany. [b] Estimate.

Source: OECDf (2002).

most widely used measures of economic development and economic growth is Gross Domestic Product (GDP). GDP is a measure of the total sum of final goods and services produced by an economy at market prices. Dividing GDP by population (GDP per capita) provides an approximate comparison of relative wealth and economic development. Table A.1 provides information on the population of the countries included in the book and two slightly different measures of GDP. Table A.2 shows two different measures of GDP per capita.[1]

There are important differences in the size of the population and the relative rate of population growth for the countries covered in this book. The USA is by far the largest country with more than 275 million people while Sweden has a population of less than 9 million. These size differences are important in shaping employment relations practices and the impact of globalisation on these practices.

The countries included in this book have each achieved a high degree of economic development. Nevertheless, there are still large differences in the relative wealth of the countries and their rates of economic growth. So, for example, while Japan has experienced slower economic growth than South Korea since the 1970s, Japan's GDP per capita remains much higher than is the case for Korea. Again it is worth considering how these differences might mediate the impact of globalisation on national patterns of employment relations.

There have been criticisms of GDP as a measure of economic development and wellbeing (see, for example, Waring 1988) One alternate measure is purchasing power parity (PPP). PPP attempts to eliminate price differences between countries by estimating the cost of the same basket of goods in different countries.[2] Table A.3 provides local currency PPPs for the countries in this book relative to the USA.

The PPP data demonstrate that despite continued growth in GDP per capita, some countries have experienced declining purchasing power since the late 1980s.

Table A.3   Purchasing power parities in terms of GDP

	Purchasing power parities (relative to $US)				
	1970	1980	1990	2000	2001
Australia	0.750	1.05	1.39	1.32	1.33
Canada	1.12	1.27	1.30	1.21	1.20
France	0.674	0.856	1.01	0.948	0.941
Germany	1.60	1.31	1.07	0.954	0.946
Italy	0.215	0.427	0.734	0.786	0.790
Japan	NA	NA	NA	NA	NA
Korea	NA	NA	NA	NA	NA
Sweden	5.71	7.05	9.34	9.55	9.53
UK	0.288	0.521	0.602	0.649	0.651
USA	1.00	1.00	1.00	1.00	1.00

NA Not available

Source: OECD PPP database (PPPs for GDP Historical Series).

Japan fits this pattern. In other cases despite relatively low or sluggish GDP growth, PPP has remained relatively strong as is the case in Sweden. Comparing the different measures of GDP and the PPP figures also demonstrates that the choice of statistical measure and measuring technique can have a significant impact on how similar or different countries seem and, therefore, that statistical comparison should be supplemented with historical and qualitative analysis.

Their economic structure is another potentially important difference between the countries; this also may influence how they experience pressures associated with globalisation. One broad measure of economic structure is the contribution of different sectors of the economy to GDP. The conventional division into the three broad categories of agriculture (including hunting, forestry and fishing), industry (including manufacturing, mining and construction) and services is based on United Nations definitions.

From the data in Table A.4 we can infer first, that there has been a decline in the contribution of the agricultural sector to GDP and a steady growth in the contribution of the service sector in all of the countries covered in this book. This decline has been taking place since well before the 1970s. In all countries except Korea, because of its more recent development, there has also been a significant decline in the contribution of industry to GDP. However, within these broad trends there are also some notable differences between countries. For example, the decline of industry has been more significant in Australia than has been the case in Canada.

These aggregates do not provide information on change within the broad categories. For example, the aggregate data does not show the extent to which there has been a shift from labour-intensive to capital-intensive manufacturing across the different countries, nor what percentage of the service sector is low skill or high skill. These factors may have important consequences for the orientation of employers and workers towards different employment relations practices. Therefore, for more detailed comparisons between countries, it may be useful to employ data on economic structure which is less aggregated.[3]

Table A.4 Gross domestic product by sector

	Sectoral % contributions to GDP by											
	Agriculture				Industry				Services[a]			
	1970	1980	1990	2000	1970	1980	1990	2000	1970	1980	1990	2000
Australia	7.3	5.3	3.8	3.5	39	36	29	26	53	58	67	70
Canada	4.7	3.8	2.8	2.6[d]	35	33	31	30[d]	60	63	66	67[d]
France	7.3	4.2	3.7	2.8	38	34	28	25	55	62	68	72
Germany[b]	3.5	2.1	1.6	1.2	48	43	37	30	48	55	61	68
Italy	8.6	5.8	3.4	2.8	40	39	32	28	51	55	64	69
Japan	5.9	3.7	2.4	1.3	44	42	38	31	50	55	60	68
Korea	27	25[c]	8.5	4.6	30	33[c]	43	43	43	43[c]	48	53
Sweden	5.5	3.4	3.3	1.7	37	31	30	27	57	66	66	71
UK	2.9	1.7	1.8	1.0	43	37	34	27	55	62	64	72
USA	3.4	2.6	2.1	1.6[e]	34	34	28	25[e]	62	63	69	74[e]

[a] Includes financial intermediation services indirectly measured (FISIM) except for Australia and the USA. [b] Data since 1991 refer to united Germany. Up to and including 1990, data concern only former West Germany. [c] 1974. [d] 1998. [e] 1999.

Source: OECDe (various years).

Table A.5   Labour force

	Total labour force (millions)			
	1970	1980	1990	2000
Australia	5.6	6.7	8.4	10
Canada	8.5	11.6	14	16
France	21	23	25	26
Germany[a]	27	28	31	40
Italy	21	23	24	24
Japan	52	56	64	68
Korea	9.7	14	19	22
Sweden	3.9	4.3	4.5	4.4
UK	25	27	29	30
USA	85	108	128	142

[a] Data after 1990 are for united Germany.

Sources: OECDb; Korean NSO.

It is worth knowing about aggregate levels of employment across countries and differences in the patterns of employment. While it is arguable that employment and its structure is a labour market *outcome*, and influenced in part by employment relations institutions and practices, there are other factors which have an impact on employment structure outside the scope of employment relations, for example, economic structure and population characteristics. Differences in national employment patterns therefore constitute a useful basis for initial comparison between countries.

Labour force participation, or the activity rate, can be calculated by dividing the working age population (normally 15–64) by the total labour force. These figures are shown in Table A.6.

As Table A.5 shows, the size of the labour force has been relatively stable in European countries (France, Italy, Sweden and the UK). However Table A.6 demonstrates that, despite apparent stability at the aggregate level, there have been significant shifts in the gender balance of the labour force, indicating significant shifts in the composition and structure of the labour force. In general these countries have witnessed a declining participation by men and increased participation by women in the workforce. It is also notable that there are still significant differences between countries in the participation by women in the labour market. Thus while 62 per cent of women of working age were part of the labour force in France in 2000, the figure for the neighbouring country, Italy, was only 46 per cent. Perhaps this apparently low participation rate for women in Italy reflects the high incidence of 'informal' employment there, especially for women, rather than a fundamentally different pattern of gender relations when compared with other European countries (Gonas 1999).

An equivalent shift from male to female participation in the workforce is evident in the other countries in the book. However these countries also exhibit increases in the labour force. While the labour force has increased more rapidly in some countries (e.g. USA), than in others (e.g. Canada and Australia), the data in Tables A.5 and A.6 demonstrate that in most cases the increase in the labour force

Table A.6 Labour force participation[a]

	Men (%)				Women (%)				Total (%)			
	1970	1980	1990	2000	1970	1980	1990	2000	1970	1980	1990	2000
Australia	94	88	85	82	47	53	62	66	71	71	73	74
Canada	86	86	85	82	43	57	68	71	65	72	77	76
France	87	82	75	75	49	55	57	62	68	69	66	68
Germany	93	84	80[b]	81	48	53	56[b]	63	69	69	69[b]	72
Italy	87	83	77[b]	74	34	39	43[b]	46	60	61	60[b]	60
Japan	89	89	83	85	55	55	57	60	72	72	70	73
Korea	76	75	76	77	43	46	50	52	59	61	63	64
Sweden	89	88	87[b]	81	59	74	83[b]	76	74	81	85[b]	79
UK	94	91	88	84	51	58	67	69	72	74	78	77
USA	87	85	86[b]	84	49	59	68[b]	71	68	72	77[b]	77

[a] Total employment divided by the working-age population. [b] Break in series.

Sources: OECDa, b (various years); Korean NSO.

is not driven by population increase alone but also by increased labour force participation. For a more detailed comparison of countries it may also be useful to disaggregate participation rates by age as well as gender. While this is likely to add greater complexity, it may also provide a more nuanced basis for comparison.[4]

More insight into the structure of employment and shifts in that structure over time can be gained from measures of the percentage of employees employed in different sectors of the economy. As might be expected, Table A.7 shows that shifts in employment structure closely match the shifts in economic structure presented in Table A.4, with declining employment in the agricultural sector and increasing employment in the service sector across all countries. Of particular interest is the decline of employment in the industry sector across most countries, given that this has been a traditional stronghold for unions. There is considerable debate about the organising propensities of workers in different sectors (e.g. Visser 1991).

The shift from full-time to part-time, atypical and temporary employment also constitutes another major shift in the structure of employment which may have significant consequences for employment relations practices. Differences in definitions of what constitutes temporary or atypical employment and inconsistencies in the collection of data make it difficult to provide a useful statistical summary of these issues. While there are similar difficulties associated with the measurement of part-time employment, comparable data on the incidence of part-time employment is more widely available.

Table A.8 demonstrates that in most countries, except Sweden and the USA, part-time employment has become increasingly important as a percentage of total employment. It also shows that in all the countries in the book, where data is available, the majority of part-time employment is undertaken by women. Using the data in Table A.6 we can infer that much of the growth of female participation in the labour force has been in part-time service work rather than full-time employment in industry.[5]

Unemployment is another labour force issue which is significant for shaping patterns of employment relations. The unemployment rate is usually defined as the percentage of the total labour force out of work, available for work and seeking work. However, there are important national differences in who is regarded as unemployed. There have also been significant changes in the official definitions of unemployment in many countries.[6]

What can we observe in terms of unemployment trends from Tables A.9 and A.10? Generally, the DMEs experienced relatively low levels of unemployment during the 1960s—although some, like Sweden and Japan, had lower levels of unemployment than others, like the USA and Korea. Since the mid-1970s these countries have faced increased levels of unemployment. This change appeared to have been precipitated by the first 'oil shock' following the OECD raising oil prices in 1973. But some associate the change with the end of a long boom in world capitalism. Since the mid-1980s, unemployment levels in the DMEs have diverged. Continental European countries have experienced increasing levels of unemployment, in some cases above 10 per cent, while the USA has experienced relatively lower levels of unemployment. The UK, Australia and Canada have been between these two poles. By the 1990s unemployment in Sweden, which during the 1980s appeared to have avoided the development of mass unemployment, reached levels similar to those of other continental European countries. Since the end of the 1990s, there have been significant reductions in unemployment levels across

Table A.7 Civilian employment by sector

	Agriculture (% of civilian employment)				Industry (% of civilian employment)				Services (% of civilian employment)			
	1970	1980	1990	2000	1970	1980	1990	2000	1970	1980	1990	2000
Australia	8.0	6.5	5.5	4.9	36	31	25	22	56	63	70	73
Canada	7.6	5.4	4.3	3.3	31	29	25	23	61	66	71	74
France	13.5	8.6	5.7	4.0	39	36	30	25	47	56	72	65
Germany[a]	8.6	5.3	3.4	2.7	49	44	39	33	42	51	58	64
Italy[b]	20.0	14.0	8.9	5.4	40	38	32	32	40	48	59	62
Japan	17.0	5.6	7.2	5.1	36	35	34	31	47	54	59	64
Korea	50.0	34.0	18.0	11.0	16	28	36	28	34	39	47	61
Sweden	8.1	5.6	3.4	2.4	38	32	29	25	54	38	68	73
UK	3.2	3.6	2.1	1.5	45	38	32	26	52	60	66	73
USA	4.5	2.6	2.9	2.6	34	31	26	23	61	66	65	70

[a] Data up to 1990 concern former West Germany only. [b] Data after 1980 have been revised.

Sources: OECDb, c (various issues), d.

Table A.8 Part-time employment

	Part-time employment[a] as % of:												Women's % share of part-time employment			
	Total employment				Male employment				Female employment							
	1973	1980	1990	2000	1973	1980	1990	2000	1973	1980	1990	2000	1973	1980	1990	2000
Australia	12	18	23	22	3.7	8.3	11	15	28	35	39	41	79	71	71	68
Canada	10	14	17	18	4.7	6.8	9.1	10	19	26	27	27	68	71	70	69
France	5.9	9.7[d]	12	14	1.7	3.2[d]	4.4	5.3	13	19[d]	22	24	82	81[d]	80	80
Germany[b]	10	13[d]	13	18	1.8	2.1[d]	2.3	4.8	24	31[d]	30	34	89	90[d]	90	85
Italy	6.4	7.8[d]	8.8	12	3.7	3.7[d]	3.9	5.7	14	17[d]	18	23	58	67[d]	71	71
Japan	14	16	19	23	6.8	7.5	9.5	12	25	29	33	39	70	71	71	70
Korea	NA	NA	4.5	7.1	NA	NA	3.1	5.1	NA	NA	6.5	9.9	NA	NA	59	57
Sweden[c]	18	25[d]	15	14	3.7	6.3[d]	5.3	7.3	39	49.5[d]	25	21	88	87[e]	81	73
UK	16	18[d]	20	23	2.3	3.3[d]	5.3	8.4	39	40[d]	40	41	91	89[d]	85	79
USA	16	14	14	13	8.6	8.1	8.3	7.9	27	22	20	18	66	68	68	68

[a] Fewer than 30 hours worked per week in the main job.   [b] Data up to and including 1990 concern former West Germany only.
[c] Break in series after 1986 and 1992.   [d] 1983.   [e] 1985.
NA Not available

Source: OECDb, d.

Table A.9 Unemployment[a]

Year	Australia	Canada	France	Germany[b]	Italy	Japan	Korea	Sweden	UK	USA
1960	1.4	6.4	1.4	1.0	5.5	1.7	4.8	1.7	1.3	5.4
1970	1.6	5.6	2.4	0.6	5.3	1.1	4.1	1.5	2.2	4.8
1980	6.0	7.5	6.2	2.9	7.5	2.0	5.2	2.0	6.4	7.0
1985	8.2	10.5	10.2	7.1	9.6	2.6	4.0	3.0	11.2	7.1
1990	6.9	8.1	8.9	4.8	10.3	2.1	2.4	1.8	6.9[c]	5.6
1991	9.5	10.3	9.4	4.2	9.9	2.1	2.3	3.3	8.8	6.8
1992	10.7	11.3	10.3	4.6	10.5	2.2	2.4	5.8	10.1	7.5
1993	10.8	11.2	11.7	7.9	10.2	2.5	2.8	9.5	10.4	6.9
1994	9.8	10.4	12.3	8.4	11.4	2.9	2.4	9.8	9.6	6.1
1995	8.6	9.5	11.6	8.2	11.9	3.1	2.0	9.2	8.8	5.6
1996	8.6	9.7	12.3	9.0	12.0	3.4	2.0	10.0	8.2	5.4
1997	8.5	9.1	12.3	9.9	11.7	3.4	2.6	9.9	7.0	4.9
1998	8.0	8.3	11.8	9.3	11.8	4.1	6.8	8.3	6.3	4.5
1999	7.2	7.6	11.2	8.6	11.3	4.7	6.3	7.2	6.1	4.2
2000	6.6	6.8	9.5	8.1	10.5	4.7	4.3	5.9	5.5	4.0
2001	6.7	7.2	8.7	7.8	9.4	5.0	3.9	4.9	5.0	4.8
2002	6.3	7.7	8.7	8.2	9.0	5.4	NA	4.9	5.1	5.8

[a] Pecentage of the labour force. [b] Up to and including 1992 data concern former West Germany only. [c] New series based on EC labour force surveys.
NA Not available.

Sources: OECDa, c, f; Korean NSO.

Table A.10 Unemployment by gender

	Women: unemployment rate (%)					Men: unemployment rate (%)				
	1970	1980	1990	2000	2002	1970	1980	1990	2000	2002
Australia	2.8	7.5	7.1	5.9	6.1	1.1	5.0	6.9	6.5	6.5
Canada	5.8	8.2	8.1	6.7	7.1	5.5	7.0	8.2	6.9	8.1
France	4.3	9.5	12.0	12.0	9.9	1.5	4.5	7.0	8.4	7.8
Germany	0.6	4.3	5.8	8.4[a]	8.0	0.5	2.6	4.1	7.8[a]	8.4
Italy	9.4	13.0	17.0	15.0	13.0[b]	3.7	4.9	7.9	8.3	7.2[b]
Japan	1.0	2.0	2.2	4.5	5.1	1.2	2.0	2.0	4.9	5.5
Korea	2.8	3.5	1.8	3.3	3.2[b]	5.3	6.2	2.9	4.6	4.4[b]
Sweden	1.7	2.6	1.8	5.4	4.5	1.4	1.9	1.8	6.3	5.3
UK	0.9	4.2	6.5	4.8	4.4[b]	2.9	6.7	7.1	6.1	5.5[b]
USA	5.9	7.4	5.5	4.1	5.6	4.2	6.9	5.7	3.9	5.9

[a] Data after 1990 are for united Germany. [b] Data for 2001

Source: OECDa, c, d, e.

Table A.11 Public expenditure on labour market programs as a percentage of GDP

| | Adult training | | | | Youth Training | | | |
| | Training for unemployed adults | | Training for employed adults | | Measures for unemployed and disadvantaged youth | | Support of apprenticeship and related training | |
	1994/95	1999/2000	1994/95	1999/2000	1994/95	1999/2000	1994/95	1999/2000
Australia	0.16	0.02	0.01	–	0.04	0.01	0.03	0.07
Canada	0.29[b]	0.17[d]	0.03[b]	–	0.01[b]	0.02[d]	–	0.01[d]
France	0.43[c]	0.25	–	0.03	0.06[c]	0.21	0.08[c]	0.19
Germany	0.38[c]	0.34[f]	–	–	0.05[c]	0.07[f]	0.01[c]	0.01[f]
Italy	0.02[a]	0.08[e]	–	0.04[e]	0.28[a]	0.01[e]	0.55[a]	0.23[e]
Japan	0.03	0.03[e]	–	–	–	–	–	–
Korea	–	0.06[f]	–	0.03[f]	–	0.01[f]	–	–
Sweden	0.75	0.30[f]	0.02	0.01[f]	–	0.02[f]	–	–
UK	0.12	0.05	0.01	0.01	0.14	0.04	0.13	0.11
USA	0.04	0.59[g]	–	–	–	0.49[g]	–	0.08[g]

[a] 1992. [b] 1995/96. [c] 1995. [d] 1997/98. [e] 1999. [f] 2000. [g] 1998/99.
– Nil (or negligible).

Source: OECDa (1996, 2001).

Figure A:1 Changes in trade openness

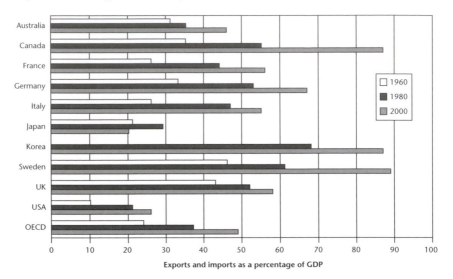

Exports and imports as a percentage of GDP

Europe including Sweden and the UK. Unemployment in Japan, while low by European standards, has reached levels unseen since the late 1950s and, in part as a consequence of the 1997 Asian financial crisis, Korea has experienced significant increases in unemployment in the second half of the 1990s.

There is a considerable literature on national differences in unemployment rates (see Bermeo 2001). However, being unemployed in Sweden is different from being unemployed in Korea, for instance. Sweden has a highly developed social welfare and unemployment insurance scheme, whereas unemployed workers in Korea have until very recently had little or no access to unemployment benefits or other forms of subsidy. Therefore, while unemployment may be lower in Korea than Sweden it may have more significance for people and for employment relations practices. National differences in state support for the unemployed is illustrated in Table A.11, which reports national expenditure on labour market programs for the unemployed.

MEASURES OF GLOBALISATION

There is extensive literature on globalisation. This section focuses on a few measures which are indicative of some of the economic changes associated with globalisation. The aim is to exemplify the extent to which changes associated with globalisation are similar in the various countries in this book, as predicted by the simple globalisation approach, or more varied as the institutionalist and integrated approaches suggest (for more discussion, see chapters 1 and 12).

The increase in international trade is one of the changes in the international economy associated with the contemporary wave of globalisation. The data in Table A.12, which show the amount of exports and imports of goods and services,

Table A.12 International trade

	Exports of goods and services as % of GDP					Imports of goods and services as % of GDP				
	1960	1970	1980	1990	2000	1960	1970	1980	1990	2000
Australia	14	13	17	17	23	17	14	18	19	23
Canada	17	23	28	26	46	18	20	27	26	41
France	14	15	21	21	29	12	26	23	22	27
Germany[a]	18	20	26	29	34	15	19	27	26	33
Italy	13	16	22	20	28	13	16	25	20	27
Japan	11	11	14	10	11	10	9.4	15	9.4	9.3
Korea	NA	14	29[b]	29	45	NA	24	39[b]	30	42
Sweden	23	24	30	30	47	23	24	31	29	42
UK	21	22	27	24	28	22	21	25	27	30
USA	5.2	5.8	10	9.7	11	4.5	5.4	11	11	15
Total OECD	12	14	18	18	24	12	13	19	18	25

[a] Up to and including 1990 data concern former West Germany only. [b] 1974.
NA Not available.

Source: OECDe (various years).

Table A.13   Borrowing on international capital markets

	$US billions				Increase 1984–1997 (%)
	1984	1988	1993	1997	
Australia	9.8	19.8	27.3	38.4	292
Canada	8.8	21.2	38.7	42.7	385
France	12.1	28.3	58	84.9	602
Germany[a]	2.1	13.5	65	222	243
Italy	6.3	14.7	31.2	30.7	387
Japan	21.3	60.9	85.4	79.2	272
Korea	NA	NA	NA	NA	NA
Sweden	NA	NA	NA	NA	NA
UK	9	75.4	51.3	181	1913
USA	33.5	61.8	125	448	1236
World	197	451	819	1769	
OECD[b]	75.8	91.1	88.9	87.4	

[a] 1984 and 1988 figures for West Germany only; percentage increase figure for period 1993–97. [b] As percentage of world.
NA Not available.

Source: Sasson (2001: 74).

Table A.14   Inward stock of foreign direct investment

	$US billions			% change	
	1980	1990	2000	1980–90	1990–2000
Australia	13	74	114	459	54
Canada	15	113	194	645	72
France	3	100	267	338	167
Germany	37	119	460	227	285
Italy	8.9	58	115	552	99
Japan	3.3	10	54	201	451
Korea	1.1	5.2	42	355	716
Sweden	2.9	12	77	331	518
UK	63	204	483	224	137
USA	83	395	1240	376	214

Source: United Nations (2000a: Annex Table B3, 303-5).

provide a simple way of measuring levels of international trade. Adding together exports and imports and expressing them as a percentage of GDP provides an approximate measure of trade openness (see Figure A.1). Figure A.1 shows changes in trade openness since 1960 across the ten DMEs.

Table A.12 and Figure A.1 illustrate a general trend towards greater levels of international trade and increased levels of trade openness. The data imply that, as Wade (1996: 62) argues, 'interconnectedness through trade has vastly increased since 1960'. The data however suggest that the impact of changes in international trade flows have not had a uniform effect across all economies. Towards one end of the spectrum, Sweden, Canada and Korea have high levels of trade openness— in 2000 more than 80 per cent. Towards the other end, international trade in goods and services accounts for less than 30 per cent of GDP in the USA and Japan. The other countries are ranged between these two poles. The implication is that forces associated with globalisation are likely to have a differential impact across these countries depending on how involved they are in international trade, which is influenced by the structure and size of the economy. The data presented here do not take into account differences in size of economy. Also, because this measure does not include transfers on the capital account (the export and import of capital) or intra-enterprise trade between subsidiaries, these figures may under-state trade for large economies. This may explain the apparently anomalous data for Japan, from which it could be inferred that the Japanese economy was less open in 2000 than it was in 1960.

Changes in the international financial system are another aspect of globalisation that have the potential to impact national patterns of employment relations (see Held et al. 1997: 189–234). Table A.13 provides one indicator of changes in the international flow of funds and the extent to which national economies are becoming linked through capital markets.

The data in Table A.13 demonstrate that there have been significant increases in borrowing on international capital markets by each of the countries since the mid-1980s. However, while each of the countries has experienced an increase in debt raised on international capital markets, consistent with the data on international trade reported above, there are important differences in the percentage increase experienced by countries in the study. The most notable increases are in the UK, USA, France and Germany. If these figures were expressed as a percentage of GDP (cf. Table A.1), the assessment would alter significantly. Nonetheless, it can be argued that each of the countries covered in this study is more exposed to pressures associated with the international financial system than they were in the early 1980s, although the extent of this exposure differs from country to country. As Jacoby (1995) notes, this increased exposure may have an impact on the labour market policies governments are prepared to pursue.

Foreign direct investment (FDI) is a third aspect of increasing inter-national inter-connectedness associated with the contemporary wave of globalisation. The extent to which FDI impacts on national patterns of employment relations is contested in the literature. On the one hand, it has been argued that subsidiaries of foreign firms tend to adopt the employment-relations practices of the host country. On the other hand, it has been suggested that there may be international diffusion of employment relations practices through subsidiaries and that affiliates of foreign firms may be at the vanguard of introducing changes in employment relations in host countries (for a review of this debate see Schuler et al. 1993). Tables A.14 and A.15 provide two different measures of the importance of FDI.

Table A.14 shows that there was an increase in FDI across all the countries in the study during the period 1980–2000. However, it also shows that there are important differences in the size and the relative growth of this investment. Thus, for example, while inward FDI has been increasing rapidly in Korea and Japan, it remains relatively less important than in countries like Australia and Canada. These data do not take into account differences in the size of the economies. While the USA had the highest amount of inward FDI in 2000, it was still fairly minor as a percentage of its overall economy.

The figures reported in Table A.15 are more interesting. They illustrate that for most of those countries where data is available, the number of foreign affiliates in the manufacturing sector is relative low. Thus, except for in the cases of Canada (29.1%) and France (13.4%), the number of foreign affiliates in manufacturing is no more than a few per cent. However, as the turnover and employment figures show, this may understate the importance of foreign affiliates in the manufacturing sector. In each of the countries foreign affiliates tend to have significantly higher turnover and employment than the industry average. This implies that foreign affiliates tend to be larger enterprises which may play an influential role in the manufacturing sector. The most extreme example of this is Sweden where only 1.8 per cent of manufacturing enterprises are foreign owned but they account for more than 20 per cent of industry turnover and employment. These enterprises probably have a disproportionate influence on national patterns of employment relations.

NATIONAL EMPLOYMENT RELATIONS INSTITUTIONS AND PRACTICES

This section provides comparative information on similarities and differences in national employment relations practices as well as indications of change over time across each of the countries.

A starting point for comparing employment relations practices across countries is to examine which of the International Labour Organisation (ILO) Conventions each country has ratified. ILO Conventions are international treaties subject to ratification by ILO member states (see chapter 12). By 2002 there were 184 Conventions. Table A.16 indicates ratification of conventions related to what are commonly regarded as core labour standards. Table A.17 focuses on the ratification of ILO conventions associated with freedom of association and employment relations.[7]

As these tables demonstrate, while most DMEs have ratified the majority of Conventions regarded as core labour standards, there is significant variation in the extent to which they have ratified ILO Conventions relating to freedom of association and employment relations issues. The USA has ratified fewer of them than any of the other countries. If a country has ratified a particular convention, however, this does not necessarily mean that it has enacted these principles in legislation or that it polices its observance. To give an example from a less developed country, Thailand has ratified the convention preventing child labour, but a significant proportion of its workforce are children (ILO 1998).

Unions are important actors in national employment relations systems and in most cases have played a major role in their development. As this book demonstrates, the development of formalised institutions of employment relations has usually been associated with the growth of collective organisation among workers. There are major differences in levels of unionisation and union strength across countries. Because of size differences between countries, aggregate membership

Table A.15 Foreign affiliates in manufacturing[a]

	Number of foreign affiliates in manufacturing	Foreign affiliates as % of all enterprises in manufacturing	Foreign affiliates as % of turnover of all manufacturing	Foreign affiliates as % of employment in manufacturing
Australia	NA	NA	NA	NA
Canada[b]	1788	29.1	50.3	NA
France	2964	13.4	31.7	27.8
Germany	1526	4.1	10.8	6
Italy[b]	1585	NA	NA	NA
Japan	286	0.1	1.8	0.8
Korea	NA	NA	NA	NA
Sweden	876	1.7	21.8	21.9
UK[b]	2462	1.5	31.4	17.8
USA	2944	NA	NA	NA

[a] 1998. [b] 1997.
NA Not available.

Source: OECD (2001).

Table A.16 Ratification of core ILO labour standards

| | Convention[a] | | | | | | | | |
| | Freedom of association | | Abolition of forced labour | | Equality | | Elimination of child labour | | |
	Right to organise (87)	Collective bargaining (98)	Forced labour (29)	Abolition of forced labour	Discrimination (111)	Equal pay (100)	Minimum age (138)	Worst forms of child labour	Number ratified
Australia	✓	✓	✓	✓	✓	✓	—	—	6
Canada	✓	—	—	✓	✓	—	—	✓	4
France	✓	✓	✓	✓	✓	✓	✓	✓	8
Germany	✓	✓	✓	✓	✓	✓	✓	✓	8
Italy	✓	✓	✓	✓	✓	✓	✓	✓	8
Japan	✓	✓	✓	—	—	✓	✓	✓	6
Korea	✓	✓	—	—	✓	✓	✓	✓	6
Sweden	✓	✓	✓	✓	✓	✓	✓	✓	8
UK	✓	✓	✓	✓	✓	✓	✓	✓	8
USA	—	—	—	✓	—	—	—	✓	2

✓ Ratified. — Not ratified.
[a] Convention number indicated in parentheses.

Source: ILOb (2002 data).

Table A.17 Ratification of ILO conventions on freedom of association and employment relations

	Convention[a]								
	Workers' representatives (135)	Rural workers (141)	Tripartite consultation (144)	Labour relations (public service) (151)	Collective bargaining (154)	Termination of employment (158)	Employment Promotion & protection against unemployment (168)	Protection of workers' claims (173)	Number ratified for each country
Australia	✓	—	✓	—	—	✓	—	✓	4
Canada	—	—	—	—	—	—	—	—	0
France	✓	✓	✓	—	—	✓	—	—	4
Germany	✓	✓	✓	✓	—	—	—	—	3
Italy	✓	—	✓	✓	—	—	—	—	3
Japan	—	—	✓	—	—	—	—	—	1
Korea	—	—	✓	—	—	—	—	—	0
Sweden	✓	✓	✓	✓	✓	✓	✓	—	7
UK	✓	✓	✓	✓	—	—	—	—	4
USA	—	—	—	—	—	—	—	—	0

✓ Ratified. — Not ratified.
[a] Convention number indicated in paretheses.

Source: ILOb (2002 data).

figures are not particularly useful for comparing union strength. Union density is a more useful measure of the strength of unions. Union density is calculated by dividing total union membership (M) by the potential (P) number of union members. Both M and P are difficult to calculate accurately and consistently.[8]

Nevertheless, we can infer from Table A.18 that the general pattern is a decline in union density. There is a large literature on the reasons for and the sources of this decline. One stream of this literature suggests declining union density is associated with structural economic change and changes in the composition of the workforce (Western 1997). Others have argued that changes in employer attitudes and legislative protections also have a significant role to play in accounting for declining density (Price & Bain 1989; Peetz 1998). Still others suggest that declining levels of unionisation may reflect generational change and post-materialist values among younger workers (see Gomez et al. 2002). It can be argued that the first two mechanisms are likely to be affected by economic changes associated with globalisation. However, the decline in union density is not uniform and has been slower in some countries than in others. Furthermore, these differences are not directly correlated to differences in the impact of pressures associated with globalisation. For example, Australia has experienced a much more dramatic decline in union density over the past two decades than Canada, despite the fact that Canada has experienced greater increases in trade openness than Australia over this period (see Figure A.1). The implication is that there are other variables, such as national institutional arrangements and social customs, which may have a more powerful influence on union density (Visser 2002).

When comparing national employment relations patterns it is important to know not only how strong unions are in terms of membership density, but also about how they are organised. It has been argued that the organisation of unions and particularly the relationship between union central federations and their affiliates has a significant impact on the direction of national economic and social policy. In one version of this thesis it is argued that union movements with a high degree of centralisation are better able to participate in social corporatism and avoid the introduction of neo-liberal economic policies (Golden et al. 1999). Mapping differences in how union movements are organised may also provide insights into the role that religious, political and ideological factors play in shaping employment relations across countries. For example, the relatively large number of central union federations in Italy and France indicates the role that political and ideological divisions play in their labour movements.

Table A.19 provides data on the number of central union federations in each country as well as information about the relative importance of the largest federation. Table A.20 presents information about the structure and sectoral composition of central union federations. It focuses on the number of affiliates to the central federation and the relative importance of a number of key groups of unions and workers. These include large unions, unions representing those working in trade-exposed sectors of the economy and unions representing public-sector workers.

These tables reveal differences in the organisation of union federations and the composition of their membership, which may be important for explaining differences in national patterns of employment relations. There are differences across countries in the number and associational strength of central union federations and they have remained relatively constant over time. While it is generally the case that large unions dominate peak union bodies, the extent of this dominance varies between countries. There are also notable variations in the relative importance of

Table A.18 Union membership

| | Union density (%) | | | | | Union density change (%) |
	1980	1985	1990	1995	2000	1990–2000
Australia	49[a]	46[b]	41	35	25	–39
Canada	35	36	35	34	31	–11
France	19	14	10	10	10[f]	stable
Germany[c]	35	34	32	29	24	–25
Italy[d]	50	42	39	38	36	–8
Japan	31	29	25	24	21	–16
Korea[g]	15	12	17	14	12	–29
Sweden	78[e]	81[e]	80	83	79	–1
UK[h]	52	43	38	32	29	–24
USA	23	18	16	15	13	–19

[a] 1982. [b] 1986. [c] Up to and including 1990 data concerning former West Germany only. [d] Italian density is underestimated, as 'autonomous' unions are excluded. [e] Based on calculations of Anders Kjellberg (see source). Includes unemployed members belonging to unions with union unemployment funds. Data for 1990 and after based on *Labour Force Surveys*, which refer only to employed workers. [f] Estimated. [g] Data from OECD Labour Force Statistics (indicators) database. [h] Excludes Northern Ireland.

Source: Adapted from Kjellberg (2002), using national labour force surveys and national statistical offices data.

Table A.19 Union peak bodies

	Number of union centres[a]			Name	Largest centre — Share in total membership[b]		
	1970–79	1980–90	1991–98		1970–79	1980–90	1991–96
Australia	2–1	1	1	ACTU	84	100	100
Canada	3	3–4	4–3	CLC	72	62	60
France	5	5	5	CGT	47	34	30
Germany	3	3	3	DGB	82	82	83
Italy	6–7	7	7	CGIL	49	46	43
Japan	4	4–2	3	Sohyo, Rengo	37	45	61
Korea	1	1–2	2	FKTU	NA	NA	61[c]
Sweden	4	4	4	LO	64	59	56
UK	1	1	1	TUC	91	87	84
USA	1	1	1	AFL-CIO	70	76	81

[a] Number of national union federations covering at least two complete one-digit ISIC sectors. Excludes public-sector federations.
[b] Share of the largest union federation of total membership. [c] 1999 estimated.
NA Not available.

Source: Adapted from Traxler et al. (2001: 41).

Table A.20   Union centre (confederation) structure and coverage[a]

	Number of affiliates[b]		Membership of three largest affiliates[c] (%)		Membership of three largest exposed-sector unions[d] (%)		Membership of three largest public-sector unions[e] (%)	
	1980–90	1991–96	1980–90	1991–96	1980–90	1991–96	1980–90	1991–96
Australia	156	81	18	28	13	25	11	NA
Canada	167	98	65	63	19	21	32	37
France	37	NA	32	33	21	18	31	30
Germany	17	16	57	57	47	42	25	29
Italy	19	17	44	46	29	27	24	20
Japan	60	74	44	33	16	27	40	20
Korea	NA	NA	NA	NA	NA	NA	NA	NA
Sweden	24	22	57	57	28	27	36	38
UK	90	71	34	43	34	35	17	25
USA	87	86	22	26	17	18	13	15
Mean	60	45	44	46	25	27	24	27

[a] Average for period. [b] Number of affiliates of the largest union centre. [c] Share of the three strongest affiliates in the largest centre's total membership. [d] Membership of the three largest exposed-sector unions as % membership of the largest centre's total membership. [e] Membership of the three largest public-sector unions as % of the largest centre's total membership. NA Not available.

Source: Adapted from Traxler et al. (2001: 46).

workers in the tradeable sector and in the public sector. In Canada, public-sector employees comprise a significant proportion of the membership of the largest federation, whereas in Germany the central federation is dominated by large unions (e.g. IG Metall) representing workers in the tradeable sector of the economy. As Swenson (1989, 1991) and others have noted, the interests of these groups of workers may differ significantly and need to be taken into account when comparing national employment relations patterns.

Growing attention has focused on the role that employers and employers' associations play in shaping employment relations patterns (Swenson & Pontusson 1996, Thelen 2000). Table A.21 provides information about national employer federations which are members of the International Organisation of Employers. This table shows that there are differences in how these employers' organisations operate and the nature and level of affiliation they enjoy. For example, there are high levels of affiliation to the BDA in Germany while affiliation to *Nikkeiren* in Japan is much more modest. While the information provided in this table is a useful point of departure, comparative assessment of the role of employers' federations in shaping employment relations policy should be based on more detailed analysis. For example, despite being numerically small, one of the most influential advocates of change in Australian employment relations has been the Business Council of Australia. It has less than 100 members but these include the CEOs of Australia's largest enterprises (see chapter 5). The increasingly important role of this type of lobby group is not captured in these aggregate statistics.

Much recent debate in comparative employment relations has focused on changes in the structure of bargaining and, particularly, on the coverage of collective bargaining. The simple globalisation approach (see chapter 1) suggests that globalisation will erode organised national systems of employment relations. Traxler et al. (2001: 194) argue that collective bargaining coverage is a key indicator of the extent to which national employment relations are organised because 'the less employees are covered by collective agreements, the more irrelevant organised industrial relations as a whole will become'.

Table A.22 indicates a complex pattern of change and continuity in collective bargaining coverage. There are a group of countries in which there has been a significant decline in collective bargaining coverage. These include Australia, Japan, the UK, and the USA. This decline has been greater in the private sector in these countries than across the economy as a whole. However, in France coverage has increased. In Canada, Germany, and Sweden, collective bargaining coverage has remained relatively stable. In general the data suggest that the higher the level of collective bargaining coverage, the less likely there is to have been a decline, although the Australian case appears to be an anomaly. As Traxler et al. (2001: 199) note, these data suggest that there is no simple relationship between changes in the international economy and erosion of collective bargaining.

Will new forms of employee representation develop in the context of changes in the international economy? Poole et al. (2001: 496–8), for example, argue that while the broader international economic environment seems unfavourable to the development of industrial democracy, factors including changes in production systems have created opportunities for the development of new forms of consultation and participation in some economies

Table A.23 illustrates that there is considerable diversity in the forms of workplace representation. Union-based representative forms remain the most typical. However, there has been a growth in the use of joint consultation committees, in

Table A.21 Profile of national employers' organisations[a]

	National employers' organisations[b]	No of enterprises covered	Type of enterprise	Workforce employed by associated members	Enterprise direct/indirect membership	Density 1996
Australia	Australian Chamber of Commerce & Industry (ACCI)	300 000/50% of total	NA	75% of labour force	Indirect	75[f]
Canada	Canadian Employers' Council (CEC)	NA	Private	Majority	Both	NA
France	Conseil national du patronat français (CNPF)	1 500 000	NA	14 Million	Indirect	74
Germany	Confederation of German Employers' Associations (BDA)	NA	Private	80% of labour force	Both	72[d,e]
Italy	dell' Industria Italiana (Confindustria)	130 000	Private or mixed	About 4 million	Indirect	40
Japan	Employers' Association (Nikkeiren)	26 000	NA	20 million	Indirect	40[f]
Korea	Korean Employers' Federation (KEF)	4 000	Private	2.5 million	Both	NA
Sweden	Swedish Employers' Confederation (SAF)	42 000	NA	1.3 million	Indirect	56
UK	Confederation of British Industry	250 000	NA	NA	Both	54[e]
USA	US Council for International Business	300	NA	NA	Direct	NA

[a] 1997. [b] National employers' organisations that are members of the International Organisation of Employers. [c] Industry and transport.
[d] West Germany. [e] 1995. [f] 1997.
NA Not available.

Sources: ILO (1998); density data from Traxler et al. (2001: 55).

Table A.22 Collective bargaining coverage

	Collective bargaining coverage[a]				Private-sector collective bargaining coverage[b]			
	1980	1985	1990	1996	1980	1985	1990	1996
Australia	88	85	80	70[h]	NA	79	72	63[h]
Canada	NA	37[f]	38	NA	NA	28	30[f]	25[h]
France	85	94	NA	95[h]	85	92	NA	93
Germany[c]	87	85	86	84	86	83	85	82
Italy	NA	NA	NA	NA	NA	NA	NA	NA
Japan	28	NA	23[g]	18[h]	27	NA	22[g]	17[h]
Korea	NA	NA	NA	NA	NA	NA	NA	NA
Sweden	92	92	92	92	88	88	88	88
UK	72[e]	67	50	37	66[e]	55	44	22
USA	26	20	18	16	23	16	13	11
Mean[d]	73	73	67	69	69	68	63	61

[a] Employees under a collective agreement as a percentage of the total number of employees entitled to conclude collective agreements.
[b] Employees under a collective agreement as a percentage of the total number of employees in the private sector. [c] West Germany.
[d] Mean of 18 selected countries (see source). [e] 1978. [f] 1986. [g] 1989. [h] 1995.
NA Not available.

Source: Traxler et al. (2001: 196).

Table A.25 The systems of employee workplace representation

| | Employee-based systems | | |
	Union bodies	Works councils	Joint committees
Australia	Union representatives C, UV		Joint consultative committees C, A
Canada	Union representatives C, UA + UV		
France	*Délégués sindicaux* S: (50), UA	*Délégués du personnel* S: 1946, 1985, 1995 (11), A *Délégation unique du personnel*, S: 1994	*Comités d'énterprise* S: 1945, 1982 (50), A
Germany	*Vertrauensleute*	*Betriebsrat* S: 1952, 1972 (5), A	
Italy	*Rappresentanze sindicale aziendali* (RSA) S: 1970 (15/5), A + (UA)/*Rappresentanze sindicale unitare* (RSU) S: 1970, PC 1993, A + UA, UV		
Japan	Union representatives C, UV Works committees C, UV		
Korea	Union representatives UV	Labour–Management Council S: 1981 (50), A, UA	
Sweden	Fortroendeman C, S: 1974, 1976; PC 1982, UV		Foretagsnamd PC: 1938, 1946 (25), 1958 (50), UV until 1977
UK	Union representatives C, UV		Joint consultative committees C, UA + UV
USA	Union representatives C, UA + UV		Joint consultative committees C, UA + U

Notes: **Modes of institutionalisation:** S = statute, PC = peak-level collective agreements, C = sectoral/local agreements; figures following S & PC indicate the year of legislation/conclusion of the agreements and of major amendments; the figures in parentheses indicate the threshold of institutionalisation in terms of number of employees required. **Mode of selection:** representatives are elected by all employees (A), by union members only (UV), or appointed by higher-level union officials (UA). If the mode of selection varies within a country, classification refers to the most common.

Source: Adapted from Traxler et al. (2001: 121).

which unions do not necessarily have a formal role. But the role and nature of joint consultation committees in Korea and Sweden, for example, differ significantly. While Table A.23 shows little evidence of the spread of works councils, it contains data only up to 1996. As mentioned in chapter 12, the introduction of the EWC directive in 1994 and its implementation in the second half of the 1990s has probably increased the prevalence of works councils. Nonetheless, there is little evidence to suggest growing uniformity in forms of workplace representation across these countries.

Cross-national variations in levels of industrial disputes have long fascinated comparative employment relations scholars. However, there are two features of data on industrial disputes which makes cross country comparison difficult. First, national definitions of industrial disputes are highly idiosyncratic. Statistics are therefore unlikely to be consistent across any two of the countries, let alone across all of them. Canada, Germany, Italy, Japan and Sweden, for example, do not take into account the working days 'lost' by workers not directly involved in the dispute. In some countries, such as the UK and the USA, a distinction is made between stoppages about 'industrial' issues and those which arise over 'political' or 'non-industrial' matters. When attempting to make comparisons, such distinctions cause more traps for the unwary. Before 1975, Italy did not count days lost due to political strikes, while France excludes certain industries from its statistics. Australia, on the other hand, includes stoppages which may last for only a few hours, as long as a total of ten working days are lost. Thus Australia counts stoppages that would not be counted either in the UK or the USA. For such reasons, Shalev (1978) cautions against 'lies, damn lies and strike statistics'. A second feature of national statistics on industrial disputes is that they are likely to change over time. In 1981, for example, the USA increased the minimum size threshold for inclusion in its strike statistics to at least a full shift and from five workers to 1000. In 1987, Canada followed suit in an attempt to counter the criticism that it was more strike prone than the USA. Hence international comparisons became even more difficult (Edwards 1983: 392). However, Canada subsequently resumed the publication of data on the pre-1987 basis (ten working days lost). Nevertheless such distinctions make it very difficult to compare the patterns of work stoppages between countries and over time.

Table A.24 shows that there has been a general decline in the level of industrial disputes e.g. working days lost due to stoppages during the 1990s. Despite this decline, some countries have much higher levels of industrial disputes than others. While working days lost to industrial disputes declined significantly in Australia and France during the 1990s, the average number of working days lost remained higher in these countries than in Japan and Germany. In several other countries levels of disputes seem to have remained relatively stable. These include Sweden and the USA. Furthermore, while Tables A.24 and A.25 do not report data for Korea, as Park and Leggett (chapter 11) note there has been a significant increase in industrial disputes in Korea since 1987. As with bargaining coverage, the relationships between international economic change and industrial conflict appear to be complex.

The comparison of industrial conflict in manufacturing and construction and the service sectors further complicates the picture. Generally we would expect to find higher rates of industrial disputes in manufacturing and building than in the service sector. The data in Table A.25 show that levels of industrial disputes are lower in the service sector in most countries. However, during the 1990s, there have been periods when industrial conflict in the service sector has been higher than in manufacturing in both France and Sweden. Therefore, it may be argued that the general declining

Table A. 24   Working days not worked per 1000 employees: all industries and services[a]

	1992	1993	1994	1995	1996	1997	1998	1999	2000	2001	Average[b]		
											1992–1996	1997–2000	1992–2001
Australia	148	100	76	79	131	77	72	88	61	50	107	69	87
Canada	184	132	137	133	280	296	196	190	125	164	174	192	183
France	37	48	39	304	58	43	52	72	114	83	97	73	84
Germany	47	18	7	8	3	2	1	2	0	1	17	1	9
Italy	180	236	238	65	137	84	40	62	59	66	172	62	116
Japan	5	2	2	1	1	2	2	2	1	1	2	1	2
Korea	NA	NA	NA	NA	NA	NA	NA	NA	NA	NA	NA	NA	NA
Sweden	7	54	15	177	17	7	0	22	0	3	54	6	30
UK	24	30	13	18	57	10	12	10	20	20	29	14	21
USA	37	36	45	51	42	38	42	16	163	9	42	54	48
OECD	69	48	62	77	51	41	46	30	90	29	61	47	54

[a] Employees in employment; some figures have been estimated.   [b] Annual average for those years within each period for which data are available, weighted for employment.
NA Not available.

Sources: Davies (2001) and Monger (2003), using ILO, Eurostat, national statistical offices and OECD data.

Table A.25 Working days not worked per 1000 employees: manufacturing and construction; service industries[a]

| | Manufacturing and construction industries | | | | | | Service industries | | | | | |
| | | | | Average[b] | | | | | | Average[b] | | |
	1990	1995	1999	1990–94	1995–99	1990–99	1990	1995	1999	1990–94	1995–99	1990–99
Australia	594	263	247	183	217	254	80	26	47	28	8	40
Canada	1378	323	293	194	217	306	96	69	163	103	161	148
France	46	112	79	275	15	154	63	279	69	130	104	82
Germany	11	19	6	0	2	13	17	1	1	0	0	7
Italy	609	92	116	62	126	186	174	44	34	59	35	72
Japan	2	2	1	1	0	1	4	2	2	1	1	2
Korea	NA	NA	NA	NA	NA	NA	NA	NA	NA	NA	NA	NA
Sweden	8	13	2	42	4	24	275	241	29	63	60	62
UK	189	115	20	20	15	18	44	20	7	20	22	22
USA	25	188	62	55	14	94	67	6	2	200	8	33
OECD	(174)	(145)	(54)	(67)	(46)	(80)	(64)	(40)	(18)	(102)	(22)	(37)

[a] Employees in employment; some figures have been estimated. [b] Annual averages for those years within each period for which data are available, weighted for employment. Paretheses indicate averages based on incomplete data. NA Not available.

Sources: Davies (2001) and Monger (2003) using ILO, Eurostat, national statistical offices and OECD data.

numbers of working days not worked due to industrial disputes is associated with the shift in employment from industry to services. Nonetheless, the examples of Sweden and France in the 1990s illustrate that there are possibilities for significant industrial action in the service sector, and that various factors help to shape national levels of industrial conflict.

Work stoppages are only one form of sanction, of course. There are many others, including working-to-rule, working without enthusiasm, banning overtime and so on, but there are no comparative data available on such forms of collective sanction. Nor are there any comparable data available on the many forms of individual sanction such as apathy, industrial sabotage and quitting.

LABOUR MARKET OUTCOMES

This section focuses on labour market outcomes which are likely to impact on either economic performance or the quality of working life.

Labour costs associated with producing goods and services are likely to impact upon economic performance. Table A.26 presents an index of the relative costs per hour of production work in manufacturing, compared to those in the USA.

The index implies that, in comparison to the USA, hourly labour costs are significantly lower in Korea, the UK, Australia and Italy but higher in Japan and Germany. However, relative to the USA, between 1990 and 2000 labour costs fell in all of the ten countries except Japan and Korea. This may reflect increasing labour costs in the USA associated with economic growth, but may also indicate the impact of increased international competition on labour costs. Nonetheless, care should be taken in drawing conclusions from these data alone because, among other things, the comparisons can be distorted by fluctuating exchange rates and they do not take into account differences in labour productivity between countries.

Labour productivity differences can be taken into account by measures of unit labour costs which provide an indication of costs of labour per unit of output. Table A.27 demonstrates that in all the countries covered in this study, except Korea, unit labour costs have increased more slowly than remuneration (compensation) since 1998. The implication is that productivity increases have partially offset wage increases. The Korean data can be explained by the end of authoritarian control of employment relations in the late 1980s and the high concentration of independent unionism in the key sectors of the economy (chapter 11). Over the period 1988–2001, increases in unit labour costs have been lowest in Germany and Japan, the two countries with the highest labour costs relative to the USA. There was also a notable reduction in the rate of increase in unit labour costs in the period 1999–2001 compared with the period 1988–98 in the UK, Sweden, Korea, Italy and Canada. These figures are consistent with the view that increased competitive pressures associated with globalisation have had a dampening effect on labour costs and wages (Jacoby 1995).

While labour costs contribute to the costs of business, wages also play a central role in determining the living standards of workers. There are a range of comparative measures of living standards. One interesting example is the annual survey by the International Metalworkers' Federation (IMF) of metalworkers' purchasing power, based on average hourly net wages (i.e. after deduction of workers' social security con-tributions), expressed in working time required for the purchase of selected consumer items.[9]

Table A.26   Hourly labour costs

	Hourly labour costs (index USA = 100)				
	1980	1985	1990	1995	2000
Australia	86	63	88	89	71
Canada	88	84	107	94	81
France	91	58	104	116	83
Germany	124[b]	73[b]	146[b]	184	116
Italy	83	59	112	94	74
Japan	56	49	86	139	111
Korea	10	10	25	42	41
Sweden	127	74	140	125	101
UK	77	48	85	80	80
USA	100	100	100	100	100

[a] These data relate to production workers in manufacturing. Costs are converted from national currency to $US at prevailing annual average exchange rates.
[b] Former West Germany only.

Source: US BLS (2001).

Let us make a few comments on Table A.27. First, the data is probably subject to less scrutiny and standardisation than that data collected by, for example, the OEDC, ILO and national statistical offices. Second, the data illustrates that Korean metal workers are paid significantly less than metal workers in all the other countries in this study and need to work longer hours to purchase a similar basket of goods (see Table A.28). However, even though workers in one country may earn significantly more than workers in another, this does not necessarily mean they are better off. This can seen by comparing the amount of working time Japanese workers need to purchase a basket of goods with the situation faced by workers in Italy, France, Canada and Australia—countries in which net hourly earnings for metalworkers are considerably lower. It is also evident from these figures that some of the necessities of life are relatively more expensive in some countries than in others. Thus, for example, paying the rent consumes almost four times more of French workers' time than is the case for German metal workers. In addition, the table demonstrates large differences in the tax burden that falls on workers. However, the figures in this table do not indicate the extent to which taxation is redistributed to workers in terms of social security and public provision of goods and services.

Working time is another labour market outcome which impacts on economic performance and the quality of working life. There are notable cross-national differences in the hours of work.

Table A.29 demonstrates that, in general, the average working week for men is longer than for women. This reflects the fact that women are more likely to be employed on a part-time basis. The length of the average working week and annual hours of work are lower in the continental European countries (France, Germany, Sweden and Italy) and highest in the Asian countries (Japan and Korea), with the Anglo-Saxon countries (UK, USA, Australia and Canada) between these two

Table A.27   Changes in labour costs in the business sector[a]

	Compensation (remuneration) per employee (annual % change)				Unit labour costs (annual % change)			
	1988–98	1999	2000	2001[c]	1988–98	1999	2000	2001[c]
Australia	4.2	2.4	3.0	4.0	2.1	0.1	2.3	2.9
Canada	3.5	2.6	3.6	3.2	2.3	0.7	1.4	2.1
France	4.8	1.6	1.8	2.8	0.8	0.3	0.7	1.6
Germany	3.5[b]	0.9	1.3	1.9	1.4[b]	0.5	-0.1	0.5
Italy	5.3	2.1	2.9	2.6	3.3	1.3	1.4	1.5
Japan	1.7	-1.1	0.1	0.3	0.3	-2.4	-1.7	0.7
Korea	10.9	12.2	8.0	6.6	6.5	2.1	2.9	2.7
Sweden	6.1	2.8	3.7	3.7	3.4	0.1	2.2	2.3
UK	5.6	4.9	4.4	4.8	4.4	3.9	2.3	2.6
USA	3.5	4.3	4.5	4.7	2.0	1.6	1.0	3.5
EU	4.6	2.5	2.8	3.2	2.7	1.4	1.2	1.7
Total OECD[d]	3.6	2.6	3.1	3.3	1.9	0.9	0.7	2.1

[a] Aggregates are calculated on the basis of 1995 GDP weights expressed in 1995 purchasing power parities.   [b] Average growth rate has been calculated by adjusting data for West Germany prior to 1992.   [c] Secretariat forecasts.   [d] Excluding high inflation countries (i.e. annual inflation of 10% or more).

Source: OECDa (June 2001).

Table A.28 The purchasing power of working time

	Bread (per kg)	Coffee (per kg)		Men's shoes (per pair)		1 litre petrol (super)	Colour TV (50 cm screen)		Rent 4 rooms[a]		Income tax[b] (annual)		Net earnings (hourly) in 2002
	mins	hrs	mins	hrs	mins	mins	hrs	mins	hrs	mins	hrs	mins	$US[c]
Australia	8.5	1	54	4	33.5	3	19	12.5	68	23.5	331	39.5	8.60
Canada	5	—	49	4	5	21.5	27	51	40	48.5	534	21.5	12.76
France	15	—	31.5	5	20.5	6	19	51	76	21	20	19.5	11.65
Germany	7.5	—	33	5	2	21.2	38	38	24	6	98	16	17.34
Italy	13	—	7.5	6	20.5	6	24	23.5	43	54.5	294	17	11.65
Japan	14.5	2	6	7	42	4	19	15	78	36	109	54	15.19
Korea	50.5	5	7.5	17	53.5	7	42	56	198	46.5	44	7.5	4.75
Sweden	7.5	—	30.5	5	6	4.5	29	45.5	42	30.5	498	25	14.59
UK	4	—	41.5	6	33	6	18	42	66	0.5	514	51	14.66
USA	9	—	33.5	4	25.6	1.5	14	45	31	21	497	20.5	13.56

[a] Four rooms including kitchen. [b] Metal workers' family of four with one income. [c] United Nations Offical Exchange Rates, March 2002.

Source: IMF (2003) using 2002 data.

Table A.29 Hours of work

	Men[a]		Women[a]		Total[a]		Annual hours of work[n]	
	1990	2000	1990	2000	1990	2000	1990	2000
Australia[a,i]	39.9	40.5[d]	33.2	33[d]	38.1	38.5[d]	1866	1855
Canada[c,m]	NA	NA	NA	NA	37.9	38.7[k]	1788	1801
France[b,m]	40.3[h]	38.8	39.5[i]	38.1	40.1[i]	38.6	1657	1590
Germany[c,e,m]	39.5[e]	38.0	38.1[e]	37.4	39.2[e]	37.9	1583[e]	1482
Italy[b,l]	41.3[i]	41.6	38.1[i]	37.9	40.4[i]	40.5	1674	1622
Japan[b,m]	49.2	47.1	38.5	37.3	45.0	43.7	2031	1821
Korea[b,m]	49.4	49.2	49.0	49.7	49.3	49.3	2514	2474
Sweden[c,m]	NA	39.1[i]	NA	36.4[i]	39.1	38.2[i]	1549	1625
UK[b,f,m]	43.4	42.0	39.1	38.9	42.3	41.3	1767	1708
USA[c,h,m]	NA	NA	NA	NA	40.8	41.6	1838	1835

[a] Manufacturing. [b] Hours actually worked. [c] Hours paid for. [d] Break in series. [e] Former West Germany only. [f] Includes overtime. Full-time employees on adult pay rates. [h] Private sector; production workers. [i] 1993. [j] 1998. [k] 1999. [l] Labour force survey. [m] Enterprise survey. [n] Total number of hours worked over the year divided by the average number of people in employment. includes part-time employment.
NA Not available.

Sources: ILOa; ILOb; OECDa.

groups.[11] Despite large increases in the amount of part-time work in most of the countries covered in this book (see Table A.8), between 1990 and 2000 there has been an increase in the average working week in Australia, Canada and Italy. Given the increase in part-time employment, annual hours of work have not decreased as much as might have been expected in many countries and have even increased in Sweden. The implication is that, during the 1990s, in most of these economies (apart from the USA) there has been a reversal of the decline in working time that had been taking place since 1945.

Several tables including Table A.30 provide information on the position of women relative to men in the labour market.

Care should be taken in interpreting the data in Table A.30. First, it reports wages in the manufacturing sector. As has been noted earlier, women's employment tends to be concentrated in the service sector of the economy. It is therefore difficult to use this data to make generalisations about the gap between women's wages and men's wages for the economy as a whole. Since many types of service sector workers are paid less than manufacturing workers, these figures may significantly understate the gender wage gap for the economy as a whole. Second, the table reports average hourly earnings. Because women are more likely to employed on a part-time basis, reporting the data in this way may again understate the relative gap between male and female earnings. Taking these factors into account, Pocock (1998: 596), for example, finds that the gender wage gap in Australia was between 65 per cent and 70 per cent during the first half of the 1990s—a much more significant gap that that reported in Table A.30. Those seeking to make more detailed comparisons of gender equity between countries covered in the study should examine figures on average weekly earnings.[10]

Despite such limitations, we can conclude from Table A.30 that women's average hourly earnings in manufacturing are lower than men's. Even in Sweden, which reports high levels of gender equity in a number of other areas, like labour force participation, women working in manufacturing tend to be paid less than men. In spite of significant differences between the ten countries compared in this book, gender continues to play a key role in structuring labour market participation and outcomes.

Access to maternity leave provisions may influence the ability of women to participate in the labour market and take part in full-time work. Table A.31 shows that Australia has the longest period of statutory maternity leave while the USA has the shortest and then only for workers in firms with more than 50 employees. However, Australia and the USA differ from the other countries in not providing statutory income replacement during maternity leave. Among the other countries, periods of paid maternity leave range from three months to six months and the levels of compensation are between 55 per cent and 100 per cent. Korea is the only country where the costs of income replacement are not integrated into the social welfare system and are borne by the employer. This may reflect the relative underdeveloped nature of the welfare system in Korea and the traditionally paternalistic tradition of employment relations there.

Another factor which influences the quality of working life is dangerous work. As with many aggregate statistics, there are limitations in the extent to which direct comparison can be made using the data in Table A.32. As can be seen from the notes that accompany the table, there are differences in the basis on which work-related deaths, injuries and illnesses are reported across countries. Furthermore, there may be differences in the *extent* to which deaths and injuries are reported in the various

394

Table A.30 Gender wage gap in manufacturing

	Women's earnings in manufacturing as % of men's (hourly earnings)						
	1970	1975	1980	1985	1990	1995	2000
Australia	64	79	79	79	82[d]	85	84[c]
Canada[g]	60	60	64	65	68	73	72[e]
France	77[a]	76	77	79	79	79	79[b]
Germany[k]	70	72	73	73	73	74	74 (74)[f]
Italy	NA	NA	NA	NA	NA	NA	NA
Japan[h]	45	48	44	42	41	56[i]	58
Korea	NA	NA	NA	47	50	54	59[h]
Sweden	80	85	90	90	89	90	91
UK	58	67	69	68	68	71	75
USA[g]	62	62	63	68	72	75[i]	76[i]

[a] 1971. [b] 1997. [c] 1998. [d] Series break in 1990. [e] New series after 1996. [f] Figure in parentheses is for united Germany. [g] Data for most countries are based on hourly earnings in manufacturing. However, data for Canada refer to average annual earnings for full-time, full-year workers; data for USA refer to median weekly earnings for full-time wage and salary workers. These data are, therefore, not directly comparable with each other, or with figures from the other countries. [h] Data for Japan are based on monthly, rather than hourly, earnings in manufacturing. Some differences will be apparent from figures used in the earlier edition of this book for which OECD adjustments of Japan's monthly figures into approximate hourly data had been used (see OECDa 1988). These were available only up to 1986; hence all figures for Japan in this edition are based on ILO monthly figures. [i] 1995 figure based on new series begun in 1994 which only includes establishments with ten or more regular employees and regular cash earnings. [j] 1995 and 2000 figures use BLS data, using the same definitions as earlier US Department of Commerce data (as explained in note g). [k] Former West Germany only. NA Not available.

Sources: ILOa; Statistics Canada, Catalogue 13-217 and 202-0102; US BLS (1997, 2002).

Table A.31 International comparisons of maternity leave, 1998

	Length of maternity leave	Wages paid in covered period (%)	Provider of coverge
Australia	1 year	0	—
Canada	17–18 wks	100	Social security
France	16–26 wks	55 for 15 wks	Social security
Germany	14 wks	100	Social security
Italy	5 months	80	Social security
Japan	14 wks	60	Social security
Korea	60 days	100	Employer
Sweden	14 wks	75[a]	Social security
UK	14–18 wks	90[b]	Social security
USA	12 wks[c]	0	—

[a] 450 days paid parental leave. 360 days at 75 per cent and 90 days at flat rate. [b] 90 per cent for 6 weeks, flat rate thereafter. [c] Applies only to workers in companies with 50 workers or more.
— No provider.

Source: United Nations (2000b)

Table A.32 Incidence rates of fatal and non-fatal occupational injuries

	Rates of injuries (men & women)			
	Fatal injuries per 100 000 employees		Non-fatal injuries per 100 000 employees	
	1990	1999	1990	1999
Australia[a]	7[h]	4	NA	2021
Canada[a]	8.5	6.7	3848[i]	3067
France[a,f]	8.4	4.5[j]	5271	4432
Germany[a,d]	5.07[c]	3.42	5440[c]	4128
Italy[a,f]	11[g]	8[k]	6199[g]	3932[k]
Japan[b,e,m]	0.01	0.01	NA	NA
Korea[a,f]	30	19	NA	NA
Sweden[b,e]	2.6[i]	1.7	1050[i]	954
UK[b]	1.4[g]	0.7	789[g]	666
	5	4	NA	NA

[a] Compensated injuries. [b] Reported injuries. [c] Former West Germany only. [d] Per 100 000 full-time equivalent workers. [e] Per 100 000 hours worked. [f] Per 100 000 workers insured. [g] 1991. [h] 1992. [i] 1993. [j] 1996. [k] 1998. [l] Excludes Victoria and Australian Capital Territory. [m] Excludes general construction.
NA Not available.

Source: ILOa (2001).

countries and under-reporting in some countries may mask differences between countries. Nonetheless, we can draw tentative conclusions. It is more dangerous to work in some countries that in others. In terms of fatal injuries, Korea has a much worse record than all the other countries. However, there are also marked differences between the more developed countries in terms of non-fatal injuries. Thus, Germany, France and Italy have much higher rates of occupational injuries than do the UK or Sweden. These figures are consistent with the academic literature on occupational health and safety (OH&S) which suggests that the incidence of occupational injuries is affected by a complex array of variables—including technical, psychological and social factors (Quinlan & Bohle 2000), factors which are likely to differ from industry to industry as well as country to country. Nevertheless, in all of the countries for which data is available there has been a reduction in fatal and non fatal injuries in the1990s. One reason for this improvement may be the spread of UK-type legislation, which focuses on consultation between employers and employees over OH&S matters rather than compliance with health and safety standards.

NOTES

Chapter 1   Introduction

1. Industrial relations may be regarded as dealing more with the macro or institutional aspects of the employment relationship, while HRM focuses on the micro or enterprise level aspects; we regard each as being complementary to the other.
2. The term employment relations is increasingly used in the literature to reflect the interconnectedness of labour-management relations, industrial relations and human resource management (see Locke et al. 1995b; Kochan et al. 1997; Gardner & Palmer 1997; Kitay & Lansbury 1997; Katz & Darbishire 2000). Giles (2000b) has recently argued for the use of the broader notion of 'work relations' to take into account issues such as self-employment, subcontracting and voluntary work.
3. There are *comparative* studies that focus, say, on two industries or establishments within one country. Although such studies can be very insightful, they do not have an *internationally* comparative dimension.
4. Reich and Higgot (quoted in Reich 1999: 305) have argued that globalisation is rapidly replacing 'Cold War' as 'the most overused and underspecified explanation for a variety of events in international relations'.
5. For a more detailed treatment, see Held et al. (1999: 27-8).
6. A more detailed discussion of these aspects of comparative analysis can be found in earlier editions of this book; see Bamber and Lansbury (1998: 2).
7. Although the MIT project recruited local teams of academics from the countries being compared. As Kitay (1997: 4) notes, this was in an effort to avoid the imposition of US values and perspectives on the issues being studied (another of the potential pitfalls of comparative analysis and one of the perceived shortcomings of Kerr et al. 1960).
8. For one recent attempt to do this, see Traxler et al. (2001: 3-9), who distinguish three dimensions of convergence.
9. There have been attempts to examine the impact of international economic change on national patterns of employment relations from a political economy perspective (see, e.g. Cox 1987, Lange et al. 1982, Gourevitch et al. 1984). See also the special issue of the *Journal of Industrial Relations* on globalisation and labour regulation, especially the contributions by Haworth and Hughes (2000), Murray et al. (2000) and Deyo (2000).

10. The growing interest in the role of institutional variables has been called the *new institutionalism* across a range of disciplines. There are different versions of the new institutionalism (for a useful overview, see Goodin 1996). This chapter focuses on views associated with what has been called *historical institutionalism* in comparative politics (see Thelen & Steinmo 1992; also, Hall & Taylor 1996; Pontusson 1995: Immergut 1998).

11. Some examples include Giles and Murray (1988), Smith and Meiskins (1995), Pontusson and Swenson (1996), Murray et al. (2000) and Wailes (2000a).

12. For a review of this literature, see Wailes (1999).

13. For an explanation of the nature of the capitalist state and its implications for industrial relations, see Giles (1989).

Chapter 2   Employment relations in Britain

1. Britain includes England, Scotland and Wales, while the UK includes Britain and Northern Ireland. Although Northern Ireland has much in common with Britain, some important elements of industrial relations are different. This chapter concentrates on Britain, although some of the cited statistics here and in the Appendix refer to the UK as a whole.

2. Unless otherwise indicated, the data from WERS relate to workplaces employing 25 or more employees.

3. The union density data in this paragraph are based on a question in the Labour Force Survey of individuals, and so are not strictly comparable with earlier data that were based on union sources.

4. Membership of the Institute of Directors is based on individuals, and tends to reflect the views of directors in small and medium-sized companies. By contrast, membership of the CBI is on a corporate basis, giving greater influence to larger companies.

5. British unions usually have unpaid union representatives at the workplace, often referred to as shop stewards or staff representatives. They may be allowed time off work to represent fellow union members in the workplace (Goodman & Whittingham 1969; Terry & Dickens 1991).

6. An unofficial strike takes place without the official approval of the union hierarchy.

7. The statute does not prevent employers voluntarily recognising non-independent unions or in-house staff associations. Doing so makes it more difficult—though not impossible—for independent unions to replace them. This approach has been adopted by a few high-profile companies (Simpson 2000).

Chapter 6   Employment relations in Italy

1. The full title is 'The protocol on incomes and employment policies, on bargaining structures, work and support for the productive system'.

2. Prior to its takeover by Sweden's Electrolux, during the 1970s and 1980s, Zanussi's main plants in Pordenone, like FIAT's at Turin, were sites of some of the most intense industrial conflict (Golden 1988).

Chapter 11   Employment relations in the Republic of Korea

1. Except in cases where the usage has long been otherwise (e.g. 'Syngman Rhee'), Koreans' names are represented according to Korean convention, i.e. family

name first followed by two hyphenated given names, the second being introduced by a lower-case initial. In the references and where necessary in the text, the second initial is retained unhyphenated (and in upper case) for consistency in this volume and to facilitate the distinction of authors with common family names.
2. An account of Korea's labour legislation, which includes a tabular summary, is provided by Park and Lee (1996).
3. For a more detailed account of labour dispute settlement machinery in Korea, see Park (1993: 153–7).

Chapter 12   Conclusions

1. ILO conventions can be deratified only 'within the year following the expiration of ten years from the date upon which the convention first comes into force', and during every tenth year thereafter. Ratification remains operative even after withdrawal from the ILO, unless and until denounced in an appropriate year.
2. For a review of such arguments, see Lee (1997) and Singh (2003).
3. For an analysis of the fate of labour standards in NAFTA, see Schoch (2000).
4. For a historical overview of the development of the international union movement and assessments of the current policy direction of the ICFTU, see Carew et al. (2000).
5. For other accounts of cross-border organising in the Americas, see, for example, Frundt (1996) and Williams (1999).

Appendix   Globalisation, employment and labour

1. Table A.2 shows GDP at (a) current prices and exchange rates and (b) current prices and PPPs. Exchange rates seldom reflect the purchasing power of different currencies. Exchange rates are often affected by influences unrelated to the values of any goods and services. These influences include among other things, currency trading and relative interest rates among countries. PPPs are interspatial indexes constructed for the purpose of comparing currencies and volumes across countries so that comparisons between countries reflect only differences in volume. For a more detailed discussion see US BLS (2001).
2. PPPs are currency conversions that allow output in different currency units to be expressed in a common unit of value. A purchasing power parity is a relative price which measures the number of units of country B's currency that are needed in country B to purchase a similar basket of goods as one unit of country A's currency will purchase in country A. In other words, PPP's eliminate the differences in price levels between countries in the process of conversion. For the tables in this book country A is the USA. For more details see OECDk.
3. One useful way of doing this is by using the International Standard Industrial Classification System (ISIC). The ISIC system provides a standard classification of economic activities of entities by arranging according to the activity they carry out. For more details on the ISIC system including major divisions and recent revisions to the classification system see United Nations Statistics Division (2003). The services category is now very heterogeneous as it includes all the industries which do not fit one of the first two categories, including public administration, finance, property and business services, community services, recreation, personal and other services and many more. Therefore, some commentators suggest that it

would be appropriate to subdivide services into further categories such as: tertiary, consisting of tangible economic services; quaternary, comprising data processing; and quinary, covering unpaid work and homework where pay is secondary, and professional services of a quasi-domestic nature (e.g. Jones 1982). However, as yet the authorities do not provide a sufficiently comprehensive set of such data, nor do we have a sufficiently well developed conceptual framework within which to gather and analyse it. As an additional complication, the distinctions between categories are not always precise due to classification difficulties and because some people work in more than one sector. Moreover, the trend towards subcontracting and the growth of employment agencies have tended to distort the data and so have exaggerated the growth of services.

4. For disaggregated labour force participation data, see OECDa and OECDb, various years.

5. For a detailed discussion of the the growth of atypical work and its gendered nature see OECDa 2002 chapter 2, see also De Grip et al. (1997) and Klausen (1999).

6. For discussion of national differences in the measurement of unemployment rates see OECDb. The OCED generally uses standardised unemployment rates based on international standards. Different methods of collecting unemployment statistics can show different results between figures of registered jobseekers and figures based on unemployment surveys and other methods. See also ILO (1995).

7. For the full text of each of the ILO conventions and details about the ILO Convention system see ILOb.

8. M may be based on survey data or on membership figures supplied by the unions themselves. Many unions simply report estimates, if they do not collect precise membership details centrally. Some include unemployed and retired members. For various purposes, moreover, they may either wish to exaggerate or understate their membership. M also depends on the working definition of a union. Does it include employee associations, as in the USA, staff associations, as in the UK, or professional organisations of doctors and lawyers, for example, which may have some union functions? The USA has also seen the growth of 'associate unions', which provide services to their members at reduced prices, but are not really labour unions in the traditional sense (Stern 1997). P depends on the definition of potential union membership. This also raises many questions. Several countries have more than one series of union density data. For instance, certain series are based on population surveys that may be limited to civilian employment, which excludes the armed forces, but such surveys also tend to show lower density in comparison with those based on union returns. Some series exclude other groups who rarely belong to unions, such as employers, the self-employed, the retired, the unemployed and those employed in agriculture, forestry and fishing in most countries.

9. On such international trade secretariats, see above chapter 12.

10. Table A.29 also illustrates that there is not a consistent relationship between average weekly hours and annual hours worked across countries. This reflects national differences in data-collection methods as well as in their customs in relation to annual leave and statutory holidays. Some countries collect data on average hours *actually worked*, while others collect data on average *hours paid for*. Hours actually worked include normal hours of work, overtime, stand-by hours at place of work, and short rest periods at the workplace including tea or

coffee breaks. Hours paid for comprise hours actually worked and, depending on varying custom and practice, may also include factors such as paid annual leave, paid public holidays, paid sick leave, meal breaks and time spent on travel from home to work and vice versa. These broad differences are indicated by the summary notes against each country in Table A.28. Relatively long annual hours in the USA are due mainly to annual leave entitlements which are nearly three weeks shorter than the European average, combined with a relatively low level of absence from work.

11. Comparative data on weekly earnings is available on the ILO's LABOURSTA online database (http://laborsta.ilo.org/). For some countries this data is disaggregated by gender.

REFERENCES

Chapter 1   Introduction

Adams, R. (1981) 'A theory of employer attitudes and behaviour towards trade unions in Western Europe and North America' in G. Dlugos & K. Weiermair in collaboration with W. Dorow eds *Management under Differing Value Systems* ——Berlin: de Gruyter
——(1988) 'Desperately seeking industrial relations theory' *International Journal of Comparative Labour Law and Industrial Relations* 4, 1, pp. 1-10

Albeda, W. (1984) 'European industrial relations in a time of crisis' in P. Drenth et al. eds *Handbook of Work and Organisational Psychology* New York: John Wiley

Bain, G.S. & Clegg, H.A. (1974) 'A strategy for industrial relations research in Great Britain' *British Journal of Industrial Relations* 12, 1, pp. 91-113

Bamber, G. & Lansbury, R. (1998) 'An Introduction to International and Comparative Employment Relations' in G. Bamber & R. Lansbury eds *International and Comparative Employment Relations: A Study in Industrialised Market Economies* 3rd edn, Sydney: Allen & Unwin

Bamber, G.J., Boreham, P. & Harley, B. (1992) 'Economic and industrial relations outcomes of different forms of flexibility in Australian industry: An analysis of the Australian Workplace Industrial Relations Survey' in *Exploring Industrial Relations: Further Analysis of AWIRS* Canberra: Department of Industrial Relations, Industrial Relations Research Series, no. 4

Bamber, G.J. & Sheldon, P. (2001) 'Collective bargaining' in R. Blanpain and C. Engels eds *Comparative Labour Law and Industrial Relations in Industrialized Market Economies*, pp. 549-84, The Hague: Kluwer

Barbash, J. & Barbash, K. eds (1989) *Theories and Concepts in Comparative Industrial Relations* Columbia: University of South Carolina Press

Bean, R. (1994) *Comparative Industrial Relations: An Introduction to Cross-National Perspectives* revised edn, London: Routledge

Bendix, R. (1970) *Embattled Reason* New York: Oxford University Press

Berger, S. (1996) 'Introduction' in S. Berger & R. Dore eds *National Diversity and Global Capitalism* Ithaca, NY: Cornell University Press

Blain, A.N. & Gennard, J. (1970) 'Industrial relations theory: A critical review' *British Journal of Industrial Relations* 8, 3, pp. 389–407

Blanpain, R. (2001) 'Comparativism in labour law and industrial relations' in R. Blanpain & C. Engels eds *Comparative Labour Law and Industrial Relations in Industrialized Market Economies* 7th edn, The Hague: Kluwer

Brown, D. & Harrison, M.J. (1978) *The Sociology of Industrialisation*, London: Macmillan

Brulin, G. & Nilsson, T. (1997) 'Sweden: The Volvo and Saab road beyond lean production' in Kochan et al. eds (1997)

Burton, J. ed. (1988) 'Review Symposium on *The Transformation of American Industrial Relations: Industrial and Labor Relations Review* 41, 3, pp. 439–55

Campbell, D. (1996) 'How have OECD trade unions fared in an interdependent world economy? Some evidence and some speculation' *Mimeo* Geneva: International Labour Organisation

Camuffo, A. & Micelli, S. (1997) 'Spain, France and Italy: Mediterranean lean production' in Kochan et al. eds (1997)

Chamberlain, N.W. (1961) 'Book review of Kerr et al.' [1960] *American Economic Review* 51, 3, pp. 475–80

Chelius, J. & Dworkin, J. (1990) *Reflections on the Transformation of Industrial Relations* Metuchen: IMLR Press/Rutgers University

Clegg, H.A. (1976) *Trade Unionism Under Collective Bargaining: A Theory Based on Comparisons of Six Countries* Oxford: Blackwell

Cochrane, J.L. (1976) 'Industrialism and industrial man in retrospect: A preliminary analysis' in J.L. Stern & B.D. Dennis eds *Proceedings of the Twenty-ninth Annual Winter Meetings, Industrial Relations Research Association Series* Madison: IRRA, pp. 274–87

Cox, R. (1987) *Production, Power, and World Order: Social Forces in the Making of History* New York: Columbia University Press

Craig, A. (1975) 'The framework for the analysis of industrial relations systems' in B. Barrett et al. eds *Industrial Relations and the Wider Society* London: Collier Macmillan, pp. 8–20

de la Graza, M. (2001) 'Converging divergences or converging through four patterns?' *Industrial and Labor Relations Review* 54, 3, pp. 694–7

Deyo, F. (2000) 'Reform, globalisation and reconstructing Thai labour' *Journal of Industrial Relations* 42, 2, pp. 258–94

Doeringer, P.B. (1981) 'Industrial relations research in international perspective' in P.B. Doeringer et al. eds *Industrial Relations in International Perspective: Essays on Research and Policy* London: Macmillan

Dore, R. (1973) *British Factory, Japanese Factory: The Origins of National Diversity in Industrial Relations* London: Allen & Unwin

Dunlop, J.T. (1958) *Industrial Relations Systems* New York: Holt, Rinehart & Winston

Evans, P. (1997) 'The eclipse of the state? Reflections on stateness in an era of globalisation' *World Politics* 50, 1, pp. 62–87

Ferner, A. & Hyman, R. (1998) 'Introduction: Towards European industrial relations?' in A. Ferner & R. Hyman eds *Changing Industrial Relations in Europe* 2nd edn, London: Blackwell

Freeman, R.B. (1989) 'On the divergence in unionism among developed countries' *Discussion Paper no. 2817*, National Bureau of Economic Research

Fucini, J. & Fucini, S. (1990) *Working for the Japanese: Inside Mazda's American Auto Plant* London: Macmillan

Gardner, M. & Palmer, G. (1997) *Employment Relations* 2nd edn, Melbourne: Macmillan

Garrett, G. (1998) 'Global markets and national policies: Collision course or virtuous circle?' *International Organisation* 52, 4, pp. 787-824.

Giles, A. (1989) 'Industrial relations theory, the state and politics' in J. Barbash & K. Barbash eds (1989)

——(2000a) 'Globalisation and industrial relations theory' *Journal of Industrial Relations* 42, 2, pp. 173-94

——(2000b) 'Industrial relations at the millennium: Beyond employment?' *Labour/Le Travail* 46, pp. 37-67

——(2000c) 'Review of Katz and Darbishire (2000), Converging divergences: worldwide changes in employment relations' *Journal of Industrial Relations* 42, 2, pp. 474-8

Giles, A. & Murray, G. (1988) 'Towards an historical understanding of industrial relations theory in Canada' *Relations Industrielles* 43, 4, pp. 780-810

——(1997) 'Industrial relations theory and critical political economy' in J. Barbash & N. Meltz eds *Theorising in Industrial Relations: Approaches and Applications* Sydney: Australian Centre for Industrial Relations Research and Training

Gill, J. (1969) 'One approach to the teaching of industrial relations' *British Journal of Industrial Relations* 7, 2, pp. 265-72

Goldthorpe, J.H. (1984) 'The end of convergence: Corporatist and dualist tendencies in modern western societies' in J.H. Goldthorpe ed. *Order and Conflict in Contemporary Capitalism: Studies in the Political Economy of Western European Nations* Oxford: Clarendon

Goodin, R. (1996) 'Institutions and their design' in R. Goodin ed. *The Theory of Institutional Design* New York: Cambridge University Press

Gould, W.B. (1984) *Japan's Reshaping of American Labor Law* Cambridge, MA: MIT Press

Gourevitch, P. et al. (1984) *Unions and Economic Crisis: Britain, West Germany and Sweden* London: Allen & Unwin

Hall, P. & Taylor, R. (1996) 'Political science and the three new institutionalisms' *Political Studies* 44, 5, pp. 936-57

Hancke, B. (2001) 'Review of Katz and Darbishire *Converging Divergences*' *British Journal of Industrial Relations* 39, 2, pp. 305-7

Haworth, H. & Hughes, S. (2000) 'Internationalisation, industrial relations theory and industrial relations' *Journal of Industrial Relations* 42, 2, pp. 195-213

Held, D., McGrew, A., Goldblatt, D. & Perraton, J. (1999) *Global Transformations: Politics, Economics and Culture* Cambridge: Polity Press

Hirst, P. & Thompson, G. (1996) *Globalisation in Question: The International Economy and the Possibilities of Governance* Cambridge: Polity Press

Hyman, R. (1975) *Industrial Relations: A Marxist Introduction* London: Macmillan

——(1980) 'Theory in industrial relations: Towards a materialist analysis' in P. Boreham & G. Dow eds *Work and Inequality, vol. 2: Ideology and Control in the Labour Process* Melbourne: Macmillan

——(1994) 'Theory and industrial relations' *British Journal of Industrial Relations* 32, 2, pp. 165-80

Immergut, E. (1998) 'The theoretical core of the new institutionalism' *Politics & Society* 26, 1, pp. 5-34

Isaac, J.E. (2003) 'Intercultural and other forces in the transfer of human resource management and industrial relations practices in globalization' *Working Paper*, p. 1: Austrian Institute of Economic Research, Vienna

Katz, H.C. (1993) 'The decentralization of collective bargaining: A literature review and comparative analysis' *International and Labor Relations Review* 47, 1, pp. 1-22

Katz, H.C. ed. (1997a) *Telecommunications: Restructuring Work and Employment Relations Worldwide* Ithaca, NY: Cornell University Press

——Katz, H. & Darbishire, O. (2000) *Converging Divergence: Worldwide Changes in Employment Systems* Ithaca, NY: Cornell University Press

Kerr, C. (1983) *The Future of Industrial Societies: Convergence or Continuing Diversity?* Cambridge, MA: Harvard University Press

Kerr, C., Dunlop, J.T., Harbison, F.H. & Myers, C.A. (1960) *Industrialism and Industrial Man: The Problems of Labour and Management in Economic Growth* London: Penguin

Kim, Dong-heon (1997) 'Works councils in Korea and Taiwan: A comparative perspective' *Working Paper* Champaign: Institute of Labour and Industrial Relations University of Illinois

Kitay, J. (1997) 'Changing patterns of employment relations: Theoretical and methodological framework for the six Australian industry studies' in Kitay & Lansbury eds (1997)

Kitay, J. & Lansbury, R.D. eds (1997) *Changing Employment Relations in Australia* Melbourne: Oxford University Press

Knudsen, H. & Markey, R. (2002), 'Works councils: lessons from Europe for Australia' in P.J.Gollan, R. Markey, and I.Ross eds, pp. 102-28, Sydney: Federation Press

Kochan, T. (1998) 'What is distinctive about industrial relations research?' in K. Whitfield & G. Strauss eds (1998) *Researching the World of Work: Strategies and Methods in Studying Industrial Relations* Ithaca, NY: Cornell University Press

Kochan, T., Katz, H. & McKersie, B. (1984) *The Transformation of American Industrial Relations* New York: Basic Books

Kochan, T.A., Lansbury, R.D. & MacDuffie, J.P. eds (1997) *After Lean Production: Evolving Employment Practices in the World Auto Industry* Ithaca, NY: Cornell University Press

Kochan, T.A., McKersie, R.B. & Cappelli, P. (1984) 'Strategic choice and industrial relations theory' *Industrial Relations* 23, 1, Winter, pp. 16-39

Lange, P., Ross, G., Vannicelli, M. & Harvard University Center for European Studies (1982) *Unions, Change and Crisis: French and Italian Unions and the Political Economy, 1945-1980* London: Allen & Unwin

Lansbury, R.D., Sandkull, B. & Hammarström, O. (1992) 'Industrial relations and productivity: Evidence from Sweden and Australia' *Economic and Industrial Democracy* 13, 3, pp. 295-330

Lewin, D. (1988) 'Industrial relations as a strategic variable', in M. Kleiner et al. eds *Human Resources and the Performance of the Firm* Madison: Industrial Relations Research Association

Linden, M. (1998) 'Doing comparative labour history: Some essential preliminaries' in J. Hagan & A. Wells eds *Australian Labour and Regional Change: Essays in Honour of R.A. Gollan* Sydney: University of Wollongong in association with Halstead Press

Locke, R.M. (1992) 'The decline of the national union in Italy: Lessons for comparative industrial relations theory' *Industrial and Labor Relations Review* 45, 2, pp. 229-49

Locke, R.M., Piore, M. & Kochan, T.A. (1995a) 'Reconceptualising comparative industrial relations: Lessons from international research' *International Labour Review* 134, 2, pp. 139-61

Locke, R.M., Kochan, T.A. & Piore, M. (1995b) *Employment Relations in a Changing World Economy* Cambridge, MA: MIT Press

Locke, R. & Thelen, K. (1995) 'Apples and oranges compared: Contextualized comparisions and the study of comparative politics' *Politics and Society* 23, 3, pp. 337–67

Mandel, E. (1969) *A Socialist Strategy for Europe* Institute for Workers' Control Pamphlet no. 10, Nottingham: IWC

Marsden, R. (1982) 'Industrial relations: A critique of empiricism' *Sociology* 16, 2, pp. 232–50

Mayo, E. (1949) *The Social Problems of an Industrial Civilization* London: Routledge

Mills, C. Wright (1959) *The Sociological Imagination* New York: Oxford University Press

Murray, G., Levesque, C. & Vallee, G. (2000) 'The re-regulation of labour in a global context: Conceptual vignettes from Canada' *Journal of Industrial Relations* 42, 2, pp. 234–57

Parker, M. & Slaughter, J. (1988) *Choosing Sides: Unions and the Team Concept* Boston: South End Press

Perraton, J. et al. (1997) 'The globalisation of economic activity' *New Political Economy* 2, 2, 257–77

Piore, M.J. (1981) 'Convergence in industrial relations? The case of France and the United States' *Working Paper no. 286* Department of Economics, Cambridge: Massachusetts Institute of Technology

Piore, M.J. & Sabel, C. (1984) *The Second Industrial Divide: Possibilities for Prosperity* New York: Harper & Row

Pontusson, J. (1995) 'From comparative public policy to political economy: Putting political institutions in their place and taking interests seriously' *Comparative Political Studies* 28, 1, pp. 117–48

Pontusson, J. & Swenson, P. (1996) 'Labor markets, production strategies and wage bargaining institutions: The Swedish employer offensive in comparative perspective' *Comparative Political Studies* 29, 2, pp. 223–51

Poole, M. (1986) *Industrial Relations: Origins and Patterns of National Diversity* London: Routledge

Regini, M. (1999) 'Comparing banks in advanced economies: The role of markets, technology, and institutions in employment relations' in Regini et al. eds (2000)

Regini, M., Kitay, J. & Baethge, J. eds (2000) *From Tellers to Sellers: Changing Employment Relations in Banks* Cambridge, MA: MIT Press

Reich, S. (1999) 'Review of Weiss, L. (1998) *The Myth of the Powerless State*' *New Political Economy* 4, 2, pp. 305–10

Rogers, J. & Streeck, W. (1995) *Works Councils: Consultation, Representation and Cooperation in Industrial Relations* Chicago IL:University of Chicago Press

Ross, A.M. & Hartman, P.T. (1960) *Changing Patterns of Industrial Conflict* New York: Wiley

Schregle, J. (1981) 'Comparative industrial relations: Pitfalls and potential' *International Labour Review* 120, 1, pp. 15–30

Seelinger, R. (1996) 'Conceptualizing and researching policy convergence' *Policy Studies Journal* 24, 2, pp. 287–306

Shalev, M. (1980) 'Industrial relations theory and the comparative study of industrial relations and industrial conflict' *British Journal of Industrial Relations* 18, 1, pp. 26–43

407

Shirai, T. ed. (1983) *Contemporary Industrial Relations in Japan* Madison: University of Wisconsin Press

Sisson, K. (1987) *The Management of Collective Bargaining: An International Comparison* Oxford: Blackwell

Sisson, K. ed. (1994) *Personnel Management* Oxford: Blackwell

Smith, C. & Meiskins, P. (1995) 'System, society and dominance effects in cross-national organisational analysis' *Work, Employment and Society* 9, 2, pp. 241-67

Strauss, G. (1992) 'Creeping toward a field of comparative industrial relations' in H. Katz ed. *The Future of Industrial Relations* Ithaca, NY: Cornell University Press

——(1997) 'Neither European nor works councils' *Economic and Industrial Democracy* 18, 2, pp. 325-38

——(1998) 'Comparative International Industrial Relations' in Whitfield & Strauss eds *Researching the World of Work: Strategies and Methods in Studying Industrial Relations* Ithaca, NY: ILR Press/Cornell University Press

——(2001) 'High equality, low activity: The contribution of the social welfare system to the stability of the German collective bargaining regime' *Industrial and Labor Relations Review* 54, 3, pp. 698-704

Streeck, W. (1988) 'Change in industrial relations: strategy and structure' *Proceedings of an International Symposium on New Systems of Industrial Relations*, 13-14 September, Tokyo: Japan Institute of Labour

Thelen, K. (1993) 'Western European labour in transition: Sweden and Germany compared' *World Politics* 46, 1, pp. 15-27

Thelen, K. & Steinmo, S. (1992) 'Historical institutionalism in comparative politics' in K. Thelen, S. Steinmo & F. Longstreth eds *Structuring Politics: Historical Institutionalism in Comparative Perspective* New York: Cambridge University Press

Tilly, C. (1995) 'Globalisation threatens labour's rights' *International Labour and Working Class History* 47, 1, pp. 1-23

Traxler, F., Blaschke, S. & Kittel, B. (2001) *National Labour Relations in Internationalised Markets: A Comparative Study of Institutions, Change and Performance* Oxford: Oxford University Press

Turner, L. (1991) *Democracy at Work: Changing World Markets and the Future of Labour Unions* Ithaca, NY: Cornell University Press

Verma, A., Kochan, T.A. & Lansbury, R.D. eds (1995) *Employment Relations in the Changing Asian Economies* London: Routledge

Wade, R. (1996) 'Globalisation and its limits: Reports of the death of the national economy are greatly exaggerated' in S. Berger & R. Dore eds *National Diversity and Global Capitalism* Ithaca, NY: Cornell University Press

Wailes, N. (1999) 'The importance of small differences: The effects of research design on the comparative study of industrial relations reform in Australia and New Zealand' *International Journal of Human Resource Management* 10, 6, pp. 1006-30

——(2000a) 'Economic change and domestic industrial relations institutions: Towards a theoretical model' *Journal of Industrial Relations* 42, 2, pp. 214-33

——(2000b) 'Review of Katz and Darbishire, *Converging divergences*' *Relations Industrielles/Industrial Relations* 55, 3, pp. 540-3

Wailes, N., Ramia, G. & Lansbury, R.D. (2003 forthcoming) 'Integrating interests and institutions: The case of industrial relations reform in Australia and New Zealand' *British Journal of Industrial Relations* December

Walker, K.F. (1967) 'The comparative study of industrial relations' *Bulletin of the International Institute for Labour Studies* 3, pp. 105–32

Weiss, L. (1998) *The Myth of the Powerless State: Governing the Economy in a Global Era* Polity Press: Cambridge

Womack, J., Jones, D. & Roos, D. (1990) *The Machine that Changed the World* New York: Rawson-Macmillan

Chapter 2 Employment relations in Britain

ACAS (annually) *Annual Report* London: Advisory, Conciliation and Arbitration Service, Her Majesty's Stationery Office

Ackers, P. & Payne, J. (1998) 'British trade unions and social partnership: Rhetoric, reality and strategy' *International Journal of Human Resource Management* 9, pp. 529–50

Annual Reports of the Certification Office, London (1980–2000)

Bain, G.S. & Price, R.J. (1983) 'Union growth in Britain: Retrospect and prospect' *British Journal of Industrial Relations* 11, 1, pp. 46–68

Barrell, P. & Pain, N. (1997) 'EU, an attractive investment', *New Economy* 4, 1

Beaumont, P.B. (1987) *The Decline of the Trade Union Organisation* London: Croom Helm

Berridge, J., Cooper, C.L. & Highley-Marchington, C. (1997) *Employee Assistance Programmes and Employee Counselling* Chichester: John Wiley & Sons

Blake, D. (2000) 'Two decades of pension reform in the UK' *Employee Relations* 22, 3, pp. 223–45

Burns, P. (2001) 'A telling intervention', *People Management* 7, 14, pp. 30–3

Claydon, T. (1989) 'Union derecognition in Britain in the 1980s' *British Journal of Industrial Relations* 27, 2, pp. 214–24

——(1998) 'Problematising partnership' in P. Sparrow & M. Marchington eds *Human Resource Management: The New Agenda* London: Financial Times/Pitman, pp. 180–92

Colling, T. (1997) 'Managing human resources in the public sector' in I. Beardwell & L. Holden eds *Human Resource Management* 2nd edn, London: Pitman Publishing, pp. 654–80

——(2000) 'Personnel management in the extended organisation' in S. Bach & K. Sisson eds *Personnel Management: A Comprehensive Guide to Theory and Practice* Oxford: Blackwell, pp. 70–90

Coupar, W. & Stevens, B. (1998) 'Towards a new model of industrial partnership: Beyond the "HRM versus industrial relations" argument' in P. Sparrow & M. Marchington eds *Human Resource Management: The New Agenda* London: Financial Times/Pitman, pp. 145–59

Cully, M., Woodland, S., O'Reilly, A. & Dix, G. (1999) *Britain at Work: As Depicted by the 1998 Workplace Employee Relations Survey* London: Routledge

Department of Trade and Industry (DTI) (1998) *Fairness at Work* Cmnd 3968, London: Her Majesty's Stationery Office

Dickens, L. (2000) 'Doing more with less: ACAS and individual conciliation' in B. Towers & W. Brown eds *Employment Relations in Britain: 25 Years of the Advisory, Conciliation and Arbitration Service* Oxford, Blackwell, pp. 67–92

Dix, G. (2000) 'Operating with style: The work of the ACAS conciliator in individual employment rights cases' in B. Towers & W. Brown eds *Employment*

Relations in Britain: 25 Years of the Advisory, Conciliation and Arbitration Service Oxford: Blackwell, pp. 93–122

Donovan, T.N. (1968) *Royal Commission on Trade Unions and Employers' Associations: Report* Cmnd 3623, London: Her Majesty's Stationery Office

Earnshaw, J. & Cooper, C.L. (1996) *Stress and Employer Liability* London: Institute of Personnel and Development

Edwards, P. (1995) 'Strikes and industrial conflict' in P. Edwards ed. *Industrial Relations: Theory and Practice in Britain* Oxford: Blackwell

Equal Opportunities Commission (EOC) (2001) *Just Pay, Report of the Equal Pay Task Force* Manchester: EOC

Fox, A. (1985) *History and Heritage: The Social Origins of the British Industrial Relations System* London: Allen & Unwin

Gall, G. & McKay, S. (1994) 'Trade union derecognition in Britain, 1988–1994' *British Journal of Industrial Relations* 32, 3, pp. 433–48

Gill, C. & Krieger, H. (1999) 'Direct and representative participation in Europe: Recent evidence' *International Journal of Human Resource Management* 10, 4, pp. 572–91

Goodman, J.F.B. (1994) 'The United Kingdom' in *Towards Social Dialogue: Tripartite Co-operation in National Economic and Social Policy-Making* Geneva: International Labour Organisation, pp. 273–96

——(2000) 'Building bridges and settling differences: Collective conciliation and arbitration under ACAS' in B. Towers & W. Brown eds *Employment Relations in Britain: 25 Years of the Advisory, Conciliation and Arbitration Service* Oxford, Blackwell, pp. 31–65

Goodman, J.F.B. & Earnshaw, J. (1995) 'New industrial rights and wrongs: The changed framework of British employment law' *New Zealand Journal of Industrial Relations* 19, 3, pp. 305–21

Goodman, J.F.B. & Whittingham, T.G. (1969) *Shop Stewards in British Industry* London: McGraw-Hill

Gospel, H.F. & Littler, C.R. (1983) *Managerial Strategies and Industrial Relations: An Historical and Comparative Study* London: Heinemann

Gottlieb, B., Kelloway, E. & Barham, E. (1998) *Flexible Work Arrangement: Managing the Work/Family Boundary* Chichester: John Wiley & Sons

Grant, D. (1997) 'Japanisation and new industrial relations' in I. Beardwell ed. *Contemporary Industrial Relations: A Critical Analysis* Oxford: Oxford University Press, pp. 201–33

Gratton, L., Hope Hailey, V., Stiles, P. & Truss, C. (1999) *Strategic Human Resource Management* Oxford: Oxford University Press

Green, F. (1992) 'Recent trends in trade union density' *British Journal of Industrial Relations* 30, 3, pp. 445–58

Grimshaw, D., Willmott, H. & Vincent, S. (forthcoming) 'Going privately: Practices of partnership in the outsourcing of services in the public sector' *Public Administration*

Guest, D. & Conway, N. (2000) *The Psychological Contract in the Public Sector* London: Chartered Institute of Personnel and Development

Guest, D. & Hoque, K. (1994) 'The good, the bad and the ugly: Employment relations in new non-union workplaces' *Human Resource Management Journal* 5, 1, pp. 1–14

Guest, D. & Peccei, R. (1998) 'The partnership company: Benchmarks for the future *The Report of the IPA Survey Principles, Practice and Performance*' London: Involvement and Participation Association

——(2001) 'Partnership at work: Mutuality and the balance of advantage' *British Journal of Industrial Relations* 39, 2, pp. 207-36

Hall, L. & Torrington, D. (1998) *The Human Resource Function: The Dynamics of Change and Development* London: Pitman

Haynes, P. & Allen, M. (2001) 'Partnership as union strategy: A preliminary evaluation' *Employee Relations* 23, 2, pp. 164-87

Heery, E. (1998) 'The relaunch of the TUC' *British Journal of Industrial Relations* 36, 3, pp.339-60

Hyman, R. (1997) 'The future of employee representation' *British Journal of Industrial Relations* 35, 3, pp. 309-36

Industrial Relations Services (1999) 'Trends in employee involvement' *IRS Employment Trends* 683, pp. 6-16

Institute for Employment Research (2001) *Projections of Occupations and Qualifications 2000/2001* London: Department for Education and Employment, no. 1

Kelly, J. (1982) *Scientific Management, Job Redesign and Work Performance* London: Academic Press

——(1996) 'Union militancy and social partnership' in P. Ackers, C. Smith & P. Smith eds *The New Workplace and Trade Unionism* London:Routledge, pp. 77-109

Kessler, S. & Bayliss, F. (1998) *Contemporary British Industrial Relations* 3rd edn, Basingstoke: Macmillan

Knell, J. (1999) 'Partnership at work' *Employment Relations Research Series* no. 7, London: Department of Trade and Industry

Kochan, T., Katz, H.C. & McKersie, R.D. (1986) *The Transformation of American Industrial Relations* New York: Basic Books

Kramer, R.J. (1998) 'Equal employment opportunities' in M. Poole & M. Warner eds *The IEBM Handbook of Human Resource Management* London: Thomson Learning, pp. 736-44

Labour Market Trends (Monthly) Central Statistical Office London: Her Majesty's Stationery Office

Lobel, S. (1996) *Work/Life and Diversity: Perspectives of Workplace Reponses* Boston, MA: Boston University, Center on Work and Family

Low Pay Commission (2000) 'The National Minimum Wage: The story so far' *Second Report of the LPC* Cmnd 4571

Marchington, M. (1995) 'Employee relations' in S. Tyson ed. *Strategic Prospects for Human Resource Management* London: Institute of Personnel and Development, pp. 81-111

——(1998) 'Partnership in context' in P. Sparrow & M. Marchington eds *Human Resource Management: The New Agenda* London: Financial Times/Pitman, pp. 208-25

——(2001) 'Employee involvement at work', in J. Storey ed. *Human Resource Management: A Critical Text* 2nd edn, London: Thomson Learning, pp. 232-52

Marchington, M. & Parker, P. (1990) *Changing Patterns of Employee Relations* Hemel Hempstead: Harvester Wheatsheaf

Marchington, M. & Wilkinson, A. (2002) *People Management and Development* London: Chartered Institute of Personnel and Development

Marchington, M., Wilkinson, A., Ackers, P. & Dundon, T. (2001) *Management Choice and Employee Voice* London: Chartered Institute of Personnel and Development

Marginson, P., Gilman, M., Jacobi, O. & Krieger, H. (1998) *Negotiating European Works Councils: An Analysis of Agreements Under Article 13* Dublin: European Foundation for the Improvement of Living and Working Conditions

McKay, S. (2001) 'Between flexibility and regulation: Rights, equality and protection at work' *British Journal of Industrial Relations* 39, 2, pp. 285-303

McLoughlin, I. & Gourlay, S. (1994) *Enterprise Without Unions: Industrial Relations in the Non-Union Firm* Buckingham: Open University Press

Metcalf, D. (1999) 'The British National Minimum Wage' *British Journal of Industrial Relations* 37, 2, pp. 171-201

Millward, N., Stevens, M., Smart, D. & Hawes, W. (1992) *Workplace Industrial Relations in Transition* Aldershot: Dartmouth Publishing

Millward, N., Bryson, A. & Forth, J. (2000) *All Change at Work? British employment Relations 1980-1998, as Portrayed by the Workplace Industrial Relations Survey Series* London: Routledge

OECD (1997) *Implementing the OECD Job Strategy: Lessons from Member Countries' Experience* Paris: Organisation for Economic Cooperation and Development

Purcell, J. & Sisson, K. (1983) 'Strategies and practice in the management of industrial relations' in G. Bain ed. *Industrial Relations in Britain* Blackwell: Oxford, pp. 95-120

Ramsay, H. (1977) 'Cycles of control: Worker participation in sociological and historical perspective' *Sociology* 11, pp. 481-506

Rubery, J., Earnshaw, J., Marchington, M., Cooke, F. & Vincent, S. (2002) 'Changing organisational forms and the employment relationship' *Journal of Management Studies* 39, pp. 645-72

Salamon, M. (2000) *Industrial Relations: Theory and Practice* 4th edn, Harlow: Financial Times/Prentice Hall

Schmid, G., Reissart, B. & Bruche, G. (1992) *Unemployment Insurance and Active Labor Market Policy* Detroit, MI: Wayne State University Press

Shephard, R.J. (1996) 'Financial aspects of employee fitness pro-grammes' in J. Kerr, A. Griffiths & T. Cox eds *Workplace Health* London: Taylor & Francis, pp. 29-54

Simpson, B. (2000) 'Trade union recognition and the law, a new approach' *Industrial Law Journal* 29, 3, pp. 193-222

Smith, P. & Morton, G. (2001) 'New Labour's reform of Britain's employment law' *British Journal of Industrial Relations* 39, 1, pp. 119-38

Stewart, J. & Walsh, K. (1992) 'Change in the management of public services' *Public Administration* 70, 4, pp. 499-518

Streeck, W. (1987) 'The uncertainty of management in the management of uncertainty: Employers, labour relations and industrial adjustments in the 1980s' *Work, Employment and Society* 1, 3, pp. 281-308

Terry, M. & Dickens, L. eds (1991) *European Employment and Industrial Relations Glossary: United Kingdom* London: Sweet and Maxwell/Luxembourg: Office for Official Publications of the European Communities

Thomas, C. & Wallis, B. (1998) 'Dwr Cymru/Welsh Water: A case study in partnership' in P. Sparrow & M. Marchington eds *Human Resource Management: The New Agenda* London: Financial Times/Pitman, pp. 160-70

Towers, B. (1997) *The Representation Gap: Change and Reform in the British and American Workplace* Oxford, Oxford University Press

Trades Union Congress (1999) *Partners in Progress: New Unionism in the Workplace* London: TUC

Turner, H.A. (1962) *Trade Union Growth, Structure and Policy: A Comparative Study of the Cotton Unions* London: Allen & Unwin

Undy, R. (1999) 'New Labour's industrial relations settlement—The Third Way' *British Journal of Industrial Relations* 37, 2, pp. 315-36

Waddington, J. (2000) 'United Kingdom: Recovering from the neo-liberal assault' in J. Waddington & R. Hoffman eds *Trade Unions in Europe: Facing Challenges and Searching for Solutions* Brussels, European Trade Union Institute, pp. 575–626

Waddington, J. & Whitson, C. (1997) 'Why do people join unions in a period of membership decline?' *British Journal of Industrial Relations* 35, 4, pp. 515–46

Wills, J. (1999) 'European works councils in British firms' *Human Resource Management Journal* 9, 4, pp. 19–38

Winchester, D. & Bach, S. (1995) 'The state: The public sector' in P. Edwards ed. *Industrial Relations: Theory and Practice in Britain* Oxford: Blackwell

Womack, J., Jones, D. & Roos, D. (1990) *The Machine that Changed the World* New York: Rawson-Macmillan

Chapter 3   Employment relations in the United States of America

Adams, R.J. (1980) *Industrial Relations Systems in Europe and North America* Hamilton, Ontario: McMaster University

Applebaum, E. & Batt, R. (1994) *The New American Workplace* Ithaca, NY: ILR Press

Barbash, J. (1967) *American Unions: Structure, Government and Politics* New York: Random House

Bernstein, I. (1970) *The Turbulent Years* Boston: Houghton Mifflin

Blau, F.D. & Kahn, L. (1996) 'International differences in male wage inequality: Institutions versus market forces' *Journal of Political Economy* 106, August, pp. 791–837

Bronfenbrenner, K. (1997) 'The role of union strategies in NLRB certification elections' *Industrial and Labor Relations Review* 50, pp. 195–212

Bureau of Labor Statistics (2001) 'Union members in 2000' *Press release* 18 January, Internet at www.stats.bls.gov/newsrels.htm

Bureau of National Affairs (1995) *Collective Bargaining Negotiations and Contracts* Washington: Bureau of National Affairs

——(2000) 'Kaiser, AFL-CIO detail contract hailed as model for health care sector' *Daily Labor Report* Washington DC, 27 September, 188: A-6

——(2001) 'Carpenters withdraw from the AFL-CIO, citing disagreement over internal policies' *Daily Labor Report* Washington DC, 30 March, 62: AA-1

Cappelli, P. (1985) 'Competitive pressures and labor relations in the airline industry' *Industrial Relations* 24, Fall, pp. 316–38

——(1999) *The New Deal at Work* Boston: Harvard Business School Press

Commons, J.R. (1909) 'American shoemakers' *Quarterly Journal of Economics* 24, November, pp. 39–81

Doeringer, P. & Piore, M. (1971) *Internal Labor Markets and Manpower Analysis* Lexington, MA: D.C. Heath

Economic Report of the President (2001) Washington, DC: US Government Printing Office

Erickson, C.L. (1992) 'Wage rule formation in the aerospace industry' *Industrial and Labor Relations Review* 45, April, pp. 507–22

——(1996) 'A re-interpretation of pattern bargaining' *Industrial and Labor Relations Review* 49, July, pp. 615–34

Farber, H.S. (1998) 'Has the rate of job loss increased in the nineties?' unpublished working paper, Industrial Relations Section, Princeton University

Feuille, P. & Wheeler, H.N. (1981) 'Will the real industrial conflict please stand up?' in J. Stieber, R.B. McKersie & D.Q. Mills eds *US Industrial Relations 1950-1080: A Critical Assessment* Madison, WI: IRRA, pp. 255-95

Foner, P.S. (1947) *History of the Labor Movement in the United States, vol. 1* New York: International Publishers

Getman, J.G. (1998) *The Betrayal of Local 14* Ithaca, NY: Cornell University Press

Gomez-Mejia, L.R., Balkin, D.B. & Cardy, R.L. (1995) *Managing Human Resources* Englewood Cliffs, NJ: Prentice Hall

Hession, C.H. & Sardy, H. (1969) *Ascent to Affluence: A History of American Economic Development* Boston: Allyn & Bacon

Jacoby, S.M. (1985) *Employing Bureaucracies* New York: Columbia University Press

——(1999) 'Are career jobs headed for extinction?' *California Management Review* 42, Fall, pp. 123-45

Juravich, T. & Bronfenbrenner, K. (1999) *Ravenswood: The Steelworkers'Victory and the Revival of the American Labor Movement* Ithaca, NY: Cornell University Press

Kassalow, E.M. (1974) 'The development of western labor movements: Some comparative considerations' in L.G. Reynolds, S.A. Masters & C. Moser eds *Readings in Labor Economics and Labor Relations* Engelwood Cliffs, NJ: Prentice-Hall

Katz, H.C. (1985) Shifting Gears Cambridge, MA: MIT Press

——(1993) 'The decentralization of collective bargaining: A literature review and comparative analysis' *Industrial and Labor Relations Review* 47, 1, pp. 3-22

Katz, H.C. & Darbishire, O. (2000) *Converging Divergences: Worldwide Changes in Employment Systems* Ithaca, NY: Cornell University Press

Katz, H.C. & Kochan, T.A. (1999) *An Introduction to Collective Bargaining and Industrial Relations* 2nd ed, New York: Irwin-McGraw Hill

Katz, H.C., Batt, R. & Keefe, J.H. (2000) 'The revitalization of the CWA: Integrating political action, organizing, and collective bargaining' March, NYSSILR-Cornell University, unpublished manuscript

Kochan, T.A., Katz, H.C. & McKersie, R.B. (1994) *The Tranformation of American Industrial Relations* 2nd edn, Ithaca, NY: Cornell University Press

Lebergott, S. (1984) *The Americans: An Economic Record* New York: W.W. Norton

Ledvinka, J. & Scarpello, V.G. (1991) *Federal Regulation of Personnnel and Human Resource Management* 2nd edn, Belmont, CA: Kent

Levy, F. & Murname, R.J. (1992) 'U.S. earnings levels and earnings inequality: A review of recent trends and proposed explanations' *Journal of Economic Literature* 30, September, pp. 1333-81

McClendon, J.A., Kriesky, J. & Eaton, A. (1995) 'Member support for union mergers: An analysis of an affiliation referendum' *Journal of Labor Research* 16, 1, pp. 9-23

Osterman, P. (1994) 'How common is workplace transformation and how can we explain who does it' *Industrial and Labor Relations Review* 47, January, pp. 175-88

——(1999) *Securing Prosperity* New York: Oxford University Press

Rosenblum, J. (1995) *Copper Crucible* Ithaca, NY: Cornell University Press

Rubinstein, S.A. & Kochan, T.A. (2001) *Learning from Saturn* Ithaca, NY: Cornell University Press

Sexton, P.C. (1991) *The War Against Labor and the Left* Boulder, CO: Westview Press

Stone, K. (1996) 'Mandatory arbitration of individual employment rights: The yellow dog contract of the 1990s' *Denver Law Review* 73, pp. 1017-34

Sturmthal, A. (1973) 'Industrial relations strategies' in A. Sturmthal & J. Scoville eds *The International Labor Movement in Transition* Urbana, IL: University of Illinois Press

Taft, P. (1964) *Organized Labor in American History* New York: Harper & Row

Turner, L., Katz, H.C. & Richard W. Hurd (2001) *Rekindling the Movement* Ithaca, NY: Cornell University Press

Wheeler, H.N. (1985) *Industrial Conflict: An Integrative Theory* Columbia: University of South Carolina Press

Chapter 4   Employment relations in Canada

Adams, G. (1995) *Canadian Labour Law* 2nd edn, Aurora, ON: Canada Law Book

Adell, B., Grant, M. & Ponak, A. (2002) *Strikes in Essential Services* Kingston, ON: Queen's University IRC Press

Akyeapong, E.B. (2000) Statistics Canada, *Special 2000 Labour Day Release*

Betcherman, G., McMullen, K., Leckie, N. & Caren, C. (1994) *The Canadian Workplace in Transition* Kingston, ON: IRC Press, Queen's University

Brown, D.J.M. & Beatty, D.M. (2001) *Canadian Labour Arbitration* 4th edn, Agincourt, ON: Canada Law Book

Chaykowski, R. & Verma, A. (1992) *Industrial Relations in Canadian Industry* Toronto: Holt, Rinehart & Winston

Craig, A.W.J. & Solomon, N. (1993) *The System of Industrial Relations in Canada* 4th edn, Scarborough, ON: Prentice-Hall

Craven, P. (1980) *'An Impartial Umpire': Industrial Relations and the Canadian State* Toronto: University of Toronto Press

Drache, D. & Glasbeeck, H. (1992) *The Changing Workplace: Reshaping Canada's Industrial Relations System* Toronto: James Lorimer

Finkelman, J. & Goldenberg, S. (1983) *Collective Bargaining in the Public Service: The Federal Experience in Canada* 2 vols, Montreal: Institute for Research on Public Policy

Godard, J. (2000) *Industrial Relations: The Economy and Society* 2nd edn, North York, ON: Captus Press

Gunderson, M., Ponak, A. & Taras, D.G. (2001) *Union–Management Relations in Canada* 4th edn, Toronto: Addison Wesley Longman

Hébert, G., Jain, H.M. & Meltz, N.M. eds (1989) *The State of the Art in Industrial Relations* Kingston: Industrial Relations Centre, Queen's University and Centre for Industrial Relations, University of Toronto

Human Resources Development Canada, Government of Canada: http://labour-travail.hrdc-drhc.gc.ca

Kaufman, B.E. & Taras, D.G. (2000) *Non-Union Employee Representation* Armonk, NY: ME Sharpe

King, W.L.M. (1918 & 1973) *Industry and Humanity* Toronto: University of Toronto Press

Kumar, P. (1993) *From Uniformity to Divergence: Industrial Relations in Canada and the United States* Kingston, ON: IRC Press, Queen's University

Labour Canada, *Strikes and Lockouts in Canada*, various issues; unpublished data, Human Resources Development Canada (HRDC) 1966–2000

——*Chronological Perspectives on Work Stoppages in Canada*, Human Resources Development Canada (HRDC)

Palmer, B.D. (1983) *Working Class Experience: The Rise and Reconstitution of Canadian Labour, 1800–1980* Toronto: Butterworths

Panitch, L. & Swartz, D. (1993) *The Assault on Trade Union Freedoms: From Wage Controls to Social Contract* Toronto: Garamond Press

Peirce, J. (2003) *Canadian Industrial Relations* 2nd edn, Scarborough, ON: Prentice Hall Canada

Sethi, A. ed. (1989) *Collective Bargaining in Canada* Scarborough, ON: Nelson Canada

Sims, A.C.L., Blouin, R. & Knopf, P. (1995) *Seeking a Balance: Canada Labour Code Review, Part 1* Ottawa: Minister of Public Works and Government Services

Statistics Canada, Government of Canada: www.statcan.ca *Special 2000 Labour Day Release*

——(2002) 'Fact-Sheet on Unionization' *Perspectives on Labour and Income*

Swimmer, G. (2001) *Public Sector Labour Relations in an Era of Restraint and Restructuring* Don Mills, ON: Oxford University Press

Swimmer, G. & Thompson, M. eds (1995) *Public Sector Collective Bargaining in Canada: The End of the Beginning or the Beginning of the End?* Kingston, ON: IRC Press, Queen's University

Verma, A. & Chaykowski, R.P. eds (1999) *Contract & Commitment: Employment Relations in the New Economy* Kingston, ON: Queen's University IRC Press

Warrian, P. (1996) *Hard Bargain: Transform Labour-Management Relations* Toronto: McGilligan Books

Weiler, P. (1980) *Reconcilable Differences* Toronto: Carswell

White, J. (1993) *Sisters and Solidarity: Women and Unions in Canada* Toronto: Thomson Educational

Woods, H.D., Carruthers, A.W.R., Crispo, J.H.G. & Dion, G. (1969) *Canadian Industrial Relations* Ottawa: Information Canada

Workplace Information Directorate, *Workplace Gazette*, vol. 3, no. 4, p. 115

——*Workplace Gazette*, vol. 5, no. 3

Chapter 5   Employment relations in Australia

Alexander, M., Green, R. & Wilson, A. (1998) 'Delegate structures and strategic unionism: Analysis of factors in union resilience' *Journal of Industrial Relations* 40, 4, pp. 663-89

Australian Bureau of Statistics (ABS)a *Australian System of National Accounts* cat. no. 5204.0, Canberra: ABS (quarterly)

—— b *Consumer Price Index* cat. no. 6401.0, Canberra: ABS (quarterly)

——(2003) Australian Labour Market Statistics

Australian Centre for Industrial Relations Research and Training (ACIRRT) (1999) *Australia at Work: Just Managing?* Sydney: Prentice Hall

Beggs, J.J. & Chapman, B.J. (1987) 'Australian strike activity in an international context: 1964-1985' *Journal of Industrial Relations* 29, 2, pp. 137-49

Bell, S. (1997) *Ungoverning the Economy: The Political Economy of Australian Economic Policy*, Melbourne: Oxford University Press

Bennett, L. (1995) 'Bargaining away the rights of the weak: Non-union agreements in the Federal Jurisdiction' in P. Ronfeldt & R. McCallum eds *Enterprise Bargaining, Trade Unions and the Law*, Sydney: Federation Press

Bray, M. & Rimmer, M. (1989) 'Voluntarism or compulsion? Public inquiries into industrial relations in New South Wales and Great Britain, 1890-4' in S. Macintyre & R. Mitchell eds (1989) pp. 50-73

Briggs, C. (1999) *The Rise and Fall of the ACTU: Maturation, Hegemony and Decline*, Unpublished PhD thesis, Sydney: Department of Industrial Relations, University of Sydney

Buchanan, J. & Briggs, C. (2002) 'Works councils and inequality at work in contemporary Australia' in P.J. Gollan et al. eds (2002) pp. 48-73

Burgess, J. & Campbell, I. (1998) 'Casual employment in Australia: Growth, characteristics, a bridge or a trap?' *Economic and Labour Relations Review* 9, 1, pp. 31-54

Callus, R., Moorehead, A., Cully, M. & Buchanan, J. (1991) *Industrial Relations at Work: The Australian Workplace Industrial Relations Survey* Canberra: Australian Government Publishing Service

Campbell, I. (2001) 'Industrial relations and intellectual challenges: Reconceptualising the recent changes to labour regulation in Australia' paper presented to *Conference on the Future of Industrial Relations*, University of Sydney

Castles, F.G. (1988) *Australian public policy and economic vulnerability: A comparative and historical perspective* Sydney: Allen & Unwin

Clegg, H.A. (1976) *Trade Unionism Under Collective Bargaining: A Theory Based on Comparisons of Six Countries* Oxford: Blackwell

Combet, G. (2001) 'Employee participation in an Australian context' *Conference on Works Councils in Australia* Melbourne: Royal Melbourne Institute of Technology

Cooper, R. (2000) 'Organise, organise, organise! The 2000 ACTU Congress' *Journal of Industrial Relations* 42, 4, pp. 582-94

——(2002) 'Trade unionism in 2001' *Journal of Industrial Relations* 44, 2, pp. 247-62

——(2003) 'Trade unionism in 2002' *Journal of Industrial Relations* 45, 2, pp. 205-23

Cooper, R., Lansbury, R.D. & Westcott, M. (2003) 'Labour revitalisation in Australia' in D. Cornfield & H. McCammon eds *Labor Revitalisation*, Research in the Sociology of Work, JAI.

Creighton, B. (1997) '*The Workplace Relations Act* in an International Perspective' *Australian Journal of Labour Law* 10, 1, pp. 31-49

Dabscheck, B. (1989) *Australian Industrial Relations in the 1980s* Melbourne: Oxford University Press

——(2000) 'The Australian waterfront dispute and theories of the state' *Journal of Industrial Relations* 42, 4, pp. 497-518

Davis, E.M. (1996) 'The 1995 ACTU congress: recruitment and retention' *Economic and Labour Relations Review* 7, 1, pp. 165-81

Denoon, D. (1983) *Settler Capitalism: The Dynamics of Dependent Development in the Southern Hemisphere*, Oxford: Clarendon Press

Ellem, B. (2001) 'Trade unionism in 2000' *Journal of Industrial Relations* 43, 2, pp. 196-218

Gardner, M. & Ronfeldt, P. (1996) 'The arbitral model: What remains?' in *Current Research in Industrial Relations: Proceedings of the 10th AIRAANZ Conference* Perth: Association of Industrial Relations Academics of Australia and New Zealand, pp. 157-66

Gollan, P.J. & Patmore, G. eds (2003) *Partnership at Work: The Challenge of Employee Democracy* Sydney: Pluto Press

Gollan, P.J., Markey, R. & Ross, I. eds (2002) *Works Councils in Australia* Sydney: Federation Press

417

Hancock, K. (1984) 'The first half century of wage policy' in B. Chapman, J. Isaac & J. Niland eds *Australian Labour Economics: Readings* Melbourne: Macmillan, pp. 44–99

Howard, W.A. (1977) 'Australian trade unions in the context of union theory' *Journal of Industrial Relations* 19, 3, pp. 255–73

Isaac, J.E. (1977) 'Wage determination and economic policy' *The Giblin Memorial Lecture* University of Melbourne

Lansbury, R.D. (1978) 'The return to arbitration: Recent trends in dispute settlement and wages policy in Australia' *International Labour Review* 117, 5, pp. 611–24

——(1985) 'The Accord: A new experiment in Australian industrial relations' *Labour and Society* 10, 2, pp. 223–35

——(1994) 'Changing patterns of industrial relations and human resources in the Australian automotive industry: Towards trans-formation?' *International Journal of Employment Studies* 2, 1, pp. 3–40

Lansbury, R.D. & Macdonald, D. eds (1992) *Workplace Industrial Relations: Australian Case Studies* Melbourne: Oxford University Press

Lansbury, R.D. & Wailes, N. (2003) 'The meaning of industrial democracy in an era of neo-liberalism' in P.J. Gollan & G. Patmore eds (2003)pp. 37–46

Ludeke, J. (1993) 'The public interest and the Australian industrial relations commission' *Journal of Industrial Relations* 34, 4, pp. 593–604

Macintyre, S. (1989) 'Neither labour nor capital: The politics of the establishment of arbitration' in S. Macintyre & R. Mitchell eds (1989) pp. 178–201

Macintyre, S. & Mitchell, R. eds (1989) *Foundations of Arbitration: The Origins and Effects of State Compulsory Arbitration, 1980–1914*, Melbourne: Oxford University Press

Mathews, T. (1994) 'Employers' associations, corporatism and the Accord: The politics of industrial relations' in S. Bell & B. Head eds *State, Economy and Public Policy in Australia* Melbourne: Oxford University Press

McCallum, R. (1997a) 'Australian workplace agreements—an analysis' *Australian Journal of Labour Law* 10, 1, pp. 50–61

——(1997b) 'Crafting a new collective labour law for Australia' *Journal of Industrial Relations* 39, 3, pp. 405–22

——(2000) *Employer Controls over Private Life* Sydney: University of New South Wales Press

McCallum, R. & Patmore, G. (2002) 'Works councils and labour law' in P.J. Gollan et al. eds (2002) pp. 74–101

Morehead, A., Steele, M., Alexander, M., Stephen, K. & Duffin, L. (1997) *Changes at Work: The 1995 Australian Industrial Relations Survey* Melbourne: Longman

Niland, J.R. (1976) *Collective Bargaining in the Context of Compulsory Arbitration* Sydney: University of New South Wales Press

O'Brien, J. & O'Donnell, M. (1999) 'Government, management and the unions: The public sector under the Workplace Relations Act' *Journal of Industrial Relations* 41, 3, pp. 446–67

Organisation for Economics Cooperation and Development (OECD) (2000) *Economic Surveys: Australia* Paris: OECD

Patmore, G. (2003) 'Industrial conciliation and arbitration in New South Wales before 1998' in G. Patmore ed. *Laying the Foundations of Industrial Justice: The Presidents of the NSW Industrial Relations Commission 1902–1998* Sydney: Federation Press

Peetz, D. (1990) 'Declining union density' *Journal of Industrial Relations* 32, 2, pp. 197–223

418

——(1998) *Unions in a Contrary World: The Future of the Australian Trade Union Movement* Melbourne: Cambridge University Press

Pittard, M. (1997) 'Collective employment relationships: Reform of arbitrated awards and certified agreements' *Australian Journal of Labour Law* 10, 1, pp. 62–88

Plowman, D. (1989) 'Forced march: The employers and arbitration' in S. Macintyre & R. Mitchell eds (1989) pp. 135–55

Ravenhill, J. (1994) 'Australia and the global economy' in S. Bell & B. Head eds *State Economy and Public Policy in Australia* Melbourne: Oxford University Press

Rimmer, M. (1987) 'Australia: New wine in old bottles' in B. Bilson ed. *Wage Restraint and the Control of Inflation: An International Survey* London: Croom Helm

Rimmer, M. & McDonald, T. (1989) 'Award restructuring and wages policy' *Growth* CEDA, 37, pp. 111–34

Schwartz, H. (1989) *In the Dominions of Debt: Historical Perspectives on Dependent Development* Ithaca, NY: Cornell University Press

Sheldon, P. & Thornthwaite, L. (1999) 'Employer matters in 1998' *Journal of Industrial Relations* 41, 1, pp. 152–69

Short, M. & Buchanan, J. (1995) 'Wages policy and wage determination in 1994' *Journal of Industrial Relations* 37, 1, pp. 119–31

Waring, P. (1999) 'The rise of individualism in Australian industrial relations' *New Zealand Journal of Industrial Relations* 24, 3, pp. 291–318

Willis, R. (1997) 'Productive employment and sustainable livelihoods' *Address to the Commission for Social Development* New York: United Nations

Wilson, K., Bradford, J. & Fitzpatrick, M. eds (2000) *Australia in Accord: An Evaluation of the Prices and Income Accord in the Hawke-Keating Years* Melbourne: South Pacific Publishing

Wooden, M. (1999) 'Individual agreement making in Australian workplaces: Incidences, trends and features' *Journal of Industrial Relations* 41, 3, pp. 417–45

——(2000) *The Transformation of Australian Industrial Relations* Sydney: Federation Press

Yerbury, D. & Isaac, J.E. (1971) 'Recent trends in collective bargaining in Australia' *International Labour Review* 110, pp. 421–52

Chapter 6   Employment relations in Italy

Alacevich, F. (1996) *Le Relazioni Industriali in Italia: Cultura e Strategie* Rome: Nuova Italia Scientifica

Baccaro, L. & Locke, R.M. (1998) 'The end of solidarity? The decline of egalitarian wage policies in Italy and Sweden' *European Journal of Industrial Relations* 4, 3, pp. 283–308

Baccaro, L., Carrieri, M. & Damiano, C. (2003) 'The resurgence of the Italian confederal unions: Will it last?' *European Journal of Industrial Relations* 9, 1, pp. 43–59.

Baglioni, G. (1991) 'An Italian mosaic: Collective bargaining patterns in the 1980s' *International Labour Review* 130, 1, pp. 81–93

Banca d'Italia (2000) *Assemblea Generale Ordinaria dei Partecipanti: Anno 1999: Considerazioni Finali* 31 May, Rome

Boldizzoni, D. & Lorenzet, A. (1996) 'Il gigante si trasforma: Il caso IBM (B)' in D. Boldizzoni, R.C.D. Nacamulli & C. Turati eds *Integrazione e Conflitto: Relazioni Sindacali, Flessibilità e Marketing del Personale* Milano: EGEA, pp. 89–112

Boldizzoni, D., Nacamulli, R.C.D. & Turati, C. eds (1996) *Integrazione e Conflitto: Relazioni Sindacali, Flessibilità e Marketing del Personale* Milano: EGEA

Bordogna, L. (1997) 'Committee appointed to assess the July 1993 tri-partite agreement' *EIROnline*, 28 September, Internet at http://www.eiro.eurofound.ie/1997/09/feature/IT9709212F.html

——(1998) 'Le relazioni sindacali nel settore pubblico' in G.P. Cella & T.Treu eds *Le Nuove Relazioni Industriali: L'Esperienza Italiana nella Prospettiva Europea* Bologna: Il Mulino

——(2000) 'La conflittualita' in Centro Studi Economici, Sociali e Sindacali (CESOS) ed. *Le Relazioni Sindacali in Italia 1997-98* Rome: CNEL, pp. 305-15

Camuffo, A. & Volpato, G. (1997) 'Italy: Changing the workplace in the auto industry' in T.A. Kochan, R.D. Lansbury & J.P. MacDuffie eds *After Lean Production: Evolving Employment Practices in the World Auto Industry* Ithaca, NY: ILR Press, pp. 155-76

Candeloro, G. (1977) *Storia dell'Italia Moderna, vol. 6: Lo Svillupo del Capitalismo e del Movimento Operaio* Milan: Feltrinelli

——(1978) *Storia dell'Italia Moderna, vol. 7: La Crisi di Fine Secolo e l'Eta Giolittiana 1896-1914* Milan: Feltrinelli

Carrieri, D. (2000) 'I sindacali non confederali' in Centro Studi Economici, Sociali e Sindacali (CESOS) ed. *Le Relazioni Sindacali* Rome: CNEL, pp. 767-74

Castronovo, V. (1980) *L'Industria Italiana dall'Ottocento a Oggi* Milan: Arnaldo Mondadori

Cella, G.P. (1990) 'The institutions in the Italian system of industrial relations' *Labour* 4, 1, pp. 9-15

Cesos ed. (2000) *Le Relazioni Sindacali* Rome: CNEL

Clark, M. (1996) *Modern Italy 1871-1995* 2nd edn, Harlow, UK: Longman

Codara, L. (2000) 'La sindacalizzazione' in Centro Studi Economici, Sociali e Sindacali (CESOS) ed. *Le Relazioni Sindacali* Rome: CNEL, pp. 316-34

Confindustria (2003) 'Chi siamo', downloaded 23 May 2003 from Internet at http://www.confindustria.it/DBImg2002.nsf/HTMLPages/ChiSiamo

Della Rocca (1998) 'Il sindicato' in G.P. Cella & T. Treu eds *Le Nouve Relazioni Industriali: L'Esperienza Italiana nella Prospettiva Europea* Bologna: Il Mulino

EIRR (*European Industrial Relations Review*) (2001) no. 333, October, p. 23

——(2002a) no. 340, May, pp. 18-21

——(2002b) no. 341, June, p. 7

Fellini, I., Mazzolari, F., Pagani, L., Lodovoci, M.S. & Semenza, R. (2001) 'La dimensione territoriale e l'articolazione del lavoro' in M.S. Lodovici & R. Semenza eds *Le Forme del Lavoro—L'Occupazione Non Standard: Italia e Lombardia nel Contesto Europeo* Milan: Franco Angeli, pp.119-46

Galli, P. & Pertegato, G. (1994) *Fiat 1980: Sindrome della Sconfitta* Rome: Ediesse

Ginsborg, P. (1990) *A History of Contemporary Italy: Society and Politics, 1943-1988*, London: Penguin

——(2001) *Italy and its Discontents 1980-2001* London: Penguin

Giugni, G. (1987) 'Social concertation and the political system in Italy' *Labour* 1, 1, pp. 3-14

Golden, M. (1988) *Labor Divided: Austerity and Working-Class Politics in Contemporary Italy* Ithaca, NY: Cornell University Press

Lanzalaco, L. (1998) 'Le associazioni imprenditoriali' in G.P. Cella & T. Treu eds *Le Relazioni Sindacali*, Bologna: Il Mulino, pp. 147-82

Mania, R. & Orioli, A. (1993) *L'Accordo di San Tommaso: I Segreti, la Storia, i Protagonisti dell'Intesa sul Costo del Lavoro* Rome: Ediesse

Maraffi, M. (1994) 'L'organizzazione degli interessi industriali in Italy, 1870–1980' in A. Martinelli ed. *L'Azione Collettiva degli Imprenditori Italiani* Milan: Edizioni di Comunita, pp. 137–96

Negrelli, S. (2000) 'Social pacts in Italy and Europe: Similar strategies and structures; different models and national stories' in G. Fjertag & P. Pochet eds *Social Pacts in Europe—New Dynamics* Brussels: Etui Ose

Negrelli, S. & Santi, E. (1990) 'Industrial relations in Italy' in G. Baglioni & C. Crouch eds *European Industrial Relations: The Challenge of Flexibility* London: Sage, pp. 154–98

Negrelli, S. & Treu, T. eds (1992) *Le Scelte dell'Impresa fra Autorità e Consenso* Milan: Angeli

Paparella, D. (1999) 'Cisl initiative leads to change in relations between unions' *EIROnline* 28 December, Internet at http://www.eiro.eurofound.ie/about/1999/12/feature/IT9912137F.html

——(2000) 'Sectoral agreement signed in telecommunications' *EIROnline* 28 July, Internet at http://www.eiro.eurofound.ie/about/2000/07/feature/IT0007158F.html

——(2001a) 'Confindustria proposes new social pact' *EIROnline* 18 April, Internet at http://www.eiro.eurofound.ie/2001/04/feature/IT0104185F.html

——(2001b) 'New metalworking collective agreement signed despite CGIL opposition' *EIROnline* 19 July, Internet at http://www.eiro.eurofound.ie/2001/07/feature/IT0107193F.html

Pedersini, R. (1997) 'Gradual alignment and discount agreements' *EIROnline* 20 June, Internet at http://www.eiro.eurofound.ie. 1997/06/feature/IT970620/F.html

——(1999) 'Privatisation and industrial relations' *EIROnline* 28 December, Internet at http://www.eiro.eurofound.ie/1999/12/Study/TN9912201S.html

——(2000) 'New president for Confindustria: A new phase in relationships between the social partners?' *EIROnline* 28 June, Internet at http://www.eiro.eurofound.ie/2000/06/feature/IT0006268F.html

Pedersini, R. & Trentini, M. (2000) '2000 Annual Review for Italy' *EIROnline* 28 December, Internet at http://www.eiro.eurofound.ie/2000/12/ feature/IT0012275F.html

——(2002) '2001 Annual Review for Italy' *EIROnline* 21 March, Internet at http://www.eiro.eurofound.ie/2002/01/feature/IT0201273F.html

Pellegrini, C. (1998) 'Employment relations in Italy' in G.J. Bamber & R.D. Lansbury eds *International and Comparative Employment Relations: A study of Industrialised Market Economies* 3rd edn, Sydney: Allen & Unwin, pp. 144–68

Procacci, G. (1991) *History of the Italian People* Harmondsworth: Penguin

Quinlan, M., Mayhew, C. & Bohle, P. (2001) 'The global expansion of precarious employment, work disorganization, and consequences for occupational health: A review of recent research' *International Journal of Health Services* 31, 2, pp. 335–414

Regalia, I. & Regini, M. (1998) 'Italy: The dual character of industrial relations' in A. Ferner & R. Hyman eds *Changing Industrial Relations in Europe* Oxford: Blackwell

Sapelli, G. (1993) *Sul Capitalismo Italiano: Trasformazione o Declino* Milano: Feltrinelli

——(1995) *Southern Europe Since 1945: Tradition and Modernity in Portugal, Spain, Italy, Greece and Turkey* London: Longman

Sheldon, P., Thornthwaite, L. & Ferrero-Regis, T. (1997) 'The Federmeccanica: Its changing commitment to collectivism and the remaking of industrial relations in Italy, 1980-1995' in D. D'Art & T. Turner eds *Collectivism and Individualism: Trends and Prospects* Dublin: Oak Tree Press, pp. 77-97

Terry, M. (1994) 'Workplace unionism: Redefining structures and objectives' in R. Hyman & A. Ferner eds *New Frontiers in European Industrial Relations* Oxford: Blackwell, pp. 223-49

Trentini, M. (2000) 'New active labour market policies introduced' *EIROnline* 20 May, Internet at http://www.eiro.eurofound.ie/2000/05/feature/IT00053 55F.html

Treu, T. (1987) 'Ten years of social concertation in Italy' *Labour and Society* 12, 3, pp. 355-66

Treu, T. & Negrelli, S. eds (1985) *I Diritti di Informazione nell'Impresa* Bologna: Il Mulino

Zanetti, M. (1999) 'Important agreement signed on restructuring the state railways' *EIROnline* 28 December, Internet at http://www.eiro.eurofound.ie/1999/12/feature/IT9912349F.html

Chapter 7   Employment relations in France

Adam, G. (1983) *Le Pouvoir Syndical en France* Paris: Dunod

Andolfatto, D. (2002) 'Syndicalisme et individualisme' Projet, n.271, automne 2002, pp. 81-9

Ardagh, J. (1982) *France in the 1980s: The Definite Book* London: Penguin

Auroux, J. (1981) *Report on the Right of Workers* Paris: Ministère du Travail

Bélier, G. (1990) *Report on Employee Representation* Paris: Ministère du Travail

Bevort, A. & Labbé, D. (1992) *La CFDT: Organisation et Audience depuis 1945* Paris: La Documentation Française

Bibes, G. & Mouriaux, R. eds (1990) *Les Syndicats Européens à l'Épreuve* Paris: FNSP

Bridgford, J. & Sterling, J. (1994) *Employee Relations in Europe* Oxford: Blackwell

Bunel, J. & Saglio J. (1984) 'Employers' associations in France' in J.P. Windmuller & A. Gladstone eds *Employers' Associations and Industrial Relations: A Comparative Study* Oxford: Clarendon Press

Caire, G. (1992) *La Négociation Collective* Paris: PUF

Coffineau, M. (1993) 'Report to the French Prime Minister on the Auroux Laws: Ten Years After' *Liaisons sociales* 29

Crouch, C. (1993) *Industrial Relations and European State Traditions* Oxford: Clarendon

Crouch, C. & Streeck, W. eds (1996) *Les Capitalismes en Europe* Paris: La Découverte

DARES 2002, 'Premières Synthèses': *Direction de l'Animation de la Recherche, des Études et des Statistiques* Ministère de l'Emploi et de la Solidarité, Décembre, no. 51.1

Delamotte, Y. (1988) 'Workers' participation and personnel policies in France' *International Labour Review* 16, pp. 59-76

Denis, J.M. (1996) *Le Groupe des Dix* working document, Paris: IRES

Despax, M. & Rojot, J. (1987) *Labour Law and Industrial Relations in France* Deventer: Kluwer

Fajetag, G. ed. (1996) *Collective Bargaining in Western Europe* Bruxelles: ETUI

Ferner, A. & Hyman, R. eds (1992) *Industrial Relations in the New Europe* Oxford: Blackwell

Gallie, D. (1978) *In Search of the New Working Class* Cambridge: Cambridge University Press

Gandois, J. (1993) *Le Choix de la Performance Globale* Paris: La Documentation Française

Gehin, J.P. & Jobert, A. (2001) 'Training and development in France' *International Journal of Training and Development* 5, 1, pp. 92-4

Goetschy, J. (1983) 'A new future for industrial democracy in France' *Economic and Industrial Democracy* 1, pp. 85-103

------(1991) 'An appraisal of French research on direct participation' in R. Russel & V. Rus eds *International Yearbook of Participation in Organizations* Oxford: OUP

------(1995) 'Major developments and changes in French industrial relations since 1980s' in M. Mesch ed. *Sozialpartnershaft und Arbeitsbeziehungen in Europa* Vienna: Manz Verlag

——(1998) 'France: the limits of reform' in A. Ferner & R. Hyman eds, *Changing Industrial Relations in Europe* Oxford: Blackwell, pp. 357-95

——(1999), 'The European employment strategy: genesis and development' *European Journal of Industrial Relations* 5, 2, pp. 117-37

Goetschy, J. & Linhart, D. (1990) *La Crise des Syndicats en Europe Occidentale* Paris: La Documentation Française

Howell, C. (1992) *Regulating Labor: The State and Industrial Relations Reform in Postwar France* Princeton, NJ: Princeton University Press

Jefferys, S. (1996) 'Down but not out: French unions after Chirac' *Work, Employment and Society* 10, 3, pp. 509-27

Jobert, A. (1990) 'La négociation collective dans les entreprises multinationales en Europe' in G. Devin ed. *Dimensions Internationales* Nanterre: Editions Européennes Erasme

——(2000) *Les Espaces de la Négociation Collective, Branches et Territoires* Toulouse: Octarès

Jobert, A. & Rozenblatt, P. et al. (1989) *Les Classifications dans l'Entreprise: Production des Hiérarchies Professionnelles et Salariales* Paris: La Documentation Française

Kesselman, M. ed. (1984) *The French Workers' Movement: Economic Crisis and Political Change* London: Allen & Unwin

Labbé, D. (1995) *Syndicats et Syndiqués en France* Paris: L'Harmattan

——(1996) *Syndicats et Syndiqués en France* Paris: L'Harmattan

Lallement, M. (1996) *Sociologie des Relations Professionnelles* Paris: La Découverte

Lane, C. (1989) *Management and Labour in Europe: The Industrial Enterprise in Germany, Britain and France* Aldershot: Edward Elgar

Lange, P., Martin, A., Ross, G. & Vannicelli, M. (1982) *Unions, Change and Crisis: French and Italian Union Strategy and Political Economy* London: Allen & Unwin

Leysink, P., Van Leemput, J. & Vilrocks, J. (1996) *The Challenge of Trade Unions in Europe* Cheltenham: Edward Elgar

Maurice, M., Sellier, F. & Sylvestre, J.J. (1986) *The Social Foundations of Industrial Power: A Comparison of France and Germany* Cambridge, MA: MIT Press

Mesh, M. ed. *Sozialpartnerschaft und Arbeitsbeziehungen in Europa* Wien: Manz Verlag

Moss, B.H. (1980) *The Origins of the French Labour Movement 1830-1914: The Socialism of Skilled Workers* Berkeley: University of California Press

——(1998) 'Industrial law reform in an era of retreat: The Auroux laws in France' *Work, Employment and Society* 2, 3, pp. 317-34

Mouriaux, R. (1994) *Le Syndicalisme en France depuis 1945* Paris: La Découverte

Murray, G., Morin, M.L. & Da Costa, I. eds (1996) *L'Etat des Relations Profession-nelles* 8th edn, Paris: Les Presses de l'Université Laval

Reynaud, J.D. (1975) *Les syndicats en France* Paris: La Découverte

Rojot, J. (1986) The developments of French employers' policy towards trade-unions' *Labour and Society* January, pp. 175-93

——(1988) 'The myth of French exceptionalism' in J. Barbash & K. Barbash eds *Theories and Concepts in Comparative Industrial Relations* Columbia: University of South Carolina Press

Rosanvallon, P. (1988) *La Question Syndicale* Paris: Seuil

Segrestin, D. (1990) 'Recent changes in France' in G. Baglioni G. & C. Crouch eds *European Industrial Relations* London: Sage

Sellier, F. (1984) *La Confrontation Sociale en France: 1936-1981* Paris: PUF

Shorter, E. & Tilly, C. (1974) *Strikes in France 1830-1968* Cambridge: Cambridge University Press

Smith, R. (1984) 'Dynamics of pluralism in France: The CGT, CFDT and industrial conflict' *British Journal of Industrial Relations* 22, March, pp. 15-33

Touraine, A. et al. (1996) *Le Grand Refus* Paris: Fayard

Visser, J. (1990) *In search of Inclusive Unionism* Deventer: Kluwer

Visser, J. & Ruysseveldt, J. (1996) *Industrial Relations in Europe* London: Sage

Chapter 8   Employment relations in Germany

Adams, R.J. (1995) *Industrial Relations under Liberal Democracy: North America in Comparative Perspective* Columbia: University of South Carolina Press

Addison, T., Schnabel, C. & Wagner, J. (1996) 'German works councils, profits, and innovation' *Kyklos* 49, pp. 555-82

——(1997) 'On the determinants of mandatory works councils in Germany' *Industrial Relations* 36, pp. 419-45

——(2000) 'Die mitbestimmungsfreie Zone aus ökonomischer Sicht' *Hamburger Jahrbuch für Wirtschafts- und Gesellschaftspolitik* 45, pp. 277-92

Arlt, H.J. & Nehls, S. eds (1999) *Bündnis für Arbeit: Konstruktion—Kritik—Karriere* Opladen: Westdeutscher Verlag

Artus, I. (2001) *Krise des deutschen Tarifsystems: Die Erosion des Flächentarifvertrags in Ost und West Opladen* in Artus, I., Schmidt, R. & Sterkel, G. (2000) *Brüchige Tarifrealität: Der schleichende Bedeutungsverlust tariflicher Normen in der ostdeutschen Industrie* Berlin: Edition Sigma

Bach, St. et al. eds (1999) *Public Service Employment Relations in Europe: Transformation, Modernization or Inertia* London: Sage

Baethge, M. & Wolf, H. (1995) 'Continuity and change in the "German model" of industrial relations' in R. Locke, T. Kochan & M. Piore eds *Employment Relations in a Changing World Economy* Cambridge: MIT Press, pp. 231-62

Bellmann, L., Ellguth, P. & Seifert, H. (1998) 'Weiße Flecken in der Tarif- und Mitbestimmungslandschaft' *Die Mitbestimmung* 44, 11, pp. 61-2

Bellmann, L., Kohaut, S. & Schnabel, C. (1999) 'Flächentarifverträge im Zeichen von Abwanderung und Widerspruch: Geltungsbereich, Einflußfaktoren und Öffnungstendenzen' in L. Bellman & V. Steiner eds *Panelanalysen zu Lohnstruktur, Qualifikation und Beschäftigungsdynamik* Nürnberg: IAB, pp. 11-40

Bertelsmann-Stiftung & Hans-Böckler-Stiftung (1998) 'Mitbestimmung und neue Unternehmenskulturen—Bilanzen und Perspektiven' *Bericht der Kommission Mitbestimmung* Gütersloh: Verlag Bertelsmann-Stiftung, pp. 53–4

Bispinck, R. (1997) 'Deregulierung, Differenzierung und Dezentralisierung des Flächentarifvertrags: Eine Bestandsaufnahme neuerer Entwicklungstendenzen der Tarifpolitik' *WSI-Mitteilungen* 50, pp. 551–61

Bispinck, R. & WSI-Tarifarchiv (2000) *Tarifhandbuch 2000* Frankfurt: Bund

Bundesmann-Jansen, J., Groß, H. & Munz, E. (2000) *Arbeitszeit '99: Ergebnisse einer repräsentativen Beschäftigtenbefragung zu traditionellen und neuen Arbeitszeitformen in der Bundesrepublik Deutschland* Köln: Ministerium für Arbeit, Soziales und Stadtentwicklung, Kultur und Sport des Landes Nordrhein-Westfalen

Bunn, R.F. (1984) 'Employers' associations in the Federal Republic of Germany' in J.P. Windmuller & A. Gladstone eds *Employers' Associations and Industrial Relations* Oxford: Clarendon Press, pp. 169–201

Calmfors, L. & Driffill, J. (1988) 'Bargaining structure, corporatism and macroeconomic performance' *Economic Policy* 6, pp. 13–61

Clarke, O., Bamber, G. & Lansbury, R. (1998) 'Conclusions: Towards a synthesis of international and comparative experience in employment relations' in G. Bamber & R. Lansbury eds *International and Comparative Employment Relations* 3rd edn, Sydney: Allen & Unwin, pp. 294–327

Clasen, L. (2000) 'Tarifentwicklung '99: Effektiv zwei Prozent mehr' *Bundesarbeitsblatt* 4, 2000, pp. 11–17

Dell'Aringa, C. & Samek Lodovici, M. (1992) 'Industrial relations and economic performance' in T. Treu ed. *Participation in Public Policy-Making* Berlin: de Gruyter, pp. 26–58

Dell'Aringa, C., Della Rocca, G. & Keller, B. eds (2001) *Strategic Choices in Reforming Public Service Employment: An International Perspective* London: Macmillan

Delsen, L. (1995) *Atypical employment: An international perspective—Causes, Consequences and Policy* Groningen: Woltersgroep Groningen

DIW (1994) 'Gesamtwirtschaftliche und unternehmerische Anpassungsfortschritte in Ostdeutschland' *DIW-Wochenbericht* 61, pp. 209–27

Dreher, C., Fleig, J., Harnischfeger, M. & Klimmer, M. (1995) 'Neue Produktionskonzepte' in *Der deutschen Industrie* Berlin: Physika-Verlag

Düll, H. & Ellguth, P. (1999) 'Atypische Beschäftigung: Arbeit ohne betriebliche Interessenvertretung? Empirische Analysen mit dem IAB-Betriebspanel zum Einfluß von Betriebsräten auf befristete und geringfügige Beschäftigung' *WSI-Mitteilungen* 52, pp. 165–76

Eaton, J. (2000) *Comparative Employment Relations: An Introduction* Oxford: Polity Press

Ebbinghaus, B. & Visser, J. (1999) 'When institutions matter: Union growth and decline in Western Europe, 1950–1995' *European Sociological Review* 15, pp. 135–58

Esping-Andersen, G. & Regini, M. (2000) 'The dilemmas of labor market regulation' in G. Esping-Andersen & M. Regini eds *Why Deregulate Labor Markets?* Oxford: Oxford University Press, pp. 11–29

Fajertag, G. & Pochet, P. eds (1997) *Social Pacts in Europe* Brussels: ETUI

——(2000) *Social Pacts in Europe—New Dynamics* Brussels: ETUC

Ferner, A. & Hyman, R. (1998) 'Introduction:Towards European industrial relations?' in A. Ferner & R. Hyman eds *Changing Industrial Relations in Europe* 2nd edn, Oxford: Blackwell, pp. 11-26

Fischer, W., Hax, H. & Schneider, H.K. eds (1996) *Treuhandanstalt:The Impossible Challenge* Berlin: Akademie Verlag

Frick, B. & Sadowski, D. (1995) 'Works councils, unions and firm performance' in F. Buttler, W. Franz & R. Schettkat eds *Institutional Frameworks and Labour Market Performance* London: Routledge, pp. 46-81

Fuchs, S. & Schettkat, R. (2000) 'Germany: A regulated flexibility' in G. Esping-Andersen & M. Regini eds *Why deregulate labor markets?* Oxford: Oxford University Press, pp. 211-44

Fürstenberg, F. (1998) 'Employment relations in Germany' in G. Bamber & R. Lansbury eds *International and Comparative Employment Relations* 3rd edn, Sydney: Allen & Unwin, pp. 201-23

Gill, C. & Krieger, H. (2000) 'Recent survey evidence on participation in Europe: Towards a European model?' *European Journal of Industrial Relations* 6, pp. 109-32

Hassel, A. (1999) 'The erosion of the German system of industrial relations' *British Journal of Industrial Relations* 37, pp. 483-505

Hege, A. (1999) 'Collective bargaining in Germany in the age of monetary union' in Ph. Pochet ed. *Monetary Union and Collective Bargaining in Europe* Brussels: Peter Lang, pp. 41-83

Henneberger, F. (1993) 'Transferstart: Organisationsdynamik und Strukturkonservatismus westdeutscher Unternehmerverbände—Aktuelle Entwicklungen unter besonderer Berücksichtigung des Aufbauprozesses in Sachsen und Thüringen' *Politische Vierteljahresschrift* 34, pp. 640-73

Hickel, R. & Kurtzke, W. (1997) *Tarifliche Lohnpolitik unter Nutzung der Härtefallregelung: Ergebnisse einer Untersuchung zur Praxis der ostdeutschen Metall- und Elektroindustrie* Köln: Bund

Iversen,T. (1999) *Contested Economic Institution:The Politics of Macroeconomics and Wage Bargaining in Advanced Democracies* Cambridge: Cambridge University Press

Jacobi, O., Keller, B. & Müller-Jentsch, W. (1998) 'Germany: Facing new challenges' in A. Ferner & R. Hyman eds *Changing Industrial Relations in Europe* 2nd edn, Oxford: Blackwell, pp. 190-238

Katz, H. (1993) 'Decentralization of collective bargaining' *Industrial and Labor Relations Review* 47, pp. 3-22

Keller, B. (1993) *Arbeitspolitik des öffentlichen Sektors* Baden-Baden: Nomos

——(1998) 'Recent shifts in public policy and industrial relations' in R. Hoffmann, O. Jacobi, B. Keller & M. Weiss eds *The German Model of Industrial Relations Between Adaptation and Erosion* Düsseldorf: Hans-Böckler-Stiftung, pp. 61-74

——(1999) 'Germany: Negotiated change, modernization and the challenge of unification' in S. Bach et al. eds *Public Service Employment Relations in Europe: Transformation, Modernization or Inertia?* London: Routledge, pp. 56-93

——(2001a) *ver.di:Triumphmarsch oder Gefangenenchor? Neustrukturierung der Interessenvertretung im Dienstleistungssektor* Hamburg:VSA

——(2001b) 'The emergence of regional systems of employment relations:The case of the European Union' *Journal of Industrial Relations* 43, pp. 3-26

——(2001c) *Europäische Arbeits- und Sozialpolitik* 2nd edn München: Oldenbourg

Keller, B. & Henneberger, F. (1999) 'Privatwirtschaft und Öffentlicher Dienst: Parallelen und Differenzen in den Arbeitspolitiken' in W. Müller-Jentsch ed. *Konfliktpartnerschaft* 3rd edn, München: Hampp, pp. 233–56

Keller, B. & Seifert, H. eds (1995) *Atypische Beschäftigung:Verbieten oder gestalten?* Köln: Bund

——(1998) *Deregulierung am Arbeitsmarkt: Eine empirische Zwischenbilanz* Hamburg: VSA

Kerckhofs, P. (2000) 'Multinationals database. Companies having installed European Works Councils' Internet at http://www.etuc.org/etui/databases/Multinationals/default.cfm

Kern, H. & Schumann, M. (1986) *Das Ende der Arbeitsteilung? Rationalisierung in der industriellen Produktion: Bestandsaufnahme, Trendbestimmung* 3rd edn, München: Beck

Kohaut, S. & Schnabel, C. (1999) 'Tarifbindung im Wandel' *iw-trends* 2, 99, pp. 63–80

Kotthoff, H. (1994) *Betriebsräte und Bürgerstatus: Wandel und Kontinuität betrieblicher Mitbestimmung* München: Hampp

Leibfried, S. & Wagschal, U. eds (2000) *Der deutsche Sozialstaat: Bilanzen—Reformen—Perspektiven* Frankfurt/Main: Campus

Manow, P. & Seils, E. (2000) 'Adjusting badly: The German welfare state, structural change, and the open economy' in F.W. Scharpf & V.A. Schmidt eds *Welfare and Work in the Open Economy, vol. II: Diverse Responses to Common Challenges* Oxford: Oxford University Press, pp. 264–307

Marginson, P., Gilman, M., Jacobi, O. & Krieger, H. (1998) *Negotiating European Works Councils: An Analysis of Agreements under Article 13* Luxembourg: Office for Official Publication of the European Commission

Marginson, P. & Sisson, K. (1998) 'European collective bargaining: A virtual prospect?' *Journal of Common Market Studies* 36, pp. 505–28

Müller-Jentsch, W. (1995) 'Germany: From collective voice to co-management' in J. Rogers & W. Streeck eds *Works Councils. Consultation, Representation, and Cooperation in Industrial Relations* Chicago: University of Chicago Press, pp. 53–78

Müller-Jentsch, W. & Ittermann, P. (2000) 'Industrielle Beziehungen: Daten, in Zeitreihen' in *Trends 1950-1999* Frankfurt: Campus

Naschold, F. (1995) *Ergebnisse, Wettbewerb, Qualitätspolitik: Entwicklungspfade des öffentlichen Sektors in Europa* Berlin: Edition Sigma

Niedenhoff, Horst-Udo (1999) *Die Praxis der betrieblichen Mitbestimmung: Zusammenarbeit von Betriebsrat und Arbeitgeber, Kosten des Betriebsverfassungsgesetzes, Betriebsrats- und Sprecherausschußwahlen* Köln: Deutscher Industrie-Verlag, pp. 157–58

OECD (1997) *Employment Outlook* Paris: OECD

——(1999) *Employment Outlook* Paris: OECD

Promberger, M., Seifert, H. & Trinczek, R. (1999) 'Experiences with the four-day week at the Volkswagen company' *Journal of Human Resource Costing & Accounting* 4, pp. 27–43

Rosdücher, J. (1997a) *Arbeitsplatzsicherheit durch Tarifvertrag: Strategien—Konzepte—Vereinbarungen* München: Hampp

——(1997b) 'Beschäftigungsorientierte Tarifpolitik: Firmentarifverträge oder Verbandstarifverträge mit Öffnungklauseln?' *WSI-Mitteilungen* 50, pp. 459–69

Ross, G. & Martin, A. (1999) 'Through a glass darkly' in A. Martin & G. Ross eds *The Brave New World of European Labor: European Unions at the Millenium* New York: Berghan Books, pp. 368–99

Schedler, K. & Proeller, I. (2000) *New Public Management* Bern: Haupt

Schmidt, R. (1998) 'The transformation of industrial relations in Eastern Germany' in R. Hoffmann, O. Jacobi, B. Keller & M. Weiss eds *The German Model of Industrial Relations between Adaptation and Erosion* Düsseldorf: Hans-Böckler-Stiftung, pp. 51–60

Schnabel, C. (2000) *Tarifautonomie und Tarifpolitik* Köln: div

Schulten, T. & Bispinck, R. eds (1999) *Tarifpolitik unter dem EURO: Perspektiven einer europäischen Koordinierung—das Beispiel Metallindustrie* Hamburg: VSA

Seifert, H. (2000) 'Negotiating employment security' in P. Berg ed. *Creating Competitive Capacity: Labor Market Institutions and Workplace Practices in Germany and the United States* Berlin: Sigma, pp. 55–71

Siaroff, A. (1999) 'Corporatism in 24 industrial democracies: Meaning and measurement' *European Journal of Political Research* 36, pp. 175–205

Silvia, S.J. (1999) 'Every which way but loose: German industrial relations since 1980' in A. Martin & G. Ross eds *The Brave New World of European Labor* New York: Berghan Books, pp. 75–124

Sinn, W. & Sinn, H.W. (1994) *Jumpstart: The Economic Unification of Germany* Cambridge: MIT Press

Soskice, D. (1990) 'Wage determination: The changing role of institutions in advanced industrialised countries' *Oxford Review of Economic Policy* 6, pp. 36–57

Streeck, W., Hilbert, J., van Kevelaer, K.H., Maier, F. & Weber, H. (1987) *The Role of the Social Partners in Vocational Training and Further Training in the Federal Republic of Germany* Berlin: Wissenschaftszentrum für Sozialforschung

Thelen, K.A. (1991) *Labor Politics in Postwar Germany* Ithaca, NY: Cornell University Press

Thelen, K. & Turner, L. (1999) 'Die deutsche Mitbestimmung im inter-nationalen Vergleich' in W. Streeck & N. Kluge eds *Mitbestimmung in Deutschland: Tradition und Effizienz* Frankfurt: Campus, pp. 135–223

Traxler, F. (1995) 'Farewell to labor market associations? Organized versus disorganized decentralization as a map for industrial relations' in C. Crouch & F. Traxler eds *Organized Industrial Relations in Europe: What future?* Aldershot: Avebury, pp. 3–19

——(1997) 'Der Flächentarifvertrag in der OECD: Entwicklungen, Bestandsbedingungen und Effekte' *Industrielle Beziehungen* 4, pp. 101–24

——(2000) 'The metamorphoses of corporatism: From classical to lean patterns' Paper presented at the 12th Annual Meeting of SASE, London

Traxler, F., Blaschke, S. & Kittel, B. (2001) *National Labor Relations in Internationalized Markets: A Comparative Study of Institutions, Change and Performance* Oxford: Oxford University Press

Turner, L. ed. (1997) *Negotiating the New Germany: Can Social Partnership Survive?* Ithaca, NY: ILR Press

Turner, L. (1998) *Defending the High Road: Labor and Politics in Unified Germany* Ithaca, NY: Cornell UP

Tüselmann, H. & Heise, A. (2000) 'The German Model of Industrial Relations at the Crossroads: Past, Present and Future' *Industrial Relations Journal* 31, pp. 162–76

Waddington, J. & Hoffmann, J. (2000) 'The German union movement in structural transition: Defensive adjustment or setting a new agenda?' in R. Hoffmann,

O. Jacobi, B. Keller & M. Weiss eds *Transnational Industrial Relations in Europe* Düsseldorf: Hans-Böckler-Stiftung, p. 133

van Waarden, F. (1995a) 'Employers and employers' associations' in J. van Ruysseveldt & J. Visser eds *Comparative Industrial & Employment Relations* London: Sage, pp. 68–108

——(1995b) 'The organizational power of employers' associations: Cohesion, comprehensiveness and organizational development' in C. Crouch & F. Traxler eds *Organized Industrial Relations in Europe: What future?* Aldershot: Ashgate, pp. 45–97

Visser, J. & van Ruysseveldt, J. (1996) 'Robust corporatism, still? Industrial relations in Germany' in J. van Ruysseveldt & J. Visser eds *Industrial Relations in Europe: Traditions and Transitions* London: Sage, pp. 124–74

Weiss, M. & Schmidt, M. (2001) *Labour Law and Industrial Relations in the Federal Republic of Germany* 3rd revised edn, Deventer: Kluwer

Wever, K.S. (1994) 'Learning from works councils: Five unspectacular cases from Germany' *Industrial Relations* 33, pp. 467–81

——(1995) *Negotiating Competitiveness: Employment Relations and Organizational Innovation in Germany and the United States* Boston: Harvard Business School Press

Windolf, P. (1989) 'Productivity coalitions and the future of European corporatism' *Industrial Relations* 28, pp. 1–20

——(1990) 'Productivity coalitions and the future of unionism: Disintegration of generalized political exchange?' in B. Marin ed. *Governance and Generalized Exchange—Self-Organizing Policy Networks in Action* Frankfurt/Main: Campus, pp. 289–313

WSI-Projektgruppe (1998) 'Ausgewählte Ergebnisse der WSI-Befragung von Betriebs-und Personalräten 1997/98' *WSI-Mitteilungen* 51, pp. 653–67

Chapter 9   Employment relations in Sweden

Bosworth, B. & Rivlin, A. eds (1987) *The Swedish Economy* Washington, DC: Brookings Institution

Brulin, G. (1995) 'Sweden: Joint councils under strong unionism' in J. Rodgers & W. Streeck eds *Works Councils* Chicago: University of Chicago Press

Brulin, G. & Nilsson, T. (1991) 'From societal to managerial corporatism: New forms of work organization as a transformation vehicle' in *Economic and Industrial Democracy* 12, 3

Delsen, L. & Van Veen, T. (1992) 'The Swedish model: Relevant for other European countries?' *British Journal of Industrial Relations* 30, 1, pp. 83–105

Edlund, S. & Nystrom, B. (1988) *Developments in Swedish Labour Law* Stockholm: The Swedish institute

Elvander, N. (1990) 'Incomes policies in the Nordic countries' *International Labour Review* 129, 1, pp. 1–21

——(1992) *Labour Market Relations in Sweden and Great Britain: A Comparative Study of Local Wage Formation in the Private Sector During the 1980s* Uppsala: Economic Studies Institute

——(2001) 'A new Swedish regime for collective bargaining and conflict resolution' Paper presented at IIRA 6th European Congress, Oslo, June

Erixon, L. (2000) *A Swedish Economic Policy: The Theory, Application and Validity of the Rehn-Meidner Model* Stockholm: Stockholm University, Department of Economics

Fry, J.A. (1986) *Towards a Democratic Rationality: Making the Case for Swedish Labour* Aldershot: Gower

Fulcher, J. (1988) 'Trade unionism in Sweden' *Economic and Industrial Democracy* 9, pp. 129–40

Fulcher, J. (1991) *Labour Movements, Employers and the State: Conflict and Cooperation in Britain and Sweden* Oxford: Clarendon Press

Graversen, G. & Lansbury, R.D. (1986) *New Technology and Industrial Relations in Scandinavia* Aldershot: Gower

Hammarström, O. (1978a) *Negotiations for Co-Determination* Stockholm: Swedish Working Life Centre

——(1978b) *On National Strategies for Industrial Democracy: Some Reflections on Ten Years of Industrial Democracy Development in Sweden* Stockholm: Swedish Working Life Centre

Hammarström, O. & Mahon, R. (1994) 'Sweden: At the turning point?' *Economic and Labour Relations Review* 5, 2, pp. 14–27

Hammarström, O. & Piotet, R. (1980) *Evaluation of the Main Trends in Work Organisation within the Context of Economic, Social and Technological Changes* Brussels: European Community

Hanami, T. & Blanpain, R. (1987) *Industrial Conflict Resolution in Market Economies: A Study of Canada, Great Britain and Sweden* Deventer: Kluwer

Higgins, W. (1996) 'The Swedish municipal workers union: A study in the new political unionism' *Economic and Industrial Democracy* 17, 2, pp. 167–98

Huzzard, T. (2000) *Labouring to Learn—Union Renewal in Swedish Manufacturing* Umeå: Boréa

Industrial Relations Services (1983) 'Sweden: Employee investment funds' *European Industrial Relations Review* 199, December, pp. 22–3

Jangenas, B. (1985) *The Swedish Approach to Labour Market Policy* Stockholm: The Swedish Institute

Johansson, Anders L. (1989) *Tillväxt och klassarbete—en studie av den svenska modellens uppkomst* Stockholm: Tiden

Johnston, T.L. (1962) *Collective Bargaining in Sweden* London: George Allen & Unwin

Jones, H.G. (1987) 'Scenarios for industrial relations: Sweden evolves a new consensus' *Long Range Planning* 20, 3, pp. 65–76

Kjellberg, A. (1992) 'Sweden: Can the model survive?' in A. Ferner & R. Hyman eds *Industrial Relations in the New Europe* Oxford: Blackwell's Business Books

Kochan, T. & Osterman, T. (1994) *The Mutual Gains Enterprise: Forging a Winning Partnership among Labor, Management and Government* Boston: Harvard Business School Press

Korpi, W. (1978) *The Working Class in Welfare Capitalism: Work, Unions and Politics in Sweden* London: Routledge & Kegan Paul

Lash, S. (1985) 'The end of new-corporatism?: The breakdown of centralised bargaining in Sweden' *British Journal of Industrial Relations* 23, 2, pp. 215–39

Meidner, R. (1983) *Strategy for Full Employment* Stockholm: PSI Symposium

National Mediation Office (2001) *The Swedish Rules on Negotiation and Mediation: A Brief Summary* Stockholm: NMO

Nilsson, T. (1996) 'Lean production and white collar work' in *Economic and Industrial Democracy* 17, 3

——(1999) *Social Partnership and Work Organisation: Boxing or Dancing for the Trade Unions in Europe? Draft Outline Research Proposal* Stockholm: Arbetslivsinstitutet

Olsen, G.M. ed. (1988) *Industrial Change and Labour Adjustment in Sweden and Canada* Toronto: Garamond Press

Olsen, G.M. (1992) *The Struggle for Economic Democracy in Sweden* Aldershot: Avebury

Olsson, A.S. (1989) *The Swedish Wage Negotiation System* Department of Sociology, University of Uppsala

——(1990) *Swedish Wage Negotiation System* Aldershot: Dartmouth

Pontusson, J. (1992) *The Limits of Social Democracy: Investment Politics in Sweden*, Ithaca, NY: Cornell University Press

Pontusson, J. & Kuruvilla, S. (1992) 'Swedish wage-earner funds: An experiment in economic democracy' *Industrial and Labor Relations Review* 45, 4, pp. 779-91

Rehn, G. & Viklund, B. (1990) 'Changes in the Swedish model' in G. Baglioni & C. Crouch eds *European Industrial Relations: The Challenge of Flexibility* London: Sage, pp. 300-25

Sandberg, A. et al. (1992) *Technological Change and Co-Determination in Sweden* Philadelphia: Temple University Press

Schmidt, F. (1976) *The Democratisation of Working Life in Sweden: A Survey of Agreements, Legislation, Experimental Activities, Research and Development* Stockholm: TCO

Swenson, P. (1985) *Unions, Pay and Politics in Sweden and West Germany* Ithaca, NY: Cornell University Press

Tilton, T. (1990) *The Political Theory of Swedish Social Democracy* Oxford: Clarendon

Chapter 10   Employment relations in Japan

Abegglen, J.C. (1958) *The Japanese Factory: Aspects of Its Social Organisation* Glencoe, IL: Free Press

——(1973) *Management and Worker: The Japanese Solution* Tokyo: Sophia University Press

Abegglen, J.C. & Stalk, G. Jr (1985) *Kaisha: The Japanese Corporation* New York: Basic Books

Aoki, M. (1988) *Information, Incentives, and Bargaining in the Japanese Economy* Cambridge: Cambridge University Press

Bank of Japan (Nihon Ginko) (1999, 2000) *Kokusai Hikaku Tokei* (International Comparative Statistics) BOJ

Chalmers, N.J. (1989) *Industrial Relations in Japan: The Peripheral Workforce* London: Routledge

Chusho Kiggyocho (Small Business Agency) (1983, 1991) *Chusho Kigyo Hakusho* (White Paper on Small Business) Ministry of Finance Printing Office

Clarke, R. (1979) *The Japanese Company* New Haven, CT: Yale University Press

Cole, R.E. (1971) *Japanese Blue Collar: The Changing Tradition* Berkeley: University of California Press

Dore, R. (1979) *British Factory-Japanese Factory: The Origin of National Diversity in Industrial Relations* London: George Allen & Unwin

——(1987) *Taking Japan Seriously* Stanford: Stanford University Press

Ford, G.W. (1983) 'Japan as a learning society' *Work and People* 9, 1, pp. 3-5

Freeman, R. & Weitzman, M. (1987) 'Bonuses and employment in Japan' *Journal of the Japanese and International Economies* 1, pp. 168-94

Fukao, K. (2002) 'Chokusetsu Tohshi to Koyo no Kudoka' (Foreign Direct Investment and Hollowing of Employment) *The Japanese Journal of Labour Studies* 44, 4, April

Gordon, A. (1985) *The Evolution of Labor Relations in Japan* Cambridge: Council on East Asian Studies, Harvard University

Gould, W.B. (1984) *Japan's Reshaping of American Labor Law* Cambridge: MIT Press

Hanami, T. (1979) *Labour Relations in Japan Today* Tokyo: Kodansha-International

Hashimoto, M. (1990) *The Japanese Labor Market in a Comparative Perspective with the United States* Kalamazoo, MI: W.E. Upjohn Institute for Employment Research

JETRO (Nihon Boeki Shinkokai) (2001) *JETRO Toshi Hakusho* (JETRO White Paper on Investment) Ministry of Finance Printing Office

JIL (1979–89) *Japanese Industrial Relations Series* 1–12, Tokyo: Japan Institute of Labour (Nihon Rodo Kenkyu Kiko)

——(1995) *Japanese Working Life Profile* Tokyo: Japan Institute of Labour (Nihon Rodo Kenkyu Kiko)

——*Japan Labor Bulletin* (monthly) Tokyo: Japan Institute of Labour (Nihon Rodo Kenkyu Kiko)

JISEA (1984) *Japan 1990: An International Comparison* Tokyo: Keizai Koho Centre (Japan Institute for Social Economic Affairs)

Keizai Kikakucho (Economic Planning Agency) (1996) *Keizai Hakusho White Paper on Economy* Tokyo: Toyo Keizai Shimpo Sha

——(1997) *Nihon no Keizai Kozo* (Economic Structure of Japan) Tokyo: Toyo Keizai Shimpo Sha

Keizai-Sangyo Sho (Ministry of Economy, Trade and Industry) (2001) *Tsusho Hakusho* (White Paper on Foreign Trade) Ministry of Finance Printing Office

Koike, K. (1988) *Understanding Industrial Relations in Modern Japan* New York: St Martin's Press

Koseisho (Ministry of Health and Welfare) (1989) *Kani Seimei Hyo* (Simplified Life Expectancy Table)

Kosei-Rodosho (Ministry of Health, Labour and Welfare) (1989) *Kosei Hakusho* (White Paper on Welfare) Ministry of Finance Printing Office

——(2001) *Rodo Kumiai Kiso Chosa* (Basic Research on Labor Unions) Ministry of Finance Printing Office

Kuwahara, Y. (1983) 'Technological change and industrial relations in Japan' *Bulletin of Comparative Labour Relations* 12, pp. 32–52

——(1985) 'Labour and management views of and their responses to microelectronics in Japan' Paper presented to the International Symposium on Microelectronics and Labour, Tokyo

——(1989) *Industrial Relations Systems in Japan: A New Interpretation* Tokyo: JIL

——(1993) 'Untied knots: Labour migration and development in Asia' *International Labour Migration in East Asia* Tokyo: The United Nations University

——(1996) 'The impact of globalization on industrial relations: Corporate governance and industrial relations in Japan' *Democratization, Globalization and the Transformation of Industrial Relations in Asian Countries* International Industrial Relations Association, 3rd Asian Regional Congress, Taipei, Taiwan, R.O.C.

——(1997) 'Japan's dilemma: Can international migration be controlled?' in M. Weiner & T. Hanami eds *Temporary Workers or Future Citizens?* New York: Macmillan, pp. 355–83

Levine, S.B. (1984) 'Employers' associations in Japan' in J.P. Windmuller & A. Gladstone eds *Employers' Associations and Industrial Relations: A Comparative Study* Oxford: Clarendon, pp. 318–56

Marsh, R.M. (1992) 'The difference between participation and power in Japanese factories' *Industrial and Labor Relations Review* 45, 2, pp. 250–7

Ministry of Finance (Zaimusho) (2001) *Foreign Direct Investment* http://www.mof.go.jp/english/files.htm

Ministry of Labour (Rodosho) (1975) *Rodo Hakusho* (White Paper on Labour) Ministry of Finance Printing Office

Ministry of Labour (1997) *White Paper on Labour 1996: Summary* Tokyo: Japan Institute of Labour

Morishima, M. (1992) 'Use of joint consultation committees by large Japanese firms' *British Journal of Industrial Relations* 30, 3, pp. 405–23

Mueller, F. (1992) 'Designing flexible teamwork: Comparing German and Japanese approaches' *Employee Relations* 14, 1, pp. 5–16

Naikakufu (Cabinet Office) (1999, 2001) *Kokumin Seikatsu nikansuru Yoron Chousa* (Opinion Polls on the Lives of the Citizens), September

Nakayama, I. (1975) *Industrialisation and Labor–Management Relations in Japan* Tokyo: Japan Institute of Labour

OECD (1977) *The Development of Industrial Relations Systems: Some Implications of Japanese Experience* Paris: OECD

Olson, M. (1982) *The Rise and Decline of Nations: Economic Growth, Stagflation, and Social Rigidities* New Haven, CT: Yale University Press

Ota, T. (1988) 'Work rules in Japan' *International Labour Review* 127, 5, pp. 627–39

Ozaki, R. (1991) *Human Capitalism* New York: Penguin

Rododaijin Kambo Seisaku Chousabu (Labour Minister's Secretariat, Policy Research Department ed.) (1996) *Nihon no Rodokumiai no Genjyo* (The Current Situation of Japanese Trade Unions) Tokyo: Okurasho Insatsukyoku

Rodosho (Ministry of Labour) (1987) *Rodo Hakusho* (White Paper on Labour) Ministry of Finance Printing Office

——(1991, 1996) *Rodo Kumiai Kihon Tokei Chosa* (The Basic Survey on Trade Unions) Tokyo: Rodosho (Ministry of Labour)

——(1995) *Rodo Sogi Tokei Chosa* (The Survey on Industrial Distputes) Tokyo: Rodosho (Ministry of Labour)

——(2000, 2001) *Rodokeizai Hakusho* (White Paper on the Labour Economy) The Japan Institute of Labour

Sako, M. (1990) *Women in the Japanese Workplace* London: Hilary Shipman

Sako, M. & Sato, H. eds (1997) *Japanese Labour and Management in Transition: Diversity, Flexibility and Participation* London:

Shimada, H. (1994) *Japan's 'Guest Workers': Issues and Public Policies* Tokyo: University of Tokyo Press

Shirai, T. ed. (1983) *Contemporary Industrial Relations in Japan* Madison, WI: University of Wisconsin Press

Somucho (General Coordination Agency) (1986) *Jigyosho Tokei* (Census of Establishments)

——(1995) *Rodoryoku Chosa* (Survey on Labour Force)

Somucho (Ministry of Public Management, Home Affairs, Posts and Telecommunications) (2001) *Rodoryoku Chosa* (Labour Force Survey) Ministry of Finance Printing Office

Sugeno, K. (1992) *Japanese Labor Law* translated by Leo Kanowitz, Tokyo: University of Tokyo Press
Sumiya, M. (1990) *The Japanese Industrial Relations Reconsidered* Tokyo: The Japan Institute of Labour
Ward, B. (1958) 'The firm in Illyria: Market syndicalism' *American Economic Review* 68, pp. 566–89
Weitzman, M.L. (1984) *The Share Economy: Conquering Stagflation* Cambridge: Harvard University Press
White, M. & Trevor, M. (1983) *Under Japanese Management* London: Heinemann
Whittaker, D.H. (1997) *Small firms in the Japanese Economy* Cambridge: Cambridge University Press

Chapter 11   Employment relations in the Republic of Korea

Bank of Korea (1990) *Economic Indicators* Seoul: Bok
Choi, J.-J. (1989) *Labor and the Authoritarian State: Labor Unions in South Korean Manufacturing Industries* Seoul: Korea University Press
Chun, B.-Y. (1985) 'Hankukjabonjooeuwa Yimnodongeu Kujobyeonhwa (Korean Capitalism and Structural Changes in Wage Labour)' *Sahyeowa Sasang Hankil* May, pp. 239–70
Chun, K.-Y. (1989) *Hankuk Nodongkyeoungjearo* (Korean Labour Economics) Seoul: Hankilsa
Deyo, F.C. (1989) *Beneath the Miracle: Labor Subordination in the New Asian Industrialism* London: University of California Press
Dore, R. (1979) 'Industrial relations in Japan and elsewhere' in A.M Craig ed. *Japan: A Comparative View* Princeton, NJ: Princeton University Press, pp. 324–70
Dunlop, J.T. (1958) *Industrial Relations Systems* New York: Holt, Rinehart & Winston
Frenkel, S.J. ed. (1993) *Organized Labor in the Asia-Pacific Region: A Comparative Study of Trade Unionism in Nine Countries* Ithaca, NY: International Labor Relations Press
Hwang, D.-S., Hur, S., Yoo, J.-S. Shim, C.-H., Yoo, T.-K. Lee, H.-Y. & Jeong, Y.-T. (1999) *Study on the Protection of Low-Income, Long-Term Unemployed Workers* Seoul: Korea Labor Institute (in Korean)
Kim, H.-J. (1993) 'The Korean union movement in transition' in S. Frenkel ed. *Organised Labour in the Asia-Pacific: A Comparative Study of Trade Unionism in Nine Countries* Ithaca, NY: International Labour Relations Press, pp. 133–61
Kim, J.-N. (1984) '*Kiyeobeu Seongjangkwa Kyeoungjaeryeog* (Growth of the corporation and managerial power)' *Monthly Chosun* February, pp. 116–23
Kim, K.-C. & Kim, S. (1989) 'Kinship group and patrimonial executives in a developing nation: A case study of Korea' *Journal of Developing Areas* 24, October, pp. 27–46
Kong, B.-H. (1992) *Chaebol (The Chaebol)* Seoul: Yemyung
Korea Labour Institute, Seoul (various issues) *Quarterly Labor Review* (in Korean)
——(various issues) *Quarterly Labor Trends*
——(1994) *The Profile of Korean Human Assets: Labor Statistics 1994* Seoul: Korea Labour Institute
——and Korea Institute of Health and Social Affairs (KLI and KIHASA) (1999) *Report of Survey Results on Unemployment and Welfare Needs* Seoul: KLI and KIHASA (in Korean)
Korean Chamber of Commerce and Industry (1988) *Hankukeu Kyeoungyeoung Nosakwankyei (Labour–Management Relations in Korea)* Seoul: KCCI

Kuk, M.-H. (1987) *The Relationship between Government and Private Companies in the Industrial Development of South Korea: A Study of Korean Way of Development* PhD thesis, Urbana-Champaign: University of Illinois

Kwon, S.-H. & Leggett, C.J. (1994) 'Industrial relations and the South Korean Chaebol' *Proceedings of the 8th Association of Industrial Relations Academics of Australia and New Zealand (AIRAANZ)* February, Sydney: AIRAANZ

Kwon, S.-H. & O'Donnell, M. (1999) 'Repression and struggle: The state, the chaebol and independent trade unions in South Korea', *Journal of Industrial Relations* 41, 2, pp. 272-93

Lee, Changwon (2000) 'Challenges facing unions in South Korea' in G.J. Bamber, F. Park, C. Lee, P. Ross & K. Broadbent eds *Employment Relations in the Asia-Pacific: Changing Approaches* Sydney: Allen & Unwin

Lee, J.-N. (1985) *Chaebol (The Chaebol)* Seoul: Hyunjae

Moon, C.-I. (1994) 'Changing patterns of business–government relations in South Korea' in A. Macintyre ed. *Business and Government in Industrialising Asia* Sydney: Allen & Unwin, pp. 142-61

Ogle, G.E. (1990) *South Korea: Dissent within the Economic Miracle* Washington, DC: Zed Books

Park, D.-J. (1992) 'Industrial relations in Korea' *International Journal of Human Resource Management* 3, 1, pp. 105-23

Park, F.-K. & Park, Y.-B. (2000) 'Changing approach to employment relations in South Korea' in G.J. Bamber, F.-K. Park, C. Lee, P. Ross & K. Broadbent eds *Employment Relations in the Asia-Pacific: Changing Approaches* Sydney: Allen & Unwin

Park, Y.-B. (1995) 'Economic development, globalization, and practices in industrial relations and human resource management in Korea' in A. Verma, T.A. Kochan & R.D. Lansbury eds *Employment Relations in the Growing Asian Economies* London: Routledge, pp. 27-61

——(1996) *Labour Trends in the 1990s in Korea* Seoul: Korea Labour Institute

——(1998) 'The financial crisis in Korea: Industrial relations connection' *Perspectives on Work* pp. 37-41

——(1999) 'Tripartite cooperation in Italy: Implications for the Korean Tripartite Commission' *Korean Journal of Industrial Relations* 8, pp. 3-24 (in Korean)

——(2000) *The Feasibility of Introducing Non-Contributory Cash Benefits System for the Unemployed in Korea* Seoul: Korea Labor Institute and the World Bank

Park, Y.-B. & Lee, C.-S. (1996) 'Labour standards and economic development in Korea' in J.S. Lee ed. *Labour Standards and Economic Development* Taipei: Chung-Hua Institution for Economic Research, pp. 173-208

Park, Y.-K. (1993) 'South Korea' in S.J. Deery & R.J. Mitchell eds *Labour Law and Industrial Relations in Asia* Melbourne: Longman-Cheshire, pp. 137-71

Ranald, P. (1999) 'Analysing, organising, resisting: Union responses to the Asian economic crisis in East Asia, South Korea and the Philippines' *Journal of Industrial Relations* 41, 2, pp. 295-325

Sharma, B. (1991) 'Industrialisation and strategy shifts in industrial relations: A comparative study of South Korea and Singapore' in C. Brewster & S. Tyson eds *International Comparisons in Human Resource Management* London: Pitman, pp. 92-102

Vogel, E.F. (1991) *The Four Little Dragons: The Spread of Industrialization in East Asia* Cambridge: Harvard University Press

Wilkinson, B. (1994) *Labour and Industry in the Asia-Pacific: Lessons from the Newly Industrialised Countries* Berlin: de Gruyter

435

Woo, S.-H. (1996) 'Approaching the 21st century: Perspectives on Korean industrial relations' *Proceedings of the International Industrial Relations Association 3rd Asian Regional Congress*, September 30–October 4, 1996, Taipei, pp. 155–76

Chapter 12   Conclusions

Addison, J. & Belfield, C. (2002) 'What do we know about the New European Works Councils? Some Preliminary Evidence From Britain' *Scottish Journal of Political Economy* 49, 4, pp. 418–44

Ambruster-Sandoval, R. (1999) 'Globalization and Cross-Border Labour Organising: The Guatemalan Maquiladora Industry and the Phillips Van Heusen Workers' Movement' *Latin American Perspectives* 26, 2, pp. 108–28

Basu, K., Horn, H., Roman, L. & Shapiro, J. eds (2003) *International Labour Standards: History Theory, Policy Options* EGDI, Blackwell Publishing

Breitenfellner, A. (1997) 'Global unionism: A potential player' *International Labour Review* 136, 4, pp. 531–55

Campbell, D. (1992) 'The globalizing firm and labour institutions' in P. Bailey et al. eds *Multinationals and Employment: The Global Economy of the 1990s* Geneva: International Labour Organisation

——(1994) 'Foreign investment, labour immobility and the quality of employment' *International Labour Review* 133, 2, pp. 185–204

Carew, A., Dreyfus, M., Van Goethem, G., Gumbrell-McCormack, R. & Van Der Linden, M. eds (2000) *The International Confederation of Free Trade Unions* Bern: Peter Lang

Carley, M. & Hall, M. (2000) 'The implementation of the European Works Councils Directive' *Industrial Law Journal* 29, 2, pp. 103–24

Carr, B. (1999) 'Globalisation from below: Labour internationalism under NAFTA' *International Social Science Journal* 51, 1, pp. 49–60

Chaykowski, R.P. & Verma, A. eds (1992) *Industrial Relations in Canadian Industry* Toronto: Dryden

Creighton, B. (1992) 'How the ILO works' *Workplace: The Australian Council of Trade Unions Magazine* Summer, pp. 36–9

Engerman, S. (2003) 'The History and Political Economy of International Labour Standards' in Basu et al. eds (2003)

Evans, P. (1997) 'The eclipse of the state? Reflections on stateness in an era of globalisation' *World Politics* 50, 1, pp. 62–87

Frundt, H. (1996) 'Trade and cross border labour strategies in the Americas' *Economic and Industrial Democracy* 17, 3, pp. 387–417

Giles, A. (2000) 'Globalisation and industrial relations theory' *Journal of Industrial Relations* 42, 2, pp. 173–94

Haworth, N. & Hughes, S. (2002) 'International regimes: Revitalising political economy in industrial relations theory' Paper presented at the *British Journal of Industrial Relations Conference on Politics and Industrial Relations*, September

Hughes, S. & Wilkinson, R. (1998) 'International Labour Standards and World Trade: No role for the World Trade Organisation' *New Political Economy* 3, 3, pp. 375–89

Jacoby, S.M. (1995) 'Social dimensions of global economic integration' in S.M. Jacoby ed. *The Workers of Nations: Industrial Relations in a Global Economy* New York: Oxford University Press, pp. 3–30

Jakobsen, K. (2001) 'Rethinking the International Confederation of Free Trade Union and its Inter-American Regional Organisation' *Antipode* 33, 3, pp. 363–83

Kahn-Freund, O. (1976) 'The European social charter' in F.G. Jacobs ed. *European Law and the Individual* Amsterdam: North-Holland, pp. 181–211

Keller, B. (2001) 'The emergence of regional systems of employment relations: The case of the European Union' *Journal of Industrial Relations* 43, 1, pp. 3–26

Knutsen, P. (1997) 'Corporatist tendencies in the Euro-polity: The EU Directive of 22 September 1994, on European Works Councils' *Economic and Industrial Democracy* 18, 2, pp. 289–323

Lee, E. (1997) 'Globalisation and labour standards: a review of the issues' *International Labour Review* 136, 2, pp.173–90

Lipsig-Mumme, C. (1989) 'Canadian and American unions respond to economic crisis' *Journal of Industrial Relations* June, 31, 2, pp. 229–56

Lucio, M. & Weston, S. (2000) 'European Works Councils and "flexible regulation": the politics of intervention' *European Journal of Industrial Relations* 6, 2, pp. 203–16

Moody, K. (1997) *Workers in a Lean World: Unions in the International Economy* London: Verso

Northrup, H. & Rowan, R.L. (1979) *Multinational Collective Bargaining Attempts: The Records, the Cases and the Prospects* Philadelphia: Industrial Research Unit, The Wharton School, University of Pennsylvania

Peetz, D. (1998) *Unions in a Contrary World: The future of the Australian Trade Union Movement* Melbourne: Cambridge University Press

Poole, M., Lansbury, R. & Wailes, N. (2001) 'A comparative analysis of developments in industrial democracy' *Industrial Relations* 40, 3, pp. 490–525

Ramsay, H. (1995) 'Euro-Unionism and the great auction: An assessment of the prospects for organised labour post-Maastricht' *Economic and Industrial Democracy* 6, 2, pp. 13–44

——(1997) 'Solidarity at last? International trade unionism approaching the millenium' *Economic and Industrial Democracy* 18, 4, pp. 504–37

Rasmussen, E. & Lamm, F. (2003) *An Introduction to New Zealand Employment Relations* Auckland: Longman Paul

Schoch, J. (2000) 'Contesting globalisation: Organised labour, NAFTA and the 1997 and 1998 fast track fights' *Politics and Society* 28, 1, pp. 119–50

Servais, J.M. (1996) 'International Labour Organisation' in R. Blanpain ed. *International Encyclopedia of Laws* The Hague: Kluwer

Singh, N. (2003) 'The impact of International Labour Standards: A survey of economic theory' in Basu et al. eds *International Labour Standards: History Theory, Policy Options* EGDI, Blackwell Publishing

Smith, F. (1984) 'What is the International Labour Organisation?' *International Labour Reports* 6, Nov/Dec., pp. 23–4

Staiger, R. (2003) 'A role for the WTO' in Basu et al. eds *International Labour Standards: History Theory, Policy Options* EGDI, Blackwell Publishing

Sterling, J. & Fitzgerald, I. (2001) 'European Works Councils: Representing workers on the periphery' *Employee Relations* 23, 1, pp. 13–25

Strange, G. (2002) 'Globalisation, regionalism and labour interests in the new international political economy' *New Political Economy* 7, 3, pp. 343–66

Streeck, W. (1997) 'Neither European nor works councils: A reply to Paul Knutsen' *Economic and Industrial Democracy* 18, 2, pp. 325–37

——(1998) 'The internationalisation of industrial relations in Europe: Prospects and problems' *Politics and Society* 26, 4, pp. 429–59

Weiss, L. (1998) *The Myth of the Powerless State: Governing the Economy in a Global Era* Cambridge: Polity Press

Wilkinson, R. (2002a) 'The World Trade Organisation' *New Political Economy* 7, 1, pp. 129–41

——(2002b) 'Peripheralising labour: The ILO, the WTO and the completion of the Bretton Woods project' in J. Harrod & R. O'Brien eds *Globalised Unions? Theory and Strategy of Organised Labour in the Global Political Economy* London: Routledge

——(2002c) 'Locked out, shut down: Worker rights and the World Trade Organisation' Paper presented to *British Journal of Industrial Relations Conference on Politics and Industrial Relations*, September

Williams, H. (1999) 'Mobile capital and trans-border labour rights mobilisation' *Politics and Society* 27, 1, pp. 139–66

Wills, J. (1998) 'Taking on the Cosmo-Corps? Experiments in transnational labour organization' *Economic Geography* 74, 2, pp. 111–31

——(2001) 'Uneven geographies of capital and labour: The lessons of European Works Councils' *Antipode: A Radical Journal of Geography* [n24]33, 3, pp. 484–509

Windmuller, J.P. (1995) 'International trade union secretariats, the industrial trade union internationals' *Foreign Labor Trends*, 47, Washington, DC: US Labor Department, Bureau of International Labor Affairs

Winters, A. (2003) 'Trade and Labour Standards: To link or not to link?' in Basu et al. eds *International Labour Standards: History Theory, Policy Options* EGDI, Blackwell Publishing

Appendix   Globalisation, labour and employment

Not all of these sources are cited explicitly in the Appendix tables. The following list includes others as an initial guide to sources of data relevant to the study of international and comparative industrial relations. The ILO and OECD also publish many useful works (including the bimonthly *International Labor Review* and *OECD Observer*, the OECD annual *Employment Outlook* and its regular half-yearly surveys of economic trends and prospects for each OECD country). Other useful sources include relevant publications from the World Bank, UN, EU, BLS, JIL, *European Industrial Relations Review*, *The Economist*, Economist Intelligence Unit, Incomes Data Services, and the Korea Labor Institute.

Anderson, V. (1991) *Alternative Economic Indicators* London: Routledge

Bain, G.S. & Price, R.J. (1980) *Profiles of Union Growth: A Comparative Statistical Portrait of Eight Countries* Oxford: Blackwell

Bermeo, N. ed. (2001) *Unemployment in the New Europe* New York: Cambridge University Press

Bamber, G.J., Ross, P.K. & Whitehouse, G. (1998) 'Employment relations and labour market indicators in ten industrialized market economies: Comparative statistics' *International Journal of Human Resource Management* 9, 2, pp.401–35

Batstone, E. (1985) 'International variations in strike activity' *European Sociological Review* 1, 1, pp. 47–64

Bean, R. ed. (1989) *International Labour Statistics: A Handbook Guide, and Recent Trends* London: Routledge

438

Blyton, P. (1989) 'Hours of work' in *International Labour Statistics: A Handbook Guide, and Recent Trends* London: Routledge, pp. 127-45

Bratt, C. (1996) 'Tables and graphs' *Labour Relations in 18 Countries* 4th edn, Stockholm: Swedish Employers' Confederation (SAF) (intermittently)

Clarke, R.O. (1980) 'Labour-management disputes: A perspective' *British Journal of Industrial Relations* 18, 1, pp. 14-25

Creigh, S.W. et al. (1982) 'Differences in strike activity between countries' *International Journal of Manpower* 3, 4, pp. 15-23

Davies, K. (2000) 'International comparisons of labour disputes in 1999' *Labour Market Trends* April, pp. 195-201

De Grip, A., Hoevenberg, J. & Willems, E. (1997) 'Atypical employment in the European Union' *International Labour Review* 136, 1, pp. 49-72

Edwards, P.K. (1983) 'The end of American strike statistics' *British Journal of Industrial Relations* 21, 3, pp. 392-4

EU *Labour Costs Survey* Brussels: Eurostat (triennially)

Economist 'Economic and financial indicators' London (weekly)

Fisher, M. (1973) *Measurement of Labour Disputes and their Economic Effects* Paris: Organisation of Economic Cooperation and Development

Golden, M., Wallerstein, M. & Lange, P. (1999) 'Postwar Trade Union Organisation and Industrial Relations in 12 Countries' in H. Kitschelt, P. Lange, G. Marks & J. Stephens eds *Continuity and Change in Contemporary Capitalism* New York: Cambridge University Press

Gomez, R., Gunderson, M. & Meltz, N. (2002) 'Comparing Youth and Adult Desire for Unionisation in Canada' *British Journal of Industrial Relations* 40, 3, pp. 521-42

Gonas, L. (1999) 'Gender and regional employment differences: An industrial relations perspective' *International Journal of Human Resource Management* 10, 6, pp. 981-95

Held, D., McGrew, A., Goldblatt, D. & Perraton, J. (1997) *Global Transformations: Politics, Economics and Culture* Oxford: Polity

ILO (1976) *International Recommendations on Labour Statistics* Geneva: International Labour Organisation

——(1995) *World Labour Report: Controversies in Labour Statistics* Geneva: International Labour Organisation

——(1996) 'Union membership rates' Geneva: International Labour Organisation, unpublished

——(1998) *World Labour Report: Industrial Relations, Democracy and Social Stability* Geneva, International Labour Organisation

—— a *Yearbook of Labour Statistics* Geneva: International Labour Organisation (annually)

—— b *Bulletin of Labour Statistics* Geneva: International Labour Organisation (quarterly)

—— c ILOLEX Database of International Labour Standards http://www.ilo.org

International Metalworkers Federation (2003) *The Purchasing Power of Working Time 2002* Geneva: International Metalworkers Federation

IMF (2000) *The Purchasing Power of Working Time: An International Comparison 1999* Geneva: International Metalworkers' Federation (annually)

Jackson, M.P. (1987) *Strikes: Industrial Conflict in Britain, USA and Australia* Brighton: Wheatsheaf/Sydney: Allen & Unwin

439

Jacoby, S. (1995) 'Social Dimensions of Global Economic Integration' in S. Jacoby ed. *The Workers of National: Industrial Relations in a Global Economy* New York: Oxford University Press

Japan Institute of Labour (JIL) (2002) *Japanese Working Life Profile: Labor Statistics* Tokyo: Japan Institute of Labour (annually)

Jones, B. (1995) *Sleepers, Wake! Technology and the Future of Work* 4th edn Melbourne: Oxford University Press

Kjellberg, A. (2002) 'Ett nytt facklight landskap—i Sverige och utomlands' *Arkiv*, no. 86-7

Klausen, J. (1999) 'The declining significance of male workers: Trade union responses to changing labour markets' in H. Kitschelt, P. Lange, G. Marks & J. Stephens eds *Continuity and Change in Contemporary Capitalism* New York: Cambridge University Press

Korpi, W. (1981) 'Sweden: Conflict, power and politics in industrial relations' in P. Doeringer et al. eds *Industrial Relations in International Perspective: Essays on Research and Policy* London: Macmillan

Labour Market Trends (monthly) Central Statistical Office London: Her Majesty's Stationery Office

Monger, J. (2003) 'International comparisons of labour disputes in 2001' *Labour Market Trends*, April, pp.181-9

OECDa *OECD Employment Outlook* Paris: Organisation for Economic Cooperation and Development (annually)

—— b *Labour Force Statistics* Paris: Organisation for Economic Cooperation and Development (annually, with a 20-year historical abstract)

—— c *Quarterly Labour Force Statistics* Paris: Organisation for Economic Cooperation and Development (quarterly)

—— d *OECD in Figures: Statistics on the Member Countries* Paris: Organisation for Economic Cooperation and Development (an invaluable set of summary tables, with most data only two years old; it is usually published as a supplement to a mid-year issue of the *OECD Observer*)

—— e *Historical Statistics* Paris: Organisation for Economic Cooperation and Development (annually)

—— f *Economic Outlook* Paris: Organisation for Economic Cooperation and Development (half-yearly; it includes OECD forecasts based on a review of each OECD member country)

—— g *National Accounts of OECD Countries: Main Aggregates, vol. 1* Paris: Organisation for Economic Cooperation and Development (annually)

—— h *Main Economic Indicators* Paris: Organisation for Cooperation and Development (monthly)

—— i *Revenue Statistics of the OECD Member Countries* Paris: Organisation for Cooperation and Development (annually)

—— j *PPP Database (PPPs for GDP—Historical Series)* www.oecd.org.std/ppp/

—— OCECD (2001) *Measuring Globalisation: The Role of Multinationals in OECD Economies, vol. 1, The Manufacturing Sector* Paris: Organisation for Economic Cooperation and Development

Peetz, D. (1998) *Unions in a Contrary World: The Future of the Australian Trade Union Movement* Melbourne: Cambridge University Press

Pocock, B. (1998) 'All change, still gendered: the Australian labour market in the 1990s' *Journal of Industrial Relations* 40, 4, pp. 580-604

Pontusson, J. & Swenson, P. (1996) 'Labor markets, production strategies, and wage bargaining institutions: The Swedish employer offensive in comparative perspective' *Comparative Political Studies* 29, 2, pp. 223–51

Poole, M., Lansbury, R. & Wailes, N. (2001) 'A comparative analysis of developments in industrial democracy' *Industrial Relations* 40, 3, pp. 490–525

Price, R. & Bain, G.S. (1989) 'The comparative analysis of union growth' in *Recent Trends in Industrial Relations Studies and Theory* Brussels: International Industrial Relations Association, pp. 99–110

Quinlan, M. & Bohle, P. (2000) *Managing Occupational Health and Safety in Australia: A Multidisciplinary Approach*, 2nd edn, Melbourne: Macmillan

Ross, A.M. & Hartman, P.T. (1960) *Changing Patterns of Industrial Conflict* New York: Wiley

Ross, P., Bamber, G. & Whitehouse, G. (1998) 'Employment, economics and industrial relations: Comparative statistics' in G. Bamber & R. Lansbury eds *International and Comparative Employment Relations: A study of industrialised market economies* 3rd edn, Sydney: Allen & Unwin

Sassen, S. (2001) *The Global City: New York, London, Tokyo* Princeton, NJ: Princeton University Press

Schuler, R., Dowling, P. & De Cieri, H. (1993) 'An integrated framework of strategic international human resource management' *International Journal of Human Resource Management* 4, pp. 717–64

Shalev, M. (1978) 'Lies, damned lies and strike statistics: The measurement of trends in industrial conflict' in C. Crouch & A. Pizzorno eds *The Resurgence of Class Conflict in Western Europe Since 1968*, vol. 1, 1978 London: Macmillan, pp. 1–20

——(1980) 'Industrial relations theory and the comparative study of industrial relations and industrial conflict' *British Journal of Industrial Relations* 18, 1, pp. 26–43

Stern, R. (1997) *Organizing for Collective Purchasing of Low Cost Services and Political Representation* Ithaca, NY: ILR–Cornell University

Swenson, P. (1989) *Fair shares: Unions, pay, and politics in Sweden and West Germany* Ithaca, New York: Cornell University Press

——(1991) 'Bringing capital back in, or social democracy reconsidered: Employer power, cross-class alliances, and centralization of industrial relations in Denmark and Sweden' *World Politics* 43, 4, pp. 513–45

Thelen, K. (2000) 'Why German employers cannot bring themselves to dismantle the German model' in T. Iversen, J. Pontusson & D. Soskice eds *Unions, Employers and Central Banks: Macro-Economic Coordination and Institutional Change in Social Market Economies* New York: Cambridge University Press

Traxler, F., Blanske, S. & Kittel, B. (2001) *National Labour Relations in Industrialised Countries: A Comparative Study of Institutions, Change and Performance* Oxford: Oxford University Press

Turvey, R. ed. (1989) *Developments in International Labour Statistics* London: Pinter

UK Department of Employment *Employment Gazette* London: Her Majesty's Stationery Office (monthly) (NB: this publication has now been incorporated into *Labour Market Trends* London: HMSO)

United Nations (1971) *Indices to the International Standard Industrial Classification of all Economic Activities* New York: Department of Economic and Social Affairs, United Nations (intermittently)

——(2000a) *World Investment Report* New York: United Nations

——(2000b) *The World's Women: Trends and Statistics* New York: United Nations, http://www.un.org/Depts/unsd/ww2000

United Nations Statistics Division (2003) *International Standard Industrial Classification of all Economic Activities* (ISIC) Revision 3, New York: United Nations

United States Bureau of Labor Statistics (US BLS) (1985) *Handbook of Labor Statistics* Washington, DC: US Bureau of Labor Statistics, Department of Labor (intermittently)

——(1996) *International Comparisons of Manufacturing Product-ivity and Unit Labor Cost Trends, 1995* Internet at http://stats.bls.gov/newsrelease/prod 4.toc.htm (released on 17 July) Washington, DC

——(1997) *Median usual weekly earnings of full-time wage and salary workers by selected characteristics, annual averages*, Internet at http://stats.bls.gov/news.release/wkyeng.t06.htm (released January)

——(2000) 'Comparative real gross domestic product per capita and per employed person: Fourteen countries 1960-98'

——(2001) *International Comparisons of Hourly Compensation Costs for Production Workers in Manufacturing, 1975-95* Report 909, Washington, DC: US Bureau of Labor Statistics

——(2002) *Median Usual Weekly Earnings of Full Time Wage and Salary Workers by Selected Characterstics, annual averages* http://www.stats.bls.gov/news.release/wkyend.t06.htm 17 January 2003

Visser, J. (1990) 'In search of inclusive unionism' *Bulletin of Comparative Labour Relations* 18, Deventer: Kluwer, pp. 245-78

——(1991) 'Trends in trade union membership' *OECD Employment Outlook*, July pp. 97-134

——(2002) 'Why fewer workers join unions in Europe: A social custom explanation of membership trends' *British Journal of Industrial Relations* 40, 3, pp. 403-30

Wade, R. (1996) 'Globalisation and its limits: Reports of the death of the national economy are greatly exaggerated' in S. Berger & R. Dore eds *National Diversity and Global Capitalism* Ithaca, NY: Cornell University Press

Waring, M. (1988) *Counting for Nothing: What Men Value and What Women Want*, Wellington: Allen & Unwin/Port Nicholson Press

Western, B. (1997) *Between Class and Market: Postwar Unionisation in the Capitalist Democracies* Princeton: Princeton University Press

World Bank (1982) *World Development Report* Washington, DC: International Bank for Reconstruction and Development

World Bank *World Bank Atlas* Washington, DC: International Bank for Reconstruction and Development (annually)

World Trade Organisation (WTO) (1997) 'World Trade Organisation' Internet at http://www.wto.org/

Websites
Up-to-date Web addresses for statistical sources can be found on the useful links page of the Website associated with this book.

INDEX

Country names are abbreviated as follows: A—Australia, C—Canada, F—France, G—Germany, I—Italy, J—Japan, K—Korea, S—Sweden, UK—Britain, US—United States. Other abbreviations are as given on pp.xix–xxvii.